D1233175

BURNING
THE
FLAG

★

BURNING THE FLAG

The Great 1989-1990
American Flag
Desecration Controversy

Robert Justin Goldstein

THE KENT STATE UNIVERSITY PRESS
Kent, Ohio, and London, England

© 1996 by The Kent State University Press, Kent, Ohio 44242
All rights reserved
Library of Congress Catalog Card Number 95-5541
ISBN 0-87338-526-8
Manufactured in the United States of America

02 01 00 99 98 97 96   5 4 3 2 1

Library of Congress Cataloging-in-Publication Data

Goldstein, Robert Justin.
   Burning the flag : the great 1989–1990 American flag desecration
controversy / Robert Justin Goldstein.
      p.   cm.
   Includes bibliographic references and index.
   ISBN 0-87338-526-8 (cloth) ∞
   1. Flags—Desecration—United States.   I. Title.
CR113.G568   1996
929.9'2'0973—DC20   95-5541
                                                                 CIP

British Library Cataloging-in-Publication data are available.

★

CONTENTS

★

PREFACE

On September 12, 1989, Representative Thomas Petri (R-Wisc.) told his House colleagues, who were then debating the merits of attempting to circumvent the 1989 Supreme Court decision in *Texas v. Johnson,* which had legalized flag burning as a form of political protest, that recently a constituent had telephoned his office "and moved my staff to tears telling how her husband had fought and died for our country and its flag, and that flag had draped his coffin and she could not imagine how we could allow anyone to desecrate the symbol for which so many had given up their lives." He added, however, that another constituent had personally visited his Capitol office and told him that "she had supported me for years, but her husband had fought and died to protect the freedom of all Americans to burn our flag if they so wished, and she could not imagine why I would undermine the freedom of speech for which the flag stands."[1]

Petri's account summed up the depths and ultimate uncompromisability of the dispute that raged in American society and politics in 1989 and 1990 in the aftermath of the *Johnson* decision. Like a small minority of his fellow Republican congressmen and a clear majority of Democratic congressmen, Petri attempted to satisfy both sides of the dispute: in 1989 he voted in favor of the Flag Protection Act (FPA) of 1989, which Congress passed in an attempt to override the *Johnson* ruling, while in 1990, he voted against a Bush administration–backed constitutional amendment designed to accomplish the same ends after the Supreme Court struck down the FPA in its June 11, 1990, *U.S. v. Eichman* decision.

The June 21, 1990, vote in the House, which sealed the fate of the constitutional amendment, came exactly one year to the day after the *Johnson* decision. During the intervening twelve months, the flag desecration controversy, which originated with a 1984 Dallas flag burning, was one of the nation's dominant political disputes. On June 26, 1990, Senator Howard Metzenbaum (D-Ohio) told the Senate that the flag dispute had "taken up more time than perhaps any other issue we have faced during this [1989–90] Congress." By the time the dispute faded away as a political issue, along with the Bush administration's proposed constitutional amendment, in June 1990 Congress had spent about one hundred hours of floor debate on it along with about a dozen days of public legislative hearings, and thousands of additional hours of members' and staff time consumed in research and private meetings. The results of this expenditure of congressional time and resources filled about four hundred pages of the *Congressional Record* (at an average cost to taxpayers of $500 per page) as well as fifteen hundred pages of published hearings, no doubt transforming the *Johnson* case (which itself was the culmination of almost five years of litigation in the Texas and federal courts, generating thousands of pages of trial transcripts, court rulings, and legal briefs) into one of the most expensive legal disputes of all time.[2]

In the end, the right to desecrate the flag for purposes of political protest was theoretically legally established (although, as will be pointed out in this book's epilogue, anyone attempting to exercise this right in practice still faced a high chance of being prosecuted for something), and the flag and the country continued to exist more or less as before. But the year-long political focus on this purely symbolic issue unquestionably contributed to the same failure of the nation's leaders to address the country's real problems which had fostered the very climate of general national uncertainty and insecurity that had originally fueled the massive negative reaction to the *Johnson* ruling (a subject that is discussed at some length at the end of this book).

As many readers will already have detected, I believe that the Supreme Court decided the flag desecration issue correctly in 1989–90. So that all readers can be fully alerted to detect and discount my biases, I believe that it is important to set out my own views on this contentious subject. From one perspective, the 1989–90 flag desecration controversy was surely one of the greatest examples of "much ado about nothing" in American, if not world, history. The United States was not overrun with mobs of flag burners in the 1980s; as the *Tampa Tribune* pointed out on June 28, 1989, "You are likely to live a lifetime, and never see a 'dissident' burn a flag, except on television where such events are greatly welcomed. All we know about flag-burners is that they are microscopically few and seriously deficient in public-relations skills." Furthermore, there is no evidence that flag desecration threatens the flag's symbolic value. Indeed, the reaction to the Supreme Court's *Johnson* ruling suggests that from the standpoint of promoting patriotism and mass flag waving, both verbal and actual, *Johnson*'s contribution was virtually unprecedented (and certainly unheralded).

Although tolerating flag desecration is hardly likely to threaten the flag's symbolic value (or anything else), forbidding flag burning as a means of peaceful political protest will surely diminish the flag's symbolic ability to represent political freedom. As Professor Arnold Loewy has written, "Perhaps the ultimate irony is that *Johnson* has done more to preserve the flag as a symbol of liberty than any prior decision, while the decision's detractors would allow real desecration of the flag by making it a symbol of poltical oppression." Although the particular incident involving *Johnson* was isolated and ultimately insignificant, the principle represented by the Supreme Court's decision was absolutely fundamental to the core values of a political democracy: the right to vigorous, vehement, and even highly offensive and upsetting peaceful dissent from government policy. As Justice William Brennan summed up this key point in his *Johnson* opinion, "If there is a bedrock principle underlying the First Amendment, it is that the Government may not prohibit the expression of an idea simply because society finds the idea itself offensive or disagreeable." Or as the late Supreme Court justice Robert Jackson declared in a 1942 case (in which the Court outlawed compulsory flag salutes and recitals of the Pledge of Allegiance in public schools), in what remains probably the most eloquent and apposite paean to democratic principles ever penned by the Court:

> Those who begin coercive elimination of dissent soon find themselves
> exterminating dissenters. Compulsory unification of opinion achieves
> only the unanimity of the graveyard. . . . The case is made difficult not
> because the principles of its decisions are obscure but because the flag
> involved is our own. . . . Freedom to differ is not limited to things that
> do not matter much. That would be a mere shadow of freedom. The test
> of its substance is the right to differ as to things that touch the heart of
> the existing order. If there is any fixed star in our constitutional constel-
> lation, it is that no official, high or petty, can prescribe what shall be
> orthodox in politics, nationalism, religion or other matters of opinion.[3]

As Justice Jackson suggests, much of the controversy over the *Johnson* ruling came not from the principles at issue but because it involved the flag, and "the flag involved is our own." No serious claim would likely be made that it should be unlawful for an opponent of the 1991 American war with Iraq to burn a newspaper copy of President George Bush's explanation for this policy. Although ultimately any flag is simply a piece of cloth or other substance with colors or designs imprinted on it, many Americans have clearly invested this fabric with highly emotionally charged values. But, again to quote Justice Jackson, "A person gets from a symbol the meaning he puts into it, and what is one man's comfort and inspiration is another's jest and scorn." If there is to be any meaning to freedom of expression in the United States, it can only be that if President Bush can wave the flag as he sends troops to Panama or Iraq, then dissenters can protest that action by burning the flag. As the great civil libertarian scholar Alexander Meiklejohn has written, the true meaning of freedom of expression is that if

> on any occasion in the United States it is allowable to say that the Constitution is a good document it is equally allowable . . . to say that the Constitution is a bad document. If a public building may be used in which to say, in time of war, that the war is justified, then the same building may be used in which to say that it is not justified. If it be publicly argued that conscription for armed service is moral and necessary, it may likewise be publicly argued that it is immoral and unnecessary. If it may be said that American political institutions are superior to those of England or Russia or Germany, it may, with equal freedom, be said that those of England or Russia or Germany are superior to ours. . . . When a question of policy is "before the house," free men choose it not with their eyes shut, but with their eyes open. To be afraid of ideas, any idea, is to be unfit for self-government.[4]

In the context of this eloquent explanation of the meaning of democracy, it cannot make any difference that a flag burner speaks symbolically rather than verbally. Common sense dictates that attempts have been made to ban flag desecration because the *message* the act conveys is disliked, not because the burning of one or even a thousand flags inflicts any concrete damage or that the government has, as Justice Brennan wrote in a 1982 Supreme Court case, an "esthetic property interest in protecting a mere aggregration of stripes and stars for its own sake." As Senator James McClure told his colleagues on July 18, 1989, the real offense committed by flag desecrators was that "no other act" could "enrage citizens of this country more during a protest situation."[5]

Although many supporters of outlawing flag desecration have argued that such dissent should not be constitutionally protected because the First Amendment refers only to freedom of "speech" and "press," whereas flag burning is a form of "conduct," this position has been rejected by the Supreme Court for over sixty years, ever since a 1931 ruling overturning attempts to ban displays of red (i.e., communist) flags; furthermore, carried to its logical conclusion, this argument would make it constitutional to forbid all forms of nonverbal communication, including pantomime, sign language, theater, music, spitting, and hissing. Indeed, such an interpretation of the First Amendment would make it legal to forbid waving the American flag, but this would be an absurdity because everyone knows that waving an American flag, or a red flag, is as purely expressive as is burning an American flag, or a red flag. (The concept of a country banning the display of its own flag is not as absurd as it sounds. For example, during the run-up to the so-called velvet revolution that overthrew the communist dictatorship in Czechoslovakia in late 1989, displaying the national flag became a form of protest that so enraged the ruling elements that wearing the national colors in the form of coat lapels was forbidden to Czech soldiers as "against the dress code." American officials themselves have not been loath to ban the national flags of other countries: after World War II, American military occupation authorities banned displays of the swastika in Germany and of the "red sun" flag of Japan.)[6]

Although some proponents of banning flag desecration concede the obvious—that it is a form of expression—many of them maintain that no real harm will be done by forbidding only *one* especially heinous (in their view) form of political communication. But if the fundamental principles of democracy can be bent to exclude one object or one subject of discussion, there could be no principled legal barrier to extending such restrictions. More fundamentally, even if it were true that restrictions on freedom of expression could, in practice, be strictly limited to outlawing flag desecration, this still could not justify such a ban in a democratic country, where the fundamental principle of government is the right to peaceful dissent, even if expressed in an outrageous and offensive manner. As Reagan administration solicitor general Charles Fried, a well-known conservative, told the Senate Judiciary Committee in 1990, "the man who says you can make [such] an exception" to the principle of freedom of expression "does not know what a principle is," just as the man who says, "Only this once let's make $2 + 2 = 5$" does not understand logic or mathematics. In short, such an "exception" would destroy the principle itself.[7]

Even if all the flags in the country suddenly magically disappear, the nation will survive with its principles intact. But if the democratic principles that are supposed to govern our political system are permanently, or even temporarily, limited, even if the number of flags is multiplied by three, our freedoms will have been irreparably damaged. In perhaps the clearest illustration of this point, *Chicago*

Tribune columnist Stephen Chapman wrote in 1989, in response to the argument made by proponents of flag desecration laws that American soldiers had literally died for the flag rather than for the principles it is supposed to represent, that he doubted that "soldiers would have deserted in droves" during the Vietnam War if Congress had changed the design of the flag. Chapman asked, "What would they have said: 'Sorry, I don't mind dying for the red, white and blue, but getting killed for this purple and gold model is too much'?"[8]

This book focuses on the 1989–90 American flag desecration controversy, and I have made no attempt to explore an important related subject, which thus far has attracted only casual scholarly attention and would require another book: how American attitudes toward the flag compare with attitudes toward the flag in other countries. Both scholarly and journalistic observers have suggested, based largely on impressionistic evidence, that American veneration of the flag is considerably more extreme than that in most, or even all, other countries. For example, my friend Whitney Smith, director of the Flag Research Center in Winchester, Massachusetts, who probably knows more about flags that anyone in human history, says that the United States has "created something unique in the world: the flag as a religion, a civil religion." He adds, "The United States goes to the greatest extreme. The flag has become our substitute for a royal family or religion. We have made an icon out of it." Similarly, cultural historian Wilbur Zelinsky has written that the American flag has "pre-empted the place, visually and otherwise, of the crucifix in older Christian lands" and that "nowhere is the observation more apt than in the United States" that modern states have made their flag into a "literally holy object, the equivalent of the cross or the communion wafer." (This is perhaps an appropriate place to note that I use the term "desecration" in the title of this book and elsewhere only because it has become a commonly accepted short-hand reference to physically damaging the American flag for the purpose of expressing political protest. Technically, an object can be "desecrated" only if it has been "consecrated," a term that applies only to religious sacred objects; I do not agree that a piece of cloth invested with political significance can be regarded as a religious or sacred object, at least in a polity that constitutionally requires that the state shall not endorse or support any particular religious beliefs and in which the fundamental principle of the state is that all ideas are open to discussion and criticism without fear of legal penalties.)[9]

My guess is that the hypothesis that the United States venerates its flag more than other nations is true but somewhat exaggerated. As of 1989, well over fifty nations, including such relatively democratic countries as Austria, Denmark, Finland, France, Germany, Israel, Italy, New Zealand, and Switzerland, penalized flag desecration, and in several countries, including Argentina, Brazil, France, Germany, Greece, India, Italy, Mexico, Spain, and Turkey, the penalty for violating such flag laws far exceeded the one-year jail term that was provided in the U.S. federal flag desecration laws of 1968 and 1989. For example, the maximum penalties for flag desecration in 1989 were two years in France and Greece, three years in India and Italy, five years in Germany, six years in Turkey and up to twelve years in Spain.[10]

In 1990, the same year that the American Supreme Court made clear that outlawing flag desecration committed as an act of political protest was unconstitutional, its German equivalent, the Federal Constitutional Court, made equally clear that the German government was entitled to forbid flag desecration. The German court held that the flag "serves as an important means of [political] integration through the principal state goals which it incorporates" and that defaming it could "injure the authority of the state which is necessary for internal peace" and might hinder "the identification of its citizens with the basic values symbolized by the flag," such as the "free democratic basic order." Similarly, in Japan, an Okinawa district court in 1993 upheld the conviction of a man for tearing down and burning the national flag, even though no law specifically barred such behavior. In the "reformed" Soviet Union of President Mikhail Gorbachev, a woman was sentenced to two years of "correctional labor" in 1991 for burning a Soviet flag, and in mainland China a June 1990 law (passed one week after the American Congress rejected the Bush flag desecration constitutional amendment) provided a three-year jail term for flag desecration.[11]

Aside from the multitude of foreign laws banning flag desecration, additional impressionistic evidence clearly suggests that flags have played and still play an important role in the politics and history of many countries other than the United States. For example, on two separate occasions the Bourbon pretender to the throne would have become king of France during the 1870s save for his refusal to accept the revolutionary French tricolor flag rather than the white Bourbon standard which symbolized prerevolutionary France. In Germany, the black-red-and-gold flag, which symbolized a united country, was regarded as so threatening to the thirty-eight states into which Germany was divided in the early nineteenth century that its display was formally forbidden in 1832; subsequent to German unification in 1871, every regime from Bismarck to Weimar to Hitler to postwar democratic Germany has forbidden desecration of the national flag. Furthermore, Germany has not only outlawed the swastika since World War II, but after right-wing groups informally adopted the World War I imperial navy flag as their symbol in the early 1990s, seven out of the sixteen German states banned display of that flag by mid-1993 (although, as a German Justice Ministry spokesman pointed out, the "problem" was "not the flag itself" but "what is behind the flag" and therefore banning its display does nothing to solve "the real problem"). In Japan, there has been continual controversy in recent years over the government's decision to reintroduce the "rising sun" flag as the national emblem.[12]

Disputes over the designs of flags caused major political crises in both Germany and South Africa during the mid-1920s and became modestly significant political issues in Australia, South Africa, Austria, and Russia in the early 1990s. Attempts to ban the display of Buddhist flags in South Vietnam and the Panama flag in the American-controlled Panana Canal Zone in the early 1960s touched off major crises which, respectively, helped to lead to the ouster of the Vietnamese government of Ngo Dinh Diem and to the ultimate American decision to withdraw from the Canal Zone. South African authorities banned the flag of the African National Congress until Nelson Mandela was freed from prison in 1990, and Israeli authorities banned display of the Palestinian Liberation Organization flag until serious negotiations over the future of the West Bank and the Gaza Strip were initiated in 1993. One of the public objections by Greece to the newly pro-claimed state of Macedonia following the breakup of Yugoslavia in the early 1990s was the claim that the Macedonia flag had incorporated a historically Greek symbol.[13] (In late 1995, Macedonia agreed to delete the contested symbol.)

Within the United States, controversy over flags has not even been limited to the national emblem. Particularly during the early 1990s, there have been repeated attempts, especially by black organizations, to stop the display of the "stars and bars" Confederate battle flag, especially where official government sanction of its display is involved (in South Carolina and, until 1993, in Alabama the Confederate flag has been flown over the state capitol, while in Mississippi and in Georgia it is incorporated into the official state flags). In many ways, the argument over the Confederate flag (or, for that matter, over the Japanese flag or over changing the design of the German flag in the 1920s or of the Australian and South African flags in the 1990s) has mirrored the American flag desecration contro-versy. Defenders of the Confederate flag praised it as a symbol of southern honor and valor (just as those who wish to ban desecration of the American flag see it as a symbol of freedom and justice), while those who wish to ban the Confederate flag or burn the American flag (or abolish the former South African flag, as hap-pened in 1994) see them as symbols of evil and oppression.

   Thus one black opponent of the display of the Confederate flag described the emblem in 1992 as a symbol of "treason, sedition, slavery and oppression towards my people," while a defender of the "Stars and Bars" declared that for him it symbolized the "nation some of my ancestors fought and died for" and "to remove the flag is to remove the heritage." Even arguments as to whether it makes sense to spend time and energy debating the Confederate flag has paralleled a similar discussion concerning the American flag desecration controversy: an NAACP official opposed to its display declared in 1992 that "flags are very important and we can't ignore the real effect they have on people," but the mayor of Atlanta declared in 1993 that more pressing matters required attention and added, "I have yet to hear anybody in the community tell me the flag flying there is going to affect their lives at all. You can spend your life fighting a symbol and miss the important things."[14]

   The organizational plan of this book is as follows: Chapter One discusses the pre-1984 origins of the modern flag desecration controversy, especially focusing on the 1890–1920 period, when what I have termed the Flag Protection Movement first arose and succeeded in obtaining passage of flag desecration laws in most of the states, and on the Vietnam War period, when flag desecration reemerged as a major political issue and the first federal flag desecration law was passed. Chapter Two discusses the 1984 Dallas flag burning and subsequent legal proceedings in Texas from 1984 to 1988, which eventually led to the 1989 Supreme Court decision in *Texas v. Johnson* which once more returned flag desecration to the national stage. Chapter Three focuses on three different disputes involving the flag which collectively catapulted flag desecration to the front pages in mid-1989: the 1988 presidential campaign controversy concerning the Pledge of Allegiance, the early 1989 dispute over Scott Tyler's art exhibit in Chicago in which a flag was placed on the floor, and the Supreme Court's consideration of and its ultimate *Johnson* decision declaring flag desecration a constitutionally protected form of political protest. Chapter Four treats the immediate and massively negative response to the *Johnson* ruling, especially the role of the press and political elites in transforming the flag desecration issue into a major political controversy. Chapter Five studies the summer–fall 1989 congressional debate on the *Johnson* decision, which ultimately centered on whether to attempt to circumvent it via legislation—the ultimately passed 1989 FPA favored by Democratic congressional leaders—or via a constitutional amendment as backed by the Bush administration and Republican congressional leadership. Chapter Six discusses the factors that led to the 1989 defeat of the amendment and the passage of the FPA. Chapter Seven examines the subsequent defiance of the FPA by various flag desecrators and the testing and rejection of the law by two federal district courts. Chapter Eight discusses the Supreme Court's consideration and constitutional rejection of the FPA in its June 11, 1990, decision in *U.S. v. Eichman*. Chapter Nine discusses the public and political reaction to the *Eichman* ruling and examines the 1990 defeat of the constitutional amendment as well as attempting to explain why the public became so agitated about the flag desecration issue in 1989–90 (and during earlier periods). An epilogue discusses the rapid (at least short-term) fading of the flag desecration issue as a national concern following the 1990 defeat of the amendment but notes the rather numerous local incidents in which flag desecration continues to lead to local prosecutions and harassment. The book concludes with some afterthoughts that seek to place the 1989–90 controversy in historical, political, and analytical perspective.

To conserve space devoted to the endnotes and to hold their number down into the hundreds, as opposed to thousands, while still providing my readers with complete documentation, I have taken the following measures: (1) notes are gathered together at the end of each paragraph or grouped together at the end of one of a series of paragraphs dealing with closely related material, rather than being attached to each individual statement; (2) when the text itself gives the exact date of a newspaper or periodical source, that source is not repeated in the notes; (3) when textual information is based on interviews conducted by the author, such is clearly indicated in the text and not repeated in the notes (as an additional source aid, an asterisk [*] precedes, in the index, the names of all persons interviewed for this book); (4) full legal documentation is provided when a court case is first referred to or quoted from but subsequent general or passing references to a case are usually not noted because the reader can obtain a full citation by consulting the index; and (5) I have frequently used abbreviations in the notes, which are keyed to a list of abbreviations printed at the beginning of the notes section.

As aids to the reader, a listing of abbreviations used in the main text is printed in the prefatory matter, and several key documents repeatedly referred to in the text are printed in full in the Appendix, namely the 1968 and 1989 federal flag desecration laws, the Bush administration's proposed 1989–90 flag desecration constitutional amendment, and the text of the 1973 Texas state law struck down in the 1989 Supreme Court *Johnson* ruling. A comprehensive collection of documents relevant to the entire history of the American flag desecration controversy is planned for 1996 publication under the present author's editorship by Syracuse University Press, under the title *The American Flag Desecration Controversy: A Collection of Key Documents.* A companion study by the present author to the present volume, which primarily focuses on the pre-1984 period and is summed up in Chapter One here, was published in early 1995 by Westview Press under the title *Saving "Old Glory": The History of the American Flag Desecration Controversy.*

★

ACKNOWLEDGMENTS

This volume could never have been written without the research assistance of several hundred newspaper, public, and university librarians, university and other archivists, lawyers, journalists, civil liberties officials, and many others, almost all of whom generously offered me assistance although their only contact with me was by telephone or mail. Any attempt to name all of them would inevitably omit some of them (many of them never told me their names), but I do need to personally acknowledge a few people who were especially helpful. First, I owe great thanks to the more than one hundred people with intimate knowledge of the Vietnam-era and 1989–90 flag desecration controversies who granted me interviews. Of these, I am above all indebted to many of the lawyers and judges in the 1989–90 flag desecration controversy: Stanley Weinberg, Douglas Skemp, Michael Gillett, Kathi Drew, David Cole, William Kunstler, U.S. Solicitor General Kevin Starr, Assistant Solicitor General John Roberts, Dallas County judge John Hendrik and Texas Court of Criminal Appeals Court judge Charles Campbell, all of whom not only granted me lengthy interviews but supplied me with thousands of pages of legal briefs, transcripts, and other court documents concerning the *Johnson* and *Eichman* cases. I am also especially indebted to the Emergency Committee Against the Flag Amendment and Laws, the 1989–90 flag burners' defense organization, which similarly gave me access to their massive and invaluable collection of news clippings from sources across the nation (and especially to committee members Nancy Kent and Bruce Bentley); and to three flag experts: Flag Research Center Director Whitney Smith, San Jose State American Studies Professor Scot Guenter, and Austin attorney Charles Spain, all of whom provided me with invaluable moral support and encouragement as well as generous amounts of advice and research assistance. Finally, I am greatly indebted to the entire staff at my publisher, Kent State University Press, and especially to my editors, Julia Morton and Linda Cuckovich, and marketing manager Susan Wakefield for unending patience, help, support, and encouragement.

Although this book would have been entirely inadequate without the assistance of the many individuals already referred to, I must regretfully and reluctantly add that many other people who could have provided assistance refused to. Above all, although the Bush administration endorsed a flag desecration constitutional amendment in both 1989 and 1990, not a single White House or Justice Department official was willing to be interviewed on the record for this book, despite literally scores of telephone calls and letters requesting such directed to dozens of officials, from President Bush and then White House Chief of Staff John Sununu on down. However, a number of White House and Justice Department officials (although not at the highest levels) did speak to me on a not-for-attribution basis, and I am confident that only Bush or Sununu (who I never expected to talk to me) could have provided me with any additional significant information. Although none of the top congressional leadership—Senate Majority Leader George Mitchell, House Speaker Tom Foley, Republican Senate leader Bob Dole, and Republican House leader Bob Michel—were willing to talk to me either, I was able to obtain interviews with about a dozen congressmen and I also interviewed (almost invariably on a not-for-attribution basis) about twenty congressional staff members who played vital roles in the congressional consideration of the flag issue in 1989–90, and I therefore am confident that no significant aspects of this subject eluded me. Outside of official circles, above all I regret that Harvard law professor Laurence Tribe, who played a critical role in promoting the Flag Protection Act of 1989, whose passage helped to block 1989 congressional approval of a constitutional amendment, refused to grant me an interview.

After the original manuscript of this book was completed in mid-1995, important new developments occurred with regard to attempts to revive the proposed 1989–90 constitutional amendment to ban flag desecration. The proposed amendment easily passed the House of Representatives in late June, but was narrowly defeated in the Senate in mid-December. These developments are discussed in an addendum to the original text, which follows the epilogue.

★

ABBREVIATIONS
USED IN TEXT

ABA	American Bar Association
ACLU	American Civil Liberties Union
AFA	American Flag Association
AIC	Art Institute of Chicago
ASNE	American Society of Newspaper Editors
CFA	Citizens Flag Alliance
DAR	Daughters of the American Revolution
DWC	Democratic National Committee
ECAFAL	Emergency Committee Against the First Amendment and Laws (successor organization to ECSCFC)
ECSCFC	Emergency Committee on the Supreme Court Flag-Burning Case
FPA	Flag Protection Act of 1989
FPM	Flag Protection Movement
GAR	Grand Army of the Republic
HJC	House Judiciary Committee
PAW	People for the American Way
RCP	Revolutionary Communist Party
RCYB	Revolutionary Communist Youth Brigade (RCP youth group)
RNC	Republican National Committee
RNCCC	Republican National Congressional Campaign Committee
RW	Revolutionary Worker (RCP newspaper)
SAIC	School of the Art Institute of Chicago
SAR	Sons of the American Revolution
SCW	Society of Colonial Wars
SJC	Senate Judiciary Committee
SMAC	Senate Military Affairs Committee
TCLU	Texas Civil Liberties Union
WLF	Washington Legal Foundation

CHAPTER 1

THE PRE-1984 ORIGINS
OF THE AMERICAN FLAG
DESECRATION CONTROVERSY

The American flag played no significant role in American life until the Civil War. It was displayed only on federal government buildings and forts and on American ships at sea. Public schools did not fly the flag, and as the director of the Betsy Ross House in Philadelphia noted during the 1989–90 flag desecration controversy, "It would have been unthinkable to fly an American flag at a private home. It simply was not done." General display of the flag and popular familiarity with it were so rare that the first full-time American flag manufacturing company began operation only after the Mexican War of 1846–48 stimulated enough demand to make such a venture financially feasible.[1]

Only the outbreak of the Civil War—begun by the firing of Confederate troops upon the flag-bedecked Fort Sumter, South Carolina—transformed the American flag into an object of public adoration (although only, of course, in the North). According to historian George Preble, the flag then suddenly appeared everywhere, "from colleges, hotels, store-fronts, and private balconies," and the demand for flags became "so great that the manufacturers could not furnish them fast enough." In the South, however, the American flag became the object of scorn and hatred, and for the first time in American history, it became the widespread target of symbolic protest. The U.S. treasury secretary in 1861 ordered the summary execution of anyone attempting to haul down the flag in New Orleans, and in 1862 in that city a military court's death sentence for treason was executed against a man convicted of pulling down, dragging through the mud, and shredding a flag that had been hoisted over the federal mint.[2]

The newly found northern love for the flag continued after the Civil War, partly fostered by a series of patriotic historical commemorations such as the 1876 revolutionary centennial. But the flag's growing popularity was not accompanied at first by any sense that it should be regarded as a sacred object or relic. The most common form in which the flag became increasingly visible in American life during the last third of the nineteenth century, in fact, was as a decorative accompaniment in the commercialization of a wide range of products, as the modern advertising industry developed amid the rapid postwar industrialization of the nation. For example, one 1878 advertisement depicted a large ham against the backdrop of a flag on which was printed across the stripes, "The Magnolia Ham is an American Institution."[3]

Origins of the Flag Protection Movement

Gradually, after 1890, what will henceforth be termed (as a form of shorthand for a loosely organized coalition of groups) the Flag Protection Movement (FPM) grew up to protest the perceived commercial debasement of the flag, which would allegedly degrade the significance of both the flag and patriotism among the general public. Thus the 1895 pamphlet that served as the FPM's opening shot complained that the "tender sentiment" properly associated with a "decent use" of the flag would be "dissipated" and "sadly marred when we see it shamefully misused" as a "costume to bedeck stilt walkers, circus clowns, prize fighters and variety players or gaiety girls."[4]

New threats to the flag were soon targeted, notably its perceived abuse by politicians and, especially after about 1900, the supposed threat posed by trade union members, immigrants, and political radicals who might use the flag to express symbolic political protest. Although politicians had printed their names, portraits, and slogans on the flag at least since 1840, in 1896 such "politicization" of the flag reached previously unknown heights when the campaign of Republican candidate William McKinley made his alleged love for the flag a central theme. Millions of flags and flag buttons were distributed, and a national Flag Day was announced in his honor to help develop the theme (strikingly similar to that of George Bush in 1988) that Republicans had a unique relationship to the flag, while the Democrats and their presidential candidate, William Jennings Bryan, were portrayed as posing a threat to the "American way of life."[5]

Not surprisingly, a few zealous Bryanites responded in scuffles in which flags were damaged. The dozen or so "flag desecration" incidents associated with the 1896 campaign reenergized the FPM and led to growing demands to ban placing any writing or pictures on the flag—not just advertising uses. Thus in pamphlets published in 1898 and 1902, leading FPM spokesman Charles Kingsbury Miller declared that the flag's "sacredness" had been equally "encroached upon" by the "great political parties and the janizaries of trade" and equally abused by "avaricious tradesmen and crafty politicians, who turn it into a campaign banner for rival political clubs, a mop for the floor of barrooms and other despicable uses."[6]

Concern about perceived "mainstream" commercial and political abuse of the flag was the primary focus of FPM complaints until about 1900. Gradually thereafter, and especially after the twin 1917 developments of American intervention in World War I and the Bolshevik Revolution, the FPM's concern shifted and increasingly focused on the alleged or potential use of the flag as a means of expressing political protest by political radicals, trade union members, and immigrants (who were often indiscriminately lumped together). In practice, however, instances in which the flag was physically damaged (as opposed to being the subject of verbal assault or, in the eyes of the FPM, insufficient reverence) to express political dissent during the 1900–1920 period, and indeed during the entire pre–Vietnam War era, were rare. For example, the only protest flag burning that appears to have occurred between 1900 and 1965 involved an eccentric socialist-pacific New York clergyman named Bouck White, who acted in 1916 on the eve of his trial for distributing a caricature that allegedly demeaned the flag. White was convicted under the New York State flag desecration law, for which the FPM had successfully lobbied, and received separate maximum sentences of thirty days in jail and $100 fines for both offenses.[7]

No doubt a major motivating force behind the FPM was a growing sense of American patriotism and nationalism as the United States became a major world industrial and political power following the Civil War and especially after 1890. However, both the composition and the rhetoric of the FPM clearly suggest that its leaders feared that "their" traditional America was being threatened by newly emerging forces, such as big business, trade unions, political radicals, and "new immigrants," all of which were perceived as threatening the traditional social and economic order. The FPM was dominated by hereditary-patriotic groups like the Sons of the American Revolution (SAR) and the Daughters of the American Revolution (DAR) and by Union veterans' groups such as the Grand Army of the Republic (GAR), whose leaderships were composed of the middle- and upper-middle-class elites that had traditionally dominated American society. As Wallace

Davies, a leading historian of such groups, has summarized, these organizations felt that they had a special claim to leadership of the country, the hereditary-patriotic groups because of their "self-appointed roles" as "guardians of the American past and interpreters of its ideals" and the Union veterans for having, in their view, "acquired a first mortgage upon the country" by virtue of their success in battle on its behalf.[8]

FPM leaders developed a campaign to turn the flag into a holy object kept "pure" from contamination and put themselves forth as the most "true blue" patriots. Thus FPM rhetoric was filled with references to the flag's "sacredness" and purity, on the one hand, and to the threat of its pollution by its perceived enemies, on the other. For example, the national commander in chief of the GAR compared the flag to the "Holy of Holies," and leading FPM pamphleteer Miller wrote of "those three sacred jewels, the Bible, the Cross and the Flag," and referred to "unscrupulous" businessmen who had "polluted" the flag, whose "sacred folds were never designed to be defaced with advertisements of beer, sourkraut candy, itch ointment, pile remedies and patent nostrums." DAR Flag Committee chairwoman Frances Saunders Kempster complained bitterly that the flag, which had been "christened and hallowed" by the "prodigal outpouring of noble blood" and should be "held free and pure and sacred as the cross," had been "contaminated by the greed of gain." Ralph Prime, the president of the American Flag Association (AFA), an organization created in 1897 to coordinate FPM efforts, attacked merchants and politicians who sought to "prostitute" the flag, saying it should be maintained as a "sacred emblem, not to be used for any unholy or mercenary or partisan purposes," but to be "kept pure by patriots."[9]

In a 1900 pamphlet, Miller warned that the country had become the "international dumping ground" for "hundreds of thousands of the lowest class of immigrants" who swelled the "populace who abuse" the flag and posed a "menace to the nation," along with the "riotous elements of the labor organizations" and assorted and apparently interchangeable "Socialists, Anarchists, Nihilists, Populists, Tramps and Criminals." AFA president Prime claimed in 1912 that those guilty of "malicious outrages" against the flag were invariably immigrants associated with "meetings and demonstrations of labor movements."[10]

Having identified the various elements that were perceived as threatening to pollute the sacred character of the flag and, by extension, of their vision of and influence in American society, FPM leaders vigorously lobbied at the state and federal levels for stringent laws to "protect" the flag against all forms of alleged "desecration" (a term that by definition means the harming of sacred religious objects). According to Miller, flag protection laws were "essential to our welfare as a nation" because disrespect for the flag "may ultimately cause the government itself to tremble on its foundations," and encouraged in the "leaders of mobs and misguided strikers" a general "spirit of lawlessness and license," rampant "out-lawry and hoodlumism," and "anarchy and murderous labor riots." According to the 1900 statement of the vice-president of a Spanish-American War veterans group, flag desecration was a "crime more heinous in its ultimate effects than theft, arson or murder, as it strikes at the root of law, order and government."[11]

Fortunately, according to FPM leaders, such massive and horrendous threats to the stability of American society could be quickly and easily lanced by simply outlawing flag desecration and fostering respect for the flag. Thus former New York congressman Cornelius Pugsley told a 1923 Flag Day celebration: "No ral-lying point should be so effective to combat evil and dangerous tendencies in our national life than respect for our flag and our country." Frances Saunders Kempster told the DAR in 1907 that flag protection legislation would deliver alike to the "illogical and visionary enthusiast," the "glib-tongued, blatant demagogue," the "crafty schemer," and the "malignant fomenter of sedition" the message to "Cease! Cease!"[12]

Early State Flag Desecration Laws and Cases

Between 1897 and 1932, lobbying by the FPM and its supporters succeeded in ob-taining passage of flag desecration laws in all forty-eight states; thirty-one states acted between 1897 and 1905 alone. The laggards were mostly former Con-federate states, where the memories of the Civil War and Reconstruction dimmed passion for the American flag, at least until the nationalistic fervor stirred up by World War I took hold. Southern opposition in Congress, at least partly based on the states'-rights grounds that flag protection was a local matter, appears to have been largely responsible for the failure of flag desecration legislation on the national level until 1968 (although flag protection bills did pass one house of Congress on nine different occasions between 1890 and 1943).[13]

Although the state flag desecration laws varied somewhat, most of them were based on a model bill published by the AFA in 1900 and therefore had basically similar provisions. In short, the laws outlawed attaching anything to or placing any marks on the flag, using the flag in any manner for advertising purposes, or physically or even verbally "harming" flags in any way, including, typically, "pub-licly" mutilating, trampling, defacing, defiling, "defying," or casting "contempt," either "by words or act," upon the flag. The laws generally defined "flag" as any-thing even remotely resembling the American flag—all objects "made of any substance whatever" and "of any size" that "evidently" purported to be either the

American flag or its representation or included the flag's colors and the "stars and the stripes in any number," such that a person seeing it "without deliberation may believe the same to represent" the flag. Most state flag desecration laws provided maximum penalties of thirty days in jail and a $100 fine, but a few were considerably more harsh, such as the World War I–era laws passed in Texas and Montana, which contained maximum sentences of twenty-five years in jail.

The earliest state flag desecration laws were quickly challenged by adversely affected commercial interests as illegally restricting property rights. Although a series of local and state court rulings between 1899 and 1904 seemed on the verge of paralyzing the FPM by upholding such claims, in 1907 the U.S. Supreme Court, in the case of *Halter v. Nebraska,* upheld Nebraska's law in sweeping terms that made clear the futility of any further immediate legal challenges. In a case involving selling bottles of "Stars and Stripes" beer with pictures of flags on the labels, the Court declared that the state was entitled to restrict property rights for the valid and worthy purpose of fostering nationalism. Although the ruling did not address free speech questions (which had not been raised by the defendants), the ruling was so broadly worded that the Court clearly would have rejected any such position, especially because before 1925 the Court consistently refused to extend First Amendment rights to individuals who challenged state, as opposed to federal, laws.

The *Halter* decision was filled with patriotic oratory, declaring, for example, that "every true American has not simply an appreciation but a deep affection" for the flag and that, as a result, "it has often occurred that insults to a flag have been the cause of war, and indignities put upon it, in the presence of those who revere it, have often been resented and sometimes punished on the spot." The Court clearly endorsed the basic orientation of the FPM, declaring that advertising which used the national emblem tended "to degrade and cheapen the flag in the estimation of the people, as well as to defeat the object of maintaining it as an emblem of national power and honor," and that "love both of the common country and of the State will diminish in proportion as respect for the flag is weakened."[14]

Because the Supreme Court did not hear another flag desecration case after its 1907 *Halter* ruling until 1969, during the interim period the constitutionality of flag desecration laws was considered beyond review by the lower courts. During these years, just as the rhetoric of the FPM shifted increasingly away from targeting perceived "mainstream" commercial and political abuses of the flag toward focusing on the supposed desecratory words and acts of perceived political malcontents, post-*Halter* flag desecration prosecutions almost invariably targeted those who were viewed as motivated by political dissent. Thus, virtually all of the pre-*Halter* prosecutions that could be uncovered involved alleged commercial misuse of the flag, while of the total of about fifty-five flag arrests uncovered between 1907 and 1964, about forty-five clearly involved perceived political dissent.[15]

The overwhelming focus of post-*Halter* flag desecration enforcement on incidents with political significance is further highlighted by the clustering of cases around the periods of World War I and the postwar Red Scare and World War II, which were times of intensified patriotic-nationalistic fervor and decreased tolerance for dissent. Thus about thirty-five of the forty-five politically related flag desecration arrests between 1907 and 1964 occurred during 1914–20 and 1939–45. Almost half of these incidents involved oral disrespect for the flag, with the largest single cluster of such prosecutions occurring during World War I. In apparently the first verbal flag desecration case considered by a state supreme court, in 1918 the Kansas high court affirmed the conviction of a man who, while in a blacksmith shop, had expressed what the court termed "a very vulgar and indecent use of the flag." In 1942, the Arkansas Supreme Court upheld a similar conviction in the case of a man who was sentenced to one day in jail and a $50 fine for calling the flag a "rag" without eyes, ears, or a mouth and refusing to salute it when he was asked to do so as an apparent condition for obtaining relief supplies. The most extreme penalty for oral flag desecration was handed down under Montana's draconian 1918 law: E. V. Starr was sentenced during World War I to ten to twenty years at hard labor in the state penitentiary, along with a $500 fine, for refusing a mob's demands that he kiss the flag (a favorite wartime vigilante punishment for the allegedly disloyal) and for terming it "nothing but a piece of cotton" with "a little paint" and "some other marks" on it which "might be covered with microbes."[16]

Slightly more than half of the forty-five politically related flag desecration cases involved physical abuse of the flag. For example, among the ten or so such arrests reported during World War I, a Trenton, New Jersey, man was jailed for six months for spitting on a flag, another New Jersey man was arrested for cutting a flag to pieces and stomping on it, a New York man was arrested after a mob had attacked him for allegedly tearing down and trampling on a flag, and two New York City women were found guilty of disorderly conduct for sticking antidraft buttons and posters onto flags.[17]

The Fuzzy Line between Outlawing Disrespect
and Compelling Obeisance to the Flag

Although a growing emphasis on suppressing political dissent is clearly apparent in the post-1900 oratory of the FPM and in post-*Halter* flag desecration prosecutions, the new focus of the FPM and its progeny also had periodic spill-over effects on the broader society which reflected the political intolerance that increasingly formed the heart of the movement and became its major long-term legacy for American politics. After about 1920, the FPM, narrowly defined, gradually dissolved, apparently because of its success in obtaining flag desecration laws in all states. By then, however, its attitudes had permeated broad sectors of American society.

During three of the periods of greatest domestic political tension in the United States between 1907 and 1945—World War I, the 1919–20 Red Scare, and the period leading up to and including U.S. participation in World War II—sentiments that the FPM had stirred up, such as the conception that the American flag was sacred, that any true American would gladly pay homage to it, and that no true American would give greater homage to any other flag, especially one associated with radicalism and "un-Americanism," led to widespread demands, often enforced by government authority, that went far beyond the command that the flag not be desecrated to include also that the flag be kissed or saluted on demand and that no flag associated with radical political opposition be displayed. That the boundary between forbidding flag desecration and requiring obeisance to the flag was always highly permeable was demonstrated by periodic arrests for failure to show sufficient respect for the flag. For example, in 1922 a Des Moines, Iowa, man was arrested (and subsequently severely beaten by his fellow inmates) for failing to remove his hat when the flag passed during a parade. In 1925 a New York man was fined $25 for a similar incident, and in 1930, two young women who ran a communist children's camp in Van Etten, New York, were sentenced to jail terms of ninety days each for "desecrating" a flag by refusing to hoist one at the order of a mob.[18]

The permeability of the boundary between outlawing disrespect and compelling respect for the flag became especially clear during periods of crisis. During World War I, hundreds of people suspected of political dissidence or merely of insufficiently enthusiastic patriotism were, as in the Starr case, attacked by mobs that sought to compel them to kiss the flag, often while government officials looked the other way or joined in. During the 1919–20 Red Scare, official requirements for acceptable behavior toward flags were expanded beyond demands for proper reverence for the American flag to include outlawing the display of flags—usually but not only defined as red flags—viewed as subversive. This ban clearly demonstrated that by 1920 flag protection etiquette in practice primarily focused on suppressing dissent.[19]

Demands for the suppression of red flags, the symbol of the international socialist (and, after 1917, the communist movement), had been gradually growing after 1900. This trend exploded during the Red Scare, when, in response to exaggerated fears of an imminent communist revolution in the United States, thirty-two states and cities such as New York and Los Angeles banned the display of such flags. The red flag laws typically carried penalties of up to $500 fines and six months in jail. Most of them were extremely vague or wide-ranging: for example, Oklahoma forbade displaying any banners "indicating disloyalty or a belief in anarchy or other political doctrines" and West Virginia banned displaying any emblem that suggested "sympathy or support of ideals, institutions, or forms of government hostile, inimical, or antagonistic to the form or spirit" of the American "constitution, laws, ideals and institutions."

During the late 1930s and the early period of American participation in World War II, hundreds of American children who refused to salute the flag (all or overwhelmingly Jehovah's Witnesses, who acted out of religious convictions) were expelled from school. In scores of incidents, mobs, often acting with official approval or assistance, physically attacked Jehovah's Witnesses because their opposition to saluting the flag was viewed as evidence of insufficient patriotism.[20]

By June 1940 disputes over the flag in schools had developed in many states, and more than two hundred children had been expelled. In an atmosphere of hysteria generated by the growing likelihood of American involvement in World War II, and as the Nazi spring offensive of June 1940 was overrunning France and the Low Countries, the United States Supreme Court greatly aggravated the situation with its decision in *Minersville School District v. Gobitis.* The Court upheld the legality of expelling children from school for refusing to salute the flag and recite the Pledge of Allegiance on the grounds that the "flag is the symbol of our national unity" and "national unity is the basis of national security." The *Gobitis* decision, along with American entry into the war in December 1941, helped to foster a new wave of expulsions of Witnesses' children and a large and often extremely violent eruption of harassment, beatings, and arrests of adult Witnesses. The American Civil Liberties Union (ACLU) reported that between May and October 1940, almost fifteen hundred Witnesses became the victims of mob violence in 355 communities in forty-four states and that no religious organization had suffered such persecution "since the days of the Mormons."[21]

In short, the FPM, which had originally sought to forbid "mainstream" political and commercial uses of the flag that were viewed as insufficiently reverential, ended up by primarily seeking to suppress political dissent and by spawning movements that demanded ritual obeisance to the flag from those who did not wish to give it and which sought to forbid any display of allegedly "subversive" flags. A movement that originally sought to protect the American flag from all forms of perceived misuse thus became a movement aimed at suppressing dissent, even when that meant forcibly compelling symbolic allegiance to a flag that the FPM honored because it stood for freedom. Ironically—but from the standpoint of constitutional democracy justly—some of the worst and most undemocratic excesses spawned by the FPM, namely the red flag and compulsory flag salute laws, led to Supreme Court decisions in 1931 and 1943, which established the basic legal principles that later logically led the Court in 1989 and 1990 to strike down all laws outlawing flag desecration.

In the 1931 case of *Stromberg v. California,* a red flag law prosecution, the Court effectively struck down all such laws on the grounds that to forbid the display of emblems used to foster even "peaceful and orderly opposition" to government was an unconstitutional violation of the First Amendment. This decision, the first Supreme Court declaration that symbolic speech (as opposed to only written or spoken remarks) was protected by the First Amendment, established the principle that symbols such as flags could be used peacefully to express political opposition and thus contained the seeds of the 1989 *Johnson* ruling. In the 1943 case of *West Virginia Board of Education v. Barnette,* the Court, citing *Stromberg* among other precedents, overruled its *Gobitis* decision of only three years earlier, striking down compulsory school flag salute and Pledge of Allegiance requirements on the grounds that a child required by state laws to attend public schools could not, without violating the First Amendment, be forced by public authorities "to utter what is not in his mind." Justice Jackson declared:

> The case is made difficult not because the principles of its decision are obscure but because the flag involved is our own. Nevertheless, we apply the limitations of the Constitution with no fear that freedom to be intellectually and spiritually diverse will disintegrate the social organization. . . . If there is any fixed star in our constitutional constellation, it is that no official, high or petty, can prescribe what shall be orthodox in politics, nationalism, religion or other matters of opinion.[22]

In the 1969 case of *Street v. New York,* the Supreme Court relied heavily on *Stromberg* and especially *Barnette* to strike down all flag desecration law provisions that outlawed verbal disrespect for the flag as violating the First Amendment. Subsequently, in the 1989–90 flag burning cases of *Johnson v. Texas* and *U.S. v. Eichman* (which are the central focus of this book), the Court declared that the same principles that forbade outlawing oral disrespect for the flag applied equally to banning physical destruction of the flag for the purpose of expressing political dissent. The line of court principles and decisions that began with *Stromberg* and *Barnette* thus led directly to *Street, Johnson,* and *Eichman.* In short, it was the very excesses of the FPM and its progeny that led the Court to establish the principles that eventually were applied to declare unconstitutional the original goal—the outlawing of flag desecration—which had given birth to the FPM one hundred years earlier.[23]

The Flag Desecration Controversy
during the Vietnam War

Between 1945 and 1965, only a scattering of flag desecration incidents were reported, and the issue virtually disappeared from American consciousness. The handful of individuals and organizations which continued to focus on the threat posed by flag desecration during this period generally gave the impression of being on the lunatic fringe or at least of being obsessed with obscure matters. For example, in a 1953 book, Gridley Adams, the director of the United States Flag Foundation (a successor organization to the American Flag Association), suggested that the use of flag stamps (which, of course, were canceled, and thus "defaced" by the billions) reflected communist infiltration of the Post Office.[24]

By 1962 objections to the use of the flag for advertising purposes had become so rare and such uses had become so generally accepted that the American Law Institute (ALI), a nongovernmental organization of prominent judges, lawyers, and professors closely intertwined with the legal establishment, proposed in its Model Penal Code (MPC) that all restrictions on commercial usage be deleted from state flag desecration laws because "whatever may have been true [previously], it is scarcely realistic today to regard commercial exploitation of the national emblem or colors as a serious affront to popular sensibilities." Even more striking in 1966 the National Conference of Commissioners on Uniform State Laws (NCCUSL—a group representing state governments, which seeks to coordinate state legislation on issues of common concern), which in 1917 had recommended that all states pass the AFA's model law that banned both commercial use of the flag and physical flag desecration, withdrew its support for flag desecration laws on the grounds that they had become "obsolete."[25]

Ironically, within a year of the NCCUSL action, flag desecration erupted into the public arena again. Just as the 1989–90 controversy was touched off by a single flag burning, the Vietnam War controversy was "ignited" by the burning of one flag, in this case in Central Park in New York during a massive antiwar demonstration on April 15, 1967. Although there had been a few scattered flag desecration incidents in the preceding year or so, the New York burning was photographed and widely publicized, and, like the 1989 *Johnson* Supreme Court decision, it triggered a wave of indignation, widespread demands for punitive legislation, and (just as in 1989) congressional passage (in 1968) of a federal flag desecration law aimed at the suppression of dissent.[26]

The 1890–1920 flag desecration controversy seemed to have become so intense because the FPM associated alleged attacks on the flag with an assault on the traditions and stability of American society. Likewise, the Vietnam-era controversy seems to have arisen because for many Americans flag burning became a symbol of events associated with the 1960s antiwar opposition which seemed to threaten the entire value system and political structure of American society, including the emergence of a "counterculture" and increases in violent crime, black militancy, and political radicalism. Thus Representative Richard Roudebush (R-Ind.), a leading sponsor of the 1968 federal flag desecration law, termed the growing wave of domestic "anarchy and disrespect for law and order" a key reason why the nation needed to preserve the flag's "respect and dignity." While dissidents were prosecuted in record numbers for unorthodox use of the flag during the 1967–74 period, millions of other Americans displayed flags, flag lapels, and flag buttons to demonstrate their patriotism. Political scientist Seymour Martin Lipset explained the flag explosion by noting, "All sorts of traditional values are being challenged. In a certain sense, by having a flag on the car, you're saying that you're not a hippie, you're against campus demonstrations and that you believe in the traditions and values that are under attack."[27]

The flag thus became the greatest single symbol of the cultural and political divide that ripped the country apart during the Vietnam War. *Time* magazine, in a lengthy cover story about the flag "civil war" on July 6, 1970, declared that the flag had "become the emblem of America's disunity" as the "defiant young blow their nose on it, sleep in it, set it afire or wear it to patch the seat of their trousers" while the response of other Americans was to "wave it with defensive pride, crack skulls in its name and fly it from their garbage trucks, police cars and skyscraper scaffolds." Not coincidentally, the Vietnam-era flag desecration controversy peaked between 1967 and 1974, the years of greatest American involvement in the war, and died down quickly thereafter. A series of flag burnings between 1979 and 1988 attracted virtually no media or political attention until the Supreme Court's 1989 *Johnson* ruling.[28]

The Debate over the 1968 Federal Flag Desecration Law

Within three weeks of the April 15, 1967, Central Park burning, which occurred at the height of Vietnam War fervor, the House Judiciary Committee (HJC) began hearings on more than one hundred bills (almost all identical) that had been introduced in its immediate aftermath. Although all fifty states retained flag desecration laws on the books and only a handful of flag desecration incidents had occurred within recent memory, New Hampshire representative Louis Wyman explained that it was "not the number of actors, it is the wideness of distribution of the public impression [via photographs] of a single act that is the crux of the problem for Congress." Within two months of the Central Park burning, the House passed a flag desecration bill after five hours of debate on June 20, 1967, by 385 to 16, as the *New York Times* reported on its front page. The Senate subsequently passed the measure by voice vote and without debate on June 24, 1968, and President Lyndon Johnson signed it into law on July 4, thereby marking the first time that Congress had passed a flag desecration law.[29]

The statute made it illegal "knowingly" to cast "contempt" upon "any flag of the United States by publicly mutilating, defacing, defiling, burning, or trampling upon it," subject to a penalty of up to $1,000 and/or one year in jail. It defined "flag" in the expansive manner typical of most of the state laws to include virtually any object such as "any picture or representation" made of "any substance" and of "any size evidently purporting" to be the flag or its representation, containing "the colors, the stars and the stripes, in any number of either thereof, or of any part or parts of either, by which the average person seeing the same without deliberation may believe the same to represent" the American "flag, standards, colors or ensign."[30]

The Vietnam-era flag desecration debate was a mini-version of the dispute that engulfed American society in 1989–90. As would be the case then, the major argument for banning flag desecration during the Vietnam era was that the flag was a unique and special symbol of America, and especially American freedom, and that although the right to dissent was sacred, burning the flag went "too far." Thus Republican representative James Quillen of Tennessee declared that the flag has "always been the symbol of freedom and liberty" but "there are bounds in which" such freedom should be exercised and "when anyone goes so far as to desecrate our beloved flag" he "has gone too far." Democratic representative Hale Boggs of Louisiana termed flag desecration "outrageous acts which go beyond protest and violate things which the overwhelming majority of Americans hold sacred." Backers of a flag desecration law rejected arguments that symbolic protests using the flag were a form of constitutionally protected expression because, they maintained, the First Amendment applied only to verbal or written expression. Thus, Representative William Randall of Missouri termed any free speech argument in defense of flag desecration "tommyrot, baloney, pure hogwash."[31]

As if echoing the earlier FPM, backers of flag desecration legislation claimed that flag burners posed a great threat to the nation. Representative Edna Kelley viewed flag burning as "a direct attack on the sovereignty of the United States," which amounted to "a form of destruction of the basic values and principles of our Government." Pennsylvania Supreme Court justice Michael Musmanno declared that those who burned the flag "apply an acetylene torch to the police stations, courthouses and Federal and state capitols."[32]

The shadow of the Vietnam War pervaded the debate. Thus in endorsing a federal flag desecration law on May 2, 1967, the House Republican Policy Committee declared that it was "strange indeed" to see in the press photographs of "American young men facing danger and death in Vietnam" alongside those of "other American young men burning their nation's flag in the safety of an American park." Many backers of a federal law declared that it was required because flag desecrators were subverting the American war effort by undermining the morale of U.S. soldiers (who were often said to be fighting and dying "for the flag") while simultaneously boosting that of the Vietnamese enemy. For example, the Louisiana legislature demanded that Congress halt the "loathsome and disgusting" acts of "seditious" flag desecrators while the "valiant defenders of Freedom" were fighting "invidious hordes of atheistic communism."[33]

As would be the case in 1989–90, for backers of the 1968 law, no description of flag burners and no penalty for their offense could be too harsh. Judge Musmanno, in his HJC testimony, termed flag burners "miserable wretches," "vile America-hating hooligans," and "treasonous" agitators "fit to conspire with Communists who would force our freedoms into the straitjacket of Bolshevistic dictatorship." "Nothing's too strong for them," declared House Armed Services Committee chairman Mendel Rivers, and Representative James Haley helpfully suggested, "Load a boat full of them and take them 500 miles out into the ocean and handcuff them, chain the anchor around their necks and throw them overboard."[34]

As in 1989, the smell of political pandering hung heavy over the congressional debate. During HJC hearings in May–June 1967, not a single congressman expressed opposition to a federal flag desecration law, and more than sixty representatives submitted oral or written testimony on its behalf. During floor debate on June 20, 1967, a few opponents of the measure spoke up, but in general, as the *Washington Post* reported, "symbol-minded members, including some who hardly ever cast a yea vote for any legislation, fell over each other grabbing for microphones to get on record in favor of the bill." Representative Lionel Van Deerlin of California openly confessed that he would vote for what he termed a "bad" and "unnecessary" law because it was "not important enough" to risk allowing "zealots and know-nothings" to make alleged "disloyalty" the "prime issue" in his reelection race." HJC chairman Representative Emmanuel Celler, a liberal, who termed the measure a "bad bill" of doubtful constitutionality, explained his ultimate support for it by declaring, "Who can vote against something like this? It's like motherhood."[35]

Just as the arguments for the 1968 law prefigured those advanced for the 1989 Flag Protection Act, so did the arguments against it resemble those to be advanced against similar proposals and constitutional amendments twenty years later (although there was far more opposition expressed in 1989 than in 1967–68). However, the Vietnam-era debate was quite different from the original 1890–1920 controversy, when the free speech issue was rarely raised by critics of flag desecration laws. In 1967–68, opponents of the flag law stressed that flag desecration, although highly distasteful, was a form of political expression protected by the First Amendment. Thus Representatives John Conyers and Don Edwards (in dissenting from the HJC majority report) protested that the proposed legislation "would do more real harm to the Nation that all the flag burners can possibly do" because it would "infringe upon what is certainly one of the most basic freedoms, the freedom to dissent," the "real 'evil' at which the bill was directed." The *Washington Post* declared that supporters of flag desecration laws were "grossly ignorant" of and sought to commit "acts and deeds unworthy" of the values, such as freedom of dissent, which the flag stood for; moreover, the *Post* added, flag burners did no more real harm than "hanging someone in effigy" because the flag's meaning did not reside in a "scrap of textile" but "in the minds of Americans."[36]

As would be the case in 1989–90, critics of the 1968 law also argued that a handful of flag burnings hardly justified congressional action; that banning such behavior would not protect anything but would only create martyrs because the flag was not the same as the country or the principles it symbolized; that it was more important to protect the substance rather than the symbol of constitutional rights; that love of country could not be compelled; and that what the country really needed was action to solve real rather than symbolic problems. For example, *Commonweal* magazine asked sarcastically, "Seeing as nothing can be done about the war in Vietnam or rampant racism here, why not at least begin with respect for the flag?" The *Christian Century* lamented, "While our Congress argues about people who burn a bit of bunting, the United States scorches land, blows up humble homes and burns thousands of people to death or until they pray to die. That, more than anything else, desecrates our flag."[37]

Flag Desecration in the Courts, 1966–1976

The 1968 federal law did not end flag desecrations; in fact, the 1968–74 period saw an explosion of flag desecration prosecutions which by far exceeded the total of all such prosecutions during all of the rest of American history. All but a hand-ful of these prosecutions, however, were brought under state laws, not the new federal law. About ten states beefed up their flag desecration laws with increased penalties during the Vietnam period—for example, Alabama, Oklahoma, and Illinois raised their penalties from a maximum of thirty days in jail and $100 fines to from two to five years in prison and fines of $3,000 to $10,000. Although it is impossible to say for certain how many such incidents were brought to trial or what percentage of them were successfully prosecuted, a 1973 *Christian Science Monitor* estimate that "some 1,000" flag desecration prosecutions had occurred during the Vietnam War period is almost certainly an underestimate inasmuch as New York ACLU attorney Burt Neuborne told a reporter in 1972 that he had personally handled more than three hundred such cases.[38]

Contemporary accounts differ wildly as to the general outcome of these pros-ecutions. My survey of the approximately sixty flag desecration prosecutions that were reported in standard legal references between 1966 and 1976 (generally meaning that they were appealed, which was probably not the case with most such prosecutions) suggests that, at least in reported cases, acquittals or dismissals ulti-mately resulted from about 60 percent of the prosecutions. Such outcomes were increasingly likely after 1972 (acquittals jumped from about 55 percent between 1966 and 1972 to almost 70 percent between 1973 and 1976), when American ground combat involvement in Vietnam had decreased markedly and there was a growing consensus that the war had been an error. Acquittals were also far more likely when the allegations involved were relatively less, literally and figuratively, inflammatory than burning the flag, such as wearing a "flag patch" on the seat of one's pants or "superimposing" over the field of stars a "peace sign" (a trident sur-rounded by an oval). Because lower court decisions were so contradictory and the Supreme Court repeatedly failed to rule squarely on the fundamental constitution-ality of flag desecration laws between 1969 and 1989, the legal status of such laws was in a state of constitutional confusion until the Court's 1989–90 rulings in the *Johnson* and *Eichman* cases.[39]

The sixty reported cases surveyed were divided into four categories: burning the flag (nine cases), wearing the flag (usually, but not only, as a trouser's seat patch, sixteen cases), superimposing symbols like the peace sign over the flag (fif-teen cases), and a wide variety of miscellaneous charges which included publishing a picture of a burning flag, driving a car painted in flag colors, pouring paint over a flag and displaying it at half-mast in an inferior position to the United Nations flag (twenty cases). Flag burning charges led to convictions two-thirds of the time, but 85 percent of cases involving "superimposition" ultimately resulted in acquittals, as did 55 percent of the "wearing" cases and 60 percent of the miscellaneous cases.

When prosecutions led to convictions, the courts frequently cited the 1907 Supreme Court *Halter* ruling as the leading authority. They also usually relied on one or both of the two interests that were to be advanced by Texas in the 1989 *Johnson* Supreme Court case as overriding any free speech rights alleged to be involved in flag desecration: protecting the flag as a symbol of the nation as furthering the state's interest in fostering unity and patriotism, and preventing breaches of the peace. For example, in the flag burning case of *Deeds v. State,* the Texas Court of Criminal Appeals (which later reversed itself in the *Johnson* case) declared that "since the flag symbolizes the entire nation, not just one particular philosophy, the state may determine that it be kept above the turmoil created by competing ideologies." In upholding flag desecration convictions as legitimate attempts to prevent breaches of the peace, even though evidence of any actual threats to the peace was rarely if ever introduced, courts often cited the *Halter* contention that insults to the flag had "often been resented and sometimes punished on the spot." For example, in the flag burning case of *Sutherland v. DeWulf,* a federal court quoted *Halter* and declared that public flag desecration had a "high likelihood" of causing a breach of the peace and was inherently an act of incitement as "fraught with danger" as if a person stood "on the street corner shouting derogatory remarks at passing pedestrians."[40]

Acquittals were based on a wide variety of reasons, a very few of which directly rejected the professed state interests just referred to, and most of which were based on other, usually narrow or technical, grounds. In the only reported case between 1965 and 1984 in which a flag burning conviction was thrown out on the grounds that such symbolic expression was a constitutionally protected right, while any alleged state interest in fostering patriotism was rejected as justifying flag desecration laws, a federal district court in *Crosson v. Silver* denied that there existed "any constitutionally recognized state power to prohibit flag desecration based on an interest in preserving loyalty or patriotism." This prosecution was brought under the Arizona state law, and Crosson was later successfully prosecuted for the same flag burning under the new federal law.[41]

Most acquittals in flag desecration cases were based on far more narrow grounds which avoided basic constitutional issues. For example, several convictions involving "wearing" of flags, "superimposition" of flags, and various other miscellaneous uses of flags were reversed on the grounds that no physical desecration had occurred, that no "contempt" had been displayed, that no real "flag" had been involved, that no clear threat to the peace had been demonstrated, or on similar narrow grounds. For example, in the 1969 case of *State v. Saionz,* which involved wearing the flag as a cape, an Ohio appeals court found that because Saionz had not physically altered the flag to turn it into a cape, there was no evidence that he had "cast contempt" on the flag, which was held to require an act of physical destruction. In the 1971 peace symbol superimposition case of *State v. Liska,* an Ohio appeals court overturned a conviction on the grounds that Liska was simply expressing his "aspiration for peace" and that this was "not a contemptuous act." In another peace symbol flag case, *State v. Nicola,* the North Dakota Supreme Court ruled in 1971 that because Nicola's flag had been manufactured with the peace symbol in place of the field of stars, that he was not guilty because he had never physically desecrated it, and moreover, Nicola's flag had never been the object of the state's law, which protected real American flags as opposed to "any flag which may happen to have a prevailing scheme or idea of red and white stripes."[42]

Flag desecration laws in about half a dozen states were struck down between 1970 and 1976 on the somewhat broader grounds that they were unconstitutional in whole or in part because of vagueness or overbreadth (outlawing clearly legal as well as possibly illegal behavior)—but not on the more fundamental free speech grounds cited by the federal district court in the *Crosson* case. For example, in *Parker v. Morgan,* a case involving wearing a jacket with a sewn-on flag which had the words "Give peace a chance" superimposed on it, a federal court found North Carolina's law unconstitutionally vague by virtue of its typically expansive definition of flag. The court declared that the state law's definition of flag was "simply unbelievable" and "a manifest absurdity," which "read literally" might make it "dangerous in North Carolina to possess anything red, white and blue." The court added, "It seems to us that red, white and blue trousers, with or without stars, are trousers and not a flag, and that it is beyond the state's competence to dictate color and design of clothing, even bad taste clothing." In *Long Island Vietnam Moratorium Committee v. Cahn,* a case involving buttons and decals which superimposed the peace sign over a portion of the flag, a federal appeals court held that the section of New York's law which banned placing any "word, figure, mark, picture, design, drawing, or any advertisement, of any nature" on the flag was unconstitutionally overbroad in violation of the First Amendment. The court held that the New York law vested law enforcement officers "with too much arbitrary discretion" in initiating prosecutions and thus "permits only that expression which local officials will tolerate; for example, it permits local officials to prosecute peace demonstrators but to allow 'patriotic' organizations and political candidates to go unprosecuted."[43]

As the *Cahn* decision and some of the others suggest, the picture presented by the flag desecration issue after 1965 was one of chaotic, highly discretionary law enforcement and contradictory court decisions. Thus in *State v. Waterman, People v. Cowgill,* and *State v. Mitchell,* wearing the flag, respectively, as a cape, a vest, and a patch on the seat of the pants led to convictions, but in *State v. Saionz, Franz v. Commonwealth,* and *People v. Vaughan* the same behaviors led to acquittals. Superimposition of a peace sign over the flag's field of stars usually led to acquittals (at least on appeal), as in *Cahn,* but in *State v. Saulino,* superimposition of a picture of Mickey Mouse led to conviction. In a 1972 case, *State v. Kasnett,* an Ohio appellate court upheld the conviction of a man who wore a flag patch sewn on his back pants pocket, partly because wearing the flag "over the anus . . . a part of the human body universally and historically considered unclean . . . was a clear act of defilement." In 1973, however, the Ohio Supreme Court overturned Kasnett's conviction on the grounds that no physical damage had been done to the flag in question and that a patch over a pants pocket was, as a matter of anatomy, not "over the anus." The Ohio Supreme Court declared that the intent of the state law was only to ban physical mutilation of the flag and suggested that applying it to the use of the flag as clothing would raise the question, "Is a flag worn by a policeman over his heart, or on his sleeve, or on his helmet permissible, and the same flag worn by a student impermissible depending upon which part of his anatomy it is upon or near?"[44]

An especially disturbing aspect of the Vietnam-era flag desecration cases, as the *Cahn* decision and some of the others suggest, was the arbitrary manner in which such prosecutions were used against "peace" demonstrators, while "establishment" and "patriotic" persons and organizations (including President Richard Nixon and the White House staff and the police departments of Boston and New York City), who wore flag lapels and placed flag decals on their windows and cars by the tens of millions, often in technical violation of flag desecration statutes, invariably were unhindered. Whitney Smith, director of the Flag Research Center, noted in 1970 that "commercial misuse" of the flag was "more extensive than its misuse by leftists or students, but this is overlooked because the business interests are part of the establishment." *Time* magazine, commenting in the same year on prosecutions for "wearing" the flag, noted that applying such logic, "Uncle Sam should be indicted first, followed by Roy Rogers and Dale

Evans [popular entertainers who had appeared on national television wearing flag costumes in a clearly patriotic cause]." New York State prosecuted one man for driving a stars-and-stripes-painted automobile along a highway that featured state billboards promoting New York potatoes and had pictures of Governor Nelson Rockefeller superimposed over the flag and potatoes replacing the stars. Occasionally such anomalies became too obvious to ignore: the charge against a Topeka, Kansas, man for having a "peace flag" decal on his car was dropped after his lawyer pointed out that city police cars bore flag decals "defaced" by the slogan "Love it or leave it."[45]

In some cases, penalties handed out as a result of Vietnam-era flag desecration prosecutions were extraordinarily harsh or simply bizarre. For example, a California youth who used the flag as a beach towel because, he said, "I didn't have anything better to lie on," was sentenced to sixty days in jail for "defiling" the flag and was compelled to write a two-thousand-word essay on "What I think and feel the flag is to this country." In several cases, flag desecrators were ordered to display public penance to avoid harsh jail terms. For example, in a 1974 incident, two teenagers were ordered to apologize publicly in newspaper advertisements for burning a flag and to attend flag raising and lowering ceremonies at city hall for a week, to observe a curfew for six months, and not to communicate with each other for a year. A Cambridge, Massachusetts, teenager was sentenced in 1970 to carry a large, fifteen-pound American flag on a three-mile march through town as an alternative to serving six months in jail for burning a flag.[46]

By far the harshest Vietnam-era flag desecration penalty was the four-year jail term given in 1970 to a nineteen-year-old Dallas man, Gary Deeds, for burning a piece of flaglike bunting in a Dallas park. Deeds testified that he had burned the bunting as a "theatrical display" because it had been "soiled by the policies of the country" and not as "an insult to the flag." He stated, "I love my country and the flag." Deeds's conviction and sentence were upheld by the Texas Court of Criminal Appeals in 1971—the court which in 1988 became the first to uphold the right of Gregory Lee Johnson to burn a flag for the purpose of expressing political dissident in the 1984 Dallas incident that eventually led to the Supreme Court's 1989 *Johnson* ruling. In another bizarre connection between the *Deeds* and *Johnson* cases, the presiding judge at Deeds's 1970 jury trial was John Vance, who was later to uphold Johnson's original 1984 Dallas conviction as a Texas Court of Appeals judge in 1986 and who subsequently, as the elected Dallas County district attorney, was Johnson's unsuccessful chief protagonist before the Texas Court of Criminal Appeals in 1988 and the U.S. Supreme Court in 1989. In seeking to uphold Johnson's convictions before those two courts, Vance would especially rely on the 1971 Texas Court of Criminal Appeals confirmation of Deeds's conviction in the case he had presided over himself.[47]

The Supreme Court and the Flag Desecration Issue during the Vietnam War Era

Much of the responsibility for the confusion in the lower courts over the flag desecration issue during the Vietnam War period, and indeed during the entire era leading up to the 1989 *Johnson* ruling, rests with the Supreme Court. Beginning with the 1931 *Stromberg* red flag ruling, the Court had held that "symbolic speech" (i.e., expression that was neither verbal nor written) was, at least in some cases and to some degree, protected under the First Amendment. Ever since the *Stromberg* ruling, however, the Court had given out highly confusing signals as to exactly what constituted "symbolic speech" and to what degree it was protected. This was especially true with the flag desecration issue, an area in which during the 1969–88 period the Court handed out a series of broad hints suggesting that it was reluctant to uphold convictions yet also repeatedly avoided confronting the fundamental First Amendment issue head-on.

Beginning with *Stromberg* and continuing through the 1943 *Barnette* compulsory flag salute case and a number of other decisions handed down before 1970, the Court had made abundantly clear that First Amendment protections extended well beyond purely verbal and written expression. In addition to using "opposition" flags to express peaceful political dissent (*Stromberg*) and refusing to salute the government's flag (*Barnette*), other examples of "symbolic speech" that had obtained Supreme Court protection by 1970 included the right to picket peacefully in labor disputes, to march in support of civil rights, and to wear black armbands to school to express opposition to the Vietnam War (an activity the Court termed "closely akin to 'pure speech'" when no disruption was involved).[48]

Although the Court thus clearly recognized that a wide variety of "symbolic speech" was protected by the First Amendment, it also indicated, in a generally vague manner that left considerable legal confusion in its wake, that such "conduct" was not as protected by the First Amendment as was oral and written expression. Thus, in a 1965 case, the Court "emphatically" rejected the "notion" that the First Amendment and other constitutional provisions afforded "the same kind of freedom to those who would communicate ideas by conduct such as patrolling, marching and picketing on streets and highways" as was provided "to those who communicate ideas by pure speech." In the 1968 case of the *U.S. v. O'Brien,* a ruling that would prove of central importance to the 1989–90 flag desecration controversy, the Court upheld a conviction for burning a draft card to protest the Vietnam War, an action that had been outlawed by Congress in 1965.[49]

Although the 1965 law sought to suppress dissent (as was especially evident because failure to possess a draft card was already illegal and the congressional debate on it was filled with references to draft card burners as filthy beatniks, communist stooges, and traitors), the Court upheld it on the highly dubious grounds that it was designed not to hinder free expression but to foster the effective functioning of the draft. Such a purpose required for its credibility the obviously untrue assumption that the draft administration retained no copies of the information contained on individuals' draft cards. After declaring, "We cannot accept the view that an apparently limitless variety of conduct can be labeled 'speech,'" the Court laid down a test that was to prove extremely vague for determining when conduct could be constitutionally regulated where it was combined with an expressive element. In short, the Court held that restrictions on mixed conduct-expression could be upheld where government regulation of the conduct was within its "constitutional power" and furthered an "important or substantial governmental interest" that was "unrelated to the suppression of free expression" and "if the incidental restriction on alleged First Amendment freedoms is no greater than is essential to the furtherance of that interest."[50]

Translated insofar as possible into ordinary English, the key point in *O'Brien* as it potentially applied to flag desecration was that if the government sought to ban such conduct out of purely suppressive motivations, the First Amendment would likely override such action, whereas, if the government had a nonsuppressive purpose, flag desecration laws would likely survive because the other aspects of the guidelines provided rather low legal hurdles. Much of the controversy over the Court's 1989 *Johnson* ruling would center around the issue of whether the Court had meant to indicate that all flag desecration prosecutions in cases involving political protest were invalid because their only possible purpose was suppressive and thus they were outside the lenient *O'Brien* guidelines, or whether a nonsuppressive motivation could legally rescue an artfully drawn flag desecration law via the *O'Brien* test. As legal scholar Randolph Collins summarized in a 1991 law review article, "As a practical matter, when the more lenient standard in *O'Brien* is applied, the statute is almost always upheld; in contrast when the more exacting scrutiny [applied when the government's motivation in regulating "conduct" is found to be purely suppressive] is used, the statute is usually struck down."[51]

In its 1989–90 flag desecration rulings, the Supreme Court would eventually make crystal clear that all politically expressive flag desecration was protected by the First Amendment because only suppressive motivations could be served by outlawing such conduct. Until then, however, the Court consistently avoided ruling squarely on this issue, and as a result the *O'Brien* decision was regarded as a key precedent for the lower courts in deciding flag desecration cases. *O'Brien*'s vagueness, however, only further muddied the already clouded legal waters: when lower courts applied it to flag desecration cases, they repeatedly ended up with contradictory results because they could not consistently decide what the key *O'Brien* phrase, "unrelated to suppression of free expression," meant. This problem is understandable as the Supreme Court had itself held that the 1965 draft card burning law thus "unrelated" even though suppression of dissent was obviously its clear intent.

While the lower courts puzzled over the meaning of the *O'Brien* ruling, the Supreme Court considered several flag desecration cases between 1969 and 1974, but it invariably avoided addressing the central constitutional issue. The 1969 case of *Street v. New York* involved a New York man, who, in the aftermath of the shooting of civil rights activist James Meredith in 1966, burned a flag to the accompaniment of oral declamations such as, "If they let this happen to Meredith, we don't need an American flag." Street was unquestionably prosecuted for the flag burning rather than for his comments (no one appears to have been charged for verbal flag disrespect alone since World War II). By a 5–4 vote, however, the Court overturned his conviction on the strained grounds that since he had been charged under a provision of the New York law which forbade casting "contempt" upon the flag by "words or acts" and evidence concerning his statements had been introduced at trial, he might have been convicted for his words alone. Any such conviction, in the absence of any evident threat to the peace or incitement to violence, was held to violate the First Amendment because "it is firmly settled that under our Constitution the public expression of ideas may not be prohibited merely because the ideas are themselves offensive to some of their hearers." Relying heavily upon and citing its 1943 *Barnette* flag salute ruling, the Court declared that "'the right to differ as to things that touch the heart of the existing order' encompass[es] the freedom to express publicly one's opinions about the flag, including those opinions which are defiant or contemptuous." The Court avoided addressing the constitutionality of banning physical flag desecration on the grounds that there was no need to decide the case "on a broader basis than the record before us imperatively requires."[52]

Although the *Street* decision evaded the key issue, it did suggest that even physical abuse of the flag that involved the "public expression of ideas" could not be prosecuted simply because the ideas were viewed as "offensive to some."

Therefore, it laid the groundwork for the Court's 1989–90 holdings that verbal and physical attacks on the flag were legally identical forms of symbolic speech; that laws outlawing physical flag desecration were motivated, just as were bans on verbal disrespect, by the desire to forbid perceived "offensive" or disagreeable expression; and that therefore attempts to ban physical flag destruction fell outside the *O'Brien* test and could not withstand First Amendment scrutiny.

Subsequent to *Street,* the Court issued several rulings in non-flag-related cases which it would also later rely on in *Johnson.* For example, in the 1969 case of *Brandenburg v. Ohio,* it held that protecting political expression was so central to democratic values that even advocacy of "the use of force or of law violation" could not be punished "except where such advocacy is directed to inciting or producing imminent lawless action and is likely to incite or produce such action." By 1969, the Court had effectively established that politically related expression could be forbidden only via the inciting "imminent lawless action" *Brandenburg* doctrine or on the grounds that such expression amounted to direct, abusive personal insults which were the equivalent of "fighting words" under the doctrine of a 1942 ruling, *Chaplinsky v. New Hampshire.* Otherwise, the Court's rulings clearly suggested, no political expression could be criminalized, no matter how unpopular or offensive. In the 1971 case of *Cohen v. California,* the Court made a legal point that was to prove highly damaging to the position advocated by many in 1989–90 that physical flag desecration was viscerally offensive in a way that verbal flag disrespect was not and therefore justified special restrictions. In overturning, on First Amendment grounds, a conviction for disturbing the peace against a man who wore a jacket bearing the words "Fuck the Draft," the *Cohen* Court noted, "One man's vulgarity is another man's lyric," and suggested that the "emotive" aspect of speech was just as constitutionally protected as its "cognitive" content, especially because, "practically speaking," the former "may often be the more important element of the overall message sought to be communicated." In the 1970 case of *Schacht v. U.S.,* the Court made clear that laws which discriminated on the basis of content of even symbolic expression could not survive First Amendment scrutiny by striking down on such grounds an obscure law that outlawed the unauthorized use of military uniforms in dramatic productions, but only when such use tended to "discredit" the military.[53]

Aside from *Street,* the Court overturned convictions in the only other two Vietnam-era flag desecration cases in which it issued substantive rulings, but again without directly addressing the validity of state interests in protecting the physical integrity of the flag. In the 1974 case of *Smith v. Goguen,* the conviction of a Massachusetts man for "contemptuously" treating the flag by wearing a flag patch on his trousers was reversed 6-3 on the grounds that the law was unconstitutionally vague. In another 1974 case, *Spence v. Washington,* a conviction for placing a "peace sign" on a flag with removable tape was also reversed by a 6-3 vote, essentially on the grounds that regardless of whether there actually existed any constitutionally valid state interest in "preserving the national flag as an unalloyed symbol of our country," no such interest could have been harmed because Spence did "not permanently disfigure the flag or destroy it."[54]

Although the *Spence* ruling was so narrowly written that it could not be applied directly to other cases, the Court sprinkled the ruling with several observations that later proved highly significant for the 1989–90 flag desecration cases. For example, the Court declared that if Washington State did have an interest in preserving the symbolic value of the flag, such an interest was "related to expression," at least "in the context of activity like that undertaken" by Spence, and therefore his prosecution would be subjected to a higher-level scrutiny than the lenient *O'Brien* test. Although this ruling did not directly address the issue of permanently damaging flags to express political protest, it suggested the position the Court would take in 1989–90 that flag burning was also protected (a conclusion that necessarily followed unless somehow temporarily and permanently altering flags were to be placed in different legal categories). The *Spence* Court "summarily" rejected an argument that had been made by the Washington Supreme Court in upholding Spence's conviction and would be resurrected in 1989–90 by foes of legalizing flag desecration, namely that the availability of alternative means of expression (i.e., written and oral speech) could mitigate depriving would-be flag desecrators of their preference for symbolic speech. Finally, another highly significant point in *Spence* was the Court's announcement of its first real test for determining what constituted symbolic "expression": the Court suggested that such occurred when "an intent to convey a particularized message was present, and in the surrounding circumstances the likelihood was great that the message would be understood by those who viewed it."[55]

Taking *Street, Goguen,* and *Spence* together, it was hard to avoid the conclusion that the Court was reluctant to convict in flag desecration cases. But ultimately the narrow scope of the Court's Vietnam-era flag desecration rulings simply fostered massive legal confusion in the lower courts by refusing squarely to address the First Amendment issue posed by inflicting permanent physical damage to flags for expressive purposes, which was compounded by the vague *O'Brien* test and by the Court's refusal to consider over a dozen other flag desecration cases between 1969 and 1984. For example, the Court refused to accept appeals in seven separate flag burning cases during this fifteen-year period, all but one of which were from convictions upheld by the lower courts.[56]

If the real attitude of the Court majority toward flag desecration laws was obscured by a thick legal haze, the views of a vociferous minority were abundantly clear. For example, Justice William Rehnquist wrote bitter dissents in the *Goguen* and *Spence* cases, which in retrospect can be seen as rehearsals for his impassioned dissent fifteen years later in the *Johnson* ruling. In *Goguen,* Rehnquist argued that the government was entitled to assert a "property interest" that could govern how individuals were allowed to treat even privately owned flags because what individuals purchased "is not merely cloth dyed red, white and blue, but also the one visible manifestation of 200 years of nationhood." In his *Spence* dissent, Rehnquist declared that attempts to protect the "character, not the cloth" of the flag no more impermissibly burdened First Amendment rights than did laws against perjury, libel, copyright infringement, incitement to riot, or "the painting of public buildings."[57]

Among the other dissents, in *Goguen* Justice Harry Blackmun argued that the "contemptuously" provision of the Massachusetts flag law was neither unconstitutionally vague nor aimed at punishing Goguen for any particular expression but simply constitutionally punished him for "harming the physical integrity of the flag by wearing it affixed to the seat of his pants." This suggestion that Blackmun would uphold a flag desecration law that was not targeted at political dissent but sought only to protect the "physical integrity of the flag" in all instances would later play a key role in the 1989–90 flag desecration controversy.[58]

The State Legislative Response
to the Vietnam-Era Flag Desecration Rulings

While judges and legal experts attempted to read the tea leaves of the Supreme Court's decisions and nondecisions, state legislatures in almost twenty states significantly revised their flag desecration statutes between 1970 and 1980. These revisions reflected attempts both to update them (by removing references to the by then massively practiced and never prosecuted use of the flag in advertising) and to overcome constitutional problems that had been suggested by various court rulings (especially those associated with vagueness and overbreadth in the definition of flags and in the conduct that was prohibited, including the near universal provisions outlawing verbal disrespect for the flag).[59]

Ironically, however, at least in retrospect, almost all of these state legislative revisions made their flag desecration laws even less constitutional than before by making more clear that they were aimed directly at suppressing political dissent. They retained bans only on forms of flag usage unambiguously associated with such expression. Thus Missouri's 1980 revised law (which was similar to post-1970 laws passed in another ten or so states and was apparently based on the 1968 federal law) read, in its entirety: "Any person who purposefully and publicly mutilates, defaces, defiles, tramples upon or otherwise desecrates the flag of the United States or the state of Missouri is guilty of the crime of flag desecration." (The great majority of states outlawed desecration of both national and state flags by 1980, and five southern states banned desecration of the Confederate flag.) An additional eight or so states made revisions that were based on the American Law Institute's 1962 Model Penal Code, which had suggested a text largely identical to the revised Delaware law, which read in its entirety: "A person is guilty of desecration if he intentionally defaces, damages, pollutes or otherwise physically mistreats any public monument or structure, any place of worship, the national flag or any other object of veneration by the public or a substantial segment thereof, in a public place and in a way which the actor knows will outrage the sensibilities of persons likely to observe or discover his actions."[60]

One of the states that adopted a revised flag desecration law based on the MPC was Texas, where a 1973 law defined "venerated objects" as including a "state or national flag," along with public monuments and places of worship or burial, and outlawed defacing, damaging, or "otherwise" physically mistreating such objects "in a way that the actor knows will seriously offend one or more persons likely to observe or discover his action." The new Texas law (which reduced the formerly draconian maximum twenty-five-year penalty to a far more typical maximum of one year in jail and a $2,000 fine) was to be invoked against Gregory Lee Johnson for the 1984 Dallas flag burning that would eventually lead to the Supreme Court's 1989 *Johnson* ruling.[61]

The post-1970 flag desecration revisions generally made the state laws more overtly unconstitutional than previously by restricting the banned activities to physical mistreatment of the flag of the sort almost exclusively used by political protesters. They were much more obviously solely intended to target dissent than had previously been the case, thus increasing the prospect that eventually the Supreme Court would find them unconstitutional as outside of the *O'Brien* guidelines. In particular, by explicitly making the offense dependent upon whether people were seriously offended or outraged by viewing or learning about it, the

MPC-based revisions clearly violated the guidelines of the Supreme Court in *Street* and other cases in which the high court had repeatedly made clear that the criminality of expressions with political significance (unlike obscenity) could not be based on such considerations. Furthermore, many of the revisions, and especially the laws like that passed in Texas in 1973 that were based on the MPC, were also even more vague than were the unrevised statutes. This was because they were typically larded with phrases that eliminated any objective definition of exactly what was being criminalized, instead making such matters dependent upon whether the actor "knows" that persons "likely to observe or discover" his action would be offended by it and, in some cases (although not in Texas), upon whether otherwise undefined "substantial" segments of the public venerated the object to begin with.

The Revolutionary Communist Party and Burning the Flag, 1979–1984

Between 1974 and 1979, as American involvement in Vietnam ended and the domestic conflict associated with the war diminished, incidents of flag desecration virtually disappeared. Between 1979 and 1988, there was a renewed spurt of flag desecration incidents, but they received relatively little publicity. In all but a handful of cases, they involved members or supporters of the small Maoist-oriented Revolutionary Communist Party (RCP), a group whose origins dated to the late 1960s. The RCP's dominant figure, "Chairman" Bob Avakian (an appellation modeled after Communist Chinese "Chairman" Mao Tse-tung), stressed during the organization's formative years the "glorious achievements" of the so-called Great Proletarian Cultural Revolution in China during the mid-1960s and early 1970s.[62]

The arrest of the Maoist-backed so-called Gang of Four in China in the mid-1970s and China's abandonment of the Cultural Revolution policies, which in the West were viewed as a chaotic, brutal wave of massive, indiscriminate terrorism and purges directed against all traces of Western influence, provoked turmoil within the RCP. The crisis ended when the RCP attacked the new Chinese government of Deng Xiao Ping as a revisionist "fascist bourgeois dictatorship" that had abandoned true communist ideals and, among other crimes, had decadently reintroduced into China Western classical music, Shakespeare, and Rembrandt. The denunciation of the Deng regime in China led to the loss of about one-third of the RCP's 1977 membership of about two thousand and inaugurated a period of greatly increased public activity in which the RCP identified itself not only with the policies of the Cultural Revolution but also with other political positions that seemed deliberately designed to repel mass public opinion in the United States. The apparent aim was to appeal to deeply alienated urban youth. Thus the RCP supported the Iranian students who seized the American embassy in Teheran in November 1979 and consistently supported the Sendero Luminoso ("Shining Path") guerrilla movement, which by all accounts has responded to brutal poverty and repression in Peru by equally brutal and indiscriminate terrorism.

By the late 1970s, the RCP was advocating violent revolution in the United States and in virtually every other country in the world, although it seems to have limited its concrete activities to oral and written agitation. It also engaged in "propaganda by the deed" incidents, which often ended with arrests and mostly involved petty vandalism, clashes with the police, and flag burnings. In early 1980, for example, five RCP members were convicted of disorderly conduct for mounting a red flag on top of the Alamo in San Antonio, two were arrested for throwing paint at Soviet and American delegates to the United Nations, and about eighty were arrested in connection with fights with police and bystanders during rowdy May Day demonstrations.[63]

Many incidents involving the RCP appear to have been designed to provoke police forces into repressive overreactions that could then become the grist for additional organizing and publicity. The police were generally happy to cooperate with these plans, and though RCP actions were often illegal and sometimes involved violence, they achieved their goal of provoking excessive and sometimes needless reactions from police who were enraged by the party's political views. For example, Los Angeles police broke up a rowdy but peaceful 1983 RCP May Day demonstration, explaining that the party's offenses had included using a bull horn and "various traffic violations, like walking against the light." Perhaps the most bizarre repression directed against the RCP came in Beckley, West Virginia, in March 1980, where police arrested more than a dozen members under the state's long obsolete and clearly unconstitutional (under the Supreme Court's 1931 *Stromberg* ruling) red flag law after an RCP demonstration was attacked by bystanders waving American flags.[64]

Beginning in late 1979, apparently inspired by the widely televised burnings of American flags by the Iranian students who took Americans hostage in Teheran, the RCP's newspaper, *Revolutionary Worker* (*RW*), glorified flag burnings. For example, the February 1, 1980, *RW* published pictures of miniature "flag burning kits," consisting of a pack of matches, a small paper flag, and an RCP button, that had been distributed during a protest in Berkeley on January 26; the paper urged its readers to "burn the flag, then pin it proudly on your chest." Presumably at least partly acting under such inspiration, RCP members were associated with at least eight flag burning incidents in the United States between 1979 and 1984, including the 1984 Dallas flag burning that led to the 1989 *Johnson* Supreme Court case. In five of the eight flag burnings, prosecutions ensued and convictions were originally obtained, but in three incidents, including Johnson's, the convictions were eventually overturned on appeal by federal courts on First Amendment grounds. Except in the Johnson case (which was the only one eventually decided by the Supreme Court), however, by the time the appeals succeeded, those convicted had already served lengthy jail terms. Altogether, in these five cases, almost a dozen people spent a total of about ten years in jail for an "offense" the Supreme Court would declare in the 1989 *Johnson* case was protected by the First Amendment.[65]

In one of the pre-*Johnson* RCP cases in which the convictions were overturned, two people were each sentenced in 1980 to the maximum one year in jail provided by the Georgia state flag desecration law for a 1979 Atlanta flag burning intended to protest American foreign policy in Iran. The Georgia Supreme Court later upheld the conviction, as did a federal district court, but it was reversed in 1984 on First Amendment grounds by the Eleventh Circuit Federal Court of Appeals in *Monroe v. State Court of Fulton County*. In 1985, the same federal appeals court reversed, on the same grounds, the convictions, again under the Georgia law, of seven RCP members resulting from a 1981 Atlanta flag burning incident, but, as in the *Monroe* case, the ruling came too late for the defendants, all of whom had by then served out one-year jail terms.

The contrasting views expressed by the Georgia Supreme Court and by the Eleventh Circuit court in the *Monroe* case provided a preview of the key legal and political arguments that were to follow in the *Johnson* case. In upholding the convictions in 1982, the Georgia Supreme Court conceded that the defendants had intended to "convey a message of displeasure" with American foreign policy, but it held that this did not "necessarily" provide them with First Amendment protections for their action because the people of Georgia and the United States had a "unique and compelling interest in protecting the flag as the symbol of our nation" and because the law's purpose was not to suppress dissent but to ban "deliberate acts of physical destruction and desecration of the flag." The court further argued that the *Monroe* case was different from the 1974 Supreme Court *Spence* case partly because in *Spence* the defendant had not permanently damaged the flag.[66]

In reversing the *Monroe* conviction on August 20, 1984 (two days before Gregory Lee Johnson was arrested for burning a flag in Dallas), a three-judge panel of the Eleventh Circuit federal appeals court unanimously declared that the state law had been unconstitutionally applied. In a ruling largely duplicated by the U.S. Supreme Court five years later in *Johnson,* the *Monroe* appeals court held that the flag burning was presumptively protected by the First Amendment as "expressive" under the *Spence* test and that neither of Georgia's professed interests (the same to be subsequently proffered by Texas in *Johnson*), to protect the symbolic value of the flag and prevent breaches of the peace, were "unrelated to the suppression of free speech" or were "so substantial" as to justify depriving Monroe of her First Amendment rights. Regarding the symbolic value of the flag, the court cited the Supreme Court's 1943 decision in the *Barnette* compulsory flag salute case and asserted that there was "no significant difference" between government attempts to "compel the expression of respect" for the flag and to "prevent the expression of disrespect." The court noted that in the 1969 *Street* case the Supreme Court had held this to be true with regard to state attempts to outlaw verbal disrespect for the flag and argued that "governmental regulation of nonverbal expression should be subject to the same limitations under the first amendment." Regarding breach of the peace, the court held that in *Monroe* the state had failed to demonstrate any "clear and present danger" of the "likelihood and imminence of public unrest," as was required in the Supreme Court's 1969 *Brandenburg* decision, or the sort of "fighting words" direct personal insults invoked in the high court's 1942 *Chaplinsky* ruling.[67]

In the only one of the 1979–84 RCP-associated flag desecration prosecutions that was brought under the 1968 federal law forbidding destructive physical acts which sought to cast "contempt" upon the flag, two RCP members, Teresa Kime and Donald Bonwell, were convicted and sentenced to eight months in jail in 1980 for a flag burning earlier that year outside the federal courthouse in Greensboro, North Carolina. In appealing the convictions, the defendants' lawyers stressed many of the arguments about the First Amendment and the deficiencies of the 1968 federal law which would lead the Supreme Court to strike down the Texas flag desecration law in 1989. For example, in an unsuccessful federal appeals court brief, the defense argued that the federal law was unconstitutional because flag desecration was a form of symbolic expression "akin to pure speech and entitled to First Amendment protection."[68]

In 1989–90 the Supreme Court would endorse this position, but in 1982 such arguments proved unavailing and the Court refused to take the case on appeal. Nevertheless, the Court's October 18, 1982, decision not to grant certiorari in the case, *U.S. v. Kime,* attracted considerable press attention because Justice William Brennan issued an extremely unusual and blistering dissent, which prefigured his opinions for the 1989–90 court majorities that effectively struck down all flag desecration laws. Brennan wrote that the defendants' convictions "violated their First Amendment rights" because the 1968 law disregarded the "vital constitutional principle forbidding government censorship of unpopular political views." He argued that it was evident that the defendants "were making a statement of political protest," and that the government's professed interest in preserving the flag's symbolic value simply amounted to an unconstitutional desire to suppress their dissent. Brennan added that the government's wish to preserve the flag's symbolic value had been held in the 1974 *Spence* Supreme Court case to be "directly related to expression" and that the government had advanced no "interest other than [the suppressive one of] enforcing respect for the flag" on behalf of the 1968 law because it claimed "no esthetic or property interest in protecting a mere aggregation of stripes and stars for its own sake" and asserted no other nonsuppressive interest such as preserving the peace or preventing arson. Brennan maintained, therefore, that, under the Court's 1968 *O'Brien* rule, because the defendants were engaged in expressive conduct and had "impaired no non-speech related governmental interest," the case, and indeed all flag desecration prosecutions, was governed by the 1969 *Street* decision protecting the right to express even "defiant or contemptuous" views about the flag.[69]

Endorsing a key defense argument, Brennan declared that the federal law was "flagrantly unconstitutional on its face" because its "contempt" provision required violators to "intend to engage in political expression—and not just any political expression, but only that espousing a particular, unpopular point of view." This, Brennan declared, made it so "narrowly drawn" that "everything it might possibly prohibit is constitutionally protected expression" because one "literally cannot violate it" without "espousing unpopular political views," a requirement that "constitutes overt content-based censorship, pure and simple," which "goes to the heart of what the First Amendment prohibits."

The 1984 Dallas Flag Burning

The flag burning that led to the Supreme Court's 1989 decision in *Texas v. Johnson* occurred on August 22, 1984, as the climax to a raucous and often disorderly demonstration by about one hundred protesters who marched for two hours through downtown Dallas in 100-degree heat to object to the planned presidential renomination there of Ronald Reagan by the Republican National Convention. The protesters made about ten stops along their march route to deliver anti-Reagan speeches and attempted to enter a variety of Dallas corporate offices to protest their alleged involvement in American foreign policy ventures and other misdeeds such as exploitation of the Third World. During the march, the protesters repeatedly held "die-ins" (in which they fell down to portray the effects of a nuclear war), chanted obscenities such as "Fuck America," overturned newspaper racks, pounded on and spray-painted building walls and windows, uprooted potted plants, and tore up bank deposit slips at buildings along the protest route, and at the Mercantile National Bank pulled down and seized one or more American flags.[70]

Although many of the protesters' acts were clearly illegal and briefly disrupted business at some of the targeted buildings, little serious damage was caused by their vandalism and there were no injuries. Dallas city spokesman Gail Cushing later explained that the large numbers of uniformed and undercover Dallas police who accompanied the march simply looked on and made no arrests during these events because the police "felt they might cause a much more difficult situation to control" if they tried to break up the moving demonstration, especially since "the demonstrators were not injuring anybody." The final destination of the marchers was the Dallas City Hall, two blocks from the Republican convention site, where a group of protesters gathered to form a circle. At approximately 2:15 P.M. an American flag was burned inside the circle. Although bystanders gathered to watch the protest, no disorders accompanied the flag burning, during which some of the protesters spit on the flag and chanted, apparently from a Revolutionary Communist Youth Brigade (RYCB) flyer handed out during the march, "Red, white and blue, we spit on you. You stand for plunder, you will go under." (Other chants on the handout included, "Reagan, [Democratic presidential nominee Walter] Mondale, which will it be? Either one means World War 3," and "1, 2, 3, 4, We don't want your fucking war, 5, 6, 7, 8, Organize to smash the state.")

After the flag burning, many of the protesters jumped into the fountain at the City Hall to cool off, while a passing Korean War veteran named Daniel Walker, angered and disturbed by the flag burning, gathered up remnants of the flag (ironically, he used a copy of the Revolutionary Communist newspaper to collect these remains), which he later buried in his back yard. Walker became something of a local hero after he was widely quoted and pictured in the Dallas media as declaring that the flag burning was a "form of suicide" because "we're all part of society. If you try to destroy it, you destroy yourself." None of the protesters interfered with Walker's activities. At the subsequent trial of Gregory Lee Johnson for burning the flag, Walker explained that although he knew that the approved means of disposing of a soiled flag was to burn it, he buried the remnants because "I didn't feel that I should reincinerate it again, you know because it had already been burned once."

Approximately thirty minutes after the flag burning, a large number of Dallas police surrounded the remaining demonstrators at City Hall (many of whom were still in the fountain) and, without any resistance other than occasional curses and chants, arrested almost one hundred people in a procedure that consumed well over an hour. The original charge in all cases was "disorderly conduct," a Class C misdemeanor carrying a $200 fine. The August 22 protest received a modest degree of national publicity, although more for the disorderly nature of the demonstration than for the flag burning. For example, the August 23 *New York Times* carried a short account of the protest on page 26, accompanied by the picture of an unidentified man being arrested. This man, later identified as Gregory Lee Johnson, was formally charged at about 5 P.M. on August 22 with "disorderly conduct," for "using abusive, obscene language in a public place causing a crowd to gather."

The disorderly conduct charges were soon dropped, but new charges were placed against Johnson and seven other protesters, who were apparently the only demonstrators against whom the police had individual grounds for charging illegal conduct. Testimony by witnesses for both the defense and the prosecution at Johnson's trial clearly indicated that some of those originally arrested had had nothing to do with the protest but were simply rounded up along with the demonstrators. In a 1990 interview, Dallas assistant district attorney Michael Gillett, who was chief of the misdemeanor division in 1984 and who personally prosecuted Johnson for flag desecration, explained, "Those that were committing offenses that the police could identify were filed on, and those that the police couldn't identify weren't filed on."

Four of the protesters were charged with felony criminal mischief in connection with incidents of vandalism, while the other four were charged with the Class A misdemeanor offense of "desecration of a venerated object" in connection with the City Hall flag burning, dragging the flag on the ground before the burning, and a virtually unnoticed second flag burning that had occurred during the march outside the Neiman-Marcus department store. According to Dallas police records and information provided by Gillett in 1990, of the four persons charged with flag desecration, two failed to appear for trial and forfeited bonds, and a third, Matthew Michael Dodt, age twenty-seven, of Austin, pled guilty on July 29, 1986, in connection with the Neiman-Marcus flag burning and was given a ten-day jail term. Gregory Lee Johnson eventually became famous above all because, of the four persons charged with flag desecration in connection with the August 22, 1984, Dallas protest, he alone chose to show up for trial and to fight the charge— eventually all of the way to the Supreme Court.

According to information provided by Johnson in a 1990 interview, he was born in 1956 in Richmond, Indiana. Among the factors he cited as having "shaped or pushed me in the direction of a revolutionary way out of this system" were the jailing of his father for theft when he was two years old and being exposed first to American racism and later to anti–Vietnam War sentiment within the military when he lived on army bases in the South and in West Germany after his mother remarried a soldier. According to Johnson, "I owe a lot of my thinking to a whole generation of radical GIs who went against the masters of war." After returning to the United States in 1971, Johnson related, he decided he was "for revolution and not for reform," having read a book by a black militant that he found in his Tampa, Florida, high school library. When he came into contact with the RCYB (the RCP's youth wing) shortly thereafter, he felt as though "I'd been looking my whole life for something like that."

After spending some time in the merchant marine, Johnson returned to Tampa in 1976 and became increasingly involved with the RCYB. According to a Tampa newspaper, he was arrested in Tampa almost twenty times during protests. His 1984 Dallas trial record indicates that after moving to Atlanta in 1980, Johnson was arrested and convicted about half a dozen times in Atlanta between 1981 and 1984 on relatively minor charges such as "refusal to disperse" and trespassing, for which he received a total of about $200 in fines and served nine months in jail. In a 1990 interview, Johnson's Dallas ACLU attorney Douglas Skemp characterized Johnson as a "real rabble rouser" and a "national protester for a long time" who "never backs away, goes to court, when he gets time [in jail], he doesn't run."

In his 1990 interview, Johnson said he quickly developed "enormous respect" for the RCYB because "they were revolutionary" and favored "actively preparing" to "bring down the system," ultimately through armed "war between two sections of the people." Johnson explained that the RCYB sees the American flag as "representing an imperialist system which dominates and exploits large sections of the world" and whose "crimes committed against the people of the world exceeded even what the Nazis were capable of." According to Johnson, American "wars of aggression" and Central Intelligence Agency–organized revolts have led to "six million" deaths. Therefore, he continued, the RCYB "welcomes every defeat that the U.S. suffers in the world," such as the Iranian holding of American hostages, and seeks to use such events "to hasten the day when we can actually bring down the empire."

In the 1990 interview, Johnson denied "actually igniting" the flag that was burned in Dallas in 1984, but when asked if he had poured lighter fluid on it, he responded, "Those who say don't know, those who know don't say, but I didn't actually ignite it." Nonetheless, he defended flag burning as a symbol of "total rejection of the system," which is a "powerful political statement" that speaks with "international communicability, it crosses language barriers." According to Johnson, the power of flag burning was demonstrated by how "relentlessly and feverishly" the government sought to suppress it, as well as by the fact that whenever people around the world "rise up and want to a make a statement of strong hatred and contempt for U.S. imperialism and the capitalist regimes that back up brutal dictatorships, they burn the flag."

In response to a question suggesting that flag burning alienated people, Johnson argued, "You cannot bring about any radical change, any real fucking change, any revolutionary change, without bringing forth a radical right-wing reaction." He added, "You can be overwhelmed with the majority of Americans, that's always used to bludgeon you down, anytime you begin to raise your head, they go, 'The majority thinks another way,' and you're supposed to go, 'Oooh, oooh, I guess I'm weird.' The majority of people at one time supported the Vietnam war or slavery, or McCarthyism or the incarceration of Japanese-Americans [during World War II], but that was wrong and it's a good thing that people had the courage to persevere and fight for people to see that it was wrong." The key issue involved in the flag burning controversy, Johnson argued, was "forced patriotism" reflecting government attempts to "bind people together" in preparation for "new acts of aggression internationally."

CHAPTER 2

THE TEXAS TRIALS OF GREGORY LEE JOHNSON, 1984–1988

*The 1984 Dallas Flag Burning Trial
of Gregory Lee Johnson*

The disorderly conduct charge originally lodged against Johnson was quickly dropped, but he was formally charged at 2:18 A.M. on August 23, 1984, with violating Texas's law forbidding the desecration of "venerated objects." The law outlawed intentional or knowing action that defaced, damaged, or otherwise physically mistreated "a state or national flag" in a manner "that the actor knows will seriously offend one or more persons likely to observe or discover his action." Johnson was released on August 24 on a $200 cash bond. After several postponements (partly because he suffered a broken nose during an apparent altercation in San Francisco in early November), his case, given the docket number MA8446013-H/J, came to trial in Dallas on December 10, 1984. The presiding officer was Dallas County Criminal Court judge John C. Hendrik, a native-born (in 1945) Dallasite long involved in Republican politics, who had worked short spells as a Bible and a Fuller Brush salesman before graduating from the University of Texas Law School in 1971 and spending nine years in private practice before first being elected to his judgeship in 1980. Representing Dallas was Assistant District Attorney Michael Gillett, then head of the misdemeanors division and later promoted to chief felony prosecutor. Gillett, a graduate of the University of Texas Law School and a Dallas prosecutor since 1973, notes on his vita that he has "obtained in excess of 100 life sentences," including ten life sentences each for a notorious Dallas rapist and for a repeat bank robber. Johnson was defended without charge by Dallas ACLU attorneys Stanley Weinberg (then president of the Dallas

ACLU chapter) and Douglas Skemp. Weinberg, then fifty-five years old and the
lead attorney, grew up in the Bronx and attended law school at Southern Methodist
University in Dallas. Skemp was born in 1950 and received a law degree from
Baylor University in Waco, Texas, in 1975.[1]

Johnson's fate was put in the hands of a six-person jury (the standard jury in
Texas for misdemeanors), which found him guilty on December 13 after four days
of testimony and deliberating for about two hours. After hearing additional arguments and testimony, the same jury set Johnson's punishment a few hours later at
the maximum possible of one year in jail and a $2,000 fine, without probation,
following additional deliberations taking about thirty minutes under Texas's so-
called "bifurcated" procedure in which penalties are assessed separately from the
determination of guilt or innocence.[2]

Although, aside from a brief item reporting his sentence in the December 15,
1984, *New York Times,* Johnson's trial and conviction were ignored by the national
media, it was something of a cause célèbre in Dallas and received heavy coverage
in the local press, which Johnson clearly relished. He distributed press releases
and held several news conferences in the courthouse corridors when the trial was
in recess and frequently engaged visitors, including high school students who attended the trial during field trips, in political debates. For example, in a press release he handed out over the signature of the RCYB when his trial began on
December 10, Johnson declared that he was innocent of the flag burning charge
but that he fully supported all the events of the August 22 protest and that it was
"great to see the American flag go up in flames, a symbol of international plunder
and murder reduced to ashes." Dallas officials were out for "blatant revenge" and
"want to make an example of me," Johnson told reporters during the trial.

In a 1990 interview, Skemp recalled that Johnson "loved every minute" of the
attention he received and wouldn't have "missed this for all the money in the
world." Weinberg remembered, also when interviewed in 1990, "class after class
after class [of high school students] coming up there" until "there wasn't enough
room in the courtroom" and "daily coverage, newspapers, TV, radio, there was a
lot of attention paid to it." Weinberg recalled feeling that by politicizing the trial,
Johnson risked not only getting convicted but "bopped into the maximum sentence," but he added that Johnson "was carrying himself pretty well" during the
corridor debates and that, in any case, "nothing I'm going to do could control him
if that's what he wants to do."

Perhaps the most remarkable aspect of Johnson's trial, which fills more than
eight hundred transcribed pages, was that only a tiny portion of it focused on
whether he actually burned an American flag at the Dallas City Hall plaza on

August 22, 1984, and that the evidence concerning Johnson's role in the flag burning was weak, strongly contested, and largely circumstantial. The vast majority of the evidence introduced by Dallas prosecutors focused on the rowdy and disorderly nature of the August 22 demonstration in general and on Johnson's alleged leadership role in the demonstration. Although prosecutor Gillett maintained that Johnson had personally burned the flag, he also argued in a pretrial hearing that throughout the march Johnson was "there and part of it and verbally encouraging it and participating in it," and that therefore, even if events occurred during the protest, "that the Defendant physically himself did not do," such as "spray painting the walls," because he was present "our theory is that by his conduct and participation that he would be responsible for acts of co-conspirators and was acting as a party by aiding and encouraging this type of conduct." This argument was based on Texas's so-called law of parties, which, as Judge Hendrik charged the jury in the *Johnson* case, holds that "a person is criminally responsible for an offense committed by the conduct of another if, acting with intent to promote or assist the commission of the offense, he solicits, encourages, directs, aids or attempts to aid the other person to commit the offense." Johnson himself did not testify during the guilt-innocence phase of the trial. He pled not guilty, however, and explicitly denied burning the flag during a five-minute closing argument which Judge Hendrik allowed him to deliver to the jury in the first phase of trial, as well as in direct testimony during the trial's penalty phase.

The major witnesses for the prosecution were two Dallas vice squad officers, Terri Stover and Ronald Tucker, who infiltrated the August 22 protest as undercover agents, dressed in blue jeans and tennis shoes in an attempt to "blend in" with the demonstrators. Almost all of their testimony was about the disorderly nature of the protest. They both testified that they viewed Johnson as one of the leaders of the demonstration, based, for example, on Stover's recollection of seeing him using a megaphone and on both of their recollections that Johnson had frequently engaged in what appeared to be a leadership role in "talking," "yelling," and "chanting" remarks such as "Fuck you, America" and "screw everybody." But neither Stover nor Tucker claimed to have clearly observed Johnson either encouraging or participating in any demonstrably illegal or destructive activities before the march reached the Dallas City Hall; in fact, Stover repeatedly stated that as far as she could tell all such activities appeared to have been "spontaneous" and not planned or arranged. For the period before the march reached the City Hall, the only specific information they proffered about Johnson was that after an American flag was stolen from the Mercantile Bank, by persons other than Johnson, that he had been given the flag and had stuck it under his shirt; Stover added that she had once observed him banging with his fists on a window at the Diamond Shamrock building and had also seen him participating in a "die-in" at the Southwestern Bell building, during which he "rolled on his back and was shooting the finger with both hands saying 'Fuck America.'"

Stover testified that she did not see who burned the flag at City Hall. Tucker testified that from a distance of five feet away he had clearly observed Johnson burn the flag with a cigarette lighter after dousing it with lighter fluid. Both Tucker and Stover declared that they had been "seriously" offended by the flag burning. Tucker maintained that he would "not hardly" ever forget Johnson because he had never seen an American flag burned before except "on television in Iran." The only testimony that supported Tucker's identification of Johnson was offered by a prosecution rebuttal witness, Evelyn Olsovsky, a Dallas city security guard, who said that she saw Johnson burn the flag from her vantage point inside City Hall. Her account was almost completely lacking in credibility, however, because only hours before she appeared on the stand Gillett told the court (outside the presence of the jury) that in interviews she had indicated that "she couldn't identify anyone" and in her courtroom testimony she depicted Johnson burning the flag more or less "out in the open" and "all by himself," which conflicted with testimony by all other witnesses for both sides, who declared that the flag burner was surrounded and cut off from view by a large circle of protesters.

Two defense witnesses testified unequivocally that Johnson, who had short, dark hair on the day of the protest, could not have been the flag burner because they both saw, from a short distance away, the flag burned by a person with long, blond hair. No photographic evidence was produced showing who had burned the flag, although several photos were produced by the defense which seemed to show Johnson standing on the outside of the circle within which the flag was supposedly burning. The photographer was uncertain exactly when the flag was burned in relationship to the pictures, however, and they were ultimately inconclusive.

Aside from stressing Johnson's alleged leadership role in the protest, the prosecution took every opportunity to highlight his obviously radical political views and affiliations and to appeal to the jury's sense of patriotism. Johnson fully cooperated with Gillett's endeavor to paint him as an antipatriotic communist extremist, making clear in his courtroom statements that he viewed America's self-proclaimed devotion to democratic principles as a hypocritical smoke screen. This was proved, he told the jury, by the very fact of his trial for engaging in a "very powerful act of symbolic speech." In addition, Johnson wore to court every day a T-shirt emblazoned with the words "Revolutionary Communist Youth Brigade" and bearing a depiction of a man carrying a rifle. Gillett leaped upon this attire with enthusiasm, drawing the attention of witnesses and the jury to Johnson's T-shirt on at least six different occasions and once even asking Johnson to "move out your hands, please," so that his shirt could be more easily viewed. In urging the jury to give Johnson the maximum sentence, Gillett asked them to ponder what "this man with a gun on his chest" might have done had Daniel Walker physically attempted to stop the flag burning.

Whether or not Johnson actually burned the flag, the weakness of the prosecution case against him and the well-known extraordinarily conservative political climate in Dallas make it difficult to avoid the conclusion that Johnson was convicted largely because the prosecution successfully associated him with radical political views in general and more specifically with the entirety of the August 22 protest disorders. For this reason, Johnson probably lost his case even before the trial began, when, over the vigorous and repeated objections of his attorneys ("We were objecting like hell," Weinberg recalled in 1990), Judge Hendrik agreed to allow introduction of testimony and evidence, including police and television videotapes, concerning the entire protest march. Although Johnson was not personally shown to have engaged in most of the activities portrayed, the videotapes, which were played repeatedly during the trial, depicted bizarrely dressed protesters engaged in spray painting, window pounding, and "die-ins." One brief shot showed Johnson making obscene gestures with his hands.

The videotapes apparently were especially damaging to Johnson: The jury asked to see them once more during their consideration of Johnson's guilt or innocence, and during a 1990 interview, six years after the trial, juryman Rex Skelton (the only juror who agreed to an interview) volunteered that "what really influenced everyone the most was the [video]tapes." Skelton said that although he "personally didn't have any doubt" that Johnson was involved in the flag burning, "what really ruined" Johnson was the pictures of "the physical destruction of the properties that the group was doing." He added that even though "that was not the issue, when they're sitting there ripping things apart, that's what set everybody [i.e., the jurors] wrong." In a 1990 interview, Judge Hendrik agreed that the videotapes had "a big impact" and "made most people pretty upset" because they were "pretty incendiary, if you pardon the pun." Ironically, even Gillett conceded that the videotapes were inconclusive on the subject of Johnson's guilt; he noted during pretrial proceedings, in response to Judge Hendrik's comment that after viewing the tapes the defense might decide to plead guilty, that he did not think that "these pictures are quite that good, judge."

When Johnson took the stand to plead for probation during the penalty phase of the trial, Gillett concentrated almost exclusively on bringing out Johnson's political radicalism, declaring at one point, "There's something real dangerous about you, isn't there?" Asked if he had chanted, "Fuck you America," during the protest, Johnson said that he had but declared that such remarks were not directed at "average people" but instead at the "multi-death corporations" who "carry out plunder and corporate rape of the third world, and they were directed at the U.S. government, which is a utensil or an apparatus to assist in that." At one point Johnson said, "I'm not going to stand up here and say, 'America Number One,' which is what you want to hear and I think it's disgusting." After listening to Johnson explain his views, Gillett repeatedly suggested that if Johnson did not "like the way it's [the country is] run, why don't you just leave," and he asked (revealing his lack of knowledge about the RCP, which regarded the Soviet Union as a betrayal of communism), why "you just don't move to Russia?" Johnson responded that the Soviet Union was not "any sort of society that people in the world who are striving for a future without oppression should look to," especially because, like the United States, it was stockpiling nuclear weapons. In a stinging response to Gillett that Johnson's lawyer Doug Skemp repeated almost verbatim with obvious amusement in an interview conducted six years after the trial, Johnson declared, "The people here blindly and obediently follow and look brightly into the mushroom clouds and march off and I suspect if you were in the Soviet Union you would be guilty of doing the same thing, blindly following the government in the Soviet Union. I'm asking people here today to not do that."

When Gillett asked Johnson "what the rifle up in the air on your shirt" represented, Johnson replied, "revolution," which would "take weapons" because although he did not advocate "individual violence," a situation would eventually "arise where millions of people will be confronted with the alternative of either fighting in a third world war" or else fighting to "overthrow the system that exists." Johnson repeatedly complained during Gillett's questioning that he was being tried not on the false charge of burning the flag but for being "unpatriotic" and for his "overall political beliefs," including rejecting interpreting the Constitution to mean "that you can protest just as long as you bow down before the American flag." The real message of the trial, Johnson suggested, was to tell "anyone that has unpatriotic beliefs to keep them to yourself" and to brand him a "thought criminal."

Although Johnson seems to have gone out of his way to make his political views an issue in the trial, his claim that his politics was his real "offense" was supported by the closing appeals to the jury by Gillett and another prosecuting attorney, Randy Kucera, which were filled with appeals to the jury's patriotism and references to Johnson's radicalism. In his closing argument during the guilt-innocence phase of the trial, Kucera referred to the information "flashed across the defendant's chest [on his T-shirt]," and declared that Johnson was the "leader" and the "instigator" of a "group of anarchists" who had sought to frustrate the effort of patriotic citizens of Dallas to make their city "sparkle in the national limelight" of the Republican convention. Referring to trial testimony that Johnson had chanted, "Fuck you. Fuck America," Kucera told the jury, "it's you he's talking about." Terming the flag burning the protesters' "little holocaust," Kucera declared, "thank God for people like Daniel Walker," who had the courage to "stand up" amid this "disrespect for our flag" and "this chanting of 'Red, white and blue, spit on you,' as they spat on it, stomped on it as it burned there on the ground."

Gillett's closing arguments were spiced with similar rhetoric. During his closing argument on the guilt or innocence phase of the trial, Gillett declared that his time had come to "defend the colors of our country" because the flag Daniel Walker had buried in his back yard "between two tall oak trees" could not speak, and "I'm going to speak for it." At one point Gillett exclaimed, "You know what's fantastic, watching a baby being born, not our flag being burned." Gillett stressed that although the prosecution believed that Johnson had personally burned the flag, Johnson was "guilty as sin as far as the law of parties is concerned," given the evidence concerning his leadership role in the protest, including "the shirt, who he is, the chanting, the yelling, the encouragement, the having the [mega]phone, being there, wanting this to happen, there is no question he encouraged it at all."

During his closing argument in the penalty phase of the trial, Gillett urged the jury to give Johnson the maximum punishment of a year in jail and a $2,000 fine because he had "offended the nation" and was "creating a lot of danger for a lot of people by what he does and the way he thinks." By destroying a symbol that "is the last thing given to a grieving mother or a wife from the top of the coffin" and whose red stripes were "symbolic of the units and units of blood" shed to defend it, Gillett declared, Johnson had committed a deed that was "serious" and "offensive" as "far as every American is concerned and when you go back into the jury room you represent each and every one of them and don't forget it." He told the jury that even if "you can't change [Johnson's] thinking," they needed to make clear that if anyone in Dallas burned the flag "that represents the things we love," the jurors should respond with "the full force" of the law and deliver the "message" to Johnson and "others like him, 'No more. We won't have it.'"

Although the overwhelming focus of Johnson's trial was on the events of August 22, 1984, Judge Hendrik and the lawyers for both sides understood that if Johnson were convicted, any subsequent appeals would move away from the particulars of the case and focus on the constitutionality of prohibiting flag desecration to express political protest. Both during pretrial proceedings and the trial itself, the defense lawyers unsuccessfully sought to have Judge Hendrik stop the prosecution on the grounds that the Texas "venerated objects" law posed an unconstitutional threat to freedom of speech. This argument was designed to establish the groundwork for subsequent appeals, however, because trial court judges rarely, if ever, attempt to establish fundamental constitutional precedents. Moreover, the U.S. Supreme Court had repeatedly avoided the fundamental constitutional issue involved in flag desecration laws, and in the 1972 *Deeds* case, the Texas Court of Criminal Appeals, the state's highest judicial authority, had upheld such laws based on the state's interests in promoting patriotism and preventing breaches of the peace. That defense arguments concerning the alleged unconstitutionality of the Texas law were destined largely for the eyes of future appeals court judges was made especially clear when, in response to Gillett's complaint that he could not "hear anything that's going on" while Weinberg was urging that Hendrik strike down the law, Hendrik said, "It's not going to make any difference. It's for the record."

Despite Hendrik's no doubt expected refusal to halt the trial on constitutional grounds, Johnson's lawyers, both to build a record for later appeals and in hopes of finding a sympathetic response from jurors, stressed that, though Johnson had not, in fact, burned the flag on August 22 beyond any "reasonable doubt," the flag burning had been intended to express a political point of view and therefore was protected by the First Amendment. For example, in his opening remarks, Weinberg declared, "There are two defendants in this case: Mr. Johnson and the First Amendment." Gillett objected to this remark on the grounds that Johnson was the only defendant, but Hendrik overruled him because "counsel is speaking rhetorically" and "everyone knows" that only "one human being" was on trial.

Once Hendrik had allowed the introduction of general testimony about the August 22 protest, over vigorous defense objections, Johnson's lawyers and defense witnesses stressed the political protest aspects of the march. This approach contrasted with the picture Tucker and Stover had presented of essentially mindless anarchy, marked by occasional speeches, which, according to Tucker, had consisted of "just mainly profanity." To make the point that Dallas authorities objected primarily to Johnson's political views and did not impartially enforce Texas's law banning the "desecration" of any "national" flag when such desecration would create "serious offense" among observers, Johnson's attorneys brought out uncontested evidence from witnesses for both sides that during the Republican convention an Iranian flag was also burned and that this incident set off physical clashes between different groups of Iranian protesters, but that Dallas police on the scene had taken no action. In his closing remarks during the guilt-innocence phase of the trial, Weinberg argued that the failure of police to arrest anyone for burning the Iranian flag suggested that the authorities were trying to establish "what's approved as far as speech and symbolic speech and expression" were concerned and "what is not," and "Lord help us all if that's the position we're in." Weinberg declared that the First Amendment protected even "nasty speech" and "symbolic action" that speaks "louder" than words and that therefore an acquittal would demonstrate not only "reasonable doubt" about Johnson's guilt but that "the First Amendment is alive and well in Dallas."

During interviews conducted in April 1990, shortly before the Supreme Court was to hold oral hearings on the constitutionality of the 1989 law passed by Congress in an attempt to circumvent its 1989 decision overturning Johnson's 1984 Dallas conviction, Judge Hendrik and the three main lawyers in the case retained both strong memories of the trial conducted six years earlier and strong feelings about the issue involved. Hendrik, at forty-four an extremely friendly, gregarious, and strikingly young-looking man, talked about the case in his chambers, which were decorated with classic illustrations by French caricaturist Honoré Daumier lampooning lawyers and judges. He recalled thinking that the case would "very likely" get into the federal courts, although not to the Supreme Court, because" except maybe for *Roe v. Wade* [the 1973 ruling legalizing abortion] this is probably the only misdemeanor in the history of Dallas County to get to the Supreme Court."

Although Hendrik did not express an opinion as to whether Johnson had personally burned the flag, he said that "there wasn't any question" that Johnson had been "aiding, abetting or encouraging" the flag burning and therefore was clearly guilty under the Texas law of parties. Hendrik related that Johnson impressed him as "pretty serious" and "fairly committed" in his testimony rather than "an exhibitionist" who was "just playing games," as had been his first impression. He added that Johnson's tale of seeing his father jailed at a young age and "hearing a little bit about his background made me understand that's why he might not be in love with the American system." Hendrik elaborated: "All things considered, I thought that Johnson won the 'debate'" with prosecutor Gillett during the punishment phase of the trial because "he knew his position better than Mr. Gillett knew his" and because Gillett resorted to the "tired and worn out cliché" of suggesting that Johnson leave the country if he didn't like it. Had the sentencing been up to him, Hendrik indicated that he would have given both a lower fine and a slightly lesser jail term than the maximum penalty handed out by the jury.

Hendrik reported that his impression, based on Johnson's T-shirt and general demeanor, was that Johnson would have been "very disappointed" if he had been acquitted because his attitude was that "he couldn't get a fair trial, that the whole system stinks and he had no chance." Hendrik said he did not think the T-shirt made any difference because just sticking to "the facts of case" was enough to "appeal to the community's feelings." "Anyone doing the same thing would have been found guilty" and would receive "close to the maximum [penalty] from any average Dallas County jury," given the "very staunchly conservative" nature of Dallas political attitudes. Hendrik indicated that he had never seriously considered declaring the Texas venerated objects law unconstitutional because the case Johnson's lawyers presented for doing so was only a "50/50 proposition" and trial court judges are generally "a little hesitant to declare a state law unconstitutional" unless the authority was "clear." Hendrik added that, in all candor, "there's no doubt" that "any judge who's elected [as are all judges in Texas] would have to think long and hard" before declaring a flag desecration law unconstitutional. Hendrik said that he "personally had no problem at all" with the law because the flag was a "special symbol" and a country that "won't stand up for itself and defend its symbols" is saying "that our country's not worth defending, that our values are not worth protecting." Hendrik conceded that there were "elements of expression" in flag desecration, but he maintained that outlawing such behavior would not "be a significant limitation on free speech" because "people can express their ideas and opinions without burning the flag" and because flag burning was an "extremely violent, very provocative" attempt to "cause trouble" and to "show the utmost disrespect for the American system" that "is pretty close to treason, a modified form of treason."

During Johnson's 1984 trial in Dallas, prosecutor Gillett told the jury that he "would probably get" emotional about the case, and it was clear that he still felt as strongly about it in an interview six years later. When asked if the continuing uproar over the flag desecration issue in mid-1990 had become "blown all out of proportion" to its real significance, Gillett responded, "I think if you ask the surviving family members of every person who has been lost in a war defending the rights of this country, they're going to tell you that it is important." He added, "I don't think it's going to end until the law, either through statute or constitutional amendment, prohibits the burning of the flag" and "it wouldn't bother me in the least to have a constitutional amendment."

As chief of the misdemeanors division in 1984, Gillett related, he supervised about fifty employees and about fifty thousand cases a year, and he viewed the Johnson affair as a "major case and as I result I chose to try it myself." Gillett described the march that preceded the flag burning as "kind of like a bunch of termites tearing up everything in their way" and termed the City Hall flag burning "not speech" but "conduct." Even if it was "considered speech," he added, it was no more constitutionally protected or worthwhile than going "into a theater and hollering fire" or "lewd comments made to a woman in a public place," especially because flag burning "went toward breaches of the peace." Even "an expression of an idea," Gillett argued, must be "balanced against" a public right to "order, decency, and morality," and if the "majority doesn't have the right to legislate against that," he asked, didn't that violate "what this country is about?" Gillett agreed that he "obviously" retained "pretty strong feeling" about flag desecration and added that he believed that "most Americans would feel the same way I feel, and that is, if you don't like the country, you know, pack your bags."

Johnson's lead attorney, Stanley Weinberg, in recalling the case in 1990, said, "I doubt if I'll ever get a case again involving as important an issue." Weinberg summed up his legal strategy as the "age-old" defense posture that "#1 the statute was not good and he had every right to do this thing, but #2 he didn't do it." The Texas venerated objects law was "bad on its face" because of the vagueness of the "serious offense" clause, Weinberg said; for example, "if the Ayatollah [Khomeini of Iran] had read about the Iranian flag being burned in Dallas and took serious offense at that then he could have insisted that a criminal charge be brought." Alternatively, Weinberg suggested, if a flag was burned in a deserted forest region, whether an offense had been committed might depend on whether there was a "forest ranger up on top of a mountain fifty-five miles away with a high-powered telescope, ever watchful for puffs of smoke in the forest, who saw a puff of smoke and happened to see what he thought was a flag."

As to Johnson's guilt, Weinberg argued that Dallas "had nothing really to prosecute" him on, especially because, despite media and police undercover taping of the protest, the tapes showed only a "bunch of extraneous things because nobody saw Johnson take part in any activity of damaging property," and "there isn't a bit of film of the burning of the flag." Weinberg seconded Hendrik's view that "Johnson bested Gillett" because his demeanor was "cooler than Gillett," and Johnson could "make points back that Gillett, in the fervor of getting after the guy, couldn't respond to." Weinberg characterized Gillett as "forceful," "outraged," and engaging in the kind of "typical overkill" that Dallas prosecutors were "notorious" for in an attempt to get an "emotional response" from the jury. He lamented that though the defense had taken the posture of "Come on folks, this is the fundamental bedrock principle of our government," it was "outrage which apparently carried the day, which is no surprise in Dallas."

Weinberg recalled that his relations with Johnson were frequently strained because Johnson ignored his advice to not wear the RCYB T-shirt and wanted to generally politicize the case both in the courtroom and the corridors, while

Weinberg was trying to put together a purely legal case which Johnson could win. Further, Weinberg related, Johnson frequently tried to direct his own defense; at one point during the trial, Weinberg recalled, he became so aggravated at Johnson that "I just flat turned around and told him, 'Shut the fuck up and sit down,' and Johnson looked at me and said, 'Mr. Weinberg, I'm exercising my First Amendment rights.'" Weinberg added that after that incident, Johnson "shut up and let me try the case" and that "Johnson is not really that unlikable once you get rid of the theatrics and the rhetoric."

In a 1990 interview, Johnson's second attorney, Doug Skemp, recalled Johnson as "quite effective" as a witness, especially in suggesting that Gillett would have been a loyal policeman even in a totalitarian regime ("It's so true. If you look at Gillett he'd be a patriot wherever he was born"). Skemp conceded, however, that "the jury didn't seem to care." Skemp added that he felt Gillett truly was "deeply upset" and "incensed" about the flag burning and was "a real law and order kind of guy," who will "never make any contributions to the ACLU." Gillett wanted to "make a real issue" of the incident because "it's very dear to him." Skemp termed Hendrik a "real conservative Republican, which most judges in this county are," but also a "real nice guy," who "tries to be nice to everybody" and presided over a "real fair trial as he always does," even though "his personal feelings are that he doesn't like those flag burners." Hendrik gave him the impression, in fact, that "he wanted it to go up [on appeal] and see what was going to happen with it."

Skemp recalled Johnson as a "pretty cynical guy" who was "out for every bit of publicity he could get" and was holding press conferences "right in the middle of the trial," even "during the bathroom breaks," but he also remembered him as having "genuine feelings about the way a country ought to be run." "I'm not going to say he wanted publicity personally for himself, I give him the benefit of the doubt and would say he wanted it for the issue." According to Skemp, Johnson saw the prosecution as a "no-lose situation" because "if the government put him in jail, all that he has been saying is true, we're just as totalitarian as the next country." If he was acquitted, "he's going to shake some people up and maybe make this country a better place." Like Weinberg, Skemp recalled "quite a little friction" with Johnson, but, he wryly noted, he and Weinberg "never got a dime" for their legal work in the case and "Johnson wanted us, I guess, because he didn't have anybody else who was going to do it for our price."

Skemp said that flag burning "upsets me a lot, it really hurts me," but "there's only one thing that hurts me more, to send someone to jail for doing it. The test of whether you have free speech is whether you can swallow the very offensive dissent. When you sit there and start putting restrictions on it, then to me that destroys the flag as a national symbol and not one kook out there on the street burning the flag." The attempt to overturn the Supreme Court decision in the *Johnson* case, Skemp lamented, threatened to prove "Gregory Johnson's right, that we are a repressive country like every other country, and we kind of play into his hands," while "we prove Gregory Johnson wrong by letting him do what we did."

The Johnson *Case in the* Texas Appeals Courts, 1985–1988

Although the fundamental constitutional issues raised by Johnson's prosecution were relatively minor and formal sideshows during his December 1984 Dallas trial, they moved to the fore during the five years of subsequent litigation, which culminated in the 1989 Supreme Court decision that Texas had unconstitutionally prosecuted him. Johnson was allowed to go free on a $750 cash appeal bond posted about a week after his December 13, 1984, conviction. Weinberg and Skemp immediately made preparations to appeal his case to the Court of Appeals for the Fifth Texas Supreme Judicial District, a right of appeal automatically granted to all persons convicted in Texas of criminal charges.

Following the formal notification by the Court of Appeals on May 8, 1985, that the case would be considered, Skemp and Weinberg filed their appeal brief in what was now titled *Johnson v. Texas*, case 05-85-00318-CR, on July 8, 1985. Subsequently they filed a supplemental brief on October 2, 1985, to clarify matters brought out in oral argument before the appeals court on September 26. Setting the tone for the remaining four years of litigation, their brief maintained that Johnson had been prosecuted in violation of the First Amendment and of the free speech clause of the Texas constitution because the flag burning "occurred as a symbol" during a "political protest demonstration." They argued that the flag burning clearly met the test of "expression" set out by the Supreme Court in the 1974 *Spence* flag desecration case because it was intended to "convey a particularized message" of dissatisfaction with the Reagan administration's policies and "because the flag was burned in a period of recognized protest activity, involving speeches, parades, picketing and even street theater." During the Republican convention "the likelihood that the message would be seen and understood by those who viewed it and heard about it was great." The brief relied heavily on the decision handed down a year earlier by the Eleventh Federal Circuit Court of Appeals in the *Monroe* case, in which a Georgia flag burning conviction had been overturned on First Amendment grounds. Additionally citing the 1969 Supreme Court ruling in *Street,* which struck down flag desecration laws that forbade verbal criticism of the flag, as well as other Supreme Court "symbolic speech" cases such as *Stromberg* (1931) and *Barnette* (1943), the brief argued that similar restrictions should be placed on government attempts to regulate "nonverbal expression."[3]

In addition to the brief's free speech argument, Weinberg and Skemp argued that Texas's law was especially flawed because it was unconstitutionally vague, because the "serious offense" provision failed to give adequate notice of what conduct was forbidden and thus encouraged "arbitrary and erratic arrests and convictions," and because it was unconstitutionally "overbroad" by forbidding constitutionally protected as well as unprotected activity. They also argued that Johnson's prosecution could not be upheld on grounds of maintaining the peace because no evidence had been introduced to suggest that the flag burning had incited or threatened to incite disorders. They further maintained that Johnson's case had been prejudiced by the admission of highly damaging evidence about the disruptive and illegal conduct of other persons even though "the record clearly reflects that Appellant was not personally involved in this activity" and "never encouraged, promoted or assisted the illegal activities" of others. Additionally, the brief argued that under Judge Hendrik's charge concerning the law of parties, the jury might have convicted Johnson solely for constitutionally protected verbal statements that it interpreted as encouraging the flag burning, a conviction that allegedly would have violated the Supreme Court's 1969 ruling in *Street.*

Dallas responded to the defense arguments with a brief filed in September 1985 that was authored by John D. Nation, the deputy head of the appellate division of the Dallas district attorney's office. Nation, a 1979 graduate of Bates College of Law (University of Houston), who had worked as a staff attorney in the Texas appellate courts and for the Dallas County district attorney before being appointed to his supervisory position in 1984, was the second in command of a division with slightly under twenty attorneys and in that capacity decided which attorney would handle cases reaching his office on appeal. In a 1990 interview, Nation, who left the district attorney's office for private practice in 1987, explained that as deputy in the appellate division he rated all cases on a "legal difficulty" scale of one to six; he recalled that because the *Johnson* case rated near the top of the scale at "about a five" and because the case was of considerable public interest and involved constitutional law, in which he had recently been specializing, he assigned it to himself, a step he typically took in less than twenty cases annually out of a total of about five to seven hundred cases. Nation recalled, "I knew from the day I took it that this was going to be in the Supreme Court one way or another."

Nation conceded that the Texas law was "inartfully" and "unfortunately drawn," and "that was always the part that worried me" because "you knew that a good lawyer like Stan [Weinberg] would make the most of it." Nation seemed less than convinced that Johnson had personally burned the flag, suggesting that he was "prosecuted probably because he was the most visible person" in the protest. Unlike Mike Gillett and Kathi Drew, the two Dallas prosecutors who, respectively, handled the *Johnson* case before and after he did, Nation made clear that he thought that flag burning was a form of expression rather than conduct. From the very beginning, Nation said, he took the position that "there isn't any point in denying the obvious, it's a politically motivated free speech issue" but that "there's a limit past which you cannot go and Johnson went past that limit. My position was that he could do anything he wanted to up to burning the flag," including taping another symbol over the flag as Spence did in the 1974 Supreme Court case, or "singing those funky chants," but "burning the flag is sort of the ultimate" and "at that point whatever contribution to the public good that is made by his particular statement is outweighed by the potential damage and the incremental damage it could cause."

According to Nation, "The government's interest in preserving a sort of bundle of sticks are [*sic*] the rights of everybody, which is partially preserving the flag as a symbol of national unity and partially sort of preserving the fundamental values of the country and to some extent preventing breaches of the peace." Nation made clear that his fundamental concern was that tolerating physical destruction of flags could, over a long period of time, damage American national unity and hamper a united response to some future crisis. He explained, "I never took the position that Mr. Johnson was going to bring the government crumbling to its knees. He probably causes more Republican votes than anything else." Rather, Nation continued, he viewed the harm as "incremental" because "if you allowed obvious and repeated acts of destruction of our ultimate symbol, you're going to incrementally destroy whatever it is that keeps us together," and "you will definitely have a big problem if you should need national unity" in some "emergency" in the future.

Just as the main thrust of the defense brief foretold the defense arguments during four subsequent years of litigation, Nation's response laid down the major lines of argument to be taken for the following four years by Dallas. Nation relied heavily on the leading Texas flag desecration case, the 1971 decision of Texas's highest court upholding a flag burning conviction in *Deeds v. State* and also on the case of *State v. Farrell,* in which the Iowa Supreme Court had upheld a flag burning conviction in 1974 and the U.S. Supreme Court had refused to consider the case on appeal in 1975. Accepting "for purposes of argument that the communicative aspects of appellant's conduct give rise to First Amendment protections," the brief argued that nonetheless the state had two "major interests" which provided reasons "sufficiently substantial to justify limitations" on Johnson's First Amendment rights, namely "prevention of breaches of the peace and protection of the flag as a symbol of national unity."[4]

With reference to the need to outlaw flag desecration to maintain the peace, Nation argued that there was "ample evidence" presented in Johnson's trial concerning a "potentially explosive" situation created by the flag burning, including the "sizable crowd" gathered at City Hall. Because people were chanting and spitting on the flag, the situation could have led to an "immediate physical reaction from people opposed" to the destruction of the flag. The brief contended that the need to preserve the flag as a symbol of national unity was centered on the "nation's concern with self perpetuation and self preservation," an interest that could be done "great harm" by tolerating public acts of flag desecration. Such acts would weaken the flag's "effectiveness" in serving "as a rallying point for the people's support of our country in time of peace and war" and providing "a visible representation of the stability and strength of our country." Additionally, Nation argued, the country had the right to keep the flag "above ideology" by protecting this "central symbol of our national unity" from being "appropriated by either side in the particular context of their political ideology" (an argument which, of course, assumed that "patriotic" uses of the flag were ideologically neutral). Furthermore, Nation contended that the country had a "substantial interest" in "preserving each person's sense of national identity, as represented by the flag," because "the emotions of the people of this country are integrally linked" to the flag and thus its destruction would "attack" those emotions and represent an "assault on a person's sense of national identity" and "unity with his country."

Nation denied that the "serious offense" provision made the law unconstitutionally vague because its application did "not depend on a vague notion of the sensibilities of persons likely to observe the actor's conduct," which would make even a "relatively innocent touching" or merely "reckless or negligent handling of the flag" punishable "if this conduct offended an observer." Instead, the brief maintained, the Texas law punished only "those acts of physical abuse of the flag which the actor knows are likely to seriously offend potential observers," such as "intentional and knowing" or "flagrant abuse of the flag" "designed" to "seriously offend" the "shared norms that society holds relative to treatment of the flag." The brief did not explain how every Texan could be expected to know what these norms were, especially if he did not share them, nor did it explain how flag desecrators could know if acts performed solely before a crowd of sympathizers would violate the "shared norms" of other people. While conceding that Johnson "was not seen committing any of the various acts of vandalism" reported during the August 22, 1984, protest, the brief brushed aside the law of parties issue and the introduction of evidence about illegal actions committed by others by arguing that "the State's evidence, which was obviously believed by the jury, showed that Appellant burned the flag himself" and that "the overall theory of the State's case was that" Johnson "committed the offense acting alone."

On September 26, 1985, a three-judge panel of the thirteen-member Court of Appeals for the Fifth Supreme Judicial District of Texas (Dallas), one of fourteen such appeals courts in Texas, heard oral arguments on Johnson's appeal. Each side was allocated twenty minutes, with an additional ten minutes allotted to Johnson's lawyers for rebuttal. Weinberg, Skemp, and Nation all recalled in 1990 interviews that their arguments proceeded virtually without interruption. The only remark from the bench that they recalled came in response to defense arguments that the vagueness of the "serious offense" provision of the Texas law was evident from the fact that, although it applied to the desecration of all "national" flags, Dallas police made no arrests even after the burning of an Iranian flag during the 1984 Republican convention sparked scuffling between different groups of Iranian demonstrators; presiding Judge John Vance reportedly replied to this point along the lines of "Well, maybe no one was offended."

Weinberg recalled in 1990 feeling that the lack of questions or comments from the bench reflected "minds closed" because "they were going to rule in favor of the state." Skemp, his colleague, recalled similarly concluding from the silence from the bench, which he termed "really not normal at all," that "they didn't want to hear this, they were not going to get into any kind of argument with these kooky civil liberties lawyers." Nation recalled interpreting the silence differently, as simply reflecting the judges' wishes not to interfere with the presentation of the cases because they "knew we had a lot of ground to cover," but he added that "the Dallas Court [of Appeals] is pretty conservative on crime issues, so they didn't have a prayer of winning in that forum."

On January 23, 1986, Judge Vance surprised nobody by issuing a unanimous opinion upholding Johnson's conviction as well as every position in Nation's brief. The heart of the decision was Vance's conclusion that although Johnson's flag burning did constitute "symbolic speech" and thus qualified as a form of "constitutionally-protected free speech" under the U.S. Supreme Court's 1974 *Spence* test, Texas's interests in "preventing breaches of the peace" and protecting "the flag as a symbol of national unity" were "substantial" enough to "justify infringement of Johnson's constitutional rights." Citing the 1971 decision of the Texas Court of Criminal Appeals in the *Deeds* case, Vance (who had presided over the original trial of Deeds) held that acts of flag desecration were "of themselves, so inflammatory" that Texas could forbid them, even without any showing of "objective evidence of imminent public unrest" and that the state also had a "legitimate and substantial interest in protecting the flag as a symbol of national unity."[5]

The Court of Appeals essentially followed Nation's brief in brushing aside the less fundamental defense complaints. Thus the court made no direct reference to the "serious offense" provision of the venerated objects law but rejected complaints that it was vague and overbroad because the statute "in no way" outlawed "legitimate protest activities" and in any case flag burning would "clearly constitute desecration" under it. The law of parties issue was similarly rejected because the court held that the state's case and the evidence adequately demonstrated Johnson's "guilt as a sole actor." The introduction of evidence concerning the illegal actions of other parties, including the videotapes (which the appeals court viewed), were held to be relevant as "establishing the context of the offense" but not "inherently prejudicial" to Johnson.

On February 25, 1986, the Dallas Court of Appeals denied, without any written explanation, a request for a rehearing in a brief filed by Weinberg and Skemp on February 7, 1986. The rehearing request was based on the contention that the Dallas Court of Appeals had erred in literally every sentence of its decision by rejecting all of the defense arguments. While restating all of their previous arguments, Johnson's lawyers stressed what was clearly the weakest point in the Court of Appeals decision, namely that the court had conceded that in principle Johnson's flag burning was an exercise of "constitutionally-protected free speech," yet in practice had concluded that such expression was always illegal because it inherently threatened both the public peace (an assumption denied in the brief with reference to the August 22, 1984, burning) and the symbolic value of the flag. "The Court swallows its own reasoning" on this point, the brief argued, because it simultaneously defines the same conduct as both "constitutionally protected" and a "per se violation of law. The Court can not have it both ways." In 1990 interviews, both Weinberg and Skemp recalled the court's concession that flag burning was "symbolic speech" as a major long-run victory despite their short-run defeat. Weinberg said that he was surprised that "Vance went as far as he did" on this point because he "set the downfall of the prosecution by conceding it was a speech issue. I read that and said, 'That's it, we're going up [on appeal] because I don't see how this is going to stand up.' I told Johnson we've gotten quite a bit of a way there." Skemp recalled similarly feeling that the court's ruling was hopelessly illogical because "they said on the one hand this is protected speech and on the other hand made an exception that engulfed that whole area of speech," thereby creating "an exception that is larger than the rule itself."[6]

With regard to other points in the Court of Appeals ruling, the defense rehearing brief argued that the vagueness of the "serious offense" provision made it impossible for a protester to know "when the exercise of his protected right violates the law" and that it also fostered "arbitrary and erratic arrests and convictions." Johnson's lawyers cited the failure of the police to arrest anyone for the burning of the Iranian flag, despite the simultaneous outbreaks of "physical assaults and insults before" their "very eyes" and Vance's comment at oral argument that "maybe no one was offended" by the burning as further evidence that "the statute is void for being vague."

Following the rejection by the Court of Appeals of their motion for a rehearing, on March 26, 1986, Weinberg and Skemp filed a petition for discretionary review (PDR) requesting that the Texas Court of Criminal Appeals, the highest state court for criminal cases, hear the case (although all persons convicted of crimes in Texas are entitled to an appeal before the intermediate courts of appeals, the Court of Criminal Appeals, like the United States Supreme Court, has discretion as to which cases it will hear). The PDR brief was essentially a restatement of the brief unsuccessfully requesting a rehearing in the Court of Appeals, again stressing the basic constitutional issues and the alleged deficiencies of the wording of the Texas law but also restating all the arguments made in the original briefs filed before the Court of Appeals. Thus Weinberg and Skemp argued that the Court of Appeals's reasoning had upheld a statute that prohibited activity which it simultaneously "recognizes as protected by the Constitution" and by its reasoning had created a "constitutionally protected act that is a per se violation of law." They further argued that by relying on the 1971 *Deeds* case to hold that in flag desecration cases there was an inevitable threat to the public peace and to the state's interest in protecting the symbolism of the flag which inherently overrode any claimed First Amendment rights, the Court of Appeals had "incorrectly applied" the subsequent 1974 Supreme Court decision in *Spence*. *Spence*, they argued, had made clear that when the flag was used for expressive purposes the state bore the burden of justifying restrictions on First Amendment rights by demonstrating a "substantial" particular harm to state interests in the context of its use. In the 1984 *Monroe* case, the brief argued, the *Spence* test had been appropriately and persuasively applied to hold that in the context of a flag burning during a political protest, Georgia's flag desecration law, "quite similar" to that of Texas, was "unconstitutional as applied to the protester."[7]

On March 11, 1987, almost a year after Johnson's PDR was filed, the Texas Court of Criminal Appeals agreed to hear Johnson's appeal (now given the docket number 0372-86). It largely restricted consideration to the fundamental constitutionality of the Texas venerated objects law, both facially and as applied to

Johnson. The court declined to consider almost all other issues raised by the defense, including those concerning the law of parties and the introduction of evidence about illegal conduct committed by persons other than Johnson. In a 1990 interview, Court of Criminal Appeals judge Charles Campbell, who authored the court's 1988 decision overturning Johnson's conviction on First Amendment grounds, explained that at least four of the nine judges must agree to allow the court to grant a PDR. Campbell indicated that his court grants only about 10 percent of the twelve to fourteen hundred yearly PDR petitions presented to it each year but that the *Johnson* case was likely to be heard because the court was particularly prone to review cases involving "issues of constitutional magnitude," and "it obviously involved the First Amendment. We don't get a lot of those. That was the primary thing, and then, of course, the statute under which Johnson was prosecuted obviously is not one of those, burglary or theft or murder, that's being used every day." Campbell suggested that the grant of PDR did not necessarily indicate that at least four criminal appeals judges disagreed with Vance's opinion. Rather, "because it was a constitutional issue and specifically because it was a First Amendment issue I think you're going to find that appellate judges enjoy looking into First Amendment issues and researching and writing about them, so there is an interest separate and apart from all other considerations about why you grant review."

On April 9, 1987, Weinberg and Skemp filed their brief with the Court of Criminal Appeals, repeating their previously unsuccessful arguments before the Court of Appeals. They again argued that the lower court had illogically proclaimed the Dallas flag burning to be a "constitutionally protected exercise of symbolic speech" yet also a "per se violation of law," because it "incorrectly" relied on the assertedly outdated 1971 *Deeds* case and "incorrectly" applied the principles of the 1974 Supreme Court *Spence* case to the record. They also reiterated that the Eleventh Federal Circuit Court of Appeals in the 1984 *Monroe* case had properly applied the *Spence* principles to hold that a flag burning performed in a context of a political demonstration that, like the Dallas incident, did not threaten an imminent breach of the peace and therefore could not constitutionally be prosecuted because there was no state interest, including protecting the flag's symbolic value, sufficient to justify infringing on First Amendment rights. The failure of Dallas police to arrest anyone for the burning of the Iranian flag was again cited as evidence that the "serious offense" provision of the Texas law made it unconstitutionally vague because the statute failed to "put one sufficiently on notice as to that which is proscribed" and made violations of the law not dependent "on the relevant acts alone," a point the brief declared the Court of Appeals "conveniently ignores." Johnson's lawyers also again argued that the "serious offense" provision was so vague that the practical result was to give the police "an unconstitutional scope of discretion in the application of the law, and to hand the direction of that discretion over to the receiver of the communication," who might be offended.[8]

On June 1, 1987, the Texas Court of Criminal Appeals received a response to Johnson's brief from the Dallas district attorney's office, which was officially filed, as always, under the name of the Dallas County district attorney, John Vance, who, in a bizarre twist, had been elected to that post shortly after writing the Court of Appeals decision upholding Johnson's conviction. This placed Vance in the highly unusual position of officially seeking, as an executive branch officer, to have Texas's highest criminal court uphold a decision he had himself written as a member of the judiciary. (Moreover, Vance had presided over the *Deeds* trial, which in turn had led to the 1971 Texas Court of Criminal Appeals decision upholding the Texas flag desecration law, which he had relied upon to uphold Johnson's conviction as a Court of Appeals judge. Vance declined to be interviewed for this book and failed to respond to letters posing written questions.)

Although Vance's name was on the brief, the real work in preparing it was performed by Assistant District Attorney Kathi Drew, who had just been named to replace John Nation (who had departed for private practice) as deputy chief of the appellate division. Drew held a 1977 law degree from Southern Methodist University (SMU) and began working for the Dallas district attorney's office in 1981, after several years as a research and briefing attorney for several Texas courts; she had long been active in Republican politics, for example, serving as president of SMU and Dallas Young Republicans, and was named several times as "Woman of the Year" by the National Young Republicans.

In a lengthy 1990 interview, Drew recalled being unable to understand why the Court of Criminal Appeals granted PDR in the *Johnson* case "because I felt with *Deeds* there was nothing to be decided. I couldn't imagine the Court ruling in favor of Johnson." Drew made clear that she had absolutely no doubts about the wisdom or validity of the Texas venerated objects law, although she recalled feeling hindered in making her defense of the law because she took over the case "sort of by right of inheritance." In replacing Nation, she simultaneously took over his "job, his office, his salary and his caseload." This "inheritance" came at almost exactly the same time the Criminal Appeals Court granted PDR, which meant that Drew, who had never before handled a First Amendment case, had only a couple of months to file her first brief before that court on a case that she had previously known nothing about. Drew added, however, "I really feel that under the circumstances that I did the best job I could do with it," and "if I were sitting down today to write this brief it would not be that different."

Drew indicated that, unlike Nation (although like Gillett), she personally did not view flag desecration as expression but as "conduct," partly because, in her view, flag burning did not meet the 1974 Supreme Court *Spence* test of conveying a "particularized message." Thus Gregory Johnson, she argued, was "expressing his contempt for just about everything" but not delivering a specific message. Drew lamented, however, that she felt "very angry" that she could not argue this position because she was "hampered" by the Court of Appeals decision (and later by the Criminal Appeals Court), which clearly labeled such acts as "expression." Thus, she related, in arguing before the criminal appeals court and later before the Supreme Court, her hands were "really kind of tied" because "after a great deal of soul searching and an incredible amount of advice," she concluded that the higher courts were "very unlikely to back off" on this point.

Speaking of the "serious offense" language of the Texas law, which the Supreme Court was later to point to as dooming the statute, Drew explained in 1990 that when she took on the *Johnson* case she was not "anywhere near as uncomfortable with that provision as a lot of other people seemed to be." Although "I would have hoped they [state legislators] would have chosen better language," that did not "lend itself so easily" to appearing to ban flag destruction only when it cast "contempt," she explained that she interpreted that wording as "simply the legislature's way" of indicating that the law was intended to ban public acts of "serious physical desecration" of the flag but not "to criminalize an act in somebody's basement that is out of public view." The "serious offense" language was mistakenly viewed as troublesome, Drew argued, only by those who made the incorrect although admittedly "ingrained" assumption that flag desecration is "communication," whereas in fact Texas was not seeking to "prevent communication" but to "prevent a public act with potential for a breach of the peace."

In explaining her general views on the flag and the doctrine of symbolic speech, Drew declared, "I just find it very difficult to believe that the First Amendment was done to protect a destructive act, even if you accept that it is an act with expressive content. It seems to me that this is the first time that this doctrine has been extended to something that is actually destructive in nature and I see it as really quantitatively different than any other type of symbolic speech that's protected." Asked if she would outlaw banning destruction of other symbols, such as burning copies of the Constitution or smashing models of the Alamo, however, she demurred. "The flag is simply different from anything else, it is unique" and "you simply cannot make an adequate analogy, and believe me,

I've been trying." The flag is a "special" and "unique entity," Drew declared, which "really belongs to the nation as a whole" and therefore deserved protection even if an "extra category" of law, created if necessary by a constitutional amendment, was required.

Asked what damage to the flag's symbolic value was caused by an act of flag burning, Drew responded, "The act of burning a single flag is not inconsequential" because "anytime you have a symbol, the symbol's viability only lasts as long as it remains untarnished and the symbol can lose its meaning over a period of time through neglect, through abuse, through acts of destruction." Oral criticism of the flag could be tolerated but physical destruction could not, she maintained, "because it's not going to cause the same symbolic damage." She related, "One of my children said, 'Mom, if you burn a flag you don't have any more freedom because there's nothing to show that we're free.' It's really kind of true because this stands for everything I believe in."

The brief Drew filed on June 1, 1987, with the Texas Court of Criminal Appeals (officially under Vance's name) argued that the Dallas Court of Appeals decision (authored by Vance) had been correct in every particular. The brief rejected Johnson's challenge to the "serious offense" provision of the Texas venerated objects law by repeating the argument previously successfully made before the Court of Appeals that the law's meaning was clear in that it only forbade acts of "flagrant" flag desecration that were knowingly "designed" to offend society's "shared norms" with regard to flag etiquette and that its meaning therefore did not depend upon the desecrator's "assessment of the sensibilities of those who observe" his actions. The brief noted that the same court now considering Johnson's appeal had ruled in the 1971 *Deeds* case that public flag burning "constitutes the type of hard-core conduct which would be prohibited under any construction which we might give the statute." Concerning whether the state had interests that justified restricting constitutional rights, the brief quoted directly from the Court of Appeals decision for over four pages and endorsed that court's position that maintaining the peace and protecting the symbolic value of the flag constituted sufficient such interests.[9]

The *Spence* case was rejected as determining the outcome of the *Johnson* case on the grounds that Spence had displayed a flag with a removable peace symbol taped onto it from the window of his home for a short time and thus, unlike Johnson, had neither permanently damaged the flag nor used it amid an excited crowd of people in a public place. Similarly, the *Monroe* case was rejected as not controlling because it was a federal circuit court opinion not binding on the Texas courts; because Johnson's act posed a clear likelihood of public unrest lacking in

Monroe; and because the *Monroe* opinion was lacking in "force and logic" by relying on the 1943 Supreme Court *Barnette* case, which forbade compelling people to show respect for the flag unwillingly and therefore improperly confounded compulsory flag salute laws with laws that did not require any coerced behavior but only outlawed acts of flag desecration. "Requiring a person to refrain from wantonly destroying the flag is not the same as compelling respect for the flag," Dallas argued.

With regard to Texas's right to protect the "effectiveness of the flag as a symbol revered by the vast majority of Americans," the brief cited *Deeds* and other court decisions at length to restate the argument that Nation had earlier successfully advanced before the Court of Appeals. Concerning the state's interest in banning flag desecration as a means of protecting the peace, the brief declared that even if evidence "demonstrating imminence of a breach of the peace" was required to justify restricting Johnson's rights on such grounds, the trial record showed "ample evidence" of a "potentially explosive" situation, including the presence of a "gang of protesters" who had attracted a "sizable crowd" at the Dallas City Hall and the burning of a flag "during a time of increased public attention and presence."

On September 16, 1987, the Texas Civil Liberties Union (TCLU) filed an "amicus" or "friend of the court" brief with the criminal appeals court on Johnson's behalf, which was written by TCLU attorney Kerry McGrath. The TCLU brief appears to have significantly influenced the decision of the Texas court and ultimately the U.S. Supreme Court that Johnson had been unconstitutionally prosecuted, especially in its stress on the practical importance of symbolic protest and on the implications of allowing the government to determine how symbols could or could not be used. The brief presciently declared that the case would likely "define and shape the boundaries of free expression in this country" and declared that the *Monroe* court had properly held that the First Amendment protected the right to express "defiant or contemptuous opinions about the flag," including symbolic expressions of such opinions through acts such as flag burning. McGrath's brief added that "especially in this era of electronic media and journalism," symbolic action was often far more effective than "mere words" and that in practice "symbolic activity for a thirty-second news spot has become a more effective message than a thirty-page treatise."[10]

McGrath supported Johnson's argument that there was no evidence indicating that the Dallas flag burning or flag burnings in general threatened to create a disturbance of the peace and suggested instead that the state was "simply" and unconstitutionally punishing Johnson because it found his views "offensive." The brief rejected Dallas's contention that Johnson had engaged in an "assault on the marketplace of ideas," instead contending that he was participating in that marketplace, "albeit more crudely than the state would prefer," while it was Dallas that was "assaulting that marketplace" by seeking to punish Johnson for his political expression. The heart of the TCLU brief, which was later echoed in the decisions of the Texas Court of Criminal Appeals and the U.S. Supreme Court, was the argument that since the state punished "only critical use of the flag," while tolerating and encouraging flag usage for "patriotic or popular purposes," flag desecration laws effectively established an officially approved form of political discourse from which its citizens could not dissent and created a precedent with an unlimited potential for a subsequent legal "slippery slope" toward government regulation of expression. The brief declared:

> The State would have this court decree that a potent and highly visible symbol of this country and its government cannot be used to express dissenting or unpopular ideas. A holding that certain symbols could not be used to express critical ideas would undermine the foundation of our constitutional guarantee of free expression. If the flag can be withdrawn from public discourse, other symbols can be similarly withdrawn. There is no principled way to distinguish between certain symbols that the state may control and other symbols placed beyond its control by the constitution. This Court can draw the line in only one place: peaceful expression of opinion, whether by symbols or otherwise, may not be suppressed.

In a 1990 interview, TCLU legal director James Harrington explained his organization's intervention in the case by declaring that even though flag burning was "asinine" and politically "counterproductive," in the context of the Dallas flag burning it was also "pure, pure protest and that's what America's about even if you may not think that's the way to do it." He added, "To me, it's just classic symbolic speech, just a textbook case. Burning the flag is a way of expressing political protest in a nonviolent, nonthreatening way. To me, it's almost ultimately what the First Amendment is about." Asked to respond to arguments that flag burning threatened national unity, Harrington responded, "If that's true, it doesn't say much about the symbol or about our national unity if it's so easily torn asunder. I can't believe that the country is that weak, but it's not the flag that holds us together, it's the Constitution and the principle of liberty that's in it." Harrington declared that a country that tolerated "only certain forms of political expression" will have "lost the Constitution." Harrington added that he understood from personal experience the strong feeling that flag burning aroused: "When my folks found out that I was involved in this case, it was a terrible experience. I thought they were never going to talk to me again in my life."

On September 16, 1987, oral arguments on the *Johnson* appeal were heard by the Texas Court of Criminal Appeals. In a 1990 interview, Weinberg recalled that he began his presentation by declaring that the prosecution was "a classic case of 'If you don't like the message, kill the messenger. The state is trying to kill the messenger.'" Skemp recalled an incident during Drew's presentation, when she quoted the court's opinion in the *Deeds* case to back up her argument and then responded that *Deeds* dated from 1971, when Judge Sam Houston Clinton, a well-known liberal and former ACLU lawyer, asked her, "When was the *Deeds* case decided anyway?" As Skemp remembered what he clearly regarded as a devastating retort from Clinton, "He just looked at her, there's these nine judges and they are all sitting up high, he just looked up and down, looked at everybody and said, 'I sure hope we've done a little growing up since then.'" Drew also remembered the incident and, noting Clinton's ACLU background, added, "I wasn't the least surprised by his particular views." Otherwise, she recalled of the oral argument, "I had no indication that the Court would reverse in this case."

On April 20, 1988, the Texas Court of Criminal Appeals handed down a stunning decision, which by a 5–4 vote declared that the Texas venerated objects law had been unconstitutionally used to prosecute Johnson by violating his First Amendment right to engage in peaceful symbolic political protest. Rejecting its own earlier analysis in *Deeds* as inadequate because of subsequent Supreme Court decisions, notably the 1974 *Spence* case, Texas's highest criminal court agreed with the Court of Appeals that Johnson had engaged in "symbolic speech" presumptively protected by the First Amendment but rejected the lower court's conclusion that Texas's interests were compelling enough to justify overriding Johnson's constitutional rights. With regard to Dallas's asserted need to outlaw flag desecration to preserve the peace, the court held that the Texas law was "too broad for First Amendment purposes" to be used properly for that reason in the case at hand (and, by implication, in general) because by banning all flag desecration that caused merely "serious offense," it outlawed "protected conduct which has no propensity to result in breaches of the peace." The court specifically found, in a direct rejection of Dallas's claims, that although the *Johnson* trial testimony revealed that the flag burning had caused "serious offense," "there was no breach of peace" or any "potentially explosive" situation. In a footnote that suggested that Dallas was not enforcing the venerated objects law in an evenhanded manner, the court pointed out that although a "physical brawl" had erupted when the Iranian flag was burned during the same period as the Johnson flag burning, no arrests had been effected even though the law specifically applied to the desecration of any "national flag."[11]

Relying heavily on the 1943 Supreme Court compulsory flag salute case of *West Virginia Board of Education v. Barnette,* the court also clearly rejected Texas's claimed interest in preserving the flag as a symbol of unity as not adequate to justify the compromising of Johnson's First Amendment rights. The court quoted extensively from *Barnette,* including its key phrase: "If there is any fixed star in our constitutional constellation, it is that no official, high or petty, can prescribe what shall be orthodox in politics, nationalism, religion or other matters of opinion or force citizens to confess by word or act their faith therein." The court built on this argument and also appears to have been heavily influenced by the TCLU brief in constructing the heart of its analysis:

> Recognizing that the right to differ is the centerpiece of our First Amendment freedoms, a government cannot mandate by fiat a feeling of unity in its citizens. Therefore, that very same government cannot carve out a symbol of unity and prescribe a set of approved messages to be associated with that symbol when it cannot mandate the status or feeling the symbol purports to represent. If the state has a legitimate interest in promoting a State approved symbol of unity, that interest is not so compelling as to essentially license the flag's use for only the promotion of the governmental status quo.

The court further declared, citing *Barnette*, that for Texas to override Johnson's First Amendment rights in furtherance of its interest in promoting national unity it would have to demonstrate that Johnson's action posed a "grave and immediate danger" that the flag would lose its ability to "rouse feelings of unity or patriotism" and become devalued "into a meaningless piece of cloth." "We do not believe such a danger is present," the court concluded, and therefore declared that the venerated objects law was unconstitutional when "used to punish acts of flag desecration when such conduct falls within the protections of the First Amendment." The court declined to address the question of whether Texas could prosecute flag desecration that did "not constitute speech under the First Amendment" and therefore declined to respond to Johnson's urging that the statute be found facially invalid on grounds of vagueness, declaring instead that "our holding that the statute is unconstitutional as applied to this appellant renders a facial determination unnecessary." Having overturned Johnson's conviction on the basis of the First Amendment to the federal Constitution, the court did not address whether the

venerated objects law also violated the free speech provision of the Texas constitution (Article 1, Section 8).

In a 1990 interview, Stanley Weinberg, Johnson's lawyer, reported that
sources close to the court told him that the court did not address the question of the
constitutionality of the law under the Texas constitution so as to reserve the right to
strike it down on such grounds if the Supreme Court overruled its decision on federal constitutionality (the Supreme Court cannot overrule decisions of state courts
concerning interpretations of state constitutions). Separate court sources indicated
that a majority was also available to declare the entire law *facially* unconstitutional
on First Amendment grounds, rather than merely as *applied* to political protesters,
but that the narrower ruling was ultimately issued in hope of attracting the vote of a
sixth judge, who eventually voted against even the narrower ruling.

Opposing the decision of the five-man Court of Criminal Appeals majority
(Judges Charles Campbell, Sam Houston Clinton, Bill White, M. P. "Rusty"
Duncan, and Marvin Teague) were presiding Judge John Onion and Judges W. C.
Davis, Michael McCormick, and Charles Miller. Only Miller wrote a substantial
dissent, arguing that the 1971 criminal appeals decision in *Deeds* was "viable and
highly persuasive" in support of the "valid state interest of preserving the flag as a
symbol of national unity," which "supersedes whatever first amendment right"
Johnson sought to assert.[12]

The Aftermath to the Texas Court
of Criminal Appeals Ruling

Virtually everyone associated with the *Johnson* case was shocked at the Texas
Court of Criminal Appeals ruling because that court was almost universally regarded within the Texas legal community as highly conservative and because two
of the judges in the majority, Campbell, and, above all, White, were former elected
district attorneys who were viewed as especially conservative. Thus in 1990 interviews, Drew termed the court "extremely conservative" and recalled being "flab-
bergasted" and unable to come up with any explanation for the ruling, while
Nation said he was "very surprised" at the decision, which was "very much
unlike" the court's track record. Weinberg remembered counting on only Judges
Clinton, Teague, and Duncan, all of whom had formerly been defense lawyers. It
"just surprised the heck out of me" that White was among the majority, he added,
noting that he was also "surprised at who wrote it" because, to understate the case,
"I would not classify Campbell as being a firebrand." Even Judge Hendrik, who

differed with the court's ruling, expressed admiration for its courage, declaring that he was "quite a bit surprised" at the decision, which "took a bit of political courage" and "had to increase my respect" for the court.

In a lengthy 1990 interview on a hot spring day in the Texas Court of Criminal Appeals conference room in Austin, Judge Campbell, attired in shorts and a T-shirt, spoke at length about the *Johnson* case. Explaining that the writing of opinions for the Court of Criminal Appeals is assigned at random by drawing "little plastic balls" with numbers on them, even before the majority position of the court is established, he declared, "I'm the lucky fellow who drew Gregory Johnson." Campbell related that after reading the briefs and hearing oral argument he was not completely decided about the case; however, he continued, after asking his assistant, Charles Stanfield, to research the legal issues and precedents involved and discussing the case with Stanfield and another staff aide, it was "crystal clear" that Johnson's conviction had to be overturned, and it "didn't seem like a tremendously difficult issue to address."

Campbell indicated that the Supreme Court rulings in the 1974 cases of *Goguen,* overturning on grounds of vagueness a conviction for "contemptuously" wearing a rear-end flag patch, and (especially) *Spence,* overturning a conviction for superimposing a peace sign on the flag, played a particularly important role in his thinking because they were "pretty clear" precedents. "It just was not that different from the peace symbol on the flag or the flag sown on the seat of the pants," he argued. Although the Supreme Court had not specifically decided any case "where there had been complete destruction of the flag," Campbell continued, "there was no way to distinguish it, unless you just wanted to make up some kind of magical distinction without a difference."

Campbell also stressed the 1943 Supreme Court *Barnette* ruling outlawing compulsory school flag salutes to bolster his contention that "Supreme Court precedent in this area was crystal clear, and to write it in any other way was just to completely ignore precedent with everything the Supreme Court has ever said about the First Amendment. As a judge, what I feel about the law personally cannot enter into how I interpret it from an objective standpoint." Campbell declared that flag burning is "symbolic speech" just as much as "putting the peace symbol on the flag. Gregory Johnson was symbolically disagreeing with his government, which I think the First Amendment gives him the right to do. He doesn't have to stand out there and shout. He can express it through symbolic means and that's what he was doing."

Campbell explained that after Stanfield drafted an opinion under his direction, it was circulated to the other judges. "It was not easy at all" to convince enough of his fellow judges "to see it that way," he recalled, and discussions within the court were "heated, no doubt about it." Campbell added that once the voting was taken "that was it," and after the Supreme Court upheld his decision "everybody came by and shook my hand and said congratulations, even the dissenters." Campbell made clear that fears of adverse political reaction to the decision were discussed among the judges, all of whom are elected, and that he was himself concerned because "I thought it would probably make the papers but more than anything else as an elected official I felt it would make all the VFW halls and the American Legion halls. That's where I knew it would be discussed or, more accurately, cussed." Campbell added, "We discussed it [the political implications of the ruling] and I'm not going to say that we didn't because that would be fudging the truth. I was aware that it was gonna cause me some problems with the veterans' groups and folks like that. We discussed it and finally I decided that it was written correctly, that it was the correct interpretation of the law. One of the things that you better be aware of before you ever come up here is that you're going to have cases like this, and if you're not prepared to decide them honestly then you probably shouldn't be in this building, probably you ought to be looking for a job somewhere else."

According to Campbell and others involved in the *Johnson* case, the ruling did attract a fair amount of press coverage and aroused considerable adverse reaction in Texas, although nothing like the criticism in Texas and across the nation provoked by the 1989 Supreme Court ruling upholding his decision. Public reaction was "heavier than in any case" in his eight years on the court, Campbell related, and it "was all of one mind," with "hundreds" of letters and phone calls and not "one single letter" supporting the ruling. As he expected, Campbell indicated, reaction was particularly strong among veterans, who organized a letter-writing campaign to protest the ruling. Some of the letters were "abusive and threatening," he recalled, "although only in the sense of 'You can forget about being reelected next time, Charley,' that kind of thing, not physically threatening, certainly abusive in the sense that 'You're wacko, a communist' or whatever. 'I fought for my country and I can't believe you'd stoop to something that bad.'" Nonetheless, only seven months after the April ruling, Campbell was reelected to his judgeship.

The criminal appeals ruling clearly stunned the Dallas district attorney's office and above all Vance, whose own Court of Appeals ruling had been rejected. On May 3, 1988, Drew filed a brief asking the criminal appeals court to rehear the case, which contained language that clearly reflected the astonishment of Vance's office at the ruling. In her concluding statements, Drew argued that the "public burning of a United States flag simply cannot constitute protected speech, be it 'symbolic speech' or not," and the state "must be permitted to regulate in this area." The brief incorporated Vance's earlier judicial concession that flag desecration was at least potentially a form of protected expression, while reiterating Dallas's position that the need to protect both the peace and the flag's symbolic value were "compelling state interests which permit the state to regulate in areas in which an individual might, in certain factual situations, be possessed of some First Amendment rights."[13]

Drew argued that with regard to the state's interest in preserving the peace, the court had misconstrued the law by requiring evidence of "actual violence" rather than imminent or clearly threatened potential violence and also ignored the facts by overlooking the "potentially explosive and inherently inflammatory" situation that had been created by the "gang of protesters," led by Johnson, who had "invaded several businesses, damaged and destroyed chattels real and personal and chanted inflammatory slogans such as 'Fuck you, America,' before burning the flag" before a "sizable crowd" on "public property during a time of increased public attention and presence." It was "merely fortuitous that no undue public disorder actually occurred," Drew argued, "yet this is precisely the sort of situation that the State of Texas must be permitted to prevent." On this point, Drew tried to turn the Iranian flag burning incident to her advantage by arguing that the accompanying brawl demonstrated that burning a national flag and especially the American flag might well "lead to a breach of the peace."

Drew complained that the court had "summarily" dismissed the state's argument concerning its interest in protecting the flag's symbolic value and even appeared to "question whether the protection of the United States flag as a symbol of national unity is a state interest at all." She argued that reliance on *Barnette* was misplaced because "compelling respect" for the flag was far different from promoting national unity by "prohibiting its wanton destruction in a public place." Drew also rejected the court's argument that "some sort of a threat to a symbol is necessary" to outlaw its destruction because the Texas legislature had determined that the flag was a venerated object per se and beyond that "nothing need be done to prove" its value or that it was "entitled to additional protection."

Dallas district attorney Vance's office was joined in asking the criminal appeals court to reconsider its decision in a brief filed on April 29, 1988, by state prosecuting attorney Robert Huttash, whose office is appointed by the same court to act as a quasi-independent agency representing the interests of the people of Texas. In a 1992 interview, Huttash said that he intervened because "we thought this law was constitutional. We saw little difference between this law and forbidding Lee Harvey Oswald from shooting President Kennedy to express a political opinion." Huttash's brief anticipated a major political defense of flag desecration legislation during the 1989–90 debate following the Supreme Court's *Johnson* ruling, namely the contention that flag desecration was an "overt physical act" and that outlawing it was a regulation of conduct that only "incidentally restricts 'symbolic speech.'" Huttash maintained that the venerated objects law was "no more narrowly directed against speech than laws against political assassination, criminal conspiracy, murder, kidnapping, arson and the like, insofar as a person, in committing these offenses, also desires to communicate a message." Huttash contended that just as the state could punish conduct that might have expressive components, such as defacing graves or public buildings, so the legislature could forbid flag desecrations in the form of "overt physical acts that it deems offensive to the people, even though 'pure speech' is also intermingled with those acts."[14]

Again foreseeing a major defense of flag desecration legislation during the 1989–90 national debate, Huttash also argued that because the Texas law banned only "overt physical acts" as opposed to written or verbal abuse of the flag, Johnson was not prevented from expressing his views in other ways, "just as John Wilkes Booth could have expressed his anger against President Lincoln without assassinating him." Gliding over the "serious offense" provision of the Texas law, Huttash foreshadowed yet another defense later to be made of flag desecration legislation by arguing that the state statute did not "take sides," as the criminal appeals court suggested, but was entirely "content neutral," because it outlawed "overt physical acts," whether the flag is "burnt out of love or hate, patriotism or treason, agreement or protest, or forbearance or anger."

On June 8, 1988, the Texas Court of Criminal Appeals refused to reconsider its decision in the *Johnson* case by a 5-4 vote; only the four dissenters in the original decision voted to rehear the case. This ruling left District Attorney Vance with the options of either dropping the case or asking the U.S. Supreme Court to grant a writ of certiorari and thus agree to review the Texas court's ruling, a decision that would require the affirmative vote of four of the nine Supreme Court justices. On July 26, Dallas filed a petition for certiorari with the Supreme Court, accompanied by the required $200 filing fee, which was docketed by the Supreme Court as *Texas v. Johnson,* No. 88-155, the following day. In a 1990 interview, Johnson's lead attorney, Stanley Weinberg, recalled asking Jeffrey Keck, the head of Vance's appellate division, "Why are you wasting my [taxpayer's] money to take this silly thing to the Supreme Court?" and that Keck replied, "Judge Vance insisted."

Dallas's petition for certiorari, primarily authored again by Kathi Drew, stressed its long-standing argument that the twin state interests of preserving the peace and protecting the symbolic value of the flag justified restricting flag desecration. The brief summarized its case for urging the Supreme Court to grant certiorari as follows: "The Texas Court of Criminal Appeals has decided an important question of law under the First Amendment which has not been, but which should be, resolved by [the Supreme Court], specifically whether an act of flagburning, which occurred at the climax of a turbulent, destructive and potentially violent demonstration during the 1984 Republican convention constitutes 'speech' entitled to First Amendment protection." Drew answered this question by arguing that "the act of flagburning does not rise to the level of speech, or, in the alternative . . . Texas is vested with sufficient compelling state interests to justify minimal infringement of a flagburner's First Amendment rights."[15]

The Dallas brief combined the two briefs that had unsuccessfully called upon the Texas high court to reconsider its decision, with the resultant ambiguity concerning whether flag burning should be considered "speech" entitled to any presumption of constitutional protection (although the brief conceded that before the Texas court "all parties assumed" that the Dallas flag burning did constitute "symbolic speech"). Drawing from Huttash's earlier brief, Drew's petition, in a section headed "Flagburning Is Conduct," argued that the Texas law outlawed only "overt physical acts" involving "physical mistreatment of flags" and other venerated objects but not any forms of speech or writing, that the forbidden acts were outlawed on a "content-neutral" basis "regardless of the message" intended by their perpetrators, and that the Texas legislature could properly outlaw such acts "that it deems offensive and/or harmful to society . . . even if some speech aspects are involved."

Otherwise, the brief repeated arguments made by Dallas in asking the Texas criminal appeals court to reconsider its decision. Thus Drew maintained that the Texas court, by allegedly requiring a showing of "actual violence" to justify restricting flag desecration on the grounds of maintaining the peace, had wrongly created a standard not previously recognized by the Supreme Court or "any court of which the State is aware" and had ignored both the state's legitimate interest in advance "prevention" of disturbances and the evidence that "imminent public unrest" and a "potentially explosive" situation existed as a result of the Dallas flag burning. Drew's brief cited past opinions endorsing the concept of the flag's symbolic value issued by variety of courts, including the Supreme Court's 1907 *Halter* decision and dissents from the Court's Vietnam-era rulings by four Supreme Court justices, including those by Chief Justice Rehnquist in the *Goguen* and *Spence* cases. Attempting to distinguish the *Johnson* case from the 1943 *Barnette* compulsory flag salute case, the brief maintained that although Texas might lack any "compelling interest in compelling respect for the flag," it did have a "substantial and compelling interest" in protecting the flag as a "symbol of national unity."

Therefore, and because Texas sought only to deny Johnson "the use of the flag for physical destruction" but had not attempted to deny his right to dissent publicly through "any legitimate protest activities," the brief argued, the state could properly punish him "for trying to destroy the flag as a symbol revered by the vast majority of Americans."

On September 28, 1988, Stanley Weinberg, the TCLU, and the ACLU Foundation of New York filed a joint response, on Johnson's behalf, to Drew's petition, asking the Supreme Court not to grant certiorari. Johnson's brief endorsed the ruling of the Texas Court of Criminal Appeals and argued that the decision was "entirely consistent" with almost all other lower court decisions that postdated the 1974 *Spence* case (the last major Supreme Court flag desecration decision), such as the two most recently reported federal appeals court flag burning decisions, namely the 1984 *Monroe* ruling and the subsequent ruling in a 1985 case striking down RCP-related flag burning convictions under Georgia's flag desecration law. Therefore, the brief argued, the basic issues involved in the *Johnson* case were now "well-settled constitutional doctrine," and Dallas had "presented no reason warranting review" by the Supreme Court. Citing the *Spence* ruling, Johnson's lawyers rejected any suggestion that the Dallas flag burning was not "symbolic political speech" and quoted at length from the Texas high court's key argument that when such speech was at issue the government could not constitutionally allow only a "prescribed set of approved messages" to be associated with a state "symbol of unity," any more than the state could "mandate by fiat a feeling of unity in its citizens." The Dallas contention concerning the government's interest in preserving the flag as a symbol of national unity contained no "self-limiting principle," the brief continued, and therefore "would appear to bar even critical [verbal or written] comments about the flag," in violation of the Supreme Court's 1969 decision in *Street*. Such logic would also "invite the withdrawal of other focal points of dissent" from general "public discourse," Johnson's lawyers argued, and therefore the Texas high court responded by the "only determination it could have made," concluding that "peaceful expression of opinion, whether by symbols or otherwise, may not be suppressed."[16]

In response to Dallas's argument concerning the alleged valid state interest in banning flag desecration to maintain the peace because such acts were inherently inflammatory, *Johnson*'s brief noted that the "lower courts have often reviewed" cases involving flag desecration "unaccompanied by even a threat of violence." The brief further noted and endorsed the Texas high court's rejection of the Dallas claim that the City Hall flag burning had taken place in a "potentially explosive" situation and the court's conclusion that the "serious offense" required to trigger the Texas law could not be equated with "incitement to breach the peace." Finally, Johnson's brief argued, even if the Supreme Court believed that flag burning was not "necessarily protected speech," the Texas law was an "inappropriate vehicle for review" because the "serious offense" provision would require its invalidation regardless of other considerations as it was so "plainly unconstitutional." This was so, the brief concluded, because the provision made violations of law dependent upon "what onlookers might think" rather than upon clearly defined conduct and therefore it was so vague that it threatened to "chill" protected speech by leading individuals to "steer wide of even potentially prohibited conduct" by avoiding "all conduct disrespectful of the flag in the fear that it might cause some observer a degree of displeasure that could, conceivably, be described as serious offense."

CHAPTER 3

THE FLAG CONTROVERSY
MOVES TO CENTER STAGE,
AUGUST 1988–JUNE 1989

On October 17, 1988, the United States Supreme Court announced that it would grant Dallas's request for a writ of certiorari—that is, it would agree to hear an appeal—from the Texas Court of Criminal Appeals ruling holding that the Texas venerated objects law had been unconstitutionally applied to prosecute Gregory Lee Johnson for the August 22, 1984, Dallas flag burning. According to files deposited with the Library of Congress by retired Supreme Court justice Thurgood Marshall and made public shortly after his death in early 1993, five justices (one more than the four needed to grant certiorari), all generally regarded as being in the conservative camp (Chief Justice Rehnquist and Justices Byron White, Sandra Day O'Connor, Antonin Scalia, and Anthony Kennedy), voted to hear the appeal and thus create the opportunity to reinstate Johnson's conviction in a vote taken in early October. Of these five, Scalia and Kennedy later voted to uphold the Texas high court's ruling. Four justices, including the Court's two most liberal judges (Brennan and Marshall) and two justices generally regarded as ideologically in between the Court's liberal and conservative wings (Blackmun and John Paul Stevens), voted not to grant certiorari and thus to leave unreviewed the Texas Court of Criminal Appeals ruling—in effect ensuring Johnson's freedom but not necessarily endorsing the lower court ruling. Of the four who voted against hearing an appeal, only Stevens later voted to reinstate Johnson's conviction.

Ordinarily, Supreme Court decisions to hear cases, as opposed to actual Court decisions, attract relatively little press attention outside of a handful of the most comprehensive newspapers such as the *New York Times* and the *Washington Post*, and even these outlets usually bury such news in small articles on the inside pages. The Supreme Court's decision to hear the *Johnson* case, however, received extraordinarily wide and prominent media attention. For example, the *Washington Post* and the *Dallas Times-Herald* both published stories about the Court's action on the front page, and many other newspapers, such as the *Washington Times*, the *Dallas Morning News*, the *Los Angeles Times*, the *New York Times*, *USA Today*, the *Chicago Tribune*, and the *San Francisco Chronicle*, published lengthy and prominent articles about the Court's decision to hear the case in their October 18 issues.

This unusually heavy media attention to a procedural Supreme Court decision can be explained for the Dallas media simply by the "local angle" and to a small extent can be understood for the rest of the media by the emotional nature of the flag desecration issue, the seeming clarity of the issues involved, and the fact that the Supreme Court had never squarely decided the flag burning question on its merits. The real explanation, however, for the extraordinary press attention given to the *Johnson* case from its very earliest Supreme Court phases is that the grant of certiorari coincided with another development that had made clear to the media the intense emotional response of many politicians and members of the public to any controversy involving supposed "disloyalty" to the flag: it was announced during the middle of a presidential election campaign in which vice-president and Republican presidential candidate George Bush had repeatedly and, apparently, with considerable political success, suggested that Democratic contender Michael Dukakis was insufficiently devoted to the flag.

The Pledge of Allegiance Issue
in the 1988 Presidential Election

Many of the news stories that reported the Supreme Court's decision to grant certiorari in the *Johnson* case linked the story to the emergence of the flag's symbolism as a major issue in the 1988 presidential campaign. For example, an October 17 United Press International report began by stating that "debate over the sanctity of the American flag" had "moved from the campaign trail to the Supreme Court" and noted that the grant of certiorari had come "in the midst of a presidential election that has focussed on patriotism and reverence for the flag." Similarly, the October 18 *Los Angeles Times* noted that the *Johnson* case raised issues "mirroring the patriotism debate of the current presidential campaign."

The flag and patriotism emerged as key issues in the presidential contest as the result of Bush's repeated criticism of an obscure veto by Dukakis in 1977, while governor of Massachusetts, of a law that would have required all public school teachers to lead daily classroom recitations of the Pledge of Allegiance to the flag. Dukakis's veto, which was later overturned by the Massachusetts legislature, mirrored identical action taken by Massachusetts Republican governor Francis Sargent in 1971 and was based on legal advice from both the Massachusetts Supreme Judicial Court and the Massachusetts attorney general that the law was unconstitutional as a result of the Supreme Court's 1943 *Barnette* decision forbidding public schools from requiring students to say the pledge. Dukakis's action was completely proper from a constitutional standpoint and did not reflect any hostility by Dukakis to either the flag or the pledge. It was also consistent with two recent court rulings ordering the reinstatement of teachers who had been fired for refusing to recite the pledge; in a 1972 case, for example, federal circuit court of appeals judge Irving Kaufman wrote, "Patriotism that is forced is a false patriotism, just as loyalty that is coerced is the very antithesis of loyalty."[1]

Nonetheless, Bush, who at the beginning of the 1988 campaign was well behind in the public opinion polls, used Dukakis's 1977 veto to impugn Dukakis's patriotism with considerable success. Bush publicly asked about his opponent, "What is it about the American flag which upsets this man so much?" A September Gallup poll suggested that one-third of all voters thought less of Dukakis because of the pledge issue. Bush stressed the pledge issue so much, in a campaign that was virtually devoid of any substantive issues, that in early October *Time* magazine declared, "Five weeks after the Republican convention, the public can be certain of two things about George Bush: he loves the flag and he believes in pledging allegiance to it every morning. But some voters may wonder what he would do with the rest of his day if he became president." The pledge issue was the focus of so many news and magazine articles that one news story referred to a media "feeding frenzy." Among the books subsequently published about the 1988 election, one was entitled *Pledging Allegiance,* and another declared that Bush made "patriotism a centerpiece issue" of his campaign, "with the American flag as its prop" and the suggestion that Republicans "had some exclusive claim to the Stars and Stripes as the symbol of their campaign." Yet another book on the campaign declared that by election day there was "much talk about whether Bush, if he won, would have a mandate to govern—other than to say the Pledge of Allegiance and not let Willie Horton out of jail," a reference to another major Bush issue, his criticism of Dukakis, as governor of Massachusetts, for superintending a prison weekend furlough program, originated during a Republican administration, in which a convicted murderer committed a rape during a furlough.[2]

Beginning with Bush's nomination at the Republican National Convention in late August, he made his criticism of the Dukakis pledge veto a central theme of his campaign, and reporters noted that crowds seemed to respond more to the pledge issue than anything else Bush said in his speeches. By general consensus, Dukakis's attempt to explain the legal basis for his decision, along with his declaration that in fact he "encourage[d] school children to say the Pledge," could not compete with Bush's appeals to patriotism, such as Bush's remarks that he "would be willing to fight those liberal judges who say that our kids can't say the Pledge" (in fact, the Supreme Court had ruled that children could not be forced to say it) and that the founding fathers would not have objected to classroom recitals of the pledge (although the Pledge had not been written until 1892). Thus *Newsweek* declared that Dukakis "had his facts right, but the Pledge was still a losing issue," and a *New York Times* reporter recalled during the 1989 controversy over the Supreme Court's *Johnson* decision that Bush had criticized Dukakis's 1977 veto during the 1988 campaign "from sea to shining sea" and Dukakis had responded by citing *Barnette,* giving an "answer that was scholarly, cogent and politically devastating."[3]

Beginning with his acceptance speech on August 17 at the Republican convention, Bush not only repeatedly criticized Dukakis on the pledge issue, but he also habitually led his audiences in mass recitals of the pledge and surrounded his campaign stops and advertisements with flags. One reporter noted wryly that "flags surround him on the stump like flowers at a mafia funeral," and another characterized his campaign as a cross-country version of the children's game "capture the flag." Eventually, Dukakis responded by similarly surrounding his campaign stops with masses of flags and even began leading rallies in recitals of the pledge. The Democratic-controlled House of Representatives changed its rules to require beginning each session with a similar recital (as Dukakis pointed out in a September 25 debate with Bush, during the latter's eight-year term as vice-president and therefore Senate president, Bush had never urged the Senate to begin its sessions by reciting the pledge). Bush's campaign stress on the flag and the pledge reached a climax with his September 16 visit to Findlay, Ohio, a city Congress had dubbed "Flag City USA," and his visit four days later to the Annin Flag Factory in Bloomfield, New Jersey.[4]

Bush's stress on the pledge issue and his visit to the flag factory attracted much criticism in the press. For example, *U.S. News & World Report* said after the visit to the factory that the Bush campaign had become a "caricature" of itself, and *Newsweek* said Bush had "seized the low ground" by stressing the issue. Despite these criticisms and a marked decline in Bush's use of the pledge issue after the flag factory visit, the political consensus was that the issue had severely damaged Dukakis, especially because Republican references to the issue were frequently linked to other largely symbolic questions which attempted to portray Dukakis as also out of the mainstream on other "hot button" issues such as "softness" on defense policy and on "law and order" issues. For example, in one speech Bush linked Dukakis's "fervent opposition to the Pledge" with his alleged opposition to the "development of every new weapons system since the slingshot," and in another speech Bush declared, "I simply can't understand the kind of thinking that lets first-degree murderers" out of jail "so they can rape and plunder again and not be willing to let the teachers lead the kids in the Pledge of Allegiance" (although the law Dukakis vetoed *required* teachers to do so under threat of criminal penalty).[5]

In two instances, leading Republicans implied that Democrats approved of flag burning. In response to criticism of vice-presidential nominee Dan Quayle for his apparent efforts to avoid the draft during the Vietnam War, Bush declared on August 22 that his running mate "did not go to Canada, he did not burn his draft card and he damn sure didn't burn the American flag." This apparent suggestion that Democrats supported flag burning was followed a few days later by a claim by Republican senator Steve Symms of Idaho that photos existed which showed Dukakis's wife burning a flag during a Vietnam-era demonstration. After Mrs. Dukakis flatly denied this allegation, Symms quickly withdrew it and admitted that he had no evidence to support it, but in the meantime it had gained wide circulation.[6]

Bush's success in using the flag issue and his deliberate and seemingly cynical and misleading manipulation of it, together with the effectiveness of so-called thirty-second negative attack ads on the Willie Horton issue, were to have profound repercussions during the subsequent *Johnson* controversy; indeed, the specter of 1988 hung over the entire flag burning debate of 1989–90. However sincere Bush's opposition to flag burning may have been, by demanding the passage of a constitutional amendment to override the Supreme Court's 1989 *Johnson* ruling, he appeared to Democrats to be attempting again to "capture the flag" for the Republican party. Thus, on the one hand, Democrats in Congress and around the country, remembering the 1988 campaign and fearing "negative" ads in their upcoming races if they supported the *Johnson* ruling, were determined not to be portrayed as less than 100 percent patriotic—as one reporter put it, "many Democrats swore they would never be outflagged again." But on the other hand, many Democrats were deeply embittered by their perception that Bush's public devotion to the flag contained a large amount of political cynicism. Therefore, some Democrats became doubly determined in 1989–90 to block a constitutional amendment, not only because they opposed in principle "tampering" with the Bill

of Rights but also because they vowed not to let Bush succeed in what they perceived as another attempt to manipulate the flag for crass political gain. The combined force of these two drives—to oppose Bush but not be portrayed as favoring
flag burning—largely explains the successful Democratic drive in 1989 to overrule the *Johnson* ruling not by a constitutional amendment but instead with a statute, the 1989 Flag Protection Act (FPA). In 1990 the Supreme Court struck down
the FPA in its *U.S. v. Eichman* ruling, and by mid-1990 enough steam had gone
out of the flag burning controversy that the revived amendment was soon again
defeated in a straight up-and-down vote in Congress. The great irony of all of this
is that had Bush not so transparently manipulated the flag issue in 1988, he might
have obtained a constitutional amendment in 1989–90; of course, he also might
not have become president in the first place.[7]

The February–March 1989 Chicago
"Flag on the Floor" Controversy

Two months after Bush was elected president and immediately preceding the
Supreme Court's scheduled March 21, 1989, oral argument in the *Johnson* case,
yet another controversy involving the flag gained national media attention. The
new controversy focused on a piece of flag-centered art which was on display in
Chicago in February and March 1989 as part of a special exhibit of seventy-two
artworks created by minority students and selected for display by a faculty jury at
the School of the Art Institute of Chicago (SAIC) (a fine arts school administra-
tively autonomous of the internationally renowned Art Institute of Chicago [AIC]
museum, although ultimately responsible to a common board of trustees).

The artwork that became the storm center of the controversy, created by
SAIC student Scott Tyler (who used the name Dread Scott in his artwork), was
titled *What Is the Proper Way to Display the American Flag?* It featured a photomontage attached to a wall, which consisted of the exhibit's title printed above
pictures of an American flag being burned by South Koreans (one of whom was
holding a sign reading, "Yankee Go Home, Son of a Bitch") and of flag-draped
coffins, presumably being shipped to the United States from Vietnam. Underneath
the photomontage was a shelf fastened to the wall which held a ledgerbook for
visitors to record their responses. An American flag was placed on the floor in
front of the shelf in a position that seemed to invite patrons to walk on it if they
wished to write in the ledger, although it was possible to approach the book from
the side and write in it without stepping on the flag or simply to pick up the book

and move it to another place before writing in it. The exhibit touched off a national storm of controversy and criticism, massive protest demonstrations by veterans and others in Chicago, condemnations by President Bush and many other politicians, and the passage of measures seeking to outlaw such exhibits by the Chicago City Council, the Illinois legislature, and the U.S. Congress, all topped off by an Illinois legislative defunding of SAIC and another state-funded arts group that supported SAIC's right to display the Tyler exhibit.[8]

Tyler himself became the center of the month-long storm of controversy following the opening of the exhibit. According to information Tyler provided in a 1990 interview—during which he wore a shirt with a picture of former Chinese communist leader Mao Tse-tung, festooned with the slogan, "Mao more than ever"—he was born in 1965 and raised in relatively comfortable surroundings in Chicago. Tyler related that he attended the prestigious Latin School, where he was one of a handful of blacks who attended what he termed a "very rich, very white and very private" institution. He recalled that despite his own middle-class background, he was exposed to racist remarks and treatment at the school, gradually became aware that most blacks lived in far less privileged circumstances than he did, and ultimately became radicalized over issues related to the possibility of nuclear warfare. "I just didn't like the thought that two people on either side of the ocean could destroy the world for their own interests," he declared.

After leaving high school before graduating, Tyler related, he entered the SAIC, "fell in love" with photography, and began trying to produce art that would be "really liberating and revolutionary for the masses." He recalled that the SAIC controversy was a surprise, partly because the same exhibit had been displayed without attracting public attention or protest at a private Chicago art gallery a few months earlier and partly because "what happened [at SAIC] never happens—you've got an artwork which becomes the center of an international controversy, you've got laws written in Illinois, Chicago, and at the federal level to outlaw that artwork, a school defunded because of refusal to take the work out, another organization defunded because they did not condemn the school, you had 2,500 troglodytes from the VFW coming out and threatening to kill me, and raising the slogan, 'The flag and the artist, hang them both high.'" Tyler said that the protests and condemnation his exhibit attracted demonstrated that "the ruling class can't tolerate any questioning, any thought or any dissent on the question of patriotism. On the other side, a lot of people, hopefully, one day, can not only burn the flag but do in the whole empire the flag represents."

Although Tyler reported receiving death threats during the SAIC controversy, he clearly was not reluctant to take advantage of the media attention focused on him. He held several press conferences in which he usually appeared in a black beret, sunglasses, and an Arab-style headdress (kaffiyeh) that made him look somewhat like a black Yassir Arafat. Tyler told a reporter for *Spin* magazine in late March 1989 that the kaffiyeh not only displayed solidarity with the Palestinian cause and "keeps my neck warm" but it attracted press attention in a society in which "image is everything. Had I gotten out there in polyester clothes . . . unfortunately as it is in this society, it's not going to carry as much weight." Referring to the celebrity the exhibit brought him, Tyler told the *Spin* reporter, "It's weird, I mean, people want my autograph now. People just want to hear every word that comes out of my mouth."

In a discussion of his political views in the 1990 interview, Tyler described himself as a supporter, although not a member, of the RCP, which he publicly thanked for "political inspiration and guidance" in an essay he authored for the June 1989 issue of *New Art Examiner.* According to Tyler, class inequalities are so ingrained in American society that "if people are going to be free, it's going to take revolution; that's cold and it's hard but it's also true. I want to work for a system that is going to put human needs above human greed. To say that American capitalism works ignores that 50 million blacks were killed during slavery, up to 800 million native Americans and south and central American Indians died [during colonization], ignores the fact that one of three women are raped, all of those would be reason enough to overthrow the system."

In a 1990 interview, SAIC president Anthony Jones recalled that SAIC officials were concerned about the Tyler exhibit from the very start. "It occurred to me immediately that we should check the legality of the exhibition of our national symbol in a very uncharacteristic position lying on the floor," Jones said. After SAIC's legal counsel reported that merely placing a flag on the floor would not violate the state and federal ban on "trampling" flags, "we elected to go ahead and show the piece" although "we recognized that there would be controversy." For example, SAIC decided to post a sign next to Tyler's display warning that under Illinois law it was illegal to "walk on, trample, mutilate, deface or defile the flag." Throughout the month-long controversy that followed, SAIC and AIC officials defended the exhibit on First Amendment grounds. Thus SAIC vice-president Tony Brown told reporters that the school felt "that the First Amendment is at stake in a very big way here," and President Jones declared that the school was "perched on a razor blade," understanding that many people were upset but also determined to "protect the First Amendment" even for an exhibit that "technically" was "not much."[9]

As Jones's remark suggests, SAIC officials frequently made clear to reporters that they were less than enthusiastic about Tyler's art, especially because the controversy paralyzed SAIC for weeks, required it to spend $250,000 for security, and cost it heavily in public relations during the middle of a major fund-raising campaign. Thus SAIC officials stressed to reporters that visitors could write in the ledgerbook without walking "on the flag" (in the 1990 interview, Jones reported that "99.9 percent of people did that"), and declared that most SAIC students "intensely dislike the way the flag is displayed but they take a strong stand on First Amendment rights." According to a lengthy article published in the *Village Voice* in April 1989, the "general feeling among the tired [SAIC] staff is that they are stuck defending a mediocre work of art by a commie artist who seeks to overthrow the government." In response to resolutions from the Illinois legislature denouncing the exhibit, SAIC declared that it would contact all persons who had protested the display, "and we are acknowledging the distress that this work caused." On June 29, a week after the Supreme Court's *Johnson* decision, the AIC trustees issued new SAIC exhibition guidelines, developed by SAIC staff and students, which authorized officials to "relocate or remove" any exhibit that might violate the law, be "disruptive to the educational process," or be "hazardous to the health and/or safety of viewers or participants."[10]

After Tyler's flag display, along with the rest of the SAIC exhibit, opened on February 17 at the school's gallery, housed in a building physically attached to but otherwise not part of the AIC, everything went peacefully until February 22, when a Chicago television station broadcast a story featuring four veterans, one of whom was in a wheelchair, removing the flag from the floor and protesting the display. Thereafter, until the exhibit closed as scheduled on March 18, the Tyler display became a cause célèbre in Chicago and eventually across the United States. No doubt one reason why the display aroused so much anger was that many people mistakenly believed that it was sponsored by the AIC (Chicago's cultural crown jewel) and displayed in AIC galleries, whereas in fact only the SAIC and its own separate gallery was involved. As SAIC president Jones lamented in a 1990 interview, "The public perception was that it was up there next to the [AIC's] Rembrandts and Renoirs" and it was "seen by many people to be particularly outrageous because it was the Art Institute, which it wasn't." Furthermore, "in order to make the protest more focused and more successful all of the protesters of course did their protesting outside the [AIC] museum, because it looks good on television, where you're standing next to the [two huge] lions [statues outside the main AIC entrance], which everybody knows symbolically are the Art Institute. So in terms of public perception, of course the Art Institute was validating the exhibition of this work," but "the museum had nothing to do with this" because "they don't teach and we don't collect."

Jones added that even if people understood that Tyler's display was part of a SAIC exhibit rather than part of the AIC museum, "it was a complete waste of

time" to try to explain to a "mob of enraged persons" that the SAIC was not endorsing Tyler's work simply because it was exhibited in SAIC space. Moreover,
Jones added, any attempt to explain that part of the function of a fine arts school
was precisely to create an atmosphere "where there's always free debate of
ideas, no matter how hostile, aggressive, confrontational, unpalatable, outrageous,
boring," only aggravated public opinion because the "very fact that this is what we
were doing and this is what we were here for made it a bloody sight worse as far
as these people were concerned."

Following the February 22 television broadcast, Tyler and the SAIC received
numerous threats of violence unless the display was ended, and the exhibit
became the target of repeated picketing and other protests. By late February, the
atmosphere surrounding the Tyler exhibit had become increasingly tumultuous, as
violent threats against the SAIC increased and as unhappy visitors repeatedly attempted to remove the flag from the floor and place it on the ledgerbook shelf.
These efforts sometimes resulted in shoving matches and left the flag so dirty that
SAIC gallery director Joyce Fernandes, who at first attempted to replace the flag
on the floor whenever it was removed, took to washing it with a heavy-duty deter-
gent. Fernandes lamented, "The building has been stormed, we've received death
threats and bomb scares." Between February 27 and March 3, the SAIC gallery
was closed to the general public, apparently to enhance security while awaiting
the outcome of a lawsuit filed on behalf of Chicago veterans who claimed that the
display violated the state ban on "trampling" on the flag. According to the
veterans' lawyer, Joseph Morris, the exhibit was even "more egregious than a flag
burning" because a flag burning was "brief," but the exhibit constituted an "on-
going" flag desecration. Other veterans termed the exhibit "tantamount to treason"
and a "slap in the face of millions of veterans who gave their lives" or had suffered
"to defend the values symbolized by the flag." One declared, "I'd like to go in and
shoot that kid who put that flag on the floor."[11]

On March 2, Cook County circuit court judge Kenneth Gillis dismissed the
suit, declaring that "merely placing the flag on a clean floor" did not violate state
law. Gillis (whom SAIC president Jones noted in his 1990 interview is a prominent Republican) declared that the "role of the flag and the artist" was to "communicate and motivate ideas and feelings and traditions. Certainly the artist here
has succeeded in this particular case of communicating ideas and feelings, and it
is good to know that the flag has not lost its ability to communicate ideas." He
added that the concept of free speech required protecting even "hateful" ideas and
that the contested exhibit was "as much an invitation to think about the flag as it is
an invitation to step on it." When the exhibit was reopened to the public shortly
after Gillis's decision, security was greatly beefed up, with six guards stationed

inside the small SAIC exhibit and uniformed Chicago police at the entrance. SAIC officials stopped replacing the flag when veterans regularly removed it from the floor and placed it on the ledger shelf, although SAIC students often did so, with the result that the flag was sometimes removed from the floor and replaced again dozens of time each day.[12]

Protest demonstrations continued, reaching their heights on March 5 and March 12, when several thousand people, mostly veterans bedecked with flags and often dressed in combat fatigues, marched in front of the main AIC entrance to voice their grievances about the SAIC exhibit. On March 12 the crowd was so large that Chicago police were forced to close Michigan Avenue, a major downtown thoroughfare, to traffic. The protesters chanted slogans such as "One, two, three, four, get the flag off the floor," recited the Pledge of Allegiance, sang patriotic songs, stomped on "Scott Tyler dolls," and waved signs with slogans like "The American flag is not a doormat." Periodically, much smaller groups of counterprotesters, including SAIC students, demonstrated in support of Tyler's right to exhibit. They chanted and carried signs with slogans like "Mandatory patriotism. We say no. The thought police have got to go!" and "Art makes us mad, makes us think, makes us act. Is this un-American?" At one point they carried empty picture frames to dramatize the threat posed by artistic censorship.

During the month-long period of the exhibit, which attracted a record attendance for a student art display and became so crowded that SAIC officials began limiting visitors to eight-minute stays each, a total of about twenty arrests occurred. These included about a dozen arrests for disorderly conduct; two SAIC students charged with criminal damage to property for painting flags on sidewalks outside the AIC early one morning in an attempt to force exhibit protesters to walk on flags (the pair was fined $400 and placed under one year of court supervision, even though sanitation workers had washed away the painted flags before any demonstrations began); and a half dozen flag desecration arrests, including four high school students accused of sitting on a flag, one person accused of using a flag to drape an effigy, and one lone exhibit visitor charged for actually stepping on Tyler's flag, a forty-year old teacher from Virginia whose lawyer reported that she had "no intention of making a protest" and who apparently mistook Tyler's ledgerbook for a guest registry.

As controversy swirled over Tyler's exhibit, reportedly fourteen thousand people wrote protest letters to veterans' groups or the AIC/SAIC, another fourteen thousand Chicago television viewers "voted" 86 percent to 14 percent in telephone calls to ban the display, and visitors filled up more than four hundred pages of Tyler's ledgerbook with comments that provided a foretaste of the public firestorm that was to follow three months later in response to the Supreme Court's *Johnson* decision. As two published accounts of the controversy noted, "at the very least" Tyler had "prodded the public to face the meaning of their own patriotism and the power of its symbol" and "whatever else its merits, few works of art in recent memory have been able so perfectly and so obviously to achieve their desired effect" of eliciting responses from viewers.[13]

Ledgerbook comments on both sides ranged from the thoughtful and polite to the bitter and vulgar; one reporter compared the comments to the "walls of a public toilet." Among the comments critical of Tyler were the following: "We have to hold something high as far as standards and this is in poor taste"; "A lot of good men have died to maintain the rights you abuse"; "Hang it proudly! Honor it, don't put it down"; "I think you are an unpatriotic son of a bitch"; "Why don't we have a Scott Tyler flag and put it on the floor where dogs can crap on it?"; "I hope you go to hell for this"; "Go back to the foreign country where you belong"; "You're a commie bastard"; and "Fuck you and your art!!!" Comments supporting Tyler included the following: "You have made a strong statement and have captured a lot of feelings—congratulations"; "What happened to freedom! I'm proud!"; "The very venom that has been spewed in this book is precisely the kind of America you are talking about—Death, Hatred, Violence, Ignorance"; "Good work at provoking a reaction. That's what art is supposed to do"; "If the First Amendment means anything, it should be obvious that it allows people to step, burn, piss and defecate on the flag if they choose to"; "We are free people! So how can anyone say that we can't step on a stupid piece of cloth"; and "Use it as a dishrag."[14]

The Tyler art exhibit, coming so soon after George Bush had been elected president proclaiming his love for the flag, presented an irresistible attraction for local politicians. The March 12 demonstration attracted, in addition to an estimated twenty-five hundred to seven thousand ordinary protesters, eleven Chicago aldermen, ten state legislators, one congressman, one member of the Cook County Board, and Edward Vrydolyak, a mayoral candidate whose campaign was lagging for the elections scheduled for April 4. Vrydolyak (who finished a dismal third despite his stress on the flag issue) and state senator Walter Dudycz (who was to run unsuccessfully for Congress in 1990) engaged in repeated and sometimes daily press conferences and flamboyant participation in protests, and both urged people to contact major contributors to the AIC to express their unhappiness with the Tyler exhibit. *Chicago Tribune* columnist Mike Royko wrote on March 15 that Chicago politicians had leaped into the controversy with glee "through the camera's first glare, while filled with hot air," speaking "through the night that our flag shouldn't be there." Royko also noted that Dudycz had himself treated the flag with disrespect in his most recent election campaign by distributing paper trash bags with flag pictures on their sides. Despite all of the uproar, one major corporate AIC sponsor reported receiving only two letters about the Tyler exhibit and only 57 out of 106,000 AIC individual memberships were canceled to protest it; an AIC donor promised to provide up to $10,000 to make up for money thereby lost.[15]

SAIC president Jones's 1990 recollections of the month-long maelstrom graphically described a nightmarish experience. He recalled that SAIC received many letters and phone calls that "were very, very violent and dangerous—'we're going to kill you.' I got death threats and any student with paint-splattered jeans who was out in Chicago got harassed and yelled at—'You're part of that scummy group that has the flag on the floor.'" He added, "I had to pull the female staff off the telephones because the level of sexual vulgarity and violence was so outrageous that they were very, very upset. There were people who had guns and knives and bomb threats and death threats and everything you could think of." Jones continued, "This went on for twenty-eight days," leaving the SAIC staff "whacked, we were all exhausted and we couldn't get anything done. It caused such incredible damage that we effectively lost eight weeks of work in the administration."

In the meantime, Jones added, a handful of students "just left and said, 'I'm an artist and I'm supposed to be here in a teaching situation, and I'm not going to be in an institution that is surrounded by these demonstrators.' The minority students were in a very difficult situation because they realized their exhibit was gone, dead, no interest in what they were doing at all, only in this flag piece, and yet they had a loyalty to a fellow minority student although many of them were very upset by what was going on. There were forty to fifty artists in the show, and some of them said to me afterward, 'Our exhibition was totally hijacked by this one work.' You won't find anyone who can remember another piece of work in this exhibition."

While the Tyler controversy raged in Chicago, a similar controversy developed in Valencia, California, over an exhibit at the California Institute for the Arts (CalArts), which was modeled on Tyler's display and designed to support him. A flag-on-the-floor/ledgerbook display put together by student Adam Greene, which was originally supposed to have been displayed between March 1 and March 10, was closed five days early, after a series of protests, when the exhibit flag was removed by two men who turned it in to the local sheriff. The latter thereupon kept the flag, he said, to investigate whether the exhibit had violated flag desecration laws. CalArts officials termed the removal of the flag an "appalling" act of theft, but Santa Clarita Sheriff's sergeant Carl Goyen maintained that the flag "was not stolen" but rather had simply been "picked up" as "evidence in an investigation" by "some good, red-blooded young men" who happened to have no official status. CalArts officials strongly supported Greene's right to display his exhibit, declaring that "controversy is what an art school is about" and that "the open exploration of ideas" was "central not only to the production of art but to the well-being of a free society."[16]

The Tyler exhibit led to new flag desecration legislation in Chicago and Illinois, state legislative defunding of the SAIC, and ultimately the inclusion of a ban on maintaining flags on the floor in Congress's October 1989 response to the Supreme Court's *Johnson* ruling. The first official reaction to the Tyler exhibit came from the Chicago City Council, which on March 8 unanimously denounced the display and asked the AIC to close the exhibit as a "gesture of respect rightly due the flag of the United States." The resolution was sponsored by Alderman George Hagopian, who declared, "I don't believe there has been a more dastardly act in the history of this city." During the council debate, Alderman George Burke played dual roles in an imaginary telephone conversation with Benjamin Franklin, in which he exclaimed on behalf of Franklin, "What! [Tyler's] got Betsy Ross's flag draped on the floor and he says that's art?" After approving the resolution, councilmen recited the Pledge of Allegiance. Resolutions denouncing the Tyler exhibit were also adopted by at least eight suburban Chicago community governments, and one local school board unanimously voted to ban all student field trips to the AIC on the grounds that the Tyler exhibit was teaching children "disrespect for our country." On March 14, legislative houses in Indiana and Illinois condemned the Tyler exhibit and called for an end to the display. The Illinois House denunciation of the exhibit, which passed by a 99-5 vote (the Illinois Senate unanimously passed a similar measure in April) demanded that the SAIC remove the exhibit and "teach its students to abide by the laws of Illinois and teach proper respect for the flag."[17]

Officials in Chicago, Springfield, and Washington moved beyond resolutions of denunciation to outlawing future displays such as Tyler's. On March 16, the day before the exhibit closed, the Chicago City Council voted unanimously to outlaw placing the flag of any country on the ground or displaying "any article or substance" bearing a representation of the flag (a provision violated by some of the resolution's supporters, who wore flag buttons and lapel pins, even as they voted for it), with penalties of up to six months in jail and a daily fine of $250. Shortly before the Supreme Court issued its *Johnson* ruling, the Illinois legislature amended the state flag desecration law to outlaw placing flags on the floor, by a vote on Flag Day of 99-6 in the House and by unanimous vote in the Senate. In support of such legislation, state representative Robert Regan declared that he was "thoroughly disgusted by these kinds of loonies hiding behind the Constitution." One of the few legislative opponents of the bill, Representative Paul Williams, declared that criminalizing doing "something to a piece of material" was "wrong and we know it" and that the measure would outlaw having a "different opinion from the government."[18]

By the time Governor James Thompson approved the bill on September 3 (hailed by Dudycz as a "great day for America"), its constitutionality had already been placed in jeopardy by the Supreme Court's June 21 *Johnson* decision. In signing the bill, Thompson suggested that flag desecrators behaved like Nazi murderers and those who defiled graves or damaged buildings like the Washington Monument and called for protecting the "sacred" flag in a "hallowed place." Thompson also signed, without comment, a budget for the Illinois Arts Council, passed by votes of 53-2 in the House and 36-18 in the Senate, reducing state assistance to the SAIC and the Illinois Arts Alliance, which had supported the SAIC's right to display the Tyler exhibit, to $1 each, from prior respective allocations of $65,000 and $20,000. State representative Ted Leverenz, chairman of the House Appropriations Committee, in discussing the funding reduction, said of the SAIC students, "Next year they can come back. If they've been good boys and girls, maybe they'll get funding." SAIC president Jones lamented the defunding, asking, "Is the legislature to punish anyone who doesn't adhere to community standards of art as determined by politicians?"[19]

Even federal officials denounced Scott Tyler's exhibit. President Bush termed the exhibit "disgraceful" on March 15, although, curiously, considering his later support for a constitutional amendment to overturn the Supreme Court's subsequent *Johnson* decision, he added that he was "very wary" of criminally punishing people for such displays because, "I'm always worried about the right of free speech." On March 16, two days before the Tyler exhibit closed and the same day that the Chicago City Council outlawed placing flags on the floor, the United States Senate, by a 97-0 vote, amended the 1968 federal flag desecration law to include a similar provision. The Senate action, which was introduced by Republican minority leader Bob Dole and cosponsored by thirty-six other senators, was taken without any committee consideration or hearings and after only about fifteen minutes of debate. Dole termed the exhibit a "disgraceful" display which showed "disrespect and contempt for our flag." He stated, "I do not know much about art, but I do know desecration when I see it." Democratic senator Alan Dixon of Illinois proclaimed that Tyler had "raised the ire and offended the sensibilities of many Americans," adding that the flag was the "first line of defense in the fight for the preservation of the rights and liberties of many at home and around the world." A provision banning maintaining flags on the floor was ultimately folded into the Flag Protection Act of 1989, passed by Congress in October 1989 in response to the Supreme Court's June 21 *Johnson* decision.[20]

One of the last protests against Tyler's exhibit was a counterexhibit, developed by a suburban Chicago art teacher, Gary Mann, titled *How to Display 'Dread' Scott Tyler.* It featured a floor picture of Tyler's face accompanied by a police homicide-style outline drawing of his body, together with a flag attached to a wall and a ledgerbook for visitors to comment in after stepping on Tyler's "body." Mann's exhibit was displayed during the spring of 1989 in more than a dozen Illinois and Indiana cities, often at veterans' halls, where, Mann reported, people "did some serious walking" on Tyler's portrait. One of Mann's exhibit sites was a children's camp, where a counselor reported that the children had been "waiting to stomp all over [Tyler] for two weeks."[21]

Just as much of the news coverage of the Supreme Court's October 17, 1988, decision to grant certiorari in the *Johnson* case had linked this decision with the politicization of the flag during the 1988 presidential election, many accounts about the Tyler controversy similarly linked it with the Supreme Court's forthcoming oral argument in *Johnson,* which was scheduled for March 21, 1989, just three days after the closing of the Tyler exhibit. For example, on March 13, 1989, the *Los Angeles Times* ran parallel lengthy stories on the two controversies.

David Cole, one of Johnson's new lawyers, similarly tied the two controversies together in a letter published in the *New York Times* on March 23, 1989, which argued that while "mainstream political candidates and commercial advertisers" were allowed to superimpose images on the flag with impunity, Tyler and Johnson were both persecuted because they had used the flag to convey "a message the government dislikes." Tyler and Johnson themselves also linked the two cases by appearing together at rallies and on several radio and TV shows, including *CBS This Morning.* Johnson, who toured the country during the winter of 1988–89 to bring attention to his case, told one reporter that until the Tyler conflict erupted, "we had difficulty getting a lot of interest." He visited Chicago in March to lend support to Tyler, praising the latter's "righteous art" and declaring there and in other statements that the "attack on Dread Scott's art and the threat of the Supreme Court to reinstate my conviction" represented "desperate steps" by a "sick and dying empire desperately clutching to its symbols" and seeking to "force patriotic obedience and allegiance." Johnson also ridiculed President Bush's references to volunteer activity as a "thousand points of light" by using the same phrase to praise international flag burnings, declaring that "it's great to see a symbol of international murder go down to ashes." Tyler repaid Johnson for the latter's visit to Chicago by traveling to Washington for the March 21 Supreme Court oral argument, where he appeared with Johnson at a rally outside the Court.[22]

By the time the Supreme Court issued its decision in the *Johnson* case on June 21, 1989, the combined press coverage of the 1988 Pledge of Allegiance controversy, the February–March 1989 Tyler art exhibit, and previous developments concerning Johnson had stimulated significant segments of the public, and especially the press and political elites, to considerable thought about the "flag desecration" issue. By March 1989, virtually all of the arguments and much of the passions that were to be featured prominently on both sides of the ensuing 1989–90 "flag firestorm" already had been voiced. For example, the major position of those who later wanted to overturn the Supreme Court's 1989–90 decisions legalizing flag burning as a form of political protest was voiced repeatedly during these controversies: because the flag was the unique symbol of the country and because burning flags and putting them on the floor were forms of protest that were deeply offensive to many Americans, especially veterans, such dissent went "too far." In any case, they argued, forbidding such actions did not infringe on freedom of expression because they amounted to "conduct" and not First Amendment–protected "speech," especially since protesters were still free to say or write anything they wanted to about the flag. For example, in a letter to the *Dallas Morning News* published on November 28, 1988, Austin resident Lawrence Cranberg, who identified himself as a TCLU member, termed flag burning a "gratuitous insult to those thousands who died" for the "worldwide symbol of freedom, democracy and civil liberties" and denounced the TCLU for defending Johnson and thus "scoffing at everything civilized people hold dear."

Although such sentiments were unquestionably the majority viewpoint, as would be demonstrated in public opinion polls concerning the subsequent Supreme Court decisions, the major themes of later supporters of the Supreme Court also emerged, especially among substantial segments of "elite" opinion as newspaper editorial writers, artists, and civil liberties organizations. The main argument of those who opposed coerced flag salutes, interference with Tyler's exhibit, and prosecution of flag burners was that the flag was simply a symbol and that under the First Amendment Americans were free to use, abuse, or ignore symbols as they wished; therefore, they could not be compelled either to pay homage to symbols if they did not want to or to refrain from displaying or even destroying them as they wished. For example, the *New Republic* quoted Justice Oliver Wendell Holmes's famous dictum that the real test of protecting free speech was a society's willingness to tolerate "the expression of opinions that we loath" in support of its argument that "an American flag that couldn't be openly burned would be a flag less worthy of allegiance." Many of those who supported the right to desecrate the flag were neither personally enthusiastic about such actions nor particularly comfortable about Johnson's and Tyler's political views. Thus one professor who heard Johnson speak at the University of Miami told a reporter, "This kid's really an ass. But the principle involved is what's important."[23]

Many supporters of the constitutional right to desecrate the flag drew parallels between attempts to suppress such acts and the widely condemned death sentence proclaimed in February 1989 against author Salman Rushdie by Iran's Ayatollah Khomeini for his alleged blasphemy of Islam in his book *The Satanic Verses*. Thus, *Miami Herald* columnist Tom Fiedler declared that the principle involved in the *Johnson* case was "the right of an individual to express an unpopular, even a blasphemous view," that the "national outrage" over Khomeini's attack "is rooted in that principle," and that "Americans were among the first to leap smugly to Rushdie's defense" but that the *Johnson* case suggested that "national smugness about our own tolerance may have been inappropriate" and that "if the Supreme Court determines that we as a nation are threatened by the expression of Johnson's bizarre views, perhaps his version of [a repressive] America is closer to reality than we know."[24]

Aside from these basic themes—that the right not to say the Pledge of Allegiance and to use the flag symbolically to protest government policy involved basic freedoms and that coercing expressions of loyalty or forbidding expressions of dissent were unworthy of a democratic society—many other arguments were put forth by supporters of the right to desecrate flags during the period leading up to the *Johnson* ruling that would later be revived. Among the most prominent of these subsidiary themes were the arguments that politicians were simply manipulating the flag for cheap partisan purposes and that the heavy concentration of political and public energy upon a purely symbolic issue was diverting the country's attention away from far more fundamental and serious matters.

For example, the *Arkansas Gazette* said that Bush's use of the pledge issue was a "sinister effort" which amounted to a "red-baiting, 1988 style," to "brand" Dukakis as "disloyal" at a time when the candidates should be explaining how they would "preserve and strengthen" American liberties. The *Ann Arbor News* sarcastically predicted that Bush would soon call upon grocery stores "to begin [their] day with the National Anthem." The *Minneapolis Star* sounded what was to become the dominant editorial theme of the 1989–90 flag burning controversy when it declared that "the best way to salute the flag is to sustain the principles for which it stands. Preserving liberty, justice, and equality is a president's first obligation."[25]

Several commentators on the Tyler flag exhibit controversy suggested that politicians were leaping on the furor to avoid dealing with more difficult but more important issues. For example, Claude Lewis, a columnist for the *Philadelphia Inquirer,* attacked Illinois state senator Dudcyz's agitation of the Tyler issue, declaring that the real desecration of the flag occurred on a "daily basis" when "we allow hungry Indians, Appalachian whites, poor blacks and jobless Mexicans to live in hopelessness and despair." Another theme among those who commented positively about Tyler's exhibit that would recur during the 1989–90 flag burning uproar was that the entire controversy was an absurd overreaction which confused symbol with substance and deified a piece of cloth for the purpose of suppressing dissent. Thus *Chicago Tribune* columnist Stephen Chapman, noting that his own newspaper printed a picture of the flag on its front page yet had not been prosecuted, even though such flags ended up "lining cat boxes," concluded that the flag could be used for "any purpose you can dream up, as long as it isn't a political message that contradicts the views of most Americans." The entire Tyler controversy was a "ludicrous overreaction," Chapman concluded, because the flag was only a "metaphor for the nation and its ideals" and "what kind of free country is it in which the government punishes people for gestures of contempt?" Responding to the argument that people had died for the flag, Chapman expressed doubt that "soldiers would have deserted in droves" during the Vietnam War if Congress had changed flags: "What would they have said? 'Sorry I don't mind dying for the red, white and blue, but getting killed for this purple and gold model is too much.'"[26]

The Supreme Court Briefs in Support of Texas in Texas v. Johnson

While the future political firestorm over the Supreme Court's forthcoming 1989 *Johnson* ruling was being publicly kindled and rehearsed during the fall of 1988 and the winter of 1988–89, the primary focus of the *Johnson* legal combatants before the scheduled March 21, 1989, oral arguments was the far more private work of writing and submitting yet another round of legal briefs—the seventh and last set of briefs to be submitted to courts considering the August 22, 1984, Dallas flag burning during almost five years of litigation.

To those familiar with the *Johnson* case, the brief submitted to the Supreme Court on November 10, 1988, by Dallas district attorney John Vance (primarily written by Kathi Drew) contained few surprises. Drew's brief began by arguing that flag burning did "not constitute 'speech' entitled to First Amendment protection because the conduct involved is essential neither to the exposition of any idea nor to the peaceful expression of opinion," particularly because the Texas venerated objects law outlawed, in a "content neutral" manner, "regardless of the message sought to be conveyed," only "overt physical acts," namely "flagrant acts of flag desecration," whether the flag was burned "out of treason or patriotism, love or hate." Especially because demonstrators were not prevented from heaping "abuse on the flag either verbally or in writing," and therefore could express their views via "an otherwise limitless arsenal" of protest tactics, the brief argued that the ban on flag desecration amounted to a neutral type of "time, place and manner regulation" previously upheld by the Supreme Court so long as a "substantial governmental interest" was involved and "alternative avenues of communication" were not "unreasonably" limited.[27]

Although this argument suggested that flag burning contained such limited and inconsequential communicative aspects that it was not really a form of speech or expression, the bulk of the brief conceded this point, while arguing that Texas had compelling overriding interests which justified forbidding such expression, especially in light of previous Supreme Court decisions that established that "expressive conduct demands less constitutional protection than does 'pure speech.'" Drew argued that the Texas law met the test of the court's 1968 *O'Brien* draft card burning decision, which justified incidental governmental restrictions on First Amendment rights where both conduct and expression were mixed together, so long as there was a sufficiently important purpose for the law directed not at restricting expression, but, as Drew maintained was true here, aimed "at reaching only the non-communicative aspects of that conduct." Even if flag desecration was found to be clearly expressive under the 1974 Supreme Court *Spence* test, which appeared to require a higher level of state interests to justify restrictions than did the *O'Brien* test, the brief reiterated previous arguments that Texas had two "compelling state interests" which superseded any First Amendment rights involved in such activity, namely preventing breaches of the peace and protection of the flag as "a unique, important," and "paramount symbol of nationhood and unity."

The brief maintained that, in violation of the holdings of many courts, dating back to the Supreme Court's 1907 *Halter* decision, the Texas Court of Criminal Appeals had required a showing of "actual as opposed to potential violence" to uphold the state's overriding interest in maintaining the peace, whereas the proper test would only require demonstrating "the potential for a breach of the peace," especially as the legitimate purpose of the Texas law was "prevention, not punishment, of a breach of the peace." Such potential for disorder had clearly been shown in the *Johnson* trial record, the brief argued, because the Dallas flag burning had occurred at the "climax of a turbulent, destructive and potentially violent demonstration" as a result of which criminal mischief, theft, and disorderly conduct charges "could doubtless have been brought," and it was "merely fortuitous that no undue public disorder or unrest actually" followed the flag burning.

Texas's interest in preserving the symbolic value of the flag, the brief argued, reflected that flag desecration would damage the flag's ability to "survive to represent and symbolize this country" as "a unique symbol, qualitatively different from any other symbol that this nation uses to express its existence." Drew rejected the argument that the 1943 Supreme Court *Barnette* opinion striking down compulsory school flag salutes required the invalidation of the Texas venerated objects law, on the grounds that Texas did not require Johnson to "salute the flag, take a pledge or oath to the flag or make any other expression of respect or belief" and even allowed him to express "any thoughts he may have concerning the flag, no matter how contemptuous," so long as he refrained from "wantonly, intentionally and totally destroying the flag in a public context."

The brief also rejected two other arguments that had been stressed by the Texas Court of Criminal Appeals. First, in response to the contention that by banning flag desecration, Texas was seeking to mandate by fiat a "feeling of unity" or to "prescribe a set of approved messages" to be associated with the flag, Drew argued that Texas was not "endorsing, protecting, avowing or prohibiting any particular philosophy" and in fact tolerated the expression of all viewpoints about the flag, but sought only to protect it "against destruction, regardless of the philosophy" behind that destruction, so that it could continue to "serve as a symbol of nationhood and unity." Second, the brief rejected the Texas court's argument that only clear showing of a "grave and immediate danger" to the flag's symbolic power could justify forbidding flag desecration, instead arguing that the "very nature" of any "wanton destruction" of the flag in public provided sufficient evidence of "potential danger to the flag as a symbol." Finally, in response to the argument that the "serious offense" provision of the Texas law was unconstitutionally vague or overbroad, Drew maintained that the statute referred to the "individual's intent and to the manner in which the conduct is effectuated, not to the reaction of the crowd" and therefore did not depend upon the flag desecrator's "assessment of the [observers'] sensibilities" but outlawed only "serious acts of physical abuse" of the flag "intentionally designed to seriously offend other individuals" and "having a high potential for creating unrest." In particular, Drew asserted, the law would therefore not forbid public destruction of a "worn flag."

Dallas's defense of the Texas venerated objects law before the Supreme Court was supported in separate amicus curiae briefs filed by the Legal Affairs Council (LAC), which described itself as a nonprofit group "dedicated to preserving the inherent and constitutional rights of the people," and by the conservative Washington Legal Foundation (WLF) on behalf of itself and the VFW, the National Flag Foundation, the AMVETS organization of World War II veterans, the Air Force Foundation, and the Allied Educational Foundation. The two amici briefs were fairly similar and essentially followed the main themes of the Dallas brief. Thus the WLF argued that, especially in the context of the August 22, 1984, Dallas demonstration, which was "short on speech or debate, and looked more like a roving band of vandals," the Johnson flag burning amounted to "mindless nihilism" rather than expression and therefore the 1974 Supreme Court *Spence* ruling suggested that it would not qualify for constitutional protection any more than would the acts of those "who spray paint 'KKK' and the swastika on synagogues in order to convey their hatred of Jews." Both briefs argued that even if the flag burning was interpreted as potentially protected expression, the state interests spelled out by Dallas justified forbidding it because the Texas law was "content and viewpoint neutral" and thus would apply equally to a flag burned by vandals, regardless of their motives, or even to a flag burned by a "person who thinks that Americans take their country and freedom too much for granted" and wished to "shock observers and stimulate feelings of patriotism."[28]

Both briefs also supported the Dallas contention that the state interest in protecting the flag's symbolic value justified restricting any symbolic speech rights belonging to flag desecrators. According to the LAC brief, since the flag was the "essence of nationhood" and the "symbol for all of the people," safeguarding "free speech and assembly" and "protecting the right to dissent," the government's interest in protecting it was identical to that in "protecting the Constitution, the Declaration of Independence, the Capitol Building or the Washington Monument." As a result of public reverence for the flag, the WLF argued, protest flag burning amounted to a form of symbolic "assault" on "most people" that was so inherently "inflammatory" that "any patriotic citizen who loves his country and cherishes the freedoms the flag stands for" would "likely intervene to protect the flag," and therefore it could be justifiably banned to keep the peace.

Conspicuously missing from the ranks of those supporting Dallas was President Reagan's solicitor general, the conservative legal scholar Charles Fried, whose office, a quasi-autonomous part of the Justice Department, represents the interests of the national government before the Supreme Court. Fried's failure to intervene, which was reported in a *Washington Times* news article on December 9, 1988, suggested that Fried, or possibly the Reagan administration in general, either viewed the entire flag desecration issue as not important enough to elicit federal concern or felt that the Texas high court decision was correct because flag desecration was deemed protected speech or because the Texas law was viewed as too deficient to defend. Fried declined to explain his position at the time and refused to comment on whether his decision had been approved by Attorney General Dick Thornburgh, who was retained in his post by Reagan's successor, Bush, and subsequently supported Bush's demand for a constitutional amendment to outlaw flag desecration in the wake of the *Johnson* ruling.

In congressional testimony in 1989–90 and in a 1990 interview, Fried (by then returned to his Harvard University law professorship) said that he had regarded the Texas law as unconstitutional when he examined it as solicitor general in late 1988, although he seemed reluctant to clearly explain his decision. In the 1990 interview, in an apparent reference to the prominence of the Pledge of Allegiance issue in the 1988 election campaign, Fried said that in deciding not to file a brief in support of the Texas law in 1988, the reason was not that "people who were all excited about flags in and about the [Justice] Department would not have been pleased by a brief," but that "it was not writable, it wasn't correct," because the statute "was clearly unconstitutional, it wasn't even a close case and that's why I couldn't support it." Pressed repeatedly to explain exactly why he reached that conclusion, Fried would only say that the "seriously offends" provision of the Texas law "plainly sank" the statute. In testimony before the House Judiciary Committee in 1989, Fried said that though he personally opposed any attempt to overturn *Johnson,* which he termed "right in principle," as solicitor general he would have defended as arguably constitutional a law that sought to ban "mistreatment of a flag in all circumstances."[29]

Johnson's Supreme Court Briefs

Soon after the Supreme Court granted Johnson certiorari on October 17, 1988, Johnson decided to change lawyers, apparently largely in hopes of increasing the legal and political profile of the case. On November 6, 1988, Johnson sent his lead Texas lawyer, Stanley Weinberg, a letter expressing "sincere gratitude" to Weinberg and Skemp for their "dedication" and "enormous amount of work" in defending him in Texas. He added, however, "because of the nature and magnitude of this case and its national significance," he had retained the assistance of New York civil liberties lawyer William Kunstler, one of the founders and a vice-president of the Center for Constitutional Rights (CCR), an organization dedicated to providing legal defenses in civil liberties cases. Kunstler was before his 1995 death perhaps the most famous lawyer in the United States associated with defending radicals in the courts; indeed, according to his law partner, Ronald Kuby, Kunstler is "the most famous lawyer in the universe, ever," which, though clearly an exaggeration, is not a great one. Kunstler's reputation was especially forged by his defense of the so-called Chicago Seven, who were charged by the federal government with interstate conspiracy to provoke rioting at the 1968 Democratic National Convention. Before the Chicago Seven trial brought him fame, Kunstler had earned a Bronze Star in the Philippines during World War II and a law degree from Columbia University, defended civil rights workers in the South for most of the 1960s, and served as a legal consultant to Martin Luther King.[30]

The primary motivation suggested in 1990 interviews with all of the participants in the case for Johnson's change of lawyers was that Kunstler's high public profile, his obvious fondness for publicity, and the media's reciprocal attraction to him made him more likely to conduct the type of public, political defense that Johnson wanted to complement the lower-profile, legal defense required in the courtroom. Kunstler recalled in 1990 that his impression was that Johnson hired him because "I'd be better known than the Texas attorneys who did a very good job for him. Also the CCR had the funds to take the case and publicize it and I think he probably thought his politics and my politics were a bit closer than the Texas lawyers." Johnson himself, in a 1990 interview, declared that though his Texas attorneys "really need to be commended" for a "very, very good" job, he decided to retain Kunstler because "this was an enormously important case and Kunstler is known throughout the world for representing radical causes."

On January 25, 1989, Kunstler and his CCR colleague David Cole filed Johnson's brief with the Supreme Court in response to the briefs from Dallas and its two amici (hereafter collectively referred to as the petitioners' briefs). While Kunstler described himself and Cole as a "very good team," in some ways they appeared to be an odd couple: not only was Kunstler, who was almost seventy in early 1989, more than twice Cole's age, but he was well known for his flamboyance in appearance (in 1990 he was sporting flowing gray sideburns) and manner, including his booming trial lawyer's voice, while Cole conveyed a modest, gentle style in speech, dress, and aura. According to all accounts, including Kunstler's, most of the research and writing of the brief was done by Cole, then a thirty-year-old attorney who had received a law degree from Yale in 1984 and quickly established a reputation as a rising star among civil liberties lawyers. Kunstler described Cole in a 1990 interview as an "absolutely brilliant brief writer," and, comparing himself to puppeteer Edgar Bergen's famous wooden friend, he added, "Cole did three-fourths of the brief. I was like Charlie McCarthy—he handed it to me and said 'Go!'"[31]

Cole's brief centered on the argument that the combination of the "serious offense" provision of the Texas law and the stress of the petitioners' briefs on the state's interest in protecting the symbolic value of the flag made it overwhelmingly clear that Texas was primarily interested in suppressing public acts of flag desecration precisely because they were unwelcome political expression. Such viewpoint-based discriminatory restrictions on expression were clearly directed against ideas rather than conduct and were not "content neutral," Cole argued, and therefore squarely violated the First Amendment. Cole maintained that as far back as the Supreme Court's 1931 *Stromberg* ruling banning red flag laws, the Court had repeatedly held that "the absence of words in no way diminishes First Amendment protection accorded to political expression" and added that, especially in "the age of broadcast media, sound bites and instantly-transmitted television images," flag burning was a particularly powerful form of dissent because its nonverbal nature "cuts across language barriers" both in the United States and abroad.[32]

Cole added that because Texas forbade only flag desecration that "seriously" offended people and sought to protect "one view" of the flag, namely that it represented "nationhood and national unity," from opposing views, such as Johnson's interpretation of the flag as standing for "oppression or imperialism," the Texas statute, both on its face and as applied to Johnson, violated numerous Supreme Court decisions which banned content-based government restrictions on expression, even if the expression potentially or actually provoked hostile popular reactions. "Whether one is compelled to respect a flag by saluting it or by observing a series of taboos concerning its use or misuse," Cole argued, "the compulsion is viewpoint-based and is presumptively unconstitutional in a society which declares itself dedicated to political toleration." Texas's content-based discrimination in regulating flag usage was especially made clear, he contended, by the state's willingness to allow those who shared its viewpoint to "burn the flag, so long as they do so ceremoniously," even though such ritual disposals might well offend political dissidents. Texas's assertion that to preserve the flag as a symbol of "national unity" it could forbid citizens to use that symbol to "express dissent" was clearly "inimical to First Amendment principles," the brief declared, and in any case Texas had never shown how flag desecration actually harmed the symbolic value of the flag, especially because "people choose to burn the flag to express dissent precisely because it is such a powerful symbol."

Cole's brief also argued that the Texas law was unconstitutionally vague because it required persons who were considering using the flag for symbolic dissent to place themselves in the "shoes of wholly unidentifiable other persons in order to gauge whether they will be 'seriously' offended, an impossible inquiry" inasmuch as individual reactions would likely depend on "the flag's particular meaning for that person." The Dallas claim that flag burning was inherently likely to breach the peace had been disproved by numerous flag desecration prosecutions in which no disorders had been demonstrated, the brief continued, and in any case a ban on all flag desecration which caused "serious offense" but not necessarily a violent reaction could not be justified, especially since Supreme Court precedents, such as *Chaplinsky* and *Brandenburg,* legitimized restricting political expression only when direct personal insults or other statements likely and intended to incite immediate violence were involved. Finally, Cole argued that, because massive evidence had been introduced at Johnson's trial concerning speech and protest activities not directly associated with the flag burning, because Judge Hendrik had told the jury that, under the law of parties, Johnson could be found guilty either for burning the flag or for encouraging others to burn it, and because prosecutor Gillett had referred to Johnson's general political views and speech activities in his closing remarks, it was entirely possible that the jury had convicted Johnson solely "for his words and associations" in violation of the Supreme Court's 1969 *Street* decision.

Three separate amici briefs were filed on Johnson's behalf: one jointly filed by the ACLU and the TCLU; a second (hereafter the artists' brief) by political cartoonist Paul Conrad and fifteen established artists; and a third (hereafter the organizations' brief) by twenty-one civic, political, professional, and trade union organizations with a combined membership of more than five hundred thousand Americans, including the pacifist Fellowship of Reconciliation, the National Lawyers Guild, the National Organization of Women, People for the American Way, the United Electrical, Radio and Machine Workers of America, and the Writers Guild of America, as well as many less well-known groups. The amici briefs primarily bolstered Cole's legal arguments, while additionally seeking to convey a political message to the Court that many reputable organizations viewed the right to use the flag symbolically for political protest as fundamental. For example, lawyer Jonathan Hines, who helped write the organizations' brief on behalf of the New York law firm of Debevoise & Plimpton, declared in a 1990 interview that his firm felt "it would be important for organizations and perhaps a law firm representing the organizations to be putting forward a brief that would let the Supreme Court know that it's not just fringe characters like Johnson who felt that this was important and that he shouldn't be prosecuted." Hines's colleague Mark Goodman added, "One of the reasons you [file an amicus brief], no question about it, is to say to the Court that [there are] . . . lots and lots of Americans from a wide variety of organizations and lifestyles who feel that burning the flag is a legitimate form of political expression," particularly with "some of the groups we represent who don't have a lot of money and who have to express themselves in ways that are powerful but aren't expensive."[33]

As Goodman's comment suggests, another point which the amici briefs sought to make to the Supreme Court was that for both "mainstream" and "fringe" groups and individuals the legal right to use the flag as a means of expression was of practical, and not just theoretical, significance. Thus Gloria C. Phares, a lawyer who served as the primary author of the artists' brief, submitted by the New York law firm of Weil, Gotshal & Manges, reported in a 1990 interview, "Just as the president used the Pledge of Allegiance as a political football, seizing a piece of artwork is an easy way for a prosecutor running for office to use something to show that he's a true patriot and to appeal to the sentimental emotions of the electorate. And it happens, so it's not a sort of speculative fear, I have actually had artists make inquiries of me [concerning potential artistic violations of flag desecration laws]."

The ACLU-TCLU amicus brief focused on the perceived fundamental constitutional flaws in the Texas law, arguing that it was unconstitutionally vague because no one could predict what conduct might "seriously offend" other people and also that it amounted to unconstitutional content-based discrimination violating fundamental democratic principles and the "settled law" of the 1943 Supreme Court *Barnette* decision that the state could not "use its coercive power to command respect for the nation and its symbols" or to engage in the "forcible suppression of one political viewpoint in favor of another." Texas's contention that Johnson could express his ideas by other means was meaningless, the TCLU-ACLU brief argued, because, as the Supreme Court had recognized in cases protecting other forms of symbolic expression, "the medium is often the message," and flag burning "added an expressive dimension that words could not supply."

The artists' and organizations' briefs emphasized that the Texas law was not only theoretically a constitutionally impermissible content-based restriction on expression but that, in practice, such laws posed a clear and present threat to their ability to function effectively. Thus the artists' brief stressed that the vagueness of the "serious offense" provision of the statute and its lack of any definition of what constituted a "flag" could pose a serious threat to the ability of artists to incorporate flag imagery in their work and therefore "limits the visual vocabulary and stifles the creative process." Faced with such a statute, the brief maintained, the only safe path for painters, sculptors, craftsmen, actors, movie directors, and others would be to censor themselves "to the point of virtually forgoing the use of a flag." As examples of actual but potentially illegal artistic uses of the flag, the brief included an appendix with two dozen illustrations, including Conrad's political cartoon "The American Way of Death," depicting a razor blade cutting lines of cocaine on a flag and Jasper Johns's frequent use of sometimes-distorted flag images in his paintings.

The organizations' brief stressed that the sponsoring groups relied "upon the constitutional guarantee of free expression," including the regular use of "political expression that is symbolic in form," and that because the flag was a "particularly potent medium for communicating opposition to government policies," if the Supreme Court were to uphold Johnson's conviction, "efforts to effect progressive social changes through the exercise of free speech would be seriously impaired." If Texas could punish those who used the flag symbolically to express dissent, the brief added, no principle would "limit even wider suppression" justified by similar claimed government interests in protecting other symbols, such as against someone who "profanes our national anthem to express dismay" at American foreign policy or against a protester who "hangs our President in effigy." The brief rejected petitioners' analogies comparing protecting flags to safeguarding government buildings, noting that, for example, because there is only one Lincoln Memorial, the "true analogy" would be between laws that protected flags and those that protected Lincoln Memorial replicas; similarly, just as damaging one Lincoln Memorial replica would in no way impair the meaning of the "real" Lincoln Memorial, neither would destroying "a particular cloth or paper rendering of the flag impair the link between our flag and our nationhood."

Under Supreme Court rules, the party who petitions the Court to review a lower court decision is entitled to file a brief in response to those of its opponents. Dallas filed such a reply brief on February 22, 1989. It primarily focused on defending the "serious offense" provision of the Texas law, an aspect of the statute that had emerged as a truly major issue for the first time in the Supreme Court briefs of Johnson and his amici. As the ultimate Supreme Court decision in the *Johnson* case was to make clear, the "serious offense" provision was the Achilles' heel in the Texas law. This was because it apparently made the crime of flag desecration solely dependent upon people's reactions to acts (or, more precisely and even more dubiously, on flag desecrators' predictions of how others would respond to their acts), rather than on any objective definition of the acts themselves, in clear violation of repeated Supreme Court decisions that invalidated banning expression because it was unpopular or offensive to others. Dallas therefore was forced in its reply brief to maintain the position that, despite the clear language of the law, the crime it proscribed "does not turn on the reaction, if any, of those who view an act of flag desecration, but on an intentional act of severe, flagrant abuse of the flag."[34]

According to Dallas, the statute focused not on whether observers might be offended by flag desecration but on the "culpable mental state" of the desecrator, who had to be engaged in "clear, severe and flagrant acts of desecration" performed in a public context "likely to create a breach of the peace." Thus Dallas argued that "no actual serious offense [to an observer] need occur in order for the statute to be violated" and also that "relatively casual touching or mishandling of the flag, such as wadding it up and tucking it under a tee shirt" could not be covered, even if it offended people, an interpretation of the statute that effectively deleted the "serious offense" clause, while adding a "threat to the peace" clause that was not in the law's text. According to Dallas, the Texas law was "viewpoint neutral," because under this interpretation it would outlaw flag burning "regardless of the message," including acts by those who sought to "proclaim a patriotic stance" (although ceremonial flag burning to dispose of worn flags was exempted in the Dallas brief), just as the same law would forbid even " 'dignified' defacement of the Alamo."

Oral Argument before the Supreme Court *in* Texas v. Johnson

At 2 P.M. on March 21, 1989, the Supreme Court held oral arguments in the case of *Texas v. Johnson,* docket No. 88-155. Defending the Texas law, Assistant Dallas district attorney Kathi Drew began her presentation by stating that, "for purposes of this argument today," the state would "assume" that Johnson's flag burning constituted "symbolic speech." She then began to outline Dallas's well-established position that Texas had two "compelling state interests" which outweighed Johnson's First Amendment rights, namely "preservation of the flag as a symbol of nationhood and national unity" and "prevention" of a breach of the peace, "as opposed to punishment" after a breach had already occurred. Justice Antonin Scalia, one of the Court's most conservative members, quickly indicated that Dallas's position was not meeting with a warm reception even among some of its presumed friends, suggesting that the Dallas flag burning did not make the flag "any less a symbol" and in fact "would have been useless unless the flag was a very good symbol." When Drew rejoined that the flag could "lose its symbolic effect" if it was "ignored or abused" over a "period of time," Scalia proclaimed, "not at all," because "when somebody does that to the flag" it "becomes even more a symbol of the country."[35]

A second conservative justice, Anthony Kennedy, who was subsequently to join Scalia and three Court liberals in supporting Johnson's position, also quickly indicated puzzlement over Drew's argument. Pointing out that Drew had already conceded that Johnson's action was, from a constitutional standpoint, "speech," Kennedy asked, "What is the juridical category you're asking us to adopt in order to punish this kind of speech?" and suggested that Drew was seeking to establish a special "[United States] flag exception of the First Amendment." Drew's reply, "To a certain extent, we have made that argument," clearly did not satisfy Kennedy, who declared, "From what I can see, the constitutional category is that we simply say the flag is different," and then forced Drew to concede that the Texas law also protected all state flags so that "your category for one flag is now expanded to 51."

When, in response to a question from Justice Sandra O'Connor, Drew said that Texas could not prohibit "burning of copies of the Constitution" because there "would not be the same" state interest in protecting symbolism, Scalia asked, "Why not?" Scalia foreshadowed his subsequent vote by declaring, to laughter in the courtroom, "I was going to ask about the state flower," and noting, "If I had to pick between the Constitution and the flag, I might well go with the Constitution." Scalia added that in any case the Supreme Court had never previously "allowed" an "item" to be declared a symbol that could be "usable symbolically only in one direction, which is essentially what you're arguing," because "you can honor it all you like, but you can't dishonor it as a sign of disrespect for the country," thus making the Texas law "sort of a one-way statute." When Drew denied this, Scalia's request that she give an example of a situation in which "somebody desecrates the flag in order to show support" for American policy elicited laughter in the courtroom, while evoking from Drew the unlikely scenario that someone might "burn a flag as an honor for all the individuals who died in Vietnam" and her contention that the Texas statute would cover such an instance.

In response to a query from O'Connor about the "serious offense" provision of the Texas law, Drew denied that the statute barred the expression of ideas merely because they offended listeners, in violation of Supreme Court precedents, because, she maintained, the offense centered on "the way in which the act is performed" and "not what an individual is trying to say, not how onlookers perceive the action, not how the crowd reacts, but how it is done." Therefore, Drew maintained, "serious offense does not have to be caused" to violate the statute. Within a few seconds of this statement, however, she seemingly contradicted her argument by declaring, "If you take your flag into your basement in the dead of night, soak it with lighter fluid and ignite it, you probably have not violated this statute, because the Texas statute is restricted to certain limited forms of flag desecration." The only aspect missing in such a situation, however, would seemingly be the "serious offense" she had just indicated was unnecessary to violate the law, as "the way in which the act is performed" was otherwise similar to what Johnson was convicted for.

Toward the end of Drew's presentation Scalia again returned to the justification for singling out the flag for protection by suggesting that her reasoning could justify protecting "Stars of David and crosses" or "Salman Rushdie's book or whatever, whatever might incite people." Drew responded by noting that the Texas law in fact did protect "public monuments" and "places of burial and worship" so that no one could "paint swastikas on the Alamo." Kennedy protested that this "example just doesn't work" because the Alamo is public property, "unless you want to say that the flag is somehow public property of us all and ignore traditional distinctions of property." Drew responded that this was so, because the flag "is this nation's cherished property" and "every individual has a certain interest" in protecting it because "it is such an important symbol of national unity." Scalia's parting shot in response to this remark, delivered to laughter, was, "I never thought that the flag I owned is your flag."

William Kunstler, representing Johnson, faced fewer interruptions and far fewer difficult or hostile questions from the justices than had Drew. He began his presentation by declaring that Dallas, in its reply brief and in Drew's oral argument, had tried to delete the "serious offense" provision from the Texas law in a futile attempt to avoid the fact that the statute squarely "singles out communicative impact for punishment." Dallas had now conceded that the Dallas incident involved "pure speech," Kunstler argued, but had failed to present any "compelling state interest that is worth consideration" to override Johnson's free speech rights. The Supreme Court had repeatedly held that expression could not be forbidden because people objected to the message that was communicated, and the 1943 *Barnette* compulsory flag salute decision, in particular, had set "to rest" any argument for suppressing expression in the name "of nationhood and national unity." Chief Justice William Rehnquist objected that the *Barnette* case had "quite different" facts because it involved school students who "were required to salute the flag" and "one could quite easily say you can't do one [require flag salutes] but you can do the other [forbid flag desecration]." Kunstler responded that in his view it was "the same" to say you "can't force them to salute the flag" and to forbid expressing "other means of disrespect for the flag," including flag burning. Kunstler conceded to Rehnquist, "I don't know if I've convinced you," to which Rehnquist responded, to laughter, "Well, you may have convinced others."

Kunstler argued that Justice Scalia was correct in maintaining that flag desecration did not harm the flag's symbolic value, and he discounted Dallas's second proffered "compelling" interest in banning such acts on the grounds that virtually no instances of flag desecration, including the *Johnson* case, had in fact involved breaches of the peace. The "serious offense" required by the Texas law was, moreover, hopelessly vague, Kunstler added, and the term "physical mistreatment" suffered from the same deficiency, creating "an undefinable statute." "Does physical mistreatment mean wearing it, twisting it, burning it?" he asked. Kunstler closed his argument by quoting from Justice Jackson's warning in *Barnette* that "compulsory unification of opinion achieves only the unanimity of the graveyard," as well as from a recent newspaper column on the Chicago SAIC flag on the floor controversy which had concluded, "Whatever pain freedom of expression may inflict, it is a principle on which we can give no ground." The *Johnson* case, Kunstler concluded, went "to the heart of the First Amendment," which protects the right "to hear things or to see things we hate" because the "things we like" had "never needed a First Amendment."

Before the March 21 oral arguments, most observers willing to predict an outcome for the *Johnson* case interpreted the Court's very willingness to grant certiorari as a clear sign that the Court would rule that flag burning was not constitutionally protected. This was especially so because, as Kunstler noted just before oral arguments, the certiorari decision could be interpreted as "part of the patriotic fervor unleashed in the fall [presidential campaign]." Reinforcing this expectation were the realities that the Rehnquist Court was clearly far more conservative than the Warren and Burger courts, which had overturned flag desecration convictions on narrow grounds in three Vietnam-era cases; and that, while granting certiorari in *Johnson,* in which a lower court had acquitted on constitutional grounds, the Court had repeatedly refused to hear appeals from flag burning convictions for the previous two decades. Even Texas Court of Criminal Appeals judge Charles Campbell, the author of the opinion up for review, stated in a 1990 interview that he had interpreted the decision to grant certiorari as portending a reversal of his opinion. "Usually when the Supreme Court grants cert[iorari] in a case like that," he declared, "it's because they're going to signal a new direction." He added, "I thought that they had decided that they were gonna change the rules and reinterpret the whole concept of what speech was under the First Amendment, [because] . . . I didn't see any reason why they would want to grant cert and then turn around and affirm me for Christ's sake, because the law was so crystal clear. I was surprised that [in the end] they took it to pretty much say the same thing that I said."[36]

More publicly and considerably further to the left, the *Progressive* magazine termed the Court's decision to grant certiorari "disturbing," and civil liberties lawyer Martin Garbus, writing in the *Nation* and *Newsday,* predicted that the Court would hold Johnson guilty by a 6–3 vote that would "seriously impair the right of free speech" and "stand as a precedent for years." Joe Cook, president of the Dallas CLU, termed the decision to grant certiorari in *Johnson* a "part of the [Court's] creeping fascism."[37]

The *Revolutionary Worker* (*RW*), the RCP's newspaper, declared in its December 5, 1988, issue that the decision by the Supreme Court, "a highly political body" which served as a "barometer of what the ruling class is doing," to hear Dallas's appeal "in the middle of the flag-waving presidential campaign" reflected the justices' decision to add their "legal endorsement and encouragement to the mindless flag waving patriotism that is being promoted by the U.S. ruling class." The *RW* made clear that the RCP viewed the *Johnson* case as an important organizing opportunity and as a virtual no-lose situation, in which allegedly either the Supreme Court would uphold Johnson's conviction and be revealed as a repressive tool of an intolerant regime, or Johnson would go free as a result of popular protest which had forced the government to retreat. Thus, in its December 5, 1988, issue the *RW* declared that a "bold and broad political and legal battle" around the case could "strengthen the pole of revolutionary communism in society" by uniting "broadly people who themselves would not burn the flag but who will defend the right to do (for many different reasons)."

Subsequently, the Emergency Committee on the Supreme Court Flag-Burning Case (ECSCFC) was organized to defend Johnson, under strong RCP influence. Although seeking to make a broad-based civil liberties appeal, the ECSCFC generally reflected the RCP's analysis, although often in toned-down terms. For example, in a brochure published in late 1988 or early 1989 the ECSCFC argued that if the Supreme Court reinstated Johnson's conviction "it will send a message that the government, with the Court's blessing, does not intend to tolerate expressions of anti-patriotism, anti-Americanism, or which challenge the fundamental order." According to the ECSCFC, such "moves towards compulsory patriotism and the acceptance of any act of government as long as it comes wrapped in the national flag recall the lessons of Nazi Germany."[38]

Following the March 21, 1989, oral argument, almost all of the writing about the *Johnson* case which suggested or predicted an outcome carried a very different tone from the coverage before the oral argument, reflecting the unexpectedly harsh questioning of Drew by Justices Scalia and Kennedy. Thus the *Chicago Tribune* reported that the Court had shown "little sympathy" for Drew's position, and even the "hometown" *Dallas Morning News* reported that Drew's best arguments "appeared to be too little" for most of the justices. A lengthy editorial in the March 27 *RW* reported that the Supreme Court had given "contemptuous treatment" to Drew and speculated that the Court might not back Texas because the "ruling class" had decided "not to risk shocking and politically alienating the broad middle classes." Similarly, Johnson declared that if the Court ruled in his favor "you can rest assured that it would be a very cold, calculated political decision" that "to try to ram this down people's throats was gonna be just too politically explosive and costly."[39]

The Supreme Court's Decision in Texas v. Johnson

On June 21, 1989, the Supreme Court upheld, by a 5-4 vote, the decision of the Texas Court of Criminal Appeals that Texas had violated Johnson's First Amendment rights by prosecuting him under its venerated objects law for burning a flag "as a means of political protest." According to the files of the late Justice Thurgood Marshall, a preliminary vote of the Court taken on March 24, three days after the oral argument, revealed a tentative vote of 6-2 to uphold the ruling of the Texas high court, with liberals Brennan and Marshall, moderate Blackmun, and conservatives Scalia, Kennedy, and O'Connor (who ended up switching her position) voting with the majority, conservatives Rehnquist and White in the minority, and moderate Stevens (who ended up dissenting) apparently not expressing an opinion. Marshall's sketchy notes of the March 24 Court conference reveal only that Brennan stressed that the case involved freedom of speech and that Marshall himself and Blackmun both suggested that the *Spence* precedent dictated their positions.

Brennan, the senior justice in the majority, subsequently volunteered to write the majority opinion and was assigned to do so by Rehnquist on April 3. Brennan circulated a first draft of an opinion—which was substantially identical to the final majority ruling—on June 3, and by June 19 Kennedy, Marshall, Scalia, and Blackmun agreed to join in. Blackmun did so in a memo declaring that before finally making up his mind he had "struggled with this difficult and distasteful little (big?) case." Conservative Chief Justice Rehnquist authored one dissent, which was joined by his fellow conservatives O'Connor and White; a separate dissent was authored by moderate John Paul Stevens.[40]

In announcing the ruling on June 21, the justices provided a small foretaste of the intense and bitter controversy that would surround it for the next year. Typically, when the Supreme Court announces a decision, the full text is handed out by the Court's press office, while, in the Court chamber, the author of the majority opinion reads aloud at most a short summary of the Court's holding; generally dissenters do not say anything. In announcing the ruling in *Texas v. Johnson,* however, both Brennan, for the majority, and Stevens, in dissent, read lengthy portions (or according to some accounts the entire text) of their opinions; Stevens's voice quivered with emotion while he read his opinion before a crowded and hushed courtroom.[41]

Brennan's majority opinion was similar to that of the Texas Court of Criminal Appeals, although it was more elaborated, more rigorous in its analysis, and more strongly rooted in previous Supreme Court decisions. From a legal standpoint, the decision was summarized in a sentence, buried deep inside the opinion, which noted that because the Dallas flag burning was purely "expressive," any distinction between "written or spoken words and nonverbal conduct" was "of no moment," and therefore the same analysis that the Court used to forbid the criminalization of speech critical of the flag in the 1969 *Street* case applied. The Court had avoided reaching this conclusion for two decades, and one of the most remarkable—but unremarked—aspects of the *Johnson* ruling was that the Court majority deliberately avoided taking advantage of an easy escape route—the *Street* doctrine narrowly applied—to keep from facing it once again. The *Johnson* trial court record suggests that the jury may well have convicted him, by applying the Texas law of parties, for encouraging, orally or otherwise, the Dallas flag burning rather than for personally burning the flag, and both Dallas prosecutor Gillett and trial judge Hendrik clearly informed the jury that a guilty verdict would be justified on such grounds. Yet the Supreme Court majority brushed aside this possibility—which was far stronger than the scraps the *Street* majority had seized upon to conclude that Street could have been convicted for speech alone—in a footnote on the grounds that it was "too unlikely" that the jury had convicted Johnson "for his words alone" to "consider reversing his conviction" on that basis.[42]

Having concluded that Johnson was convicted for "burning the flag rather than for uttering insulting words," the majority applied the Court's 1974 *Spence* case test for determining whether the flag burning constituted "expressive conduct" and thus was potentially subject to First Amendment protection, namely whether there was an "intent to convey a particularized message" and if the "likelihood was great that the message would be understood by those who viewed it." Noting the context of the Dallas protest during the 1984 Republican National Convention on the very day that President Reagan was renominated, the Court cited its past flag cases (*Stromberg, Barnette, Goguen,* and *Spence*), which had determined that flag displays could be a form of symbolic speech, and concluded that the "expressive, overtly political nature" of Johnson's conduct was "both intentional and overwhelmingly apparent."

Next, the Court considered whether what it termed the "relatively lenient standard" of the 1968 *O'Brien* draft card burning case test was applicable to determine whether Texas's claimed interests could outweigh Johnson's First Amendment rights; this test held that where "important or substantial" governmental interests are involved, the "non-speech" aspects of "conduct" which combines both "'speech' and 'non-speech' elements" can be regulated, so long as "the governmental interest is unrelated to the suppression of free expression." In considering the two interests advanced by Texas to justify forbidding concededly expressive conduct, the Court first held that, under what might be termed "maintaining the peace exceptions" to otherwise fully protected political speech, contained in the 1942 *Chaplinsky* and 1969 *Brandenburg* cases, "the state's interest in maintaining order is not implicated," and therefore such an interest was invalid in the *Johnson* case.

The Court pointed out that, despite Texas's claim of a legitimate interest in preventing a breach of the peace, "no disturbance of the peace actually occurred or threatened to occur because of Johnson's burning of the flag" and therefore, in practice, the state's position amounted to a "claim that an audience that takes serious offense at particular expression is necessarily likely to disturb the peace" and that all flag burnings "necessarily" posed a potential for breach of the peace," regardless of the actual circumstances. Brennan pointed out, however, "We have not permitted the government to assume that every expression of a provocative idea will incite a riot, but have instead required a careful consideration of the actual circumstances surrounding such expression."

Turning to Texas's second asserted interest in overcoming Johnson's First Amendment rights, "preserving the flag as a symbol of nationhood and national unity," Brennan suggested that Texas's apparent concern was that flag burning would convince people that "the flag does not stand for nationhood and national unity" or that "we do not enjoy unity as a nation." The Court pointed out, as it had previously declared in *Spence,* that such "concerns blossom only when a person's treatment of the flag communicates some message"; therefore, Brennan concluded, Texas's interest was related "to the suppression of free expression" and the "relatively lenient" *O'Brien* test was inapplicable. Instead, because Johnson's guilt depended "on the likely communicative aspect of his expressive conduct," and he was therefore "restricted because of the content of the message he conveyed," the Texas statute was held to be "content based" under the doctrine of the 1988 case of *Boos v. Barry,* which involved a law banning protests near embassies, but only when they sought to bring foreign governments into public "odium" or "disrepute." Because under the *Boos* doctrine, Brennan continued, the state's interest "in preserving the special symbolic character of the flag" was not "content neutral," as it could not be "justified without reference to the content of the regulated speech," it was subject to "the most exacting scrutiny" and must meet the "compelling" government interest standard required by the *Boos* test for laws that threatened First Amendment rights, rather than merely meet the "important or substantial" government interest test of *O'Brien.*

The Court held, however, that because Texas wished to prevent citizens from conveying "harmful" messages that "cast doubt on either the idea that nationhood and national unity are the flag's referents or that national unity actually exists," there was no "compelling" government interest to justify convicting Johnson "for engaging in political expression" because to do so would violate the "bedrock principle underlying the First Amendment" that "the Government may not prohibit expression of an idea simply because society finds the idea itself offensive or disagreeable." Brennan cited numerous precedents that established this principle and pointed out that in the *Street* case the Court had recognized no exception "even where our flag has been involved." Noting that in *Street* the Court had cited the 1943 *Barnette* compulsory flag salute case to hold that "a State may not criminally punish a person for uttering words critical of the flag," even the expression of "opinions which are defiant or contemptuous," Brennan declared flatly that Texas's attempt to distinguish the *Johnson* case from *Street* was "of no moment where the nonverbal conduct is expressive, as it is here, and where the regulation of that conduct is related to expression, as it is here." In short, Brennan maintained, echoing the Texas Court of Criminal Appeals, "nothing in our precedents suggests that a state may foster its own view of the flag by prohibiting expressive conduct relating to it" and that upholding Johnson's conviction would effectively hold that the state could "ensure that a symbol be used to express only one view of that symbol," in violation of the 1970 *Schacht* ruling striking down a government ban of the unauthorized theatrical use of military uniforms only when their use tended to "discredit" the armed forces.

Brennan added that in focusing on the "precise nature" of Johnson's expression, Texas had missed the "enduring lesson" of past Supreme Court decisions, including *Spence*, that the ban on government suppression of "expression simply because it disagrees with its message, is not dependent on the particular mode in which one chooses to express an idea" and therefore the state could not "criminally punish a person for burning a flag as a means of political protest." Addressing Rehnquist's dissenting argument that Johnson's conviction should have been upheld because he could have conveyed his views "just as forcefully in a dozen different ways," Brennan argued that this assertion sat "uneasily next to the dissent's quite correct reminder that the flag occupies a unique position in this society—which demonstrates that messages conveyed without use of the flag are not 'just as forcefu[l]' as those conveyed with it."

Brennan furthermore flatly rejected the suggestion of Texas and the Court's dissenters that, because of its unique symbolic importance and power, "a separate judicial category exists for the American flag alone," which would allow the Court to hold that the state could legally tolerate its use only to communicate "a limited set of messages." Because no constitutional text or previous cases had suggested a separate legal category for the flag, Brennan declared, such a holding would require the Court "to consult our own political preferences and impose them on the citizenry" and "would be to enter territory having no discernible or defensible boundaries. Could the Government, on this theory, prohibit the burning of state flags? Of the Constitution? In evaluating these choices under the First Amendment, how would we decide which symbols were sufficiently special to warrant this unique status?" Harking back to his previous reference to the "bedrock principle underlying the First Amendment," Brennan noted that the concept of freedom of speech did not "guarantee that other concepts virtually sacred to our Nation as a whole—such as the principle that discrimination on the basis of race is odious and destructive—will go unquestioned in the market place of ideas" and that the Court could likewise not exempt the flag from "the joust of principles protected by the First Amendment."

The Court majority also rejected the notion that flag desecration could endanger the "special role played by our flag or the feelings it inspires" or that "this one gesture of an unknown man" would "change our Nation's attitude towards its flag." Finally, the Court drew a distinction between the fundamental political freedoms involved in protecting Johnson's First Amendment rights as opposed to protecting only a symbol of such freedoms. Brennan declared that the flag's "deservedly cherished place in our community" would be bolstered by a "reaffirmation of the principles of freedom and inclusiveness" that it "best reflects," that "our toleration of criticism such as Johnson's is a sign and source of our strength," and that "we do not consecrate the flag by punishing its desecration, for in doing so we dilute the freedom that this cherished emblem represents." The proper means to preserve the flag's special role, Brennan argued, was "not to punish those who feel differently" but to "persuade them that they are wrong" and to "exploit the uniquely persuasive power of the flag" by "waving one's own" as the most "appropriate response" to the acts of a flag burner.

Justice Kennedy joined in the majority, but he also wrote a separate, concurring opinion, in which he declared that although he supported Brennan's opinion "without reservation," this position had exerted a "personal toll" on him because the "pure command of the Constitution" had forced him to reach a decision that he found "painful." He declared:

> The hard fact is that sometimes we must make decisions we do not
> like. We make them because they are right, right in the sense that the
> law and the Constitution, as we see them, compel the result. And so
> great is our commitment to the process that except, in the rare case, we

do not pause to express distaste for the result, perhaps for fear of undermining a valued principle that dictates the decision. This is one of those rare cases.

Kennedy clearly indicated that his personal sympathies were with the dissenters, but that he had concluded that the Constitution did not "give us the right to rule" thusly because Johnson's acts "were speech, in both the technical and the fundamental meaning of the Constitution," and "it is poignant but fundamental that the flag protects those who hold it in contempt."

In separate dissents, Justices Rehnquist (joined by White and O'Connor) and Stevens essentially argued that ordinary principles of law simply did not apply when the American flag was involved. Thus Stevens maintained that because the flag was "unique," "rules that apply to a host of other symbols," including state flags and "various privately promoted emblems of political or commercial identity," were not "necessarily controlling" because "even if flag burning could be considered just another species of symbolic speech under the logical application of rules that the Court has developed in its interpretation of the First Amendment in other contexts, this case has an intangible dimension that makes those rules inapplicable." (Stevens ultimately omitted part of his original dissent in which he suggested that by extending the "purely logical application of judge-made rules" developed "in other contexts" to "protect flag burning as just another species of symbolic speech," his colleagues in the majority had displayed the "souls of computers.") Similarly, Rehnquist bluntly rejected Brennan's contention that the flag could not be exempted from questioning "in the marketplace of ideas" and the "joust of principles protected by the First Amendment," instead maintaining that the flag "is not simply another 'idea' or 'point of view' competing for recognition in the marketplace of ideas" because, "millions and millions of Americans regard it with an almost mystical reverence" and a "uniquely deep awe and respect."

Both dissents made emotional pleas on behalf of the flag, focusing on its alleged unique properties and aspects, and both were much longer and stronger on appeals to national pride than rooted in applicable Supreme Court precedents (Brennan's majority opinion cited more than thrity previous rulings, but the two dissents cited only slightly over a dozen between them). Rehnquist began his dissent by quoting Justice Oliver Wendell Holmes's statement that "a page of history is worth a volume of logic," and he subsequently devoted far more space to patriotic history and poetry than to legal logic. He quoted the entire first stanza of "The Star Spangled Banner," the entirety of John Greenleaf Whittier's poem "Barbara Frietchie" about an apparently apocryphal Civil War incident (with its famous lines, "'Shoot if you must, this old grey head / But spare your country's flag' she said"), and the opening lines of Ralph Waldo Emerson's "Concord Hymn," describing the beginning of the revolutionary war. Rehnquist also devoted pages to the flag's history and symbolic importance, ranging from its inclusion "as the principal symbol on approximately 33 United States postal stamps and in the design of at least 43 more, more times than any other symbol," to the famous World War II flag raising at Iwo Jima, and the fact that two flags "are prominently placed in our courtroom." Stevens's dissent featured a similar, although much shorter, emphasis on the flag's historic role, ending with references to American patriots ranging from Patrick Henry to "the soldiers who scaled the bluff at Omaha Beach" during World War II and concluding that if "the ideas of liberty and equality" were "worth fighting for" then it could not be "true that the flag that uniquely symbolizes their power is not itself worthy of protection from unnecessary desecration." Near the end of his dissent, Rehnquist unleashed a bitter blast which made clear the depth of the breach between the majority and the dissenters: although both dissents, and above all, Rehnquist's, contained much more extended civics lectures on American patriotism than serious analyses of American constitutional law, Rehnquist characterized Brennan's statement that the proper response to flag burning should be education as a "regrettably patronizing civics lecture," which admonished American political leaders "as if they were truant school children" and placed the Court in a role of "platonic guardian" which had no "place in our system of government."

From a legal standpoint, Rehnquist essentially argued that the Dallas flag burning either should not be considered an expression at all because such acts were only "the equivalent of an inarticulate grunt or roar" that were "most likely to be indulged in not to express any particular idea, but to antagonize others" or, alternatively, that they amounted to a form of "fighting words" that should be exempted from First Amendment protection under the Supreme Court's 1942 *Chaplinsky* ruling as not being the "essential part of any exposition of ideas" and simultaneously having "a tendency to incite a breach of the peace." Furthermore, Rehnquist maintained, because Johnson could have conveyed his views "just as forcefully in a dozen different ways" other than burning the flag, including verbally or by publicly burning government leaders in effigy, depriving him of the right to burn the flag only outlawed "one rather inarticulate form of protest" while leaving him "with a full panoply of other symbols and every conceivable form of verbal expression to express his deep disapproval of national policy. . . . It was Johnson's use of this particular symbol, and not the idea that he sought to convey by it or his many other expressions, for which he was punished."

Using a similar analysis, Stevens declared that the majority was "quite wrong" in asserting that Johnson had been prosecuted for expressing political dissatisfaction, when in fact he was prosecuted only "because of the method he chose to express his dissatisfaction"; the case thus had nothing to do with "disagreeable ideas" but only with "disagreeable conduct" that would "tarnish" and "diminish" the "value of an important national asset." Neither Stevens nor Rehnquist explained why even verbal criticism of the flag should be protected given their strong emphasis on the flag's value and uniqueness.

Both Rehnquist and Stevens introduced in their dissents some extraordinarily weak arguments, which, like the "available alternative methods of expression" argument, were to be picked up and repeated endlessly during the political controversy that soon erupted. For example, confusing symbol and substance, Rehnquist suggested that one reason why the state should be able to forbid flag burning was that the government could draft its citizens to "fight and perhaps die for the flag," suggesting that troops literally fought for the flag rather than what it represented. Rehnquist also explicitly endorsed the profoundly anti-minority-rights concept that the views of popular majorities should be controlling with regard to the outlawing of expression they viewed as abhorrent; in doing so he hopelessly confused the distinction between political expression and common criminality by declaring, "Surely one of the high purposes of a democratic society is to legislate against conduct that is regarded as inherently evil and profoundly offensive to the majority of people—whether it be murder, embezzlement, pollution or flag burning." Similarly, Justice Stevens confused hurt feelings and anger—the only clear harm which could be caused by destroying one of an infinitely reproducible number of privately owned symbolic representations (i.e., flags)—with concrete physical damage to a unique, publicly owned building, by arguing that Johnson's flag burning should be treated as legally equivalent to spray painting "his message of dissatisfaction on the facade of the Lincoln Memorial."

CHAPTER 4

THE IMMEDIATE
POST-*JOHNSON*
FLAG FIRESTORM

The Assault on the Johnson *Ruling*

The June 21, 1989, *Johnson* decision touched off what *Newsday* characterized as a "firestorm of indignation" and *Newsweek* termed "stunned outrage" across the United States. Certainly no Supreme Court decision within recent memory, if ever, was so quickly, bitterly, and overwhelmingly denounced by the American public and political establishment. Representative Benjamin Gilman (R-N.Y.) declared that "probably no Supreme Court decision in our history since the infamous *Dred Scott* decision of 1857 has elicited such a spontaneous outburst of rage, anger and sadness on the part of the American people." Representative William Broomfield (R-Mich.) told the House of Representatives that during his almost twenty-five years in Congress, "I don't ever recall seeing such a high degree of unity [in opposing the *Johnson* ruling] in this body on an issue that has such a potential to divide." Senator Strom Thurmond (R-S.C.) declared that the ruling had "opened an emotional hydrant across our country demanding immediate action to overturn it," and Senator John Warner (R-Va.) said the *Johnson* decision had reached the "core of every individual's mind, heart, and soul."[1]

Within a week of the *Johnson* ruling, President Bush first denounced flag burning as "dead wrong" (on June 22) and then proposed a constitutional amendment to overturn it (on June 27). The Senate, on June 22, passed by 97–3 a resolution, cosponsored by Democratic majority leader George Mitchell and Republican minority leader Bob Dole, which expressed "profound disappointment" with the ruling and the following day approved by voice vote an attempt to overturn it legislatively. The House of Representatives voted 411-5 on June 27 to express its "profound concern" over the Court's action and followed with a highly unusual all-night session on June 28–29 devoted to speeches by about three dozen congressmen denouncing flag burners and the Court. More than two hundred senators and representatives introduced or sponsored about forty separate resolutions calling for a constitutional amendment outlawing desecration of the flag within a week of the *Johnson* ruling.[2]

By mid-July, among the twenty or so state legislatures still in session at the time of the *Johnson* decision, both legislative houses in seven states (Colorado, Texas, California, Missouri, Louisiana, Maine, and South Carolina) approved resolutions calling on Congress to pass a constitutional amendment protecting the flag and individual legislative chambers in at least another twelve states (New Jersey, Ohio, Wisconsin, New Hampshire, Illinois, Rhode Island, Pennsylvania, Massachusetts, Delaware, New York, Nevada, and North Carolina) passed resolutions either criticizing the *Johnson* decision or calling for constitutional or legislative action to overturn it. Scores of local governments across the country adopted similar measures: by September, resolutions urging passage of a flag desecration amendment were approved by governing officials in Detroit, Miami, Dallas, and at least an additional two dozen cities or counties in Maryland, Illinois, Kansas, Georgia, Texas, Missouri, Ohio, and New Jersey.[3]

Numerous polls indicated that overwhelming majorities of the public disagreed with the *Johnson* decision and favored overturning it by constitutional amendment. National polls published in *USA Today* on June 23, in the *San Francisco Examiner* on June 30, and in *Newsweek* on July 3 all indicated that 69 percent backed a constitutional amendment, and similar levels of support for an amendment were indicated in many other national, regional, and state polls published during the next few months. A poll of fourteen hundred residents of southern and border states published in the *Atlanta Constitution* on July 29 not only indicated that 71 percent favored a constitutional amendment, but that at least 60 percent favored such action regardless of sex, race, income, education, party affiliation, size of their community, or liberal/conservative ideological outlook.[4]

Less scientific samplings of public opinion also indicated massive rejection of the *Johnson* decision, especially in its immediate wake. Thus the *Chicago Sun-Times* of June 23 and the *Rocky Mountain* (Denver) *News* of June 29 each reported that about 85 percent of their readers who responded to call-in polls disagreed with the ruling. A *New York Daily News* columnist who listened to radio talk shows during the June 24–25 weekend sarcastically reported on June 27 that, among those who called in to protest the *Johnson* decision, "a lot of wimps seemed willing to settle for a constitutional amendment or impeachment" of the Court majority, but "an encouraging number held out for execution." Aside from protesting to newspapers and radio talk shows, thousands of citizens telephoned and wrote various government offices to voice their outrage. Thus, on June 22, Supreme Court spokeswoman Toni House reported that the Court was receiving calls from a "surprising number of rude callers," some of whom were "outraged to the point of profanity," and a House Judiciary Committee source said that the committee was swamped with calls from "outraged citizens."[5]

According to sources who worked for the Supreme Court in 1989 and were interviewed in 1991 on conditions of anonymity, although the justices expected the *Johnson* decision to be controversial, they were shocked by the volume and virulence of the opposition to it. One Court source reported that Brennan was "deluged with American flags [mailed in by those opposed to the ruling], they were all over the place," that the justices felt that the public and political response was an "extreme overreaction," and that they were not "prepared for all the flag waving that went on" and were surprised to find the flag desecration issue "turned into a political football." Another Court source reported that, at least in hindsight, the justices were "unbelievably blasé" about the *Johnson* issue and that as a result they were shocked by "reading the papers and seeing people shouting and screaming about it." According to the first source, despite the intense feelings reflected in the justices' written opinions, the case did not strain personal relationships among them. "They all take it in stride," the source said. "Nobody gets really excited. You don't see them running around halls and pounding on doors. They don't go around bearing grudges or glaring at each other."

The popular and political criticisms of the *Johnson* decision boiled down to the proposition that the flag, as the most well-known symbol of "freedom" and the nation, was "unique," "special," and, often, "sacred" and that, though dissent was a legitimate and critical part of the democratic process, desecrating the flag went "too far." President Bush proclaimed that "I will uphold our precious right to dissent, but burning the flag goes too far" because the flag was a "unique national symbol" that was "very, very special," that "what that flag embodies is too sacred to be abused," and that he felt "viscerally" about burning it. Attorney General Richard Thornburgh maintained that the United States tolerated dissent "more than any other society or political system in the world's history, but there has to be limits," and banning flag desecration "is the kind of limit I think the American people will recognize as proper." Senate Republican leader Dole declared that "freedom of speech is a constitutional guarantee that America holds dear, but we draw the line when it comes to our flag." Representative Douglas Applegate (D-Ohio), who was one of more than a score of House members who took the floor to denounce the *Johnson* decision on June 22, the day after it was rendered, described himself as "mad as hell," termed the ruling "the greatest travesty in the history of jurisprudence," and asked, "Are there going to be any limitations? Are they going to allow fornication in Times Square at high noon?"[6]

Georgia Governor Joe Frank Harris called for a constitutional amendment to overturn the *Johnson* decision because burning the flag was "beyond the limit." Wisconsin state representative David Zien, who traditionally campaigned by bicycling with a flag around his district ("I went through 14 or 15 flags" in 1986, he reported), declared, "Otherwise, freedom of speech is OK, but not when you're fooling with our national symbol." According to the *St. Louis Post-Dispatch* of June 29, even Justice Scalia's wife felt that he had gone "too far"; Scalia was quoted as telling a friend that in the aftermath of the *Johnson* decision, "I came down to breakfast to find my wife marching around the kitchen table singing, 'It's a Grand Old Flag.'"[7]

Like many other critics of the *Johnson* ruling, President Bush stressed that the flag had to be protected because it was a revered banner of "freedom," without apparently sensing the irony that his support of a constitutional amendment forbidding flag desecration sought to preserve a symbol of "freedom" by destroying part of the substantive freedom that he wished to honor symbolically. *Boston Herald* columnist Beverly Beckham, writing on June 23, no doubt unintentionally caricatured the position of such critics of the *Johnson* decision when she castigated the Supreme Court tribunal for declaring that freedom of speech was "more important than respecting the symbol of freedom." Many critics of the *Johnson* decision, including Bush and many congressmen, referred to the flag as "sacred." For example, California Republican assemblyman Richard Mountjoy announced he was supporting a constitutional amendment to prohibit flag burning because "some things ought to be sacred," and Representative Henry Hyde (R-Ill.) compared the flag to "the sacrament in the Catholic church" and "the holy book in other places or religions." Even the Senate resolution of June 22 which expressed "profound disappointment" with the *Johnson* ruling characterized the flag as "sacred."[8]

The decision was widely attacked, as in Chief Justice Rehnquist's dissent, as ignoring and offending the wishes of the vast majority of the country. Thus the *Indianapolis Star* asked, "Who will protect the rights of the millions who oppose destruction of the symbols of American freedom?" In addition to condemning the Court for offending and ignoring the wishes of American society, scores of congressmen and other critics of the *Johnson* ruling argued that the decision was an especial affront to American veterans, who had allegedly "died for the flag" (as Rehnquist had also declared) and had now been "slapped in the face," to use a phrase that recurred again and again. Representative C. Thomas McMillen (D-Md.) termed the *Johnson* ruling a "travesty of justice" which amounted to a "slap in the face to all Americans, especially those who have fought and died in defense of that symbol." The June 22 Senate resolution echoed these sentiments, declaring that flag burning was an "affront" to the American people and "profoundly offended" those who had "fought valiantly" and "died, to protect this sacred symbol of nationhood."[9]

Many critics of the *Johnson* decision additionally argued that allowing flag desecration would concretely harm both the symbolic value of the flag and the strength of the United States. Senate Democratic majority leader Mitchell maintained that the ruling "devalued and cheapened" the flag, while a Massachusetts past national American Legion commander similarly argued, "You're burning the country when you burn the flag." Without any apparent sense of irony, R. Jack Powell, executive director of the Paralyzed Veterans of America, called for Congress to reverse the *Johnson* decision because tolerating destruction of the flag would be a "step to destroy the idea that there is one nation on earth that allows people to express their opinions," whether they were "socialist," "neo-Nazi," or "mainstream."[10]

According to conservative commentator William Buckley, protecting the flag was an "act of dignity," and the "maintenance of the national dignity is essential to the maintenence of the national morale." California Republican assemblyman Richard Mountjoy complained that "if we say it's OK to burn" the flag, schoolchildren would grow up "without respect" for it and "there's a chance this will not be a patriotic nation." Apparently using similar reasoning, Representative Ronald Machtley (R-R.I.) declared that "there is nothing more important than having a symbol of our democracy," and Representative Christopher Cox (R-Calif.) argued that the flag had to be protected because it was "the very source" of the "right to exercise freedom of speech."[11]

Many critics of the *Johnson* ruling argued that tolerating flag desecration would especially harm the nation's unity because the heterogeneous nature of American society required a common symbol. Perhaps the most hyperbolic versions of this argument came from Mayor Robert Vigilianti of Mountainside Borough, New Jersey, who declared that the flag was "the thread that holds the country together," and from VFW commander in chief Walter Hogan, who told the Senate Judiciary Committee (SJC) that for American soldiers overseas the flag was the "single symbol that was a constant reminder and link to our nation and home." The national unity theme was especially stressed by Democratic SJC chairman Joseph Biden, who maintained that, given the country's ethnic and religious diversity, the flag served as the sole "unifying symbol" of American values and its importance in "promoting a strong sense of national unity" was like that "in no other country" and was "so critical" that protecting the flag "might even outweigh the First Amendment's freedom to speak." Biden even maintained that flag desecrators should be jailed because the flag helped to "generate the kind of tolerance that is required in such a diverse society." In a curious echo of the fear of "new" immigrants which partly motivated the turn-of-the-century Flag Protection Movement, Biden declared that protecting the flag's symbolic value would be especially important "when we live in a Nation where by the year 1995 you are going to have people of European stock being in an absolute minority."[12]

Although the vast majority of the criticism of the *Johnson* decision was emotional and political rather than legal, critics of the Court did also mount legal attacks. They argued that flag desecration was conduct rather than speech and therefore was not covered by the "freedom of speech" provision of the First Amendment. Representative Charles Stenholm (D-Tex.) proclaimed that, just as "my freedom to swing my arm ceases when it contacts my brother's nose," the *Johnson* ruling had "contacted millions upon millions, and hundreds of millions of American noses." Alabama attorney general Don Siegelman announced that he would ignore the decision as far as his state's flag desecration law was concerned because "it shouldn't take a constitutional law expert to figure out that the First Amendment protects speech, not the burning of the American flag." Syndicated columnist George Will similarly argued that the Court had failed to understand that "speech" encompassed only "language addressed to others for the purpose of communicating and persuading." The June 22 Senate resolution officially endorsed this approach by declaring that flag desecration "is clearly not 'speech' as protected by the first amendment."[13]

Legal critics of the *Johnson* decision also argued, as did the Court minority, that outlawing physical flag desecration did not really restrict anyone's rights to expression because dissidents could still verbally express their opinions and engage in many other forms of symbolic protests. Thus Senate Democratic majority leader Mitchell declared that it was precisely the "vast freedom" of dissent which Americans enjoyed that "renders so unnecessary the condoning" of flag desecration, and Republican senator Orrin Hatch argued that banning flag desecration did not prevent a "single idea or thought from being expressed" but only prevented "conduct" with respect to "one object only," while still allowing the expression of all ideas through "speech, use of placards, leaflets, newspapers and even more."[14]

Other legal critics of the Court argued, along with Justice Rehnquist, that the First Amendment had never been held to be absolute and that flag burning should be excluded from its protection as a form of expression which, like other nonprotected expression such as obscenity, perjury, and libel, served no significant social or political function. Finally, some legal critics of the *Johnson* decision pointed to federal restrictions on destroying mailboxes and federal currency, arguing that if the federal government could assume, in effect, a "property interest" in such privately owned items, it could also legally protect the flag. This argument was further extended by some Court critics who, along with the dissenting *Johnson* justices, maintained that the flag was a national "monument" and therefore could be protected, just as defacing the Lincoln Memorial or damaging or destroying other revered or especially significant places, such as historic buildings, cemeteries, and churches, could be outlawed. For example, in its June 22 resolution the Senate officially compared flag desecration to "desecrating a public monument such as the Lincoln Memorial," which "would never be tolerated as speech." Paul Kamenar, WLF executive legal director, told the HJC that the Court's reasoning was "inane" because

> The First Amendment is not an absolute and does not protect, for example, obscenity, libel, fighting words or even statements that rise to the level of treason, i.e. those which gave aid and comfort to the enemy. A civilized society must be able to say that there are certain things which are sacred and can be protected from desecration such as cemeteries and places of worship. Certainly, our nation's flag, as a revered and unique symbol, and one to which we all pledge our allegiance, should be protected as well.[15]

But such legal arguments were a minor sideshow to the much more common emotional defenses of the flag and attacks on the Court. House Veterans Affairs Committee chairman Sonny Montgomery, in announcing his sponsorship of a constitutional amendment, declared that the flag had been "consecrated through 200 years of love and sacrifice and reverence of a special, almost sacred, kind," and "we seek only to protect it, just as you'd protect any loved one under attack." Representative Jack Fields (R-Tex.) proclaimed that Gregory Johnson had gone "too far" because he was "not desecrating a piece of cloth" but "everything we believe in and everything that we stand for . . . everything America is and lives for and fights for and dies for." New Jersey Republican state assemblywoman Joanne Smith declared that the flag was "the one thing that is most important to an American," and California Republican state senator William Campbell termed the flag "more than a symbol" and "really the soul of America."[16]

The governing body of LaSalle County, Illinois, declared that the *Johnson* decision had "horrified the vast majority" of Americans, who "do not consider our nation's flag to be just a piece of cloth that various revolutionaries and subversive activists can destroy," and demanded that Congress endorse a corrective constitutional amendment to "guarantee that our nation remain free." The Texas legislature, in similarly memorializing Congress, declared:

> Whatever legal arguments may be offered to support [the *Johnson* decision], the incineration or other mutilation of the flag . . . is repugnant to all those who have saluted it, paraded beneath it on the Fourth of July, been saluted by its half-mast configuration or raised it inspirationally in remote corners of the globe where they have defended the ideals of which it is representative; and . . . this legislature concurs with the court minority that the Stars and Stripes is deserving of a unique sanctity, free to wave in perpetuity over the spacious skies where our bald eagles fly, the fruited plain above which our mountain majesties soar, and the venerable heights to which our melting pot of peoples and their posterity aspire.

Arguing for a constitutional amendment on the Senate floor, Senate Republican leader Dole declared: "The need for this amendment will not be found in a textbook or a treatise on constitutional law. No, it will be found in the emotions of the heart, emotions deeply rooted in the real-life experiences of millions of Americans, and emotions that are crying out today to give the flag real and lasting protection."[17]

During an all-night June 28–29 session of the House of Representatives held to denounce the *Johnson* decision, dozens of congressmen engaged in what Representative Jon Kyl (R-Ariz.) sympathetically described as "emotional stories" about the flag and "personal experiences and things that we have witnessed," and which the *Raleigh News and Observer* less kindly described as "stem-winding oratory on their close personal relationships with the flag." The representatives talked for nine straight hours, regaling each other with patriotic stories such as how proudly they had raised the flag while schoolchildren, how much their spirits had been raised by seeing a flag after foreign travels, and how much they enjoyed and remembered participating in flag ceremonies while in the military and in celebration of patriotic holidays. For example, Representative George Sangmeister (D-Ill.) revealed that as a youngster he had felt "like I had just committed a crime" when a flag he was raising at school fell and landed on the ground. Representative Robert Dornan (R-Calif.) and Representative Charles Wilson (D-Tex.) engaged in one colloquy in which Dornan asked Wilson if he had ever gotten "bored with seeing Old Glory go by" during his training at the Naval Academy. Wilson proudly declared, "Never," and added that "anybody who burns that flag around me had better have fighting clothes on." Dornan subsequently revealed that if his father "had ever seen the flag burned in front of him," he "would have gone into action. He was a welter-weight boxer." Moreover, even his mother "would be in a fight instantly" in such an event because, Dornan announced, "she loved the American flag" and "not by any stretch of the imagination would she have stood around and watched someone defile it or disgrace it."[18]

The spirit of the all-night session was evident in subsequent congressional debate. Representative Thomas Downey (D-N.Y.) announced that he liked the flag so much that he displayed it both inside and outside of his office, Senator Alphonse D'Amato (R-N.Y.) proudly told his colleagues that he was sponsoring two different constitutional amendments to overturn the *Johnson* ruling, and Representative Norman Lent (R-N.Y.) declared that he was sponsoring three such amendments. On June 29, the House adopted, by voice vote, a resolution terming July 4 "Take Pride in the Flag Day," to be marked by "appropriate programs and activities," in response to what the resolution termed the reaction of many Americans to "a recent Supreme Court decision affecting the flag." During the brief debate on the resolution, which was sponsored by Representative Joe Skeen (R-N.M.), Representative Andrew Jacobs (D-Ind.) queried why the resolution did not "make every day 'Take Pride in Flag Day'" because to "designate only 1 day a year makes you wonder about the 364, in a way, does it not?" Jacobs later decided that even such an alteration would not be enough and, instead, because people already respected the flag "every day, maybe the resolution should ask that we respect it twice every day." During the 1990 congressional revisitation of the flag desecration issue, Skeen inserted in the *Congressional Record* the announcement that he had supported all ten constitutional amendments introduced in the House which sought to outlaw flag desecration.[19]

Much, although by no means all, of the popular and political criticism of the *Johnson* decision, especially immediately after June 21, was couched in highly vitriolic terms. Republican Representative Ron Marlenee termed the decision "treasonous" and, referring to the six marines depicted in the Iwo Jima Memorial, declared, "These six brave soldiers were symbolically shot in the back by five men in black robes." Dozens of other congressmen joined in a virtual orgy of assaults upon the Court, seemingly ransacking their thesauri to come up with different words to proclaim their anger; among the terms they used to describe their reaction to the ruling were "outraged," "appalled," "repulsed," "disgusted," "shocked," "sickened," "numbed," and "astonished," while the decision itself was variously termed "unbelievable," "incredible," "inconceivable," "reprehensible," "terrible," "ludicrous," "weird," "ridiculous," "misguided," and "unthinkable." Although most congressmen limited themselves to one or two adverbs and adjectives to describe their feelings, some used a full panoply of colorful terms. Representative John Rhodes (R-Ariz.) managed to cram into a few sentences characterizations of the *Johnson* ruling as "preposterous," "tragic," "absolutely unbelievable," and a "travesty of justice."[20]

Vitriolic critiques of the *Johnson* ruling also flowed freely outside of Capitol Hill. Alf Slobodin, head of the conservative WLF's legal studies department, termed the decision "flaky" and said it reflected a Supreme Court that was not "for veterans and flag lovers" but for "the Ku Klux Klan and the Nazis," while his colleague Paul Kamenar complained that "for all the Court cares," Americans could use the flag "for toilet paper." Mayor Robert Price of Sharon, Pennsylvania, said that the ruling "shows just how stupid the Supreme Court is" because "our forefathers never meant free speech to mean having Commies burning the flag." The Illinois AMVETS department adopted a resolution declaring that, like Pearl Harbor Day, June 21, 1989, would "ever live in infamy." Miami Beach mayor Alex Daoud called for the impeachment of the Supreme Court majority and termed the decision an act of "absolute insanity." The chairman of the South Carolina Joint Veterans Council called on Americans to write to their elected officials to demand that "this crap" be stopped. Conservative columnist Pat Buchanan termed the decision an "atrocity" and labeled the Court a "renegade tribunal" to which the American people should respond by "open defiance" such as putting "a fist in their face." News stories reporting "street" reaction to the *Johnson* ruling quoted one man as declaring that the "degree of senility among these judges is greater than most people think" and another as declaiming that "they should wrap these five justices up in a flag and burn them; I wouldn't mind putting a match to it myself." A letter to a Texas newspaper, which Representative Joe Barton (R-Tex.) reprinted in the *Congressional Record,* termed the *Johnson* ruling "nothing but treason" and declared that by treating the flag as a "worthless rag" and favoring a "dirty communist" over the "American people" the Supreme Court was supplying "the Reds with shovels" with which to "bury us" and had "given the Communist Party a strong foothold in America to further demoralize the country."[21]

Most of the minority of newspapers that criticized the Court's decision did so in relatively respectful terms. For example, the June 27 *Springfield* (Illinois) *State Journal Register* said that "in a theoretical sense" the ruling was "eminently defensible because it can be viewed as democracy's finest hour" and that therefore the majority's motives should not be impugned, but it maintained that the dissents were "far more persuasive." Other newspaper critiques of the *Johnson* ruling were far less kind. For example, the June 23 *Washington Times* termed Brennan's opinion "tedious pedantry" that would help to "weaken the psychic and emotional substratum on which American freedom rests" and would facilitate "the further subversion of our nation's characteristic ideas through calculated insults to their symbols." The June 23 *New York Daily News,* in an editorial headed, "Okay, go on, burn their robes!" termed the *Johnson* decision "dumb" and declared that it put the court in "naked contempt" of the American people and displayed "pompous insensitivity to the most beloved symbol of the most benevolent form of government ever to appear on this Earth"; an accompanying cartoon depicted a figure resembling President Bush pouring gas on a pile of law books forming a pyre below five bound judges who were bearing copies of the "flag case," with the caption, "Anybody got a match?" The *Dallas Time Herald* cartoon of June 23 repeated this theme but with the Iwo Jima Memorial the object of an imminent burning, while five judges raised glasses as a toast. The June 28 *Park Ridge* (Illinois) *Herald,* termed the Court's decision a "stab in the back," especially to "veterans who will spend the rest of their lives in hospitals because of injuries they sustained defending that flag" and to the "mothers, wives and children of men who died for that flag and all it represents." *Newsday* published a cartoon on July 1 which depicted a dirtied flag being used as a doormat outside the entrance to the Supreme Court, and the *New Jersey Record* cartoon of July 4 portrayed Supreme Court justices roasting marshmallows by a flag fire.

Not surprisingly, flag burners came in for even more bitter criticism than did the five majority justices. Miami Beach's mayor Daoud declared, "People who burn the flag should be shot." A San Francisco veteran said if anyone tried to "burn [a flag] in front of me, I'd kill the sonofabitch," and a New York man declared, "If someone burned a flag in front of me, I'd kill them, shoot them right down. I got a flag on my motorcycle, my car and my camper and I'm putting one on my boat. . . . From now on, whatever I'm driving, there's going to be a flag on it—that's my protest."[22]

Many critics of the *Johnson* decision suggested that flag burners should either voluntarily leave the country or be forced to do so. Thus Senator Dole said that if dissidents "don't like our flag, they ought to go find one they do like," and Representative Carroll Hubbard (D-Ky.) urged flag burners to move to "Iran, China or Cuba, where burning the American flag is not only legal but is encouraged." Among the terms used to describe Johnson and flag burners in general, in remarks either made by congressmen or reprinted in the *Congressional Record,* were "publicity seeking miscreants," "pukeheads," "political jackasses," "contemptible maggots," "pathetic morons," and "insensitive cretins." Johnson himself reported in early July that he had been subjected to personal insults and to so many death threats that he was afraid even to go to the bathroom without taking security precautions for fear that some "Rambo maniac" would attack him.[23]

Johnson's own reaction to the ruling that bore his name, at a June 21 news conference and in subsequent remarks to reporters, was that it was "an important victory" that would "inspire people to fight." He maintained, however, that the government was not "backing off from forcing the flag on people" and "working to create an atmosphere of compulsory patriotism" but did not "want to look too dictatorial in the way they do it." According to Johnson, the government had decided that upholding his conviction was "not a 'cost-effective' way of suppressing anti-patriotism" because it feared that imprisoning him would reveal "just how much of a sham 'freedom of expression' is" in the United States at a time when Soviet Premier Gorbachev's reforms were giving the "appearance of a greater openness for political dissent in the Soviet Union." Chicago artist "Dread" Scott Tyler welcomed the *Johnson* decision with a press conference in front of the Chicago Art Institute on June 22, at which he urged people to "really use" the right to burn flags and to "spread the contagion of anti-patriotism" as "part of overall preparations for revolution." Tyler also warned "all you piggies out there" to "think twice about arresting anyone making some righteous bonfires."[24]

Symbolic Responses to the Johnson Ruling

On June 22, some of Johnson's fellow RCYB members celebrated the decision by burning dozens of miniature paper flags and several larger flags in San Francisco's Mission District and at the University of California at Berkeley. In New York, eight demonstrators who said they were RCP members were arrested for disorderly conduct and resisting arrest on June 23, when, according to police, they blocked traffic after burning a flag and attracting a hostile crowd. Another New York flag burning incident was reported on June 24, amid a rowdy gay rights protest over the recent murders of two homosexuals, during which demonstrators blocked traffic, vandalized police cars, and pelted a police station with debris, breaking two windows.[25]

Also on June 24, a burned flag was discovered draped on a concrete eagle outside a VFW building in Janesville, Wisconsin; a local VFW officer termed the incident "like a slap in the face to us" and declared, "If you did that in China, they'd take you out in the square there and shoot you. It's a privilege to live in this country." In Rushville, Indiana, a man was arrested for flag desecration on June 26 for running over a flag with his car, but the charge was later dismissed by the local prosecutor after defense lawyers convinced him that the *Johnson* ruling had invalidated the state flag desecration law. In Findlay, Ohio (dubbed Flag City by Congress), police prevented a man from burning a flag after threatening him with arrest for violating the city's open burning law on June 29, and in Tiverton, Rhode Island, on June 30, fifty-seven flags were discovered stolen from the graves of war veterans and burned.[26]

The minor rash of immediate post-*Johnson* flag burnings in late June was followed by a considerably larger flurry of flag burnings in July, almost all of which centered around the July 4 holiday. Some of these were presented as "patriotic," as when American Legion groups burned worn flags to "retire" them on July 4 in Manchester, Massachusetts, Muncie, Indiana, and Mesquite, Texas. In Texas, a Legion spokesman explained, "In light of the concerns of flag burning in the last few weeks, we wanted to let people know that the flag can be burned in an honorable and respectful way." "Protest" flag burnings or attempted burnings occurred on July 4 or thereabouts in more than a dozen cities. Many of the "protest" flag burnings were conducted by abortion rights groups seeking to protest a July 3 Supreme Court ruling that upheld a Missouri law which imposed restrictions on obtaining abortions.[27]

Some of the July 4 protest incidents, as in Seattle, Chicago, and Atlanta, were largely uneventful. In Washington a man was arrested for burning a flag in violation of laws banning open burning on park property; in North Andover, Massachusetts, a man was charged with willful and malicious burning of property after allegedly burning a flag he took from the flagpole of his former employer; and in Catawissa, Pennsylvania, a man was sentenced to six months in jail and fined $200 for violating the state's still-enforced flag desecration law for allegedly drunkenly yanking up miniature flags planted along a street for a July 4 celebration. In other July 4 protest flag burnings minor fights erupted or were barely averted. For example, in Albany, veterans prevented a man from burning a flag by knocking away his lighter, in Minneapolis abortion rights advocates were attacked by three waiters from a topless bar who seized the flag they had begun to burn, and in Iowa City a brief scuffle broke out between a flag burner and an anti-abortion picketer over gaining the attention of TV cameras. In Austin, a group of college students planning to burn a flag on the state capitol steps on July 4 were confronted by a group of Vietnam veterans who, coincidentally, were there to protest reductions in veterans' benefits; a skirmish was barely averted, but the would-be flag burners had to give up when they could not get the flags, which were made of synthetic material, to catch fire.

A July 2 flag burning in Salt Lake City, conducted by Grant Sperry, a former University of Utah student body vice-president, to protest "politicians who wrap themselves in flags" and to decry "patriotic fanaticism," was itself uneventful; however, a former navy pilot who had been held captive for more than four years after his plane was shot down in Vietnam later came to Sperry's house and allegedly assaulted him and threatened him with a gun while telling Sperry, "You deserve to die for what you did." Charges against the veteran for assault and possession of a deadly weapon with intent to assault were postponed on the understanding that they would be dropped after a year on condition that he avoid trouble and obtain counseling for post-traumatic stress syndrome. Sperry told reporters that he would not burn any more flags because he objected to people "killing and dying for the flag" and "it would be hopelessly ironic for me to die for the very thing I was protesting."[28]

The most serious disturbances connected with the July 4 flag burnings occurred in Little Rock and in New York City. In New York, plans by a group of activists to burn flags in Washington Square Park in celebration of the *Johnson* decision and to protest mistreatment of the homeless were halted when they were attacked and at least one man was bloodied by forty right-wing "skinheads," many of whom sported flag tattoos and reportedly chanted, "Burn the flag and we'll burn a fag [homosexual]." In Little Rock, black activist Robert McIntosh and his supporters were prevented from burning a flag on July 4 by a crowd of several hundred hecklers, some of whom shouted, "Burn that nigger, not the flag" and "go back to Africa." Police arrested five people while breaking up fights that nearly turned into a race riot. McIntosh, who was known as the "Black Santa Claus" of Little Rock for giving away food and other gifts to the poor, said that he wanted to burn a flag to protest the failure of the country to live "up to the American flag, justice for all," especially the lack of attention to problems of crime and drugs among the poor. Holding up a flag, McIntosh asked reporters from inside the capitol, where police had escorted him to escape the mob, "How can you love the flag and want to kill a human being? This [flag] ain't God. This is a piece of rag that came from Taiwan." U.S. Representative Tommy Robinson (R-Ark.) responded shortly afterward that if McIntosh wanted to "do something for the benefit of the country, he should burn himself" and that he would "like to hit [McIntosh] real hard, like with a baseball bat."[29]

Unquestionably the most bizarre "flag burning" incident in the month following the *Johnson* decision occurred on the Supreme Court steps in Washington on

July 20 in response to what turned out to be a false rumor that Johnson himself was planning to burn a flag there. After alerting members of the news media to their plans, a group of about a dozen Republican congressmen who favored a flag desecration constitutional amendment gathered on the steps equipped with fire extinguishers and buckets of water, while two fire trucks from the Washington fire department stood by. When Johnson failed to appear, the congressmen doused an effigy of Johnson, an action one reporter dryly noted may have been "the first time someone was doused in effigy." The congressmen also recited the Pledge of Allegiance and sang patriotic songs but had to give up on "It's a Grand Old Flag" when it turned out that they didn't know the words. Commenting on the episode, columnist Murray Kempton, noting that one of the "fire brigade" congressmen, California representative Dana Rohrabacher, had advised Americans to "follow our example" and to "take care of [flag burners] any way they can," suggested that Americans should "carry a bucket everywhere in case they run into a congressman. That way, when they tell him to go soak his head, there would be something available."[30]

With the major exception of this July 20 incident, the flag burnings during the month following the *Johnson* decision were completely or largely ignored by all but local media, in a strange contrast to the national media uproar about the ruling itself. Apparently, to the media at least, the abstract right to burn flags was a matter of great national importance but the actual burning of flags was insignificant. One enterprising newspaper, however, was able to obtain critical reactions to the July 4 incidents from both left and right, with an American Legion spokesman sarcastically declaring, "If this keeps up burning the flag won't mean much and people may have to use English to express themselves," and an ACLU lawyer suggesting that if flag burners stopped being "provocative" and critics of the *Johnson* ruling stayed silent, flag burning "would go away."[31]

In other symbolic responses to the *Johnson* decision, several government officials announced that they would arrest flag burners nonetheless. For example, the acting police chief of San Juan Batista, California, declared that "first they will be arrested for violating the city ordinance for illegal burning, second they will be charged with litter bugging, and third they will be charged with resisting arrest." The sheriff of Monroe County, Indiana, declared that he would arrest flag burners for disorderly conduct on the grounds that such acts interfered with other Americans by "trampling" on their First Amendment rights to "collective expression" of their "positive feelings for the flag." Two Illinois cities, Sesser and Murphysboro, passed their own flag desecration laws shortly after the *Johnson* ruling, even though Murphysboro's mayor conceded that it would be struck down in court and was mostly passed as a form of symbolic protest. In Orange, Connecticut, police chief Russell McLean ordered his police to wear American flag pins to protest the *Johnson* decision and instructed his officers in writing that "if you are not, you should be infuriated by the ruling."

Many other critics of the *Johnson* decision also called for or used symbolic protests—often involving the flag—to declare that Johnson should have no such right. Thus conservative groups burned symbolic judges' robes to protest the ruling on the Supreme Court steps on June 22, and scores of politicians and members of the general public unhappy with it proposed flying, or flew, flags upside down, at half-mast, or more often than usual to protest the decision (often in violation of the provisions of the voluntary flag code passed by Congress in 1942). On June 22, for example, the mayor of Memphis, terming the *Johnson* decision a "disgrace," ordered all city flags flown at half-staff. All three July 4 TV network evening newscasts carried film reports on mass upside-down flag displays in Nokesville, Virginia, in protest of the *Johnson* ruling; VRW officer Fred Fees explained (just as Vietnam War protesters who had been prosecuted twenty years earlier for similar acts had) that flying the flag upside down was a "symbol of distress" and "we had to do something to call the nation's attention to the fact that we think we're in trouble."[32]

In Manchester, Massachusetts, members of the American Legion announced that their long-planned July 4 burning of worn-out flags—a symbolic action which they clearly regarded as patriotic—would be dedicated to protesting the Supreme Court's ruling, which held, in short, that people could legally have unpatriotic thoughts in their heads while performing identical symbolic acts. In New Jersey, the Cartaret Savings Bank purchased thirteen thousand flags to give away as a protest against the Supreme Court.[33]

No doubt the most common symbolic means used to protest the *Johnson* decision was that promoted by the Cartaret bank, which was also the method recommended by Justice Brennan for Americans to express their patriotism: increased flag waving and flag flying. Indeed, the clearest concrete result of the Supreme Court's ruling was a massive upsurge in patriotism, rather than the threat to American unity foreseen by Senator Biden and others, and it was manifested most obviously by a huge increase in flag sales. Thus at the same time that he was introducing a constitutional amendment to protect the flag, presumably because it was somehow threatened, Republican House leader Bob Michel declared that Johnson's flag burning "woke us up to the meaning of the flag in our national life."[34]

The *Austin-American Statesman* reported on July 7 that if the *Johnson* decision had "some people seeing red," flag retailers were "seeing green." Greg Wald, the president of the National Independent Flag Dealers Association, a trade group, reported in early July that the *Johnson* decision had "really picked up enthusiasm" for flag sales and that flag "dealers across the country are reporting sell-outs." A saleswoman at Festival Flags in Richmond reported selling flags "like crazy" in early July, at a rate twelve times higher than during the previous year. Several flag dealers reported that their policy was to refuse to sell flags to people who were planning to burn them, although one such merchant in Texas conceded, "Of course, we really don't have a way of knowing without asking. But we're definitely opposed to anyone who would harm the flag."[35]

Several enterprising capitalists sold fireproof flags to citizens who wanted to take no chances with wandering flag burners. Thus Skipp Porteous of Great Barrington, Massachusetts, announced, just in time for July 4, that he was selling flags treated with a flame retardant known as "cease fire" for $10 each. Porteous said he supported the *Johnson* decision, but that though "you can burn the flag, you can't burn my flag." Servpro Industries of Tennessee announced it would fireproof already purchased flags by spraying them with a flame retardant guaranteed to work at temperatures exceeding 3,000 degrees Fahrenheit. The company promised that with "one or two sprays a year, the flag can be protected forever." The fireproof flags posed one dilemma, however: the officially recommended means of disposing of worn flags was by burning, but such flags apparently could never be discarded in an approved manner.[36]

Country singer Merle Haggard expressed his discontent with the *Johnson* decision by writing and singing a new song, "Me and Crippled Soldiers." Haggard, who had become well known for a 1969 song, "Okie from Muscogee," which attacked Vietnam War protesters, sang in his new song, "Now that it's all right to burn the Stars and Stripes / guess nobody really needs old Uncle Sam / might as well burn the Bill of Rights as well / and let the country go to hell, only me and crippled soldiers give a damn." Many other songs and poetry denouncing flag burning, usually of truly appalling quality, were placed in the *Congressional Record*. Representative Ileana Ros-Lehtinen (R-Fla.) inserted a poem by a Miami constituent, which included the lines, "Honored by many, disgraced by few / It should be a crime for one to burn you." (Some equally appalling poems were penned on the other side; Johnson's lawyer, William Kunstler, recited for reporters his own handiwork, written after Congress passed a law in October 1989, which sought to overturn the *Johnson* ruling, with the lines, "The Founding Fathers' ghosts have sadly learned / It was the First Amendment that was burned.")[37]

Other critics of the Supreme Court expressed their patriotism during July with unusual flag displays, many of which would have violated both former and proposed flag desecration laws. Even President Bush apparently enjoyed watching

some flag desecration: among the July 4 fireworks he observed at his Kenne-
bunkport home was a truly "burning" flag. The July 3 *New York Post* featured a
picture of a New Jersey waitress who was proudly kneeling on a huge crocheted
flag that was so large it could be displayed only on the ground. The July 3 *San
Francisco Examiner* included a photograph of an Arizona man who had sculpted
a flag image into his haircut, and the August 1989 issue of *Life* magazine included
a photo of shrubbery upon which a man had painted a flag image along with the
slogan "Don't burn our flag." The *Examiner* posed questions about the haircut that
equally applied to the shrubbery: "When he gets his next haircut, will that desecrate the flag? Or what if he fails to keep it neatly trimmed?" On June 29,
Representative Frank Annunzio (D-Ill.) proudly placed in the *Congressional
Record* a Flag Day address by Harwood Heights, Illinois, village president Ray
Willas, which lauded the proliferation of flag fashions as patriotic and provided a
list of such items that was virtually identical to the lists used to attack flag commercialization at the turn of the century: "Today we see the Red, White and Blue
everywhere. In our clothes, in our advertisements, wallpaper, bathing suits, floral
arrangements. The Stars and Stripes have become our country's favorite advertising media campaign. It tells everyone that the product being sold is 'All American.'" A *Los Angeles Times* story about the flag fashion phenomenon reassured
readers that "unlike the '60s when designers worked the flag into fashion as a political protest, designers now are flaunting the image" in "a synchronized burst of
patriotism."[38]

Several symbolic protests against the *Johnson* decision aroused controversy.
Thus a Massachusetts VFW official, when informed about the upside-down flag
flying by a veteran, declared, "If I ever came across someone flying the flag upside
down, I'd give them a good kick." Decisions by city officials in Jefferson County,
Missouri, and in Columbus, Georgia, to use unorthodox flag displays to protest the
Johnson ruling led to heated arguments. In Columbus, for example, the mayor
canceled an upside-down flag flying planned for July 4, which had been proposed
by city councilman Bobby Peters and unanimously approved by the city council,
after city officials were flooded with phone calls from veterans' organizations and
outraged citizens who termed the proposed action as disrespectful as flag burning.
Chagrined city councilman Stephen Hyles termed the fiasco a "mess" and lamented, "I think we ought to fly Bobby Peters upside down."[39]

Aside from a massive and obvious upsurge in patriotism and the hardly no-
ticed flurry of flag burnings, the *Johnson* decision also had the short-term concrete
result of freeing one imprisoned flag burner and leading to the dismissal of
charges against another. During a July 2 news interview, Attorney General Thorn-

burgh conceded that the parallels between the Texas law invalidated in *Johnson*, at least when used to prosecute political protesters, and the 1968 federal flag desecration law was so clear that he regarded the federal law as presumptively invalid, with the result that all persons jailed under it were probably entitled to relief. A search of federal jails uncovered precisely one person then imprisoned under the federal law, Puerto Rican Carlos Mendoza-Lugo, who had been given the maximum one-year sentence for burning a flag to demand independence for his homeland. By the time federal authorities moved to free him, however, he had already been released (on June 30) because a judge had ordered on June 27 that his sentence be shortened to his already served seven months. On November 6, 1989, a disorderly conduct prosecution resulting from an April 21, 1989, flag burning at Wayne State University was dropped against two protesters as a result of the *Johnson* ruling; one of the defendants, RYCB member Monte Dickenson, celebrated by handing out wooden matches with tiny attached flags.[40]

The Defense of the Johnson *Ruling*

Although the overwhelming majority of Americans unquestionably disagreed with the *Johnson* decision, polls indicated that a substantial minority of about 15 to 25 percent supported the Court's action. The decision was also supported by the American Society of Newspaper Editors (ASNE) and a clear majority of the literally thousands of newspaper editorials, cartoons, and political columns that commented on the case; by the ACLU and other civil liberties organizations; by the American Bar Association and an overwhelming majority of legal commentators, who churned out scores of law journal articles about the issue; and by a small handful of politicians. In the latter category, only eight congressmen (Democratic senators Edward Kennedy and Howard Metzenbaum, Republican senator Gordon Humphrey, and Democratic representatives William Clay, William Crockett, Ronald Dellums, Gus Savage, and Ted Weiss), out of 535 senators and representatives, voted against resolutions denouncing the *Johnson* decision in its immediate aftermath. They were joined by a similarly small percentage of state legislators and other politicians. For example, Georgia's attorney general Michael Bowers wrote in the July 2 *Atlanta Constitution* that though he personally could not understand how anyone could desecrate the flag, such an act was clearly a form of "free speech" which needed and deserved protection, just as offensive, shocking, and unpopular expression always needed legal protection, rather than popular or unimportant speech, which nobody objected to. Bowers wrote, "By upholding freedom, even the freedom to be obnoxious and offensive in burning the flag as a symbolic political act, we honor ourselves, and, in doing so, the flag."

Almost invariably, the defenders of the *Johnson* decision, like Bowers, focused on what they viewed as the fundamental democratic principle of freedom of dissent at stake, on their perception that the Court had properly valued this substantive concern over the protection of a symbol of that principle, and on the corresponding conclusion that critics of the Court were confusing symbol with substance by valuing the flag over the freedoms it stood for. Senator Metzenbaum put the case for the *Johnson* decision in a nutshell when he asked the SJC: "What example is more American, more faithful to American values? Jailing flag burners or tolerating them? Deep down, we know that tolerating even outrageous protests is truer to our tradition than jailing those who offend us." Steve Bates, the president of the South Carolina ACLU, spoke for almost all civil liberties groups and lawyers in hailing the *Johnson* ruling on the grounds that the flag symbolized freedom, including the freedom to dislike it, and that therefore flag burning "represents the exercise of the highest liberty for which it stands."[41]

Virtually every other defense of the *Johnson* decision was a variation along these basic themes. For example, in a July 2 column in the *Chicago Tribune,* Stephen Chapman declared that "America would be America with a different flag or no flag at all. It wouldn't be America without the U.S. Constitution and the freedoms it protects. . . . The most important of which is the right to think and communicate without the approval of the state. Those who support [overturning the *Johnson* decision] are trying to save the symbol by torching the substance."

Northwestern University law professor Martin Redish argued that if the Constitution protected only "freedom to agree with the majority, that's not much freedom. Even in Nazi Germany, you had the freedom to agree with the majority. . . . When I hear veterans talk about all those who died for the flag, I wonder what they think the flag stands for. It's a right to challenge our basic notions, to disagree without having tanks rolling over you. That's what people have fought for for 200 years." A letter to the editor from a veteran published in the June 28 *Washington Post* averred,

> I did not serve my country to defend a hunk of cloth [but to] protect the right of minorities to dissent, freedom of assembly and the right to redress—no matter how offensive to me that might be. . . . The blood of the Chinese students [killed in early June 1989 pro-democracy demonstrations] is barely dry and we have forgotten already that we cried for their right to dissent because that is what we as a country supposedly believe in.[42]

Former Vietnam prisoner of war James Warner told the SJC, in explaining his support for the *Johnson* decision, that to "pay honor to the flag" the most important thing was "to live in freedom, to set the example, to show the world what freedom means by our every public act." Syndicated columnist Jim Fain compared attempts to outlaw flag burning to a famous statement by an American officer involving the American destruction of a village during the Vietnam War: "We save the flag by destroying what it stands for." This same point was made in *Los Angeles Times* cartoons which showed President Bush burning the Bill of Rights while declaring, "Burning the flag goes too far" and depicted a red, white, and blue noose threatening American liberties. The *Salt Lake Tribune*'s cartoon of July 5 ridiculed Bush for abandoning basic democratic principles by depicting him as a founding father changing a draft of the First Amendment to exempt from its protection "flag burning or anything else that is unpopular and makes a lot of voters unhappy."[43]

As in the comments just quoted, the most common points made by the overwhelming majority of newspaper editorials and editorial columns which supported the *Johnson* decision all focused on the fundamental "free speech" argument: they frequently highlighted that both conservative and liberal justices had joined the majority opinion as an indication that the basic principle involved was so clear that it transcended ideology; they noted that Americans had universally hailed the recent use of "symbolic speech" by protesting Chinese students who had created a statue of the "Goddess of Democracy" and approvingly contrasted the Supreme Court's protection of dissidents' rights with the brutal suppression of the Chinese students at Tiananmen Square in Beijing; and they repeatedly paraphrased, cited, or quoted Justice Brennan's declaration that the "bedrock principle underlying the First Amendment" was that government could not "prohibit expression of an idea simply because society finds the idea itself offensive or disagreeable." For example, the June 23 *Los Angeles Times* editorial in support of the Court was titled "A Bedrock Principle," and the June 26 editorial in the *Christian Science Monitor* averred that the "unusual" conservative-liberal Court coalition "shows that the grand idea of free speech is not the property of the left or the right, but is the bedrock value of the American vision."

The *New York Times* editorially declared on June 23 that although flag burning was "despicable," the *Johnson* ruling, by placing "such a high value on free expression," had delivered a "message for patriotic Americans to be proud of" that would allow the flag to "wave more proudly than ever." Similarly, *Atlanta Constitution* editorial page editor Tom Teepen, in a July 4 column, argued, "We honor our flag by the quality of the nation we create for it to symbolize, not by the number of citizens we imprison in its name." The *Los Angeles Times* on June 28 editorialized that it would be a "tragic paradox" if attempts to "protect the symbol of the American nation become, in fact an assault on the most substantial foundation of its liberties." Syndicated columnist Clarence Page suggested that if the government was allowed to restrain political expression simply because it offended many people, the country would be adopting the "reasoning of Ayatollah Khomeini or the justice of Beijing." The *Washington Post*'s June 27 editorial also drew on Chinese developments to respond to those who, like Senator Dole, suggested that flag burners leave the country: "If all those legislators don't like a system of government that gives you a lot of room for free expression, irreverence and dissent, they could go and find one they do like. How about China? No flag burning there these days."[44]

Many critics of the drive to pass a flag "desecration" amendment or law to overturn the *Johnson* decision argued that supporters of the movement were unconstitutionally seeking to make the flag an "icon" and were guilty of "idolatry" because the concept of "desecration" applied only to religious objects, whereas the Constitution barred the establishment of a state religion. Thus an article in the religiously oriented journal *Christianity Today* termed attempts to outlaw flag "desecration" misguided efforts to make the flag "sacred" by fiat although it was not a religious object. In an article in the Autumn 1989 *Journal of Church and State*, James Wood argued that imbuing the flag with language that "would make it a sacred symbol" amounted to "idolatry" and distorted "the basic meaning of the flag and the nature of America's nationhood, which is secular and not sacred, human and not divine."[45]

A letter writer to the *Melbourne* (Australia) *Age*, which carried extensive coverage of the flag controversy, concluded that "presumably well-educated Americans customarily display towards their flag the same sort of fetishism that used to characterize so-called primitive tribes." University of California law professor Robert Cole expanded on this argument in a statement submitted to the HJC, which also rebutted the argument that protecting the flag was needed to foster national unity:

> Each U.S. flag, big or little, hand stitched or mass produced . . . can be transformed into something sacred only if it is literally taken to be the physical embodiment of virtue. A mystical and subtle thing in religion, this is nothing but primitive totemism in public affairs. To regard every U.S. flag as the incarnation of the nation is what our distant ancestors did when they ate a lion's heart to be brave. In a free, modern society, such totemism as the grounds for government suppression of political activity is bizarre. . . . The alternative to a frank confession of primitive

> totemism as the true basis [for outlawing flag desecration] is to claim
> that protecting U.S. flags is a unique means for unifying the country. In
> fact, no one symbol can unify a huge pluralistic country like ours. . . .
> More important than the patent improbability that prohibiting burning
> U.S. flags will unify the nation is the obnoxious principle involved.
> What kind of unity is built on official repression of a tiny handful of
> people? . . . Feelings of patriotism . . . unify a community because they
> are voluntary and personal.[46]

The "slippery slope" argument made by Justice Brennan that a "flag exception" to the fundamental principles of free speech would open the way for other exceptions was widely supported by defenders of the Court. Senator Kennedy, for example, warned that the Constitution was "the seamless fabric of our liberties" and that "if we pull one thread, other freedoms will began to unravel, too," because "once we abandon the broad tolerance that the Constitution requires, there is no fair way to draw the line." Similarly, the *Progressive* magazine warned that "chipping away" at the First Amendment to protect the flag "will make it easier to chip away at it again" until "we're all wearing gags in public." ACLU executive director Ira Glasser elaborated on this argument:

> The minute you establish the principle that there can be exceptions to
> the First Amendment for offensive speech, there's no practical way to
> limit it. The first exception will not be the last. Someone adds an exception for derogatory racial remarks. If you're a woman you want an
> exception for Playboy. If you're a Jew you want an exception for Nazis
> marching. Pretty soon you don't have a First Amendment.[47]

A variant of the "slippery slope" critique (asking, tongue-in-cheek, why other symbols should not also be protected) spawned numerous satirical essays. For example, syndicated columnist Mike Royko asked why nothing was done to protect the dignity of the national anthem, which he declared was, by far, more frequently insulted by inattention and improper behavior at athletic events than the flag was threatened by burnings. After describing a litany of such sins, Royko proposed a corrective constitutional amendment to make it a crime "during the singing of the national anthem in any public place" to "drink any beverage, chew gum, talk, whisper, scratch, yawn, pick your nose, gawk, leer or slouch" or to "fail to sing," with mutes "required to sing in sign language." *New York Times* satirist Russell Baker demanded protection for all of America's "precious" symbols, including "spacious skies, purple mountain majesties, shining seas, the fruited plain and plenty more," especially inasmuch as all of these were being threatened by acid rain, strip mining, industrial pollution and tons of asphalt.[48]

Dallas-Times Herald and *Arizona Daily Star* satirists Molly Ivins and Tom Beal suggested, respectively, in their June 29 columns, that constitutional amendments might next be proposed to "stop anyone from holding his nose when the flag goes by" and to "make it unconstitutional for kids to talk back to their moms, or not visit them on holidays." *Austin American-Statesman* columnist Mike Kelley, in an allusion to the general perception that fears of being viewed as "unpatriotic" were driving some politicians' behavior during the flag controversy, suggested a constitutional amendment "requiring the presence of connected vertebrae as a prerequisite for elected office"; he declared that if opinion polls showed that voters approved of yellow fever, politicians would soon be "demanding bigger and better mosquitoes." Other satirists suggested that a punishment "slippery slope" might well result from political grandstanding over the flag burning issue: according to Dave Barry's round-up of the "summer's top stories" in the September 3 *Boston Globe*, the penalty for flag burning "is now execution without trial," and Gerald Nachman, writing in the September 19 *San Francisco Chronicle,* reported that "premeditated flag abuse in Alabama may well become a hanging offense."[49]

Although most support for the *Johnson* ruling reflected ideological commitment to civil liberties in the abstract, some of it related to more practical concerns. For example, part of the reason why the vast majority of the press opposed any encroachment on First Amendment rights, even one directed against fringe radicals, was undoubtedly fear of creating a precedent for subsequent curbs on the mainstream press. Thus in endorsing the call of the American Society of Newspaper Editors (ASNE) in September 1989 for editorial opposition to any congressional efforts to override *Johnson,* the leading media trade journal *Editor and Publisher* declared on October 7 that "the right of dissent is the cornerstone of our First Amendment guarantees of freedom of speech and of the press" and that the Constitution "does not provide any exceptions" to this right and "we do not need to start defining exceptions now." A column in the August 1989 issue of *Business Marketing* drew the connection between suppressing flag desecration and far more direct threats to mainstream expression, warning that "a society and its government accepting restrictions of free political speech will soon demand new encumbrances on advertising" and asking, if flag burning could be outlawed, "Who will defend junk mail or TV commercial breaks against a public majority rabidly seeking relief from advertising clutter." Similarly, a column in the November 1989 *Field & Stream,* a journal not normally noted for its attention to constitutional issues, warned that amending the Constitution to ban flag burning could "come back to haunt gun owners" because what would then stop "a bunch of opportunistic pols [politicians] from rewriting the Second Amendment [which guarantees the right to bear arms]?"

Why Did the Flag Burning Controversy Get So Hot?

That the *Johnson* decision provoked an enormous, prolonged, and overwhelmingly negative reaction in the United States is obvious, but why this reaction became so great, and especially why the flag desecration issue consumed enormous amounts of political and public energy for an entire year is, at least in historical retrospect, a considerable mystery. The United States was not besieged by flag burners in mid-1989, and on the few occasions when they occurred during the fifteen previous years and on the more numerous occasions when they occurred during the following year, they attracted, with a few exceptions, hardly any media or public attention. Furthermore, although a strong argument could be made that flag burning, however offensive to the vast majority, was exactly the sort of exercise of dissent that was supposed to be at the heart of American freedoms, no one could demonstrate any clear and concrete harm that flag burnings did either to the country or to American patriotism. In fact, the most obvious result of the *Johnson* decision was probably the greatest upsurge in flag patriotism in American history since the Civil War. Indeed, *Houston Post* columnist Larry Ashby satirically suggested that perhaps Gregory Lee Johnson was secretly "a deep and devoted patriot" who had set out to do his best to "rejuvenate" America's "flabby" spirit. What especially makes the bona fides of the flag furor of 1989–90 historically suspect is that, after the Supreme Court's June 11, 1990, *Eichman* decision striking down the 1989 FPA (Congress's ultimate legislative response to the *Johnson* case), and the immediately subsequent second failure in Congress of the constitutional amendment, the entire issue virtually disappeared from the public and political arena overnight after having been one of the most dominant issues for a year.[50]

The answer to this mystery—how an essentially symbolic issue could attract so much attention and be attributed so much importance for a year and then suddenly disappear—is highly complex. Probably the most important contributor to this phenomenon is that the importance of the issue, at least in practical terms (as opposed to abstract intellectual theorizing about the limits of First Amendment rights), was grossly and artificially exaggerated out of all proportion by press and political elites. It must be added, however, that in an age in which American elites often focused on symbolic rather than substantive issues, the public was unusually receptive to press and political manipulation of this seemingly clear-cut symbolic issue; this was especially so because it offered up flag burners (as well as the Supreme Court) as "anger scapegoats" for the venting of a growing psychological distress for the increasing percentage of the population who perceived that their country was becoming a declining international power, losing both economic competitiveness and political clout abroad, while simultaneously seemingly unable to solve domestic problems such as urban decay, racism, drugs, crimes, and a slow but steady collapse of the nation's physical and educational infrastructure. Furthermore, for many Americans, the flag burning issue seems to have taken on exaggerated importance because it symbolically reminded them of the bitter cultural and political divisions of the 1960s, even reprising the same struggle over the symbolic use and importance of the flag which had proved so emotionally divisive twenty-five years earlier. The role of press and political elites in stoking the fires of the flag controversy in 1989 will be discussed in the remainder of this chapter; the receptivity of the public to this issue will be discussed at the close of this book.

The Role of the Press

The first element in transforming the *Johnson* decision from what the conservative British news magazine *The Economist* termed a "routine reaffirmation of free speech" into the focus of an enormous year-long ruckus was unquestionably the massive press attention to the ruling and the distorted impression of it which was (probably mostly) unwittingly conveyed by segments of the press. These two factors virtually guaranteed a massive public reaction. Nearly every major American newspaper headlined the *Johnson* decision on June 22, and two of the three television networks (ABC and CBS)—the prime source of news for most Americans—led with the flag burning story on their June 21 evening news.[51]

Given the infrequent number of flag burnings in recent American history, the complete lack of any evidence that flag burnings had any real effect on anything, the recent American celebration of the use of symbolic protest by Chinese students whose demands for democracy had been brutally suppressed by a totalitarian regime only three weeks earlier, and the arguably clear and logical derivation of the *Johnson* decision from past Court holdings such as *Barnette* and *Street,* it is difficult to understand why the press chose to highlight the *Johnson* case as much as it did. Certainly the Court's action warranted significant press coverage, but it hardly demanded the massive media attention that it received.

Press treatment of the *Johnson* ruling probably reflected a combination of circumstances. First was the purely accidental happenstance that, since the Chinese crackdown, there had been few major news developments, and thus there was little "news competition" for space and attention. As Washington reporter Alan Schlein, who published a critique of press coverage of the flag controversy in late 1989, noted in a 1992 interview, "What becomes news in this country is a function as much of whether the stars are in the right orbit as of legitimate factors." A second element that helped generate massive media coverage of the *Johnson* ruling was that both the heartfelt eloquence of Brennan's opinion and the anguished dissents of Rehnquist and Stevens, along with Stevens's unusual decision to read his dissent aloud, signaled to Supreme Court reporters that the decision was likely to be highly controversial and thus extremely newsworthy. In a 1990 interview, *Washington Post* Supreme Court reporter Ruth Marcus said that the opinions made clear that the issue was "extremely emotional" for the justices and when "they feel strongly enough about it for them to dissent from the bench, that's generally a pretty good barometer for us, for our news judgment, and I think the language on both sides really both captured and foreshadowed the debate that ensued."[52]

An additional factor that prompted the intense news coverage was simply that the ruling was a "good" if not truly important news story from the sensationalist standpoint that inevitably and subtly affects all news decisions: it was correctly perceived by the media as having enormous potential for arousing great public interest because it was a Supreme Court decision (the Texas Court of Criminal Appeals ruling upheld by the Court received no national publicity); because it concerned the flag, arguably the country's most important and certainly a highly emotive symbol; because the 1988 Pledge of Allegiance and the earlier 1989 "flag on the floor" disputes had made clear its potential for arousing controversy; because the issue had apparently clear-cut and easily understandable positions on both sides that, at least superficially, all Americans could presumably relate and react to; because highly charged symbolic issues, especially related to "values questions," had been increasingly stressed by both media and political elites and this repetition validated such topics as important news stories; and because, at least for TV, the flag burning issue naturally lent itself to graphic and literally "inflammatory" accompanying "visuals" depicting flag desecration in action.

Some journalists who were interviewed for this book flatly rejected the argument that the press overplayed the flag desecration controversy. For example, in a 1992 interview, *Fort Wayne Journal Gazette* editor Craig Klugman, who as ASNE president in 1989 helped to organize editorial opposition to attempts to overturn *Johnson,* termed such suggestions "mostly bullshit" because "the press did not create that furor, the Supreme Court created it." Many reporters, however, indicated considerable ambiguity over the role played by the press. For example, Washington reporter Schlein suggested in a 1992 interview that compared to the massive savings and loan (S&L) and Bank of Credit and Commerce International (BCCI) financial collapse scandals, which were developing at the same time and had a greater effect on far more Americans, "Flag burning is a simple story, everybody has an opinion, everybody understands it, it's much more symbolic and much more on the surface. BCCI is a nightmare [by comparison for journalists]." CBS Supreme Court reporter Rita Braver, in a 1990 interview, said that she concluded that the *Johnson* ruling would be a "big story because of the soaring quality of the language" of the Court's opinions, but she originally viewed it as "important in a major way as a human interest story" but not as a legal story "because people really care about the flag and because the justices so passionately cared." She added that, in news judgments, "outrageousness seems to take precedence and sometimes the pictures [of flag burnings] tell you more of the story than is really maybe right for them to tell you."

ABC congressional correspondent Cokie Roberts suggested in a 1990 interview that the "inflammatory" nature of the repeated scenes of flag burning shown on television played an important role in provoking political and public outrage. In television, she noted, "the pictures are so much more powerful than the words that the television spots on this subject are [anti-flag-desecration] propaganda. The wallpaper [pictures] is all flag burning and it's literally incendiary." She felt that the press had overplayed the story:

> The media is constantly saying, "Why doesn't Congress handle the serious issues, here they are dealing with the flag when the S&Ls are causing the country to go down the tubes." Well, why wouldn't they talk about the flag when that's what we lead with and we give the time to? We missed the S&L story when it was in congressional committees all over Capitol Hill. We didn't know it was a sexy story, so we've had one of those stories [the flag controversy] that everybody understands, that gets a sort of gut American reaction and we all like covering it, all of us are political reporters.

Marcia Coyle, Supreme Court reporter for the *National Law Journal,* noted in a 1990 interview that her publication, a lawyers' trade magazine, paid little attention to *Johnson* because it represented little in the way of a legal departure, but she agreed that the massive general media coverage flowed from the fact that "it's such an easy-to-grab issue" because "everybody relates to the flag" and reporters didn't have "to worry about boring the public trying to explain exactly what happened."

From the standpoint of the media consumer, because the nature of the American news media is to stress not only the important but also the unexpected, the unusual, and even the bizarre, the massive press coverage undoubtedly conveyed the message that the Supreme Court had handed down a very strange decision. In his June 21 ABC network news broadcast, anchor Peter Jennings, who devoted almost one-fifth of his program to the *Johnson* ruling, all but told his audience that the Court had behaved oddly and that they should get upset about it. He declared that the ruling had come from a "supposedly conservative court," that debate over the ruling (which had hardly begun yet) "deeply divides the country," and that "there are very few" Court rulings "which we can imagine evoking such a gut reaction as this one." In an accompanying piece, correspondent Jeff Greenfield suggested that flag burnings were "deliberately designed to provoke" and would "always" do so, much as a "parade of swastikas stirs memories of horror."

Although the CBS evening news coverage on June 21 was shorter and more restrained, it featured a highly inflammatory excerpt from a news conference by Johnson, who was shown sporting a goatee and wearing a bandanna over his shoulders and his RCYB T-shirt featuring a man with a rifle, while proclaiming his joy in seeing the flag, "a symbol of international plunder and murder, go up in flames and be reduced to ashes." In a 1990 interview, CBS reporter Braver recalled that as she prepared her story, her editor, upon viewing the Johnson footage, told her, "People are going to go berserk over this because Gregory Johnson looks so awful. He is going to be frightening to people, they're going to hate it, they're going to go crazy." Braver recalled, "What happened was exactly what my editor predicted [because] . . . the very idea that this kind of person, who many would consider the scum of the earth," was involved and "was going to make it a highly charged issue." She added that the press did not create the story. "It was more that we put out what was there," including the "incredibly passionate language" of the Court's ruling and "putting this guy on TV and then it kind of took off. The very sight of it got people's passions going." NBC's coverage was more restrained than that of the other two networks (it reported the story well into the broadcast instead of as the lead), but like its competitors NBC prominently featured film of flag burnings—apparently all from the 1984 Dallas incident—that were to be shown repeatedly during the next few days, thereby giving the incorrect impression that such events were a common occurrence.

In the print press, aside from the exaggerated importance given the *Johnson* ruling by its almost universal display as the lead front-page story, a substantial minority of newspapers gave a highly distorted impression of the decision by incorrectly suggesting that the Court had affirmatively endorsed or approved of flag burning, as opposed to its very different actual holding that such conduct was a constitutionally valid, if obnoxious, form of political expression. This highly important distinction meant the difference between portraying the Court's decision as focusing essentially on the emotional question of whether flag desecration was "good"—a question with a guaranteed negative popular response—or instead focusing on the far more complex and less impassioned question as to whether it was constitutionally protected. By far the most inflammatory and seemingly deliberately distorted headline accounts of the ruling appeared in the June 22 editions of the *Salt Lake City Tribune* and the *New York Post,* which respectively bannered, "Court Hands Match to Flag Burners" and "Supreme Court Gives Protesters OK to Burn This Flag" (accompanied in the *Post* with pictures of Johnson displaying a scorched flag and a separate story giving Johnson's reaction to his victory under the headline, "Revolting Communist Sneers at the Verdict"). Many other headlines also conveyed, in less distorted form, that the Supreme Court said flag burning was "OK," a conception that quickly gained general popular and political currency. For example, the June 22 editions of *Newsday* and the *San Jose Mercury News* respectively headlined, "Top Court OKs Flag-Burning" and "Flag Burning Ruled OK."

In fairness to the print press, most of the "OK"-type headlines probably resulted more from space constraints than deliberate distortions, and many newspaper headlines were far more accurate, as in the respective June 22 banners in the *Dallas Times-Herald* and the *Newark Star-Ledger* reading, "Burning of U.S. Flag Legal, Court Rules in Dallas," and "Justices Rule Flag Burning Is a Right of Free Speech." Nonetheless, repeated comments made in the following days to the effect that the Supreme Court had "okayed" flag burning suggest that a large percentage of the population obtained a distorted impression of the *Johnson* decision from the news media. Unquestionably the framing of the flag desecration issue in a substantial proportion of the public's mind as centering on whether or not flag burning was good, rather than whether it was constitutionally protected, helped both to intensify and to prolong the subsequent controversy.

National Law Journal reporter Marcia Coyle suggested, in a 1990 interview, that the widespread perception that the Supreme Court had "okayed" flag burning was the result not only of distorted headlines but of the failure of most media reports to fully explain the Court's reasoning and especially how it logically flowed from past rulings on symbolic speech (only leading newspapers such as the *New York Times* and the *Washington Post* printed extensive texts of the opinions; the accounts in most papers and in the broadcast media generally were far too sketchy to convey the legal context of the majority opinion). She added:

I really didn't think the coverage conveyed the rationale for the decision as clearly as it could have and didn't fully put it into the perspective of the First Amendment. Brennan's reasoning got a little lost
in the political reaction to the decision. People really have a hard time
understanding why the Court could have done what it did and it was a
great opportunity to give people another lesson in what this country
stands for, and I don't think it came across.

This distorted conception of the *Johnson* decision was by no means limited to
members of the general public. For example, California Republican assemblyman
Tim Leslie asked, "What kind of message are we sending our children when we
say it's OK to burn the flag?" and in testimony before a HJC subcommittee,
Representative Sonny Montgomery and American Legion national commander
"Sparky" Gierke characterized the *Johnson* decision in the same manner. Some
Republican politicians and officials appear to have deliberately fostered the impression that the Supreme Court, along with anyone who supported the *Johnson*
ruling or who opposed a constitutional amendment to overturn it, approved of flag
burning. For example, Attorney General Thornburgh told a national television
audience on July 2 that the ruling amounted to the statement that "it's all right" to
burn the flag. Republican Congressional Campaign Committee chairman Ed
Rollins said, in discussing the prospects for a constitutional amendment, that he
thought Democrats would not be "stupid enough to argue for the flag burners" and
that if they argued against an amendment because "they think it's OK to desecrate
the flag, we're going to win on that issue."[53]

Although the *Johnson* decision surely would have aroused controversy even
if the media coverage had been less extensive and, in some cases, misleading, the
extraordinary attention given to the story during the first two weeks following
the ruling certainly helped to create a self-fulfilling prophecy: in short, the coverage helped to generate massive public reaction, thereby "proving" that the story
deserved massive coverage because the public was so interested in it. For example, the Times Mirror Center for the People and the Press reported that the
Johnson decision had attracted more interest than any other Washington news
story and was among the top ten stories of all kinds in attracting public interest
since the beginning of its surveys in 1986. Although this finding might suggest
that the media simply gave heavy coverage to a story the public was greatly interested in, as will be pointed out below, as soon as the media coverage dropped off
after about July 4, public interest also significantly declined, suggesting that press
coverage drove public interest rather than the other way around.[54]

Not surprisingly, during the height of the 1989 controversy, the press virtually ignored its own role in stirring up the flag burning hornet's nest, even though most newspapers were soon editorializing that politicians were making far too much of the controversy and ignoring far more important matters. One lone press voice in the wilderness was *Newsday* columnist Thomas Collins, who wrote on July 6 that it "was hard to think of any other country where the flag and one's allegiance to it could become such a monumental and threatening issue" or one "in which the press would jump in with both feet, adding to the uproar," and that if President Bush could be criticized for waving the flag at the expense of more important issues, "the same might be said of the media." In a 1990 interview, a White House aide who was involved in the Bush administration's handling of the constitutional amendment partly echoed this view, complaining that the early massive press coverage helped to spur an administration and legislative response, but that then the press began attacking those who sought an amendment. He complained that the national media "kind of jumped on the bandwagon" originally but then "turned tail from the initial days and portrayed it exclusively as all politics, that no one really wanted to protect the flag. It was just day and night."

The Role of President Bush

The flag burning controversy might have quickly faded away if President Bush had not announced on June 27 that he favored a constitutional amendment to overturn the *Johnson* decision. The issue had disappeared from the front page of most newspapers by the weekend of June 24–25, and, after June 21, it was steadily given less prominent and lengthy treatment by the television networks until it disappeared entirely from the three network evening news programs by June 26. This trend was immediately and radically reversed by President Bush's June 27 morning news conference announcement that he intended to sponsor a constitutional amendment to overturn the *Johnson* decision. This announcement was followed by a media extravaganza on June 30 at which Bush formally introduced the text of the proposed amendment, making a special trip to do so at the Iwo Jima Memorial at Arlington National Cemetery in Virginia, accompanied by masses of flags, the Marine Corps Band, Secretary of Defense Dick Cheney, and the joint chiefs of staff. Essentially arguing that forbidding flag desecration was designed to advance American liberties, Bush maintained that the "surest way to preserve liberty is to protect the spirit that sustains it" and that therefore the flag must be protected because it "has guaranteed and nurtured" the "precious rights" of the nation, including free speech. "What that flag embodies is too sacred to be abused," he maintained.[55]

The news media widely reported the operative text of the proposed amendment, which Bush read aloud at the Iwo Jima Memorial: "The Congress and the States shall have power to prohibit the physical desecration of the flag of the United States." The general press virtually never reported the preamble to the amendment, however, or the circumstances that surrounded the drafting of the amendment text and preamble. The key phrase in the preamble defined "physical desecration" as including, but "not limited to, such acts as burning, mutilating, defacing, defiling or trampling on the flag, or displaying the flag in a contemptuous manner." The vagueness of the "contemptuous manner" clause was to become one of many aspects of the amendment which led to heated contention in Congress.[56]

The unusual inclusion of a preamble along with the operative text of the amendment reflected backstage maneuvering between the White House and the Republican congressional leadership, which was only hinted at in the general press. On the morning of June 28, White House press secretary Marlin Fitzwater stated that President Bush would announce the text of a proposed amendment later that day. A few hours later, however, Fitzwater suddenly said that the text would "not be ready today" because the White House was "working with members of Congress to develop appropriate language."[57]

According to congressional and White House sources interviewed in 1990 on conditions of anonymity, when Republican Senate leader Dole and House leader Michel learned of Bush's intention to announce his own amendment language on the morning of June 28, they vigorously protested to the White House because since June 22 they had been drafting their own amendment and they wanted to be credited for authoring any text endorsed by Bush. Thus, according to an administration source, although the office of White House counsel C. Boyden Gray originated the idea for a constitutional amendment within the White House and convinced Bush to support it and that any statutory attempt to override the *Johnson* ruling "absolutely would not work," when Gray's office finished drafting language and the White House made its original June 28 statement, Dole and Michel "made clear they wanted their own language" and "wanted to be able to say they wrote the damn thing." Therefore, he added, Bush issued orders "to work with the Hill and not push the President's version," at least partly because such an approach might make the amendment less of a "political issue" by tying it somewhat less closely to him. A Capitol Hill source confirmed that because the Republican congressional leadership had already been at it for a day or two before the White House became involved, there was some tension because there was already pride of authorship [by Dole and Michel]. The word was kind of out [on Capitol Hill] that these two were going to do this and then the president steps in. There was some tension between wanting the president's help, because everybody understood that unless Bush was extremely involved in this it wasn't going to happen, and not wanting him to come in at the last minute and take what Michel or Dole had done and suddenly turn that into the president's amendment.

According to White House, congressional, and Justice Department sources, the final text of the amendment was worked out at a series of highly contentious meetings, described variously as a "real tussle" and "hard negotiations," at which the key players were Brent Hatch, an assistant to White House counsel Gray; Dennis Shea, Senator Dole's counsel; and Charlene Vanlier, Michel's counsel. The major bone of contention at the meetings, according to the sources, was Dole's original insistence that the amendment's text list specific forms of flag desecration that would be outlawed, as opposed to Michel's position that the amendment should provide only a general authorization to ban flag desecration, leaving the details of implementing this up to the federal and state legislatures.

According to the sources, Dole's stance reflected his desire to make certain that putting flags on the floor, as in the Scott Tyler SAIC exhibit four months earlier, would be outlawed. They added that Michel was insistent that including a detailed list of types of forbidden flag desecration in the amendment's text would make it inconsistent with the existing style of constitutional provisions, which generally authorized broad grants of government authority but avoided specific details, and that, moreover, no list could ever be comprehensive and therefore unforeseen types of future flag desecration might require further constitutional amendments under the Dole approach. Eventually, according to the sources, a "compromise" was reached in which the operative text of the proposed amendment was close to Michel's proposal, while the preamble reflected the Dole position. According to a White House source, Dole and Michel "were adamant and it was difficult to incorporate their very different amendments" and final agreement could be reached only by "getting people to sit on their egos a bit" while "still allowing each to claim they wrote it."

Bush's endorsement of an amendment and his Iwo Jima speech brought the flag burning issue back to newspaper headlines across the country, usually accompanied by large pictures of Bush standing before the Iwo Jima statue. The flag desecration issue was the lead story on eight of the twelve evening news programs broadcast by the three networks between June 27 and June 30. CBS and NBC both devoted an extraordinary one-third of their June 27 broadcast to the controversy, while ABC spent one-fifth of its June 30 program on the issue. When the Pennsylvania VFW met in convention on June 29, Republican Senator Arlen Spector told the gathering that flag desecration was "the number one topic in this country today," and Democratic governor Robert Casey backed Bush's position, declaring that Pennsylvania "takes a back seat to no other state in loyalty to this country."[58]

As Casey's remark suggests, Bush's public espousal of a constitutional amendment placed strong pressure on Democrats to demonstrate their patriotism, and key Democratic congressional leaders apparently felt forced to set the wheels in motion to ensure that Congress would take formal action to, in Senate majority leader Mitchell's words, "correct" the Court's ruling in the *Johnson* case. The Democratic reaction to Bush's sponsorship of a constitutional amendment, and especially to his ballyhooed visit to the Iwo Jima Memorial, was an extraordinary mixture of rage and fear. Bush's endorsement of an amendment reincarnated Democratic memories of his manipulation of the Pledge of Allegiance issue during the 1988 campaign, which had helped create in many of their minds an image of Bush as a deeply cynical man, who, even more than most politicians, would stop at nothing for short- or long-term political gain. Therefore, his endorsement of a constitutional amendment on yet another flag-related issue was widely interpreted by Democrats as a cynical political maneuver; they viewed it as designed to force Democrats with civil liberties scruples about supporting such a measure to appear as "anti-flag," and this perception further embittered their dark mental picture of Bush. Moreover, Bush's amendment endorsement was seen as an even more cynical, more serious, and more dangerous political ploy than the pledge affair because while the latter could be somewhat excused as designed for the short-term effect of getting elected president during a political campaign, now he was viewed by many Democrats as willing to permanently tarnish the crown jewel of American democracy—the First Amendment and the Bill of Rights—for his perceived sordid political ends. Democratic National Committee (DNC) communications director Michael McCurry reflected the reaction of many Democrats to the Iwo Jima speech when he declared, "The heroes of Iwo Jima didn't die so they could become a backdrop for some political photo opportunity."[59]

This Democratic mental picture of a cynical Bush was greatly enhanced because his original response on June 22 to the *Johnson* decision was moderate and in no way suggested that he would seek to overturn it; therefore, his switch on June 27, was viewed as a pure political ploy especially as it was widely attributed to a June 26 meeting held between Bush and his 1988 campaign director and subsequent choice as Republican National Committee (RNC) chairman Lee Atwater, who was widely regarded as the shrewd but cynical genius most responsible for developing the pledge and Willie Horton issues. In his original June 22 remarks about the *Johnson* decision, Bush had declared that his "personal, emotional response" was that flag burning was "wrong—dead wrong," but he had also seemingly gone out of his way to dampen public criticism of the Court and to indicate that he would not seek to challenge its ruling by stating, "I understand the legal basis for that decision, and I respect the Supreme Court. And as President of the United States, I will see that the law of the land is fully supported."[60]

In subsequent days, as the polls and other indicators of adverse public reaction to the *Johnson* decision mounted, scores of congressmen introduced or supported constitutional amendments designed to reverse it. On June 22, for example, seventeen proposed amendments were introduced in the House, and pressure soon mounted from Republican congressional leaders for Bush to support such action. When Bush suddenly endorsed a constitutional amendment at a hastily called morning press conference on June 27, on the grounds that a statute "cannot correct" the Court's ruling and that somehow an amendment would "in no way limit" the right to protest, he failed to explain (then or ever) why he had departed from his earlier pledge to "see that the law of the land is fully supported."[61]

When it became known that Bush had lunched with Atwater on June 26, many Democrats became convinced that Atwater and Bush had conspired for cynical partisan reasons to replay the pledge issue on a grander and, in their eyes, far more damaging scale (although both Bush and Atwater denied discussing the flag issue). Thus Senator Kennedy, one of the few congressional defenders of the *Johnson* decision, told the SJC on August 1 that Bush had "failed" a "critical test of leadership" when, after his initial decision to "acquiesce" to the Court, he decided to "launch a high-profile campaign" to overturn *Johnson* "after lunch with Lee Atwater," in an attempt to repeat his 1988 "partisan political campaign around the flag." Similarly, in a 1991 interview Representative David Skaggs (D-Colo.) recalled "how impressed" he was "with the president's initial reaction to the *Johnson* decision, in which his untutored instincts were to recognize that the Supreme Court has a tough job and to respect their judgment. It was only after the political handlers got hold of him that he ended up at Iwo Jima."[62]

Not surprisingly, Bush administration officials and supporters vigorously denied that Bush, who had been shot down while piloting a plane during World War II, was motivated by anything but a sincere love for the flag. For example, in 1990 a White House assistant who was involved in handling the amendment vigorously insisted in an interview that last year everything I saw come from the White House stood against the claim we were playing politics. There's no doubt that Atwater and others probably saw strong political benefits to backing the amendment, and there probably was, but the president made a very clear attempt to stay above that. He gave clear marching orders not to make a partisan effort because he felt strongly about this as a moral issue and not something to play games with. I've heard him get really pissed off about charges that he wrapped himself in the flag. He felt very, very strongly about this, going back to his days in the military.

Possibly because of the widespread criticism that he was acting for political ends, Bush made only the most fleeting public references in 1989 to the flag issue after his Iwo Jima speech, thereby sparking private complaints from the right—ironically echoing those from the left, but based on an opposite evaluation of the amendment's merits—that he was engaged only in political posturing. For example, in a 1991 interview, former Representative Charles Douglas, a leading amendment backer (who no doubt felt more free to speak than did most incumbents by virtue of losing his New Hampshire House seat in the 1990 elections), bitterly complained that "there never was any White House commitment for assistance" to congressional supporters of the amendment and that, "had they really felt strongly on the flag issue, rather than just political posturing, I think they would have done something."

Whatever motivated Bush's decision to endorse the amendment, the image of Bush as desiring to repeat his successful 1988 manipulation of the flag issue became deeply ingrained in the Democratic interpretation of the 1989–90 flag desecration controversy and obtained considerable resonance in the press and among civil liberties groups and segments of the broader public. Thus *Washington Post* columnist Richard Cohen wrote, concerning Bush's trip to the Iwo Jima Memorial, that it was a "wonder he didn't row across [the Potomac River] in a little boat," and popular comedian Jay Leno's joke that Bush wanted to ban flag burning because "if you're going to wrap yourself up in the flag you don't want anyone burning it" was endlessly recycled. William Schneider, a political analyst at the conservative American Enterprise Institute, expressed the dominant press interpretation of Republican motivations shortly after Bush endorsed an amendment: "The Republicans have been trying for years to ideologize state and local elections and this gives them a wedge to do it. They want to turn every Democrat into a liberal flag-burner—like they did to Michael Dukakis." Similarly, on the June 27 network newscasts, ABC White House correspondent Brit Hume reported that Bush's endorsement of the amendment was "not surprising for a man who made the flag the centerpiece of his last campaign," and CBS White House reporter Leslie Stahl declared that Bush had "learned in the campaign that this is an issue that works for him."[63]

Many opponents of the amendment blamed Bush not only for seeking political mileage out of the flag desecration issue but for reviving the controversy at a time when it appeared to be dying down and therefore leading Congress, the press, and the public to spend months debating the issue in 1989–90. For example, in a 1990 interview, Democratic HJC Civil Liberties Subcommittee chair Don Edwards of California, who conducted hearings on possible responses to the *Johnson* ruling in July 1989, referred to the Washington flag desecration "frenzy, the hysteria that the president, to his discredit, caused," especially when Bush "did that outrageous thing and went over to Iwo Jima with bands and flags waving, he almost shot guns off into the air." Similarly, when asked in a 1990 interview to explain why the flag desecration controversy became such a major issue, Morton Halperin, the head of the ACLU's Washington office, said, "The answer is just two words—George Bush. If he had said the right thing and opposed an amendment, or if he had even said nothing, the issue would have gone away." Gloria Phares, who helped to write the artists' amicus brief opposing flag desecration laws in both the 1989 and 1990 Supreme Court cases, similarly blamed Bush in a 1990 interview for stoking up the flag controversy, declaring that he had "figured out that he made a lot of political hay over the Pledge of Allegiance [and] . . . just looked at the polls and went for it."

Democratic anger at Bush's endorsement of a constitutional amendment only increased when other Republican spokesmen publicly interpreted the flag burning issue in political terms. For example, shortly before Bush endorsed an amendment, House minority whip Newt Gingrich declared that if Democrats opposed an amendment, "they can go to the country and explain why," while at the Bush Iwo Jima ceremony Senate Republican leader Dole, in a clear political threat, invited opponents to "vote against the amendment, voice your opposition" as "part of the wonderful process we call democracy." Other statements from leading Republicans which suggested political motivations behind Bush's call for a constitutional amendment included comments by House leader Michel, who told reporters that White House chief of staff John Sununu had urged Republicans to push the flag amendment because it was a "wedge" issue that would divide the Democrats; by National Republican Congressional Campaign Committee spokesman John Buckley, who said it would be a "very long campaign season" for those "on the wrong side" of the amendment controversy; and by Atwater, who said that Republicans "don't intend to make this a partisan issue," but Democrats who "choose not to support an amendment" would create one. During the June 28 consideration in the Colorado House of Representatives of a resolution urging congressional passage of a constitutional amendment to protect what it termed the "sacred symbol" of the country, Republican representative Charles Duke declared, "It's a pro-American vote to vote for this resolution. A vote against this resolution, in my opinion, is a vote against America."[64]

Although the perception of naked partisanship as motivating Bush and most Republican congressmen and state legislators to support a flag amendment became a staple of much of the press and Democratic interpretation of the 1989–90 controversy, many observers, including congressmen in both parties who voted against the amendment, agreed in 1990 and 1991 interviews that this was an overly simplistic picture because at least some Republicans genuinely viewed the *Johnson* ruling as constitutionally in error or honestly believed that protecting the flag was more important than the free speech rights of flag desecrators. For example, in a 1991 interview, Democratic representative David Skaggs, who helped lead opposition to the amendment, said that although "many" Republicans were "absolutely delighted" at the prospects of "hoisting Democrats by their constitutional petards," others "were genuine in their feelings about the sanctity of the flag." Similarly, in a 1990 interview Democratic House assistant whip David Bonior, another anti-amendment leader, said, "I wouldn't characterize everybody who was for an amendment as being politically expedient and into the politics of cynicism. I think there were people, Republicans and Democrats, who really believed in the need for an amendment." Bonior added, however, "I don't think that crowd, quite frankly, was very large, and I would think they were outnumbered by those who saw it more in political terms." Republican representative John Porter, who voted against the amendment in 1990, said in a 1991 interview that though some Republicans might "take a certain degree of satisfaction in making the Democrats vote in a way they think they could take advantage of, I don't think that was a primary motivating factor of any significant percentage of people in my party."

The Role of the Democrats

Although many congressional Democrats were enraged at what they viewed as Bush's cynical and partisan decision to seek, for the first time, to amend the Bill of Rights, they were also deeply frightened at the prospect of once again, as in 1988, being perceived as politically deployed on the "wrong" side of the emotional "flag issue." The shadow of the 1988 pledge issue and especially the fear of being depicted as "unpatriotic" in "thirty-second negative campaign ads" were major factors in leading key congressional Democrats to decide that their party could not be perceived as supporting the *Johnson* decision, an orientation which together with Bush's endorsement of a constitutional amendment ensured that the issue would not quickly go away.

Even before Bush made his June 27 announcement, many congressional Democrats were clearly running scared. Thus virtually all Senate Democrats voted on June 22 and June 23 first to condemn the Court's decision and then to override it legislatively. In fact, according to Democratic SJC staff sources interviewed in 1990, SJC chair Biden's legislative proposal to overturn the *Johnson* ruling, which passed the Senate 97-3 on the evening of June 23 after a few minutes of debate and without any committee consideration, barely averted a strong movement to pass a constitutional amendment immediately. According to one source, "If you were on the Senate floor that Friday night as I was, you would know the speed that train had. The Constitution was about to be amended on the floor of the U.S. Senate with no hearings, no nothing."

Democratic senator John Breaux of Louisiana, the chairman of his party's Senatorial Campaign Committee, told reporters on June 23 that "Dukakis left a message" and "it's a matter of our learning and reacting very positively to it. Democrats love the flag too." On June 25, House majority leader Richard Gephardt told reporters who asked about the flag issue that Democrats didn't take a "back seat to the Republicans in those values and those ideas." A story carried by Knight-Ridder newspapers across the country on June 25 reported that at least "some" congressional Democrats were already conjuring up mental scenarios in which their opponents would run negative ads with "footage of a scruffy, long-haired protester stomping on the American flag and burning it. Then a photograph of a congressman comes on screen and the announcer says, 'He thinks this kind of behavior is just fine.'" According to a Democratic SJC staffer who was asked in a 1990 interview about such widely reported fears of "negative thirty-second spots" in the immediate aftermath of the Johnson ruling, " Politicians are always fighting the last battle and people had on their mind that Dukakis had lost because he was bad on the flag. That factor hung over the entire process up here. If this had been 1987 instead of 1989 it would have been entirely different."[65]

HJC civil liberties subcommittee chair Edwards (who, in a 1990 interview, still retained fresh in his mind the strong conviction that he had lost thousands of votes twenty years earlier for voting against the 1967 Vietnam-era flag desecration bill) told reporters shortly after the *Johnson* ruling that he had "never seen more panic among members." In a 1990 interview, *Washington Post* reporter Don Phillips similarly recalled:

> I've worked on the Hill a long, long time, since 1973, and I don't think I've ever seen a time when people were so scared of their own shadows and where they paid so little attention to the consequences of their actions. The Democrats were determined that the Republicans were not going to outflag them this time. The [1988 Bush campaign] visit to the flag factory and the Pledge of Allegiance issue was all very fresh at that time, so naturally many of them had only one thing in mind, and that was to prevent political damage.

Or, as an anonymous Democratic legislative aide was quoted immediately after the *Johnson* ruling, Democrats viewed the flag desecration issue as "a live grenade," and the question of the moment was how it could be kept "from exploding in your tent."[66]

If many congressional Democrats were already fearful, or even terrified, of the political harm a flag desecration "grenade" might cause them even before Bush endorsed a constitutional amendment on June 27, after his decision the Democratic leadership and most congressional Democrats became convinced that both symbolic and concrete steps had to be taken immediately to protect the party from being "burned" by the issue. Within hours of Bush's June 27 statement, House Speaker Tom Foley announced that he had directed the HJC to hold hearings on possible legislative responses to the *Johnson* ruling and the DNC issued a circular to congressional Democrats which declared that the flag "must be protected," announced that DNC chairman Ron Brown was encouraging "all Democrats to fly the American flag for the entire month of July," and reported that the House was expected to approve later that day a "Democratic resolution" condemning flag desecration. Virtually simultaneously, HJC chairman Jack Brooks, a cigar-chomping former marine, circulated a statement promising post–Independence Day hearings to "explore thoroughly what the Congress and the Federal Government must do to protect the flag from desecration," along with the text of the resolution referred to in the DNC circular, which expressed "profound concern" over the Johnson decision, condemned flag desecration and urged Americans to continue to "proudly" fly the flag. In introducing the resolution on the House floor on the evening of June 27, Brooks underlined that the forthcoming hearings would not focus on *whether*, but only on *how*, to attempt to override the *Johnson* ruling, and specifically whether to do so via "a constitutional amendment or possible statutory remedies." The resolution attacking the *Johnson* decision was passed by a 411-5 vote on the evening of June 27, with 98 percent of all Democrats supporting it; while President Bush spoke at the Iwo Jima Memorial on June 30, the DNC headquarters was bedecked with scores of flags.[67]

In short, as the *Washington Post* reported on June 28, congressional Demo-crats were talking "bar-room tough, essentially saying no Republican had better call them soft on the flag." Senator Metzenbaum, one of the few public congres-sional defenders of the *Johnson* decision, testified before the Senate and House Judiciary Committees that the parties were "engaged in a crude form of political one-upmanship, a crass competition about who loves the flag more," that reduced the "political debate to shameful and crass demagoguery, all with a cold eye toward the next election." Congress was considering "cutting back on the first amend-ment," Metzenbaum charged, simply to "avoid giving our opponents an issue in the next elections" and especially out of "fears of negative 30-second TV spots."[68]

Democrats across the country as well as those in Washington were affected by political fears over being caught on the "wrong" side of the flag issue. Thus Ohio Democratic chairman and national DNC vice-chairman Jim Ruvolo predicted on June 28 that there would not be "a lot of Democrats who will oppose" a consti-tutional amendment because otherwise the "flag factory" would return in Re-publican commercials. Kentucky Democratic state Senator Roger Noe voiced similar concerns: "Given the kind of mud-slinging being used these days, I can en-vision seeing campaign ads with opponents who were not strongly supportive of the amendment being pictured as communist or pinko or un-American." In Texas, Democratic state senator Gonzalo Barrientos lamented that some of his colleagues would vote for a resolution endorsing a constitutional amendment "simply be-cause the Republican Party will put into the can 30-second TV spots to hit them over the head." California State Senate Democratic majority leader Barry Keene, who was part of the 30-6 majority that voted on July 13 to support a constitutional amendment, said that he backed the measure to avoid what he termed a "deathtrap for Democrats," even though the "chief desecrators" of the flag were George Bush and "his socio-pathic sidekick" RNC chairman Atwater. The real desecration of the flag, Keene charged, was the "shameful, cynical, tawdry, manipulative exploi-tation of the flag for political purposes," but he lamented that "their political trick will work because we can't take the risk of being thought unpatriotic."[69]

In almost every state legislature that considered resolutions condemning flag desecration or supporting a constitutional amendment in 1989 (many legislatures had already adjourned by the time of the *Johnson* ruling), such measures were overwhelmingly approved by members of both parties, usually without hearings or extended discussion. Thus both houses of the South Carolina legislature called for a constitutional amendment within twenty-four hours of the decision, and when the Colorado House approved a similar resolution by a 50-11 vote on June 28, all but three members admitted that they had not read the ruling. The

Massachusetts Senate called for a constitutional amendment on June 26 by a 32-1 vote, and the California Assembly acted similarly on the same day by 58-2, with former leading anti–Vietnam War radical Tom Hayden among those voting in the majority. California Senate approval (by a 30-6 vote) was delayed for a few days so that its Rules Committee could devise a procedure to allow scores of competing senators to claim coauthorship. The New Jersey Assembly called for an amendment by a 75-0 vote; the Pennsylvania Senate vote was 49-1.[70]

Only a handful of Democrats opposed such resolutions in state legislatures. Among them were New Hampshire representatives Tick Trombly and Deborah Arneson, who respectively declared that the flag stood "for our right to speak in any manner we choose" and that "we are not Iran. We do not have an Ayatollah Khomeini who wants to kill someone who disagrees with him." In Texas, Democratic state senator Craig Washington succeeded in briefly blocking senate endorsement of a constitutional amendment, which ultimately passed with only two negative votes, by engaging in a filibuster, during which he spoke for twelve consecutive hours under rules which required that he could not sit down or leave for any purpose if he wished to retain the floor. During his filibuster, while colleagues massaged his legs and supporters provided him with food, Washington wore miniature flags on his coat lapels, high-tech basketball shoes on his feet, and a special device around his waist known as "the bag" so that, as one journalist put it, he could "abide by the rules of the senate without violating the rules of nature."[71]

Although Washington's filibuster failed to block the Senate's passage of the resolution, it did spark an unusual amount of debate about the merits of the measure. Washington termed the proposal "political tripe, pure and simple," that resembled "what Hitler did in Nazi Germany," and declared, "Our flag is not nearly as important as our Constitution, but we're going to change our Constitution because of our flag, which doesn't make sense to me. I love our flag but it's not a god. . . . The Bible says that you should not have false gods, and I think people are making a false god out of a flag." Washington was apparently not politically damaged by his filibuster; he was elected to Congress a few months later in a special election called to fill the seat left vacant by the death of Representative Mickey Leland, and he helped lead the successful 1990 congressional fight against a constitutional amendment. In a 1990 interview, he recalled filibustering against the Texas resolution because it was "silly and nonsensical, it makes me barf," because the "Congress of the United States was not waiting to see what the Texas legislature thought before they decided what they were going to do about flag burning and I saw it as the worst sort of opportunism."

One of the few state legislative bodies in which hasty approval of a resolution urging passage of a flag desecration amendment was successfully blocked in 1989 was the Wisconsin Senate (the state Assembly passed such a measure). A motion to adjourn until October was passed there by a 17-15 vote on June 30, before the proposed resolution reached the floor, after many legislators expressed opposition to debating the proposal without hearings. Democratic senator Robert Jauch, who voted for the adjournment, declared that he had fought in Vietnam "not for the flag, but for freedom," and argued that although no legislator favored laws allowing people to desecrate the flag, "a lot of people are getting blind-sided by their own emotions."[72]

CHAPTER 5

THE 1989 CONGRESSIONAL FLAG DESECRATION DEBATE:
To Overturn *Johnson* by Law or by Constitutional Amendment

Media attention and signs of intense public interest in the flag issue died down considerably after Bush's June 30 Iwo Jima Memorial speech and even further after the July 4 holiday. Although all three evening network broadcasts prominently featured the controversy on their Independence Day programs, thereafter their coverage of the flag issue became extremely sketchy and intermittent for two months. It was not until September 12, when the House of Representatives passed a statutory (as opposed to constitutional) attempt to overturn the *Johnson* decision, that all three networks' evening news shows again mentioned the flag desecration issue on the same day.

Nonetheless, as a result of what leading Democrats perceived to be the political realities that had been created by the president's support of a constitutional amendment, after Bush's endorsement the only real debate in Washington quickly became, not whether Congress should attempt to override the *Johnson* decision but only whether it would be possible to circumvent it by law, a position eventually adopted by most Democrats, or whether a constitutional amendment would be required to do so, a position taken by President Bush and most Republicans. As accurately summed up by Assistant Attorney General William Barr, the leading Bush administration spokesperson before congressional committees, the only real question was "not whether to provide protection for the Flag, but how to provide that protection." Leading congressional Democrats agreed with this analysis. Thus SJC chairman Biden noted that the only debate was about "the best way to accomplish our purpose," which he defined as determining exactly how to "protect the flag."[1]

Significant numbers of congressmen, especially Democrats, who believed that neither an amendment nor a law was really desirable, felt compelled for political reasons to support at least one of these approaches. Thus freshman Democratic representative Peter Hoagland of Nebraska, who had narrowly been elected to a traditionally Republican seat in 1988, privately said (according to a book about him published in 1991), "You shouldn't go to jail for burning a piece of cloth," yet he voted for the 1989 Flag Protection Act (FPA) which contained precisely this penalty. Similarly, when Harvard law professor and former solicitor general Charles Fried told a HJC subcommittee on July 19 that the *Johnson* decision was correct and that the best congressional response would be to "bravely do nothing," subcommittee chairman Don Edwards replied, "Your point of view is the correct point of view, but it's such a [political] loser." Edwards told Fried that his recommendation was the choice that "I am sure a majority of this committee would much rather have," but that the only practical alternative was choosing between a statute and an amendment because Congress's freedom to act "was taken away from us by the President." Edwards, who had voted against a federal flag desecration law in 1967 but cosponsored what became the FPA, added on July 20 that the HJC was "forced" into this restricted choice by President Bush's sudden decision to go "over to the monument at Iwo Jima," which had "set this emotional matter into full speed," and as a result of which "the votes aren't here just to do nothing." Representative Pat Schroeder (D-Colo.), who eventually voted against both the statute and the amendment, similarly told Fried that in a "purist world" his advice was correct because devoting so much time to the flag burning issue was like "chasing a gnat around the light bulb as the planet is burning down," but that since Bush "changed his position when Atwater went up and had lunch," a "political ball [began] rolling" and "we are not talking about the best of all possible worlds; we are talking about a political environment."[2]

The Edwards-Schroeder analysis was unquestionably the dominant mind-set on Capitol Hill in the summer and fall of 1989. A key House Democratic congressional aide, in a 1990 interview, recalled that Fried's "bravely do nothing" approach "was just in the minds of the vast majority of members not feasible given the way the choices were structured in their view. The choice was between a statute and a constitutional amendment." The aide added that, in retrospect, public excitement over the flag desecration issue died down far faster than many Democrats expected and "some people realized that they had been put into a stupid and unnecessary position and that they could have withstood it. But when the choice was do nothing, amend the Constitution or pass the statute, passing the statute was the easy way out. You had the ability to say, 'I can defend the flag and I support the Constitution.'"

The HJC and SJC witness lists reflected the predetermined outcome of endorsing either a statute or an amendment to overrule the *Johnson* decision. Even though SJC chairman Biden told the HJC on July 13 that most "leading constitutional experts in this country" whom he had spoken to did not want Congress to do "anything," of the more than forty separate witnesses who appeared before the two judiciary committees (about ten of whom testified before both groups), about 75 percent recommended either a statute, an amendment, or both, and only 25 percent endorsed Fried's "bravely do nothing" position.[3]

The Argument for "Bravely Doing Nothing"

Although the "realpolitik" debate in the summer and fall of 1989 focused on how to circumvent the *Johnson* ruling, a handful of congressmen did oppose taking any action. This small group received support from the American Bar Association (ABA), the ASNE, and most newspaper editorials, editorial columnists, and cartoonists. They continued to make the arguments summarized earlier in support of the *Johnson* decision, stressing that flag desecration was a form of political expression, even if highly distasteful, and that the substance of freedom deserved far more protection than the symbol of freedom. Three additional major arguments for taking no action were added to their repertoire once the amendment/law debate began: that the entire issue was being driven on both sides by political opportunism and fear rather than any real concern over damage to the country caused by occasional flag burnings; that because flag burners posed no real threat, the entire issue was a huge and absurd diversion of the country's time and energy from more pressing matters; and that no statute or constitutional amendment would ever be able to satisfactorily define such terms as "flag" and "desecration," and therefore the main long-term result of passing either would be an endless morass of litigation.

The first of these new arguments, that the issue had primarily become an opportunity for political pandering, usually focused on President Bush, who was criticized for trying to repeat his 1988 presidential campaign strategy. Congressional Democrats and other liberals who supported either a constitutional or statutory approach to overturning the *Johnson* ruling also came under frequent assaults, usually for hypocrisy and political cowardice.

Typical of the attacks on Bush were a cartoon in the June 30 *Washington Post,* which depicted a flag reading "politics first" hoisted over the American flag atop the White House, and a July 2 *Salt Lake Tribune* cartoon depicting Bush as naked except for the flag. Some of the criticisms of Bush were as emotional as were many of the criticisms of the *Johnson* decision. For example, in a June 29 *Dallas Times-Herald* column, Molly Ivins termed Bush's endorsement of a constitutional amendment "cheap, political grandstanding" and "shameless pandering to an ill-informed national snit" that "makes me want to vomit; but of course that would be symbolic political speech and symbolic political speech should be punishable by law, shouldn't it?" She added, "I would rather see [the flag] burned by a passionate protester than exploited by a sleazy politician for his own cynical ambition." Poet Allen Ginsberg declared that "vicious persons, including President Bush, are attacking the Bill of Rights, attempting to deface the laws of freedom that are American's pride, for the cheapest, vulgarest, political, slobbish, un-American motives since the Ku Klux Klan put on white sheets and burned crosses."[4]

Democrats who supported attempts to overturn the *Johnson* ruling also came in for criticism. The *Philadelphia Inquirer* of July 2 published a cartoon that showed a Republican elephant and a Democratic donkey tearing a flag to shreds in a tug-of-war. Democratic representative Gary Ackerman told the HJC that the proposed Democratic statutory alternative to a constitutional amendment amounted to political hypocrisy—"a political solution imposed upon a moral dilemma for something that people don't feel is right to do [i.e., overturning the *Johnson* decision] in the first place and they are looking to soften the blow."[5]

Liberal political commentator Michael Kinsley wrote that although Democrats were backing a statute in an attempt to "get this ridiculous issue" out of the way and to avoid both putting "trivia" into the Constitution and being subjected to 1988-style flag-waving "demagoguery" again, they all realized that their own proposal amounted to "trashing the Constitution" by attempting to suppress dissent. *Washington Post* columnist William Raspberry characterized both Democratic and Republican congressmen as being motivated on the flag issue by a "stomach-turning combination of cowardice and demagogy." Civil liberties columnist Nat Hentoff denounced the Democratic statutory alternative as a "dishonest and unconstitutional" measure which was "contemptuous of the First Amendment," reflecting a loss of "courage and the ability to think clearly" in an attempt to "show the country that the eyes of Democrats glisten, too, when the flag goes by."[6]

Several journalists and civil liberties activists interviewed in 1990 argued that although most attacks for political manipulation of the flag issue in 1989 focused on Bush and other Republicans, in fact the Democrats were even more politically hypocritical than were the Republicans. They based this position on the perception that most Republicans either did not care whether flag burning was a form of constitutionally protected speech or genuinely believed it should not be and therefore acted in accordance with their private convictions, as well as in a politically popular manner, whereas most Democrats either privately agreed with the *Johnson* ruling or were not much exercised by it but felt that either for personal political reasons or to head off a constitutional amendment they had to take a public position that violated their private convictions. For example, John Gomperts, People for the American Way (PAW) legislative counsel in 1989–90, recalled:

> I expect Republicans, at least some Republicans, to be at fault [on civil liberties issues]. People like Reagan and Bush don't understand the basic beauty of the Constitution. I don't think that stuff means anything to Bush whereas the flag genuinely does mean something to him. I don't expect Democratic leaders to be at fault. Many Democrats were incredibly intellectually dishonest and very disappointingly so. There were a number of very serious minded, good politicians who said things about the Supreme Court that were completely out of line and out of character. The Democrats poured into the issue all of their anxieties over issues of patriotism. Remove the politics from that and there was nothing there. All of this activity is so incredibly cynical. Nobody will just stand up and say, "Ladies and gentlemen, this [entire controversy] is ridiculous."

Although Democrats as a whole were attacked by many observers as displaying hypocrisy and cowardice for supporting attempts to overturn the *Johnson* decision, fire was especially concentrated on liberal Democrats, such as SJC chairman Biden, and constitutional lawyers with reputations as civil libertarians, especially Harvard law professor Laurence Tribe; the latter were generally expected to oppose as unwise and unconstitutional any attempt to outlaw symbolic flag dissent, but in the 1989 post-*Johnson* climate, they argued for a "content neutral" statutory ban on flag desecration on the grounds that the Supreme Court would likely uphold such a measure if it were carefully drawn. Although the prime motivation for overt or tacit support for a statute by many such liberals probably was to head off the perceived certain alternative of a constitutional amendment, their position exposed them to widespread charges, from a variety of ideological vantage points, of bartering their principles to advance the short-term goals of the Democratic party. This was especially so in the case of Tribe, who had explicitly declared in a 1988 book that flag desecration statutes were inherently unconstitutional as singling out unpopular expression for government suppression. Former solicitor general and unsuccessful Supreme Court nominee Robert Bork sarcastically told the HJC that "all of the people who might have been expected to be hired to challenge [the constitutionality of the proposed] statute have now testified that it's constitutional." Ranking HJC subcommittee minority member James Sensenbrenner, in a clear jab at Tribe, referred to professors who have to put their "views on constitutional law in a looseleaf binder where old worn-out views get replaced with a new page when a position has to change."[7]

Even more frequently, criticism of liberals like Biden and Tribe as hypocrites for supporting the statute came from the left. For example, legal writer Stuart Taylor lamented that although Bush's endorsement of an amendment won the prize for "the most grotesque exercise in cynicism, gutlessness and trivialization of the Constitution," such behavior by Republicans was "nothing new," while to see Democratic liberals like Biden and "eminent constitutionalists" like Tribe clamoring for a "civil blasphemy statute instead of standing up for the First Amendment" could only be explained by "raw political panic" and a "desperate search" for some means of "political self-preservation," which had led them down the path of "voodoo constitutional law." Radical lawyer William Kunstler, who defended Johnson before the Supreme Court and would represent other flag burning defendants in the 1990 *Eichman* case, wrote that what had "shocked" him "most profoundly" about the entire flag controversy was that "formerly unremitting defenders of the First Amendment," such as Tribe, in attempts to "head off a dangerous constitutional amendment," offered "various suggestions" to make violation of the First Amendment "legally palatable" in ways that permitted "the same damage to free expression."[8]

Aside from challenging the perceived political motivations of backers of both constitutional and statutory attempts to overturn the *Johnson* decision, a second new critique of any such attempts which emerged during the summer and fall of 1989 was that the issue was an absurd diversion of the country's energy and time away from real problems, especially given what defenders of the ruling maintained was the lack of any real threat to the country posed by flag burners. For example, the *Seattle Times* editorialized, shortly after Congress passed the F PA in October:

> Into a nation plagued by inadequate housing, rampant drug abuse, a
> mammoth federal budget deficit and the growing specter of AIDS,
> those wonderful folks in Washington, D.C. have introduced a flag

> law. . . . The real desecration of democracy occurs when people don't
> have places to live or work or adequate health insurance. . . . Those
> kind of issues don't seem to play well in the nation's capital. Maybe
> it's because they require real statecraft and that's in a lot shorter supply
> than the hype and rhetoric that's been conjured up around a non-issue
> like flag burning.

Similarly, George Mason University history professor and veteran civil rights activist Roger Wilkins termed it "absurd" and "ridiculous" that "all these politicians are jumping up and down" trying to protect the flag when the nation faced true crises such as a "budget deficit that is going to lower the standards of living of all of our children," babies dying of AIDS, "drugs ripping up our cities," and schools "failing a large chunk of our children."[9]

Senator Bob Kerrey (D-Neb.), one of the handful of senators who voted in 1989 against both the statute and the amendment, asked, "Where does it lead? When you're all done arguing, what have you got? Have you built a house? Have you helped somebody? Have you created a better world? . . . It seems to me there's nothing produced from it and you've divided the nation." California state legislator Dick Floyd noted, even as he voted for a resolution urging Congress to pass a flag desecration amendment, that President Bush probably had more important things to work on but "it keeps everybody's minds off the real problems in this country, doesn't it?" Along the same lines, a humor column by Cactus Pryor in the July 13 *Austin-American Statesman* described an imaginary Texas legislator, who, when asked a detailed question about allegations of personal corruption, responded, "We've got to stop these traitors from burning the United States flag!" An August 8 *New York Daily News* cartoon made the same point by depicting politicians scrambling to get under a "flag amendment" tent to avoid a rainy downpour of "issues." The *New Jersey Record* of July 12 portrayed a flag-covered bandwagon crowded with politicians and led by President Bush, with an attached sign reading, "Free ride for all politicians!! Tried of controversial issues? Hop aboard! No Risk!! Photo-ops galore!!"[10]

New Republic columnist Hendrik Hertzberg offered perhaps the most cogent argument for the position that the controversy was absurd for the simple reason that "a" flag could be burned, but it was impossible to burn "the" flag because it consisted of ideas rather than cloth and therefore was impervious to physical damage. But though the flag was thus "fireproof," Hertzberg continued, the Constitution could be "damaged quite effectively" by amendments such as Bush's proposal, which are "foreign to its spirit and hostile to its purposes." Whitney

Smith, the director of the Flag Research Center, made the same point, arguing that the "biggest flag is in our hearts and minds" and concluding that the solution to flag burning was "education, not criminal codes" that would punish society by "having our liberties cut back," especially when the "instant revulsion" which flag burners generated was "all you need" to deal with them. Former senator Charles Mathias similarly told the SJC that the greatest punishment the nation could inflict on flag burners was to ignore them, much as a great ocean liner's course remained unaffected by the "slugs and snails and slimy creatures" in the sea.[11]

In addition to criticizing politicians for pursuing crass partisan ends and diverting public attention from more pressing needs, a third new criticism of the drive to circumvent the Supreme Court which emerged in the summer of 1989 was that there would be no way satisfactorily to define such terms as "flag" and "desecrate" in either legislation or a constitutional amendment. For example, former Johnson and Nixon administration solicitor general Erwin Griswold pointed out to the SJC that the U.S. Post Office was the world-champion flag desecrator by daily canceling millions of flag stamps; he also queried how someone who used a flag as an emergency tourniquet and got blood smeared on it would be affected. Among congressmen, Republican senator Humphrey and Democratic representatives Schroeder and Ackerman especially championed the argument that definitional problems would bog down any attempt to ban flag desecration in an endless legal morass. For example, Schroeder, who had come under criticism from the American Legion in 1988 for appearing on the cover of *Ms.* magazine draped in a flag, brought a collection of photographs and articles showing various commercial and fashion uses of the flag to an HJC hearing to make the point that defining key terms would be a hopeless quagmire for any flag desecration efforts. At one point she held up a picture of first lady Barbara Bush wearing a flag scarf next to the controversial *Ms.* cover and declared, "I really wonder how we know which of these is desecration and which isn't." Humphrey asked how the concept of flag desecration would apply to such items as "American flag patches we see on the fannies of some people's levis" or various other clothing made out of "a material and pattern that resembles the American flag," and concluded that "if we are going to get into this kind of arcane minutia" Congress would embark upon "an endless riddle." Representative Ackerman brought a collection of flag clothing and other items to the HJC, which he displayed while asking if it would be flag desecration to "wipe your face or blow your nose" with flag napkins, to "dump your spaghetti sauce all over" or to burn paper plates with flag depictions, or to put "dirty" as opposed to "clean" feet into flag-patterned socks. Displaying a flag-patterned bathing suit, he inquired if such an item "gets caught up in the tumbler of your washer or drier, have you desecrated the flag?"[12]

The difficulties of defining flag desecration inspired a raft of essays with an even more satiric tone. A columnist in the *Wall Street Journal* of July 24 reported coming across a "flag" flower bed in New York's City Hall Park and wondered if it would be allowable to "spray pesticide the flag," if not having a flower bed flag blooming by Flag Day would lead to charges of "disloyalty," and what the legal significance would be if an inept gardener "allows slugs to eat holes in the flag?" A satirical column in the July 23 *Washington Post* suggested that all possibilities be covered by defining "desecration" to mean "subjecting the flag to damage, disrespect or funny business" and that anyone who, with regard to a flag, "misfolds, improperly launders, shreds, deep-fat-fries . . . sneezes at, whips-chops-and-purees, wears a hat in the whereabouts of . . . [or] fails to get kinda misty at," be sentenced to making license plates in jail, which would be emblazoned with the motto "Land of the Free, Home of the Symbolically Obedient." The column also proposed the establishment of a commission on "Symbolico-Devotional Malfeasance" to advise the government on "properly reverent behavior towards the Flag and Related Textile Entities."

Time magazine essayist Frank Tippett asked in an August 28 column how bans on flag desecration would apply to stomping on a flag jewelry pin, obscenely wagging a finger at the flag, burning a congressman in effigy if the effigy wore a tiny flag lapel pin, or electrocuting a prisoner who had a flag tattoo. Perhaps the most comprehensive list of ontological and etymological puzzles defining flag desecration appeared in the December issue of *Harpers* magazine, which listed twenty scenarios involving potential flag desecration, including burning a two-sided color photographic reproduction of the flag, projecting a picture of a flag on a wall and then hurling mud on the image, "burning" an indestructible metallic flag by soaking it in flammable liquid and lighting a match, and creating a flag by sewing together already burned pieces of red, white, and blue cloth.

Some critics of attempts to overturn the *Johnson* decision focused on another definitional question, arguing, in a no doubt unknowing echo of the original turn-of-the-century concerns over flag desecration, that the real debasement of the flag came from its commercial exploitation, not from its use for political communication, yet the entire controversy was focused on attempting to suppress political dissent. For example, in a column in the July 10 issue of the *New Jersey Record,* Stephanie Schorow complained that the flag had been "shamelessly exploited in commercial advertisements for years" and that equating patriotism with "eating the right kind of yogurt" and similar attempts by businessmen to use flag images to "slather some patriotic prestige on their product" decreased the flag's value "far more than an isolated act of conflagration." Similarly, marketing consultant Stanley Marcus asked in the August 8 *Dallas Morning News* why those who wanted to ensure proper respect for the flag did not simply ban "the usage of the flag for any purposes other than on the battlefield or its display on federal and state buildings? Why don't they prohibit it from being used for lapel buttons, decorations for conventions, product advertising, chorus girl costumes, shoulder patches for nightclub security guards and replication by Navajo Indians?"

The Argument for Overturning the Johnson Ruling by Statute

In the Washington political climate of the summer and fall of 1989, those who argued for the "bravely do nothing" option of former solicitor general Fried, although numerous and vocal in the media, were few and spoke mostly in whispers in the vicinity of Capitol Hill. From a political standpoint, the concept of overturning the *Johnson* decision by statute reflected an attempt by many congressmen, mostly, but not all Democrats, to reconcile their reluctance to support amending the Bill of Rights for the first time in American history with their fear of the political consequences of being perceived as supporting flag burners. The mixture of Democratic rage and fear about the political implications of the *Johnson* decision and the inevitable mixed messages that many Democrats transmitted as a result was perhaps best reflected by House Speaker Foley, who immediately labeled the ruling "deeply offensive" and declared that "everyone condemns" flag burning, while simultaneously terming amending the Bill of Rights "unwise" and promising that he would be "extra slow" to change "the heart of our constitutional liberties and freedoms." On June 27, the day Bush endorsed an amendment, Foley, who rarely overtly showed passion about anything, angrily declared, "I am sure there will be people trying to play politics with [the flag issue]. Anyone who suggests that there is a party difference in respect for the American flag is using the deep affection of Americans, twisting it, manipulating it, using it for the most base and crass political purposes."[13]

In short, many Democrats, who were both enraged at what they perceived as President Bush's tawdry political manipulation of the flag desecration issue and terrified of the political results of not registering opposition to the *Johnson* decision, believed that support for a legislative override, which was passed by Congress in October as the F PA, would allow them to oppose both *Johnson* and Bush. As PAW legislative counsel John Gomperts noted in a 1990 interview, by supporting a statute that had as its "whole purpose not to have a constitutional amendment," Democrats felt they could have it "both ways." Or as a key House

Democratic staff member put it in another 1990 interview, the F PA provided its supporters with the ability to say, "I can defend the flag and I support the Constitution." F PA backers felt that they could save both their political skins and the First Amendment because the overwhelming Washington political consensus following Bush's June 30 Iwo Jima Memorial speech was that a constitutional amendment was a certainty unless some "middle way" could be found to permit opposition both to the *Johnson* ruling and to an amendment. Thus New York University law professor and ACLU president Norman Dorsen recalled, in a 1990 interview, that when he talked to Democratic Senate majority leader Mitchell and SJC chair Biden in July 1989, "they both felt that it was quite clear that if there was no statute there would be a constitutional amendment."

Assistant House Democratic whip David Bonior, in a 1990 interview, characterized F PA backers as having "mixed" motives but agreed that the statutory approach was above all "a strategy to block a constitutional amendment at all costs." Bonior added that it was a "fair characterization" that many who backed the F PA did not necessarily think it was good or even constitutional but backed it because they felt the perceived certain alternative was "so awful." He continued, "The fact of the matter is it [the F PA] undoubtedly saved amending the constitution [in 1989]." Representative Edwards, who chaired the HJC subcommittee hearings on possible congressional responses to the *Johnson* decision in July 1989 and then cosponsored the F PA, termed the statute "marginally constitutional" in a 1990 interview but added that its backers succeeded because they convinced enough congressmen that by supporting it "they would look just as patriotic" as if they voted for the amendment. Edwards agreed with Bonior that "if we hadn't done that [sponsored the F PA], today that constitutional amendment would be a part of the Constitution very easily" because the F PA had halted the "frenzy" and "hysteria" on Capitol Hill after Bush's Iwo Jima Memorial speech.

Although blocking a constitutional amendment was clearly a foremost goal of F PA backers, at least some F PA supporters also felt, for legal reasons to be discussed below, that there was good reason to believe that a statute would not only head off an amendment but would also legitimately achieve the same ends while avoiding tampering with the Bill of Rights. According to a top House Democratic leadership aide interviewed in 1990, F PA backers were a coalition of three groups: one that would vote for "anything" that would overturn the *Johnson* ruling, either out of genuine outrage or political posturing; a second that viewed the F PA as a strategy "to avoid a constitutional amendment, but who weren't necessarily for the statute on substance grounds"; and a third for whom the F PA "made a lot of sense" on both legal and political grounds. Similarly, ABA president Stanley Chauvin, who lobbied against both the F PA and the amendment, said in a 1990 interview that his impression was that F PA backers included those who "thought there could be a statute and that it was a valid exercise of legislative authority," those who were "outraged" at the prospects of amending the Constitution and "thought that the statute might slow it down," and those "who were just outright frauds in the deal and said, 'Hell, here's a good chance to make some thirty-second clips out of the deal.'" Chauvin added that he felt that the overwhelming vote for the F PA in both houses of Congress in 1989 and the subsequent majority (but not the required two-thirds) vote for an amendment in 1990 "wasn't a sincere test of what Congress really feels. I think the reflection of a lot of them was, 'Look, there's enough going on without my taking some additional heat on this. I'm running against this viper in November and I'm not going to make his TV spots for him.' I think if the vote had been in a dark room it would have been totally different."

In addition to providing a politically "safe" alternative to a constitutional amendment, F PA backers accurately, as it turned out, believed that the time required for congressional hearings to consider both alternatives would delay any votes and thus provide a "cooling-off" period during which the intensity of public and media interest in the flag desecration issue would die down. Thus Representative Skaggs, who was one of only seventeen Democrats who voted against the F PA in September 1989, said in a 1990 interview that although there were some F PA supporters "who sincerely believed they had crafted a constitutional statute," "many more had serious questions about the constitutionality but made the practical and tactical judgment that the ultimate goal of preserving the Bill of Rights would be served by buying time with the statutory approach and letting the country's emotions cool and, if it was ultimately held unconstitutional, they believed that we would face that issue in a more thoughtful atmosphere whenever that occurred than in the summer of 1989." In a 1990 interview, a key House Democratic leadership aide said that Speaker Foley in particular was convinced that the issue "would play out over time. The basic strategic decision was that if time was allowed to work, the pressure would decrease, the hysteria would decrease and the atmosphere would get more normal and if the statute were held unconstitutional you would be able to position yourself as a defender of the freedoms that Americans hold dear instead of as a patriotism issue." In a 1990 interview, ACLU president Dorsen recalled that in July 1989, Senate Democratic leader Mitchell, whom he termed a personal friend, was "basically saying, 'I'm going to head off a constitutional amendment [with the F PA] and we'll see about the [constitutionality of the] statute, we'll worry about it later.'"

New York University law professor Burt Neuborne, a former ACLU legal director, expressed admiration in a 1991 interview for what he also perceived as the delaying strategy at the heart of the F PA. Neuborne declared that the Democratic leadership "wanted to buy a year and they did," and he termed the strategy "intellectually dishonest but politically brilliant." He added, with reference to Harvard professor Tribe's key role in endorsing the legal basis of the F PA, "I can't believe Tribe would ever have voted to uphold the statute, but politically I have nothing but admiration for his motivation [of seeking to block the amendment]. I think he was playing a very sophisticated political game. As long as he could make an argument for the statute that could pass the 'embarrassment test' [an argument that was not so weak that it was embarrassing to make] it was very important to buy the time."

The Democratic strategy of hoping to cool off fervor for a flag amendment via a combined strategy of delay and putting forth a statutory alternative was broadly hinted at numerous times in the summer of 1989. Even before Bush endorsed an amendment, for example, House Speaker Foley declared that he would be "extraordinarily slow" to consider an amendment to the "heart of our constitutional liberties and freedom," and he urged his colleagues not to "rush in in a highly emotional atmosphere and throw out to the states" such "red meat" in the immediate aftermath of the *Johnson* ruling. Immediately after Bush's June 27 endorsement of an amendment, Foley announced that the HJC would hold hearings to ensure that consideration of responses to the *Johnson* ruling, including possible statutory alternatives to an amendment, would be "conducted calmly in the spirit of deliberation and care." HJC subcommittee chairman Edwards told reporters in mid-July that he hoped that the hearings would "cool the fires" of the controversy, noting that, with time, "these kinds of emotional issues have a way of clearing up" and that the best outcome would be that the entire issue would "go away." On July 14, Senate Democratic leader Mitchell announced that the Senate would vote on both a statute and an amendment but not until October, thereby allowing consideration of a "serious matter of importance to all Americans" in a "serious, mature, deliberate way."[14]

The legal argument on behalf of the statutory approach was based on a highly technical and highly strained interpretation of a few phrases in the *Johnson* decision. The overwhelming thrust and stress of the majority opinion had clearly been, as Brennan put it, to hold that the government could not either "criminally punish a person for burning a flag as a means of political protest" or "foster its own view of the flag by prohibiting expressive conduct relating to it" because such a ban would violate the "bedrock principle" that "the Government may not prohibit the expression of an idea because society finds the idea itself offensive or disagreeable." Every news account of the *Johnson* decision reported it in these terms. For example, the (conservative) *Washington Times* of June 22 summarized the decision as holding that "the Constitution protects burning the American flag as political expression," and the (liberal) *New York Times* began its story by report-ing that "the Supreme Court ruled today that no laws could prohibit political pro-testers from burning the American flag." The minority opinion, written by Rehnquist and joined by White and O'Connor, also interpreted the majority opin-ion as a general ban on restrictions on dissident expression that symbolically used flags: Rehnquist clearly indicated that he interpreted it as overruling not only the Texas flag desecration law but also the 1968 federal statute and the then existing forty-eight state flag desecration laws.[15]

The argument for the constitutionality of a legislative override ignored the major thrust of the majority opinion and the overwhelmingly consensual interpre-tation of it by the news media, the vast majority of legal commentators, and the Court's own minority opinion and instead focused on a few phrases in Brennan's lengthy opinion to suggest that the ruling had struck down the Texas law only be-cause of its peculiar and particular phraseology and therefore that it would not in-validate more carefully phrased statutes. The key phrases F PA backers pointed to were Brennan's statement that the Court's decision was "bounded by the particular facts of this case and by the statute under which Johnson was convicted"; a foot-note which stated that the "prosecution of a [flag desecrator] who had not engaged in expressive conduct," such as dragging a flag in the mud simply because one was tired, would pose a "different case"; and above all a comment that the Texas law was clearly unconstitutional because it overtly discriminated against expression on the basis of content, because it was "not aimed at protecting the physical integrity of the flag in all circumstances, but is designed instead to protect it only against impairments that would cause serious offense to others." This latter comment was accompanied by a footnote reference to Justice Blackmun's dissent in the 1974 Supreme Court *Goguen* case (which had overturned the Massachusetts flag des-ecration law as unconstitutionally vague), in which Blackmun had argued that the Massachusetts law was constitutional because, among other reasons, it outlawed all acts that "harmed the physical integrity of the flag" and was therefore not de-signed to punish "speech—a communicative element."[16]

This footnote reference to Blackmun's opinion in *Goguen* and the accompa-nying text was viewed by proponents of a statute as especially significant, in both a legal and "Supreme Court political" sense, because Blackmun had joined the 5-4 majority in *Johnson*. They interpreted it as suggesting that Blackmun, and perhaps even others in the majority, would join the minority and uphold a law that simply outlawed *all* acts of physical flag desecration, omitting any reference to motive or impact, such as the "serious offense" provision of the Texas law or the provision in the 1968 federal law which outlawed desecration only when

committed to "knowingly cast contempt" upon the flag. Such a law, its proponents argued, would be a "content-neutral" statute, with the "non-speech-related"
interest of preserving the "physical integrity" of the flag under all circumstances
(as somehow opposed to suppressing dissent); therefore, they contended, it would
be upheld by the Supreme Court under the relatively lenient standard of the 1968
O'Brien draft card burning case, which required only an "important or substantial
government interest" to uphold government regulations "unrelated to the suppression of free expression," as opposed to the virtually impossible-to-meet "compelling" interest and "most exacting scrutiny" required under the *Johnson* ruling if
the government interest behind a law was to restrict expression "because of the
content of the message."

Ultimately, supporting this position required accepting the credulity-straining
argument that the government could conceivably have any interest in protecting
the physical integrity of all existing American flags that was not related to attempting to suppress uses of the flag that might be interpreted as damaging its symbolic
value. In fact, supporters of the constitutionality of a statutory approach were
never able to come up with any such interest—which, among other things, would
seem to require that either all flags be preserved in perpetuity or, at the least, that
for every flag removed from service because of wear another be manufactured.
Although the October 1989 enactment of the FPA did, as intended, help assure the
failure of the 1989 drive to pass a constitutional amendment, the inability of statute supporters to demonstrate any nonsuppressive interest in protecting the physical integrity of all flags ensured that the FPA would be eventually struck down by
the Supreme Court on the basis of the *Johnson* ruling, as it did in its 1990 *U.S. v.
Eichman* decision.

The concept that a law could override the *Johnson* decision was originally
raised by SJC chairman Biden, who introduced a so-called content-neutral flag
desecration statute on the Senate floor on June 23. Biden's statute essentially
stripped from the 1968 federal law its "cast contempt" language, deleted previous
language which included "defiling" the flag as an offense, and added new language outlawing displaying a flag on the floor so that the federal flag desecration
statute would henceforth encompass anyone, regardless of purpose, who "knowingly and publicly mutilates, burns, displays on the floor or ground or tramples
upon any flag." Biden's proposal, which was attached to a pending child care proposal, was passed on June 23 by Senate voice vote in ten minutes, without any
hearings, largely to head off a strong movement within the Senate to vote on a
constitutional amendment under similar hurried conditions. In explaining the proposal, Biden made the argument that others favoring a statute would subsequently

elaborate, namely that, unlike the Texas law and the 1968 federal law, such a provision would be constitutional because it would in a "content-neutral" manner outlaw all forms of flag desecration and would not single out, in Biden's words, only those acts "intended to offend others or cast contempt" on the flag.[17]

The Supreme Court "might very well" uphold such a law, Biden argued, although at the same time, in an apparent attempt to satisfy veterans' groups who traditionally conducted ceremonial flag burnings to retire worn flags, he interpreted his proposal as exempting such ceremonies by noting that this was the "preferred" method of retiring worn flags under the 1942 flag code. This attempt to appease veterans' groups, however, which was explicitly written into the final text of the 1989 FPA, clearly suggested that the real purpose of a statute was to suppress only "unpatriotic" flag desecration, rather than Biden's claimed purpose of protecting the flag's physical integrity under all circumstances. Furthermore, the *Johnson* ruling had clearly indicated that any such exemption in a flag desecration law would render it unconstitutional:

> If we were to hold that a State may forbid flag-burning where it is likely to endanger the flag's symbolic role, but allow it wherever burning a flag promotes that role—as where, for example, a person ceremoniously burns a dirty flag—we would be saying that when it comes to impairing the flag's physical integrity, the flag itself may be used as a symbol . . . only in one direction. . . . that one may burn the flag to convey one's attitude toward it and its referents only if one does not endanger the flag's representation of nationhood and national unity. We never before have held that the Government may ensure that a symbol be used only to express only one view of that symbol or its referents. . . . To conclude that the Government may permit designated symbols to communicate only a limited set of messages would be to enter territory having no discernible or defensible boundaries.[18]

The Biden statute was not taken very seriously when the Senate passed it on June 23 for a variety of reasons, including its clearly symbolic intent as an expression of Senate opinion, the lack of hearings or serious debate on it, the lack of any public endorsement of its legal theory by prominent constitutional lawyers, and, from a practical standpoint, because under the rules of the House of Representatives such a nongermane provision almost certainly could not be attached to a child care bill. But, Biden's argument received powerful credibility and support on July 3, when Harvard University law professor Tribe, generally regarded as the most prominent constitutional lawyer in the country, published an "op ed" essay in the *New York Times* which endorsed the statutory approach and laid down the legal and political position its backers would follow for the next four months. As a key Senate Democratic leadership aide recalled in a 1990 interview, Tribe's opinion "played a major role" in the minds of congressmen with "an overriding desire not to amend the Constitution," because his views and the similar views, subsequently expressed, of other "reputable legal scholars" lent considerable credence to the argument that it was "arguably constitutional" to overturn the *Johnson* ruling by statute.

In his July 3 *New York Times* essay, Tribe argued that "properly understood" the *Johnson* decision by no means banned all flag desecration laws but required only that "Government protection of the flag be separated from Government suppression of detested views." So long as the "point" of flag desecration legislation was to "give force to the community's shared sense that the object is worthy of special protection," without regard to "the presence or absence of any message" or any intent to "censor the views" of desecrators, Tribe argued, the Court would uphold a statute, just as gravesites could be protected regardless of the motivation of those who might want to disturb them. If Congress saw "in the flag such intrinsic value that it chooses to put all American flags beyond the reach of physical abuse," whether "in public or private," thus avoiding singling out "occasions on which such objects are destroyed publicly [to convey a message] or in a manner that expresses contempt," Tribe added, "nothing in the First Amendment need stand in the way." Furthermore, he maintained, in what was to become a mantra for many of those advocating the statutory approach, it would be "folly to reach for the heavy artillery" of a constitutional amendment when a law would do the job, especially since a statute would "take only days" whereas the constitutional amendment process "might take months or years." In subsequent congressional testimony, Tribe declared that a "simple statute, capable of being easily and quickly enacted," could overturn the *Johnson* decision, and therefore it would be "folly" to "reach for the heavy artillery of the amending process," which would take months and amount to using a "sledgehammer" when a "scalpel" would solve the problem. This argument, like all others for a statutory circumvention of the *Johnson* ruling, inevitably removed most or all freedom of speech principles from the controversy, as was especially made clear by his closing suggestion in his July 3 article that a constitutional amendment would be acceptable as a "last resort."[19]

According to Tribe and other promoters of a statute, their proposal would ban flag burning in a way that the Supreme Court would uphold and therefore it would negate the effect of the *Johnson* ruling just as effectively as a constitutional amendment and would take effect much more quickly and avoid "tinkering" with the Constitution. Thereby, they argued, it would avoid creating a "slippery slope" for subsequent infringements of the First Amendment. Democratic House Speaker

Foley coupled such arguments with the suggestion that amendment backers sought primarily to gain partisan advantage by telling reporters that he could not "imagine why anyone" (meaning Bush and Republican supporters of an amendment) would "lightly and frivolously" rush to amend the Constitution "unnecessarily, without reason or purpose, if a statute can accomplish all of the [same] objectives." Of course, because proponents of a statute openly proclaimed that its advantage would be to bring about more quickly the same result as a constitutional amendment, it could also be argued that the statute would itself open up a path for evading, by legislative subterfuge, other unpopular Supreme Court decisions upholding constitutional rights.[20]

Since the key public defense of the statute ultimately boiled down to the argument that it would accomplish the ends of the constitutional amendment, only more quickly and supposedly without permanently changing the Bill of Rights, its supporters could not, with any consistency, make any principled defense of the rights at issue in the *Johnson* decision. In fact, many of them, including HJC chairman Brooks and SJC chairman Biden, publicly declared that they would back a constitutional amendment if the statutory approach failed in the Supreme Court, in what amounted to admissions that only tactics and not fundamental democratic principles were at issue for them. Thus, just as Tribe had stated in his July 3 *New York Times* essay, the SJC in favorably recommending the FPA in October 1989, stressed that "the amendment process should be invoked as a last—not as a first—resort," an argument that was less than a ringing endorsement of the basic right of unpopular dissent which supposedly was a fundamental principle of American democracy. Ultimately, just as many proponents of a constitutional amendment seemed determined to protect the flag's symbolism at the expense of its substance, many backers of the statute seemed equally adamant about protecting the *symbolism* of the Bill of Rights by keeping it undamaged in appearance, while in practice undercutting its *substance* by legislatively undermining the same right which amendment proponents would have eviscerated in a more overt and formal manner.[21]

The proponents of a statute clearly had a "Supreme Court political" as well as a legal strategy. This strategy was not only the obvious one of attempting to fend off pressure for an amendment while still presenting a patriotic face to the public but also placing enough pressure on the Supreme Court through passage of the FPA to cause at least one justice (and especially Justice Blackmun) to defect from the *Johnson* majority and uphold a supposedly "content-neutral" law. Statute proponents viewed this as a real possibility both because the Supreme Court would realize that the alternative of a constitutional amendment was looming and because of the footnoted reference in Brennan's opinion to Blackmun's 1974 *Goguen* dissent.

To an extraordinary extent, in fact, the drafting of the FPA was shaped by this single fleeting footnote as evidence that it was primarily the "serious offense" provision of the Texas law which had made it unconstitutional as aimed at the suppression of dissent. Thus House of Representatives legal counsel Steve Ross, in a 1990 amicus brief urging the Supreme Court to uphold the FPA, declared that in crafting the statute, Congress had paid "the most acute attention" to this footnote, which it termed "Justice Blackmun's signal pronouncement." In a 1990 interview, PAW legislative counsel John Gomperts described the terms of the statute and the legislative reports that supported and explained it as amounting to a letter to Blackmun which read, "Dear Harry: We did what you said in *Smith v. Goguen*. Now tell us it's okay." Similarly, in a 1991 interview, a legislative aide to a Republican senator who supported both the FPA and the amendment in 1989 said that much of the FPA congressional floor debate amounted to "kind of signaling or winking to the Supreme Court that, 'You damn well better uphold this statute if there's any way to do it because if you don't we're coming back with a constitutional amendment.'"[22]

The SJC majority report virtually announced a strategy of targeting Blackmun and generally putting political pressure on the Court, not only by pointing to Blackmun's *Goguen* position as justifying the constitutionality of the FPA but also by quoting the submitted testimony of Columbia law school professor Henry Monaghan:

> *Texas v. Johnson* is far too unstable a precedent to permit a confident conclusion that a majority of the Court would reach such a result [striking down all flag desecration statutes]. *Johnson* itself was 5-4 and the minority seems adamant. Thus, the fundamental question is whether the proposed legislation is sufficiently different to detach one or more members of the majority. As a predictive matter, that seems to me a fair possibility.

Similarly, the SJC majority quoted two other law professors as predicting that "for at least one of the Justices in the 5-4 majority" a legislatively "content-neutral, at least on its face [conceding even if not in reality?]" statute "might be sufficient[ly different from the Texas law] to distinguish and validate" it.[23]

By the time hearings on possible responses to the *Johnson* decision were held by the HJC in mid-July and by the SJC in early August and mid-September, the flag desecration controversy had moved off the front pages and largely disappeared from the network evening news. But Republican support of a constitutional amendment and the political fears of Democrats that had committed most party leaders by mid-July to supporting a statutory alternative remained unchanged. Tribe was the key witness before both judiciary committees on behalf of those who argued that a "content-neutral" statute, which banned all forms of physical flag desecration in public or private, could pass constitutional muster. His conclusion was supported by Duke University law professor Walter Dellinger and University of Chicago law dean Geoffrey Stone, who, like Tribe, were constitutional law experts generally associated with liberal political views and strong civil liberties sentiments. Tribe confidently told the HJC that it could not be "responsibly" doubted that "at least six" and "perhaps seven" Supreme Court justices would uphold a "neutrally-drawn physical-integrity-of-the-flag law on its face, and as applied, as long as it's not used just to target dissenters in a politically motivated way." Two weeks later before the SJC, Tribe upped his count of certain positive votes to "at least seven."[24]

Before the HJC, Tribe clearly went beyond arguing that the Supreme Court would uphold such a statute to personally endorsing one, just as he did in his July 3 *New York Times* essay, in which he argued against an amendment by asking, "Why pursue a path that might take years when one is available that would only take days?" He told the HJC that to say that "the flag deserves protection from being desecrated" was simply to "recognize that fact" and that "it is hard to see what could be a better way of protecting the flag than to pass a simple statute making it a crime to destroy a flag or mutilate it in any way." Before the SJC two weeks later, Tribe drew back from personally endorsing a statute, stating his preference was that the Constitution would be "interpreted to mean that no emblem of the Nation may ever be placed on a sacrosanct pedestal."

Dellinger and Stone testified, respectively, that a "neutral" flag desecration law would "quite likely" be, or had "a reasonable possibility" of being, upheld by the Supreme Court. Dellinger also said in his written statement (but not in his oral testimony) that such a law "is" (in his HJC testimony) or "may be" (in his SJC testimony) "insufficiently tolerant of dissenting views." Stone indicated in both his written and oral SJC testimony that he felt the *Johnson* decision was "premised upon a sound understanding of well-settled principles of first amendment jurisprudence." These brief statements of personal qualms were overwhelmed by the clear thrust of both of their presentations, which, like Tribe's, was that there was good reason to believe that the Supreme Court would uphold a carefully drawn statute and that, in Stone's words, such an approach was "more sound" and "more responsible" than passing a constitutional amendment, which, in Dellinger's words, would be a "truly terrible idea." Because, politically, the choices in Washington had been defined by mid-July as either a statute or an amendment, the practical effect of such testimony was to urge Congress to pass a statute, a posture that was also taken by hundreds of other law professors and by leading civil liberties organizations, including the ACLU and the PAW, for fear that the inevitable alternative was amending the Bill of Rights.

Because those who argued that a statute would survive constitutional scrutiny also maintained that it would be just as effective as an amendment, F PA proponents could not with any consistency attack the proposed amendment primarily as a threat to fundamental rights but instead were forced to stress the essentially tactical argument that the F PA could be more quickly implemented, along with the position that a constitutional amendment was far too solemn and serious a remedy for a relatively infrequent and minor problem and would therefore trivialize the Constitution. Thus Stone told the SJC that the amendment would "clutter, trivialize and, indeed, denigrate the Constitution and the broad principles for which it stands," because flag desecration was a matter of "secondary importance to the overall scheme of American government." Professor Dellinger compared amending the Constitution, when a statutory remedy was available, to "going nuclear" and warned that it would make the nation "look just a little silly and a little less brave and a little less free." Journalists and editorial cartoonists joined in arguing that a constitutional amendment was an absurd overreaction to the flag burning problem. For example, an *Atlanta Constitution* cartoon depicted President Bush as a fireman on a huge, flag-bedecked, speeding fire engine labeled "constitutional amendment," explaining to a pedestrian, "We got a report of a flag on fire!!" *Chicago Tribune* columnist Mike Royko termed the amendment an attempt to use "an axe to peel a grape," and other columnists compared it to "tripling the defense budget on the grounds that Burma has just added a new blowgun to its arsenal" and to "using a howitzer to blast a flea."[25]

In addition to arguing that a statute would be a quicker and more appropriately measured response to the *Johnson* decision than an amendment, proponents of the statute maintained that another advantage was that if the F PA contained minor errors, it could be easily repealed or modified, whereas a flawed amendment would be extremely difficult to correct. Thus Tribe told the SJC that the flaws of a statute could be "rapidly repaired" with corrective legislation, or even with repeal if the country chose to do so in "calmer times," but an amendment "would be a far more permanent fixture" and "calling back or correcting such an amendment once it had been sent forth into history would be a monumental task."

Another argument against the amendment, put forth most vehemently by Dellinger but supported by several other constitutional experts, was that its operative text ("The Congress and the States shall have power to prohibit the physical desecration of the flag of the United States") was so vague that it would be interpreted by the courts either as meaningless or else as overriding all provisions of the Constitution, including due process rights, in flag desecration cases. The basis for this argument was that the amendment's text did not specifically state that flag desecration laws would override the First Amendment and that its sponsors made conflicting statements concerning exactly what it sought to amend. For example, Republican House Minority Leader Michel and Representative Montgomery, the leading House cosponsors, maintained that the proposal would amend "the Constitution as a whole" and not "one part of it." By contrast, the leading Bush administration spokesman at the congressional hearings, Assistant Attorney General William Barr, said that the amendment would "remove" contemptuous flag burning from the protection of the "Bill of Rights" and thus "affect" Supreme Court "analysis of the First Amendment," and HJC civil liberties subcommittee ranking Republican Sensenbrenner said the amendment would carve a small "exception out of the First Amendment, to hold our honored and revered flag above all else."[26]

According to a 1990 interview with a participant in the late June 1989 meetings at which the text of the constitutional amendment was drafted, a deliberate decision was made not to mention the First Amendment because otherwise amendment drafters would be making a "clear, obvious, flat-out statement" that they were "amending the First Amendment" and

> that's not really how they saw it and that's not really how they wanted it to be seen. They were taking the First Amendment back to the way it had been interpreted before 1989 and so from their perspective the Constitution had been screwed up and they were putting it back the way it was. They were not gutting the First Amendment, they were changing the Constitution as a whole, there had been this balance and they were putting this balance back, but they were not going to do surgery on the First Amendment.

Dellinger and others who supported his position maintained, however, that if the amendment was specifically directed to the First Amendment, flag desecration laws would still be limited by the First Amendment, like laws passed under other grants of constitutional authority, and the Supreme Court would likely strike them down, thereby rendering the amendment meaningless. Alternatively, Dellinger maintained, if the amendment was meant to affect the entire Constitution, then conceivably laws might be passed and upheld which deprived alleged flag desecrators of procedural protections such as the right to a jury trial or protection against warrantless searches. Similarly, Tribe argued that "nobody knows" what the proposed amendment text meant and that therefore "what it adds up to" amounted to "little more than a blank check authorizing unspecified withdrawals from America's most precious heritage, the Bill of Rights."

The Justice Department subsequently rejected this argument in a statement that was inserted into the *Congressional Record* on October 18, 1989, during Senate debate on the amendment. The statement conceded that the amendment would alter the First Amendment by declaring that the "context" in which it was debated would demonstrate to the courts that it was intended only to establish that the government's interest in protecting flags is "sufficiently compelling to out-weigh an individual's First Amendment interests in desecrating the flag" and that it would as a result "have no effect on other provisions of the Bill of Rights. . . . It is therefore untenable to suggest that the proposed amendment either would not affect the *Johnson* decision or would trump all the guarantees of the Bill of Rights."[27]

Two additional arguments made against the amendment by FPA proponents were that it posed insurmountable definitional problems and would open up a "slippery slope" for subsequent erosions of constitutional freedoms, but these arguments were largely inapposite for the simple reason that they could equally apply to the statute. The definitional critique of the amendment centered on its textual authorization for the states, as well as Congress, to ban "physical desecration of the flag" and its preamble definition of "physical desecration" as including "displaying the flag in a contemptuous manner." Amendment critics argued that these provisions would result in massive confusion and litigation. For example, they argued that each state and, potentially, each locality within the states might pass laws with different and even conflicting restrictions and that the "contemptuous manner" provision of the preamble opened the way for states to forbid highly unpopular groups from displaying the flag at all. For example, Representative Pat Schroeder expressed alarm that "clothing or artistic symbols could be illegal" in one state but "OK" in another, with the result that "you may have to have a dress code as you go across the State lines" and it might be illegal "to mail magazines over State lines." SJC chair Biden suggested that the "contemptuous manner" provision could be used to ban flying the flag at a state Republican convention if the state was "controlled by [a] Democratic legislature" or to forbid flag displays "on the day that moose season opens" in Maine. During Barr's appearance before the SJC, Senator Kennedy acidly asked him if the "contemptuous manner" provision would apply to "politicians wrapping themselves in the flag."[28]

The definitional critique of the amendment was given considerable weight by the ambiguous and conflicting statements on the subject made by its backers. Barr told congressional committees that any punishment of "physical desecration" of the flag under the amendment would have to involve "abusive physical contact" and "contemptuous conduct" with a flag and could not involve merely "words or gestures" or considerations based on the "moral worth of individuals" or a belief that "the particular surroundings [of the flag] were unfitting." He also suggested, however, that the amendment could punish conduct that "impairs the symbolic value of the Flag" without damaging any actual flag, such as "painting a wall-sized mural or billboard of the Flag with a swastika superimposed over it." Former solicitor general Bork maintained that wearing a flag "on the seat of your pants" would unquestionably be "included in the definition of physical desecration," but another amendment proponent, WLF director Kamenar, argued that to be considered "desecration" conduct would "have to go to actual burning it, mutilating, tearing it apart, throwing mud on it" and that prosecutors would use "some common sense" and would not "be running out prosecuting everybody who has a flag sewn on their pants." Attorney General Thornburgh, in one of his rare comments on the flag controversy, told a television interviewer on July 2 that whether "wearing" the flag would be considered desecration under the Bush amendment would depend on "how it's worn, where it's worn, under what circumstances, what the intent is."[29]

But while criticism of the definitional problems of the amendment and the likelihood that it would produce scores of conflicting state laws were common, exactly the same criticisms applied equally to the FPA, which, as passed by Congress, defined *flag* in a hopelessly ambiguous manner as "any flag of the United States, or any part thereof, made of any substance, of any size, in a form that is commonly displayed." Furthermore, if the FPA had been upheld by the Supreme Court, most states would likely have enacted similar, but not identical, supposedly "content-neutral" flag desecration laws, and the result would have been the same morass of litigation that marked the Vietnam War era. In fact, at least eight states (Arkansas, Tennessee, New Hampshire, Texas, Illinois, Maryland, Indiana, and South Dakota) modified their flag desecration laws in 1989 and 1990 in slightly varying ways that were clearly influenced by the FPA and were generally supported with the same arguments as those made by congressional Democrats.[30]

For example, Arkansas passed a new flag desecration law modeled on the FPA in November 1989 after its then relatively obscure Democratic governor, Bill Clinton, endorsed a "content-neutral" statute on July 14 (with an exception allowing the burning of worn flags). He characterized his approach as "a lot quicker [than an amendment] and there's no direct infringement of the First Amendment."

Using similar arguments as those proferred by Tribe and other backers of the F PA, Clinton maintained that a "generic" ban on flag desecration, whatever the reason for such action, no more infringed upon political dissent than did prosecuting people who disrobed in public, under indecent exposure laws, even if they did so for political reasons. Clinton said the proposed law would still allow dissenters to express their views in other ways without destroying the country's "symbol of unity and sacrifice" and that outlawing such action was important because "people feel their values are under assault" as a result of problems like drugs and crime, and flag burning was perceived as "tearing at the framework that holds us together." The Clinton proposal was approved by a 33-1 vote in the Arkansas Senate and by a 91-0 vote in the Arkansas House.

Just as, ultimately, the definitional critique of the amendment by supporters of a statute carried little logical force (whatever its actual impact), similarly lacking was the accompanying assault by F PA backers on the amendment on the grounds that a statute would avoid the "slippery slope" of paving the way for future frequent infringements of the First Amendment. Because F PA proponents openly proclaimed that its major advantage would be to ban flag burning more quickly than a constitutional amendment, the logical conclusion was that its passage and legitimation by the Supreme Court might well create a truly greased "slippery slope" for evading unpopular Supreme Court decisions that supported constitutional rights by means of arcane legislative maneuvering—for example, outlawing the burning "for any reason" of pictures of American politicians, destroying "for any reason" replicas of the Declaration of Independence, or even picketing government buildings "for any reason." As Republican senator Orrin Hatch, a supporter of an amendment, noted, "how a statute which prohibits flag desecration in all or some instances is not a threat to the first amendment while a constitutional amendment achieving the same thing is such a threat" was by no means clear, especially since federal statutes required only majorities in both houses of Congress, whereas amendments required two-thirds backing in both houses of Congress plus ratification by three-fourths of the state legislatures.[31]

Nobody who backed the F PA but opposed the amendment in 1989 ever gave a coherent answer to the question posed by Hatch. In interviews conducted in 1990, however, congressional aides to Democratic congressmen who took that position gave an explanation which, if not very convincing logically, no doubt made sense to politicians in 1989 who wanted to voice opposition to the *Johnson* ruling yet did not want to amend the Bill of Rights. For example, an aide to a Democratic senator who voted for the F PA but helped lead the fight against the amendment said that most congressmen genuinely believed that "flag burning was not a good thing, and if it could be prevented by law, great, but if that didn't work" an amendment was viewed "as another question entirely," because it was "screwing around with a fundamental principle of the democratic system" and therefore viewed as an "extreme remedy and overreaction." In short, the aide said, the FPA was "partly strategy to avoid an amendment, but it was also something that a lot of senators believed in." A House Democratic leadership aide gave a similar interpretation:

> You have to understand that most congressmen are genuinely repulsed at flag burners, so the thing in their mind was not so much protecting the rights of flag burners but the notion that they were protecting the Bill of Rights, something that had never been amended. They didn't want to take the Constitution, the sacred basic document of our whole country, especially the Bill of Rights, and subject it to this kind of petty political attack and that's what was most important about the flag issue. There weren't that many people who were arguing you should have the right to burn the flag, they were arguing about things like the meaning and values of the flag and not getting distracted and letting a few crazy flag burners who want to degrade the flag in that way rush us into changing our Bill of Rights.

However sincere the motives of those who backed the FPA but opposed an amendment, because so many FPA supporters were apparently little concerned about outlawing a highly unpopular form of dissent, especially if by so doing they could protect themselves politically, and because so many of them appeared to be far more concerned about the symbolism than the substance of the First Amendment, the potential for subsequent congressional abridgment of constitutional rights through legislative flimflammery would have loomed very high had the Supreme Court upheld the 1989 FPA. Given the difficulty of amending the Constitution and the arguably "unique" nature of the flag, however, the position of amendment proponents that passing it could *not* create any "slippery slope" was at least reasonably convincing. Perhaps the strongest case for this position was made by former solicitor general Bork, who rejected "slippery slope" arguments before the SJC because

> no other object remotely resembles the flag as the symbol of our identity as a Nation. . . . Forty-eight states have not enacted statutes prohibiting the burning of copies of the Constitution. Copies of the Constitution do not fly over our public buildings. . . . Nobody pledges

> allegiance to the Presidential Seal. Marines did not fight across Iwo
> Jima and up Mount Suribachi to raise the flag of Rhode Island, to raise
> a copy of the Constitution or of the Presidential seal.[32]

Evidence also existed, although critics of the amendment never pointed to it, that suggested that the flag might not be such a unique object of Americans' symbolic devotion after all, thus bolstering the "slippery slope" position. For example, in a 1965 Gallup Poll more Americans (31 percent) named the bald eagle as the most important national symbol than cited the flag (19 percent), and in a 1986 Roper Poll (in which respondents could choose two answers) the flag was designated the best symbol of America less often (46 percent) than the Statue of Liberty (57 percent), which was then the subject of one hundredth anniversary celebrations. In a follow-up Roper Poll in 1989, however, conducted amid the flag burning controversy, the flag triumphed over the Statue of Liberty by 83 percent to 55 percent.[33]

The Argument for the Amendment

Former solicitor general Bork and others who urged passage of a constitutional amendment in 1989 essentially argued that no flag desecration statute could withstand Supreme Court scrutiny under the principles established by the *Johnson* decision. Therefore, they maintained, enacting the FPA would only result in its being struck down after lengthy legal procedures, thereby inevitably leading Congress back to reconsidering an amendment as the only viable alternative. According to Bork, "After several years of litigation, we would certainly be right where we are today if a statutory route is attempted." In addition, proponents of the amendment made clear that they did not want to deal with flag desecration in the "content-neutral" manner proposed in the FPA but instead wanted to authorize Congress and the states to use considerable discretion in regulating use of the flag. They stressed that they wanted to be able to punish a wide variety of "undesirable" forms of flag usage, while still protecting "patriotic" flag uses, even if the latter involved damaging flags, such as burning worn flags or pinning battle decorations to flags. Amendment supporters argued that only an amendment could allow the government to discriminate among objectively similar types of physical damage to flags because no law that authorized such "content discrimination" could possibly satisfy the principles established in the *Johnson* ruling.[34]

The key witness for the Bush administration before the judiciary committees was Assistant Attorney General William Barr, who headed the Justice Department's Office of Legal Counsel. Barr argued, above all, that no law which sought to outlaw flag desecration, even in a facially "content-neutral" manner, could withstand Supreme Court scrutiny under the *Johnson* standards (an argument that proved correct when the Supreme Court struck down the FPA in the 1990 *Eichman* decision). Barr told the committees that the only possible government interest in seeking to protect the physical integrity of flags was to "protect the flag as the symbol of the Nation" and that the Court had made clear in *Johnson* that because this interest implied an attempt to suppress presumptively First Amendment–protected expression harmful to the flag's symbolic value, it could not meet the "compelling interest" and "exacting scrutiny" standards required to justify suppressing political dissent. Barr summarized his argument by declaring that the *Johnson* ruling had clearly established that

> whenever someone burns the Flag for expressive purposes, that conduct is protected by the First Amendment; that to prohibit such conduct, the Government must have a compelling reason that is unrelated to expression; that the Government's reason for protecting the flag (to preserve it as a symbol of national unity) is inherently and necessarily related to expression; and that the Government's interest in protecting the flag as a symbol of our national unity can never be sufficiently compelling to overcome an individual's First Amendment interest in burning the Flag for communicative purposes. This reasoning plainly would extend to any Flag desecration statute enacted to protect the Flag as a symbol of our Nation.[35]

Barr rejected any comparisons of a "neutral" flag statute to laws that protected government monuments and animals from physical damage, regardless of what motivated such assaults, as "false analogies" because such targets of special protection were "inherently rare and irreplaceable" and therefore had value beyond and above any valued symbolism. He argued that the flag is, by contrast, "inherently reproducible" and the only reason to seek to protect it "is because of its symbolic value," an interest "inherently related to expression." For example, Barr maintained, the government could protect the Statue of Liberty because it is "both unique, one of a kind, and it is symbolic," but, as was the case with the flag, without a constitutional amendment the government could not validly forbid people to "build an exact replica of the Statue of Liberty in their front yard and blow it up" because the only possible government interest in outlawing such conduct would be to suppress political dissent.

Barr and others who supported his position argued that any claim by F PA backers that the government had some interest in protecting the physical integrity of flags divorced from seeking to suppress expression, and therefore requiring only that the government meet the less demanding (than *Johnson* standards) "important or substantial governmental interest" test of the 1965 *O'Brien* draft card burning case, would be immediately seen as false by the Supreme Court. HJC subcommittee ranking Republican Sensenbrenner termed such arguments by F PA proponents an attempt to play a futile "game of cat and mouse with the Supreme Court" and to "obfuscate the issues with legal mumble jumble and delaying tactics," while Barr termed them "intellectually dishonest," "absurd," "chicanery," a "pretext," and a "weird contortion," that the "Court is not going to be fooled by."[36]

Even if a "content-neutral" statute could be crafted that the Supreme Court would uphold, Barr and other amendment advocates argued that the results would not be desirable. Barr maintained that only an amendment could constitutionally allow the government to single out for punishment "in a narrow and focussed manner" those who "are really acting contemptuously toward the flag, who really want to harm the flag and harm the symbol." The statute, however, he said, would, in an "intellectually dishonest" manner, punish "every form of conduct [physically damaging the flag], regardless of intent" so as to "get to" flag desecrators who behaved in ways that "the American people are upset about." "We make no bones about the fact that what we are trying to do is to protect the symbolic value of the flag," Barr stated. But he argued that the proposed "neutral" statute would prohibit throwing away paper cups with flag pictures on them, punish those who placed "patriotic inscriptions on flags" just as much as those who placed swastikas on them, punish "a child who innocently steps on a flag," and jail movie producers who showed flags being damaged in films about American military history, even though their intent was "to honor the flag."

In any case, Barr added, Biden's proposed F PA text was clearly flawed, even in its alleged "neutrality," because flying the flag in high winds or in battle, where "its physical integrity can be affected," was not outlawed, yet maintaining a flag on the floor was forbidden even though the "safest" place for a flag would be on a "living room floor under plexiglass." Furthermore, he maintained, any attempt to allow, in a supposedly "content-neutral" statute, the "dignified or respectful" destruction of worn flags to let veterans continue their traditional disposal ceremonies would only further weaken its claims to a "purported neutrality." In fact, Barr aptly concluded, the only truly "neutral approach" to the flag "would say either everyone can use it [however they wanted to] or no one can."

Barr's arguments were supported by other amendment proponents. For example, Sensenbrenner declared that, to be "perfectly blunt," what he wanted was to allow for "content censorship" because, "the American people do not like what Gregory Lee Johnson did in Texas, and they want Congress to put a stop to it." Former assistant attorney general Charles Cooper similarly declared that he did not "really want a neutral flag desecration statute" because he didn't want to punish conduct that physically damaged the flag if such behavior was "dignified and respectful," as in the case of a soldier who wished to be cremated with a flag or Boy Scouts who wished to destroy worn flags in a "dignified way by burning." But any attempt to exempt destroying worn flags from a statute, Cooper maintained, would create the insurmountable problem of how to determine "when a flag is a former flag" and how to protect such a "former flag" from descending "to the status of say a towel" which could be "disposed of" in a "contemptuous way."[37]

Amendment proponents leveled a withering critique at the proposed statute; in fact, especially the presentation made by Barr was largely adopted subsequently both by the lawyers who attacked the ultimately enacted F PA before the Supreme Court and by the Court itself. According to a Justice Department source interviewed in 1990, Barr's presentation was prepared as "basically a legal brief" and

> every word in that testimony was measured and carefully considered as if it were a Supreme Court opinion, which is somewhat unusual for testimony on the Hill. We made the decision here to present it in that way rather than in the typical testimony format because we knew that every law professor in America would be looking at it and trying to attack it. We had to come up with a legal analysis in the middle of a hotly contested political issue and it was a tribute to our work that the Supreme Court later adopted that analysis [in *Eichman*].

In response to the arguments of Barr and other F PA critics, Tribe, Biden, and other F PA proponents argued that allowing the disposal of worn flags would pose no legal problem because such material would no longer be "flags" in the true sense; that the other examples of "respectful" flag desecration that Barr and others had objected would be criminalized by the F PA were trivial matters; and that, at least arguably, if, admittedly uncertainly, there was a valid government interest in protecting the physical integrity of flags which could be differentiated from attempts to suppress dissent. Thus F PA supporters argued that the disposal of worn flags during respectful ceremonial burnings could be exempted from its provisions because, as Duke law professor Dellinger put it, such objects were "no longer a flag within the meaning of the statute—maybe a flag emeritus or a former flag, but it's no longer a flag." Tribe adopted the same position, arguing that old flags could perhaps be disposed of through the establishment of a "Federal respository institution maybe run by veterans to which one would have to send worn-out flags." He suggested that moviemakers who wanted to depict flags being damaged during battles could use "special effects" or not use a "real flag," and he argued that a veteran who "really cares about the country" would not find it "too much of a sacrifice" to give up being cremated with the flag in order to have a "neutral law," which would not allow anyone to destroy a "still usable flag," even to "express reverence for the country."[38]

The greatest difficulty facing those who argued that a statute would be upheld by the Supreme Court was to articulate a government interest in protecting the "physical integrity" of flags which reflected motives other than seeking to suppress dissent. Dellinger, who based his prediction that the Court would uphold a "neutral" statute primarily on Blackmun's dissent in the 1974 *Goguen* case, bluntly admitted that he could not articulate what rationale the Court could give in doing so because "it is very difficult to articulate what that legitimate [i.e., nonsuppressive] government interest is." Tribe made the most sustained argument that the government had a legitimate nonsuppressive interest in protecting the physical integrity of all flags, although his position was muddled and, at points, contradictory. Among the "nonsuppressive" interests he cited in his congressional testimony were protecting those who learned about a flag desecration from a "sense of hurt" or from resulting "mental distress," regardless of why the desecration occurred, expressing a feeling of "sympathy for the flags that are burning" rather than "out of a desire to censor those who burn them," and preventing a "sense of injury to the Nation, when any flag" was damaged. Tribe maintained that such "nonsuppressive interests" would be applicable even if flag desecrations "happen to occur in the dead of night in Gregory Lee Johnson's darkened garage." He failed to explain, however, how anyone would feel "mental distress" or how the nation would be injured by such an act if no one learned about it, or how such interests could square with Brennan's declaration in *Johnson* that the First Amendment's "bedrock principle" was that the government could not ban expression "simply because society finds the idea itself offensive or disagreeable."

Tribe explained that in his 1988 book he had mistakenly argued that a "neutral" flag law would be unconstitutional because he had "failed to consider" that government "often bans conduct precisely because a majority finds such conduct deeply offensive or reprehensible in itself, without thereby intending to punish the offensive message that the conduct might or might not be meant to express." Citing, as parallels, laws that outlawed the desecration of gravesites, the destruction of government property or of privately owned historic landmarks, and the killing of American eagles, Tribe argued that it "just does not follow" that attempting to protect revered objects was "solely, or even primarily" designed to

> censor, suppress or punish whatever the destroyer of such objects might wish to express by such conduct. . . . The sentiment reflected in a law designed to protect a physical symbol may often be a sentiment of sympathy for what the symbol embodies and represents, not a sentiment of censorship of what the symbol-destroyer expresses. . . . Such laws are justifiable not because there is a scarcity of gravesites or of historic landmarks, but because the people, acting through democratic principles, have the right to designate particularly significant things or places as off-limits to physical assault.

If Tribe's explanation of how a "neutral" flag desecration statute could have a "nonsuppressive purpose" was unconvincing, at times incoherent, and often deeply at odds with the *Johnson* decision, he was on much stronger grounds in arguing that the explicit "content censorship" which supporters of the amendment wished to authorize contradicted fundamental principles of American democracy. Tribe argued that passing laws aimed at the "specific political message" of flag desecrators would "rip the heart out of the first amendment, whose most central truth" was that "in this country we do not go after people just because we do not like their message." Similarly, Biden told the SJC that it "scares the living devil out of me" to learn that the amendment specifically sought to "get folks who say bad things about America."[39]

CHAPTER 6

THE 1989 DECLINE AND FALL
OF THE CONSTITUTIONAL AMENDMENT
AND THE PASSAGE OF THE
FLAG PROTECTION ACT

Amid the near-hysterical reaction immediately following the June 21 *Johnson* decision, it was widely and almost universally predicted that a constitutional amendment to outlaw flag desecration would quickly pass both houses of Congress and be ratified by the states in record time. Thus on June 22, American University law professor Herman Schwartz assessed the chances of a constitutional amendment as "pretty good" because allowing flag burning would be "like prohibiting Americans from eating apple pie," and on June 24, three days before Bush endorsed an amendment, HJC civil liberties subcommittee chair Edwards said that only "10 or 20 votes" would be cast against a constitutional amendment if the House voted immediately. Bush's June 27 amendment endorsement, followed by his heavily publicized June 30 Iwo Jima Memorial appearance, only increased such predictions. Thus former Democratic presidential candidate Walter Mondale's 1984 campaign manager Bob Beckel told a reporter that only politicians who liked to get "in front of railroad trains" would "enjoy" opposing an amendment, and Duke University law professor Walter Dellinger predicted that "any amendment that comes out of the Congress will be ratified faster than any amendment on record."[1]

Among state legislators questioned in early July, Republican Kansas Senate president Paul Burke predicted that a constitutional amendment would whip through both of his state's legislative houses "like a thunderstorm through

Kansas"; Utah Republican House majority leader Craig Moody declared, "If there are two or three votes against it, I'll be surprised"; and Alaska Senate president Tim Kelly said an amendment would be approved "within 30 days" because a few "whining" liberals would be "overwhelmed" by legislative and public opinion. CBS White House correspondent Leslie Stahl reported on June 27 that the amendment was "a steamroller going downhill and nobody is going to stop it," and *U.S. News & World Report* stated bluntly in its July 10 issue that "opposition [to an amendment] now seem suicidal."[2]

The Role of the Veterans' Organization in Supporting the Amendment

Besides the endorsement of a constitutional amendment by President Bush and the Republican congressional leadership (along with most rank-and-file congressional Republicans and many such Democrats) and the apparent strong public support demonstrated by the polls, an additional reason why most political observers at first believed Congress would pass an amendment was that the American Legion and the Veterans of Foreign Wars, the two leading organizations in the extremely powerful veterans' lobby, made clear that they regarded its passage as a major priority. Legion and VFW officials, who claimed a total of almost seven million members (including auxiliary organizations), testified for the amendment at both judiciary committees' hearings and kept up a steady stream of often highly emotional press releases, phone calls, and letters to congressmen, along with numerous messages to their memberships, demanding passage of the measure. According to a 1992 interview with a Democratic congressional source who attended many closed-door meetings dealing with the flag desecration issue and who closely follows veterans' affairs, many congressmen "fall down in a dead faint when veterans say anything" and it is "amazing how powerful veterans are on the Hill, it is astonishing. Surely there was legitimate personal outrage among individual congressmen over the *Johnson* decision, but that dies fairly quickly as the next issue arises. You need something to keep an issue on the front burner, to keep a continuance of the outrage, and that's what some of the vets' groups really did. It got to the point where congressional offices weren't counting their mail [demanding an amendment to ban flag burning], they were weighing it."

American Legion national commander "Sparky" Gierke, a sitting North Dakota Supreme Court justice and a former president of that state's bar association, repeatedly characterized the *Johnson* decision as holding that "it's okay to burn our flag," and he told Congress that he felt "angry, disgusted and sick" about the ruling and that his organization was "dumbfounded" because "we know in our gut that this is wrong." In a September 22 letter to Legion officials, Miles Epling, the new national commander, told his officers to make the amendment their "top priority issue" and declared, "What we won't stand for is even one more flag burner insulting our country and disparaging the memory of those who died for it by burning our flag with legal impunity."[3]

Among its other activities, the Legion commissioned a special Gallup Poll on the controversy (which reported in mid-July that 67 percent of a national sample favored a constitutional amendment), sold "Don't Burn Our Flag" T-shirts and buttons (which used flag designs in technical violation of many state flag desecration laws), and organized a massive petition-signing campaign to back passage of an amendment. On August 31, the Legion submitted to Congress a claimed one million such signatures. At the VFW's annual August national convention, twenty-seven separate resolutions denouncing flag desecration were consolidated into a unanimously adopted resolution which demanded a constitutional amendment as the organization's "number one priority goal." The resolution termed the *Johnson* decision a "gross travesty of justice" which had "totally appalled" the VFW and called upon VFW officials to make "known" to politicians that support of an amendment would be "among the requisites" for obtaining VFW financial contributions.[4]

Also supporting a constitutional amendment were two of the patriotic-hereditary organizations that had been in the forefront of the original turn-of-the-century flag desecration movement. Meeting in convention on July 4 in San Francisco, the SAR endorsed the amendment, citing its role as a "leader" in fighting flag desecration for "nearly a century"; the DAR passed a similar resolution at its April 1990 national convention.[5]

The Braking of the Drive for the Amendment

Given the almost universal expectation in late June and early July, especially among Washington political circles, that a constitutional amendment to ban flag desecration would be quickly and overwhelmingly passed in Congress and ratified by the states, any analysis of the 1989 flag burning debate must attempt to explain why, by the time the Senate voted on a constitutional amendment on October 19, it received only fifty-one votes (far short of the required two-thirds vote of sixty-seven if all one hundred senators voted) and was therefore killed for the 1989 congressional session. The basic explanation for this outcome can be divided into three parts: (1) a number of key conservatives and others whose patriotism could not be assailed spoke out against the amendment in late June and early July, thereby helping to disrupt the overwhelming momentum it otherwise likely would have developed; (2) the delay in voting on a constitutional amendment, which inevitably resulted from the normal and reasonable, but also deliberate, decision of Democratic congressional leaders to schedule committee hearings on possible responses to the *Johnson* decision, resulted in moving the flag desecration issue off the front pages and out of the public spotlight, which in turn led both to a considerable diminution of public interest in and pressure for an amendment and also to a gradual increase in both public and congressional unease over changing the Bill of Rights; and (3) the Democratic FPA legislative alternative provided a political "cover" for congressmen, and especially for many Democrats, who either privately approved of the *Johnson* decision (or were not exercised about it) or had grave doubts about "tampering" with the Bill of Rights but felt that they could not vote against an amendment without some alternative means of publicly recording their "flag patriotism."

The Role of Conservative Opposition
to the Amendment

One of the earliest signs that a flag amendment steamroller might not be inevitable was that three of the country's most influential conservative political commentators and columnists, James Kilpatrick, George Will, and William Safire, denounced the idea in nationally syndicated columns. Although conservative columnists Pat Buchanan and William Buckley supported the amendment, their columns were carried in far fewer newspapers and they were regarded as far less "mainstream" and influential. Although almost all of the major liberal and moderate columnists (with the exception of *Washington Post* columnist David Broder) opposed the amendment, because conservative opposition was considered far more surprising, the views of Will, Kilpatrick, and Safire appear to have had much greater political impact.[6]

Kilpatrick quoted Brennan's "bedrock principle" statement, termed Bush "dead wrong" because the Court had correctly protected flag burning as "the expression of an idea" that the "nation has done something gravely wrong," and declared that the nation could in any case easily "survive the puny assaults of such contemptible maggots as Gregory Lee Johnson." Will termed the Court majority "five confused men in robes" who had erred by failing to draw "lines asserting the general claims of the community against the claims of extreme individualism," but argued that conservatives out for political gain "should content themselves with saying that liberals want to read pornography by the light of burning flags," while keeping their "hands off Mr. Madison's document" because "there is no flag-burning problem sufficient to justify the radical step of amending the Constitution." Safire wrote that advocates of a constitutional amendment were confusing political symbols, which could not be desecrated because they were not sacred, with religious objects, and also were confusing the flag's symbolism, which could only "gain new glory in our tolerance of dissent and in our secure shrug of unconcern for childish disrespect and political temper tantrums," with the substantive freedoms it represented. Above all, Safire wrote, his first principle was to "never touch the Bill of Rights," or, put more graphically, to "keep your cotton-pickin' fingers off the time-honored list of freedoms demanded by our Founders" because any change would "erode" all basic rights.

The impact of the opposition of conservative columnists was no doubt bolstered by the overwhelming opposition to an amendment by editorials and editorial cartoons in newspapers of all political views. The opposition of such liberal major metropolitan newspapers as the *Washington Post* and the *New York Times* was not a surprise. But they were joined by many conservative papers such as the *Washington Times,* which, in a June 28 editorial, condemned the *Johnson* decision but also warned that if the Constitution were amended to correct "every hare brained theory advanced by the court in recent years, our founding document would be thousands of pages long" and, even "more abominable than the court's reasoning," conservatives would set a "horrible precedent by turning the Constitution into a political tool." Many small and medium-sized newspapers also added their voices to the opposition to an amendment. By mid-October, shortly before the Senate defeated the constitutional amendment, Louisiana's Democratic senator John Breaux reported, in tones of astonishment, that he was "starting to get some editorials from conservative papers in Louisiana saying we shouldn't do a constitutional amendment."[7]

The overwhelming opposition of columnists and newspapers of all political stripes to a constitutional amendment drew widespread comment from all sides of the political spectrum. From the liberal position, Thomas Mann, director of government studies at the Brookings Institution, declared in early July that Bush had been "utterly battered" by the "devastating critique" that conservative columnists had leveled at the amendment. From a far more conservative perspective, columnist Thomas Sowell complained that the "united chorus of the media" concerning the amendment, with the exception of a "few brave souls such as Pat Buchanan," reflected above all the fears of elites that ordinary citizens would "make their values the values of this country," instead of leaving such matters to the "intelligentsia and the morally anointed." In a little-noticed interview with Knight-Ridder newspapers in late July, even President Bush complained about "a lot of columnists piling on now" and rejected what he said was their argument "that people have thought about [an amendment] now and they don't think it's a good idea." In a 1990 interview, ABC congressional reporter Cokie Roberts declared that the "conservative columnists made a big difference" in providing "a tremendous amount of political coverage" for congressmen who wanted to oppose the amendment but feared being attacked for such a vote. PAW legislative counsel John Gomperts similarly recalled in a 1990 interview that the views of the conservative columnists "landed very hard in Washington" and clearly helped to brake the amendment steamroller.[8]

Augmenting the impact of the views of conservative newspapers and columnists was the widely publicized opposition to an amendment (and, by implication, to the statute also) expressed in mid-July by two veterans whose patriotism could hardly be challenged. On July 11, the *Washington Post* published an "op ed" essay by James Warner, a Washington attorney, former Reagan White House staffer, and decorated Vietnam War pilot who had been imprisoned in North Vietnam. Warner wrote that during an interrogation by his captors, he was shown a picture of American war protesters burning a flag and was told that the photo proved that he was "wrong" because "people in your country are against your cause." Warner recalled that when he responded that in fact the picture proved that he was right because "in my country we are not afraid of freedom, even if it means that people disagree with us," his interrogator's face turned "purple with rage" as fear and pain shone in his eyes, and he "smashed his fist onto the table and screamed at me to shut up." Warner continued, "I have never forgotten that look, nor have I forgotten the satisfaction I felt at using his tool, the picture of the burning flag, against him." After this experience, Warner concluded, "I cannot compromise on freedom," and in any case there was no need to because freedom "is the best weapon we have."

A week after Warner's essay appeared, Senator Bob Kerrey, a Congressional Medal of Honor winner who had lost part of a leg as a result of a Vietnam War injury, delivered a lengthy address on the Senate floor, in which he declared that although at first he was "outraged" by news reports about the *Johnson* decision, he had concluded that the majority argument was "reasonable, understandable and consistent with those values that I believe make America so wonderful."

Kerrey suggested that "there is no need for us to do anything" because the Supreme Court had merely followed a long line of decisions protecting symbolic expression and "there is simply no line of Americans queuing up to burn our flag." Kerrey directly rejected the argument made by Chief Justice Rehnquist in his dissent and by many others that too many veterans had fought for the flag to permit its desecration, declaring that during his war experience, "I do not remember feeling this way . . . I don't remember giving the safety of our flag anywhere near the thought that I gave the safety of my men."[9]

Both Warner and Kerrey were unusually eloquent, but their positions had special impact because they were both decorated veterans and thus politically unassailable and also because, until they spoke, the veterans' lobby had so vociferously argued for an amendment that the impression had been created that all veterans favored the amendment and therefore to oppose it might not only be interpreted as antiflag but also as antiveteran. Their statements were repeatedly cited and reprinted during the next few months and gave considerable political "cover" to those who wished to oppose the amendment. For example, a syndicated column by Sandy Grady about Kerrey's speech appeared in the August 9 *Atlanta Constitution* under the headline, "Kerrey's Words Marked Shift in Flag-Burning Flap." Grady concluded his column by declaring, "Bob Kerrey lost a leg, not his heart or head." Warner was invited to testify before both the House and Senate judiciary committees, and his essay was frequently cited in congressional debate.

PAW legislative counsel Gomperts recalled, in a 1990 interview, that the Kerrey speech made a "big splash and changed the dynamic of the debate" and that the Warner column was "quoted a million times" and "landed very heavily. It had a huge effect. Washington was buzzing about Warner's article. I spent the whole day talking about it." In another 1990 interview, *Washington Post* congressional reporter Don Phillips also recalled the Warner column as having a "big impact. All of a sudden there was another side to patriotism, so a patriot doesn't have to wrap himself in the flag, a patriot can also see the flag as a piece of cloth which isn't that important, it's what that stands for. I think that got picked up and repeated all over the place."

The Role of the "Cooling Off Period"

While opposition from conservative commentators like George Will and "politically invulnerable" veterans like Senator Kerrey helped to slow down what seemed an unstoppable momentum toward passage of a constitutional amendment, the passage of time had the same effect. As the flag desecration issue disappeared from the headlines and the network news and moved into the congressional committee rooms by mid-July, many congressmen saw the intensity of public interest in the issue diminishing and public doubts about the wisdom of passing an amendment slowly growing, especially given the availability of the FPA as an alternate option. For example, HJC subcommittee chair Edwards reported in mid-July that his mail had at first favored an amendment, but opposition had grown steadily since, until his letters had become "a steady three to one against an amendment" because "it really shocks people" to consider "weakening the Bill of Rights." House Speaker Foley similarly declared in several widely publicized statements to reporters in mid-July that there was "no firestorm of fervor" for an amendment, that the "country as a whole seems to be taking this in a calmer way" than Congress, and that "there is growing opinion that a statute is preferable to a constitutional amendment." In early August, SJC chair Biden told his colleagues that "the more people reflect on this, the less enthusiasm there is for amending the Constitution"; by late September, Biden reported that "there is not a single senator who's come up to me in the last three weeks and said, 'Hey, how about the critical issue of the burning flag?'"[10]

An additional suggestion that public interest in the flag controversy diminished rapidly after July 4 was that flag "desecration" incidents declined precipitously for almost four months thereafter (until congressional passage of the FPA stirred up renewed flag burnings as a protest response in late October). In one of only a handful of such incidents reported between July 4 and October 27, a group of artists held a month-long exhibit beginning in mid-September at Jersey City State College in New Jersey titled "Flagging Our Freedom" and consisting of artworks featuring actual flags or flag designs, to protest proposed restrictions on the use of the flag and on government funding of controversial art. Art displays in the exhibit included portrayals of the Statue of Liberty giving a Nazi salute against the backdrop of an American flag, a blindfolded bald eagle perched on a flag, a swastika decorated with stars and stripes, and American soldiers marching over a flag with a baby's head in the background to suggest the devastation wrought by war. According to exhibit curator Orlando Cuevas, the artists sought to raise concern about where limits on expression would stop because "what begins as an attempt to protect the flag may finish by restricting how artists express themselves through other symbols" and eventually it could become illegal even to desecrate "an image of an image," such as a photograph or painting of a flag. Gregory Lee Johnson attended the exhibit's opening, where he handed out buttons that depicted a flag and read, "Burn, baby, burn."[11]

In another art exhibit, artist Gene Elder displayed a series of four actual flags, entitled *Dangerous Ideas,* upon which he had painted or drawn designs (including a large tomato) and political slogans (such as "Know the truth and the truth shall set you free") in a San Antonio gallery. Although the exhibit opened September 1, the same day that a new Texas flag desecration law (modeled on the FPA), which outlawed damaging, defacing, or mutilating the flag, was scheduled to take effect, Elder was not prosecuted. The display did become the target of angry phone calls and at least one bomb threat. To celebrate the exhibit's opening, a huge cake with a flag design was cut and served, in what was termed a "flag defecation event," in an allusion to the inevitable ultimate fate of the flag frosting. Elder, who declared that the Texas legislature was composed of "Nazis in cowboy hats," maintained that he was not desecrating the flag but rather was "liberating it from conservative, neurotic, possessive, pseudo-patriots who insist on wrapping themselves in the flag and ignoring the First Amendment." In response, Texas Republican state representative Sam Johnson, who had coauthored the new law, proclaimed, "If people don't like this country, or can't respect the flag, then they should just get out of it."[12]

In other early fall 1989 flag "desecration" incidents, an Ohio man was arrested on September 5 for theft and disorderly conduct in connection with stealing a flag from outside a bank. Local officials pondered adding a flag desecration charge, but he died shortly after his arrest. In the only actual flag burning incident reported for almost four months after July 4, University of Pennsylvania communications professor Carolyn Marvin stirred a brief uproar at her campus by burning a flag on September 13 during a class on freedom of expression. She declared that her action was an "educational decision" that reinforced "the most basic values which the flag represents, free speech and democratic government," and had not been meant to "denigrate the United States or the flag," but rather to "stimulate debate on an issue of public policy that is now before Congress." Marvin's flag burning aroused protests from some students and attracted widespread publicity in Pennsylvania. Although university president Sheldon Hackney defended Marvin's act as a form of academic freedom, on March 21, 1990, the Pennsylvania House of Representatives voted 189-4 to condemn her for an "outrageous act of desecration."[13]

The apparent rapid diminishment of public interest in the flag issue in general and in a constitutional amendment in particular became especially clear to many congressmen during a lengthy recess in August, during which most visited their home districts. Several Democratic congressmen, including Kerrey, Representative Mike Synar (D-Okla.), and Representative Beryl Anthony (D-Ark.), reported that during the recess none or virtually none of their constituents had brought up the flag desecration issue; Synar added that "momentum to build up to a constitutional amendment has diminished substantially" and that even veterans' groups were telling him "right now they think a statute's sufficient." According to a Democratic HJC source, by August, "We started getting a lot of mail reflecting second thoughts of people, letters from vets saying, 'Gee, I didn't fight for a piece of cloth, I fought for the freedom of dissent. I spent 25 years in the military and I didn't like flag burning when I was in the military and I don't like it now, but I was in the military to protect others' right to dissent.' When people started realizing that there was a prospect of amending the First Amendment, they started saying, 'Hey, wait a minute, this is something significant.'"[14]

Even Republican backers of an amendment reported a substantial diminution of interest and support for such action by midsummer. Senator Arlen Specter offered an unusual anecdote to back up his conclusion that the initial post-*Johnson* "outrage" and "very strong" demands from his constituents for an amendment had turned, by mid-August and September, into a "more reflective" attitude which had led many to have a "second thought" about the issue and become increasingly receptive to a statute. He told the SJC that immediately after the *Johnson* decision, when he attended the Pennsylvania state VFW convention, feeling was "very, very high," but that, at a more recent meeting with constituents, a VFW group listened to a young man read a long statement opposing an amendment "with peace and tranquility. I think had that statement been read . . . 2 months earlier there would have been bedlam if not mayhem in that particular setting."[15]

By scheduling hearings on possible responses to the *Johnson* decision and then by postponing all floor votes until September and October, the Democratic congressional leadership deliberately sought to gain precisely such a diminution in public interest and pressure over the flag issue in general and an amendment in particular. When the HJC civil liberties subcommittee began hearings in mid-July, Chairman Edwards told Republican House leader Michel, who appeared as one of the first witnesses in support of the amendment, that, "if you had had your way," with congressional and state legislative voting during the immediate post-*Johnson* "period of high emotion," an amendment would have been ratified in "two or three months." Representative Weiss, one of only eight congressmen who voted against all proposals critical of the *Johnson* decision, congratulated Edwards on July 20 for holding hearings that allowed congressmen to "slowly and deliberately" consider the issues, to "slow down and think about where they are," and to engage in "sober rethinking."[16]

Whatever perceptions individual congressmen had picked up by mid-July and August which suggested that public pressure for a constitutional amendment was gradually dying down were strongly bolstered by a series of news stories, editorials, and columns with this theme beginning in mid-July. Probably the most influential of these articles, because it was printed on the front page of the *Washington Post,* a newspaper universally read on Capitol Hill, appeared on July 25: "Support Lags for Amendment to Prohibit Flag Burning, Voters Seen Opposing Change in Constitution." The article reported a considerable decline in constituent mail to congressmen about the flag issue and that though many congressional offices indicated that their constituents still wanted the flag protected, they did not differentiate between doing so by law or by constitutional amendment. The article also reported that a recent national poll indicated that Americans of both parties and in all sections of the country preferred to overturn the *Johnson* decision by law, as opposed to an amendment, by 51 to 31 percent. PAW legislative counsel John Gomperts, in a 1990 interview, recalled the *Post* article as a "big hit in Washington," especially among those who wanted "not to have a constitutional amendment." Similarly, according to a Democratic SJC source interviewed in 1991, the *Post* article was "very significant" because it helped many congressmen tell themselves, "Gee, it's not just my anecdotal experience, but others didn't hear anything [from their constituents about the flag issue during the August recess] either."

Supporters of an amendment were by no means oblivious to the hopes of their opponents that the issue would die down with time, and they sought, with clear alarm, to combat the growing perception that public interest was cooling off. Thus HJC subcommittee ranking minority member Sensenbrenner complained on July 20 that supporters of the statutory approach were "in favor of thinking about this issue for a while, like maybe a year or two or, even better, forever." American Legion commander "Sparky" Gierke told the SJC in mid-September that although the flag controversy "is no longer carried as a front page item or as a lead story by the nation's media, I can assure you that the American public continues to be outraged" by the *Johnson* decision. On July 26, the day after the *Washington Post* article, Republican Senate leader Dole took the floor to accuse the *Post* of engaging in "self-deception" because the paper "wants desperately to believe that the American people do not care about the so-called flag issue."[17]

The Role of the Flag Protection Act

A third major reason for the failure of the amendment in the fall of 1989 was the Democrats' floating of the FPA as a statutory alternative. The FPA was perceived by many Democrats as providing "political cover" for a vote against the amendment that might be perceived as a vote "for" flagburners, which could leave them politically vulnerable. The FPA alternative was therefore especially attractive for fearful Democrats who were reluctant as a matter of principle to amend the Bill of Rights, or were determined to frustrate what was seen as Bush's attempt to repeat, on a grander scale, his 1988 flag-bashing of Democrats, or felt that the *Johnson* ruling was either legally correct or not worth getting excited about, at least on a constitutional scale.

The clearest indication that the FPA played a critical role in leading to the amendment's demise in 1989 is that in the Senate, which, unlike the House, voted on both alternatives in 1989, thirty-three (60 percent) of the fifty-five Democratic senators voted against the amendment but for the statute (only ten, or slightly over 20 percent, of the forty-five Republican senators displayed a similar voting pattern). As a result, the FPA passed in the Senate by 91-9, but the amendment fell far short of the required two-thirds majority, receiving fifty-one positive votes and forty-eight negative votes. Had all senators who voted for the FPA also voted for the amendment in 1989, the latter would have obtained ninety-four votes instead of the fifty-one it actually received.[18]

In the House, where only the FPA was voted on in 1989 and it passed by 380-38, about 135 (almost 55 percent) of the total Democratic contingent of about 255 voted for it but subsequently voted against a constitutional amendment in 1990; only 16 (slightly under 10 percent) of the over 175 House Republicans cast similar pairs of votes in 1989–90. The amendment failed to obtain the required two-thirds of the House votes in 1990, receiving 254 positive votes and 177 negative votes under the changed circumstances from 1989 created by the intervening June 11, 1990, Supreme Court *Eichman* ruling; this decision struck down the FPA as unconstitutional when applied to political protesters and therefore, unlike the situation in 1989, left an amendment as the only viable means of casting a vote to ban flag desecration. Had all those who voted for the FPA in the House in 1989 supported the amendment in 1990, the latter would have received well over 400 votes.[19]

Because, as VFW commander in chief Walter Hogan aptly noted in an October 19 press release, it was difficult to understand how, if "some legislators truly believe that free speech is limited by preventing flag desecration," they could "favor such a limitation statutorily" yet "be opposed to a constitutional amendment on free speech grounds," it is clear that political considerations were at least as important as logical, legal, or constitutional ones for many of those who voted for the FPA but against the amendment. Perhaps the strongest evidence that the amendment was seen as a certain winner absent the passage of the FPA, and also that the FPA was therefore primarily favored by many of its backers for its "negative" rather than its positive virtues, was that so many prominent liberal constitutional lawyers and both of the two most influential American civil liberties organizations effectively lobbied for the FPA, even though they almost certainly did not really favor it. For example, like many Democrats, there is little doubt that Professor Tribe developed his argument for the constitutionality of an FPA in the hopes of helping the Democratic party avoid the perceived Scylla and Charybdis dilemma of either supporting Bush and the constitutional amendment (which was seen as fraught with the danger of opening up a First Amendment Pandora's box, as well as rewarding the president's perceived cynical disdain for constitutional liberties), or else being portrayed as favoring flag burning (which was seen as fraught with political catastrophe). Tribe, in fact, publicly declared in late June, only a few days before his July 3 *New York Times* article promoting an FPA, that he doubted there was "any politically credible way" to oppose a constitutional amendment and that an amendment would be the only way to overturn the *Johnson* decision because the only purpose of a circumventing statute would be the illegal one of suppressing dissent; this was the same position he had previously taken and explained at great length in a 1988 treatise on constitutional law. "What does the flag stand for," Tribe asked a reporter in late June 1989, if the government sought to say "it cannot be used to express derision?"[20]

Given this background, clearly the statute that Tribe promoted in his July 3 essay had more to do with attempting to find a "politically credible" way to oppose a constitutional amendment than it did with legal scholarship. In fact, after the FPA, for which Tribe served as the primary legal godfather, was passed in October 1989 and the proposed constitutional amendment it was designed to block was defeated, Tribe switched back to his former position and derided the FPA as unconstitutional after all; subsequently, Tribe praised the 1990 Supreme Court decision which struck the FPA down as an "extremely hopeful sign for the future of free speech" and confessed that his position in 1989 had "probably" been unprincipled. Tribe was by no means alone in either advocating the FPA or, at the least, arguing that it was presumptively constitutional, under circumstances which suggested that he was motivated more by attempting to block an amendment and/or help provide political cover to Democrats rather than truly believing in either the FPA's desirability or constitutionality. During the summer and fall of 1989, three separate groups of constitutional lawyers, law professors, college presidents, and other distinguished Americans submitted petitions to Congress which made free speech arguments seemingly applicable to both the FPA and the amendment but which formally opposed only the amendment and either remained strangely silent about the FPA or argued for its presumptive constitutionality.[21]

Under the existing political circumstances, the petition signers could hardly have failed to realize that such a position translated into, at the least, a coded urging that Congress defeat the amendment by voting for the FPA. For example, on September 21, 1989, shortly after the House had approved the FPA and several weeks before the Senate was scheduled for a decisive consideration of both the FPA and the amendment, 511 constitutional law professors representing 158 law schools from 46 states, who called themselves Constitutional Law Professors against a Constitutional Amendment, urged Congress to reject the amendment as "unwise and inconsistent with the basic premises of the Bill of Rights," in particular the First Amendment's "core purpose" of protecting "unpopular speech from suppression by the political majority." The statement made no reference to the FPA, which clearly was intended to suppress the same "unpopular speech" targeted by the amendment. Another group that opposed the amendment, the Emergency Committee to Defend the First Amendment, included two dozen prominent Americans, including college presidents (such as those of Harvard, Chicago, Stanford, Yale, and Virginia), former high-ranking government officials (including former Carter administration attorney general Benjamin Civiletti), and prominent lawyers (including three past presidents of the ABA). In a September 29 letter to Congress, the Emergency Committee urged defeat of the amendment on the grounds that, by criminalizing symbolic speech "because it is offensive to a large majority of Americans," the proposal would violate the "well-established principle that an unpopular speaker may not be silenced because of his views." Yet, even though the FPA, which was clearly intended to accomplish this same result, had just passed the House and was about to be considered in the Senate, the committee told Congress it had "taken no position on the statute related to flag desecration." In yet a third similar petition, sent to Congress on October 12, the very day that the House approved some minor Senate amendments to the FPA and sent it to President Bush, more than one hundred law professors, organized by Harvard's Tribe and Duke's Dellinger, urged rejection of the amendment as "inappropriate" because there was a "reasonable basis" for believing that the Supreme Court "will find" the FPA constitutional. The petition offered no opinions about the substantive advisability of either the FPA or the amendment, stating only that the signers had "differing views" about the *Johnson* ruling but were in agreement that, since "at least five [Supreme Court] justices might well uphold" the FPA, "which will accomplish the only legitimate objectives" of a flag desecration amendment, Congress should not "restrict the Bill of Rights" by amendment while awaiting a Court ruling.

America's two most influential civil liberties organizations, People for the American Way and the American Civil Liberties Union, strongly opposed the amendment, but took highly equivocal stands concerning the FPA that, in practice, amounted to encouraging congressmen to vote for it as a "lesser evil" means of defeating the amendment. Thus, although PAW president Arthur Kropp hailed the *Johnson* decision on the day it was handed down as a "victory for free speech," PAW never took any public position on the FPA, though it strongly denounced the amendment in a statement submitted to the SJC which primarily focused on free speech grounds that seemingly would have applied to the FPA also. For example, the statement opposed the amendment as a "frontal attack" on "freedom of expression," a right especially focused on protecting "unpopular opinions and expression from suppression from the political majority," which was at the "heart of our democratic government" and which made the United States the "envy of the world, an example and inspiration for democratic movements around the world." Despite this eloquent statement, one well-informed civil liberties activist reported in a 1990 interview that, in private, PAW lobbyists expressed a clear understanding of the political realities that led many congressmen to vote for the FPA as a means of defeating the amendment. According to the activist, the PAW position was "Don't do it, but we know you have to do it politically." He added:

> PAW tried to do a few things to make the statute less odious, but that was about it, and we said when we were talking to congressmen that we understood politically what they felt needed to be done and that protecting the sanctity of the Constitution had to be the ultimate goal. We never said anything official about the statute, but our whole point was "Don't pass the constitutional amendment." The understood message of that was, "If you think you need to pass the statute for political reasons, go ahead and do that, make it as least bad as possible, but don't ever amend the Constitution."[22]

One clear reflection of this strategy was a letter from PAW chairman John Buchanon which was inserted into the *Congressional Record* on October 18, on the eve of the Senate vote on the amendment. It urged the Senate to vote against the amendment "to preserve the sanctity of the Bill of Rights" and because Congress had already "passed a flag protection act" which made it "unnecessary" to "limit the First Amendment." Despite this virtual admission that the FPA would accomplish the same ends as the amendment, Buchanon never criticized the FPA, while opposing the amendment on the grounds that the country should not "diminish our most cherished freedoms in an effort to protect the symbol of those freedoms." Also reflecting the PAW's strategy of tacitly encouraging votes for the FPA as a means of blocking the amendment was what one well-informed civil liberties activist termed the organization's "behind the scenes role" in organizing the petition to Congress of the 511 constitutional law professors who strongly opposed the amendment but never mentioned the FPA, shortly before the Senate was scheduled to vote on both alternatives.

The ACLU's role during this same period was, if anything, even more politically determined and hypocritical than PAW's. The ACLU, unlike PAW, formally opposed both the amendment and the FPA, yet, according to congressional and other sources who were privy to backstage negotiations, ACLU lobbyists actively urged congressmen to vote for the statute so as to defeat the amendment. Thus, in a 1990 interview, one participant in many Capitol Hill meetings concerning the flag controversy described the ACLU's role as "actively supporting" and acting as "a cheerleader for the statute." The participant termed the ACLU's role "incredibly disingenuous" and "intellectually dishonest," as well as "truly eye-opening to me because I never thought that would be the case."

Numerous other sources confirmed the ACLU's role in effectively backing the statute, although some of them praised the organization for following a sophisticated strategy that helped block the amendment. For example, a top Democratic staffer who played a key role in the legislative strategy of the House leadership recalled in a 1990 interview that "the ACLU understood that you had to have a statute" to block the amendment. He added, "Whether they were for it purely strategically or thought it was good policy was unclear, but the reality was that they were for a statute and we probably could not have done a statute without that." Although reiterating that the ACLU's role was "one of the reasons we won," the source noted that the ACLU membership did not know about the organization's real role: "It happens with interest groups all the time, they ask us to do the work, they want our members to take a courageous stand, and they want to hide." A key Democratic SJC staff source, in a 1991 interview, confirmed that the ACLU "understood the only way to beat the amendment was with the statute, they're pretty savvy." Another key Democratic Senate staff source summarized the ACLU's 1989 role in a 1990 interview as "the same as PAW, which was encouraging people to vote for the statute."

The ACLU's strategy was an open secret because the organization circulated a large briefing book on the flag desecration controversy on Capitol Hill in the summer and fall of 1989 which was formally titled, "The Case against a Constitutional Amendment on Flag Desecration." Like the PAW's congressional statement, the ACLU's briefing book (bizarrely, the ACLU never testified or even submitted written material to the congressional hearings) stressed freedom of speech arguments that seemingly would have also applied to a statute. The ACLU policy statement in the briefing book contained only one brief reference to the

FPA: "The ACLU opposes the statute on flag destruction now being considered by the Congress. However, a number of witnesses have testified that there is a reasonable chance that the Supreme Court will uphold the statute. In light of that, it would be inappropriate to consider amending the Constitution until and unless the statute is declared unconstitutional."

Other bits of evidence supporting the conclusion that the ACLU in practice backed the FPA are that the ACLU's Washington office was used to coordinate and mail the initiatives of two of the petitions discussed above—those of the Emergency Committee to Defend the First Amendment and of the Tribe-Dellinger group, both of which opposed the amendment but which, in the former case, took no position on the FPA and, in the latter, said only that there was a "reasonable basis" for believing that the Supreme Court would uphold the FPA. According to one participant interviewed in 1990, during a 1989 meeting with ACLU Washington director Mort Halperin and other ACLU staff, "Mort was saying that this [the Tribe-Dellinger letter] was one of the things that the ACLU was going to do to make people comfortable in voting for the statute, by telling them that it might be constitutional."

As will be discussed in more detail below, after the amendment had been defeated in 1989 and test cases involving the FPA were scheduled for consideration before the Supreme Court in the spring of 1990, both the PAW and the ACLU, as if feeling pangs of guilt for having abandoned a principled civil liberties position in the summer and fall of 1989, filed amici briefs urging the Court to strike down the same FPA they had essentially urged congressmen to vote for only months earlier. In fact, when ACLU executive director Glasser wrote to ACLU members in April 1990, he labeled the FPA as "equally disgraceful" as the proposed amendment and accomplishing the "same thing," a position that certainly reflected both logic and official ACLU policy, but that in practice had been abandoned by the ACLU for pragmatic political reasons during the previous year.

In a 1990 interview, ACLU Washington office director Halperin denied that his organization had urged congressmen to vote for the FPA, but he did so in a "for the record" manner which resembled the organization's formal, but obviously less-than-vigorous, opposition to the statute expressed in the 1989 briefing book. According to Halperin:

> We opposed the statute. We did not urge people to vote for the statute. We did tell people that our judgment was that if the statute was not enacted that a constitutional amendment would be enacted and we made it clear to people that we were far more concerned about a consti-

tutional amendment than we were about a statute. Those were the
sentences which we gave to everybody and they could draw whatever
conclusions they wanted. We told them that we were against a statute
and that we thought the statute was unconstitutional. But the focus of
our energies was not on the statute.

When asked if congressmen might conclude from such a position that the ACLU
would not be upset if they voted for the statute, Halperin responded, "I think our
friends on the Hill would say they hear from us in opposition to different things
and they can tell the difference between different kinds of opposition."

Halperin added that

the main reason we devoted our energies to the amendment was that it
was my judgment that there was no way to block the statute and if
somehow that happened by a miracle there would be no way to stop an
amendment. We had to ask ourselves what's more important to do in
terms of how bad the thing is and what is the likelihood of winning.
The amendment in our view was far worse and the prospects of beating it were far better.

Under these circumstances, Halperin continued (speaking a month before the
Supreme Court struck down the FPA in 1990 and the constitutional amendment
was killed in Congress), "We hoped we would get the best of both worlds—the
statute passes and that holds off the constitutional amendment, the statute is held
unconstitutional and then we have enough time to calm people down and we
defeat the amendment."

The PAW and the ACLU were not alone in concluding that only an FPA
could prevent congressional passage of a constitutional amendment in late 1989;
observers from all shades of the political spectrum concluded that, in fact, passage of the FPA played the key role in blocking it. For example, shortly after the
Senate passed the FPA by a 91-9 vote on October 5 and it became clear that the
Senate was about to defeat the amendment, SJC chairman Biden, the leading
Senate FPA proponent, asked a group of reporters if any of them "doubted if this
statute had not been passed the Senate would have passed a constitutional amendment." *Washington Post* liberal columnist William Raspberry, an opponent of
both measures, wrote that although the FPA was clearly a "constitutional dead
duck," politically it was a "brilliant stroke" because, as a result of a "stomach-
turning combination of cowardice and demagogy" the only practical alternative
was the amendment, rather than the "sensible" path of educating voters about "the

meaning of freedom of speech." Conservative analysts also agreed that the FPA played a key role in leading to the amendment's demise. Thus an American Legion official termed the FPA a "shrewd move to defuse the issue."[23]

In interviews in 1990 and 1991, respectively, New York University law professor and ACLU president Norman Dorsen and Duke law professor Walter Dellinger, both of whom helped to organize petitions to Congress opposing the amendment but taking no stand concerning the FPA's merits, essentially supported Halperin's position that there was no point in energetically opposing the statute, first because its passage seemed certain and second because the amendment was viewed as the greater threat and passage of the FPA was seen as helping to block it. Dorsen said that although the ACLU relied primarily on Halperin to formulate legislative strategy, he personally visited Washington in mid-July 1989 and because "it was obvious" that without the statute the amendment would be enacted, "we [he and Halperin] told them [Senate majority leader Mitchell and SJC chair Biden] that we didn't like the idea of a statute but we told them even more forcefully that we didn't like the idea of a constitutional amendment."

Dellinger, like Tribe, testified before congressional committees that the Supreme Court would likely uphold the FPA, and he also joined Tribe in soliciting other law professors to sign their ACLU-facilitated petition to Congress urging defeat of the amendment on those grounds. Not surprisingly, therefore, because, like Tribe, Dellinger had a reputation as a strong civil libertarian, he also came under criticism for allegedly letting his desire to block an amendment compromise his scholarly integrity in predicting that the FPA would be upheld. For example, in a 1990 law review article, written before the Supreme Court struck down the FPA, author R. Neil Taylor argued that the position that the Court would uphold the statute was based on "such questionable support that it should not be deemed worthy of the backing of such scholars as Tribe and Dellinger," summarized their view as arguing that the FPA "was at least preferable to a constitutional amendment," and expressed the hope that "in the future Tribe, Dellinger and other scholars will not see fit to resort to clever political posturing but will support and defend the Constitution because of the values it represents." Similarly, in a 1992 law review article, Charles Tiefer, deputy House of Representatives legal counsel, who actively defended the FPA's constitutionality in the federal courts, lumped Dellinger together with Tribe as among "several leading academic defenders of civil liberties" who had given "vigorous" support to the FPA (a characterization which, even if widespread, clearly distorted Dellinger's position).[24]

In a lengthy 1991 interview, Dellinger conceded that in retrospect it was a "fair assessment" to argue that, given the political climate in the summer and fall of 1989, his testimony that the Supreme Court would likely uphold the FPA "might well be seen as an encouragement of Congress to enact such a statute." Dellinger noted, however, that he had never endorsed the FPA, instead restricting his testimony to predicting that the Court would likely uphold it, and that he had briefly indicated his personal opposition to the statute in a footnote to his written (although not spoken) congressional remarks. He added, "I never supported the passage of any version of the FPA and never said anything supporting it privately or publicly, but I believed there was a basis for believing that the Court would sustain it." He conceded that his position had "understandably got merged in the public mind" with Tribe's view, which he described as not only predicting that the Supreme Court would uphold the FPA but as "actually advocating" a statute in his July 3 *New York Times* article.

Dellinger added that "it's very tough to distinguish between your own view that it's unconstitutional and that it's not entirely phony to believe that the Court might uphold it. The more you state the act is unconstitutional [in your personal view], the more people think you're saying there's no basis upon which the Court could uphold it." Dellinger added that, faced this with "painful dilemma," he had "understated" his opposition to the FPA in his congressional testimony because the FPA's passage was "an absolutely foregone conclusion" in the summer of 1989

> and the only question in doubt was whether Congress would also propose a constitutional amendment to be sent to the states for ratification. There was no question that a flag statute was going to be passed and there was no point dwelling on the pros or cons of it. Those who were supporting the amendment knew that there was no argument for it if there was any basis at all for thinking that the Supreme Court might sustain the FPA. It was going to be almost impossible to get thirty-four votes [to block an amendment] in the Senate in 1989 if the judgment had been that any statute was going to have utterly ridiculous prospects before the Court.

Dellinger said that he personally "didn't see any particular [nonsuppressive governmental] interest" that the Court could use to uphold the FPA under the 1968 *O'Brien* draft card burning precedent and that, in particular, the idea of a valid government interest in protecting the flag's physical integrity in all circumstances is an "incoherent notion"; nonetheless, he maintained, the Court appeared to disagree, and Brennan's reference to Blackmun's *Goguen* dissent suggested that a majority would uphold a statute. Therefore, he continued, he felt it was "not inappropriate for Congress to take the Court at face value, rather than take the drastic step of passing a constitutional amendment" because even though the argument for the FPA's constitutionality was "not very plausible, it's an argument that comes out of" the Court's *Johnson* ruling.

Under the circumstances that existed in the summer of 1989, Dellinger continued, because many Republicans were arguing that "it makes no sense to delay proposing the constitutional amendment" on the grounds that it was a "ridiculous idea" that the Court would sustain an FPA, and because he genuinely believed that there "was a reasonable basis to say that the Court might uphold it," testifying to that effect was a "correct and not unuseful thing to say." Dellinger added that he was concerned that had he made his opposition to the FPA even

> more clear, while it would have been of some benefit to me personally in the progressive fraternity, it would have confused the argument that I was trying to make, that there really was a basis in *Johnson* for thinking the court would sustain such a statute. Launching an all-out attack on the constitutionality of the statute was just going to weaken the case against an amendment, and it was important to note that it wasn't a totally ridiculous idea to think the Court might sustain a statute and thus provide a basis for postponing the idea of an amendment. It seemed to me that holding off an amendment was far more important than making a wholly futile argument against passage of a statute that was sure to pass.

Although in retrospect, Dellinger said, "I wish I had been more emphatic about my opposition to the statute, in the end I am comforted by the fact that I didn't say anything I don't believe and in fact we now have neither an amendment nor an FPA—and with two very fine Court decisions on the First Amendment as a net outcome." Like many other vocal opponents of the amendment, Dellinger declared, "Without any question, without an FPA a constitutional amendment would have passed in 1989."

Because it is impossible to play out alternative historical scenarios, there is no way of knowing whether the apparent diminishment of public interest in the flag desecration issue and the growing general opposition to an amendment might have led to the defeat of the amendment in 1989, even without the FPA alternative. Such an up-and-down defeat of the amendment in Congress occurred in June 1990, following the Supreme Court's striking down of the FPA, and that defeat came in an election year, unlike 1989; however, the memories of the 1988 pledge and the 1989 "flag on the floor" controversies were much stronger in 1989 than they were a year later. What does seem clear is that the common conclusions of the Democratic leadership, of leading civil libertarians like Tribe and Dellinger, and of the PAW and the ACLU that passage of either the FPA or the amendment was inevitable and that the FPA was the lesser of two evils virtually foreclosed any possibility of "bravely doing nothing" in response to the *Johnson* decision in 1989. With the veterans and the overwhelming percentage of Republicans, led by President Bush, supporting an amendment, and the Democratic leadership and the nation's leading civil liberties lawyers and organizations either overtly or tacitly supporting FPA, there was virtually no significant organized support for just accepting, if not celebrating, a Supreme Court decision that upheld the most fundamental of all democratic principles—the right to peaceful political dissent—even on behalf of the most unpopular ideas and performed in the most obnoxious manner.

In looking back at the 1989 roles of the ACLU and the PAW in a 1990 interview, PAW legislative counsel Gomperts lamented, "More than anything this was a testament to the political hysteria of the moment, that two organizations that are as absolutist [in behalf of civil liberties] as the ACLU and PAW did not speak out strongly against this statute. That ultimately had a large effect on the political dynamic, it helped to frame the debate. There was essentially no one who was standing up and saying, 'Do nothing!' That's the position that is supposed to be occupied by the PAW and the ACLU, that 'We deplore flag burning but it's protected speech and you have to abide this to have the freedoms that all of us cherish.' We didn't do that." In contrast to Gomperts, ACLU Washington director Halperin, in a 1990 interview, expressed no regrets over his organization's role in, at best, only formally opposing the FPA during the previous year. "I think it was the right strategy and I'd do it again exactly the same way. To celebrate the two hundredth anniversary of the Bill of Rights with, for the first time, amending that right, would not only be a disgrace, but it would open up the possibility of further amendments of the same kind. I told people that I don't want on my tombstone that, 'While he was in charge of the ACLU Washington Office the First Amendment was amended.'"

Ironically, the only two major mainstream organizations that forthrightly supported the *Johnson* decision and vehemently opposed any attempts to override it were the American Bar Association and the American Society of Newspaper Editors, both of which traditionally had leaned more in the conservative than the liberal direction. A majority of the ASNE's member newspapers had consistently endorsed Republican presidential candidates, including Bush, for example; the

ABA had supported the early flag protection movement with a formal, unanimously approved, resolution at its 1918 convention urging all states to pass flag desecration laws and, during the McCarthy period, had called for the expulsion from the ABA and the disbarment by the states of all communists, solely for their political beliefs.[25]

At its August 1989 convention, however, the ABA's governing House of Delegates overwhelmingly approved by voice vote, after a heated two-hour debate, a report opposing passage of either the FPA or the amendment, which had been unanimously submitted by a distinguished eight-member ABA committee that included former secretary of state Cyrus Vance and former solicitor general Griswold. Apparently out of concern about possible adverse public reaction to endorsing the report, the delegates added to it a condemnation of flag desecration and voted to begin all future meetings with the Pledge of Allegiance.

The ABA committee report declared that the *Johnson* decision had been properly decided because "the principle that expression of an idea may not be penalized simply because the idea is offensive or disagreeable" was at the "core" of freedom of speech and that the FPA would violate this principle just as much as an amendment would. The flag commanded "respect and love" because the country adhered to "its values and its promise of freedom, not because of fiat and criminal law," the report concluded, whereas throughout history, as in Nazi Germany, "tyrannies have tried to enforce obedience by prohibiting disrespect for the symbols of their power." Among the leading defenders of the committee report at the convention was Supreme Court justice Brennan's son, William J. Brennan III, a New Jersey lawyer and former president of his state's bar association, who told the delegates that the *Johnson* ruling "was compelled" by previous Court decisions. The ASNE also forthrightly condemned both the FPA and the amendment in a sample editorial that accompanied a "press alert," sent to all member newspapers on September 28, which approvingly quoted from the ABA resolution and declared that by "allowing protesters to desecrate the flag, we are reaffirming our belief that the right to dissent is essential to freedom."[26]

In interviews in 1990 and 1991, Stanley Chauvin and Craig Klugman, who respectively served in 1989 as incoming ABA president and chairman of the ASNE's Freedom of Information Committee, both agreed that their organizations' decisions to oppose any attempt to overturn the *Johnson* ruling was somewhat unusual but reflected the intense concerns that the congressional proposals aroused because they were perceived as threatening fundamental American freedoms of great importance to lawyers and journalists. Klugman recalled that although the ASNE occasionally communicated its views to member newspapers, "this was unusual because it was written as an editorial and could be used as such." Chauvin readily agreed that the ABA's unyielding 1989 opposition to both the FPA and the amendment was in considerable contrast to the organization's past conservative reputation. He attributed this not only to concerns that attempts to overturn the *Johnson* ruling might serve as a "harbinger of an attack" that might start a "completely out of control" assault on constitutional freedoms but also to a "dramatic" change in the demographic composition of the legal profession in recent years which has made the ABA "infinitely more reflective" of groups other than the "well-to-do white males" who formerly dominated the bar and the courts. Chauvin suggested that, along with the fact that an entire new generation of lawyers and judges had grown up with both the heightened civil liberties standards established by the post–World War II Warren Supreme Court and the increased distrust of government fostered by such developments as Vietnam and Watergate, this change in demographics had resulted in leading lawyers emphasizing social change and individual rights and no longer viewing government as a "holy" and "all-wise arbiter of everything that comes along."

The "mainstream" ABA and ASNE were, not surprisingly, joined in their vigorous opposition to both the FPA and the proposed amendment by the RCP and the heavily RCP-influenced Emergency Committee to Stop the Flag Amendment and Laws (ECSFAL), a successor organization to Johnson's defense group (ECSCFC). The RCP's newspaper, in its issues of July 17 and September 18, labeled both the FPA and the amendment "fascist." ECSFAL proclaimed in its September newsletter that the two major parties were engaged in a "good cop/bad cop" routine, with Democrats "pushing the flag statute as the kinder and gentler of two repressive evils."

Approval of the Flag Protection Act in the House of Representatives

On July 14, the day after the HJC began hearings on possible congressional responses to the *Johnson* decision, Senate majority leader Mitchell announced an agreement with Minority Leader Dole for the Senate to vote on both a statute and the amendment in October, following SJC hearings and reports on both proposals to be submitted to the Senate by September 22. The announcement reflected a compromise between the two party leaders, in which Dole agreed to let the statute come up for a vote first, a procedure Democrats hoped would diminish support for the amendment if the FPA was approved, while Mitchell in turn assured Republicans that the Senate would have a chance to vote on the amendment. Thus Dole declared that the agreement satisfied Republican concerns that "we might pass a statute and say, 'Well, that's the end of it.'"[27]

In the House, where Democrats held a much stronger majority then in the Senate and where traditionally the majority party is less constrained by the need to make concessions to the minority, Democratic leaders operated with a far more bared-teeth approach. The first clear public indication that Democrats felt that the tide had turned against the amendment and that they could defeat it with a combination of hardball tactics and the statutory alternative came on July 27, when the FPA was favorably reported to the House floor by 28-6 HJC vote. The HJC action came after two days of public and often rancorous partisan bickering at committee "mark up" sessions on July 26 and 27, during which Chairman Brooks, over bitter Republican protests, repeatedly ruled out of order all attempts to bring the amendment up for discussion and consideration. Faced with a situation in which, as amendment supporter Representative Romano Mazzoli (D-Ky.) noted, the statute was the "only game in town" and in which, as House Republican leader Michel later noted, "there are a number of members who want to vote for most anything [to protect the flag]," all but one of the fourteen HJC Republicans and fifteen out of twenty Democrats voted for the FPA.[28]

Most HJC Republicans, however, both during the mark up sessions and in a subsequent written report which ten of them signed, stated that they were voting for the FPA solely to "show support for protecting the flag" and that they viewed it as an unconstitutional "charade." This was because, the Republicans wrote, as Assistant Attorney General Barr and other FPA critics had explained at the HJC hearings, the only possible government justification for the statute, that of "protecting the symbolic value of the flag," was clearly related to "the suppression of expression" and therefore could not, under the *Johnson* ruling, constitutionally override the free speech rights of flag burners. Therefore, the ten Republicans argued, if "the desire is to overturn" the *Johnson* ruling, "as it surely must be," the Supreme Court's interpretation of the First Amendment "must be altered" through the process of a constitutional amendment.

In a separate report, eight of the same ten HJC Republicans suggested that at least some amendment supporters saw the flag burning issue as essentially refighting the culture wars of the 1960s. They asked, "Why are we so reluctant to amend the Constitution to demand that flag desecration be prohibited? Is it too much to ask that those who call themselves Americans be required to have respect for the flag? In this day and age, when it seems that perversion is accepted and morality a taboo religion, perhaps this small mandate for freedom is not asking too much!" Representative Chuck Douglas (R-N.H.), the only Republican HJC member to vote against the FPA, took special exception to the provision exempting the disposal of "soiled" flags, which Chairman Brooks and subcommittee chairman Edwards included in the proposal they submitted for HJC consideration on July 26. He argued that the exception would effectively turn the FPA into a "Flag Burner Protection Act" because dissidents could first soil a flag without physically destroying it and then burn it "in full compliance" with the FPA.

For the Democrats, Brooks argued that the FPA would provide a "quick and effective solution" to the flag desecration problem, but he promised that, if "by some rare chance" the Supreme Court struck it down, he would personally introduce a constitutional amendment. Edwards, who along with Brooks formally co-sponsored the FPA, lamented that the "wisest course of action, the one truest to the Constitution and to the values of the country, is to do nothing," especially as the "passage of time would have a calming effect on us all." But he added, "doing nothing is [politically] not an option open to us" and "we do not have the luxury of time and must act"; therefore, he was sponsoring the FPA as the alternative that "causes the least violence to the First Amendment." Representative John Conyers (R-Mich.), one of five HJC Democrats who voted against the FPA on July 27, argued that by "doing nothing" the HJC would best protect the "substance of what the flag stands for." But he complained that instead the committee appeared more concerned about "protecting the symbol," especially since no one seemed to be "rushing" to reverse recent Supreme Court decisions that were "stripping away the rights of millions" of minorities and women "a mile a minute." At one point Conyers was answered with complete silence when he asked if any HJC members knew "how many instances of flag burning are reported annually"; the same response greeted his query as to whether anyone could remember learning of any recent flag burnings. Although the atmosphere at the mark up sessions was filled with political tension, at one point comic relief was provided when Representative Dan Glickman (D-Kan.), drew a flag to illustrate a question about defining "flag." He explained that he had meant the stripes to "be red but they started out blue and I colored them red afterwards," which led Brooks to respond, "Are you color blind?" Representative Barney Frank (D-Mass.), referring to a developing controversy over National Endowment for the Arts (NEA) funding of sexually explicit art, declared that the HJC should make clear that the NEA "has made no grants to Mr. Glickman for these purposes."

As introduced by Brooks and Edwards and approved by the HJC on July 27, the heart of the FPA consisted of language similar to that submitted by SJC chairman Biden in his July 13 HJC testimony, which was almost identical to his proposal that had passed the Senate as an amendment to a child care bill on June 22.

The Biden-based language amended the 1968 federal flag desecration law by providing a jail term of up to one year and a fine of up to $1,000 for anyone who "knowingly mutilates, defaces, burns, or tramples upon any flag of the United States." By omitting the "cast contempt," "publicly," and "defiling" provisions of the 1968 law, the FPA sought, in the words of the HJC majority report, to comply with the *Johnson* ruling by making the 1968 law "content-neutral," by forbidding flag desecration so as to carry out the "national interest" in protecting "the physical integrity of all American flags in all circumstances," while focusing "exclusively on the conduct of the actor, irrespective of any expressive message he or she might be intending to convey." The majority report asserted that this "interest" was "unrelated to the suppression of free expression" because the FPA sought to protect the flag "not because it represents any one idea" but to recognize the "diverse and deeply held feelings of the vast majority of citizens for the flag" and to reflect "the government's power to honor those sentiments through the protection of a venerated object in the same manner that protection is afforded to gravesites or historic buildings."

In response to concerns raised at the HJC hearings that it might take years to determine the FPA's constitutionality and therefore, if it was struck down, Congress would have wasted time, the Brooks-Edwards proposal added to the Biden language an unprecedented provision for expedited and mandatory Supreme Court review of the FPA's constitutionality as soon as any prosecution was initiated under it—even before any trial was held. The Brooks-Edwards FPA also added to Biden's bill language that specifically exempted "any conduct consisting of the disposal of the flag when it has become worn or soiled," in response to concerns that veterans participating in flag "retirement" burnings would be prosecuted. This provision was justified in the HJC majority report on the grounds that "worn or soiled" flags were "no longer a fitting emblem for display" so that the "governmental interest in protecting the physical integrity no longer applies." But the report did not indicate how it would be determined, presumably after the fact, whether a burned flag was sufficiently "worn or soiled" to be exempted from the FPA's criminal provisions.

In response to concerns expressed about definitional problems, the Brooks-Edwards additions to the Biden bill also redefined the definition of "flag" in the 1968 law to encompass "any flag of the United States, or any part thereof, made of any substance, of any size, in a form that is commonly displayed." According to explanations provided to HJC members at the mark up sessions and spelled out in the majority HJC report, this language was intended to narrow the 1968 definition to exclude objects that were "not actual flags in that they are not commonly displayed as flags and have other uses" so that no government interest was involved in "protecting their physical integrity." Among the examples of such "nonflags" given in the report were "depictions such as photographs of flags on magazine covers," products such as paper cups or napkins with "flags printed on them," and other "decorative representations of flags" such as "a cake in the shape of a flag," flag designs "on clothing, artistic renditions of flags in publications, and commercial and political uses of the flag." The intent of this definition seemed to be, as Representative William Hughes (D-N.J.) explained at the mark up sessions, to include only materials that both looked like flags and could be flown as flags, but because the actual text of the FPA's definition included "parts" of flags, flags made "of any substance," and flags of "any size" and never explained what "commonly displayed" meant, this apparent intent was hopelessly muddled by the text's ambiguity and vagueness. Even FPA cosponsor Edwards seemed to be baffled by the "any part" provision; he asked, "What are we talking about?" and expressed concern that people might be jailed for "let's say, cutting up four stars that they might just happen to be carrying around with them, or stripes."

Following the long August congressional recess, during which it became increasingly clear that public and press interest in the flag desecration issue had considerably diminished, the House of Representatives debated and passed the Biden-Brooks-Edwards FPA on September 12 by a vote of 380-38. Only 21 Republicans and 17 Democrats voted against it, almost all of the former on grounds that only a constitutional amendment could legally protect the flag and all of the latter on the grounds that it was unwise and unneeded. Voting for the FPA on September 12 were 230 Democrats and 150 Republicans.[29]

The House Democratic leadership called up the FPA on September 12 under a suspension of the rules procedure which made it impossible to consider any amendments from the floor, thereby protecting Democrats from being forced to vote against proposed changes that might have "strengthened" the FPA (for example, by outlawing all "contemptuous" displays using the flag) in ways that would have been politically difficult to oppose, but, if approved, would have made the FPA transparently unconstitutional under the *Johnson* ruling. But the rules suspension procedure also required a two-thirds majority for the FPA to pass, rather than the usual simple majority, and the Democratic leadership therefore could not pass it without Republican votes. To make certain that the FPA would obtain the needed Republican votes, Speaker Foley agreed to bring the constitutional amendment to a floor vote later in 1989. But Foley's promise might not have been needed because, as Representative Edwards noted, "It's pretty hard for politicians to vote against protecting the flag."[30]

The September 12 House debate occurred in a much calmer atmosphere than that surrounding the flag desecration issue several months before. During the debate, for example, only a handful of members were on the floor, and the marked decrease in media interest was clear when the three network newscasts that evening devoted a combined total of less than one minute to reporting the House action.

Speaking for the Democratic leadership, HJC chairman Brooks lashed out at Republicans who sought to gain political advantage by linking them with flag burners; he denounced those who would use the flag as a "wedge to divide us" by either "desecrating it or exploiting it" as deserving "nothing but our utter contempt." Brooks declared that the FPA should be given a "chance to work," that the Bill of Rights should not be amended unless it was "shown to be absolutely, undeniably necessary," and that it would therefore be "irresponsible" to do so without "first determining that that was the only option available." Edwards warned that defeat of the FPA would "almost surely" lead to a constitutional amendment which would leave the nation "less free" and heading toward a "slippery slope" of further amendments that would threaten "other freedoms in response to every unpopular Supreme Court decision." House majority leader Richard Gephardt devoted much of his speech to a bitter attack on President Bush, in which he referred to those who engaged in the "legal flag abuse" of "wrapping themselves in the flag, or touring a flag factory or even coopting the pledge of allegiance," or who generally sought to "tear the flag apart" by "pretending that our flag is somehow the exclusive province of one party."

Speaking for a substantial block of Democrats who, at least publicly, were more skeptical supporters of the FPA, Douglas Applegate declared that although the FPA was "weak" and "will ultimately be ruled unconstitutional, it is the only game in town." Among Republicans who supported the FPA, Thomas Petri of Wisconsin asked, "Why not try the easy road first and see if it gets us where we want to go?" Among Republicans who opposed the FPA as an unconstitutional diversionary and delaying tactic designed to block an amendment, Bill Schuette of Michigan denounced it as "a sham, a cover-up," that "just won't fly," while HJC ranking Republican Sensenbrenner denounced it for establishing an absolute "dirty flag defense" for "any political protester who feels the need to torch Old Glory" and for placing the Bill of Rights in "far more jeopardy" than an amendment by attempting "to amend the Constitution" by statute and thus short-circuiting the "cumbersome and lengthy" amendment process.

Among the seventeen House Democrats who opposed the FPA as fundamentally unwise, William Clay expressed sympathy for "liberal friends" such as Edwards who supported the FPA as a means of "foreclosing more drastic action" but declared that the fear that "extremists who vehemently oppose the desecration of the flag will violently desecrate the Constitution is not sufficient rationale to support this legislation." Rod Chandler, one of only three Republicans to oppose the FPA on First Amendment grounds, asked how Americans could condemn the Chinese government for repressing millions of its citizens, "when we cannot tolerate the isolated actions of a single, petty protester who burns the flag?" Following the House passage of the FPA, White House spokesman Marlin Fitzwater repeated the position that Bush had first enunciated at his June 27 press conference and which he subsequently reiterated at press conferences on July 28 and August 23, namely that the administration continued to support a constitutional amendment because the FPA was "insufficient to provide the protection we seek."[31]

Senate Passage of the Flag Protection Act

On September 21, ten days after the House passed the FPA and a week after the SJC completed four days of hearings on the flag controversy, the committee met to make recommendations to the entire Senate. After a heated and often partisan discussion, the committee voted to endorse the original, intact Biden FPA, by a vote of 9-5, and then recommended against passage of the amendment by 8-6.[32]

During the SJC debate, Democratic chairman Biden declared that the Bush amendment did "violence to the First Amendment because it is so broad," and Republican Hatch argued for it on the grounds that the Supreme Court simply would not "buy off" on the FPA. Democratic senator Kennedy voiced opposition to either alternative on the grounds that both attempted to "prevent desecration of the flag by desecrating the Constitution" and that freedom of speech required tolerance "for the views that we hate." His party colleague Senator Metzenbaum argued that only "politics and fear" were driving the flag controversy and that basic freedoms were being "held hostage" by legislators' fear of "negative advertising spots in the next election."

Following its September 21 meeting, the SJC issued two parallel reports on the FPA and the amendment. The essential argument of the majority was that "the amendment process should be invoked as a last—not as a first—resort" and—citing James Madison—that amendments should be reserved for "great and extraordinary occasions." They argued that such action was as yet unnecessary because the FPA could both adequately protect the "physical integrity of flag in all circumstances" and withstand Supreme Court scrutiny. Unlike both the Texas law struck down in *Johnson* and the 1968 federal flag law, it would focus "solely and exclusively on the conduct of the actor," without targeting the "message of whoever threatens" the flag, consistent with Congress's alleged right to "protect symbols" just as it could protect historical landmarks. The majority maintained that protection of the flag's physical integrity because "of what it expresses and represents" as the "unique and unalloyed symbol of the nation" would pose no First Amendment problems because such protection was not designed to "censor or suppress the person who might attack it." According to the SJC majority, "When it comes to the American flag—that one symbol of the spirit of our democracy—we care more about protecting its physical integrity than about determining why its integrity has been threatened."

With no apparent sense of irony, the SJC majority approvingly quoted Chairman Biden's remark that protecting the flag—by jailing those with a different viewpoint toward it—was needed to bring Americans "together" and to "generate a kind of tolerance that is required in such a diverse society." Even if the FPA proved unconstitutional, the majority contended, the Bush amendment was hopelessly flawed because its meaning in general, and the meaning of "physical desecration" in particular, was "entirely uncertain" and therefore the only certain outcome of adopting it would be a "generation of litigation." Furthermore, the majority argued that the amendment would "undermine the spirit and structure of the Constitution" by authorizing Congress and the states, "for the first time in our history," to criminalize conduct based on whether "that conduct contains an idea or a message of which the legislature does not approve."

The SJC majority stressed Blackmun's *Goguen* dissent as supporting the proposition that the FPA could gain the support of at least five Supreme Court justices. Senator Specter repeatedly suggested, with unusually brutal political frankness, what the SJC majority only hinted at: during the SJC hearings, on the Senate floor, and in his own written report giving his "supplemental views" to the SJC majority, he pointed to past instances in which widespread public discontent with Supreme Court decisions seemed to have resulted in quick changes in the Court's direction, and he suggested that the evidence showed that historically the Court sometimes "follows the election returns." It "does not function in such a lofty ivory tower that the Justices do not hear what goes on in the streets of America or what goes on right across the park [from the Supreme Court chambers], in the Congress of the United States."

In "additional views" accompanying the majority report opposing the amendment, Metzenbaum was joined by Kennedy in arguing that the 1984 Dallas flag burning was a "mindless, infantile act" by "an obscure protester," which "was a tiny blip on the screen of history," and that the Congress would simply "magnify it a thousand fold if it stampedes us into eroding the majesty of the Constitution." Warning against creating a constitutional "slippery slope," Metzenbaum and Kennedy argued that "if one thread" of the "seamless fabric of our liberties" that the Constitution represented was pulled, "other freedoms will unravel" also, and that the demand for an amendment illustrated the "ease with which unpopular forms of protected expression can be swept away by a political whirlwind."

In a minority report on the FPA, Senators Hatch and Charles Grassley maintained that the Supreme Court would surely strike it down under the *Johnson* precedent because its clear purpose was to "prohibit expressive conduct" and to "protect the flag as a symbol." "No one claims that we are interested in protecting the material, the thread and the dye in the flag." They declared that a constitutional amendment would not impair free expression because "numerous" means of dissent other than physical flag desecration would still be allowed, and they denied that any "slippery slope" would be created "because there is simply nothing else like our flag." Furthermore, they continued, because the amendment and the FPA both outlawed the same acts, claims by FPA supporters that the amendment threatened fundamental rights, while the statute did not, were "difficult to square," and, in any case, an amendment was the "safest, surest and most permanent way of achieving the protection of the flag" that FPA supporters "claim they favor."

On October 4, the Senate began debate on the FPA, after Biden decided to bring up the version approved by the House on September 12 (with the flag disposal exemption and the expedited review provision), rather than his original language which had been approved by the SJC on September 21. After eight hours of debate, the Senate approved a slightly amended version of the House bill on October 5 by a 91-9 vote. Media coverage of the Senate vote suggested a further sharp drop-off in press interest: for example, two of the three network broadcasts failed to mention it that evening, and the *Los Angeles Times* reported that the political atmosphere surrounding the controversy had become "far less superheated" and quoted Senator Specter as declaring that flag desecration was "no longer a burning issue."[33]

Among those who supported the statute but indicated opposition to an amendment during Senate floor debate, majority leader Mitchell termed the FPA a "full, adequate and sufficient response" to the *Johnson* ruling that would both protect the flag and make an amendment "unnecessary." Senator Patrick Leahy urged the Senate to pass the FPA and then proceed to the more serious and "very pressing needs of the country;" he declared that there was no need either for "any more public exhibitions on who is the fairest patriot in the land" or for "tampering with the Constitution" simply to respond to "the idiotic actions of one publicity-seeking jerk in Texas." Republican senator William Cohen urged giving the FPA a "chance to work" because it was "quick, easy," and "contains no risk" and thus made it "unwise and unnecessary" to amend the Constitution.

Taking the opposite position, Republican leader Dole argued that the American people "do not want a quick fix" and that the FPA "will simply not do the trick," both because it would be found unconstitutional and because it would "criminalize even acts of patriotism" under the "guise" of "content neutrality," such as the "mother, who, while mourning the loss of her dead son, pins her son's medals on the flag." "I will make no bones about it," Dole declared. "I want a statute [*sic* for constitutional amendment] that protects the cherished values that the flag symbolizes, not a statute that views the flag neutrally—as if it were some rock."

Among those who supported both the FPA and the amendment, Republican William Roth said he would vote for both alternatives because "reasonable men" differed over the constitutionality of the FPA but there was "no controversy about our desire to protect the flag." Speaking for those who opposed both alternatives as violating free speech principles, Senator Kerrey declared that the country faced no threat posed by "lines of people preparing to burn the American flag" but needed most to "encourage our people to be less afraid, speaking what they believe."

Two amendments to the House FPA were approved by Senate voice vote, with little controversy and with the endorsement of Biden, who acted as FPA floor manager. The first was an amendment proposed by Dole, which, harking back to the early 1989 Chicago "flag on the floor" uproar, added maintaining "a flag on the floor or ground" to the acts forbidden by the House version. The second noncontroversial amendment modified the House's expedited review language, replacing what Biden termed a potentially unconstitutional provision (which required that any FPA prosecution be referred immediately for mandatory and expedited Supreme Court constitutional review without any lower court proceedings) with language calling for Supreme Court review only after the completion of federal district court proceedings. The amended provision still short-circuited the ordinary intermediate appellate review and required extraordinary mandatory and expedited Supreme Court review, a requirement that had previously been included only in a handful of laws in American history, including the 1985 Gramm-Rudman budget deficit act.

Two other proposed amendments provoked considerable Senate controversy, with Republicans generally supporting them as needed to improve the FPA and many Democrats expressing concern that they were designed to gut the "content neutrality" aspect of the statute so that the Supreme Court would be forced to strike it, thereby politically paving the path to a constitutional amendment. The first of these amendments would have forbidden only "public" acts of flag desecration. Its sponsor, Dole, argued that the government had no legitimate interest in what people did with flags in the privacy of their homes, and otherwise the

FPA would require a "flag protection police snooping about in the privacy of our homes." Opponents of this amendment succeeding in killing it by a 53-47 vote after Biden argued that to punish only public acts would suggest that the government was not interested in preserving the "physical integrity" of all flags but only in punishing dissent, and therefore the provision might "diminish the overwhelming possibilities that this will be viewed as a constitutionally valid statute."

The second contested amendment, introduced by Republican Senator Pete Wilson, proposed to add "physically defiles" to the forbidden acts concerning the flag. It was approved by a 76-24 vote after a heated and bewildering debate that centered on the etymological and bordered on the surreal and the metaphysical. Wilson argued that the provision was needed to punish people who threw mud on flags, rubbed them with soluble grease, or otherwise soiled them in ways that did not "permanently damage" them. Biden objected that, on the one hand, such acts were already banned under the "defaces" or "mutilates" provisions, on the other hand, that "defiles" was not "clearly definable," and (apparently finding a third hand) that above all the term seemed, in violation of "content neutrality," to be "dealing with communicative impact" rather than "simply protecting the flag period, in and of itself," such as the provision that "if you burn that sucker, you go to jail." During a long, bizarre colloquy that followed, concerning the definitions of terms such as "deface" and "defile," Wilson maintained that, especially if the acts that he was concerned about were already covered by the FPA, "physically defiles" was no different from "defaces" or "mutilates," and therefore if Biden's analysis was correct the FPA was already "content-laden" and constitutionally doomed, whereas if Biden was wrong, adding "physically defiles" could do no harm. After a lengthy colloquy, Biden said that he would cease trying to explain the difference between the terms so as not to "frighten" night-shift working television viewers who had just "turned on C-SPAN and hear this argument and think that maybe they have gotten to Saturday Night Live early and they are late to work." After preliminary voting on October 5 made clear that the Wilson amendment would pass, several senators who at first had voted against it switched their votes; they later told reporters they did so to avoid an unnecessary political risk in a lost cause.[34]

Final Approval of the Flag Protection Act by the House of Representatives

On October 12 the House of Representatives took up and approved the Senate amendments to the FPA by a 371-43 vote after one hour of debate conducted before a largely empty chamber. Voting for the revised FPA were 217 Democrats and 154 Republicans; 25 Democrats and 18 Republicans voted against it. NBC reported the House action in a fairly lengthy story in its evening newscast, but the other two networks devoted a combined total of fifty seconds to the story, and most newspapers reported it on their inside pages.[35]

The only significant discussion during the October 12 House debate amounted to a reprise of the arcane Senate discussion concerning the meaning of "physically defiles." Ranking HJC Republican Sensenbrenner, noting that an attempt to add "defiles" to the FPA had been defeated at the HJC mark-up session on the grounds that it might damage the measure's "content neutrality," argued that the Senate addition had made the FPA "clearly unconstitutional." Any attempt to distinguish between "defiles" and "physically defiles," Sensenbrenner maintained, would be "splitting hairs" because both terms outlawed the "same type of expression." Edwards disagreed, arguing that "physically defiles" was very different from the constitutionally suspect "defiles" because, like other forms of banned "conduct," the term simply clarified that "all forms of injury to the physical integrity of a flag are prohibited" and that "one does not have to permanently destroy or damage a flag to violate the statute." Democratic representative William Hughes supported Edwards, arguing that "there is a vast difference" between "defiles" and "physically defiles" and that the latter term was only "another way" of banning "conduct already prohibited" by "language referring to mutilating and defacing." Republican Charles Douglas, however, who had sponsored the failed "defiles" amendment at the HJC mark up, denounced HJC Democrats who had voted against his proposal earlier but "suddenly find it is a neat idea when it comes back from the Senate."

Democratic representative David Skaggs, who had voted against the original FPA on free speech grounds, supported Sensenbrenner (although from a very different political perspective) on the grounds that "the real purpose" of the FPA had always been to outlaw voicing of the "kind of offensive minority views that the first amendment is there to guarantee" and that the Senate amendments had rendered the "claim" and "pretense" of seeking "merely to protect" the flag's physical integrity "ever more empty." To argue that one could "defile something in a neutral way, without implying a hostile sentiment," Skaggs declared, "is like saying you can love something without caring for it." Democrat Ted Weiss, another free speech opponent of the FPA, argued that FPA proponents were forced to indulge in "verbal acrobatics" to "try to explain away" that "what clearly is expressive conduct as held by a long line of Supreme Court decisions, is not expressive conduct."

The House passage of the amended FPA sent the statute to the White House, where, by general consensus, it posed a political dilemma for President Bush:

signing a bill the White House had repeatedly termed unconstitutional would be awkward, but vetoing a flag protection measure could pose even more problems. At a press conference on October 13, the day following the final House approval, Bush announced that he would avoid either alternative by simply letting the FPA become law without his signature, under the constitutional provision that automatically gives effect to legislation approved by Congress, if, when Congress is in session, the president fails either to sign or veto it within ten working days after it is officially transmitted to him. Bush told reporters that he would not sign the bill in order to "signal our belief that a constitutional amendment is the best way" to provide "the most lasting and legally correct means of protection" for the flag. Bush rejected a reporter's suggestion that he was "politically afraid" to veto the FPA; rather, he maintained, he was not vetoing it out of appreciation for the "overwhelming expression on the part of Congress to do something about protection of the flag," although its action was not "enough."[36]

Bush's decision to let the FPA become law without his signature attracted relatively little media reaction. In one exception, the October 16 *Atlanta Constitution* said that Bush "didn't dare veto" the FPA "for fear that all of the layers of bunting in which he has wrapped himself wouldn't protect him from the veto being misunderstood and used against him." The newspaper also issued a prediction of coming attractions that was to prove accurate: after declaring that what the FPA was "really supposed" to do was to block the drive for an amendment, the editorial forecast that once it became law "someone, somewhere will sure enough burn a flag," that a consequent constitutional test of the FPA would end with the Supreme Court rejecting it, and then "with luck" a further attempt to amend the Constitution would fail because politicians and public alike would have "regained their poise and realized it is better to live with an occasional flag-burner than to take risks that go with amending the Bill of Rights for the first time in its two centuries of history."

The 1989 Senate Defeat
of the Constitutional Amendment

Despite congressional approval of the FPA and the president's decision to let it become law, the Senate began consideration of the proposed constitutional amendment on October 16, pursuant to the bipartisan leadership agreement announced on July 14. Following more than ten hours of debate spread over four days, the Senate killed the amendment, at least for 1989, on October 19, with fifty-one senators voting for it and forty-eight against, thereby falling fifteen votes short of the two-thirds approval required for a constitutional amendment. Thirty-three Republicans joined eighteen Democrats (over half of whom were from the South), in supporting the amendment; eleven Republicans, almost all of them moderates from the Northeast and the Northwest, joined thirty-seven Democrats in defeating it. SJC chairman Biden hailed the outcome: "We protected the flag [via the FPA] and the Bill of Rights." Republican senator Dole termed it a "loss to the American people." The October 19 Senate vote was reported on newspapers' front pages across the country, as well as on all three evening network broadcasts, marking only the third time since July 4 that the three networks reported on the flag story on the same day.[37]

The amendment's defeat was virtually assured by floor announcements on October 17 by two Republicans, John Danforth of Missouri and Warren Rudman of New Hampshire, who had both been among the amendment's original cosponsors, that they had changed their minds, at least partly because, in Rudman's words, the enactment of the FPA had convinced them that "there is no need at this time to tamper with the Bill of Rights." Danforth's dramatic rhetorical style in declaring that he had been "just plain wrong" and had made a "mistake of the heart" by sponsoring the amendment attracted enormous media and political attention: *U.S. News & World Report* characterized his announcement as symbolizing the "sudden downfall of a movement that seemed a sure winner a scant four months ago." PAW legislative counsel John Gomperts, in a 1990 interview, recalled Danforth's pronouncement as "an extraordinary moment" which placed "the nail in the coffin" of the drive for the amendment.[38]

The fifty-one Senate votes cast for the amendment on October 19 decisively demonstrated that the drive for the amendment had stalled ever since it had been formally introduced in the Senate on July 18 by Republican leader Dole, with an accompanying list of fifty-two cosponsors. Conversely, according to running tallies of likely votes maintained by Democratic SJC staff members, the number of senators opposed to the amendment grew steadily to the forty-eight votes cast against it on October 19 from an August 1 compilation of only fourteen committed negative votes and another twenty leaning in that direction. According to numerous press accounts published during the October 16–19 Senate debate, support for the amendment lagged not only because of lessened public interest in the flag issue and the Democratic success in passing the FPA but also because the White House expended little political muscle on its behalf (for example, Bush reportedly made no telephone calls to senators to lobby for it). According to press speculation, the seeming White House disinterest may have partly reflected the emergence of other issues, such as a looming budget crisis and increasing tensions with Panama (which culminated in an American invasion three months later), not to mention a massive earthquake that struck the San Francisco area on October 17. After the defeat of the amendment, an American Legion official lamented, "Bush was unwilling to put on pressure" and "Congress was diverted by the deficit, Panama and the earthquake."[39]

Whatever his private efforts, after his June 30 Iwo Jima Memorial speech, Bush made virtually no visible attempt to whip up public support for the amendment, restricting his comments on the flag controversy to a few brief and scattered remarks in a couple of speeches on other subjects and in response to reporters' questions. Especially as none of these post–Iwo Jima remarks were extensive or otherwise newsworthy, they generally went unreported in the media. During the Senate amendment debate, senators on both sides referred to the White House as disinterested in the issue. Senator Kennedy declared that the "silence from the White House over the past few days has been deafening," and Republican leader Dole issued a rare public complaint that the issue "wasn't the highest priority at the White House" and "there hasn't been much done in the last few days."[40]

Aside from the Danforth and Rudman announcements, the Senate debate over the amendment traveled well-worn argumentative paths. Democratic senator Brock Adams summarized the basic argument of most critics of the amendment by declaring that the FPA would "uphold the dignity of the flag without decimating the Bill of Rights," that the First Amendment was "hallowed ground" that should not be "tampered" with in the absence of a "dire emergency," and that "in our effort to show disdain for burning the flag, we must not destroy the freedoms which the flag represents." Senator Sanford was one of several senators who referred to the revolutionary movement that was emerging in Eastern Europe in mid-October as yet another reason to reject an amendment that would "damage" American freedoms that had proved an inspiration for others around the world. "If we begin to whittle away at these freedoms," Sanford argued, the "wrong message" would be sent "at a time when all over the world there is a wave now for the freedoms for which we have stood for 200 years."

SJC chairman Biden offered the most detailed attack on the amendment, arguing that there was every reason to believe that the FPA would ban flag desecration without tampering with the First Amendment and that the Bush amendment was hopelessly deficient because it was too vague, because it violated American free speech traditions by openly seeking to censor expression based on its content, and because, by authorizing the states as well as Congress to pass flag desecration laws, it would lead to a confusing patchwork of conflicting laws and endless litigation. Under the proposed amendment, he maintained, the Bush administration had made clear that, in violation of the "essence of the first amendment," it wanted the government to be able to treat the same acts differently, depending upon its perception of whether the political expression involved was "offensive," so that a "long-haired college dropout with torn jeans and an earring who burned the flag" could be jailed, while a "well-kept businessman in a three-piece Brooks Brothers suit" who did the same thing might not. "Our statute punishes all flag burners" and thus "goes much further in protecting the flag," Biden declared, whereas the administration sought to change the Constitution to "allow the government to do what it has never been allowed to do in 200 years, and that is, censor views it does not like."

Furthermore, Biden charged, because the states would be given complete discretion by the amendment to define, outlaw, and punish "physical desecration" of the flag as they wished, and because the amendment might be interpreted as overriding all existing constitutional provisions, the ultimate result could be a "hodgepodge of 50 different" state laws; thus some states might forbid foreign car dealerships, socialists, or blacks from flying the flag, some might outlaw cutting cakes with flag representations on them or ban scraping flag stickers off cars, and some might even declare that "if you burn the flag, you lose your hand." Some states might ban "extremely revealing" flag bathing suits but allow "full length, old-fashioned" bathing outfits, Biden continued, or forbid such swimwear only if the suit had "stars across the top and the stripes on the bottom." Although such examples sounded extreme, Biden continued, "We have all been in state legislative bodies" and know that "screwy things happen."

Defenders of the amendment argued that only an amendment could provide certain protection for the flag in view of the dubious constitutionality of the FPA; that the FPA was far too broad and would punish many patriotic actions whereas only those who treated the flag contemptuously should be punished; that the amendment would overturn the *Johnson* ruling but otherwise not affect the Constitution or in any way diminish free speech rights because flag desecration was "conduct" and not "speech"; that the wording of the amendment was no more vague than other provisions of the Constitution, and if it spawned litigation, that was a normal aspect of American constitutional law; and that the FPA was just as likely as an amendment to spawn divergent state flag desecration laws and that differing such laws had been in effect for decades without destroying free speech rights or causing any other major problems.

Republican senator Rudy Boschwitz termed the amendment a needed "back-up plan of sorts" in case the FPA might be found unconstitutional. His party

colleague Trent Lott predicted that the statute would be struck down and that therefore the real question was, "Do we want the flag of the United States to be burned
and mutilated, destroyed, or not?" Republican leader Dole praised the amendment
for allowing punishment only for those who treated the flag with "contempt,"
rather than lumping "the innocent" in with "the likes of Gregory Johnson." If
"physical desecration" was a vague term, Dole argued, this was also true of words
like "defiles," "defaces," and "mutilates" contained in the FPA, not to mention
such phrases as "speedy trial," "unreasonable search and seizure," and "due
process of law," which filled the Constitution. Senator Alan Simpson likewise rejected Biden's arguments as a "parade of horribles" which posed "interesting
hypothetical cases for our nation's law school classrooms" but had no "basis in
reality."

Republican senator Hatch, who delivered the most lengthy and detailed defense of the amendment, rejected the FPA as an "empty" and "ineffectual" gesture
and ridiculed the argument that the amendment would infringe on free speech
rights. He maintained that means of expressing ideas would not be hindered by restricting "conduct" with respect to "one object and one object only" and that traditionally the First Amendment had never been "deemed absolute" because some
types of speech such as obscenity and libel had long been punishable. In specific
rebuttal to some of Biden's points, Hatch argued that the amendment's text and
legislative history demonstrated that it was an "obvious response" to the *Johnson*
decision and was not designed to override any other parts of the Constitution, such
as the ban on cruel and unusual punishments, and that, by authorizing the outlawing of only "physical" desecration, the amendment could not possibly be construed to punish "mere words or gestures of any sort" or to forbid the flag's
"proper display by particular individuals defined by their viewpoint, or the surroundings in which it is flown, or the day on which it is flown." Hatch maintained
that passing the amendment would not spawn new state flag desecration laws but
would only validate the "various differing" existing state laws that had long been
on the books without causing a "single problem." He warned, however, that if the
amendment failed, the FPA would spawn a "whole round of new, no doubt differing state statutes" because, if Congress could circumvent the *Johnson* ruling by
legislation, "then so can every state legislature and every city council." Therefore,
Hatch argued, the FPA would spawn far more litigation than the amendment, until
it "is finally held to be unconstitutional," with scores of court cases likely to arise
just to determine "how much soiling is necessary before a flag is no longer a flag
and lawfully may be burned for disposal purposes?"

If the general outlines of the Senate's debate on the amendment were predictable, the level of overt, partisan invective was unusually high and widespread, es-

pecially among Democrats, who apparently felt somewhat liberated as their impending triumph became increasingly certain. For example, Senate majority leader Mitchell, who had remained virtually silent on the flag controversy for almost four months after denouncing the *Johnson* ruling in a June 22 statement, for the first time issued several blistering denunciations of Bush for sponsoring the amendment during and after the Senate debate. Following the climactic October 19 vote, Mitchell told reporters that "the most distressing aspect" of the flag controversy had been "the eagerness with which the president sought to exploit the flag for political purposes," based on "public opinion polls and short-term political gains."[41]

About a dozen other Democrats bitterly attacked Bush for partisan manipulation of the flag during Senate floor speeches. Senator Leahy attacked those who, in a "travesty of patriotism," identified "patriotic fervor" with "who has the best 30-second ad, who films themselves with the most flags or who has the greatest band playing," as during the 1988 campaign, when symbols were "manipulated and brandished for raw political gain." Senator Dale Bumpers charged that "matters of political convenience" were "mostly at work" in the drive to amend a document which he characterized as "second only to the Holy Bible as the most sacred possession in the hands of mankind," and he bitterly denounced the "underlying suggestion" that amendment opponents did not "quite love America enough." Senator John Kerry similarly denounced, as "hungry politicians," those who "abused" the flag and the Constitution for "partisan politics" and who, by "so brazenly" asserting a "proprietary political patriotism," diminished the "real definition of patriotism." Senator Robert Kerrey declared that both houses of Congress had thus far debated an "essentially non-existent" threat from flag desecrators for more than fifty hours, largely because of "panic" and "terror" induced by President Bush's "call to action" and the "thought of negative 30-second commercials."

Republicans also got in some partisan licks. For example, after the final vote, Senate minority leader Dole denounced Democrats for "playing politics," seeking to "bash Bush," and turning a "cold shoulder" to veterans' groups. He declared that "the flag ought to be flying at half-staff because of this vote," a suggestion that would have violated the 1942 voluntary flag code approved by Congress, which restricted such displays of the flag to commemorating the death of national leaders. As the amendment's defeat was clearly looming during the Senate debate, Dole, who had lost the use of his right arm because of a World War II injury, bitterly told his colleagues that it was "not too late" to listen to the American Legion, the VFW, and other "real Americans" who "sent us here" and who, although they were not lawyers, "did not go to Harvard," and "do not read Supreme Court decisions," were "willing to fight and die for their country."

In response to such arguments, opponents of the amendment successfully encouraged many veterans to speak out against it, and in the final vote almost as many Senate veterans voted against the amendment as voted for it. On October 18, for example, Senator Tom Harkins declared that, "as a veteran, I will never desecrate the flag, but as a veteran I also do not want to do anything that would desecrate what our flag represents." Harkins termed flag burning a "very sick and violent act," which had aroused "hot passions in me" and at first had led him to want to "take those people who burned the flag and strip them of their citizenship and expel them from the country." He added, however, that just as his own feelings had changed upon reflection, of the 320 evenly divided letters he had received from constituents about the amendment, most people who had contacted him immediately after the *Johnson* ruling supported it, but most of his more recent mail urged its defeat. Harkins urged defeat of the amendment to avoid destroying the "basic and fundamental constitutional freedoms" that "our flag represents," to avoid falling "prey to the easy demagoguery of wrapping oneself in the flag to prove one's patriotism," and to demonstrate that "there is a difference between America and China, and that difference is freedom."

CHAPTER 7

THE FLAG PROTECTION ACT
AND THE FEDERAL DISTRICT COURTS,
OCTOBER 1989–FEBRUARY 1990

Defying the Flag Protection Act

On October 26, 1989, President Bush formalized his earlier news conference announcement of his decision to allow the FPA to become law without his signature. In a published statement, he reiterated that the Justice Department had advised him that the courts would likely find the FPA unconstitutional. He added, "Because this bill is intended to achieve our mutual goal of protecting our Nation's greatest symbol, and its constitutionality must ultimately be decided by the courts, I have decided to allow it to become law without my signature. I remain convinced, however, that a constitutional amendment is the only way to ensure that our flag is protected from desecration."[1]

Bush's decision meant that the FPA would take effect at midnight on the evening of October 27–28. On October 27, just hours before the law took effect, flags were burned during anti-FPA protests at Colorado State University in Fort Collins and at the University of California at Berkeley. At Berkeley, members of the RCYB and of ECSFAL burned several large cloth flags, as well as postage-stamp-sized flags. At Colorado State, a mini-version of the congressional flag debate was played out as a counterprotester put out the flames of a burning flag by blowing on it and then squelching the fire with his bare hands, while shouting, "My father served in World War II. I'm not going to let what he did go by the wayside." Jamie Krutz, one of the demonstration organizers, responded, "That's what your father fought for, the Constitution and freedom of the United States." According to a leaflet the flag burners handed out, "Obviously Americans do not agree on the flag issue. When Americans disagree, they talk about it. They exercise their right of free speech. They don't lock each other up."[2]

Shortly after the FPA took effect at midnight on the morning of October 28, additional flag burning protests occurred in New York City and Seattle. The New York City protest, led by Gregory Lee Johnson and attended by about 150 people, was uneventful and virtually unreported in the press. The Seattle protest, however, was widely reported (including on two network broadcasts that evening) and was marked by minor fights and vandalism; plainclothes Seattle police and FBI agents who were present took no action to stop either the flag burning or the disorders. The Seattle demonstration included the burning of an estimated one thousand small paper flags and the well-photographed and widely publicized lowering, burning, and then reraising, while still on fire, of a large flag that had been flying over the post office in the city's Capitol Hill district. The Seattle incident led to four arrests several weeks later which ultimately became part of the 1990 Supreme Court *Eichman* test case of the FPA.[3]

The Seattle protest was organized by Vietnam Veterans Against the War–Anti-Imperialist (VVAW-AI), which had advertised the protest with flyers depicting a burning flag. The handout "warned" that "this flyer will be illegal as of Oct. 28th" and called for a "festival of defiance" at the post office ("You know what to bring. You know what to do") to protest the "fascist" FPA, which it suggested was "not an 'exception' to the concept of free speech" but a "precedent for the future." The flyer declared, "Blind patriotism must not be the law of the land" and "anti-patriotism is a duty, not a crime."

On October 30, by a truly bizarre coincidence, the 1984 Dallas flag burning case of Gregory Lee Johnson, which had touched off the 1989 flag firestorm, finally came to a formal end, while simultaneously the first arrests were made under the FPA resulting from a new flag burning in which Johnson was involved. On that day, in a legally required formality, Dallas County criminal court judge John Hendrik, the original trial court judge in the *Johnson* case, acting in response to a directive from the Texas Court of Criminal Appeals in accordance with the 1989 Supreme Court ruling, officially dismissed the 1984 Dallas flag desecration charges against Johnson. Hendrik publicly termed his action the "most distasteful duty of my nine-year judicial career" and one which he was implementing "only because my oath to follow the law requires me to obey the mandate of a superior court." Hendrik termed it a "great day for the enemies of the United States, but a sad day for those of us who love our country" and expressed fear that dismissing the charges against Johnson would only encourage people like him "who seek to destroy the very freedoms they abuse."[4]

In fact, Johnson, who surely did not learn of Hendrik's order until much later (if ever, because it was almost completely unreported in the press), was encouraged to try to break the law on the same day that the 1984 charges were dismissed, not by Hendrik's action but by the very passage of the FPA, a law designed to defend what Hendrik termed the country's "precious symbols." Johnson, along with three companions—"Dread" Scott Tyler of Chicago art exhibit fame, Shawn Eichman, a RCP member and self-described "revolutionary artist," and David Blalock, a VVAW-AI member—participated in a flag burning protest of the FPA shortly after noon on October 30 on the Capitol steps in Washington before a crowd of reporters and photographers. As the group burned flags, they shouted, "Burn, baby, burn" and "Stop the fascist flag law." According to press accounts, at least one flag was ripped and three flags were burned before Capitol police seized and arrested the four protesters pending their arraignment the next day on preliminary charges of violating the FPA, demonstrating without a permit, and disorderly conduct.[5]

During the protest, ECSFAL spokeswoman Nancy Kent read a statement which challenged government officials to "arrest us" and "try once again to claim it is all consistent with your constitutional standards of free speech." Kent said that the FPA represented "compulsory patriotism" which sought forcefully to suppress "political dissent as part of a much larger and vicious agenda" to "shut people up" in the "name of the red, white and blue." William Kunstler, Johnson's attorney in the 1989 Supreme Court case, who was soon to represent those arrested in Washington and those arrested subsequently for the Seattle flag burning, told reporters, "Congress wanted a swift case. They're going to get it." He added that "the only thing I ever agreed with Bush on in my life" was that the FPA was "wholly unconstitutional."

Republican Senate leader Dole welcomed the arrests and predicted that he would soon be making an "I-told-you-so" speech because the FPA was only "legal hocus-pocus" and a "gimmick cooked up by lawyers to fool the American people into believing that the flag was now protected." He added that "this issue will simply not go away" and that before long Congress would come "back to a constitutional amendment" and pass it to give the flag "permanent" protection. Reporting on the new rash of flag burnings, *Time* magazine quoted Johnson as declaring, "We're back," and concluded that until the FPA was passed, "flag burning had virtually gone out of style as a means of radical protest," but that Congress had "restored its cachet by making it a criminal offense," and "now desecrating the Stars and Stripes has become a bit of a fad." In fact, probably the only flag burning prevented by the FPA was a ceremonial flag disposal planned for Veterans Day by firefighters in Plymouth, Connecticut, which was canceled because, according to a spokesman, "Since we planned this, the situation has changed so dramatically in terms of feeling about the flag that you don't even dare try to destroy them for fear that it will be misinterpreted."[6]

Although the October 30 Capitol protest received massive publicity, including short filmed reports on all three network newscasts that evening and prominent accounts, often accompanied by large photographs, in the newspapers, another flag burning that day, at the University of Washington in Seattle, received only regional press coverage. In a protest advertised in advance and organized by Tom Warner, a student newspaper editor, at the university's so-called red square (so named for the color of the surrounding campus buildings rather than for political reasons), about a dozen demonstrators burned twelve small flags and one large flag before a crowd of several hundred onlookers. Warner declared at the protest that the FPA was "an attack on freedom of speech" and that if the flag "doesn't stand for freedom, we'll burn it." One counterdemonstrator, who shouted, "This is wrong—you're just a bunch of fucking commies," unsuccessfully attempted to douse the flames with a bucket of water. University police and FBI agents at the scene took down the names of some of the flag burners and gathered up scorched sticks that had held the small flags as evidence but otherwise took no action.[7]

On October 31, the day following the Washington, D.C., and (second) Seattle flag burnings, a coincidental juxtaposition of events provided a symbolic precursor of the FPA's ultimate fate before the Supreme Court: three of the Capitol steps flag burners, including Tyler, were formally charged with violating the FPA, while a Chicago judge issued a preliminary injunction, subsequently made permanent on March 2, 1990, which declared unconstitutional that city's flag desecration law that had been passed seven months earlier in response to the "flag on the floor" controversy which centered on Tyler's art exhibit. Chicago judge Kenneth Gillis relied on the *Johnson* decision to forbid the city from attempting to use the law to ban an exhibit of ten works of "flag art," including a remounting of Tyler's famous (or infamous) work, on the grounds that the Chicago law was so sweeping that it unconstitutionally had a "deterrent effect on freedom of expression." Gillis added that the statute was so broad that it might even outlaw the *Chicago Tribune*'s daily practice of publishing flag representations on its front page or forbid selling clothes with union labels which contained pictures of the flag to demonstrate their American origin.[8]

Meanwhile, in an ironic twist, of the Capitol steps flag burners, only Tyler, Blalock, and Eichman were charged with violating the FPA (the preliminary charges of disorderly conduct and demonstrating without a permit were not pressed), but proceedings against Gregory Lee Johnson were dropped because, according to U.S. Attorney Jay Stephens, there was "insufficient evidence" against him. As for the others, Stephens declared that even though "there are substantial doubts" about the FPA's constitutionality, "it is our responsibility to enforce that law" to "vindicate the deep offense that Americans feel at desecration of their national emblem" and "to seek resolution of the constitutional implications." U.S. magistrate Deborah Robinson released the three charged defendants on their own recognizance, pending trial in Washington federal district court.[9]

Johnson, who earlier had claimed to have been falsely prosecuted for the 1984 Dallas flag burning, bitterly protested at the October 31 arraignment that he was now *not* being prosecuted for political reasons when he actually had burned a flag, or, at any rate, "was there" at the burning. Johnson said that he was "outraged" and charged that the government's failure to prosecute him reflected "profound cowardice" and was a "miscarriage of justice." In an affidavit submitted in Washington federal district court on January 9, 1990, Capitol police Sergeant Edward Bailor declared that he had seized a flag from Johnson's hands "before he ignited it." In a May 1990 interview, Johnson conceded that the flag he had tried to burn "didn't get going, but it had scorch marks"; he added that the authorities did not want to prosecute him "because it weakens their case to try to distinguish this statute [the FPA] from *Texas v. Johnson* if the same defendant is involved." Johnson subsequently told a reporter that the policeman who arrested him told him that he (the officer) had been able to spot him and stop the flag burning because "he saw me on [the Phil] 'Donahue' [television program]."[10]

The American Legion cited the Capitol arrests as requiring that House Speaker Foley honor his October 5 commitment to bring the proposed constitutional amendment to a House vote on the grounds that the FPA would likely be struck down and that therefore the amendment "should not now be put 'on hold' while awaiting a Supreme Court ruling." On November 16, however, Republican House leader Michel agreed not to press for a vote on the amendment (which had been defeated a month earlier in the Senate) until 1990 because of the press of legislation as Congress neared its 1989 adjournment.[11]

On November 27, the three Washington, D.C., defendants were given legal company when federal authorities in Seattle filed charges against seven persons, including three "John Does" who were never located, in connection with the burning of the post office flag during the October 28 protest there. The Seattle defendants were charged with destruction of government property as well as with violation of the FPA. In response to the charges, the Seattle VVAW-AI, which had organized the October 28 protest, issued a statement on November 30 which termed the FPA an "attempt to beat down dissent, mandate patriotism and

generally fan the fascist wind they so desperately want to blow across the land."
The VVAW-AI also hailed other recent flag burnings "in cities and on campuses
across the country" as a sign that "the people refuse to goose step into the future!"[12]

In referring to recent flag burnings, the November 30 VVAW-AI statement
cited several of about a dozen additional flag desecration incidents which occurred in the interim between the late October protests that led to the filing of the
Washington and Seattle charges, and the resulting federal district court rulings in
late February and early March 1990 that the FPA had been unconstitutionally
applied to suppress political dissent in both cases, in violation of the *Johnson*
precedent. Virtually all of these additional cases were reported only in local
newspapers, and although such news accounts almost invariably indicated that
the FBI had been notified of the incidents or was actively investigating them,
none of them resulted in additional prosecutions under the federal FPA. For example, on October 31 a group of students at Hiram College in Ohio attempted to
burn a flag to protest a visit by former Reagan administration national security
adviser Robert McFarlane, who had been implicated in the Iran-Contra scandal.
Counterprotesters twice extinguished the flames by stomping on the burning flag,
then seized it from a protester and themselves burned it "properly" to dispose of
it; subsequently one of the counterprotesters paid the original flag burners $20 to
reimburse them for the cost of purchasing the flag, as demonstrated by a receipt.
Also on October 31, a Telluride, Colorado, man, Patrick Ray, was arrested for
tearing down and ripping up a flag from the local post office (while ducking a
pitcher of water which a woman dumped on him from a third-story window in a
futile effort to stop him). Although federal authorities declined to prosecute Ray,
he was prosecuted under the Colorado state flag desecration law (which was
almost certainly unconstitutional under the *Johnson* ruling because it closely resembled the 1973 Texas law). Ray was convicted and was sentenced in January
1990 in the San Miguel County Court to pay $56 in fines and costs, plus $12.10
to compensate the government for the cost of the flag. Ray, a local eccentric who
lived in a teepee in the woods near Telluride, declared shortly after his arrest,
"They tie up all the law enforcement over such a silly issue as a symbol. What
about the environment? The earth?"[13]

On November 3, at the University of California at Berkeley, a crowd of about
five hundred people, many of them chanting, "Burn, baby, burn," witnessed or
participated in the burning of three large cloth flags and several tiny paper flags, as
well as several large flag posters and a cardboard caricature of President Bush.
About thirty university police were present, and officers extinguished two of the
burning cloth flags and arrested one student for obstructing and assaulting a police

officer. Police reported that no one was charged in connection with the flag burnings because they could not identify which people were responsible for them.[14]

On November 8, a protest at Princeton University was briefly foiled when a female student suddenly ran up, grabbed a large cloth flag out of the hands of two students as they prepared to burn it, and then disappeared. The protesters quickly pulled out and burned two placemat-sized flags that they had held in reserve, as about sixty supporters and another two hundred onlookers watched. The student who grabbed the flag, sophomore rugby player Alexandra Di Campi, soon became a local celebrity. Newspapers published pictures and articles about her, and the Trenton, New Jersey, branch of the Marine Corps League, a veterans' group, gave her a framed citation and made her an honorary member in a special ceremony.[15]

On November 30, another rally was held on the Princeton campus, this time organized by the New Jersey chapter of the American Association of Ex-Prisoners of War, to protest the earlier flag burning. About one hundred people attended the rally, which featured patriotic speeches, tributes to Di Campi (who was invited but did not appear), and enthusiastic flag waving. One of the speakers, a member of the Disabled Veterans of America, told the crowd, "If you can't respect the Stars and Stripes, then leave the U.S. and see what you've got overseas in communist-controlled countries." After the rally ended, Oleg Urminsky, one of the November 8 flag burners, who had been watching and taking notes, was invited by some of the veterans to give his point of view. As he began to explain that his actions were "in no way anti-American, anti-flag or anti-veteran" and that although his homeland of Czechoslovakia jailed flag burners, "we don't need that here," Urminsky was heckled with jeers of "Go back home," "I'll murder the SOB," and "Get a job, bum." One of the veterans, Cliff Larsen, shook his fist at Urminsky and was restrained by other veterans from attempting to punch him, while shouting "You burn this flag, I bury you right here."

In the interim between the two contentious rallies in Princeton, about twenty students at Wesleyan College in Middletown, Connecticut, burned a flag on November 17 before a crowd of about four hundred students and veterans, who reacted with a mixture of cheering, booing, and singing of "The Star Spangled Banner." Local police quickly doused the flag with a fire extinguisher (following arrangements made in advance with the protesters), filmed the incident, and confiscated the damaged flag, but made no arrests, explaining that they were turning over the evidence to the FBI and would leave any prosecution up to federal authorities.[16]

Two protesters burned a flag at Oberlin College in Ohio on January 5 to protest the December 20, 1989, American invasion of Panama. Despite the usual press reports of an FBI investigation, they were never charged with violating the

FPA, but they were subsequently tried and acquitted in August 1990 for allegedly having stolen the flag involved.[17]

All of the other flag desecration incidents reported between late November and mid-February occurred in California. In early December, a minor fight erupted at a high school in Healdsburg, California, after two foreign exchange students reportedly threatened to burn a flag during a debate about the flag controversy, during which most students voted in favor of the right to burn the flag. Following the incident, students who believed in the right to burn the flag made plans to wear images of a half-charred flag to school, and the exchange students issued a written apology, explaining that they had merely sought to "exercise the freedom of expression" without intending any offense because this right meant to them that "your country is so strong in its democratic principles that it can withstand the burning of its symbol." In Sonoma, California, Jim Byrd, an antiwar Vietnam veteran, burned a flag in the downtown plaza on December 12 as what he termed a "spiritual matter" to protest American policy in Central America, as well as "200 years of continuous deadly and unjust" government actions which had led to the "deaths of millions of persons worldwide." Byrd, who was cited by Sonoma police for violating the city's open burning law, explained his action by declaring that soiled flags were supposed to be disposed of by burning and that the flag "couldn't be more soiled" by American policy in Central America, which had made it a symbol for "murder and mayhem in my name."[18]

On January 2, Timothy Babbidge, a San Francisco middle school teacher, burned small paper flags before five social studies classes to protest the American invasion of Panama. Babbidge was subsequently suspended for several days without pay because, San Francisco school superintendent Ramon Cortines explained, "Flag burning is not part of the district-approved curriculum for social science." Cortines added that no further action was planned. Additional San Francisco flag burnings occurred during a January 23 demonstration against American policy in El Salvador and a February 7 visit by President Bush. During the Bush visit, demonstrators protesting American policy in Panama and El Salvador burned him in effigy and also torched both large and small flags, while police looked on without taking any action. According to one police official, arresting the flag burners would "just have started a bigger confrontation than there was."[19]

Among the California incidents, FBI investigations were reported by newspapers to have been begun in the Byrd, Babbidge, and January 23 demonstration cases. For example, the FBI requested photographs of the Byrd incident from a Sonoma newspaper, and a grand jury was convened to investigate the January 23 incident and a local free-lance photographer was subpoenaed and ordered to produce all photographs and original negatives of the flag burning. But none of the

California FBI investigations resulted in prosecutions for violation of the FPA, and, along with all other similar inquiries, they were dropped when the Supreme Court ruled the FPA unconstitutional as applied to political protesters in June 1990.

In connection with the Babbidge flag burning, on February 1, eight FBI agents spent more than two hours interviewing over one hundred of his students at the Horace Mann Middle School. The local ACLU chapter and U.S. representative Nancy Pelossi, whose district includes the Horace Mann school, both wrote letters to the FBI to protest that the investigation had been unnecessarily insensitive, intrusive, and intimidating of the students. ACLU attorney Margaret Crosby termed the agency investigation an "extraordinary" and "overzealous" effort which amounted to "an affront to one of the enduring values symbolized by the flag: freedom of political belief." Crosby reported that "many parents have said that their children felt intimidated and upset by the interrogation," which had probed their beliefs in an "extraordinarily sensitive, constitutionally protected area," in a manner that made parents and children alike feel "that their loyalty and patriotism were questioned by the FBI." Crosby concluded, "The FBI interrogation was an unfortunate civics lesson for students" and "one that they will not soon forget." In response, San Francisco head FBI agent Richard Held maintained that allegations concerning an atmosphere intimidating to the students "do not apply since there were no allegations of wrongdoing by students or parents" and the FBI investigation was limited to investigating possible violation of the FPA "and nothing more."

The Flag Protection Act in the Federal District Courts, February–March 1990

Because virtually none of the flag burnings in the late fall and early winter of 1989–90 were reported in the national news media or resulted in prosecutions under the FPA, the flag desecration controversy essentially disappeared from the national press for over three months following the October 28 Seattle flag burning and the October 30 Capitol steps incident. In the only instance involving the post-October incidents in which a Justice Department official publicly announced and explained a decision not to prosecute, Stanley Twardy, the U.S. attorney in Hartford, told reporters in late December that there would be no indictments in connection with the Wesleyan University protest because an FBI investigation had determined that the flag involved, which authorities had quickly doused with a fire extinguisher after it had been soaked in lighter fluid and set alight, had not been "burned, singed or defaced in anyway." Twardy declared, "If the flag's not burned, we're not going to prosecute. When you're dealing with criminal prosecution, you don't prosecute for violating the spirit of the law."[20]

According to Justice Department and FBI sources involved with enforcing the FPA who were interviewed in 1990, because of the enormous publicity associated with the Seattle and Capitol steps protests and the fact that the Seattle incident involved the burning of a government flag, the Justice Department could hardly fail to prosecute in those cases without appearing to abdicate its responsibility to uphold the law. They clearly suggested, however, that many officials within the Justice Department opposed any further prosecutions until the Supreme Court ruled on the FPA because they felt it was unconstitutional and almost certain to be doomed in the courts and also because they were loath to expend scarce resources to prosecute an offense they viewed as minor. Thus one Justice Department source reported that some of his colleagues felt that "the whole issue was idiotic and hoped it would go away," especially because from "our point of view, there are always so many things that seem more important." Another department source, who was interviewed in 1990 after the FPA was declared unconstitutional by the Supreme Court and renewed attempts to pass a flag desecration constitutional amendment failed, declared, "It all turned out well. Everybody's happy. The amendment was defeated. Now we can move on to more important things."

According to a Justice Department source who was involved in the case, the Capitol flag burning incident could "hardly not be prosecuted, since it was on videotape and on national TV in front of the Capitol." He added that because the incident occurred so soon after the FPA became effective, officials in the U.S. attorney's office for the District of Columbia had to scramble to find a copy of the new law. "Nobody had it in their books," he recalled. "Nobody had a copy, everybody was desperately searching." He added that although normally the local U.S. attorney would decide whether to prosecute a misdemeanor without checking with the national Justice Department offices in Washington, because of the legal and political sensitivity of the flag burning issue, both the Seattle and Capitol steps incidents were coordinated and cleared with "main Justice" in "great detail," with the Justice Department's Office of Legal Counsel, headed by William Barr, acting as the key office for such coordination. Another department source stated that "no serious consideration" was given to not prosecuting in the Capitol case or to not defending the FPA because, whatever doubts were harbored about the FPA's constitutionality, "The Department has an obligation to defend acts of Congress unless they are clearly and unequivocally unconstitutional and in that mission it accords the appropriate deference to the Congress's judgment."

In a comment that was consistent with "not for attribution" information provided by other Justice Department and FBI sources, Mark Bartlett, assistant U.S.

attorney in Seattle, explained in a 1991 interview that the reason for the decision to prosecute the October 28 Seattle post office demonstrators but not to pursue the protesters who burned flags two days later on the campus of the University of Washington was that the former incident had involved destroying government property while the latter involved solely the burning of "their own flags." According to Bartlett, "There are decisions to be made as to whether resources are going to be put in. We knew this was going to be a sensitive area and we felt that a single prosecution would answer the [constitutional] questions we had, and with the one group that destroyed the post office flag, there could be no rationalization as to why you would not prosecute them." Therefore, Bartlett added, only those involved in personally burning the post office flag were prosecuted, even though this meant that none of the VVAW-AI leaders who organized the protest were pursued. Explaining the failure to prosecute any of the San Francisco flag burners, San Francisco FBI special agent Kathleen Puckett, in a 1991 interview, reported that the FBI investigated all reported FPA violations but that the local U.S. attorney, who made decisions about prosecutions, had decided not to pursue them because they "were just not considered worth the effort" pending a Supreme Court ruling on the FPA. "U.S. attorneys have so many things presented to them daily," she said, "and so many serious violations of life or civil rights causing damage to something other than a symbol, that higher priority was given to other cases."

While the flag desecration controversy disappeared from the press for over three months following the October 30, 1989, Capitol steps incident, government and defense attorneys began writing legal briefs in preparation for pretrial hearings in the Seattle and Washington, D.C., cases. The two cases were scheduled for separate February 1990 federal district court hearings, which by joint agreement were to be solely focused on the issue of the FPA's constitutionality (rather than on the question of guilt or innocence because a finding of unconstitutionality would render trials on the facts moot). Because normally each local U.S. attorney writes his own briefs, especially in misdemeanor cases such as the FPA prosecutions, the obvious coordination and ultimate control of the two cases by "main Justice," as evidenced by the filing of identical Justice Department briefs in Washington and Seattle, clearly reflected the intense public interest in and the political sensitivity of the flag burning issue.[21]

According to Justice Department sources interviewed in 1990 and 1991, the briefs were primarily written by Craig Iscoe, assistant U.S. attorney for the District of Columbia, and then reviewed and approved by the Justice Department's Office of Legal Counsel. In a 1990 interview, Deputy Solicitor General John Roberts noted that "they [the Office of Legal Counsel] just sent a copy of the [Iscoe] brief out to the people in Seattle. It seemed to make sense, particularly given the way that everything was going to be going immediately to the Supreme Court [under the FPA's expedited review provision, following any constitutional ruling by the district courts], so that we didn't have any problem with different positions [taken with regard to the FPA by the U.S. attorneys in Washington, D.C., and Seattle]." According to Justice Department sources interviewed in 1990, Roberts's boss, U.S. Solicitor General Kenneth Starr, whose office represents the federal government before the Supreme Court, reviewed the Justice Department district court briefs before they were submitted so that, as one source put it, nothing would be included that might "damage his later arguments before the Supreme Court." Starr confirmed in a 1990 interview that his office had been in "close consultation" in the writing of the brief. "We weren't drafting anything, but we were consulted," Starr added.

The lead defense attorneys in both cases were William Kunstler and David Cole of the New York Center for Constitutional Rights, who had earlier defended Gregory Johnson before the Supreme Court. In both prosecutions, the defense attorneys filed identical briefs for dismissal of the charges on the grounds that, under the Supreme Court's *Johnson* decision, the FPA was unconstitutional, both on its face and as applied to the defendants, because the "sole governmental interest" advanced by the statute was protection of the symbolic value of the flag and because the Court had clearly held that such a purpose reflected a government desire to suppress political expression that could not override First Amendment rights. The 1989 congressional testimony of Assistant Attorney General Barr was cited at length in the briefs to demonstrate that even the very Justice Department which was now prosecuting the Seattle and Washington, D.C., defendants had conceded that under the *Johnson* ruling, in Barr's words, "it cannot be seriously maintained that a statute aimed at protecting the Flag would be constitutional."

The brief added that although Congress had asserted that it sought to protect the "physical integrity of the flag in all circumstances," the sole congressional "interest" reflected by the FPA was an attempt to "protect the flag as a symbol," an interest the Supreme Court had held in *Johnson* was "related to expression" because the flag's symbolic value could only be harmed by expressive acts that threatened its meaning. Aside from seeking to suppress such expression, the brief continued, there was no other government interest which motivated the FPA because, unlike gravesites, churches, historical buildings, and bald eagles, the flag was an object that could be both "infinitely replicated and privately created or owned," and therefore "physical destruction of one of a symbol's infinite physical representations can do the symbol no harm except by virtue of the message it communicates."

Because the government's sole interest in suppressing flag desecration was "related to expression," the defense attorneys argued, the *Johnson* decision had made clear that the government had to, but could not, demonstrate "compelling interests" to overcome the First Amendment rights of the defendants; it would not suffice for the government to meet the lesser 1968 *O'Brien* draft card burning case standard of only "important and substantial" interests sufficient where nonsuppressive motivations could be shown to have motivated the passage of the law involved. Unless the FPA were declared unconstitutional, the brief continued, the "slippery slope" which the *Johnson* ruling had warned about could emerge because the government could, based on similar unfounded "physical integrity" claims, forbid burning or "maintaining on the floor" copies of the Constitution, pictures of President Bush, or even "symbols of the Republican and Democratic parties."

Moving on to less central points, the defense brief rejected the argument that banning flag desecration imposed little hindrance on expression, because the same dissent could be communicated via other means, on the grounds that in symbolic expression the "medium is the message" and that in the *Johnson* and earlier Supreme Court opinions, the Court had explicitly rejected such reasoning and held that "the means of expressing an idea are often as important as the idea's cognitive content." The claim that the FPA was "content neutral" because it protected the flag's "physical integrity" in all circumstances was also rejected by the defense because, as Barr had testified, in fact the statute outlawed only acts such as "defacing" and "mutilating" the flag (as well as maintaining a flag on the floor, which would not necessarily affect its physical integrity but could express dissent) "that people commonly do to show disrespect" to the flag but did not forbid conduct such as flying flags in high winds, which might damage the flag but was not viewed as "unpatriotic." The exemption for legal disposal of soiled flags further compromised the FPA's alleged content neutrality, the defense contended.

A "truly neutral" flag law, the defense attorneys argued, would not permit "flagwaving, while barring flag burning," but, as Assistant Attorney General Barr had testified, "would say either everyone can use it [as they wish] or no one can use it." Finally, the brief maintained, the FPA was unconstitutionally vague in its definition of "flag" as including any flag that was "in a form" that was "commonly displayed" and by exempting "worn or soiled" flags, without defining such terms. Without a clarifying definition of "commonly displayed," the brief concluded, which flags were covered by the FPA "is anyone's guess," and because "the distinction between a soiled and an unsoiled flag" was "wholly evanescent," it was equally unclear which flags were excluded, especially inasmuch as "any flag that has ever flown" in any urban area "is soiled" to some extent, and therefore the FPA could be interpreted to ban only the "burning of flags that have never been touched by human hands or flown in polluted air."

The identical Justice Department briefs submitted in Seattle and Washington in response to the defense briefs, though virtually unreported in the press, raised eyebrows among Washington insiders who were closely following the cases because they virtually accepted the defense's position and relied even more heavily than the defense had on Assistant Attorney General Barr's congressional testimony that, under the *Johnson* ruling, no flag desecration law could pass constitutional muster. The Justice Department brief stated that although Congress had attempted to create a "content-neutral" flag desecration law by forbidding "nonexpressive as well as expressive conduct," such a "broadened ban" would truly be "content-neutral" only if "it is justified by reference to an interest wholly unrelated to expression—for example, a conservation interest (e.g. the protection of monuments, gravesites, eagles or other endangered species, historic homes and the like) or an administrative interest (e.g. the protection of mailboxes, draftcards or money [i.e. to allow for the efficient delivery of mail, administration of the draft and regulation of the economy])." When such conservation or administrative interests were lacking and the government acted only "because of the communicative value" of the protected object, "as with the flag statute here," the government brief added, Barr had testified that the government's real motive could not be "obscured by asserting that the government's interest is merely in protecting the physical integrity of the flag." Therefore, the brief noted, Barr told Congress that the FPA or any other flag desecration law could not "evade strict scrutiny" and, under the *Johnson* guidelines, "would be unconstitutional," and this position "continues to represent the views of the Department of Justice."

Although the Justice Department brief thus clearly maintained that under the *Johnson* ruling the FPA was unconstitutional and flatly rejected the major proffered congressional defense of the FPA as "content neutral," it concluded by urging the district courts to nonetheless uphold the FPA by finding that the Supreme Court in *Johnson* had "wrongly decided" that the government lacked "compelling interests" to override the First Amendment rights threatened by forbidding expressive flag desecration. While reiterating that the government's "interest in protecting the symbolic value of the Flag is the only conceivable interest the government has in protecting the physical integrity of the Flag," the brief argued that such an interest was "sufficiently compelling" to survive exacting scrutiny because the flag embodied the American "commitment to freedom and democracy" and "holds in sacred trust the spirit of the American people." While recognizing that a federal district court "cannot overrule" the Supreme Court, the

Justice Department argued that the FPA case could be distinguished from *Johnson* on the grounds that "the President [by endorsing an amendment] and the Congress of the United States [by passing the FPA] have now categorically affirmed the interest of the Nation in protecting our Flag, in direct response to the bare assertion by the Supreme Court in *Texas v. Johnson* that there was no such compelling interest" and that "the President and Congress, not state legislatures [a reference to the Texas state law at issue in *Johnson*], clearly are the most competent to determine the need for protecting our national symbol." Although the brief concluded that such reasoning would give the district court a "principled way to sustain" the FPA, this argument suggested that the courts should overturn the *Johnson* decision because it had proved unpopular, which in turn amounted to asking the courts to abandon their critical role of protecting the basic constitutional rights of minorities from majoritarian assaults.

The Justice Department brief stated that the department continued to believe that the FPA was unconstitutional under the *Johnson* ruling, yet it simultaneously and confusingly asked the district courts to hold that it was constitutional. Furthermore, the proffered basis for this requested action was that the Supreme Court had erred in ruling that the government lacked "compelling interests" in protecting the flag, yet the department simultaneously admitted that district courts could not overrule the Supreme Court. The Justice brief led to almost universal head-scratching among those who read it, with opinions generally divided into three camps: those who felt that the department had written a weak brief for whatever reasons; those who felt the department had been caught in the bind of attempting to square the circle of fulfilling its legal obligation to defend the FPA without repudiating its previously stated position that the statute was unconstitutional; and those who felt that the department was, in effect, taking a "legal dive" in hopes that the courts would strike the FPA and pressure would then mount again for passage of a constitutional amendment, just in time to make flag desecration a "burning" issue in the 1990 elections.

The first camp was represented by the comments of *Congressional Quarterly* reporter Joan Biskupic, who, in a 1990 interview, termed the briefs "feeble" and the apparent result of "half-assed Justice Department work." The two other views were summarized, in a 1990 interview, by *Washington Post* Supreme Court reporter Ruth Marcus (who declined to give her own personal verdict). She characterized one view as the "straightforward, let's give them the benefit of the doubt" approach, which interpreted the briefs as reflecting the dilemma created by the Barr testimony combined with the Justice Department's legal obligation to defend the FPA, and concluded that the department was trying to be "intellectually honest" and make the best case it could while simultaneously conveying its true belief that the FPA was constitutionally inadequate. "The other way to look at it," she continued, "is the completely cynical way," namely that "as a political matter the administration and the Republican party are much better off if they lose this case, and cynics look at the brief and look at the argument and see ulterior motives in the whole thing."

Because Justice Department sources who were interviewed in 1990 were reticent to speak about internal department communications, no clear answer could be obtained to the question of what motivated the department to produce its weak district court defenses of the FPA. One very well-informed department source, however, who was willing to speak guardedly, conceded that the briefs did not provide "a vigorous defense" of the FPA, that anyone reading them would conclude, "You can't expect to win with this," and that they "seemed to be saying, 'We [Justice] agree it's unconstitutional.'" But he maintained that the department was motivated only by a desire to be "intellectually honest" because it was "obviously not true" that the FPA was designed only to defend the flag's physical integrity rather than its symbolic value, and above all because it was "confined by Barr's testimony," especially because if the department abandoned the position Barr had taken only a few months earlier before Congress it would hurt the department's "congressional credibility." Under these circumstances, he said, virtually the only options open to the department, given its obligation to defend any law that was not "absolutely clearly unconstitutional," was to reiterate Barr's position and then to conclude, "We don't think it's constitutional, but the courts should defer to Congress." The source added that it would be "overstating the effect of the brief to argue that it was designed to lose in district court" because "whatever was argued in district court, the FPA was not likely to get upheld." The source added that he personally had no desire to "lose" the case to foster a return of the drive for a constitutional amendment, which he characterized as motivated only by a desire "to make political hay" by politicians who otherwise "don't care about flag burning."

House of Representatives legal counsel Steve Ross joined in the district court cases to defend the FPA, as did the Senate, in a brief submitted by Senate legal counsel Michael Davidson. Both of the congressional briefs argued that the district courts should uphold the FPA, in tones considerably more enthusiastic than those of the Justice Department, while using arguments that drastically differed not only from the Justice brief but also from each other. Davidson's office was authorized to file an amicus brief by formal action of the entire Senate (on the request of Democratic leader Mitchell) on November 19, 1989, well before the

Justice Department brief was filed, while the House brief was authorized by the House Democratic leadership after the Justice brief was filed and, as Ross made clear in a May 1990 interview, in response to what was perceived as a hopelessly weak argument put forth by the executive branch. Even before the filing of the Justice brief, congressional Democrats were apprehensive that the department might deliberately seek to lose the case in an attempt to force congressional reconsideration of the amendment during an election year, thereby placing them in a politically difficult spot. For example, on October 12, while the FPA was being debated in the House, cosponsor Don Edwards declared that the House would "seek to intervene if necessary" to defend the statute "if the Justice Department for some political reasons, cynically chose not to defend" it. Democratic suspicions that the Bush administration and congressional Republicans did not want the FPA upheld were only increased by the refusal of House Republican leaders to join in the House brief.[22]

The Senate amicus brief provided a straightforward "content neutrality" and "physical integrity interest" argument along by-then well-established lines. While the defense and Justice briefs had agreed that the *Johnson* precedent suggested that all flag desecration laws were inherently unconstitutional, at least if used to prosecute political protesters, the Senate brief maintained that the Supreme Court majority had "crafted" its decision to "point the way for the drafting of a constitutional statute"; in particular, it argued that the Court had signaled that a majority of justices, namely the four *Johnson* dissenters plus at least Justice Blackmun, would uphold a statute, which, unlike the Texas law considered in the *Johnson* case, "protects the integrity of the flag in all circumstances." The FPA "honors the Supreme Court's guidance" and provided a "faithful and constitutional" response to such signals in the *Johnson* ruling, the Senate brief maintained. Further, the brief argued, the FPA was "narrowly tailored" to protect the "physical integrity of this one special national emblem" and, even then, affected only those "flags that are part of a historic tradition" because it allegedly did not concern itself with "representations of the flag" on such items as "paper cups and flags" and thus could not portend any future "parade of horribles" involving "models of bald eagles and copies of the Constitution" conjured up by the defense because "no other object even remotely resembles the flag" as the nation's symbol.

By protecting the flag's physical integrity in "all circumstances," "irrespective of any view the actor may intend to communicate" and "without regard to the communicative impact of his conduct," the Senate argued, Congress had enacted a "content-neutral restriction." The purpose of the FPA was not related to the "suppression of free expression," the brief maintained, but rather sought to ratify (quoting from the SJC majority) the "unique status conferred upon the flag by virtue of its historic function as the emblem of this nation" to achieve such goals as assuring that the flag's symbolism could "be of service to the preservation of the nation"; to provide "an overreaching symbol under which a pluralistic society can strive to find common ground"; and to "serve notice that anyone can speak his or her mind under the protection of the flag." Therefore, the FPA allegedly did not have to meet the "exacting scrutiny" and "compelling interest" standards of the *Johnson* ruling but instead had to satisfy only the lesser level of scrutiny and the less stringent "important and substantial" interests required by the *O'Brien* test.

Addressing some of the less fundamental defense arguments, the Senate brief argued that the "soiled" flag exemption did not jeopardize the content-neutrality of the law but simply reflected a "practical decision not to criminalize waste disposal." It also rejected defense arguments that the FPA was either under- or over-inclusive in ways unrelated to any reasonable government interest; for example, it contended that the ban on even private destruction of flags simply demonstrated the genuineness of the law's motivation, that there was no need to ban flying flags in bad weather because all-weather flags were available, and that the ban on maintaining flags on the floor reflected the rational conclusion that such conduct could expose flags to "such harm as dirt and people trampling upon" them.

If the Senate's brief followed predictable lines, the House brief focused on an argument that had never previously surfaced during the entire 1989–90 flag desecration controversy. Its central thrust was an attempt to establish a government interest behind the FPA that was more convincingly "non-suppressive" than the "physical integrity" protection argument proffered by the Senate so as to convince the courts to assess the new law by the relatively lenient *O'Brien* standards. According to the House brief, a clearly "non-suppressive" government interest fostered by the FPA was the preservation of the flag's ability to represent, in a practical sense, the nation's sovereignty, for example, in demarcating national boundaries and identifying forts and ships at sea. "While the public may generally look at the flag as symbolizing values such as patriotism," the brief declared, "and the defendants may look at it with opposing values in mind, the government has in the flag an incident of sovereignty, with definite concrete legal significance."

The House brief argued that the history of the flag demonstrated that the framers of the Constitution and their successors had adopted the flag and sought to protect its "physical integrity, with the sovereignty interest in mind [as demonstrated, for example, by such historical instances as the inauguration of the Civil War with the Confederate firing on the American flag at Fort Sumter and government protests over foreign insults to the flag], quite distinct from any asserted ideological interests in the flag as a symbol of liberty, unity, patriotism or otherwise that would assertedly constitute an interest in suppressing expression." The brief dug deeply into over three hundred years of American history, dating back to colonial days, and was festooned with citations to rare books and obscure archival material to document that flags had historically served as "an incident of sovereignty" which had "concrete legal significance and practical importance" and provided "very practical advantages" for the nation and its citizens in connection with such matters as "control over bodies of water, or ships and of commerce."

The House brief was a historical tour de force and, in the unlikely event of its success in convincing the courts, it might well have been regarded as a stroke of genius. But many observers viewed it as almost irrelevant, and the courts treated it as such because the flag's ability to represent American sovereignty was an undisputed but still symbolic function that had never been previously mentioned as a justification for the FPA and above all because how flag desecration could threaten the flag's ability to identify American ships at sea required an almost unfathomable leap of imagination. One indication of just how peculiar the House brief seemed to many of the numerous "flag junkies," who followed every twist and turn of the controversy, was that Roy Englert, a Washington lawyer who helped write a Supreme Court brief defending the constitutionality of the FPA, publicly termed the House argument (which was repeated in a later House Supreme Court brief) "a little odd" and "far-fetched." Most other comments proffered about the House brief were equally unkind: in a 1990 interview, a Justice Department lawyer involved in the district court proceedings termed it "completely absurd."[23]

House counsel Ross defended the district court brief and the similar brief that he later submitted to the Supreme Court in a lengthy 1990 interview, conducted after the district courts struck down the FPA as unconstitutional when applied to political protesters in February but before the Supreme Court acted likewise in June. Although he was aware that his brief had attracted considerable criticism—in one aside, he casually referred to it as representing a "novel or oddball theory," in what seemed to be his summary of how others viewed it—Ross maintained that protecting the flag's ability to represent the nation's sovereignty was a valid "supplemental nonexpressive interest" reflected by the FPA, along with the similar interest in protecting the flag's "physical integrity," which Ross maintained a Supreme Court majority had "subscribed to at all times." According to Ross, Assistant Attorney General Barr had put the alleged inability of the FPA to meet the *O'Brien* test of serving a "non-suppressive" purpose "on the table as the 600-pound gorilla" that could not be legally overcome, and "what we were doing was challenging what Barr was putting forward as the administration position, which was also adopted by those [flag burners] challenging the law." Ross made clear that he felt that the district court briefs, as well as Solicitor General Kenneth

Starr's original Supreme Court brief (although not Starr's subsequent, substantially different, Supreme Court oral argument) represented an inadequate and tepid defense of the FPA. Thus he noted that his office generally filed court briefs only in the rare instance when "the Justice Department has abdicated its role of defending" laws enacted by Congress and declared that had the department presented "from day one" in district court the "full-fledged and vigorous defense" of the FPA made by Starr in the mid-May 1990 Supreme Court oral arguments, "I don't know that we would have even been in the case."

Noting that the Supreme Court in *O'Brien* had upheld the right of Congress to forbid draft card burning, Ross declared that

> there's every bit as much an appropriate government interest in preventing burning of the flag as there was in preventing the burning of draft cards. It's a case that bears a considerable likeness because you're talking about burning things as part of a protest, and the Court was able to find a supplemental [nonsuppressive] interest [to any interest in banning dissent in *O'Brien*, namely facilitating the operation of the draft administration], and having found that supplemental interest, said, "That's enough." I think we have offered the Court a supplemental non-suppressive interest in protecting the flag.

With regard to the critique that protecting the flag as a representation of sovereignty was identical to protecting the flag as a symbol, Ross responded that because the flag was originally designed as an emblem of sovereignty and this function predated "American patriotic attachment and iconization," it was still valid to argue that protecting its sovereignty function was not a suppressive interest. He maintained "The human experience is such that everything has some communicative aspects to it, but the Court has seemed to draw a line in *O'Brien*, and the flag is no more a device of communication than a piece of paper with something written on it, which is what the draft card is." With regard to the argument that flag burning did not pose any real threat to the flag's ability to represent the nation, Ross again returned to *O'Brien*, arguing that

> I truly doubt that the majority of the Supreme Court believed that the Selective Service System was about to grind to a halt because a handful of demonstrators had burned their draft card. That was not the only piece of paper in the world with that information on it. It strains credulity to think that had O'Brien had a conversion he would have been unable to find the army. The Court has accepted a fairly limited nature of injury. With regard to the administrative inconvenience injury that

was found to exist in *O'Brien*, the Court never specifically said that it was a prerequisite that there be a palpable [rather than a potential] injury. Really the test is not that there is an interest that is injured, but is there an interest that ought to be protected? In terms of what that interest is, I believe that the burning and destruction of flags represents [a potential of] an injury to the claim of legitimacy of the government.

The last of the five briefs filed in the district court test cases of the FPA was submitted by defense attorneys in response to the Justice Department, Senate, and House briefs. In essence, Cole and Kunstler argued that all three briefs boiled down to conceding that the FPA was designed to protect the symbolic value of the flag but that the Supreme Court had made clear in *Johnson* that such a government interest was inherently related to "suppression of expression" and therefore could not survive the "exacting scrutiny" and "compelling" interests required when First Amendment rights were threatened. The defense noted that both the Justice Department and Senate briefs had explicitly conceded that the FPA sought to protect the flag's symbolic value, and their brief contended that the House argument concerning protecting the flag's "physical integrity" as an "incident of sovereignty" in practice amounted to a similar concession because the flag's sovereignty function could be threatened "only by acts that communicate disrespect" for it.[24]

Turning to the Justice Department argument that presidential and congressional determinations to protect the flag constituted evidence that the government had a "compelling interest" in such action, the defense brief noted that the very purpose of the Bill of Rights and the courts was to "provide legal protection from the political inclinations of the majority when they trample upon the freedoms" of minorities. According to the defense, the House brief had provided "rich historical detail" dating back to "just short of time immemorial," but its argument could be "disregarded" because "not a sentence from the voluminous legislative history" of the FPA had propounded such a "sovereignty interest" in protecting the flag's physical integrity, because only expressive acts protected by the First Amendment could even theoretically threaten any such interest, and because "the House never explains how an act of flagburning undermines" such an interest. The brief archly inquired if Johnson's 1984 flag burning, Tyler's 1989 art exhibit, or Vietnam-era incidents of flag destruction created a situation in which "the United States flag no longer serves its function in demarcating geographical boundaries" or diminished "the function the flag serves on a ship in the Persian Gulf." Turning to the Senate brief, the defense termed any claim that the FPA sought only to protect the flag rather than to suppress dissent a matter of "mere semantics" and maintained that attempts to make analogies to protecting "cemeteries, national monuments and historic landmarks in part because of what they symbolize" failed because the flag was purely communicative whereas the other objects also had nonexpressive functions or were rare or unique. The brief also declared that the Senate claim that only by protecting the flag could it shield the right of "anyone to speak his or her mind" was ironic because the flag could hardly serve such a function "if we incarcerate people for expressing political opposition through flag burning."

Oral Argument before the District Courts

On February 14 and February 22, respectively, oral arguments on the constitutionality of the FPA were held before federal district court judges Barbara Rothstein in Seattle and June Green in Washington, D.C.; on February 21 and March 5, respectively, the two judges each ruled that under the principles of the *Johnson* decision the FPA had been unconstitutionally applied to political protesters who desecrated the flag. Although the Seattle ruling (known as the *Haggerty* case, for lead defendant Mark Haggerty) was issued one day before oral arguments were heard in the Washington case (known as the *Eichman* case, for lead defendant Shawn Eichman), both the oral arguments and the decisions in the two cases closely paralleled each other and they will be discussed together here. During both approximately hour-long oral hearings, lawyers Cole and Kunstler spoke for the defendants, while representatives of the local U.S. attorney's office and of the legal counsel's offices of both the Senate and House spoke for the prosecution.[25]

Kunstler noted in his oral arguments that he had never before participated in a case "where one arm of the government [the Justice Department] says this statute is unconstitutional, and the other arm of the government [Congress] says it is not." Any claim that the FPA was "content neutral" was absurd, Kunstler argued, because the sorts of activities supposedly impartially forbidden to everyone, such as "defacing," "trampling," and "burning" the flag, "are not things people do when they are using the flag in a positive way normally" but were "indicative of protest activities." In short, Kunstler argued, the FPA "permits flag waving, permits all sorts of activities that extol the flag, but not flag burning," and therefore it was "impermissibly one-sided."

Cole added that the FPA's professed purpose of impartially protecting the flag's physical integrity was further suspect because it failed to protect the flag in all circumstances, for example, not banning patriotic acts like "flying it in wartime, where it could be bombed, where it could be shot," yet outlawed protest acts like "maintaining a flag on the floor of your closet," which posed no physical danger to it. In response to the Justice Department's urging of deference to Congress, Cole characterized this position as amounting to declaring that "because Congress passes a law it's constitutional," which "would take the courts out of business altogether." In response to the Senate's content-neutrality argument, Cole said a statute that protected the "physical integrity of the flag in all circumstances" was imaginable but that "the only neutral way to do that would be to prohibit all use of the flag, period. You can't wave it, you can't burn it, you can't temporarily put a piece of dirt on it, you can't use it in any way whatsoever." The message of the *Johnson* decision, Cole argued, was that if people "are free to wave it, you also have to let people be free to burn it." Responding to the House "sovereignty" argument, Cole maintained that "there is just no showing that the fact that somebody burns the flag or puts a flag on their floor in their closet, has any effect whatever on the government's ability to identify its ships." Cole concluded by arguing that people "are no longer free" if the government "compels respect for the flag by prohibiting conduct that would essentially show disrespect."

Representing the Justice Department, assistant district attorneys Mark Bartlett in Seattle and Craig Iscoe in Washington, D.C., both maintained that the FPA should be upheld because Congress was traditionally entitled to a "strong presumption" of constitutionality when it carefully considered constitutional issues in the process of passing a law. Moreover, in the *Johnson* case only a "state pronouncement" about the flag's importance was involved, whereas congressional passage of the FPA "indicated the serious national interest in protecting the flag," implemented "via a national pronouncement on compelling interest."

House deputy legal counsel Charles Tiefer reiterated before both district courts the House position that Congress had an interest in protecting the flag as an indicator of sovereignty that had "real and major consequences"—for example, so that American sailors displaying the flag would not be "treated as pirates"—and that this interest reflected a "government justification apart from the suppression of expression." Representing the Senate, assistant legal counsel Claire Sylvia stressed that the FPA met what she maintained was the Supreme Court's suggestion in *Johnson* that a "content-neutral" flag protection law would be upheld under the *O'Brien* standards. She rejected arguments that the Senate had conceded that the FPA sought to protect the flag as a "political symbol," declaring that there was "nothing political about protecting a symbol that is valued because of its historical role and representing the United States and the nation, of preserving the memory of relatives who died in battle, or sustaining prisoners during their captivity."

The Federal District Court Rulings

In their respective rulings in late February and early March, Judges Rothstein and Green each endorsed the defense position, both in its general outlines and in most of its nuances. The *Johnson* case was controlling, they both held, because the defendants were all engaged in expressive conduct requiring strict First Amendment scrutiny, and because, as Judge Rothstein wrote, the underlying government interest was found to be that of "protecting the symbolic value of the flag" and such an interest could not "survive the exacting scrutiny which this court must apply." Judge Rothstein stated that the three government briefs were "curiously split" but concluded that they all ultimately agreed that the FPA's "underlying purpose" was "to preserve the flag's symbolic value," and because, under established Supreme Court doctrine, the "test of content-neutrality is whether the regulation is justified without reference to the content of the regulated speech," the FPA was clearly "content-based and subject to strict scrutiny." Both judges rejected the vigorous contentions of the House and Senate that the FPA could be justified on non-speech-regulation grounds, thereby qualifying for the more lenient *O'Brien* test; Judge Rothstein archly noted that, by so "strenuously" arguing this point, Congress implicitly conceded that "the Act cannot survive the more stringent standards applied in *Johnson*."[26]

The Senate's argument that the FPA was "content neutral" because it had the allegedly non-speech-related interest of seeking to protect the "physical integrity of the flag" by banning certain conduct regardless of the intended message or its communicative impact was rejected as based on a desire to suppress expression, such as, Judge Green noted, "those viewpoints which are expressed through the symbolic destruction of the flag." Judge Rothstein declared that the FPA was not, in fact, content neutral because it outlawed only conduct "generally associated with disrespect for the flag," while allowing conduct that threatened the flag's physical integrity but did not "communicate a negative or disrespectful message," such as "flying the flag in inclement weather or carrying it into battle." The House argument, that the government had a non-speech-related interest in shielding "the flag as an incident of sovereignty with a specific legal significance aside from its symbolic value," was similarly rejected as groundless. Both judges pointed out that there was nothing in the law's legislative history to indicate any concern for protection of a nonsymbolic "sovereignty interest" and also that as a representation of sovereignty the flag was still used in a symbolic way. Therefore, Judge Rothstein found, any government interest in protecting such a "sovereignty interest" could only be directed at suppressing expression that amounted to a "rejection of United States sovereignty," which therefore made the interest subject to the *Johnson* rather than the *O'Brien* test. Judge Rothstein added that, in any case, the House never explained "how the governmental interest in preserving the flag as an incident of sovereignty would be harmed by defendants' act of flagburning."

Both judges also summarily rejected the Justice Department position that the government's interests in protecting the flag's symbolic value were sufficiently compelling to survive strict scrutiny, even though the Supreme Court had rejected this position in *Johnson*. Noting that the Justice Department had taken this position on the grounds that "both the Congress and the Executive have pronounced the protection of the flag as a necessary policy goal," Judge Green declared, "However compelling the government may see its interests, they cannot justify restrictions on speech which shake the very cornerstone of the First Amendment." Judge Rothstein penned an equally eloquent defense of the First Amendment, noting that "in order for the flag to endure as a symbol of freedom, we must protect with equal vigor the right to wave it and the right to destroy it." In a clear reference to the recent democratic revolutions in Eastern Europe, she added, "This is an inspiring time for those of us who treasure freedom" and declared that freedom of speech "is the crucial foundation without which other democratic values cannot flourish." Judge Rothstein concluded:

> Burning the flag as an expression of political dissent, while repellant to many Americans, does not jeopardize the freedoms which we hold dear. What would threaten our liberty is allowing the government to encroach on our right to political protest. It is with the firm belief that this decision strengthens what our flag stands for that this court finds the Flag Protection Act unconstitutional as applied to defendants' conduct in burning the flag.

CHAPTER 8

THE SUPREME COURT
AND FLAG BURNING, ROUND TWO,
MARCH–JUNE 1990

The Reaction to the District Court Rulings

The twin district court rulings declaring the FPA unconstitutional when applied to political protesters were well-publicized, especially the first (Seattle) ruling. For example, on February 22, all three network evening newscasts carried *lengthy* stories on the flag desecration issue for the first time since July 4, 1989 (although none of them ran stories on the second district court ruling from Judge Green in Washington, D.C.).

The reactions to the district court holdings were highly predictable. Advocates of the FPA argued that the rulings were not worrisome because the statute remained valid until and unless the Supreme Court held otherwise, and they contended that the high court would uphold it on appeal. For example, House Speaker Foley and HJC chairman Brooks both predicted that the Supreme Court would uphold the FPA, although Foley added, "Whatever the outcome is, I do not favor a constitutional amendment."[1]

The flag burning defendants hailed the district court rulings as evidence of their triumph over government attempts at political repression. For example, three of the Seattle defendants, Carlos Garza, Jennifer Campbell, and Darius Strong, issued a statement on February 21 which termed Judge Rothstein's decision "a real victory for righteous people everywhere," which posed a "serious setback" for the government's attempts "to stifle dissent and mandate patriotism" and to "create a climate of fear and intimidation." Strong, a leather-jacketed self-described "street youth with a mohawk [haircut]," celebrated the ruling on the

Seattle federal courthouse steps by burning and spitting on a flag he had been wearing on the back of his jacket, just as he had earlier marked the February 14 hearing. Although pictures of both flag burnings appeared in the *Seattle Times*, Strong was not further prosecuted. Following the March 5 Washington, D.C., ruling, defendant Blalock warned that any attempt to counter the decisions by passing a constitutional amendment would be met with flag burnings "from sea to shining sea," and defense lawyer Kunstler expressed satisfaction, adding that he was not at all surprised because nobody "with a grain of sense could look at that statute and think it's constitutional."[2]

Proponents of a constitutional amendment pointed to the district court rulings as evidence that their arguments that the FPA would prove inadequate were correct and demanded both a quick government appeal to the Supreme Court and rapid congressional reconsideration of the amendment. Thus White House spokesman Marlin Fitzwater declared, "We've always believed that a constitutional amendment was the correct approach to protecting the flag and have always believed that it would be ultimately necessary." Senate Republican leader Dole declared that the rulings demonstrated that the FPA "completely flunks the constitutionality test" and had only "encouraged the flagburners to commit their outrages, to show their contempt" for Congress's attempt to wave "a magic wand over the flag desecration problem" with a "hocus pocus statute."[3]

On February 23, two days after the Seattle ruling, the Justice Department announced that it would defend the FPA on appeal by asking for expedited Supreme Court review of the decision "as soon as possible" and definitely before the Court adjourned in June until the following October. A similar announcement was issued within twenty-four hours after the second district court ruling was announced on March 5. Decisions by the federal government to ask the Supreme Court to hear appeals are generally determined by the United States solicitor general, an official within the Justice Department who is both appointed by and removable by the president, but who by long-established custom normally (although not in every instance) operates independently of the rest of both the department and of the executive branch. Given the congressional determination, as expressed in the FPA itself, to obtain a Supreme Court review concerning its constitutionality, it would have been virtually impossible for Bush administration solicitor general Kenneth Starr to make any decision other than to seek a Supreme Court appeal. In any event, Starr related in a 1990 interview that though he enjoyed a "very close working relationship" with Attorney General Thornburgh, his decision to appeal was reached without any consultation with higher-ups, adding that he "literally signed off" on the decision, with "no automatic pen, I used my own pen to sign the authorization."

In a separate 1990 interview, Starr's deputy, John Roberts, confirmed that, so far as he was aware, Starr had acted without "any communications from on high [i.e., Thornburgh or Bush] at any point in the case."

Starr said, in the 1990 interview, that the 1989 congressional testimony of Assistant Attorney General William Barr, to the effect that any flag desecration statute would be unconstitutional in light of the *Johnson* decision, had posed no problems for his decision to ask the Supreme Court to reach a different judgment. He said that he had "chatted" with Barr before Barr's congressional appearance and thus was "keenly personally aware of what Bill had testified to," but that he (Starr) was not in "a position [in which he had any function] of approving testimony," and, in any case, the Barr testimony "was entirely irrelevant" to his own subsequent responsibilities and decisions. According to Starr, this was because Barr's views had been offered as "part of the congressional deliberative process," in which the Justice Department carried out its "responsibility to provide, pursuant to Congress's invitation, our views, our legal advice," but once Congress had "worked its will" and passed the statute, an entirely new legal situation was created. In this new situation, Starr continued, it was now the duty of the president "to faithfully execute the laws" and "ultimately the responsibility of this office to defend the constitutionality of the statute. That we [the Justice Department] had views, institutionally, previously, was, as a legal matter, utterly irrelevant."

With reference to Barr's testimony, Roberts, Starr's deputy, said, "The fact that Bill [Barr] concluded, as an objective matter, as a decision maker, as a counselor, in giving advice to the Congress, that this would be unconstitutional, certainly doesn't mean there are not creditable, legitimate arguments that can be raised on the other side and it's our job to raise them once Congress had acted. So sure, we looked at and thought about it [the Barr testimony] and we determined, Ken [Starr] determined, he's the ultimate decision maker, and, for what it's worth, I agree with him completely, that there were credible, reasonable arguments that could be advanced and that we had the obligation to make them." Roberts added that Starr was "heavily involved" personally in handling the FPA appeal from the very beginning, both because of the legal importance of the issues involved and the "heightened degree" of general interest associated with the flag controversy. According to Roberts, the solicitor general's office includes about twenty-five lawyers and is a leading party or amicus in about seventy-five cases before the Supreme Court each year. Of these, he added, Starr typically became heavily involved, including personally appearing before the Court for oral argument, in only about "six or seven cases a year," but the FPA appeal was "clearly one he'd be arguing. It was an important act of Congress that had been struck down as unconstitutional. Congress had provided for immediate, expedited [Supreme Court] review to highlight its importance. We needed the government's top litigator on it and that was Ken."

The Fight over the Timing of
the Supreme Court's FPA Consideration

Starr filed formal appeal papers with the Supreme Court on March 13, in which he asked the Court to consolidate the two district court FPA cases and to hear oral argument, on a drastically expedited schedule, on April 25. Because, in the FPA, Congress had explicitly directed the Supreme Court to "accept jurisdiction" over any appeal from a district court ruling on the statute (skipping the normal intermediate appeals court stage) and to "advance on the docket and expedite [such an appeal] to the greatest extent possible," the only real question concerning the Court's response to Starr was not *whether* it would consider the cases on appeal, but rather what turned out to be the highly politically sensitive question of *when* it would hear the case and render a verdict. Under ordinary procedures, any appeal to the Court made after early February, if accepted for consideration, would not have been scheduled for a hearing until after the next Supreme Court term began in October and no decision could be handed down until after the November 1990 congressional elections; but if the Court exceptionally scheduled the appeal for argument before its scheduled summer recess at the end of April, a decision would be expected well before the elections.[4]

Almost everyone who was closely following the flag desecration issue expected, at least privately, that the Court would uphold the district courts' decisions and thus strike down the FPA. Therefore, the general Washington political consensus was that a preelection decision would place enormous pressure on Congress to reconsider and pass a constitutional amendment under the threat of "thirty-second negative ads" directed at members running for reelection who voted against it and that, moreover, the amendment would also likely become a hot issue in 1990 state legislative races because a congressionally endorsed amendment would require state legislative ratification. Furthermore, the state elections were viewed as unusually critical politically because the newly elected state legislatures would control the congressional and state legislative redistrictings that would be required once the 1990 census results were available, decisions that were often of crucial importance for the fates of both parties in general and individual legislators in particular. For example, Duke law professor Walter Dellinger predicted that if the Court overturned the FPA before the elections "flag politics" would become "an issue in every state legislative election in 1990."[5]

In short, Washington insiders viewed a preelection Supreme Court ruling as likely to be especially helpful to those who favored a constitutional amendment and to Republican electoral interests, whereas a postelection decision was seen as better for Democrats and amendment opponents. Thus, in 1990 interviews, PAW legislative counsel John Gomperts and ACLU Washington office director Morton Halperin both stated that they had unsuccessfully tried to convince potential flag burners not to test the FPA immediately, precisely to avoid bringing an amendment back before Congress in an election year, and several Democratic congressional aides who helped to organize support for the statute as a means of blocking the amendment said that they had both hoped and expected that the Supreme Court would not decide a test case until after the 1990 elections. Halperin said the ACLU had "frankly hoped" that flag burners would "wait a few months" so that the Supreme Court would not hear any appeal "before the [1990] elections" and that any future proposed amendment would be considered by "Congress in a non-election year." Gomperts recalled that he had "implored them to burn something else to make the point that their flag is just another thing," but "those guys were no help in defeating the amendment."

Whether or not all of the key actors in the legal and political wings of both sides of the flag desecration controversy consciously tried to control the timing of the Supreme Court's consideration of the FPA appeal for political reasons, in practice all parties almost invariably acted as though they were doing so. In late March, the intense politicization attached to the flag controversy, and especially to the timing of the Supreme Court's consideration of the FPA appeal, sparked an extraordinary and explosive debate in the House of Representatives after the House Democratic leadership urged the Court to wait until October to hear the case and Republicans howled in outrage that such a request violated the urgency suggested by the expedited review provision of the FPA.

This political explosion in the House in late March originated with Starr's March 13 request that the Supreme Court grant the FPA appeal and hear oral arguments by no later than April. In his filing, Starr presented an argument that, at most, only slightly bolstered the weak and unsuccessful case presented by the Justice Department in the district courts. As was the case with the Justice Department's district court briefs, Starr ostentatiously failed to give any support to the congressional argument that, as a "content-neutral law," the FPA complied with the *Johnson* ruling. Therefore, he was reduced to the weak legal position espoused earlier by the Justice Department in the district courts, namely that the Supreme Court should simply confess error and overrule its own decision of only nine months earlier.[6]

Starr summarized his position by declaring that the Court should uphold the FPA "because of Congress's determination regarding the weight of the government interest at stake and because the proscribed conduct should not fall within the protection of the First Amendment." In short, Starr argued that the Court had both overvalued the constitutional protection that "the narrow category of expressive conduct at stake" in flag desecration deserved under the First Amendment and "undervalued the compelling government interests that lie at the core of the statute: the preservation of the flag as the unique symbol of our nation." Introducing one argument not previously advanced by the Justice Department, Starr urged the Court to "reconsider" its *Johnson* finding that flag desecration, even if carried out in a political protest context, was a form of protected expression, instead maintaining that like obscenity, libel, and so-called fighting words (personal insults designed to incite direct physical retaliation), such behavior was not entitled to "full First Amendment protection." While conceding that flag desecration "constitutes expressive conduct," Starr argued that, based on Supreme Court precedents, such "narrowly and precisely defined" expression could be excluded from First Amendment protection when its value to society was "outweighed by its demonstrable destructive effect on society as a whole" and when "suitable alternative means" were available to the speaker to express "whatever protected expression may be part of the intended message."

In addition, Starr reiterated the fundamental—and fundamentally weak—argument of the district court briefs that even if political flag desecration was a form of protected expression, the Court should jettison its *Johnson* holding and find that the government had "compelling" overriding interests. Such interests had been demonstrated, Starr argued, when the "people's elected representatives"—the Congress through the FPA and the president by endorsing an amendment—had expressed "with one voice" their "considered decision that the physical desecration of the flag is—uniquely—anathema to the nation's values" and that the flag "as the unique symbol of the Nation, merits protection not accorded other national emblems" because such acts posed the "substantial potential harm" of "weakening" the "shared values that bind our national community." Starr concluded by conceding that his position was "in tension" with the *Johnson* decision, but he urged that "to the extent" that the Court had then accorded flag burning "full First Amendment protections," the FPA appeal presented an "appropriate occasion for the Court to consider more fully that analysis."

Because it was a foregone conclusion that the Court would agree to hear the case, the most intense interest provoked by Starr's filing focused on his appeal for an extraordinarily rapid Supreme Court hearing, which he justified by noting that the FPA had specifically urged the Court to hear and expedite any appeal "to the greatest extent possible." Although normally the Court grants thirty days for the opposing party to respond to a request that it hear an appeal (i.e., until April 13), Starr asked the Court to reduce this period to ten days, and Starr requested an April 25 oral hearing. Finally, Starr asked that the Court issue a decision to hear the case at its scheduled March 30 conference and that thereafter the ordinary subsequent seventy-five-plus-day period for exchange of all briefs be collapsed into twenty-five days.

In a preliminary response on March 14 to Starr's filing, attorney David Cole opposed Starr's timing requests but indicated no opposition to his request that the Court hear the appeal. Cole asked the Court to grant the defense the "ordinary 30 days" to fully respond to Starr's filing and to set the cases for argument on "the first Monday of the October term," on the grounds that such a schedule would be expedited because "the cases would be heard ahead of those cases already accepted" for the next term, yet would also "permit the full briefing and careful consideration that an issue of this constitutional significance deserves." Cole argued that the schedule proposed by Starr would "gravely and unnecessarily restrict" defense abilities to research and write their brief and characterized it as "rash" because the FPA case did not present "the type of national emergency" involved in the "handful" of past cases for which the Court had extraordinarily expedited review. Cole also clearly, if politely, hinted that extraneous political considerations were involved by questioning "where the Government's extreme sense of urgency derives from."[7]

On March 16, the Supreme Court rejected Cole's request for thirty days to make a formal response to Starr's March 13 filing, but, instead of accepting Starr's suggestion for a March 23 deadline, granted Cole until March 26. In his formal response to Starr (which was filed on March 23), Cole briefly summarized the defense arguments earlier advanced before the district courts, noted that Judges Rothstein and Green had "agreed" that the *Johnson* ruling "compelled" dismissing the FPA prosecutions, and recalled that Assistant Attorney General Barr had told Congress that "it cannot seriously be maintained" that, in light of *Johnson,* any "statute aimed at protecting the Flag would be constitutional." In light of the Court's "clear pronouncement less than one year ago in *Johnson,* and the two well-reasoned decisions below," Cole wrote, the district court rulings might be "suitable for summary affirmance" by the Court without any further formal proceedings. He added, however, that in keeping with the "spirit of Congress's statutory directive, the constitutional implications of the case and the strong public interest in the issues," he supported Starr's request that the Court grant a full review, including oral arguments and a regular exchange of briefs. Cole stated that in view of Starr's "unprecedented theory" that flag burning should be "deemed unprotected activity," the government's concession that its position was "in tension" with the *Johnson* ruling was "something of an understatement." As in his preliminary response, Cole again argued that the hearing and briefing schedule proposed by Starr "gravely infringes" on the "due process rights" of defendants who faced up to a year in jail. Without suggesting any specific alternative schedule to that proposed by Starr, Cole asked that the Court allow "the matters to be briefed with the care and consideration that they deserve."[8]

On March 15, the House Democratic leadership, represented by House legal counsel Steven Ross, filed a brief in support of Starr's request that the Court hear the FPA appeal but in opposition to Starr's proposed hearing and briefing schedule, which, it declared, sought a "degree of haste scarcely compatible with the serious presentation" of the issues involved. Ross declared that Starr's filing was "not the only official defense" the FPA warranted because it failed to adopt the congressional position that there was a "sharply drawn contrast" between the "non-neutral statute" involved in *Johnson* and the "neutral" FPA, which aimed at protecting the flag's "physical integrity" in "all circumstances" and, in the view of the House, as an "incident of sovereignty" rather than as a "suppression of expression." Because fully developing the House position required extensive research in "difficult-to-obtain sources," the brief continued, and because the issues involved were "controversial, difficult and subtle," adequate time for a "full briefing of the important questions" involved was required, in keeping with the "importance of the legislation under review with the alternative of a constitutional amendment, and the Justice Department's position on the merits, which has been to ask this Court to reconsider *Texas v. Johnson*." Therefore, the House brief requested that the Court give the case "priority when it devises its argument schedule for October" to reflect Congress's wish to have the FPA evaluated by the Court without a lengthy delay while still providing an opportunity for a regular exchange of briefs and adequate time for research and responses.[9]

The House brief touched off an extraordinary political brawl which clearly indicated that the flag desecration issue had lost none of its political sensitivity and implications since the October passage of the FPA. Republican Senate leader Dole was the first to sound an alarm over the brief, charging in a floor speech on March 20 that the House Democratic leadership and House counsel Ross had interpreted the phrase "expedited review" in the FPA to mean "delayed consideration" and had conveyed the impression that the "Justices should go home, take a vacation and let the flag burners enjoy the summer holidays." He charged that the brief reflected the "political intentions" of the "House [Democratic] lawyers" to ask the Court to "delay consideration" of the FPA until "after the November 1990 elections."[10]

Dole's charges were supported with a vengeance by about half a dozen House Republicans in a bitter debate on March 22, which apparently marked the first time in the history of the House that the details of a court brief submitted by the House leadership were debated, disputed, and ultimately repudiated by the entire chamber. House Republican leader Michel touched off a partisan brawl by presenting a motion which declared that the brief's proposed FPA hearing schedule was "wholly inconsistent" with a "plain reading" of the FPA, complained that Republicans had not been consulted about the brief, and directed that the brief be withdrawn and referred to a "full and proper review" by the bipartisan House legal advisory panel. HJC ranking Republican Sensenbrenner supported Michel, declaring that the House brief sought to "delay and delay this matter until after the November election," when the plain intent of the expedited review language was that Congress should know "before we break for the election" whether it was necessary "to pass a constitutional amendment and send that matter to the States for their hopeful speedy ratification." His party colleague and fellow HJC member Chuck Douglas declared that what was "terrifying" Democrats was the fear that the Court would strike down the FPA "before the Fourth of July."[11]

In response to the Republican assault, Democratic leaders denied any intent to misrepresent the views of the House and stated that they had not consulted with Republicans about the brief because, at the time that the House district court amicus brief was being fashioned, Republican leaders had indicated that they wanted nothing to do with any attempt to defend the FPA legally. House Democrats also denied any political motivations in wanting the Court to schedule an October hearing on the FPA appeal, instead maintaining that they sought only the time needed to make a strong case for the FPA's constitutionality, especially in light of their perception that the Justice Department's defense of the statute was feeble at best. Thus Majority Leader Richard Gephardt declared that Solicitor General Starr's March 13 filing amounted to little more than saying to the Supreme Court, "Change your mind," a position that had led House lawyers to feel that they needed "time to do the research, to consult the books, to get the experts" to "give us the best possible case." HJC civil liberties subcommittee chairman Edwards supported Gephardt, declaring that House lawyers especially needed additional time for their research because Starr "in essence, is not in favor of the FPA" and the Justice Department district court posture had not been "very effective." The problem about timing had been caused, Edwards charged, because Starr had not been content with requesting a reasonable form of expedited review but had requested "this ridiculous superexpedited treatment."

The debate ended with the adoption of Michel's motion by a 309–101 vote. A few hours after the tumultuous March 22 House debate on Ross's brief concluded, the House's bipartisan legal advisory panel agreed to resubmit it to the Supreme Court but stripped of all references to scheduling. The extraordinary vote amounted to a repudiation of the Democratic leadership, not only by virtually all Republicans but also by a majority of Democrats. The *New York Times* reported on March 31 that members had grown increasingly convinced the issue scheduling fracas had taken "on the overtones of a test vote on the flag-burning issue itself" and that therefore a vote against the Michel proposal could come back to haunt them politically with dreaded "30 second attack ads." *Baltimore Sun* reporter Lyle Denniston similarly declared, in a 1990 interview, that "everybody understood that this was the first test of [voting on] a constitutional amendment to protect the flag and that you better get on record right on this issue because somebody's going to sound-bite you." According to Denniston, the congressional Republicans viewed themselves as a "permanent minority" and therefore were "passionately looking for a magic touchstone" like the flag issue that would "allow them not only to win a majority in Congress but to get a majority in the state legislatures so they can control redistricting after the 1990 census. The flag amendment is all tied up with redistricting in the Republican mind. Anyone who tells you it is not is smoking something."

In a lengthy 1990 interview, conducted the day after the Supreme Court heard oral arguments in the FPA appeal in mid-May, House legal counsel Ross, who served as the leading lightning rod for Republican criticism of the House brief, vehemently denied that political considerations played any role in his decision to ask the Court not to hear the case until October. According to Ross,

> This was *sui generis* in that if somebody sneezes in this case, people attribute political motivations to it. My view was that if the Court decided it before the 1990 election and struck down the statute there will be a political controversy in the 1990 election, and if they decide it after the 1990 election and strike it down, there will be a political controversy in the 1992 election. I don't see how one gets out of it being a political controversy.

Although Ross praised the position Starr ultimately took at oral argument as a "full fledged and vigorous" defense of the FPA, he said that he was particularly concerned that, based on the Justice Department district court briefs and Starr's

March 13 filing, Starr was "simply going to march in and say [in later briefs and oral argument], 'We think you made a mistake last year and you should change your mind.'" Although such a brief could be "written fairly quickly," Ross continued, the "sovereignty" argument that he wanted to develop and advance required considerable time to "research the material, especially because so much of it is historically related." Since the Court was scheduled to recess in April and "I did not presume to suggest that they come back and have a special session" for the FPA appeal before the next term began in October, Ross continued, asking the Court to hear the case at the beginning of the October term was not hatching a "plot to get past the elections" but rather asking for the earliest possible date that would allow adequate time to draw up a brief. In a brief follow-up interview in 1992, Ross recalled that in the more than one hundred briefs his office had filed since he became House counsel in 1984, the FPA brief was the only one the House had ordered withdrawn and amended.

On March 30, the Supreme Court ended the suspense about the timing of its consideration of the FPA appeal by announcing that it would review the case under a schedule which promised a preelection decision. According to previously secret records revealed after the death of Justice Marshall in 1993, all nine justices agreed to consider the case; four (Brennan, Marshall, Blackmun, and Stevens) voted summarily to affirm the district court rulings without reading briefs or hearing oral argument, while the other five justices (Rehnquist, White, O'Connor, Scalia, and Kennedy) voted to give it full consideration, thus suggesting a potential willingness to overturn the lower courts (ultimately the court ruled 5–4 to affirm, with Brennan, Marshall, Blackmun, Scalia, and Kennedy in the majority). The Court publicly announced on March 30 that it would hear oral arguments on May 14 at a special sitting, thereby suggesting a decision no later than July. Whereas the usual schedule allowed a total of seventy-five or more days for the exchange of briefs once the Court agreed to hear a case, the Court mandated forty days for the FPA appeal. The scheduling of a special post-April session to hear the FPA appeal marked only the fourth time that the Court had made such an unusual accommodation to requests for a rapid decision: the other three occasions had involved monumental controversies which had demanded more urgent consideration, as in the 1974 Nixon tapes case (involving a major constitutional crisis and the likely impeachment of a president).

Press coverage of the Court's March 30 announcement stressed the political implications of the Court's hearing schedule. For example, a front-page *New York Times* story reported that a decision striking down the FPA, "which many constitutional scholars consider likely, would renew political pressure for a constitutional amendment" and "inject the issue into the fall campaigns for Congress and state legislatures." Following the Court announcement, House Speaker Foley promised to schedule a vote on the Bush constitutional amendment within thirty days of any decision declaring the FPA unconstitutional.[12]

Reaction to the Court's announcement broke along political lines which reflected the electoral implications that had been earlier attached to the scheduling controversy. Thus Republican Senate leader Dole welcomed the decision, declaring that if the Court struck down the FPA by July as he expected, there would be "plenty of time to act" on a constitutional amendment "before we adjourn" prior to the November elections. Defense lawyer David Cole declared that no "national emergency" required such urgent consideration and that "the push to have it decided quickly can only be politically motivated" because the Bush administration "fully expects to lose [in Starr's defense of the FPA before the Supreme Court]" and "would like to lose before the elections so they can push the amendment."

Relatively few editorials and columns commented on the Court's decision. Satirist Art Buchwald wrote in his syndicated column that an informant had told him that President Bush felt the threat of flag burnings was so urgent that he "sleeps with a fire extinguisher in his bed" and that resolving the issue was especially critical because "every Republican congressman's election depends on it." The New York Times suggested on April 11 that "it shouldn't take the justices long to affirm" the district court rulings but lamented that such a ruling would make it "sadly likely that politicians, who have so far been egged on by President Bush, will play low politics with the flag this fall," potentially resulting in a constitutional amendment that would amount to burning something "more precious than an individual flag, all out of fury at a few punks."[13]

In response to this editorial, which also termed flag burners "tinhorn rabble rousers," "vandals," and "small-minded dissidents," and was typical of many editorials and columns that vehemently attacked flag burners while defending their constitutional rights, defense lawyer William Kunstler suggested, in a letter to the editor, that the Times was indulging in liberal hypocrisy by engaging in the same kind of flag-waving patriotism that it criticized the Bush administration for to provide itself with "cover" for its opposition to a constitutional amendment. Kunstler wrote that the flag burners he was "privileged to represent" hardly deserved such "vitriol" because they had risked their liberty to test a repressive law and noted that recently Americans had hailed, rather than condemned, Eastern Europeans who had desecrated flags to protest communist tyranny. Also, as if to answer the Times editorial, on May 15 USA Today published a column by economist and writer Juliane Malveaux, which, uniquely among literally thousands of editorials and columns defending the constitutional rights of flag burners, argued that flag burning could actually be a useful and needed form of political expression. She wrote that most flag burners were idealists and might be among "our staunchest patriots," who would "hold us to the highest standard" and "goad the rest of us into action." For example, she argued, those who burned flags to protest the Vietnam War "did us a service" by demonstrating "how thoughtlessly we had incinerated our ideals" and "for almost no reason" caused the deaths of fifty thousand Americans. She concluded, "When we pledge the flag, we verbalize our nation's promise and potential. When we burn the flag, we dramatize the fact that too many of those promises have been broken."[14]

The Supreme Court Flag Protection Act Appeal Briefs

While the flag burning issue largely disappeared from the press for six weeks following the Supreme Court's March 30 announcement that it would hear the FPA case, the lawyers and amici in the two consolidated Justice Department appeals from the district court rulings, now known as the case of *U.S. v. Eichman*, docket numbers 89-1433 and 89-1434, began writing and submitting their briefs. Solicitor General Starr's April 17 brief largely fleshed out the position he had sketched in his March 13 filing. Starr conceded that he was asking the Court to "reconsider" and "abandon" its *Johnson* ruling, which he summarized as holding that "flag burning is a form of expressive conduct meriting full First Amendment protection," and thereby striking down all laws that banned such conduct as violative of the First Amendment. Although Starr gave a lengthy exposition of Congress's claim that it had satisfied the *Johnson* ruling by passing a "content-neutral" flag desecration law which was motivated by considerations "unrelated to the suppression of free expression," he clearly indicated that he rejected this argument in a footnote endorsing the district courts' conclusion that the FPA was not content neutral because it reflected the "view that the flag stands for something valuable, and should be safeguarded because of that value." Instead, Starr reiterated his earlier position that the Court should uphold the law because of "Congress's determination regarding the weight of the governmental interest at stake and because the proscribed conduct, even when undertaken for communicative purposes, should not fall within the protection of the First Amendment."[15]

Although Starr conceded that flag burning was a form of "expressive conduct," he argued that it also constituted a "violent assault" upon the "shared values that bind our national community" and upon the "most deeply shared experiences of the American people, including the sacrifice of our fellow citizens in defense of the nation and the preservation of liberty." Flag burning, Starr maintained, imposed an "injury that society should not be called upon to bear" because it "goes beyond that level of decency, civility and respect in discourse which merits constitutional protection" and assaulted "the memory of those who have sacrificed for the national community." Therefore, he argued, and especially because Congress had made a "considered decision" that flag desecration was "uniquely—anathema to the nation's values," the Court should place flag burning outside of full First Amendment protection. Such an exclusion, Starr contended, would merely parallel past Court decisions to exclude certain "narrowly and precisely defined" forms of expression, such as obscenity, child pornography, defamation, incitement to violence, and "fighting words."

Aside from asking the Court to "reconsider" its holding that flag burning was fully protected First Amendment activity, Starr reiterated that the Court should reconsider its *Johnson* finding that the government's interest were not strong enough to overcome any expressive rights which flag burners might have, in light of the "representative consensus articulated by the Congress and the President" in 1989 that the government had a "compelling" interest in "preservation of the flag as the unique symbol of the nation." Passage of the FPA created a different situation from that existing at the time of the *Johnson* ruling, Starr argued, because the law reflected a "considered" congressional determination, "as opposed to that of a single state legislature [i.e., Texas]," that the flag is a "unique national symbol deserving special protection." Even if the Court did not agree with Congress that flag burning presented "such serious dangers," Starr maintained, the Court should "defer to the considered judgment of the elected branches on the question of how important it is to the Nation to protect the flag from physical attack."

Although a total of five amicus briefs were filed in support of Starr's contention that the FPA should be upheld, not one of them completely supported Starr's position. To varying degrees, the amici all stressed that one major basis for such a decision should be that the FPA was "content neutral" and not directed at suppressing expression and thus that it met the constitutional standards of the *Johnson* ruling; Starr, in contrast, had rejected the "content-neutral" argument and therefore had asked the Court to "revisit," rather than to apply, the *Johnson* doctrine.[16]

A brief filed by SJC chairmen Biden, though mostly focusing on the "content-neutrality" argument, also stressed the need for Court "deference" to Congress, a position Starr had also strongly emphasized. According to Biden, the "deference" owed by the Court to Congress "was at its zenith" when Congress, "by overwhelming majorities," makes the "inherently legislative judgment" that the government has a "powerful" interest in protecting the flag's physical integrity. Furthermore, Biden argued, the Court should "not lightly second guess" Congress's additional determination that the FPA protected that interest with the "very statute" that the Court had suggested would be constitutional in *Johnson*, namely one that was "content neutral" and was not aimed at suppressing expression but simply tried "in an even handed way to preserve the flag for everyone."

A brief filed by New York's Democratic governor Mario Cuomo also focused on the "content-neutrality" argument but differed from all others filed in the FPA appeal in his explicit, "non-legal" warning to the Court that the flag desecration issue was politically explosive and that striking down the FPA might well lead to pressure to pass a constitutional amendment. In an extraordinary footnote, the Cuomo brief stated that, although the Court "should not let its ruling be based on projected political reactions," if the Court struck down the statute, "there will be a serious and profound impact on New York and other states because such a ruling would almost certainly trigger a divisive battle in Congress and in the states over whether a constitutional amendment to permit a ban on flag burning should be passed."

The House Democratic leadership and the Senate also submitted briefs urging the Court to uphold the FPA, but despite their common support of the "content-neutrality" argument, the two congressional briefs mainly presented distinct, lengthy analyses of the history of the flag and flag protection legislation which sought, via very different routes and arguments, to demonstrate that the FPA was justified on additional, nonsuppressive grounds. As in the district court considerations, this was a critical point because if the FPA's justification was accepted by the Court as nonsuppressive, the statute would arguably be subject only to the relatively lenient *O'Brien* test of meeting an "important or substantial" government interest, rather than the "compelling" interest standard of the *Johnson* doctrine, in determining whether the government could override the First Amendment rights of flag desecrators.

The House brief (which Republican House leaders again declined to join) reiterated the argument of the earlier House district court briefs, namely that the flag was originally established as an "important incident of sovereignty before it was used for symbolic purposes by patriots and others"; that the flag's primary function originally was "to obtain proper treatment for the United States as a sovereign nation," such as the "right of its seamen not to be hanged by the English"; and that attempts to protect the flag, up to and including the FPA, always had served the "non-suppressive intent" of protecting its continued ability to function in this manner, as in the identification function served by the post office flag the Seattle defendants had burned on October 28, 1989. In short, the House argued, the flag and its protection had served from its origins until the present the "framers' original non-suppressive intent" of "obtaining proper treatment for the country and its citizens," and claims that "ideology or viewpoint suppression" was the "sole possible governmental interest" behind the FPA were in error.

While the House brief focused on the history of the flag itself, the Senate brief stressed the history of flag protection legislation. The essential thrust of the Senate brief was that such legislation was originally motivated at the turn of the century by a desire to end commercial and political misuse of the flag and was "not directed at suppressing political dissent" and that, similarly, the FPA sought to protect the flag without any suppressive intention. According to the Senate brief, the history of flag protection legislation demonstrated a "persistent desire" by supporters "neither to favor nor to disserve any group or point of view in the course of protecting the flag" but only to "preserve the flag's value as the nation's salient symbol." The Senate brief maintained that the FPA was motivated solely by the desire to prevent, in a content-neutral manner that complied with the *Johnson* ruling, the "serious harm" caused to the nation by "the destruction of the flag itself," regardless of the "actor's purpose"; in particular, the brief continued, the statute was not motivated by concern over any "harm that results from expression of an offending message," as was demonstrated by its banning even the private destruction of flags, while leaving available "limitless alternative means of communication, many of which involve the flag," such as the display of the flag with "temporary symbols attached to it."

In a 1990 interview, Senate legal counsel Michael Davidson explained that in the brief he was seeking to be "complementary" to the other briefs by filling a void and providing a "legal depth" to the case by giving the Court "a sense of what experience" flag desecration legislation had emerged from, which he characterized as a "history without intent to suppress dissent, which was mindful of free speech." But although the Senate brief accurately portrayed the origins of the flag desecration movement as directed largely at commercial and patriotic/political flag "misuse" rather than at political dissent, it downplayed or ignored the reality that subsequently flag desecration laws had been almost entirely motivated by attempts to suppress political dissent and were almost exclusively applied for this purpose, and it presented a highly selective interpretation of the motivations behind passage of the FPA, which was the only legally relevant issue.

As in the 1989 *Johnson* case, the main brief for the defense was filed by David Cole and William Kunstler and was primarily researched and written by Cole. Cole argued that Judges Rothstein and Green had correctly held that

Johnson governed the current case because despite the differences in wording between the FPA and the Texas statute at issue in *Johnson*, the same principle applied to both laws, namely that both sought to protect the symbolic value of the flag and that such a government interest "did not justify criminally punishing respondents for their politically motivated flagburnings." According to Cole, the correctness of the district courts' ruling that the FPA sought only to protect the symbolic value of the flag was clear because "the flag" was not really a "physical object but an infinitely reproducible symbol" and therefore destroying any particular one of its "infinite material representations" could only harm it symbolically. This purpose alone doomed the FPA, the brief argued, because as Assistant Attorney General Barr had testified, the *Johnson* ruling established that such a government interest was subject to stringent First Amendment scrutiny: it aimed at the "communicative content of the proscribed flag conduct," and the *Johnson* opinion had found that this interest was "insufficiently compelling" to "justify criminal punishment of politically expressive conduct."[17]

Although the very purpose of the FPA doomed it, no matter how it was worded, Cole continued, the claims made in the briefs submitted by Biden and others that the statute was "content neutral" because it sought to protect the flag's "physical integrity" under all circumstances could not withstand scrutiny. Thus, he argued, the very act of singling out the flag for special protection made the law "content based," as would be immediately apparent if the statute had forbidden desecrating the "emblem of the Democratic party" instead of the flag. Furthermore, Cole added, the act's alleged content neutrality was clearly compromised by the fact that it allowed "patriotic" conduct that imperiled the flag, such as flying it in a storm or in battle or burning it to "respectfully" retire worn flags, yet the FPA banned "virtually all conduct associated with dissent," even acts that would not physically harm it, such as maintaining a flag on the floor under a glass cover or "physically defiling" a flag but causing it no permanent damage.

Cole rejected all of the various other arguments put forth in the briefs of Starr and his amici. Starr's contention that flag burning should be excluded from full First Amendment protection, he argued, not only had been flatly rejected by the Court in *Johnson,* but it illogically sought to analogize political expression to expression like pornography and "fighting words" which had no "serious political value," as well as contradicting numerous Court precedents which held that "offensiveness" could not be used to outlaw speech in a political context. Cole also rejected Starr's and Biden's urging that the Court defer to the judgment of Congress concerning the constitutionality of the FPA on the grounds that such reasoning would "leave the Bill of Rights to the whims of legislators," thus violating a key purpose of the Constitution and the courts, which was to provide "legal protection from the political inclinations of the majority when they trample upon the freedoms" of minorities.

Responding to the House argument that Congress had a nonsuppressive interest in protecting the flag as an "incident of sovereignty," Cole maintained that this alleged purpose had never surfaced in congressional consideration of the FPA and that such an interest was still speech-related and thus constitutionally invalid because flag desecration could pose only a symbolic threat to it. Moreover, Cole maintained, the "sovereignty" argument was irrelevant because burning a flag could not threaten its "function in demarcating boundaries and identifying ships," and, even if it could, the government's "interest in having a symbol to mark ships cannot justify jailing its citizens for burning reproductions of that symbol." In response to the Senate's brief, the defense declared that, even if flag desecration laws had originated in response to perceived commercial and partisan misuse of the flag rather than as an attempt to stifle political dissent, in practice such laws "have invariably been enforced against critics of the government" and, in any case, such an original intent was constitutionally impermissible because it sought to maintain the flag's symbolic value by suppressing "the message of disrespect" conveyed by advertising and political uses of the emblem.

In addition to Cole's brief, the attack on the FPA was supported by a separate brief filed by Charles Hamilton, a lawyer representing Darius Strong, one of the Seattle defendants; an amicus brief filed on behalf of movie director Oliver Stone, editorial cartoonist Paul Conrad, and fourteen prominent artists, including Jasper Johns and Claes Oldenburg (hereafter the "artists' brief"); and five additional amicus briefs representing a total of forty-six political, civil liberties, legal, and public interest groups, including the ABA, the ACLU, PAW, the ASNE, and the NAACP. From a legal standpoint, these briefs reinforced Cole's arguments rather than making substantial additional arguments (no doubt because Cole's brief covered all the legal bases). Of the seven supporting briefs, the one filed on behalf of the national ACLU, the Washington State and Washington, D.C., ACLU chapters, and the American Jewish Congress attracted by far the most attention among those who closely followed the flag desecration controversy. Partly this was because it was a strong and well-written brief, but even more so because it was written by two of Laurence Tribe's professorial colleagues at Harvard Law School: Kathleen Sullivan, generally regarded as a leading protégé of Tribe, and Charles Fried, the conservative former Reagan administration solicitor general, who had refused to file an amicus brief in support of Texas in the *Johnson* case and had later told Congress that no action should be taken to overturn the *Johnson* ruling. Because

Tribe was viewed as the intellectual "godfather" of the FPA, opponents of the statute openly spoke of their success in getting Sullivan and Fried to coauthor a brief opposing it as something of a "coup."

The Fried-Sullivan brief argued that any claim of a nonsuppressive interest behind the FPA was meaningless because the flag was "nothing but a symbol," with no administrative or other noncommunicative function (unlike draft cards, currency, gravesites, or bald eagles); therefore desecrating a flag was nothing but a statement "without words—as a picture, a melody, a statue, or a dance, a mime or a string of semaphore flags." Claims that the FPA merely sought nonsuppressively to protect the flag's "physical integrity" were transparent, the brief added, as would be immediately evident if the government claimed a similar interest in protecting the "physical integrity" of all photographs of the president, because the only conceivable purpose behind protecting a "symbol against symbolic attack" was the suppression of "offensive expression." Furthermore, Fried-Sullivan argued, precisely because the flag was only a symbol, destruction of what it stood for, which the government sought to punish, was "conceptually impossible" because burning one or more "physical instantiations of the flag's symbolism cannot obliterate its symbolic value." The brief further rejected what it termed Starr's attempt to banish flag desecration to the "fringes of the First Amendment," along with defamation, obscenity, and "fighting words." Unlike such expressions, the brief contended, which were legally categorized as making no substantial contribution to the "exchange of ideas" because they respectively included only reckless falsehoods and provocations to sexual arousal and fisticuffs, flag desecration deserved the strongest possible constitutional protection because it was a form of dissident "political speech" and therefore was "located at the very core" of First Amendment–protected expression, just like "a speech, a pamphlet or a satiric cartoon." Moreover, where public, political speech was at issue, "dainty rules of etiquette and paternalistic protection of vulnerable sensibilities have long since been ruled out."

Most of the amicus briefs supported Cole's legal analysis and also focused on the practical consequences of outlawing flag desecration. For example, the brief submitted by the PAW, the ASNE, and four other organizations argued that if the Court accepted the principle that highly offensive political expression could be outlawed by legislative majorities, then "no defensible principle" would remain to bar future laws that might outlaw other forms of symbolic and verbal criticism of additional national symbols and even of "the nation and the government for which those symbols stand." The artists' brief focused on the perceived threat to artistic expression posed by the FPA, maintaining that the FPA threatened to "inhibit the creative process of artists" because it was so vague that "artists seeking to avoid prosecution are likely to censor" themselves and "refrain from creating even protected works." The brief stressed that in particular the FPA definition of "flag," which included all flags "or any part thereof, made of any substance, of any size, in a form that is commonly displayed," was so vague that artists could only "speculate whether their work risks criminal prosecution." Indeed, the brief added, as interpreted by the HJC majority report, the FPA illogically and arbitrarily appeared to cover all "three dimensional" but not any "two dimensional" flags, so that "a picture of a flag on a magazine cover is not a flag, but becomes one when cut out and attached to a stick."

The NAACP brief also focused on the practical impact of the FPA. It declared that even though many NAACP members were "appalled" by flag burnings, the First Amendment had been a "primary instrument" used by the NACCP in struggling to "make a reality of the rights" symbolized by the flag, and that the organization therefore "must take great interest in protecting the broad interpretation of the First Amendment clauses which allow civil dissent." The brief warned that forbidding any form of expressive nonviolent protest limited the "ability of the holders of minority viewpoints to dramatically express their ideas to the public at large." The amicus brief filed on behalf of thirty-four political, educational, artistic, legal, religious, and other organizations (including the Association of Art Museum Directors and the Modern Language Association—hereafter termed the "organizations' brief"), with a combined membership of over 250,000 Americans, similarly stressed that "symbolic political expression" was a key medium for expressing "messages of political and social significance." It warned that "any retreat" from the Supreme Court's "hitherto vigorous enforcement" of First Amendment rights would "seriously impair" opportunities to "effect political and social change through the exercise of free speech" and, if the government's argument urging the Court to defer to Congress was accepted, such a ruling would transform the Court into a rubber stamp that merely endorsed the legislative results of passing outbursts of "fervor and passion," whereas the Court's charge was to protect minorities against the "ebb and flow" of the "political tide of majoritarian sentiment."

The ABA brief especially stressed that if the Court upheld the FPA it would deliver a heavy blow to the forces of freedom all over the world at a time when Eastern European democracies were still in an embryonic state. "Since flag burning is a familiar form of political dissent everywhere," the ABA contended, and, even in Gorbachev's Soviet Union, protesters had been allowed to march in Moscow's Red Square with red flags shorn of their hammer and sickle, the Court's ruling would be "carefully noted by friends of democracy and supporters of dictatorship throughout the world." Therefore, the ABA contended that by upholding the FPA, the Court would likely lead oppressive governments to seize upon such a precedent to "stifle political expression under the guise of 'neutral' restrictions" or to otherwise outlaw expression viewed as offensive, just as the Ayatollah Khomenei had decreed death for author Salman Rushdie for writing *The Satanic Verses;* indeed, "except for the severity of punishment, what is the difference?" the ABA asked.

Oral Argument before the Supreme Court

Solicitor General Starr was given an opportunity to respond to the various defense briefs both in a written reply brief and, since he was the first speaker at oral argument, during the half-hour allotted to him before the Supreme Court on May 14, 1990. In these arguments, Starr presented a case for the constitutionality of the FPA that amounted to a considerable shift from the positions previously presented both by the Justice Department in the district courts and by himself in his prior Supreme Court briefs (although the vast majority of press accounts completely overlooked this). Whereas both Starr and the Justice Department district court briefs had previously dismissed the "content-neutral" argument as lacking in substance, in his reply brief and even more in his oral argument Starr made this position the central point of his defense of the FPA's constitutionality. Thus he maintained that in the FPA Congress had carefully followed the *Johnson* guidelines to create a "viewpoint-neutral" law free of "content-laden language," which protected the physical integrity of the flag without "singling out certain viewpoints for disfavored treatment." Instead, Congress had simply sought to protect the flag, admittedly "because of its symbolic value," but "not from criticism"—rather only from "physical destruction or mutilation" which amounted to a "physical, violent assault on the most deeply shared experiences of the American people," much as governments could protect "houses of worship" or "the bald eagle" against destruction, without seeking to suppress any point of view. Clear evidence that the FPA was "content neutral" could be seen, Starr added, in the fact that one could be prosecuted for "patriotically" desecrating the flag, such as emblazoning it with the message, "I love the Supreme Court."[18]

Whereas earlier the Justice Department had urged Court deference to Congress simply on the grounds that the passage of the FPA in itself demonstrated the government's "compelling" interests in banning flag desecration, Starr's reply brief and oral argument drastically transformed the "deference argument" into the position that the Court should uphold the FPA because Congress had already deferred to the Court by "very carefully, very respectfully" responding to the Court's "various intimations" in *Johnson* and earlier decisions that a law protecting the flag's "physical integrity" in "all circumstances" would pass constitutional muster. Such Court action should follow, Starr continued, especially because the FPA's "highly specific, narrowly tailored" prohibitions of "certain forms of conduct" still permitted "robust and uninhibited speech to continue unabated." In expressing fears that the FPA would lead to further encroachments on expression, Starr declared, the defense and its amici were "crying wolf" because the flag was "sui generis."

Additionally, and especially in his oral argument, Starr seemed, somewhat ambiguously, to abandon the position that flag desecration was clearly expression, which the Justice Department had taken in the district courts and which in his briefs he had modified somewhat to argue that such acts were "expressive conduct" although not entitled to "full First Amendment protection." In his oral argument, Starr seemed to argue that flag burning was not "expression" at all because it failed to meet the Court's 1974 *Spence* test, which required the transmission of a "particularized message" to qualify as expression." Instead, he maintained, such acts left a "major message gap" and were meaningless without accompanying "speech that is incident or tied to the conduct." Therefore, Starr argued, flag burnings amounted to "mindless nihilism," as the Seattle flag burners had demonstrated by also burning a "McDonald's golden arches flag," and were no more expressive than were mere attention-getting devices like "burning any" object or "shouting or screaming or using a loudspeaker at full blast."

The response to Starr's new tack at oral argument by at least two justices who had voted with the *Johnson* majority suggested (correctly, it soon turned out) that he had not changed their minds. In response to his argument that flag burning did not convey a particularized message, Justice Kennedy termed such conduct an "internationally recognized form of protest," and Justice Scalia said that the message clearly was, "I am in opposition to this country," and that, in any case, even with verbal expression, "you don't have to be precise to be protected do you?" Scalia also issued a devastating critique of Starr's claim that the FPA was "viewpoint neutral." Citing the text of the law, Scalia declared, "If I get a spot on my tie, I don't say, gee I've defiled my tie . . . or if I tear my jacket I don't say, my, I've mutilated my jacket. These are words of—cast contempt upon."

William Kunstler, speaking for the defense at oral argument, noted that Starr's position was "dramatically" changed from the previous government stance, but he responded with a summation of previous defense arguments, namely that the *Johnson* ruling dictated that the FPA be found unconstitutional as a content-based statute which "singles out one particular political symbol" for protection in an attempt to suppress expression that was "anathema" to government officials. The FPA was clearly content-based, Kunstler argued, because it allowed "patriotic" conduct which imperiled the flag, like flying it in battle, but forbade all conduct that would cast it "in a bad light." In response to Starr's oral argument that flag burning did not deliver a "particularized message," Kunstler told the Court, "That's true of all non-verbal communication. . . . You can't relegate non-verbal expression to the scrap heap." Kunstler argued that although Starr had suggested that a flag burning "by itself carries no message," in fact it did communicate that the actor "doesn't like something the United States is doing," and the specifics could be explained in accompanying flyers. A skeptical Justice Stevens responded by characterizing this scenario as, "call this number and we'll tell you why we burned the flag."

Responding to Starr's analogizing of flag desecration with child pornography or defamation as not warranting full First Amendment protection, Kunstler suggested that this was a "last resort" attempt by the government to "carve out" a new exception to the First Amendment to "get around" the *Johnson* ruling. He argued, however, "In the area of political speech, the government cannot make judgments of what is overly offensive or unimportant," and the courts had the constitutional responsibility of forestalling the government's "inclination to suppress" what it deemed "offensive at any one time or another." Kunstler concluded by declaring that the government was seeking to turn the flag into a "golden image" that must be worshiped, but "once people are compelled to respect a political symbol, then they are no longer free and their respect for the flag is quite meaningless. To criminalize flag burning is to deny what the First Amendment stands for."

Flag Burning Scenarios:
Washington during the Spring of 1990

Both immediately before and after the May 14 Supreme Court oral arguments, Washington was awash with speculation by politicians and political observers concerning the likely outcome of the FPA case and its potential ramifications. The overwhelming—indeed, virtually unanimous—prediction of politicians, lawyers, lobbyists, journalists, and others who followed the flag desecration controversy was that the Court would strike down the FPA and that the result would be the almost immediate endorsement of a constitutional amendment by Congress and its subsequent rapid ratification by state legislatures as politicians across the country, fearful of electoral retribution in November if they failed to support it, scrambled to get on a flag-waving bandwagon. Veteran *Baltimore Sun* Supreme Court reporter Lyle Denniston, in an interview in mid-May, voiced the "conventional wisdom" in Washington as the Court's opinion was awaited: he predicted the Court would strike down the FPA, following which a "constitutional amendment will have passed both Houses [of Congress] sometime before the August recess. Before the end of next spring, three-fourths of the state legislatures will approve." Similarly, PAW legislative counsel John Gomperts expressed fear that a "political wildfire" might erupt following the expected decision invalidating the FPA, with Congress endorsing an amendment by August and then state governments across the country convening special legislative sessions and legislators "zooming back to state capitols to vote for this God-damned thing so that they can use it in their state elections. In the worst-case scenario, the issue gets completely out of control and we have a constitutional amendment by the November elections." According to a 1990 interview with a Supreme Court clerk, even the justices themselves expected that striking down the FPA would lead to the rapid enactment of an amendment to overturn their decision.

Such privately voiced predictions were reflected in virtually all of the press coverage that preceded and followed the oral argument. For example, the headline of the *Washington Post*'s May 14 story, which appeared on the morning of the Court hearing, read, "'Old Glory' May Wave in Fall Campaign Winds." It accompanied a report which declared that "many legal observers," as well as congressional Democrats who had backed the FPA, expected the Court to strike it down and that the Democrats feared being placed under "enormous pressure" on the issue in the November elections. Virtually all press speculation following the oral argument suggested that Starr's presentation had not changed the Court's mind (even though Justice Blackmun, who was generally considered the only likely *Johnson* majority defector, had remained silent at oral argument). Thus in their May 15 accounts of the oral argument, *USA Today* headlined, "High Court Skeptical of Flag Law," and *Newsday* bannered, "Flag Burning Law May Not Fly." The *Miami Herald*'s May 15 report reflected the "conventional wisdom" in noting that "many legal experts" expected the FPA to be overturned and that "Republicans and the Bush administration hope to push the constitutional amendment through Congress and send it to the states in time to help them in election contests this fall," including state legislative races, which would be "particularly critical because the parties in control of state legislatures will redraw congressional and legislative boundaries based on new census data."

An article in the May 28 *Legal Times,* by legal observer Tony Mauro, which was headlined "Flag-Case Forecast: No Switch in Nine," reflected the perceptions of many present during the oral argument that Starr had made a good presentation of a hopelessly flawed position. Both before and after the May 14 oral argument, predictions that the Court would strike down the FPA came not only from the general and the legal press but, not surprisingly, also both from the right by supporters of a constitutional amendment and from the left by Cole and Kunstler. Thus on May 12 an American Legion spokesman termed the FPA "doomed," and in an interview conducted three days before the oral argument, Cole said that he was "pretty confident that we'll win" but expressed some concern that although "it's a hard case to lose legally, I think politically we could lose it."[19]

Beyond such expected responses, even a leading FPA backer and two of the three major constitutional experts who had told Congress in the summer of 1989 that the Court might or would definitely uphold the FPA had changed their tunes considerably by May 1990 (perhaps influenced by the fact that the constitutional amendment that they had feared a year earlier had in the meantime been defeated in the Senate in October 1989). Democratic Representative Don Edwards, a co-sponsor of the FPA, conceded, shortly before the Supreme Court oral argument, that it would fail, but he also suggested that the FPA had succeeded in its key objective—delaying and derailing the constitutional amendment in the immediate post-*Johnson* period. He told a reporter that the FPA had "bought us a year" and "we loved that" because "now the hysteria [for an amendment] is largely gone." Meanwhile, Chicago law school dean Geoffrey Stone, who had told the SJC in August that there was at least a "reasonable" chance that the Court would uphold the FPA and who subsequently authored a law review article to that effect, told a reporter in May that he would be "hard pressed" to write such a legal opinion.[20]

Even more startlingly, Harvard professor Laurence Tribe, who had intellectually authored the FPA and had consistently defended it as "content neutral," declared in May 1990 that the Court should strike down the law because its "real purpose" was "censorship" and it was not "viewpoint neutral." Tribe claimed that the inclusion of the "physically defiles" provision in the final version of the statute, as the result of Senate floor action in early October 1989, had been a "constitutional poison pill," which had led him to stop supporting the FPA because it had amounted to the "thirteenth chime of the clock that makes the first twelve ring hollow [with regard to the content-neutrality argument]." Tribe seemed to have forgotten by mid-1990 that he had written to Congress on October 12, 1989, *after* the FPA had been passed in this final form, to urge defeat of the amendment because there was a "reasonable basis" for believing that the Court "will" or "might well" uphold the FPA. (Even more absurdly, after the Court struck down the FPA and the constitutional amendment was defeated in Congress in June 1990, Tribe declared that he hoped to "get as little credit as possible" for the FPA, which he now termed an "abomination." In September 1990 Tribe publicly confessed that his role in backing the FPA in 1989 had "probably" been unprincipled and characterized the 1990 Supreme Court ruling "an extremely hopeful sign for the future of free speech.")[21]

The overwhelming consensus that the Court would strike down the FPA was based on the perception that the FPA could not possibly pass constitutional muster because it was so obviously intended to suppress dissent rather than to protect the flag's "physical integrity" (whatever that could mean as a "nonsuppressive" congressional concern) and because, additionally, its key terms were so vague and it so clearly was not "content neutral," for example, by excluding "patriotic" flag burning but including maintaining flags on the floor, even under protective glass. In this context, most legal observers felt that the inherent weaknesses in the FPA were devastatingly highlighted by the defense briefs. Cole's lead brief especially was viewed as extremely comprehensive, well-written, and effective. Thus a *New York Times* legal reporter wrote that Cole's brief was "dazzling" and quoted one of Solicitor General Starr's assistants as characterizing it as "the best he'd ever read," and a *Legal Times* analysis of the FPA appeal said that the Cole brief had "methodically dispatched each thin argument left to be made on behalf on the ailing statute."[22]

Although the flag burners' briefs were viewed as bolstering an inherently strong case against the FPA, the general perception was that the legal arguments of those defending a congenitally deficient statute only further weakened the case for it because their arguments seemed to be transparently incorrect, irrelevant, or grasping at legal straws, as well as often in almost chaotic conflict with each other. The wildly varying positions taken by the amicus briefs in support of the FPA were widely viewed as a clear sign of the fundamental weakness of the government's case, as was Starr's original brief, which essentially asked the Court to repudiate its barely year-old *Johnson* ruling and find the FPA constitutional largely because Congress had passed it and because flag desecration should be excluded from First Amendment protection. In a May 1990 interview and a November 1990 published article, *Baltimore Sun* reporter Lyle Denniston termed Starr's position "desperate" and "nearly hopeless" and declared completely "unrealistic" Starr's apparent hope that the Court would find flag desecration not protected expression, less than a year after that position had been "lost." Former House of Representatives legal counsel Stanley Brand publicly characterized Starr's original brief in May 1990 as "outrageous" because the Bush administration had a "job to do" (i.e., to defend the FPA), which, if carried out in good faith, required more than a "wink" and a decision to only "sort of defend the law."[23]

In a 1990 interview, lawyers from the New York law firm of Debevoise & Plimpton, which submitted the organizations' brief in support of the flag burners, denounced Starr's argument as asking the Court to abandon its role of judicial review and automatically to uphold all congressional enactments. Thus Andrew Montgomery argued that what Starr was "really saying is the enactment of the statute presents a compelling interest to the Court in the form of a national consensus," but "if you take that argument seriously the next step is to uphold every statute ever passed by Congress and not vetoed by the President." Similarly, Montgomery's legal colleague James Goodale termed Starr's position a "radical" and "absolutely shocking" repudiation of the doctrine of judicial review and one that was "inconsistent with the notion of three separate but equal branches of government and inconsistent with everything the flag stands for."

With the quasi-exception of the Biden amicus brief, which made the strongest "content-neutrality" argument for the FPA's constitutionality and which a *Legal Times* account termed the "most cogent" defense of the law, most of the pro-FPA amicus briefs attracted only scorn from both independent and partisan observers of the flag desecration controversy. For example, in a 1990 interview, a Justice Department official who was involved in the legal defense of the FPA characterized the Senate brief as "much worse" than the previous Senate district court brief, labeled the House brief "completely absurd," and termed it "ironic" that none of the three government briefs in support of the FPA (the two congressional briefs plus Starr's original brief) had stressed the "content-neutrality" position that was supposed to have been the basic legal justification for the statute. This source added that the content-neutrality defense was a "bullshit argument that wouldn't have changed anything, but it was the strongest argument available."

With regard to New York governor Cuomo's brief, which urged the Supreme Court to uphold the FPA to avoid a constitutional amendment, *Baltimore Sun* reporter Denniston, in a 1990 interview, termed such an overt political argument "a little clumsy." The July 23, 1990, issue of *Legal Times* quoted a legal observer who requested anonymity as terming the ten-page Cuomo brief a "press release" that was the "best evidence" yet that the New York governor was "still interested in the presidency." Similarly, defense lawyer Kunstler, in a 1991 interview, said that Cuomo had been "just whoring around, trying to get on the 'right' side of the issue. It was a terrible brief, simply awful as a legal document."

In an extraordinary article previewing the oral argument, the May 14 issue of *Legal Times* presented a devastating account of the confusion in the ranks of the FPA's legal defenders. The article reported that they had been "plunged into disarray" and "continuing chaos," their "arguments rendered contradictory and its advocates set to squabbling among themselves." The article indicated that the House and Senate legal counsels were barely talking to each other as the result of a "long-running, low temperature feud" and that the law firm that wrote Biden's brief was not consulted by either of the congressional lawyers. Asked about the varying legal theories advanced by the pro-FPA briefs, Senate counsel Davidson could only respond, "If you put a group of lawyers in separate rooms to defend the same law, you get five different products. That's just how it goes."

One of the strangest aspects of the media coverage of the FPA appeal was that, with very few exceptions, such as the coverage in the *Legal Times,* virtually no press accounts even reported, much less commented on, how dramatically the government's defense of the statute had changed over time, from a complete rejection of its constitutionality by Assistant Attorney General Barr, to its eventual complete embrace by Solicitor General Starr ("from Barr to Starr"). In particular, the press virtually ignored how Starr, who had at first rejected the "content-neutrality" argument while urging the Supreme Court to "revisit" the *Johnson* ruling and to defer to Congress, stressed the "content-neutrality" defense at oral argument and urged the Court to uphold the FPA on the grounds that Congress had deferred to the Court in drafting it. Thus House legal counsel Steven Ross, in an interview on the day following the May 14 oral argument, declared:

> To my mind, nobody had picked up yet on the biggest story on the defense of the statute which is the incredible evolution of the Justice Department's position. You start with Day One, which is Bill Barr saying there's no way a statute can be constitutional all the way over to what has to be considered a full-fledged and vigorous defense of the statute by Ken Starr [at oral argument], including advocating down the line the congressional position that Congress sought and was successful in enacting a content-neutral protection of the physical integrity of the flag consistent with *Texas v. Johnson* and the earlier flag cases. The evolution of the department's position continued up to and including yesterday, as they were much more supportive of the congressional position than even their briefs were, and that to me is truly strange.

In a 1990 interview conducted shortly after the Supreme Court struck down the FPA and the House of Representatives rejected the proposed flag desecration constitutional amendment, Solicitor General Starr agreed that his position on the FPA had changed considerably over time. "My thinking did evolve," Starr said, adding that this "should come as no surprise. Doctrines evolve. Sometimes it takes the Court twenty and thirty years to reach these doctrines. We didn't have much time at all, and we're in the situation of having to move forward on about one hundred fronts at the same time." He stated that, although at first he was not convinced that the statute was a truly "content-neutral" law, over time he became convinced that it was a "sincere," "respectful," and constitutionally adequate congressional response to various "caveats and disclaimers" that the Court had included in *Texas v. Johnson*, which "didn't need" to be there if the justices had intended to indicate that all flag desecrations laws were invalid.

Starr indicated that he had modified his thinking considerably because he was heavily influenced by the congressional and the Biden amicus briefs and also because his original briefs had suffered from the press of time and other business in his office, especially as his staff had little or no experience in handling flag desecration cases and "there was not the opportunity for much institutional deliberation." Starr contrasted the "relative novelty" of the flag desecration issue for his office with cases that more typically arose, involving "areas of law in which you're dealing time after time—antitrust, environmental law—where we have reservoirs of expertise, the benefit of people who have just thought deeply, reflected deeply, and been through a lot of cases. So we were new, this was a new issue, we had a very short period of time."

Under these circumstances, Starr continued, he heavily modified his thinking about the case, especially as the result of his reading the House, Senate, and Biden briefs. "I took all that work product very, very seriously, reflected deeply, and profited from it," he said. Starr added that he personally favored flag desecration legislation, and that, from a constitutional standpoint, he viewed flag desecration as differing from protected First Amendment expression, above all because it was "conduct," which did not deserve the same protection as "speech," and because such acts did not provide the "particularized" message the Supreme Court's 1974 *Spence* ruling suggested was required for full constitutional treatment as "expression." "If I were a legislator," he related, "I would be inclined to protect the physical integrity of the flag, even though believing fervently in the First Amendment. It does seem to me that there is a fairly powerful distinction between conduct and speech" and that it "certainly has been the law traditionally" that government interests in regulating conduct have been regarded as stronger than in restricting speech. Starr termed the flag "that one symbol of unity in a terribly fractured society with so many points of friction" and "the only symbol that does in fact draw us together," and therefore he termed it "understandable" that the community would view flag desecration as "morally offensive."

Essentially adopting the constitutional theory originated by Harvard law professor Laurence Tribe to defend the FPA, Starr added, "My own thinking is that Congress should have the power to protect the physical integrity of things that are special to us, not to protect them from criticism," but because flags, like churches, gravesites, and bald eagles, are

> special to us and Congress doesn't need a health and public safety reason to justify protecting the moral sensibilities of the community against conduct, against action. I can embrace the proposition that Congress can neutrally protect things that are important to us, as long as they don't care what the thinking [of the "desecrator"] is, whether it is mindless spitting on the Tomb of the Unknown Soldier, whether you do it as an act of protest or just as an act of extraordinary insensitivity or just mindlessness. "We don't want you doing that because it's important to us. We don't want you shooting the bald eagle for sport or as an expression of protest. We don't want people desecrating graves and houses of worship for mindlessly nihilistic reasons or because of their very well thought out views that this is the way to effectively express their disapproval." All that Congress is saying [in the FPA] is, "Please, say anything you want, be as vile as you want, but don't burn the flag."

When asked how flag desecration could be analogized to the destruction of churches or bald eagles because destroying infinitely reproducible flags seems "purely expressive," rather than involving damage to unique objects, Starr responded, "In looking at the great [Supreme Court] symbolic speech cases, I took rather seriously—and I don't think the Court did [in striking the FPA down]—a limitation in the law that I think is very sensible, and that is that there must be an intent to convey a particularized message." According to Starr, the 1990 defendants had attempted, according to their own statements, to express a "remarkable cacophony of views" and were "just railing about everything under the sun, seemingly, including things about which the government has no responsibility." In the face of such conduct, Starr continued, "I just sort of throw up my hands and say, 'This is nihilistic.'" Such flag burnings amounted to little more than an "attention-getting device," he contended, so that people will "come over and then they may listen to what you have to say," rather than the expression of any particular views.

Asked if a similar argument could not also justify the banning of all "unclear" forms of expression, including ordinary speech and writing, Starr maintained,

"This is conduct, we're in a different [legal] world than pure speech, pure communications, the written word or the spoken word." He added that he had "no problem" with the 1943 *Barnette* ruling, which outlawed compulsory flag salutes in public schools, but maintained that this precedent was not applicable to flag desecration legislation because "I draw a very clear doctrinal difference between government compulsion—'You must do something'—as opposed to 'You must not do something.'" With regard to whether a key rationale for the *Barnette* doctrine—that popular outrage could not justify outlawing highly unpopular expression—posed problems for his argument that the Supreme Court should be swayed by the very fact that Congress had enacted the FPA, Starr maintained that his position reflected both "my sense of institutional respect" and the Court's own past suggestions that congressional determinations of constitutionality were entitled to considerable deference. "When one reads the legislative record," he added, "one cannot but be taken by the fact that there was very thoughtful scholarly comment, and scholarly debate within Congress itself, that 'We really are not doing violence at all to our system of free expression. It is completely consistent with that system of free expression to protect the physical integrity of the flag.' That was the judgment made by the Congress, and the Court, I think, would be wise to give great respect to that judgment."

In a separate interview conducted on the same day that Starr was interviewed, his deputy solicitor general, John Roberts, termed the flag burning case "very interesting," "fascinating," and "fun," but added, "Like every case, I was disappointed because we didn't win," especially because "I had actually become convinced that we had a very good chance of changing the [Supreme Court] lineup [in comparison with the *Johnson* outcome]." Roberts said that he felt that Starr's office had done a "very good job" in "vigorously" defending the FPA, especially in the "delicate" and "very difficult" situation created by Barr's 1989 congressional testimony against it. Roberts termed the 1990 case "institutionally fascinating because of the fact that the Department had counseled against it and then was defending it" and politically and doctrinally "interesting" because of the "cloud on the horizon of a constitutional amendment" and "what was going on up on the [Capitol] hill." He added, "The whole thing I just found interesting as a political science matter."

Roberts said that his only regret was that former solicitor general Charles Fried had not filed an amicus brief in support of the Texas law at issue in the *Johnson* case because such an intervention "may have been enough to get just that one more [Supreme Court] vote," while "coming in later when things are sort of chiseled in stone" and having "a pretty damning precedent [of *Texas v. Johnson*] staring us in the face" created "a much heavier burden," and "it was hard to figure out how you dislodge one more vote to get it to turn around."

With regard to Starr's argument that passage of the FPA demonstrated a "compelling" government interest in protecting the flag, Roberts contended that the point was not that the Court should simply rubber-stamp all acts of Congress, but rather that the FPA reflected a national legislative consensus (as opposed to the state law involved in *Johnson*) and also that it provided a response to the Court's statement in *Johnson* that it had no way of determining "which symbols were sufficiently special" to warrant a "unique status," especially since the Constitution established no "separate juridical category" for the "American flag alone." According to Roberts:

> The Court can probably second-guess typical sort of cost-benefit analysis that goes into a lot of regulations, but when it's the importance to the nation of a unifying symbol that represents shared values, Congress is the body together with the president to determine what's important to the nation and I think the message they sent was quite clear: "Protecting the flag from defilement is important to this nation. Now you Court tell us whether or not we can do that under the Constitution, and that's emphatically the duty and province of the courts to say what the law is, but don't think that in your analysis that you can explain it away by just saying it's not a big deal, it's not important. In the scales, we're telling you that this is important, you may tell us that it doesn't matter because the First Amendment is more important, to oversimplify, but don't say that this isn't important to us."

In general, Roberts (unsurprisingly) agreed with most of the views expressed by his boss (Starr). For example, he endorsed the argument that flag desecration was "quite ambiguous expressive conduct" because "we don't really know what these people are trying to say," and the "speech component of this conduct is very minimal," therefore limiting its communicative content to "getting your attention, sort of like drumming up business." Roberts also expressed his personal views about the wisdom of outlawing flag desecration in terms similar to Starr's, declaring:

> To me, flag burning is like if you were to take a picture out of your wallet with your wife and kids and I was just to spit on it and stamp on it. That's not an invitation to argument, to discussion, to debate, it's an invitation to fight and I think we ought as a nation to be able to protect that one symbol of what we mean as a nation.

Despite his general agreement with Starr, on several points Roberts offered significantly different views. For example, although Starr clearly indicated that he felt that his efforts were harmed by the very expedited briefing and hearing schedule that he had requested, Roberts said, "We had plenty of time to develop our arguments. It didn't strike me as the sort of thing that would benefit from further percolation." Also, although Starr readily agreed that his thinking about the FPA, and especially about its alleged "content neutrality," had "evolved" considerably over time, Roberts said he was "not sure" that "evolution" was "quite accurate" as an explanation of the changing stress in Starr's briefs, as opposed to emphasizing

> different approaches at different times. It's not unusual, for example, to think that one line or argument is more compelling written, and to emphasize that in your brief, and then in oral argument decide that it may be more important to hit on another theme. I don't know that that means that one approach has won over the other argument as that it's a different presentation of both of them.

Roberts also seemed somewhat skeptical of the force of the "content-neutrality" argument that Starr indicated he had grown to accept. Thus, in explaining why Starr had brushed aside this argument in his original briefs, Roberts said, "If you read a lot of the testimony, the content-neutrality argument has some serious vulnerabilities and there's always a danger that if you lead with a main argument that has at least some troubling aspects to it that you're going to get into trouble." Roberts added that he was "not saying at all that I disagree" with the argument, but "I'm saying that it's problematic enough that I can see a decision being made not to highlight it." Finally, although Starr had mentioned, in his Supreme Court oral arguments, the burning of a McDonald's flag by the Seattle flag burners as evidence that they were engaged more in "mindless nihilism" than in serious political expression, Roberts expressed a more relaxed point of view, declaring with a broad smile, "One thing that really made my blood boil was when they actually burned the McDonald's flag. That's going too far under any system."

Although most of those who followed the flag controversy carefully were convinced that, at least if legal grounds proved controlling, the Supreme Court would strike down the FPA and that a politically charged congressional endorsement of a constitutional amendment would quickly follow, during the period between the mid-May oral argument and the Court's announcement of its decision four weeks later the political atmosphere in Washington was thick with bizarre scenarios suggesting that both sides in the flag desecration controversy were, or, at any rate, should be, plotting devious paths toward their real objectives. For example, in a May 21 *New York Times* article, Supreme Court reporter Linda Greenhouse spelled out publicly what Washington insiders were saying privately: she declared that the flag desecration controversy was becoming like a "plunge down the rabbit hole into an Alice in Wonderland where nothing is quite what it seems and everything becomes curiouser and curiouser." Greenhouse noted that supposedly it was conservatives and Republicans who most wanted to protect the flag, yet in fact many of them hoped that the Court would strike down the FPA so that Congress would approve the constitutional amendment and send it to the states "in time to make ratification an issue in state legislative races in the fall." Conversely, she noted, liberals and Democrats supposedly were most concerned about civil liberties and were publicly calling upon the Court to strike down the statute, yet many of them secretly hoped that the Court would uphold the FPA to avoid those same expected political consequences. The Greenhouse scenario was largely seconded in comments offered in May 1990 by a well-informed civil liberties activist who reported that many of his liberal friends "on the [Capitol] hill are hoping the Supreme Court upholds the statute because they think the [1968 federal flag desecration] statute wasn't a big factor in life before *Johnson* and won't be after, but what will be a factor will be the constitutional amendment that's threatening, plus we might really get drilled politically."

Speculation about how the political pressures surrounding the flag protection controversy might affect the Court was one of the most common subjects of conversation in political circles during May and early June. Thus Harvard law professor Alan Dershovitz wrote that he could "easily imagine" that one of the justices in the *Johnson* majority would vote to uphold the FPA "thinking that a constitutional amendment would be even worse." Georgetown University law professors Louis Seidman and Mark Tushnet suggested that, primarily as a result of political considerations, there might even be a wholesale switch on the Court, with those who had struck down the Texas law voting for the FPA (which they privately would view as unconstitutional) to stave off the alternative of an amendment (which they would see as legally and politically far worse) and the *Johnson* dissenters voting against the FPA (which they privately would applaud) in hopes of spurring the drive for an amendment (which they would see as a stronger political victory).[24]

Few observers felt that the Court would be so evidently and overtly affected by crass political considerations, but most of those who followed the Court closely suggested that the justices would not be entirely oblivious to the political implications of their forthcoming decision. For example, in a May 1990 interview,

National Law Journal Supreme Court reporter Marcia Coyle suggested that political controversy inevitably has "some impact" on the Court because "every justice on the Court is aware that their power and their authority relies so much on the respect of the American public" and therefore "they have to stay in touch with what the people think and feel." Coyle added, "it doesn't mean they have to rubber stamp," especially because "they truly are there for life and pretty well insulated from the mob. I'm sure they'd be concerned, but I don't think it would determine what direction they took."

Some observers speculated that the Court would be negatively affected by the overtones of political intimidation implied in the attempt to overturn the *Johnson* ruling via the FPA with the threat of an amendment in the background if the Court failed to uphold it. For example, in late May, *Legal Times* Supreme Court reporter Tony Mauro suggested, only half-jokingly, that the Court would be so insulted by what he viewed as the legally threadbare arguments advanced to uphold the FPA that the justices might even hand down a one-line decision striking it down, with the addendum, "For more information, please see *Texas v. Johnson*."[25]

Similarly, two attorneys associated with the New York law firm of Debevoise & Plimpton, who had helped to write the 1989 and 1990 Supreme Court organizations' amicus briefs supporting the constitutional rights of flag burners, suggested in a May 1990 interview that the Court would surely strike down the FPA, if only to uphold its own independence, as well as the principles of precedent and consistency in legal interpretation. James Goodale said that a decision to uphold the FPA would be almost inconceivable because for the Court to "completely disregard" its own precedent, "less than a year after deciding exactly this issue and using what would have to be seen as a technicality," would so clearly indicate that the Court collapsed under political pressure that it would mark a "low point in the Court's history" and create a "disastrous constitutional crisis." For this reason, Goodale added, he had heard speculation about a possible 9-0 decision striking down the FPA because some observers felt that "those who dissented last year will have to join the Court because now there is something else at issue, not just whether or not this statute is constitutional, but how the Court interprets its own precedents that are less than a year old."

Goodale's legal colleague Andrew Montgomery similarly declared that upholding the FPA would be so "completely unprincipled" that it would "fly in the face of basic principles of civics that we live by" and "introduce an element of anarchy" into the legal system. Montgomery added, "I'll go on record as one of those who entertains the possibility of a 9-0 decision reaffirming the principles in *Johnson*." Even some supporters of the FPA harbored similar fears. Thus in an interview conducted in June 1991, one year after the Court had struck down the

FPA by a 5-4 vote, a key Democratic SJC staffer who had helped organize support for the statute confessed, in response to a query if he had feared that the Court might react negatively to feeling "pushed around," "My fear was that the Court would feel that way and would vote 9-0 to strike the statute. That was my nightmare, and we [the Democratic congressional leadership] would have been badly embarrassed by that."

Although some observers thus suggested that the Supreme Court might incline in one direction or another as a result of the political controversy surrounding the FPA case, *Baltimore Sun* Supreme Court reporter Lyle Denniston, who has covered the Court since 1958, contended in a May 1990 interview conducted in the Court's basement press room that the justices would be unaffected by such pressures. Denniston declared:

> Most judges that I know, and I think the ones upstairs, who I know fairly well, don't think politically much of the time. It's astounding to me at times how apolitical they are. I think most of them have, at least in my conversations with them, a kind of ninth grade civics appreciation of the American polity. I would bet if you sat down with any justice and said, "I can tell you right now that if you strike down the FPA there's going to be a constitutional amendment, and maybe before the end of next year," the reaction would be, "Interesting, but not my bag [concern]." If you told them that members of Congress were going to vote on this issue primarily and maybe exclusively because of the threat of a thirty-second soundbite by an opponent who could say, "You're not in favor of the flag," they would think you were describing another political order, not this one. I am as convinced as much as I am of anything that the soundbite phenomenon is going to make a difference in amending the Constitution for the first time to take away a form of political freedom, but they wouldn't believe you upstairs if you told them that because it's not ninth grade civics. They expect that senators are going to vote as attentive, careful, considerate members of the nation's legislature and you can't disabuse them of that.

News from the Flag Burning Fronts, February–June 1990

While attorneys Starr and Kunstler presented their positions on the FPA to the Supreme Court justices on May 14, small groups of supporters and opponents of the flag burners demonstrated outside the court, outnumbered by police, reporters, and photographers, in what the *Los Angeles Times* characterized as a "carnival" atmosphere. The two sides exchanged taunts and slogans and the flag burners' supporters engaged in a wide variety of acts of flag desecration such as the burning of small paper flags and the trampling of cloth flags. No legal consequences followed, even though the picture of one demonstrator chewing on the pieces of a ripped-up flag appeared on the front pages of newspapers across the country on May 15, complete with her name. Some of the opponents of the flag burners, representing the conservative Young Americans for Freedom, wore red plastic fire hats and carried buckets of water (presumably to ward off flag burnings), flags, and large signs proclaiming slogans such as "Flagburning is a hate crime" and "Flagburning is not ecological." They also periodically sang "God Bless America" and shouted at their opponents slogans such as "Communists go home!" and "We love America, how about you?" Meanwhile, their opponents, most of whom seem to have been affiliated with the RCP, the RCYB, or ECAFAL, responded with chants like "The flag is their gag but it can't keep us silent" and "Red, white and blue, we spit on you."[26]

Aside from the flag desecration incidents associated with the May 14 Supreme Court hearing, there were only a scattering of such incidents and court proceedings related to flag desecration between the period of the district court hearings in mid-February and the Supreme Court's decision striking down the FPA on June 11. On February 26, a federal appeals court in St. Louis upheld, by a 2-1 vote, the conviction of and already served three-month jail term of former navy reservist William Cary for violating the 1968 federal flag desecration law (since amended by the 1989 FPA) by throwing a burning flag at a Minneapolis federal building during a March 1988 demonstration against American policy in Central America. According to witnesses at the demonstration, five other flags were also burned, but none of the others was accompanied by violence (or led to prosecutions). Although the appeals court held that Cary's act occurred within a "context of violence" and therefore was unaffected by the *Johnson* ruling, the decision was bewildering because it was virtually universally agreed by politicians and legal observers that, whatever the fate of the 1989 FPA, the 1968 federal law had been rendered unconstitutional under the *Johnson* decision because it outlawed only acts of flag desecration intended to "cast contempt" on the flag. Dissenting Judge Theodore McMillan voted to overturn the conviction on exactly such grounds, arguing that the 1968 law was clearly "aimed at suppressing" dissenting "communication." His dissent was eventually upheld in October 1990, when the Supreme Court effectively ordered that the case be dismissed in compliance with its June 1990 *U.S. v. Eichman* ruling striking down the FPA.[27]

Among new flag desecration incidents reported during the first five months of 1990, three youths were arrested in Midland, Texas, in late February for violating Texas's 1989 post-*Johnson* "content-neutral" flag desecration law for allegedly writing and painting obscenities and heavy-metal rock band symbols on Texas and U.S. flags. After the *Eichman* decision, one of them was prosecuted to test the continued legality of the Texas law, but the case was dismissed by the Texas courts, and in October 1992, the U.S. Supreme Court refused to hear an appeal from the lower court rulings. On March 28, four students at Indiana University in Bloomington burned a flag after a visit by Scott Tyler, the Chicago "flag on the floor" artist and defendant in the *Eichman* case. Flag burnings were also reported during protests against visits by President Bush to Dearborn, Michigan, on April 3, and to Portland, Oregon, on May 21, and, in connection with a racially charged murder trial in New York on May 8 and May 15. The May 8 New York flag burning, which was featured on the front page of the May 9 *New York Daily News,* apparently involved RCP members, thirteen of whom were arrested on the same day on various charges for blocking a courthouse entrance. The May 15 New York incident involved a man who identified himself only as "the Reparation and Compensation for Slavery Man." At the request of photographers, he burned a flag on two separate occasions as he shouted slogans against racism, while the police looked on without taking any action.[28]

On April 17, an attempt by ten to fifteen atheists at the University of Texas in Austin to burn a flag was foiled by four hundred angry counterdemonstrators, who were armed with fire extinguishers, water bottles, and signs bearing slogans like "Pray for Rain" and "America—Love It or Leave It." The counterdemonstrators blasted the protesters with their fire extinguishers and wrested the flag from the atheists' hands as they tried to ignite it, in what became a near-riot which ended only when police escorted both groups of demonstrators away from the scene. Perhaps the most unusual incident of flag desecration during the first half of 1990 was reported in mid-May in Chicago, where on several occasions so-called free speech guerrillas placed "outlaw" rolls of toilet paper in city hall bathrooms. The toilet paper bore pictures of flags, along with the texts of the First Amendment and the city's own overturned 1989 flag desecration law.[29]

In Chicago, an echo of the 1989 "flag on the floor" controversy suggested—ambiguously but correctly, as it turned out—that public interest in the flag desecration controversy had significantly diminished. SAIC president Anthony Jones announced in late April 1990 that Scott Tyler's 1989 flag exhibit would be banned from inclusion in a special display of art by graduating SAIC students on the grounds that "it is no longer a First Amendment issue" but rather a matter of not allowing "the same piece to disrupt an exhibit showing the work of 165 other students." In a June 1990 interview, Jones said that the "prevailing argument was the right of the student body to have its work shown in an environment where there was not a disruption of the academic process." According to Jones:

> I got some students stopping me on the street, and parents too, saying that they didn't agree with my decision but they understood exactly why I had done it, but the bulk of the commentary was that it was the right thing to do. The tone set last year had changed. It's a classic, "That was then and this is now." I would say that 99.9 percent of the people with whom I'm in contact before making the decision and after have understood the decision.

Although on the surface, Jones's decision might be interpreted as reflecting an increasingly repressive climate concerning the flag desecration issue—Tyler's exhibit had been allowed and defended by SAIC a year earlier—probably the real significance of the SAIC "flag on the floor flap II" was that it barely rated a mention in the local press, was entirely ignored by the national press, and aroused only a statement of "regret" but "understanding" from the same SAIC faculty and student leaders who had vociferously defended Tyler's exhibition rights during the previous commotion. Jones said, in the June 1990 interview, that he thought much of the public disinterest was reflected by a reporter who told him, "'I'm sick and tired of Scott Tyler and that damn flag.' People just got sick and tired of it." This reaction provided a foretaste of what was to come in response to the Supreme Court's *Eichman* ruling in early June: as with the Tyler furor, the second time around the flag burning controversy was treated by much of the public as a summer "rerun" that simply did not arouse the same intensity of interest as had the original controversy.[30]

Several state legislative actions in early 1990 suggested that interest and sentiment about flag burning was still running high in some quarters. In Pennsylvania, where the Senate had endorsed a flag desecration constitutional amendment by a 49–1 vote in June 1989, the House of Representatives acted likewise by a 181–11 vote on March 21, 1990, and at the same time approved, by a 189–4 vote, a formal resolution condemning Carolyn Marvin, the University of Pennsylvania professor who had burned a flag during her civil liberties class in September. But a proposal by a Democratic member of the Pennsylvania House to make assaulting a flag desecrator subject only to a $1 fine (instead of the normal maximum penalty for assault of ten years in jail and a $25,000 fine) got nowhere after another Democratic state legislator said passing the proposal would make the House "a laughingstock." Similar measures also failed in the Colorado, Georgia, and Tennessee legislatures, but in Louisiana, a proposal to lower to $25 the fine for assaulting flag desecrators (as opposed to the ordinary penalty for "simple battery" of six months in jail and a $500 fine) passed the House by a 54-39 vote in late May. Among the leading backers of the Louisiana bill was Republican representative David Duke, a former Ku Klux Klan leader who later became an unsuccessful 1992 candidate for governor of Louisiana and president of the United States. The bill's author, Democratic representative James David Cain, explained, "I'm tired of marijuana-puffing hippies desecrating our flag," and his Democratic colleague Frank Patti complained that the bill failed to go far enough; "If I saw somebody burning the flag, I would stomp the hell out of him" and "they ought to be deported."[31]

Supreme Court Strikes Down
the Flag Protection Act

On June 11, 1990, the Supreme Court handed down its decision in *U.S. v. Eichman*, upholding the two district court FPA rulings by a 5-4 vote and thus striking down the statute as applied to political protesters. The ruling came less than a month after the May 14 oral argument (considerably faster than most Court opinions and reflecting a vote taken at a Court conference on May 17). The justices remained divided into the same two camps as they were in the *Johnson* holding. The majority decision—once again written by Brennan, who read portions of his opinion for six minutes before a hushed and crowded courtroom—was only about one-third as lengthy as his *Johnson* decision, which, taken together with the speed of the ruling and the hostile questions directed at Starr in the oral argument, suggested to some observers that the Court majority was truly unimpressed with the government's arguments. For example, in a June 11 newscast, National Public Radio Supreme Court reporter Nina Totenberg noted that the "second go-round" over the flag desecration controversy had apparently not been "difficult" for the Court. She added that typically the justices required three to nine months to decide a case, whereas in the *Eichman* decision the Court took less than four weeks to say in effect, "We meant what we said last year," that "we can't put people in jail for expressing their political protest with flag burning." In a 1990 interview conducted soon after the *Eichman* ruling was handed down, even Deputy Solicitor General John Roberts admitted to having been a "little bit" surprised by the speed of the decision. He commented, "I guess the Court took seriously, as we did, the directive from Congress to expedite things, because they certainly did."

According to a 1991 interview with a Supreme Court clerk who served at the time of the *Eichman* ruling, the quickness of the decision did not imply any particular rebuke to the government but simply reflected the "normal course" of trying to wind up the Court's business by the end of June. The justices didn't need "months to play" with a case that was "the second time around," he said, because the *Johnson* ruling had "certainly raised similar issues." The former Court clerk added that his impression was that the justices fully expected their ruling to result in the enactment of a flag desecration constitutional amendment, "but I don't think there was any justice for which that kind of consideration would affect the way they would vote. It was just treated as another case: 'That's it and we'll let the rest of the country worry about whether it's important.' My sense is that extraneous political factors were not involved."

Brennan's *Eichman* opinion followed the outlines of his *Johnson* ruling and the two district court FPA opinions. Brennan first declared that the Court majority declined to accept Starr's invitation to "reconsider our rejection in *Johnson* of the claim that flag burning as a mode of expression, like obscenity or 'fighting words' does not enjoy the full protection of the First Amendment." Next, he wrote that the government's asserted interests in the FPA of protecting the flag's "status as a symbol of our Nation and certain national ideals" was related "to the suppression of free expression" and that therefore this interest could not justify "infringement on First Amendment rights" unless the statute could survive the "most exacting scrutiny" and "compelling" government interest tests spelled out in the 1988 case of *Boos v. Barry* as the hurdle that such infringements must meet to survive constitutionally. While conceding that the new law, unlike the Texas statute at issue in *Johnson* with its "seriously offends" language, "contains no explicit content-based limitation on the scope of prohibited conduct," the majority held that the law must nonetheless be tested by this high level of scrutiny because it suffered from "the same fundamental flaw" that doomed the Texas law: "It suppresses expression out of concern for its likely communicative impact," and this suppression could not be "justified without reference to the content of the regulated speech."[32]

The Court majority held that the FPA's suppressive purpose was clear, not only from the government's own asserted interest in protecting the flag's symbolic value but also from the "precise language" of the law. Brennan said that this language "confirms Congress's interest in the communicative impact of flag destruction" by outlawing only conduct, such as mutilating and defiling flags, which "unmistakably connotes disrespectful treatment of the flag and suggests a focus on those acts likely to damage the flag's symbolic value," while simultaneously exempting disposal of worn flags in ways "traditionally associated with patriotic respect for the flag," as well as allowing the flying of flags in storms and "other conduct that threatens the physical integrity of the flag, albeit in an indirect manner unlikely to communicate disrespect." While accepting the House of Representatives argument that the flag is "emblematic of the Nation as a sovereign entity" and that the government had a legitimate interest in preserving this function, the Court declared that the House "does not, and cannot, explain" how the law "is designed to advance this asserted interest in maintaining the association between the flag and the Nation" because flag burning "does not threaten to interfere with this association in any way."

In rejecting the government's "invitation" to reconsider its key *Johnson* holding—namely that the government's interest in protecting the symbolic value of the flag could not justify infringing First Amendment rights—in view of "Congress' recent recognition of a purported 'national consensus' favoring a prohibition against flag burning," Brennan bluntly declared that "any suggestion that the Government's interest in suppressing speech becomes more weighty as popular opposition to that speech grows is foreign to the First Amendment." Recognizing that flag desecration is "deeply offensive to many," he pointed out that the same could be said about "virulent ethnic and religious epithets," "vulgar repudiations of the draft," and "scurrilous caricatures," all of which the Court had previously held to be constitutionally protected forms of expression. Brennan concluded the majority opinion by quoting his own statement from *Johnson:* "If there is any bedrock principle underlying the First Amendment, it is that the Government may not prohibit the expression of an idea simply because society finds the idea itself offensive or disagreeable." He added, "Punishing desecration of the flag dilutes the very freedom that makes this emblem so revered, and worth revering."

Justice Stevens wrote a dissent on behalf of himself and his three colleagues in the minority (Rehnquist, O'Connor, and White). Although Stevens's dissent was considerably more tempered than had been his and Rehnquist's dissents in *Johnson,* it reiterated the basic claim offered earlier that the unique importance of the flag, such as its role in symbolizing "the ideas of liberty, equality and tolerance," justified infringing upon political expression to protect its "symbolic value," especially when there was no "interference with the speaker's freedom to express his or her ideas by other means." Stevens also maintained that the FPA was not directed at the suppression of expression because while the expressions of flag desecrators were "various and often ambiguous," the government's "legitimate interest in preserving the symbolic value of the flag is, however, essentially the same" and was not dependent upon "the specific content of the flag burners' speech."

In comparison with the *Johnson* dissents, Stevens's *Eichman* dissent was far calmer in tone, going well beyond even its omission of patriotic poetry and discursions into flag history (morever, he chose not to read the dissent aloud when it was handed down by the Court, in contrast to his highly unusual and emotional reading of his *Johnson* dissent). For example, unlike the near-hysterical tone of Rehnquist's *Johnson* dissent (Rehnquist did not write a separate dissent in *Eichman*), Stevens concluded in his *Eichman* dissent that the case "comes down to a question of judgment" and conceded that "reasonable judges may differ with respect" to the questions raised by flag desecration laws. Moreover, although in his *Johnson* dissent, Stevens had compared flag desecration to placing "graffiti on the Washington Monument," and Justice Rehnquist had compared flag burning to murder and embezzlement, in his *Eichman* dissent Stevens clearly repudiated such analogies by declaring that burning a privately owned flag "is not, of course, equivalent to burning a public building" because it "causes no physical harm to other persons or to their property" and its impact is "purely symbolic." Finally, the *Eichman* dissent delivered an extraordinary and unmistakable rebuke to President Bush and others who had appeared to seek political gain from the 1988 Pledge of Allegiance controversy and from attempts to overturn the *Johnson* ruling. Stevens lamented that the flag's integrity and value had been damaged, not only by what he termed "this Court's decision [in *Johnson*] to place its stamp of approval on the act of flag burning," but also by "those leaders who seem to advocate compulsory worship of the flag even by individuals whom it offends, or who seem to manipulate the symbol of national purpose into a pretext for partisan disputes about meaner ends."

As a result of the Eichman ruling, the charges of flag desecration brought under the FPA against the three Washington D.C., and the four Seattle defendants were dropped, but federal officials continued to press charges of destruction of federal property against the Seattle defendants in connection with their burning of the post office flag. In November 1990, the four Seattle defendants all pleaded guilty; Mark Haggerty and Jennifer Campbell were fined $100 each, while Darius Strong and Carlos Garza were each fined $225 and sentenced to three days in jail. These sentences, which represented the coda to the 1989–90 flag desecration uproar, were not even reported in the national news media, which, as discussed below, completely lost interest in the entire issue following the June 1990 congressional defeat of attempts to resurrect the failed the 1989 constitutional amendment to ban flag desecration.[33]

★

CHAPTER 9

FLAG BURNING: THE SEQUEL, JUNE 1990

The Immediate Public and Political Reaction to the Eichman *Ruling*

The *Eichman* decision touched off what some observers termed "Flag Burning: The Sequel" or "Flag Burning II," namely a renewed struggle in Congress on whether to pass a constitutional amendment to ban flag desecration. Almost all of the press accounts of the *Eichman* decision stressed its political implications. The June 12 *Chicago Tribune* account, for example, was headlined "Burning Issue for '90 Elections Is Ignited by Court's Flag Ruling," and the June 13 *Christian Science Monitor* story was bannered "Flag Desecration a Burning Issue Again in Washington." Within an hour after the *Eichman* ruling was announced, President Bush renewed his call for a constitutional amendment to prohibit flag desecration. He reiterated this position the following day, declaring that flag burning "endangers the fabric of our country" and that what the flag "encapsules is too sacred to be abused." He added, "I am all for free speech, but I am for protecting the flag from desecration. The law books are full of restrictions on free speech, and we ought to have this be one of them." Bush was quickly joined by the Republican leadership; for example, Senate Republican leader Dole endorsed the president's June 12 demand that Congress vote on the amendment before the July 4 recess and even suggested that a vote within seventy-two hours of the Court's ruling would be an appropriate Flag Day (June 14) gesture.[1]

In the House of Representatives, 171 of the 290 votes needed for the two-thirds majority required to endorse an amendment were reported committed within hours of the *Eichman* ruling, and, according to an Associated Press story distributed on June 19, 255 representatives had signed on by June 18; among senators, 34 of the needed two-thirds majority of 67 were reportedly committed immediately after the Court ruling, and the AP reported the total had reached 54 by June 18. Public opinion polls indicated strong and possibly growing support for a flag desecration amendment: a *New York Times* poll published on June 12, but conducted three weeks earlier, indicated that 83 percent wanted to outlaw flag burning, although only 50 percent indicated willingness to support a constitutional amendment, while two national polls conducted immediately following the *Eichman* ruling suggested that almost 70 percent supported an amendment.[2]

Reports from state legislatures following the *Eichman* ruling suggested strong support for an amendment in more than thirty states, out of the thirty-eight needed to ratify an amendment, with some signs of opposition in about fifteen states; however, these reports were preliminary because most state legislatures had adjourned for the year and therefore could not take up any amendment, absent special legislative sessions, until early 1991. According to an American Legion tally, by June 1990, both houses of fourteen state legislatures had urged Congress to pass an amendment, and similar proposals were pending in nine additional states. Most state legislators quoted by reporters immediately after the *Eichman* ruling indicated either strong support for the amendment or an unwillingness to buck perceived political pressures by voting against it. Washington State Republican Senate leader Jeannette Hayner said it would be "pretty hard for people to vote against it"; Kentucky Republican state Senate caucus leader Jack Trevey and Pennsylvania House Republican minority leader Robert J. Mellow both predicted easy passage in their states because the vote would be like "motherhood and apple pie." Pennsylvania House Democratic majority leader H. William DeWeese said that he would vote reluctantly for an amendment, but he admitted it would be a "political vote," which "lacks political integrity."[3]

In Louisiana, a state Senate committee responded to the *Eichman* ruling by endorsing the House-passed proposal to reduce the penalty for assaulting a flag burner to $25. In Romeoville, Illinois, the city government unanimously passed a similar resolution, which provided a $1 penalty for assaulting flag burners; however, after the ACLU threatened to challenge the measure, local officials repealed it. The Romeoville police chief reported that he had never heard of a flag burning in his twenty-one years of police work in the town, but he declared that if he ever saw any flag burners he would first "ask them to put it [the flag] down," then try to "grab it away," and if these two tactics failed, "I'd punch them."[4]

Although Democratic congressional leaders quickly indicated that they would oppose an amendment, relatively few voices were raised in active support of the *Eichman* ruling. Among them, naturally, were lawyers for the flag burners, such as

David Cole, who declared that the defense was "overjoyed" because the Court had "essentially said that the First Amendment means what it says." The flag burning defendants also hailed the ruling: Shawn Eichman termed her namesake decision "a victory, not just for the defendants, but for all those who are against forced patriotism." On Capitol Hill, for the most part only the handful of Democrats who had voted against the FPA praised the *Eichman* ruling: Senator Metzenbaum said it was "great" and "right on the mark."[5]

In the immediate aftermath of the *Eichman* ruling, most, although not all, press reports, as well as the vast majority of predictions by backers of the amendment and by independent political observers, suggested that the amendment would pass handily and rapidly. For example, a long story in the June 16 *Congressional Quarterly,* a weekly journal focused on Capitol Hill which is generally regarded as extremely reliable, was typical of the tone of most early press reports: it reported that opposition to the amendment would be "political suicide," and the headline read, "Congress Snaps to Attention Over New Flag Proposal: Proposed Constitutional Amendment on Fast Track, Could Get Through Both Chambers by July 4." On the day of the *Eichman* decision, Republican congressional leaders Dole and Michel each predicted that both houses of Congress would endorse the amendment. Michel rhetorically inquired, "Who wants to be against the flag, mother and apple pie?" Similar predictions came from a number of Democrats, including consultant Brian Lunde, who urged Democrats not to "get on the wrong side of a powerful symbol like the flag" because "down in the political trenches you don't have a chance by opposing the amendment" and "you can't possibly explain in 30 seconds." Conservative legal analyst and amendment opponent Bruce Fein termed its passage "inevitable" on June 11, while his ideological colleague and fellow columnist James Kilpatrick warned on June 14 that, absent a rapid mobilization of the "forces of reason," constitution lovers were about to be "run over" by a "stampede of bellowing politicians, out to preserve 1) the flag and 2) their jobs." Kilpatrick reported that the congressmen he had talked to wanted to oppose the amendment and viewed it as chipping away at the Bill of Rights, "but politically they dare not."[6]

Numerous opponents of the amendment suggested, like Kilpatrick, that many congressmen who personally did not like the amendment were too politically scared to oppose it, especially given the potential for "thirty-second negative ads" that could cast doubt on the patriotism of anyone who voted against it. For example, Representative Robert Matsui (D-Calif.), an amendment opponent, declared that "the 30-second TV commercial and the damage it could do to a candidate during an election year is what's motivating members to vote for the constitutional amendment" and was "almost immobilizing" Democrats and thus helping to create "almost a bankruptcy of beliefs and positions and principles and values." Democratic HJC subcommittee chairman Edwards similarly lamented that "hardly any" of his colleagues really supported the amendment, but "they are just afraid." He added, "There's a mindless stampede out there," and predicted that if Congress endorsed the amendment "the states will step all over themselves to ratify it."[7]

One Republican Philadelphia-based media consultant characterized Democrats as "absolutely freaked-out" with fear over voting against the amendment; he described them as "like they're on methamphetamines." An aide to a Democratic New Jersey congressman offered a lengthy explanation for such fears, characterizing the flag controversy as a "defining issue" and the amendment as requiring support because Republicans had in the past so successfully defined Democrats as "out of the mainstream." He added: "We have the stomach to play politics here. Only a small number of people—the ACLU, the academics—will have heart attacks if we amend the Bill of Rights. But they're not the swing voters . . . you sacrifice the flag-burners in order to stay in office and fight for child care, the homeless, the whole agenda. But it stinks."[8]

The arguments offered in 1990 for passage of an amendment were largely the same as in 1989. Amendment backers stressed that if the overwhelming majorities in both parties and both houses of Congress who voted for the FPA in 1989 truly wanted to protect the flag the only alternative left was the amendment. Voting for the amendment, its supporters argued, was not a matter of politics but of "drawing the line" at unacceptable conduct, defending the honor of the unique emblem of American liberty and all that it represented, and preventing serious harm to American society. Thus Senator Hatch said that the amendment would simply establish that "there are certain parameters we are not going to let you go beyond." According to Acting Assistant Attorney General J. Michael Luttig, who had replaced William Barr as head of the Justice Department's Office of Legal Counsel and as chief administration spokesman for the amendment, flag desecration could "break the spirit and thus cripple the cause" represented by the flag and pose "in the long run" a threat to the American "social and political fabric."[9]

The amendment would not limit First Amendment freedoms, Republican Senate leader Dole argued, because flag desecration was not speech "but conduct; malicious, stupid, irresponsible conduct." Therefore, forbidding it was little different, Representative Douglas Applegate suggested, than outlawing "chipping away at the tombstones in Arlington Cemetery." According to Senator Richard Lugar (R-Ind.), flag burnings were "wanton destructive acts" and not "an articulation of free speech" because they lacked "verbalizing" and were "not a logical exercise that comes forth with words, orally or in print." Even if flag desecration was considered a form of speech, amendment backers argued, many forms of speech, such as libel, obscenity, and "fighting words" were not protected by the First Amendment, and adding one additional exception, for what Senator Jesse Helms termed "an unlawful, unwarranted and unacceptable assault on the very meaning of America," would not seriously limit free expression. According to chief administration spokesman Luttig, the amendment would not have "any measurable impact on free speech" because it was "almost laser-like" in "only affecting the First Amendment" as interpreted in the two recent Supreme Court flag burning rulings and therefore would otherwise not affect any constitutional rights.[10]

Amendment backers maintained that its minimal impact on free speech and the lack of any problem that might be caused by authorizing each state to pass its own statute had been clearly demonstrated by the almost one-hundred-year history of state flag desecration laws. During that period, Senator Slade Gorton argued, the laws "succeeded in meeting their goals without limiting free speech in general, or vigorous and free political debate in particular." Luttig similarly declared that "no one suggests that there was a lack of robust debate" during the past century or that America "was a crazy-quilt of varying and incomprehensible" or "vague or tyrannical" flag desecration laws. If outlawing flag desecration seriously injured constitutional rights, amendment supporters asked, then why did overwhelming majorities in both parties support the FPA in 1989, and if it did not, then how could anyone consistently vote for the FPA and oppose the amendment? Thus Democratic Representative Harold Volkmer argued that it was "completely inconsistent" for those who voted for the FPA but opposed the amendment to "say last year that freedom of speech did not protect flag burning" and "this year to say that it does."[11]

Amendment supporters also attacked the "slippery slope" argument, maintaining that the flag was so unique that a flag protection amendment could not possibly pave the way for any future amendments. Thus Dole declared that no one pledged allegiance to "the Constitution or to the Presidential seal," no national holiday or national anthem honored any symbols but the flag, flags traditionally had been the only symbols whose desecration had been forbidden, and the states had "been getting along pretty well for all these years" in doing so.[12]

The 1990 Defeat of the Constitutional Amendment

Despite early, widespread predictions that the *Eichman* ruling would lead to swift congressional endorsement of a constitutional amendment, on June 21, 1990, precisely one year from the *Johnson* ruling, the amendment was killed in the House of Representatives by a vote of 254 for and 177 against (with 159 Republicans and 95 Democrats voting for the amendment and 160 Democrats and 17 Republicans voting against it), thus falling 34 votes short of the required two-thirds majority. The climactic vote followed eight hours of debate, during which almost 200 representatives spoke. When the magic number of 146 negative votes required to block a constitutional amendment registered on the House's electronic vote board at approximately 6:50 P.M., ten minutes into the allowed fifteen-minute voting period, opponents of the amendment engaged in an unusual display of exuberant emotion on the House floor, cheering, slapping each other on the back, and even hugging. Outside the House chamber, according to a 1990 interview with PAW legislative counsel John Gomperts, lobbyists opposed to the amendment similarly indulged themselves. Gomperts recalled, "There was all this hugging and backslapping going on, [conservative former solicitor general] Charles Fried hugging liberal activists, liberal activists clapping Charles Fried on the back, and we're all saying congratulations and smiles as big as your whole face. It was really extraordinary, it was really a great scene."[13]

On June 26, in a truly anticlimactic event, the amendment also failed in the Senate by a 58-42 vote (with thirty-eight Republicans and twenty Democrats voting for and thirty-five Democrats and seven Republicans voting against), thus falling nine votes short of the required two-thirds. The Senate vote followed ten hours of debate which featured repeated complaints from Democrats that Republicans were insisting on forcing a completely pointless vote on an already-dead proposal solely so that, in the words of Senator James Exon (who voted for the amendment), "the stuff of which negative 30-second commercials are used to attempt to destroy an individual" could be created "for partisan political advantage." SJC chairman Biden told his colleagues at the beginning of the debate on June 25 that the Senate was about to engage in a "futile exercise" over a "dead issue" and that he wished to "apologize to my mother for—if she is watching—wasting the taxpayers' money."[14]

The 1990 defeat of the constitutional amendment took place with extraordinary speed, with only ten days separating the June 11 *Eichman* ruling from the June 21 House vote. In fact, the pace of developments was so fast that by the time letters sent by the ACLU and the ECAFAL urging their supporters to oppose the amendment arrived in the mail the amendment had already been killed. Even as the climactic June 21 House vote was occurring, SJC chairman Biden was concluding a lengthy hearing on the Bush amendment and on his own proposal for a supposedly "content-neutral" constitutional amendment along the lines of the

1989 FPA. The Biden proposal, which received embarrassingly little support from witnesses at the hearing, was designed to forbid anyone from physically damaging the flag for any reason (aside from disposal of worn flags), as opposed to the Bush proposal, which would have authorized, according to administration officials, banning "disrespectful" damage to flags while still allowing "patriotic" damage such as pinning war medals to flags. When the results of the House vote reached Biden and he announced it to the hearing, witness Stephen Presser, a law professor at Northwestern University and supporter of the Bush proposal, lamented, "This cancels an op-ed piece that the [*Chicago*] *Tribune* editor promised to run if the amendment passes. I am sad to hear it."[15]

The Biden proposal, along with several other alternatives to the Bush amendment, was easily and quickly disposed of in Congress, as members apparently decided, after their experience with the FPA, to focus their attention on an up-or-down vote on the Bush proposal. Thus all other proposals, which were designed to attract more votes than the Bush amendment by putting forth language less directly offensive to civil libertarians, were overwhelmingly crushed by an alliance of conservatives who opposed any weakening of the Bush measure and liberals who were determined not to support any proposal which they saw as damaging First Amendment rights under camouflage designed to gain political support. For example, in various Senate votes on June 26, Biden's proposed amendment was defeated by a 93-7 vote and a proposal by Senator Thurmond to take away the Supreme Court's jurisdiction over flag desecration issues was rejected by 90-10.[16]

In the House shortly after the Bush amendment was rejected on June 21, a last-minute bill sponsored by three Democrats entitled the Flag Protection Act of 1990 was rejected 236-179; this new FPA would have outlawed flag desecration intended and "reasonably" likely to "produce imminent violence," along with stealing and damaging flags belonging to the federal government and stealing and destroying, on federal land, flags belonging to other persons. The proposal, which was supported almost exclusively by Democrats—with 105 of the 179 favorable votes coming from the 160 Democrats who voted against the Bush amendment—was accurately lampooned by Republicans as a transparent attempt to provide political "cover" for those who feared being attacked as "anti-flag" for voting against the amendment; this was especially clear because all of the acts it would forbid were already illegal under existing statutes forbidding theft and incitement to riot. Thus Representative Sensenbrenner termed the new proposed FPA a "political cop-out, a figleaf for those who are attempting to get some political cover," and House Republican leader Michel denounced the measure as "crazy" and a "sham," which outlawed acts "that are already illegal" but failed to reach most acts of flag desecration.[17]

From one perspective, "Flag Burning II" amounted to a highly condensed version of the previous year's congressional battle, simply taking ten days to defeat the amendment in 1990 instead of consuming four months as in 1989. But the lack of a serious "middle ground" FPA alternative in 1990 and the fact that the amendment was defeated only because a two-thirds "supermajority" was required, makes such a one-sentence comparison deceptive. Ultimately, the fundamental reality in both 1989 and 1990 was that in each year the president of the United States, four justices of the Supreme Court, and a majority of about 60 percent or more of both houses of Congress all indicated a willingness to repress the most fundamental of American freedoms, the right to dissent, when they found such dissent offensive personally and politically. As House assistant majority whip David Bonior noted in a 1990 interview, in both 1989 and 1990 "there was still a majority" who supported a constitutional amendment and "in essence it was the Constitution itself which saved the Bill of Rights, the fact that you needed a two-thirds vote." Therefore, American civil liberties suffered a moral defeat in both years; however, from a practical standpoint, in 1989 civil liberties also suffered a legal defeat with the passage of the FPA, if not nearly so permanent a one as an amendment would have ensured, while in 1990 the up-or-down vote and supermajority requirement for the amendment led to a legal victory for civil liberties.

This is perhaps too harsh a summary because unquestionably the tone of the congressional debate in 1990 was far less hysterical than in 1989, and, given the long-standing and widespread perception that a Supreme Court decision striking down the 1989 FPA would quickly lead to enactment of a constitutional amendment, there is no doubt that to many the defeat of the amendment felt like a moral as well as a political victory. In any case, the defeat of the amendment, given the strong, widespread, and long-lasting predictions for its passage under these circumstances, cries out for explanation. At least six major, in some cases, interrelated, factors can be pointed to for such an explanation: (1) the entire flag desecration controversy was successfully "framed" by the Democratic congressional leadership in 1990 in a manner far more favorable toward a positive civil liberties outcome than in 1989, when the Democratic leadership and leading civil liberties groups essentially threw in the civil liberties towel from the start; (2) the collapse of communism in Europe and the widespread and generally acclaimed incidents of Eastern European flag desecration between the two congressional flag debates both reduced the sense of threat posed by flag burners and made obvious that flag desecration was a powerful form of political expression; (3) Republican agitation for the amendment in 1990 was far more overtly and clumsily partisan than it had been in 1989 and this approach badly backfired on the proponents of the amendment; (4) opponents of the amendment, including key congressional Democrats, the press, and the civil liberties groups, far outorganized amendment backers in 1990, while the two most powerful elements in the pro-amendment movement, President Bush and the veterans' groups, were far less vocal and effective than they had been in 1989; (5) public interest in the flag desecration "rerun" of 1990 was far less than in 1989, and the balance of public opinion that made itself known was significantly more opposed to the amendment; and (6) particularly in the last few days before the key 1990 vote occurred in the House, a significant number of congressmen underwent an unusually searching self-examination of the sort that many felt was unnecessary in 1989 and ultimately concluded that they simply could not abide voting to, in their view, permanently stain the Constitution with a provision which their consciences told them was a violation of its spirit.

The Reframing of the
Flag Desecration Controversy in 1990

Perhaps the single greatest factor that paved the way for the defeat of the Bush amendment in June 1990 was that, largely owing to the posture of the Democratic congressional leadership, the flag desecration controversy was framed in 1990 for public and congressional consumption far differently than it had been the previous year, in a manner that made the case for "bravely doing nothing" far more intellectually and politically appealing. In 1989, when most Republicans supported the amendment and the Democratic congressional leadership supported the FPA, the issue was effectively framed, as leading Democratic liberal Don Edwards told his HJC subcommittee colleagues on July 13, as determining "just how we can ensure consistent with our constitutional freedoms that this symbol of our liberty can be protected from harm." With the issue framed this way, the concept that the flag could not or should not be "protected from harm" without violating traditional "constitutional freedoms" hardly even entered the political arena in 1989; therefore the congressional debate was effectively reduced to determining *how* a particular form of political expression would be suppressed—by constitutional amendment or by law—an agenda that, of course, guaranteed some form of suppressive outcome in advance.[18]

In contrast with this framing in 1989, following the 1990 *Eichman* decision, with the statutory option effectively eliminated, opponents of an amendment, including many who had shown no compunction about legislatively diminishing freedom of expression the year before, got "constitutional religion." Supporters of the amendment attempted to frame the 1990 question as, in Republican House leader Michel's words, "Does the Congress really want to protect the flag from desecration?" or, as *Congressional Quarterly* put it, as "flag burners vs. flag protectors." For example, Republican National Congressional Campaign Committee (RNCCC) cochairman Ed Rollins told a national television audience on June 13, "It's not a complex issue, it's a simple issue: Do you care about the flag, do you want to protect the flag or are you gonna be on the side of the flag burners?" Republicans were effectively "outframed," however, in 1990 by opponents of the amendment, who reframed the issue as a battle between two sacred, competing icons: the symbolic representation of liberty (the flag) versus the substance of liberty (the Constitution and especially the Bill of Rights). Therefore, whereas in 1989 the effective question became *how*, not *whether*, to "protect" the flag, in 1990 it instead became, "Which is more important, the flag or the Constitution?"—a formulation which, needless to say, was far more favorable to a civil liberties victory. Thus in a 1990 interview conducted shortly after the Supreme Court ruled in the *Eichman* case, Democratic representative Craig Washington, who helped lead the fight against the amendment, declared, "There's no comparing the Bill of Rights to the flag, it's like comparing a locomotive to a wagon or to a piece of wood or a rock. They're not even in the same league, phylum, class, order, species, genus." Similarly, Democratic representative Mike Synar told a national CNN television audience on June 13 that the issue was "not about the patriotism of any American" or even about flag burning, because "all of us find these stupid hooligans who burn the flag commit a repugnant act," but rather, "what this debate is about is whether after two hundred years we're going to amend the Bill of Rights for the first time, and particularly the most important amendment of that Bill of Rights, the right to protect private speech."[19]

In a 1990 interview, *Washington Post* congressional reporter Helen Dewar termed the repeated stress of 1990 Democratic amendment opponents on putting forth the Bill of Rights as a superior countericon to the flag reflected "conscious" strategy because "every Democratic speaker has taken up this theme, they're almost one-upping each other in terms of articulating it, and I keep getting the feeling that they're shaping 30-second spots themselves." PAW legislative counsel John Gomperts, supported this interpretation in another 1990 interview, noting that in 1989 Democrats "lacked an effective countersymbol" to Republicans who championed a flag amendment, whereas in 1990 Democratic foes of the amendment found this in the "magical quality" contained in the very words "the Bill of

Rights." HJC subcommittee chairman Don Edwards, who had cosponsored the 1989 FPA but led the fight in 1990 against the amendment, claimed credit for the Democratic strategy in another 1990 interview, declaring, "The magical slogan this time was one I thought up, which was, 'Leave the Bill of Rights alone.' You almost have to have a slogan around here to beat something like that [amendment]."

Democratic congressmen unquestionably effectively and repeatedly framed the 1990 debate in this manner as soon as the *Eichman* decision was handed down. Senate Democratic leader Mitchell declared that the issue was "not the flag" but "whether we are going to amend the Bill of Rights," and Senator Kennedy proclaimed, "We don't need to destroy the First Amendment to save the American flag." Subsequently, scores of Democrats developed this theme. Senator Dale Bumpers declared, "We don't need to singe the Constitution to punish the few who torch a symbol"; Representative Louis Stokes thundered that he had not risked his life in combat for "a piece of red, white and blue cloth" but "for the freedoms" it represented; and Senator John Glenn maintained that "retreating from the principles for which that flag stands" would do "more damage to the fabric of our nation than 1,000 torched flags could ever do." During the climactic House floor debate on June 21, Representative John Dingell displayed a flag and a copy of the Constitution, and declared, "The flag is precious—the Constitution is even more so." After eight hours of debate, the last words uttered were Speaker Foley's plea urging members, "Defeat this amendment. Protect the Bill of Rights."[20]

The Democratic reframing of the flag issue in 1990 found considerable resonance in the press as well as among some Republicans. Republican Representative Jim Leach explained his opposition to the amendment by declaring that the "First Amendment is the cornerstone of the Bill of Rights" and "shouldn't be toyed with," and his House and party colleague Paul Henry demanded, "Why should we burn the Bill of Rights to stop burning the flag?" In its June 12 report on the *Eichman* ruling, the *Atlanta Constitution* banner headline read, "It's Old Glory vs. First Amendment"; the June 15 *Boston Globe* characterized the debate as featuring "two of the most powerful symbols of American history—the flag and the Constitution"; and in reporting the House defeat of the amendment on June 22, *USA Today* began its story with the words, "The House put the Bill of Rights before the Stars and Stripes." Numerous editorial cartoons portrayed Bush denouncing flag burning while setting the Constitution on fire: for example, different cartoons with this same theme appeared in the June 15 editions of the *Boston Globe* and the *Seattle Post-Intelligencer* and in the June 19 *Baltimore Sun*. The depiction of the flag desecration issue in 1990 along these lines was so pervasive and so powerful that one Republican amendment proponent, Representative Frank

Horton, complained on the House floor that the debate was being unfairly "framed as one dividing political opportunists seeking to wave the flag in an election year against those acting as courageous guardians of the Constitution" and that the media had "contributed largely to the simple framing of this issue."[21]

In many cases Democratic opponents of the amendment termed the Bill of Rights "sacred" and summoned up the Constitution as a virtually untouchable and unexaminable symbol—as opposed to focusing on its *contents,* which some of these same Democrats had been willing to undercut with the FPA the previous year—just as many backers of the amendment used the flag as a "sacred" symbol while enthusiastically undercutting what it was supposed to stand for. Thus in keeping with what *Congressional Quarterly* termed the Democrats' "principal strategy" of shifting the "focus" off the flag and onto the "sanctity of the Bill of Rights," House Speaker Foley declared that though he was "repulsed" by flag burning, "this is not a time when we should rush to tamper with the most sacred political document of our country's tradition." Perhaps the most elaborated opposition to the amendment on such grounds came from Democratic Senate leader Mitchell, who delivered a lengthy statement which termed the *Eichman* ruling as "wrong" as the *Johnson* decision and labeled flag burning "offensive and obnoxious," but announced his opposition to the amendment because

> across the whole sweep of human history, there is no better, clearer, more concise, more eloquent or effective statement of the right of citizens to be free of the dictates of government than the American Bill of Rights. For 200 years it has protected the liberties of generations of Americans. During that time, the Bill of Rights has never been changed or amended. Not once. Ever. It stands today, word for word, exactly as it did when adopted two centuries ago. . . . I do not believe we should ever, under any circumstances, for any reason amend the Bill of Rights.[22]

The use of sacred constitutional images to oppose the flag desecration amendment was so common that Democratic representative C. Thomas McMillen, an amendment supporter, declared that arguments based on the concept that the Constitution should never be "tampered" with ignored the fact that the Bill of Rights was itself a series of constitutional amendments and that the Constitution provided a process for its own amendment, indicating that the "Founding Fathers obviously felt no inflexible reverence for the document they wrote." Therefore, he maintained, "the debate should revolve around the issue at hand" and "not around the sanctity of the Constitution. If this amendment is not worthy of adoption, then it should be voted down on the merits of the issue." The right-wing *National Review* similarly complained that amendment critics were "wrapping themselves in the First Amendment" and that any discussion of the flag burning question had been lifted "above rational criticism or political argument" by "liberal indignation at the laying of impious hands on the sacred texts. Merely discussing the Bill of Rights has become for liberals what burning the flag is to many conservatives: a secular version of sacrilege." A few more detached observers reached similar conclusions: Harvard law professor Mary Ann Glendon argued that it would be "inappropriate to give talismanic quasi-religious significance" to either the flag or the Bill of Rights.[23]

Some opponents of the amendment did focus on the "merits." For example, Senate SJC chairman Biden and several other congressmen repeated many of the arguments made against the amendment in 1989, such as that for the first time it would authorize the government to outlaw the expression of opinion based on its content, that the amendment might be interpreted as overriding all provisions of the Bill of Rights because it did not specifically state that it was intended to modify the First Amendment; and that the lack of any clear definition of what constituted "physical desecration" and the "blank check" allegedly granted states to pass flag desecration laws would lead to what Biden predicted would be "years of litigation trying to decide what all of this means" because the states would pass varying, conflicting, and potentially absurd and arbitrary flag desecration statutes.[24]

Harvard law professor and former solicitor general Fried rejected the arguments of amendment supporters that the proposal would barely affect freedom of expression, because protection of "expressions we hate is at the heart of the First Amendment, not on the fringes" and to make "just this one exception" could not be done "without endangering our immortal soul as a nation. The man who says you can make an exception to this principle does not know what a principle is," just as the man who says, "'Only this once let's make 2+2=5,' does not know what it is to count." Although many votes in Congress understandably reflected political compromises, Fried added, this one could not because any congressman who voted to draw a "moustache on the Mona Lisa of our liberties" would create a "piece of vandalism" that would stand as his "monument for as long as this country endures." Similarly, Duke law professor Walter Dellinger warned that the flag amendment was a "truly terrible idea" that "strikes at the core of the first amendment" and would undermine its "moral legitimacy" by lowering the threshold for changing the Constitution "whenever there was a popular majority that favored restricting minority rights," thus destroying the principle that "freedom of dissenting expression is a fundamental liberty." Uniquely among the approximately two hundred representatives who spoke during the June 21 House debate, Republican representative Rod Chandler suggested that flag burning could even serve a useful purpose, declaring that had someone "resorted" to such a "dramatic demonstration" amid the "war fever" that led to the detention of more than one hundred thousand Japanese-Americans without charges or trials during World War II, it would have expressed the "absolutely correct voice of reason."[25]

The "slippery slope" argument was frequently cited in 1990, as in 1989, as an especial reason to fear an amendment. Thus Representative Washington warned that if the amendment was passed, soon "they will tell us what religion we can engage in" and next "how we may assemble and who will assemble," and Senator Mitchell suggested that no principled distinction could be drawn between the flag amendment and outlawing burning copies of the Constitution or the Declaration of Independence. Other arguments which were made again in 1990 were that outlawing flag burning was an absurd overreaction to a small number of protesters which would only grant them martyrdom and that all the time devoted to the issue diverted attention away from more pressing problems. Thus Democratic Senator Patrick Leahy, who had voted for the FPA, termed the amendment both an "unnecessary, unprecedented and ill-advised" response to the "despicable acts of a handful of publicity seekers" and an attempt to "distract and deceive" the American people from the "serious challenges" and the "realities" that posed a much greater problem than "talking about symbols," such as growing child poverty and the collapse of the savings and loan industry. The "diversion argument" was frequently reflected in editorial cartoons. For example, the June 24 *Cleveland Plain Dealer* depicted a politician sweeping issues like drugs, crime, and the homeless under a flag, and the June 20 *Miami Herald* portrayed "Representative Dertball" reading about the flag controversy and proclaiming, "Whew! I was afraid I'd have to answer questions on the savings and loan bailout!" The June 21 *Boston Globe* pictured Bush as a psychiatrist, responding to a patient expressing worry "about my job, my health, my kids' education, crime, taxes," with the diagnosis, "Ah, yes, I see . . . deep-seated anger about flag-burning."[26]

Although some amendment opponents did focus on, or at least mention, the substantive rights at issue, just as many, if not more, figuratively waved the Constitution as an icon. This was especially clear whenever congressmen who had voted for the FPA in 1989 tried to explain why they were voting against the amendment in 1990, even though, as Biden conceded during his June 21 SJC hearing, had the Supreme Court upheld the FPA, the "impact on an individual would be no different" and "his or her rights would have been equally as much curtailed" had Congress passed the Bush "amendment that did precisely what the statute was intended to do." Bereft of their key 1989 argument—that given the seriousness of changing the Bill of Rights the amendment should not be passed without first constitutionally testing the FPA—1989 FPA backers who opposed the amendment in 1990 often resorted to appeals to the "sacred" or mystical character of the Bill of Rights and avoided confronting the fact that the same fundamental principle— the bedrock constitutional right to dissent in unpopular and even offensive ways— was at stake no matter how it was undermined. Thus among 1989 Democratic FPA supporters, Representatives William Ford, Mary Rose Oakar, and Jim Cooper all compared the Bill of Rights to the Bible or the Ten Commandments to explain their opposition to the amendment, Representative John Tanner termed the Bill of Rights "the most perfect government policy ever written," and Representative John Dingell topped even that description by terming the Bill of Rights "perhaps the most sacred and perfect document which has ever been set forth in the entire history of mankind." Representative Barbara Boxer maintained that "there is a difference between voting for a law to ban flag burning and voting to change the Constitution to ban flag burning," but her only explanation of this difference was that the Bill of Rights was "sacred" and the "greatest document of freedom in the world."[27]

The Impact of East European and Soviet Developments

The successful Democratic reframing of the flag desecration controversy in 1990 was considerably enhanced in its appeal by events abroad, in particular the East European democratic revolutions of 1989 and the continuing liberalization in Gorbachev's Soviet Union, for at least three distinct, if interrelated, reasons. First, these developments virtually eliminated the perception that the nation, and there- fore its symbolic representation, the flag, needed defense against the traditional main foe of communism. Second, as the former communist lands became more free, opponents of the amendment could argue that these and other countries were looking to the United States for democratic guidance and that it would be a great and tragic irony for the United States to reduce its freedoms just when the American tradition of liberty was spurring democracy abroad. Third, and probably most powerful, the democratic movement in Eastern Europe and the Soviet Union had featured the widespread popular alteration of national flags to tear out their hated emblems of communism, such as red stars and the hammer and sickle, and this widely publicized flag desecration not only made obvious that such acts were powerful forms of the very political expression that was supposed to be at the protected heart of American democracy but were widely hailed in the United States as acts of great courage. Flag desecration was so prominent an aspect of the reform movement in the former communist lands that one book published in 1990 about recent developments in Romania was titled, *The Hole in the Flag*.[28]

References to the developments in Eastern Europe and their relationship to the American flag desecration controversy were frequent in the press throughout 1990. For example, in a March 1990 article, political analyst Robert Scheer declared that "this has been a pretty good year for flag burners, especially in the communist countries," but he lamented that "as each totalitarian regime crumbles" and at a time when "people throughout the world risk life and limb to obtain a Bill of Rights," President Bush seemed bent on "demeaning our most valuable export" by seeking to treat the American flag as a "religious shroud" and to jail American flag burners. A May 28 *Legal Times* analysis of the May 14 Supreme Court oral argument noted that Justice Kennedy had referred to Eastern European flag desecration incidents as evidence that such conduct was an "internationally recognized form of protest" and argued that such events "may have done more to dignify flag-burning than anything that has happened on this side of the Atlantic." Shortly after the *Eichman* ruling, columnist John Hughes wrote that it would be "too bad if the hate-mongers succeeded in diluting those freedoms that have long been a cornerstone of the American ideal" at the very time that, in other lands, dissidents "with our encouragement" were "desecrating their own flags."[29]

Critics of the amendment were quick to make arguments related to these themes in the judicial and political arenas. For example, in a 1990 interview, Jonathan Hines, a lawyer for the New York firm of Debevoise & Plimpton, which submitted the organizations' amicus brief opposing the flag desecration law in the 1989 and 1990 Supreme Court cases, suggested that the "virtual evaporation" of the perceived threat posed to the United States by the "world communist conspiracy" had taken some of the steam out of the drive to protect the flag and that recent incidents of East European flag desecration had weakened the case for outlawing such acts in the United States. Hines added:

> To me, what happened in Eastern Europe, in particular the images one had on the TV screen of Romanian flags flown with the hole in the middle—we even saw that in Moscow—only underscored ten times the importance of the *Johnson* decision and of maintaining that decision, of not prosecuting people who do things to our flag, because this country ought to stand for just the principle that's being fought for in East Europe.

During the 1990 congressional debate, many amendment opponents similarly referred to developments abroad to bolster their case. For example, during the June 21 SJC hearing, Republican senator Humphrey termed it "preposterous" that the Bush administration wanted to outlaw "the very same thing that we exulted in when it took place in Eastern Europe."[30]

The Backlash against Perceived Politicization of the Amendment

Along with the successful reframing of the flag controversy in 1990 as pitting the flag versus the Bill of the Rights and the boost given that argument by the use of flag desecration as an obvious and widely praised form of political expression in Eastern Europe, opponents of the Bush amendment in 1990 also were considerably strengthened by a backlash against repeated and overt references by its Republican backers which suggested motives more partisan than principled, including salivating at the prospects of politically pillorying anyone who dared vote against it. Although similar comments had been made by Republicans in 1989, they had been relatively restrained and, in public at least, rather rare; however, following the *Eichman* ruling, numerous Republican spokesmen, along with some representatives of veterans' groups backing the amendment, repeatedly and overtly threatened political consequences for anyone who voted the "wrong way."

For example, Republican Senate leader Dole twice commented after the *Eichman* ruling that a vote against a constitutional amendment "would make a pretty good 30-second spot" during the 1990 elections, especially because "real people," as opposed to "some of the academicians, and maybe some of the constitutional lawyers and some of the liberal politicians," would support the amendment. According to an "issue alert" circulated to Republicans by the RNCCC shortly after the *Eichman* ruling, the flag controversy was an especially "great campaign issue" because it was "clear and simple," required "no elaborate explanations and it is understood by everyone," and was "easy to use this time of year" as Flag Day (June 14) and July 4 approached. Some of the statements issued by veterans' groups that supported the amendment also contained overt political threats. For example, American Legion commander Miles Epling warned that "contrary to beliefs of some politicians, the memory of the American people is not short" and that if politicians "think they can abandon the flag in June, kiss babies in September and be re-elected in November, they are mistaken."[31]

Aside from Dole's references to "thirty-second spots," three Republican comments related to the political potential of the flag issue particularly attracted the attention, and often the amazement, of Washington insiders and deeply angered many Democrats. On June 11, NRCCC Chairman Rollins told reporters that the flag controversy was a "good value-defining issue" because if "your opponent is for flag-burning [thereby, of course, identifying opposing the amendment with being for flag burning] then he's got to go through a very sophisticated explanation of why he is." On June 13, the *Washington Post* reported that a White House aide had declared that President Bush felt "strongly" about the flag issue but was "not to going to demagogue on this" because "that's what he's got Dole for." Perhaps most astounding, Republican House assistant minority leader Newt Gingrich, who declared on June 14 that the flag issue would be a "definitional question" in the upcoming elections, told a reporter that if he were the "mythical Republican strategist, I would want the amendment to lose by one vote" because then all Republican congressional candidates could argue that their election might make the difference in a future vote.[32]

As many of these comments suggest, in the immediate aftermath of the *Eichman* ruling many Republican candidates and strategists indicated that they planned to stress the flag issue in the upcoming elections, and the press was filled with predictions that it would become a major campaign issue. For example, a spokesman for Republican Iowa Senate candidate representative Tom Tauke declared that the flag controversy would be "an arrow in our quiver" against Democratic incumbent Tom Harkins in the fall; in an Idaho congressional district, Republican candidate "Skip" Smyser asked whether his Democratic opponent who opposed an amendment was "as wholeheartedly behind America as Skip is." Even as the House was voting to kill the amendment on June 21, Republican officials in Washington, operating out of a headquarters building that was bedecked with flags for the occasion, were faxing press releases across the country attacking Democratic congressional candidates who opposed it.[33]

Despite such widespread indications of Republicans' plans to exploit the flag controversy, even some Republican observers (correctly, as it turned out) expressed doubt that the issue would have much impact on the elections. Thus former Reagan aide Lyn Nofziger told a reporter that he doubted if "anybody is going to win or lose an election on this" because the entire issue was "petering out," and it was "not like there is a lot of flagburning going on to keep it alive." Republican consultant Eddie Mahe reached the same conclusion via a considerably different argument, lamenting that although Republicans were on the "right side" of the flag issue, it might not prove useful politically because "in those districts where the issue is going to cut, the Democrats are [also] for [the amendment]." In fact, in the June 21 House vote that killed the amendment, among Democratic representatives who had won their 1988 race by the relatively comfortable margin of 55 percent or more, about two-thirds voted against the amendment, but among those who had been elected with thinner margins, two-thirds voted for it. In the contest in the eleventh congressional district in Illinois, Republican state senator Walter Dudcyz, who had led the protests against the 1989 "flag on the floor" Chicago SAIC exhibit, built his ultimately unsuccessful campaign around his love for the flag, only to discover that incumbent Democrat Frank Annunzio supported the amendment. Similarly, in the five most important gubernatorial races (in California, Texas, Illinois, Florida, and Michigan) both major party candidates backed the amendment within days of the *Eichman* ruling.[34]

The fear of thirty-second soundbites unquestionably was a major concern of many potential opponents of the amendment. Even Democratic senator Robert Kerrey, who was generally regarded as immune from attacks on his patriotism because of his status as a war hero, told a reporter, "I can see it now. 'Bob Kerrey votes for gun control and he won't vote to protect the flag.' It's a great 30-second spot." Democratic pollster Harrison Hickman complained that the threat and fear of thirty-second negative campaign commercials was such a major factor in the flag controversy that the amendment should be known as the "thirty-second video amendment." Part of the Democrats' fear was that, even though public clamor for the amendment seemed to have dropped off considerably since 1989, it was impossible to know if, during some unpredictably changed future political climate, a vote against the amendment might be dredged up for use against them. Thus Democratic amendment opponent representative Pat Schroeder declared that she was "absolutely appalled" by the "statements of politicians" that voting for the amendment would provide "asbestos underwear to cover your backside from getting burned in the next election." Her party colleague Representative Robert Wise, who ended up voting for the amendment after first expressing uncertainty about it, told a reporter, "People have to be wondering if this is a political AIDS virus that you will always carry and won't know when it will be activated."[35]

Despite such fears, both the constant reiteration and the blatant nature of the 1990 Republican political threats backfired overall, "turning off" many Americans already cynical about the motives of politicians, evoking sharp criticism from both sides of the political aisle, and generating massive numbers of editorials, cartoons, and editorial columns which attacked Republicans for putting political considerations first. For example, a June 14 *Miami Herald* cartoon showed Bush and his elephant friend standing before a flag and pledging "allegiance" to the flag, the country, and "to the politics with which we slam, one temptation to demagogue, irresistible, with elections and 30-second spot campaign commercials for all." A June 19 *Washington Post* cartoon pictured a congressman walking up the Capitol steps, facing a choice between "The Bill of Rights 1791," represented by pictures of the founding fathers, and "Flag-Factory Politics 1988–90," represented by portraits of Bush, Dole, and Gingrich.

A number of Republicans, including some prominent supporters of the amendment, found their party's increasingly overt politicization of the flag issue offensive, or, at any rate, harmful to the amendment's prospects. For example, Representative Charles Douglas, one of the leading Republican backers of the amendment, who was interviewed in 1991 after losing his seat in the 1990 elections, termed the comments of Dole and Gingrich "counterproductive," if only because the amendment needed Democratic votes to succeed. "If they want to make them in closed-door meetings as strategists, fine," Douglas said, "but not out in public." In a 1990 interview, Republican Representative John Porter, who was one of only seventeen members of his party to vote against the amendment in the 1990 House vote, said comments like those of Dole and Gingrich "lose [the votes of] me or others like me" because "I approach a decision on amending the Constitution with a great deal of reverence and I don't want it belittled by politics." An angry and red-faced Republican House leader Michel, whose frequent differences over tactics with House whip Gingrich were an open secret, bitterly denounced Republicans who sought to politicize the flag desecration issue during a vehement June 21 floor speech; he claimed that such persons were not "any official leaders" of the Republican party but only some "campaign operatives out there saying things they had no right to say," especially because there "was no way to win on the strength of politicizing the issue." Michel later told reporters, "I personally have never politicized this thing and I'm ticked off at those who are doing it." Republican senator John Danforth, in a blistering Flag Day attack on President Bush, denounced the latter's June 12 claim that flag burning "endangered the fabric" of the nation; one clear "hypothetical" that demonstrated the falsity of this claim, Danforth suggested, was that if a politician running for office burned a flag his opponent would not grieve that the nation was endangered but instead openly exult that he had "won the election" and that he was "running against a crackpot."[36]

Although Democrats feared the political consequences of opposing the Bush amendment, many of them reacted to the overt politicization of the flag controversy in 1990 with outrage and with the apparently accurate prediction that such tactics would backfire. For example, Democratic National Committee (DNC) chairman Ron Brown declared on June 12, "Those who seek political advantage from the flag and the Bill of Rights slander the memory of every man or woman who fought for this land. To drag the flag through cheap politics is every bit as offensive as burning it." Scores of other Democratic congressmen also denounced Republicans for seeking to make political capital out of the flag issue, and they frequently attacked Dole and Gingrich by name or transparent allusion. For example, assistant Senate majority leader Alan Cranston declared that "veiled threats about 30-second ads demean not only the flag but the political process itself." Senator Bill Bradley declared that the purpose of the amendment was to "gain political advantage" and, "as the minority leader [Dole] has admitted, is to provide a launching pad for vicious attacks on the integrity and patriotism of those who vote against it." Similarly, Representative Frank McCloskey declared that the "driving engine" of the controversy was a "partisan political agenda," as had been demonstrated by "highly placed political operatives" who had "talked repeatedly about the potential for devastating 30-second attack ads" and had suggested that the "best scenario would be for the amendment to lose by one vote" to facilitate later political exploitation of the issue. Senator Sam Nunn, who voted for the Bush amendment, suggested that the only purpose of Republicans in forcing a Senate vote after the House had killed the amendment was to "provide ammunition for 30-second campaign spots" and "political fodder for demagoguery back home on the campaign trail."[37]

Several Democratic opponents of the amendment directly or implicitly attacked some of their own party colleagues for political cowardice for not joining with them. For example, Representative John Bryant reported that based on what he heard during conversations in congressional "cloakrooms or over lunch":

> The Republicans believe that they have found an issue that they can use to win elections, and they are so anxious to win that they are willing to damage the Constitution and the Bill of Rights to do it. The Republican leadership has openly gloated about the effect their 30-second political commercials will have on upcoming political elections, and the vast majority of Democrats who will follow them are doing so because they are so fearful of not being reelected that they are willing to let the Constitution and the Bill of Rights be damaged . . . that is cowardice equally as bad as the Republicans' greed to win a majority with this issue.[38]

Several Democrats threatened to come out swinging if anyone attacked them for voting against the amendment. For example, a spokesman for Senator Harkins warned that if attempts were made to "question his patriotism" for voting against the amendment, Harkins's record of "five years as a Navy fighter pilot during Vietnam" would be stressed, and his opponent, who had not served in the military, would be "nailed to the wall." DNC communications director Michael McCurry suggested several possible "30-second counterattack ads" to respond to any attacks over the flag issue: one scenario would feature a "phony, blow-dried politician wrapping himself in the flag and blathering" with a "voice-over" proclaiming that "when politicians start wrapping themselves in the flag, it means they've got nothing better to do"; another would declare that "that guy wrapping himself in the flag is trying to pee on the Constitution."[39]

Democratic congressmen and other opponents of the amendment who were interviewed in 1990 following its defeat unanimously agreed that the increased Republican politicization of the flag controversy had redounded to their benefit. Thus assistant majority House whip David Bonior declared, "Dole and Gingrich exposed themselves [as out for political gain] at a very favorable time to us, the press was very much on our side and they saw it as a cheap political ploy." Similarly, Representative Charles Stenholm, a deeply conservative Texan who had originally cosponsored the Bush amendment and whose ultimate vote against it stunned many congressional observers, said that comments such as those of Dole and Gingrich had "cut the heart out of the argument" for the amendment. Another original Democratic amendment cosponsor who ultimately voted against it, Representative Tim Valentine, agreed that the repeated Republican threats issued in 1990 had been counterproductive, because "after awhile you kind of get your back up. I think this kind of happened here."

Democratic congressional aides who played key roles in helping to defeat the amendment in 1990 and were interviewed soon afterward had similar views. One House leadership aide declared that Dole's comments especially "exposed how crass and cynical their efforts to use the amendment was, and I think that hurt them tremendously." A key Senate Democratic aide termed the politically oriented statements of Republicans

> a bit crass and kind of gleeful in terms of celebrating what they thought were positive political implications of the issue. That back-fired to a certain extent and that backfiring sort of dovetailed with a fairly strong anti-politician sentiment that is out there right now, a feeling of cynicism among the American people. People [in Congress] therefore felt a little better about saying [by voting against the amendment], "I'm standing up for a principle here, not just what the next poll says."

The Superior Organization of the
Anti-Amendment Forces in 1990

In addition to the political boosts provided to amendment opponents by their successful reframing of the flag controversy, by developments in Eastern Europe, and by the overt politicization of the flag controversy by amendment proponents, another factor that aided the cause of antiamendment forces in 1990 was their higher level of organizational skills. This was clearly reflected both in organizational efforts within Congress and among interest groups who sought to influence members of Congress.

At about the time that the Supreme Court announced on March 30, 1990, that it would hear the FPA appeal, both parties in the House organized "flag" task forces to prepare their responses to the expected decision striking down the FPA and the revived fight over the amendment which was sure to follow. By all accounts, the Democratic task force was far more effective than its GOP counterpart, at least partly because House Republicans were divided over tactics and strategy between those who favored House Republican leader Michel's attempts to work with the Democratic leadership whenever possible and those more aligned with the frontal combat tactics favored by assistant Republican leader Gingrich. Thus Republican House task force cochair Charles Douglas, who was freed by his 1990 election defeat from the need to pull any punches, declared in a 1991 interview, "Had we had the united approach on the Republican side, it would have made a difference. Instead we were going down two roads."[40]

Douglas described the "split in approach" as between Michel, who

> felt that this could be done on a calm, low key bipartisan basis and those of us who felt the reality was that this wasn't going to happen, that it couldn't be done in a low key manner, that we had to keep the pressure on. Michel, being more of an accommodationist guy, played into their [the Democratic leadership's hand], never made it a priority on his screen, nor did the White House. There were many opportunities [to push more strongly for the amendment], even if you wouldn't do it at a crass [political] level, but they seized none of them. There were those of us who were very sincere and didn't use it for political purposes, but the Republican leadership was trying to work with the [Democratic] leadership and get any crumbs that should be thrown them, so it [fighting for the amendment] was left to a task force that really had no punch behind it. Those of us on the task force were never met with and talked with about how we get this thing moving and get a game plan.

A key House Republican aide from the Michel faction confirmed the split that Douglas described, in a 1990 interview, but characterized it, quite differently, as between the "bombthrowers, who viewed this as the greatest political issue in the world," and those, who, like Michel, sincerely wanted to protect the flag. According to the aide, the result was

> tension from the beginning between the Republican leader, who was going for the finish line, and people who were going for more immediate enjoyment, and that tension never really ended. I spent a great deal of time with a number of our members, really trying to rein them in and have them be a little more faithful to Bob Michel's long-term goal, rather than the short-term political gain. I spent a lot of time playing the clergyman on the political gain issue, and I was not a popular person for it.

In addition to splits within the ranks of Republican congressmen, many observers felt that the pro-amendment efforts were hurt in 1990 by the lack of visible White House support. Although Bush publicly urged passage of the amendment on June 11 and again on June 12, those were virtually the only public comments he offered, reportedly because the White House feared being attacked for politicizing the issue, as he had been during the previous two years. Whereas Bush's 1989 Iwo Jima Memorial trip had been a public relations extravaganza featuring a large crowd, masses of flags, and a military band, the comparatively scaled-down nature of administration support for the amendment in 1990 was extraordinarily well symbolized when Bush delivered his only substantial remarks on its behalf on June 12: he also did while accepting a small model of the Iwo Jima monument from the architect, which was presented to him at the White House before a handful of reporters and in the presence of a single flag, attached to his lectern with a small pole. In its June 13 account of this event, the *Los Angeles Times* captured the seemingly diminished scale of White House enthusiasm for the amendment with a headline that read, "Bush Urges Flag Amendment, but Does It with Less Fanfare." In contrast to the vigorous and continuous anti-amendment lobbying on Capitol Hill carried out by Speaker Foley and House Democrats, press reports suggested that although Bush did some telephone lobbying for the amendment, it was limited and tardy; thus, according to a *Congressional Quarterly* account, by the time Bush contacted several originally undecided Democrats a few days before the June 21 House vote, they had "already been contacted a number of times by colleagues from the [Democratic] flag task force" and "it was too late."[41]

In a 1991 interview, House Republican flag task force member Douglas lamented that his group was not even given the name of a White House official to contact to coordinate planning. Douglas added:

> If you can find him, let me know, because maybe there is such a person but he must have been dumb, deaf, and blind because we couldn't communicate with them. There was no activity, the president didn't develop a strategy. He didn't keep the issue highlighted in a way that could have happened in 1990 when you had Flag Day, Memorial Day, the Fourth of July. We weren't getting any help or support from the White House.

Even some Republicans aligned with the Michel faction felt abandoned by the White House during the 1990 controversy. One such aide lamented in a 1990 interview that "there were no presidential statements in the last week" before the June 21 House vote, and "the only way we could have won was for this to be an issue outside the [Washington freeway] beltway and within the short time frame [after the June 11 *Eichman* ruling] it never got outside the beltway."

Another organizational shortfall by 1990 amendment proponents, which congressmen and observers on all sides of the flag issue in 1990 agreed hindered the pro-amendment cause, was the markedly less noticeable and effective effort by members of veterans' groups compared to 1989. While veterans' organizations led by the American Legion and VFW publicly urged support for the amendment, mail and phone calls from these groups, and above all their physical presence on Capitol Hill was markedly less than in 1989. One civil liberties activist involved in fighting the amendment in both 1989 and 1990 recalled, in a 1990 interview, that during the previous year Congress had been "mobbed with 'hat people'" (a reference to the distinctive military-style hats typically worn by members of the veterans' groups) on days when the flag desecration issue was being debated, but in 1990 amendment opponents found themselves asking, "Where are the 'hat people'? Where in the hell are they? It's astonishing."

Spokesmen for the largest and most influential veterans' groups, the American Legion and VFW, generally maintained that their efforts in no way slackened in 1990 and that public opinion had not fundamentally changed either, but that Congress had simply chosen to defy public and veterans' wishes and had deliberately short-circuited the efforts of amendment opponents to mobilize by rushing to a vote. American Legion national commander Miles Epling declared on June 22 that the amendment's defeat was "an insult to the American people" because "the will of the majority has been ignored." In a June 19 press release, the VFW protested the plans of the House leadership to bring the amendment to a vote with "blinding speed" and demanded a "reasonable delay" to allow "all interested persons adequate time" to "contact members [of Congress] and the American people." Legion public relations head Lew Wood declared in a 1990 interview conducted following the amendment's defeat that his organization's mobilization was "just as strong this year as last year." Citing a 1990 Legion-sponsored Gallup Poll that indicated 71 percent of the public supported an amendment, he declared, "When almost three-quarters of the American public say they favor an amendment, Congress has protected the American people against an amendment, by deciding that they know best and the people don't."[42]

While by virtually all accounts the pro-amendment forces in 1990 were in a state of disarray, the efforts of the Democratic leadership (especially in the House) and their supporters outside Congress who opposed the amendment were highly organized and effective. For example, whereas during the immediate post-*Johnson* period in 1989, virtually every congressman who spoke out attacked the Supreme Court, during the 1990 Flag Day congressional debates almost as many representatives and senators defended the Supreme Court, or attacked the amendment, as spoke for the amendment.[43]

PAW legislative counsel Gomperts related in a 1990 interview that after the *Eichman* ruling amendment opponents

> were ready with speakers to go to the floor, instead of staying up all night condemning the Supreme Court decision, people were ready to make speeches in favor of the Bill of Rights. Instead of it being 97-3 [a reference to the June 22, 1989, Senate vote condemning the *Johnson* ruling] it was even, every time somebody stood up on their side somebody stood up on our side, so this thing never got rolling, there was no big snowball effect, if there was any snowball effect it was our way. Flag Day turned out to be an extraordinary day for us.

The House Democratic flag task force was by all accounts especially effective in organizing opposition to the amendment. According to 1990 interviews with task force members David Bonior, Don Edwards, David Skaggs, and Craig Washington, the group met two or three times a week during May and June to develop strategies and themes to fight the amendment. Bonior said that one "secret of our success" was that the group worked "very, very quietly" in lobbying members as well as "contacting all the [newspaper] editorial writers, the 'op-ed' people to get things written." According to Skaggs, the task force was "successful in many cases" in identifying potential "swing vote" Democrats and then "working them hard" and obtaining their votes.

One small but telling indication of the task force's success was that during the post-*Eichman* ruling period, House amendment opponents, largely organized by the group, blitzed their fellow congressmen with far more "dear colleague" letters than backers of the amendment generated. As one key House Republican leadership source lamented in a 1990 interview, "There must have been about thirty to forty of those things, everybody's [mail]boxes have been flooded with them. They must have out 'dear colleagued' us 40-3." Furthermore, owing to the task force's efforts in lobbying and closely monitoring the feelings of House members, the House Democratic leadership knew almost immediately following the *Eichman* ruling that the widespread press reports suggesting inevitable passage of the amendment were wrong; therefore, Speaker Foley, while on the surface simply responding to Republican demands for a quick vote on the amendment, was able to waive normal House procedures and move the amendment to the floor with lightning speed with considerable confidence (if not absolute certainty at first) that it would fail.

In a 1990 interview, Bonior said that the decision of the House Democratic leaders to schedule the vote on June 21 was made shortly after the June 11 *Eichman* ruling, when they were confident they had a "good chance" to prevail, and, above all, was determined by the calendar: Speaker Foley had earlier promised a vote within thirty days of a Supreme Court ruling striking down the FPA, and the June 11 ruling therefore required a vote before Congress took a week-long recess for the July 4 holiday. Within the resultant three-week legislative "window," Bonior explained, the vote was scheduled for a time "most favorable to us" because June 21 was farthest removed both from Flag Day and an immediate pre–July 4 vote, dates which were seen as lending themselves to emotional outbursts of flag waving. Foley considerably aided the efforts of the task force with an intensive personal lobbying campaign directed at at least thirty wavering House Democrats, which was characterized in a *National Journal* account as "his most aggressive" stance on any issue in his first year as Speaker and as having a "stunning impact."[44]

Foley reportedly convinced many Democrats both that they would not want to go down in history as supporting a weakening of the First Amendment and that the political risks of opposing the amendment had been greatly exaggerated. According to House majority leader Richard Gephardt, the amendment's defeat "would not have happened without Tom Foley." DNC chairman Ron Brown agreed, declaring that Foley "had turned this thing around" in his "quiet, persuasive, strong way." In a 1990 interview, House Democratic whip Bonior singled out Senate Democratic leader George Mitchell for also playing a key role in fostering the House defeat of the amendment. "Mitchell became very engrossed and active in lobbying [House] members on this issue," Bonior recalled. "Senator Mitchell was calling down to my office twice a day and asking about who he could talk to in the last week [preceding the June 21 House vote]."[45]

Although the House Democratic leadership scheduled the critical floor vote on the amendment for June 21 with reasonable confidence, Republican flag task force member Charles Douglas lamented in a 1991 interview that his group "never did a very good body count on the Democratic side," which left them largely blinded to the growing House sentiment against the amendment. In fact, although Republican leaders such as Dole, Bush, and Douglas had originally demanded a quick congressional vote on the amendment following the *Eichman* ruling, House Republicans soon discovered that they were short of votes. Therefore, some quickly found themselves in the embarrassing position of switching gears and demanding a delay in the floor vote scheduled by the House Democratic leadership for June 21 via a suspension of the rules (for example, of the usual requirement of a three-day legislative layover following a 19-17 vote by the House Judiciary Committee on June 19 to report the amendment, without any recommended action, for consideration by the full House).

Although House Republican whip Gingrich threatened to make the Democrats' refusal to postpone the vote the "first twelve seconds of the thirty-second commercials," these Republican complaints had little resonance with the press or public, both because they involved highly complicated and difficult-to-explain legislative technicalities and because so many Republicans had earlier been demanding a quick vote. Moreover, Republicans displayed considerable disarray over the scheduling issue: for example, Republican HJC member Sensenbrenner undercut his colleagues' complaints by publicly admitting, "If you have the votes you want to vote, if you don't have the votes, you want to talk." Moreover, even while many House Republicans were demanding a vote delay, House leader Michel declared on June 18 that a June 21 House vote would be "fine," and the White House issued a June 19 statement urging "prompt" action on the amendment.[46]

The embarrassment and bitterness that some Republicans felt over the June 21 scheduling was publicly displayed in a bizarre scene on the House floor on June 20, when Republican representative Gerald Solomon, an arch-conservative proponent of the amendment, accused the Democratic leadership of "deliberately gagging" veterans' groups and "kowtowing" to the "Communist Youth Brigade" by their plans to vote the next day. These comments sparked objections from

Democratic representative Barbara Boxer, a request by Solomon to withdraw his comment about "kowtowing," and a formal ruling that his comments were in violation of House rules. In a 1991 interview, Solomon said he had apologized because "I was in no way trying to impugn the integrity or patriotism of Speaker Foley as a individual but I felt what they were doing was kowtowing to communists, as in past turndowns of aid to the [Nicaraguan] contras."[47]

The effective organizational work done on Capitol Hill by Speaker Foley and the House Democratic task force was considerably augmented in 1990 by strong and unified opposition to the amendment by the ACLU and the PAW, the nation's two most important national civil liberties organizations, and by almost unanimous attacks on the proposal by the country's editorial voices. Unencumbered by the ambiguities created in 1989 by the FPA option, the ACLU and the PAW vigorously joined with the Democratic congressional leadership in 1990 in opposing the amendment. By all indications, moreover, their lobbying was far more intense and effective, both in Congress and (especially for the PAW) in attempts to organize grass-roots support for their position, than were the countervailing efforts of the veterans' groups. One small but clear indication of this came at the June 19 HJC meeting called to discuss the amendment, when the meeting room was dotted with people wearing PAW- and ACLU-supplied buttons reading "Don't Burn the Bill of Rights" and "Respect the Flag, Defeat the Amendment," while there was relatively little evidence of the presence of the veterans' groups.

In 1990 interviews, ACLU Washington office director Morton Halperin, PAW legislative counsel John Gomperts, and PAW field coordinator Joseph Sternlieb all characterized antiamendment efforts as the central focus of their energies during the immediate pre- and post-*Eichman* ruling period. Halperin reported that his entire staff of almost a dozen workers was assigned to lobbying on Capitol Hill against the amendment and that he personally was devoting "an enormous amount" of time to such efforts. Gomperts said that during the two months preceding the *Eichman* ruling, he spent "50 percent of my time" organizing antiamendment forces, with the result that "We were really ready. We had materials prepared. We had our field staff prepared. We knew who our targets were. We were literally doing things on Monday afternoon [June 11, the day of the *Eichman* ruling]." Sternlieb reported, for example, that the PAW ordered antiamendment buttons on Tuesday, June 12, and "we had them in packets to go to the [Capitol] Hill on Wednesday night, 2,000 of them. They were all over the Hill, on Thursday, Flag Day."

Gomperts reported that the PAW sent out four mailings to Congress within eight days of the *Eichman* ruling, including suggestions for speeches and arguments against the amendment, poll data suggesting that the political costs of opposing it would not be high, and even draft texts of possible "thirty-second spots" defending antiamendment votes, all designed to convince uncertain members that they could "talk about this issue and come out on top." The PAW material argued that the nation was "hardly beset" by flag burnings, that those which had occurred had not "dampened our love of country or flag," that "prohibiting dissent is the hallmark of oppressive regimes," and that when the "walls of oppression are crumbling all over Eastern Europe, it would be a travesty for America to compromise its position as a model open society by restricting the freedom of speech." The PAW also sent wavering congressmen scenarios for possible "spot" ads defending an antiamendment vote. For example, one proposed ad script depicted Senate Republican leader Dole threatening to "make a good 30-second spot" to attack amendment opponents, followed by comments from a "blue collar guy" named "Jim Smith," who, amid patriotic music and pictures, identified himself as a flag-loving veteran who respected the "guts" reflected in his congressman's vote against the amendment and who termed those who "wrap themselves in the flag" to get votes "almost as bad as burnin' it." In the script, "Smith" concludes, "I'm glad I have a Congressmen who isn't so afraid of a 30 second TV spot that he'd throw away 200 years of American Freedom. I'm glad I have a Congressman with guts."[48]

According to Gomperts and Sternlieb, PAW's direct lobbying of about thirty wavering members of Congress was supplemented with a massive effort, including the placing of over a thousand phone calls and the mailing of fifteen thousand postcards, to lobby them indirectly by organizing grass-roots opposition to the amendment in their districts. According to Gomperts:

> One part of our strategy was to get lawyers and law professors to write letters. Congressmen are and see themselves not as members of American Legion halls, but more like law professors or law partners. They are and see themselves as intelligent people who care about the Constitution—obviously they care about the flag, too. And to hear from respected members of the community and of the legal community, that people understand that this is a really tough vote but sometimes you just have to do what's right. We thought that could cancel out the impact of the anticipated hundreds of thousands of postcards [for the amendment]. But the postcards never came. We won the mail. There were thousands of letters from people who had actually thought about this issue, who really loved the Constitution and told the members to vote against the damn amendment.

Gomperts and Sternlieb reported similar success in encouraging amendment opponents to telephone and telegraph Capitol Hill to express their views. "We were able to get forty to fifty calls into a congressman's office within a couple of hours," Gomperts declared. "We heard that members were literally counting calls to decide what to do. There were twenty to thirty people who were undecided and ultimately almost all of them voted against the amendment." According to Sternlieb, "Some of the offices were telling me their mail was running five to one, ten to one against the amendment, even from conservative Republican districts."

The organizational efforts of the ACLU, PAW, the House Democratic task force, Speaker Foley, and other congressional opponents of the amendment were considerably bolstered in 1990 by press opposition to the amendment, which was even more massive and unanimous than it had been in 1989. With a literal handful of exceptions, such as the *Wall Street Journal* and the *Columbus Dispatch,* every major newspaper, as well as hundreds of newspapers in smaller cities across the country, editorialized against the amendment. NPR congressional reporter Cokie Roberts noted in a 1990 interview that "even little town newspapers" were editorializing against the amendment, and "that gives members of Congress a tremendous amount" of political protection. Even in Republican Senate leader Dole's home state of Kansas, opposition to the amendment from small and large newspapers was so massive that Dole told the Senate that, judging from their editorials, he was casting "one of the toughest votes of my career." Among the comments offered in these editorials about Dole's widely reported "thirty-second spot" threats, the *Kansas City Star* termed them a "vicious assault on honorable politics" and a "devaluation of the meaning of patriotism" that itself amounted to "flag desecration," while the *Wichita Eagle* accused Dole of "leading the lynch mob" against the First Amendment.[49]

Aside from reiterating the theme that preserving the substance of the Bill of Rights' outweighed the importance of protecting the physical fabric of individual flags, newspaper editorials across the country, as in Kansas, overwhelmingly denounced Dole and other Republicans—especially Bush and Gingrich—for allegedly attempting to destroy basic American freedoms for crass political reasons. For example, *Boston Globe* syndicated columnist Thomas Oliphant said Dole was Bush's "designated demagogue" and declared that "Dole & Co." were turning to "yahooism" and "sophomoric trivializing of the issue" in their crusade for the amendment. *Denver Post* columnist Bob Ewegen wrote that Gingrich was "dreaming of a scummy round of cheap 30-second political spots challenging the patriotism" of Democrats who opposed the amendment, and *Chicago Tribune* columnist Stephen Chapman declared that Republicans were "bravely prepared to protect the flag, even if it means the loss of Democratic seats in Congress," and that most Republicans, "if asked to sell their immortal souls for short-term political advantage, would reply: What's the catch?"[50]

Aside from criticizing the motives and tactics of amendment proponents, newspapers across the country blasted them for gutting American freedoms to protect the symbol of such freedoms, for diverting public attention away from real problems while overreacting to a minor or nonexistent one, and for shaming the country at a time when countries around the world were struggling to gain more freedoms. The June 13 *Kansas City Star* declared that "the glorification of the American flag should hardly take precedence over the fundamental democratic rights for which it stands"; the June 12 *USA Today* argued that the amendment would dilute "one of the freedoms that distinguish our democracy from other ways of life" and that a "divisive campaign" for it would "divert attention from serious problems" like the environment, racial discrimination, and drugs, especially because flag burning was "not a serious problem" and posed "no threat to anybody"; and the June 13 *Quincy* (Massachusetts), *Patriot Ledger* noted that Americans had cheered protests that had "toppled both the symbols and the substance" of East European communist regimes and that it would be "contradictory" to support a flag amendment that would limit "the scope of political dissent" in the United States while applauding those who dissented abroad.

As in 1989, political columnists as well as newspaper editorials were overwhelmingly opposed to the amendment, including such prominent conservatives such as legal analyst Bruce Fein and columnists James Kilpatrick, Joseph Sobran, and William Safire. For example, Safire charged that Bush was "wrapping himself" in the flag to "assault" the Bill of Rights in an "unprecedented, unconscionable and wholly unnecessary" attempt at partisan gain that amounted to an "abandonment of conservative principles." Virtually the only well-known commentator who backed the amendment was far-right columnist Pat Buchanan, who termed Supreme Court Justice Brennan a "fool" for writing the *Eichman* decision and declared that the amendment should be used as a vehicle for giving "people who hate America" and "unelected ideologues," who had "hijacked" the Constitution and engaged in First Amendment "idolatry," the "kind of beating that is long overdue."[51]

The intense press opposition to the 1990 amendment was not only expressed on the editorial pages but also clearly colored some news stories and news analyses of the controversy, which, to a far greater degree than in 1989, portrayed Republican support for the amendment as primarily political. For example, the

June 25 issues of all three major American news magazines published "news stories" that were extraordinarily opinionated and hostile to the amendment. Thus *Newsweek* reported that if "naked cynicism were a crime, a number of Republicans [such as Dole] would be arrested" and declared that "tampering" with the First Amendment would endanger the "American birthright" of political tolerance; a *Time* article, titled "Hiding in the Flag," termed the issue a "paradigm of the age of escapist politics" and warned that changing the Constitution "would do more to desecrate the flag than any misguided arsonist could, for without the liberties for which it stands, the Stars and Stripes would become little more than colors on a cloth"; and *U.S. News & World Report* said that the "main purpose" of the amendment was to "gain political advantage." A June 13 *Miami Herald* news article reported that Republicans were "smacking [their] lips" with "gusto" over the prospects of politically exploiting the flag controversy, and a June 14 *Washington Post* story similarly reported that Republicans were "salivating" over their anticipated political gains.

Similar portrayals of Republican backers of the amendment were also frequent in the broadcast media. For example on the June 13 NBC evening news, anchor Tom Brokaw introduced a lengthy report by stating, "It is a standard political tactic, wrap yourself in the flag whenever possible," and congressional reporter Andrea Mitchell described the issue as a conflict between the "conscience" and "principle" of amendment opponents on the one hand and the "politics" of amendment backers on the other. NPR congressional reporter Cokie Roberts told her audience on June 14 that the flag controversy was "one of a series of issues" that Republicans planned to use "to paint Democrats as kooky liberals out of touch with common sense American values."

Both sides in the 1990 fight agreed that press hostility toward the amendment was much more overt and intense than in 1989, which led amendment opponents to be grateful but generated bitter complaints from amendment backers. Thus House assistant Democratic whip Bonior, in a 1990 interview, said, "The press was very much on our side. They saw [the amendment] as a cheap political ploy and almost universally supported our efforts to kill the amendment. The press was very active and visible on this." A key House Democratic leadership aide, also interviewed in 1990, declared that as the critical House vote approached,

> The news coverage tended to marginalize amendment supporters, it tended to posture them more and more as people playing politics and to marginalize the issue as not a serious issue. We knew there was an anti-incumbency thing out there, and the American public was really ready

to be told that this was just politicians playing around. That's an image
that the press was to communicate.

Amendment backers viewed the press coverage in much the same manner but
evaluated it in a very different perspective. For example, in congressional floor
speeches, Dole charged that he could not "stand up for the flag without being accused of being a demagogue by some liberal editorial writer or political opportu-
nist," and House Republican Henry Hyde complained about the "slings and
arrows of the media, which has relentlessly condemned us as cultural lags, and
yahoos, and political pygmies." In a 1991 interview, leading Democratic House
amendment sponsor and Veterans Committee Chairman Sonny Montgomery lamented, "The newspaper editors just killed us."[52]

The Cooling of Public Passions

Another factor distinguishing 1990 from 1989 in a manner adverse to amendment
proponents was that general public support for an amendment appeared to be far
less both in scope and (especially) in intensity following the *Eichman* ruling. This
factor was probably a critical element in bolstering the courage of wavering congressmen who wanted to vote against the amendment but were fearful of the potential political consequences. Thus Representative Montgomery, the leading
Democratic House supporter of the Bush amendment, noted shortly before the
June 21 House vote that the outcome would all depend "on the folks back home
and how much interest there is."[53]
   Although 1990 public opinion polls showed support for a constitutional
amendment at around the same 70 percent level displayed in 1989, the intensity
and volume of such support, at least as expressed in public protests and letters to
newspapers and Congress, appears to have been markedly less. Thus shortly
before the June 21 House vote, *New York Times* editorial writer John MacKenzie
declared that "the news so far is the lack of groundswell" for the amendment.
University of Virginia law professor Dick Howard similarly concluded, "There is
a great deal less wind in the sails than there was a year ago." Newspaper letters to
the editor in 1990 supported such impressions. For example, the *Philadelphia
Inquirer* published half a page of letters on the flag controversy in its June 21 issue
under the headline "Most Letter Writers Oppose a Flag Amendment," and the June
24 *Los Angeles Times* reported receiving 223 letters opposed to the amendment
and only 46 which supported it. On June 21, a Florida poll was published which

was the first survey since the *Johnson* ruling that reported a clear majority opposed to a constitutional amendment, including over 50 percent of both sexes,
both parties, and every geographic, racial, and ethnic group in the state. Among
age groups, those over sixty backed the amendment by 48-45, while those
between thirty and forty-four opposed it 60-37, a clear indication of generational
difference in attitudes toward the flag which also was suggested in other polls.
(Justice Stevens, in his *Eichman* dissent, had suggested such a generation gap existed when he wrote that "the symbolic value of the American flag is not the same
today as it was yesterday" because "events during the last three decades [such as
Vietnam, Watergate, and the Iran-Contra scandal] have altered the country's image
in the eyes of numerous Americans, and some now have difficulty understanding
the message that the flag conveyed to their parents and grandparents.")[54]

Among the other signs that public anger over the *Eichman* ruling seemed to be
considerably less intense than that displayed in the aftermath of the *Johnson* decision was that, unlike in 1989, there were very few overt indications of public
protest, such as the flying of flags in the upside-down or half-staff position.
Compared to 1989, there was also a much lower volume of mail to Congress urging
support for an amendment, together with a far higher percentage, and in some
cases a clear majority, of mail urging the opposite position. Thus, according to a
June 19 *Washington Post* story, Democratic representative Richard Durbin of
Ohio, who listed himself undecided but eventually voted against the amendment,
reported, "The phone isn't ringing, the mail isn't coming in. The intensity of this is
much lower than a year ago." Similarly, Democratic representative Dennis Eckart
of Ohio, who was committed to supporting the amendment, declared, "There is nowhere near the [mail] volume" as in 1989. Democratic amendment opponent senator Thomas Dodd reported receiving only 120 letters on the flag issue by June 21
and 75 percent of them backed his stand, while SJC chairman Biden reported that
he was being criticized in his home state of Delaware "by a factor of 10 or 20 to
one" for supporting even a "content-neutral" amendment and that "the popular position is my state is not to be for" any flag desecration amendment.[55]

Even 1990 amendment supporters conceded that the flag issue had lost much
of its popular appeal. Thus the June 19 *Washington Post* quoted conservative
fund-raiser Richard Viguerie as concluding, "There is nothing driving this issue
other than Washington politicians," and quoted an anonymous high-level Republican operative as lamenting, "This an issue whose time has come and gone."
In one clear indication of the success of the Democratic reframing campaign, a
June 23 *Congressional Quarterly* account quoted a congressional aide to a Republican amendment supporter as reporting that in 1989 the theme in constituent

mail was that the *Johnson* ruling was "such a disgrace," but in 1990 correspondents were urging, "Don't tamper with the Constitution." In 1991 interviews, Representative Montgomery concluded that the amendment was defeated in 1990 because "people lost interest in it," and American Legion national legislative director Phil Riggins agreed that public interest had declined considerably but added, "The American people don't stay stirred up over any issue for an extended period of time, but I don't believe that they changed their fundamental views."

Probably a number of interconnected reasons explain why an issue which one Washington reporter termed as "hot as a magnesium flare" in the summer of 1989 had become "politically lukewarm" by the late spring and early summer of 1990. Although, superficially, the FPA's proponents had failed because the Supreme Court struck down the law in *Eichman,* the deeper strategy of at least some of the statute's less enthusiastic backers, which was to put off serious consideration of a constitutional amendment in the hopes that passions would cool, succeeded remarkably well. Almost certainly one reason why public interest declined was that people had become bored with the flag issue: not only had the controversy dragged on for a year in an age of decreasing media and public attention spans, but in a political climate in which television had become increasingly dominant—witness the furor and fear centering on thirty-second negative TV ads—"Flag Burning II" was very much like a summer television rerun, a formula notorious for killing public interest. Thus PAW chairman John Buchanon, in an essay written for newspaper syndication, compared the 1990 flag dispute to a "tired sequel to a movie not worth seeing in the first place." ASNE president Burl Osborne wrote that the controversy reminded him of a country song titled "Here I Go Down That Wrong Road Again."[56]

New York University law professor and former ACLU legal director Burt Neuborne, in a 1991 interview, argued that "issues involving speech with powerful emotional overtones" are like a "flash fire, they go off and have a lot of heat and light, but have no staying power." The flag issue "disappeared from the public arena" quickly, Neuborne added, because "it was bullshit, there was nothing to it except fanning people's emotions." Similarly, in another 1991 interview, Democratic representative David Skaggs, one of the few congressional opponents of both the FPA and the amendment, concluded that the latter was defeated in 1990 because "the half-life [the time it takes to diminish by 50 percent] of political passion over any given issue in this country is a couple of months," and, additionally, the cooling-off period provided by the FPA's passage "provided the opportunity for an awful lot of people, prodded I think by the press, to reflect and to have their intellect evaluate the whole thing differently than they did in the immediate aftermath [of *Johnson*]." In a 1990 interview, Democratic representative Tim Valentine, who originally cosponsored the Bush amendment but ultimately voted against it, agreed with Skaggs's analysis. He stated:

> At the beginning, there was every reason to believe that it would be a hard position politically to oppose the amendment. But I don't think it turned out that way. As time went on, thinking people began to see the other desecration, the possible desecration of the Constitution. Then, I think, most people were able to distinguish between the importance of the Constitution to this nation, and the symbolism of the flag.

The "half-life" or "rerun" phenomenon of declining public interest was perhaps especially the case with the flag desecration issue because most Americans had never seen anyone burn a flag except on TV and were hardly affected in their daily lives by flag burners. Thus National Public Radio Supreme Court reporter Nina Totenberg, in a 1990 interview, noted that flag burning "doesn't really change the status quo on a daily basis" for the vast majority of people. "It's not like their children aren't going to school or they can't get an abortion," she added, "and people aren't burning flags on every downtown street corner."

Many of the factors previously discussed no doubt also helped to bring about a change in public attitudes concerning the flag controversy between 1989 and 1990. In particular, the reframing of the issue as the Bill of Rights versus the flag without the confusing distraction of the FPA, seems to have energized civil libertarians and to have caused second thoughts among Americans who had not before pondered the significance of limiting First Amendment rights; the developments in Eastern Europe probably heightened many Americans' appreciation of the fragility and importance of such rights; and the better organization of and overwhelming media support given to amendment opponents gave them a boost, while the overt politicization of the amendment by its backers during a period of growing public disillusionment with politicians hurt their cause with the public. Thus a Justice Department official suggested, in a 1990 interview, that public support for the amendment dropped off in 1990 not only because "it's not such a sensation as last time [1989]" and people "realize it's not the end of the world" but also because they "realize more that it's purely a political issue, purely an election issue—they're cynical and worn-out."

In another 1990 interview, House assistant majority whip Bonior suggested that the "concept of spending so much time on this issue versus the other pressing problems of this nation" was a further explanation for "letting the air out of the balloon." PAW legislative counsel John Gomperts, also interviewed in 1990, suggested that another reason for the calmer tone of the flag controversy in 1990 was that Stevens's relatively moderate dissent in *Eichman* "meant that the issue started at a much less hysterical level," whereas the virulent and incendiary tone of Rehnquist's 1989 *Johnson* dissent had "started this whole thing."

Former Reagan administration political consultant Lyn Nofziger suggested yet another reason for what he termed the "petering off" of the flag issue in 1990 by noting that there had not been "a lot of flag burning going on to keep it alive"— although it was probably more accurate to state that the national press did not report most flag burning incidents that did occur. In any case, in fact even flag-burners appear to have lost interest, at least relative to 1989, during the mid-June height of the 1990 controversy. The *Johnson* ruling had been followed within two weeks by at least a score of flag burnings, yet despite the call of Shawn Eichman, the successful lead defendant in the 1990 Supreme Court case, to make June 14 "flag desecration day," only five isolated flag burning protests were reported (in New York, Minneapolis, Iowa City, Chicago, and Seattle) between the June 11 *Eichman* decision and the June 21 House defeat of the amendment. Of these 1990 incidents, only one led to any serious disorders or to any significant police or media interest: in Seattle, about 15 people were arrested on the night of June 12, following minor fighting and shouting matches between 150 flag burners and their supporters and a group of 20 counterprotesters who sang the national anthem, waved flags, carried signs with slogans like "Don't burn our flag, hippie scum!" and chanted "No more burning." One observer remarked, "I can't tell the fascists from the communists."[57]

The largest single flag burning during the mid-June period may have been in Detroit on June 16, where a group of veterans ceremonially disposed of fifty flags in what they termed the "right way," which involved separating the stars from the flag with scissors, then soaking the remnants in kerosene and igniting them in a bonfire while a bugler played "Taps." One of the participants said such flag burning was "such a moving thing when it's done properly," while another said he viewed the event as a protest against the *Eichman* decision because the flag "should not, in any manner, shape or form, be desecrated and abused." Shortly before this ceremonial flag burning took place in Detroit, a weekly Washington, D.C., newspaper published a long article detailing what it termed the American Legion's "special recipe for tattered old glories." The article described the elaborate burning ceremony, complete with a special prayer, color guard, and bugle salute used by the Legion to "retire" worn flags. American Legion judge advocate Bill Lowman asked the paper's reporter, "Did you ever try to burn one of those new rayon flags? Those suckers don't burn, they melt. It all turns into this hot black goop that smells terrible. That's why the old cloth flags are still the best to burn." Lowman added, "We try to stay away from the term 'flag-burning.' This is a flag disposal. We don't want to make it sound like the Legion's just going around burning flags."[58]

The Impact of Last-Minute Congressional Introspection

A final factor that appears to have played a significant role in the 1990 defeat of the amendment was that many (especially Democratic) congressmen, faced with a straight up-or-down vote on it without the "easy out" provided in 1989 by the FPA, decided during their final deliberations that they could not live with themselves if they voted to limit the Bill of Rights. The vast majority of congressmen who were initially undecided in the wake of the *Eichman* ruling ended up voting against the amendment. An Associated Press poll published on June 19, based on surveys of Congress conducted June 15–18, reported that 243 House members were planning to vote for the amendment and another 11 were leaning toward it, that 108 opposed the amendment and 6 were leaning against it, that 54 members were undecided and 11 could not be contacted (of these latter two categories combined, about 85 percent were Democrats). Yet during the June 21 House vote, 254 representatives voted for the amendment and 177 voted against it; 80 percent of the group that was originally undecided or could not be reached voted "no." Similarly, the AP poll indicated 58 senators favoring or leaning toward the amendment, 24 opposed or leaning against, and 18 undecided (of whom 15 were Democrats), but the June 26 Senate vote was only 58-42 for the amendment.[59]

Numerous accounts suggest that a substantial number of "no" votes resulted from last-minute decisions and that some were the products of highly unusual, prolonged periods of intense introspection which led congressmen (almost all Democrats) into the painful conclusion that their consciences would not permit them to act otherwise. Thus, although representatives Mary Rose Oakar (D-Ohio) and William Coyne (D-Pa.) were listed as, respectively, leaning toward the amendment and undecided in the AP survey, both voted against it on June 21. Coyne announced that he would "vote against this amendment because it would be hard for me to sleep at night knowing that I had caved in to some reprehensible malcontents who would burn the flag—or to some politicians and commentators who would demagog this issue to high heavens." Oakar told a reporter that although "I know it sounds corny," she had decided to oppose the amendment after staying up and reading "a biography of Patrick Henry and the Bill of Rights" on the night before the House vote, even though her constituents "go psycho" if they "see some guy on television burning the flag" and "I was really going to vote for that amendment."[60]

In five cases, representatives who had originally cosponsored the Bush amendment announced changes of heart during the June 21 House floor debate. For example, Representative John Tanner (D-Tenn.) attributed his decision to withdraw to a "deep and agonizing reflection" that had led him to conclude that American patriotism must be "fueled by guaranteed individual freedoms, not by a coercive government that demands tribute from a subjected people." Perhaps the most dramatic withdrawal of amendment sponsorship came from Representative Tim Valentine (D-N.C.), who told his colleagues that "over the rhetoric of the past few days I have finally heard the voice of my own conscience." In a 1990 interview, Valentine said that at first, "I did not fully comprehend the significance of all of the ramifications which were inherent in our amending the Constitution," but that

> as I went through the process of listening, speaking with other members [of Congress] and talking to constituents and reading our mail, I became concerned about the prospect of amending the Bill of Rights for the first time in 200 years, what the consequences of that might be down the road. It was an evolutionary process, moving from day to day. I found myself at one point thinking I would still support the amendment but hoping it would fail, and I finally reached the conclusion to vote against it without regard to the political consequences. I just decided there are some things in our work where politics has to or should take a back seat.[61]

Another original amendment sponsor, Representative Glenn Poshard (D-Ill.), told the House on June 21 that he had not been "able to sleep well while I have supported the amendment, and when that happens on any issue, I know I'm wrong." Poshard added that he had decided to vote against the amendment after visiting Independence Hall in Philadelphia, the Jefferson Memorial in Washington, and other historical sites over the previous weekend and after concluding that "it should be the purpose of the flag, as it is the Constitution, to invite respect and love but not to command it because that violates the free will of the individual, and love and respect not freely given cannot be real." In a 1990 interview, Poshard termed his consideration of the issue a "gut-wrenching" process and said that "the hardest thing" was that he had to write again to all his constituents who had expressed their views in the flag controversy and "tell them I had changed my mind." He said his visit to historic sites had led to "an emotional experience, to be honest," adding that, "I began to feel the weight of those Bill of Rights, and I could not support the amendment after that."[62]

One of the most stunning changes of mind announced on June 21 came from Representative Charles Stenholm, a conservative Texas Democrat, whose original response to the *Johnson* ruling had been to denounce the Supreme Court on the House floor for "humiliating the flag" and to demand rhetorically, "What in God's name is going on?" In his June 21 House address, Stenholm declared, "I do love the flag because it symbolizes the United States, but I love the ideals put into words by the U.S. Constitution even more than the flag." In a 1991 interview, Stenholm said that in his original response to the *Johnson* ruling he had been "caught up in the emotional reaction" and that supporting an amendment "seemed like the thing to do," but that after a "lot of research" and listening to a "lot of people," he reached the conclusion that "every nation has a flag, but only the U.S. has a Bill of Rights [*sic*]." Nonetheless, Stenholm continued, "what made it so tough for me" was that "I don't make a habit of going against my [congressional] district, but I know I did on this vote."

Among other last-minute voters against the amendment, Representative Peter Hoagland (D-Neb.), who had voted for the FPA in 1989 and was listed as undecided in the June 15–18 AP survey, told a reporter that he made his decision because "I didn't want my tombstone inscription to be that I supported an amendment to weaken the Constitution." Although Hoagland had been elected in 1988 by a razor-thin 51 percent margin and was advised by his staff to support the amendment, he explained, "A vote like this one is closely associated with self-respect. In the past, there have been a few times that I have tilted more towards political considerations than I should have. And I lived to regret that." Illinois representative John Porter, whose first reaction to the *Johnson* ruling had been that "it's outrageous that the Supreme Court would not protect the symbol of our freedom," but who ended up as one of only seventeen Republican representatives who voted against the amendment, said in a 1991 interview that he regarded the amendment as "an entirely different" matter than the FPA (which he had voted for) because an amendment would remove from the issue "the entire judicial branch of government that is the guardian of our civil liberties." Porter added, "Frankly, I was under a lot of pressure [to support the amendment], but I felt that I made the correct decision for our country and the Constitution. I made a decision a long time ago that I have to do what I think is right, and if I can't convince my voters that I'm right then they can vote [against me]."[63]

Although the public comments of those voting against the amendment might be discounted as self-serving dramatizations, independent evidence suggests that many of the last-minute vote announcements were genuine and reflected real and unusual conscience-grappling experiences by many congressmen. For example, in a 1991 interview, Representative David Skaggs recalled of the June 21, 1990, House vote:

> I will never forget when the debate was finished many of my colleagues came up in the course of the vote, people in the undecided column, and said, "David, I've thought about this and I just can't vote for it [the amendment]." It was an expression of conscience and anguish and hard thinking. I think it was one of those rare occasions in which an appeal to what's best in people's galaxy of political principles paid off.

Similarly, a key House Democratic leadership aide who was deeply involved in fighting the amendment said, in a 1990 interview, that the issue was

> one of the most remarkable things I've ever worked on. It was a matter of each individual member really wrestling with their conscience, what the Constitution and the Bill of Rights meant to them, how they could balance this mix of values and the political pressures, but in the end for most of them they weaned away the political pressures and it became a question for each member of how they could explain the values of the country to their constituents. It was quite remarkable. Congress has such a bad reputation—people don't understand the struggle members really go through—and this was just one of those cases where you felt like, "My God, this is why I do this." This was really a deep soul-searching kind of thing, this was real "profiles in courage" type stuff.

★

EPILOGUE AND AFTERTHOUGHTS:
THE FLAG DESECRATION CONTROVERSY
IN THE POST-*EICHMAN* ERA,
MID-1990 TO MID-1995

If one were to believe the predictions of most backers of the flag desecration constitutional amendment (often implicitly seconded by media accounts), the defeat of the amendment in June 1990 was bound to lead to the following developments: (1) the flag desecration controversy and, in particular, the dispute over the wisdom of an amendment would remain a continual and "burning issue" for months and possibly years to follow and would become a central issue in the 1990 congressional elections, with amendment opponents likely to suffer severe retribution at the polls; (2) until and unless an amendment was passed, Americans' love for the flag would be imperiled as they were forced to witness legally unfettered physical assaults upon the flag; and (3) such assaults would increase because with no legal penalty, anyone who wished to desecrate the flag would feel free to do so. Each of these intertwined predictions proved false during the four years following the defeat of the amendment, although following the 1994 congressional elections in which Republicans gained control of both houses of Congress for the first time in over forty years, backers of an amendment revived the issue in Congress, and prospects for its endorsement by at least the House of Representatives appeared to be strong by mid-1995. Until this 1995 resurrection of the amendment, however, the flag desecration controversy had nearly faded away completely from media coverage and public and political attention almost immediately after the defeat of the amendment in 1990; the issue arose only in a handful of 1990 congressional

races and did not figure prominently in the defeat of even a single amendment opponent; the fervor of flag waving that accompanied the Persian Gulf War of 1991
and a new burst of popular flag-based fashions in 1990–91 demonstrated that
Americans' love for the flag was undiminished by the legalization of flag desecration. Compared to the period in 1989–90 when the FPA temporarily made flag desecration illegal, such incidents markedly decreased after the *Eichman* ruling again
made such conduct legal; and finally, and perhaps most revealing of all concerning
unfettered feelings about the flag and the reluctance of political officials to uphold
the law, the handful of people who engaged in flag desecration, or acts that were
viewed by others as flag desecration, after June 1990 often continued to face legal
reprisals, sometimes under obviously unconstitutional state flag desecration laws
and sometimes under other legal or administrative pretexts.

The Flag Desecration Issue
Suddenly Disappears: Post-June 1990

With truly stunning rapidity and completeness, the flag desecration issue disappeared from the mass media and from apparent general public and political attention shortly after the congressional defeat of the constitutional amendment in June
1990. Perhaps symbolic of this sudden loss of interest was a bizarre development
in the Louisiana legislature, where on July 8 the entire provisions of the bill originally designed to reduce the penalty for assault, where flag burners were the target,
from the usual six months in jail and a $500 fine to only a fine of $25 were stripped
from the proposal by a legislative maneuver and replaced with language that imposed new restrictions on abortion. Although an angered Planned Parenthood
spokeswoman spluttered, "Only in Louisiana could you have a flag-burning bill
become an abortion bill," this legislative twist clearly captured the sudden and dramatic general loss of interest concerning the entire flag desecration issue.[1]

The almost complete disappearance of the flag desecration controversy from
general press, political, and public attention after June 1990 was especially surprising because for months Republican and veterans' groups' spokesmen and
news stories had hammered home the twin themes that the issue would be a major
focus in the 1990 congressional elections and that any incumbent who voted
against the amendment would pay dearly at the polls in November. Such predictions continued to be common even after the defeat of the constitutional amendment in the House on June 21. Thus, shortly after the vote, assistant Republican
House leader Gingrich declared that pressing for an amendment would become "a

key campaign promise of every [Republican] candidate this fall," and in a June 29 front-page story headlined "GOP Strategists See the Flag Issue as a Sure-Fire Winner," the *Christian Science Monitor* reported that Republicans were planning to "make flag burning a high-profile issue in dozens of congressional races across the country" and that party officials were convinced that the issue was a "sure-fire winner" that "could help them in 20 to 30 closely-contested House races."[2]

One especially clear indication that the flag desecration controversy was quickly disappearing came in September 1990 when David Souter, the nominated successor to retiring Supreme Court justice William Brennan, was never asked about his views about flag desecration during his successful Senate confirmation hearings. During the 1990 congressional campaigns, flag desecration became a significant issue in only a handful of races; thus *Congressional Quarterly* reported that the issue had proved to be "strictly flash-in-the-pan" and that "hardly a peep on the flag was heard" during the campaign. In every instance of the few congressional races where the issue was stressed—almost invariably by a Republican critic of an incumbent Democrat who had voted against the amendment—the candidate who emphasized it lost. Furthermore, the Democratic Party as a whole clearly did not suffer from its congressional leadership's opposition to the flag desecration amendment, as overall the party gained about ten seats in Congress.[3]

Among the 96 percent of all incumbent House candidates who won reelection in 1990 were about half-a-dozen who were subjected to moderate to intense attacks upon their vote against the flag desecration amendment. For example, North Carolina representative Tim Valentine, who reversed course to vote against the amendment, recalled in a December 1990 interview that his opponent in the state's second district had "sent me a waffle and a flag" and "accused me of waffling" on the flag desecration issue, but added that "we ate" the waffle and the attack on his vote "petered out after the first burst of that sort of thing," during which he "caught hell" for a while. "But I don't think it turned out to be a major issue in the end," Valentine added. "I got 75 percent of the vote."[4]

Democratic assistant House majority whip David Bonior, who was ultimately reelected with 66 percent support in 1990 (compared to 54 percent in 1988) in the blue-collar twelfth congressional district of Michigan, faced opposition from Republican Jim Dingeman, who campaigned by handing out small flags bearing a flyer reading, "Protecting our flag. Jim Dingeman for Congress." In an interview conducted shortly after the election, Bonior said that Dingeman's literature had suggested that he (Bonior) "supported" flag burning but that he had successfully defused the issue by expressing "my outrage" over such assertions and by telling constituents that:

I had served my country in the military for four years, loved the flag and that for which it stood and got no bigger pleasure than in giving flags to civic groups and schools. I then mentioned that basically we were talking about amending the Constitution, but more than that, one of the most sacred documents in civil liberties known to Western civilization. I tried to explain in an emotional way how many of my constituents, relatives and ancestors in Eastern Europe had been fighting for those rights.

In the twenty-second Illinois congressional district, Representative Glenn Poshard, who had originally supported the amendment in 1989, won reelection in 1990 with 84 percent of the vote against a Republican challenger (who technically ran as an independent after missing the Republican filing deadline) who made Poshard's vote against the amendment a central focus of his campaign. In an interview conducted three weeks after the November 6, 1990, election, Poshard said that his conservative district, which he described as "part of the Bible belt," "came almost full circle" on the amendment after a "pretty sound debate" which persisted for about six months. Although at first, Poshard related, he was deluged with "thousands of letters literally from a broad cross section" of his constituents denouncing his vote, eventually increasing numbers of voters were convinced by his argument that "love is only real, respect is only real, if we in effect have the right not to respect and not to love." Poshard added that throughout the election onlookers who had just been furnished by his opponent with flags and literature attacking him for his vote awaited him at parades. He related, "When I came through for these parades these people were defiantly waving the flag in my face with these flyers and that got to be pretty hard, it got to the point where my wife wouldn't go to parades with me."

During the first four years following the 1990 congressional elections, the flag desecration controversy showed no signs of resurfacing as a significant national issue (although it did lead to heated local disputes and prosecutions, and the American Legion quietly but successfully lobbied for support for an amendment from the majority of the country's state legislatures) and members of all three branches of the national government displayed little interest in reviving it. The issue virtually disappeared from congressional discussion and barely surfaced anywhere during the 1992 and 1994 congressional elections, and President Bush never sought to resurrect the flag desecration issue after mid-1990. During his unsuccessful 1992 reelection bid, Bush referred to the controversy only once and then simply to praise his opponent, Bill Clinton, for an American Legion speech in which Clinton had expressed pride in successfully sponsoring anti-flag-desecration legislation modeled on the FPA in 1989 as governor of Arkansas.[5]

In decisions that were barely reported in the national news media, the Supreme Court firmly refused to reopen or reconsider its 1989–90 flag burning rulings in October 1992 and again in March 1994 by refusing to hear appeals from lower court rulings that had vacated flag-desecration prosecutions on the basis of Supreme Court precedents. The Court refused to consider the appeals even though only four votes were required to hear them and all four dissenting members of the *Johnson* and *Eichman* Supreme Courts were still serving. An unusually direct and public clue that the Court's reluctance to reopen the issue was conscious and politically influenced was offered by Justice Stevens, the author of dissents in both flag desecration cases, who bluntly told the ABA in August 1990 that the Court "should never have" agreed to hear the Johnson case because "had we just allowed the [Texas] state court judgment [overturning Gregory Lee Johnson's 1984 Dallas flag desecration conviction] to stand" the result would have been "a lot of ink and a lot of heartache saved."[6]

Exactly why the flag desecration issue went away so quickly and completely, at least temporarily and as a national issue, can be explained only in a tentative and speculative manner. Most likely its rapid disappearance reflected a combination of the same factors that resulted in the comparative diminishment of interest in the issue in 1990 as compared to 1989 plus the additional ingredient of developments in the second half of 1990, which directed media, political, and public interest in new directions. Among the factors contributing to diminished interest or support for banning flag desecration in 1990 compared to the previous year and which continued to move currents in the same direction after June 1990 were the rerun (or, put more plainly, the boredom) factor; the growing sense that the issue had been seized upon primarily for partisan ends by Republicans; the symbolic power of the Constitution as a countervailing icon to the flag; the growing consensus that more substantive issues demanded attention and that flag desecration was a purely symbolic concern; and the sense that flag desecration, at least in Eastern Europe, could serve a positive function. After June 1990, these factors in lowering the fervor for a flag amendment were significantly supplemented by a shift in attention to at least three highly substantive concerns that, unlike flag desecration, directly affected many Americans in the course of their daily lives: increasing indications that the country was slipping into a recession; growing concern over the budget deficit and adverse reaction to President Bush's abandonment, during the summer of 1990, of his highly publicized 1988 campaign pledge never to raise taxes; and above all, during the last third of 1990, growing indications that the

United States was about to go to war in response to the August invasion of Kuwait by Iraq. Compared to these continuing and growing crises, which did or conceivably could raise Americans' taxes or cost them their jobs or their lives, concern about flag desecration, which had already been rapidly diminishing, soon faded away as a matter of significant national media, public, or political attention.

Flag Fashion and Flag-Waving Fervor, 1990–1995

Although flag desecration disappeared as a national issue after June 1990, during the subsequent year there was plenty of evidence that the legalization of flag desecration in no way diminished Americans' love for the flag, contrary to many assertions and predictions made by those who disagreed with the Supreme Court's rulings. During the second half of 1990 and especially during the Gulf War fervor of early 1991, flag fashions, flag sales, and flag displays attained extraordinary popularity, perhaps unprecedented in American history. Ironically, many of the flag fashions and the patriotic Gulf War flag displays would have violated flag desecration laws had they still been in effect—in fact, very similar sorts of clothing and displays had led to numerous prosecutions during the Vietnam War, when they were viewed as ridiculing the flag instead of being patriotic. As the *Seattle Times* reported in a 1991 story about the wave of flag fashions and displays, "What was then desecration is now decoration." Similarly, *Time* magazine, in reporting in 1990 on the rapid sales of $57.50 New Glory flag shirts at New York's fashionable Saks Fifth Avenue store, noted that "the shirt's success might have surprised [former Yippie leader] Abbie Hoffman," who was "once charged with flag desecration for wearing a shirt like Saks' best-seller."[7]

The increasing popularity of flag fashions, which was already apparent in 1989 and early 1990, became ever more clear in late 1990 and 1991 as clothing designers introduced a seemingly endless number of flag-oriented lines. Commenting on the fashion phenomenon in its lead editorial published on July 4, 1990, two weeks after the 1990 defeat of the constitutional amendment, the *New York Times* noted, "Fashion watchers aren't sure why, but Americans are immersed in flag chic. Beyond shirts, stores offer flag-motif bikinis, shorts, tube tops, socks, scarves, sweaters and evening gowns." As the prospects for American military intervention in the Persian Gulf mounted in late 1990 and then became a reality in early 1991, flag fashions attained ever greater popularity, leading several New York City stores to open special "flag boutiques" which gathered together in one convenient place all of their flag-oriented merchandise. Thus Macy's established special flag merchandise areas that sold objects ranging from a $5 flag-decorated tie rack to $1,600 flag jewelry, with items priced in between, including boxer shorts, headbands, and nightshirts, not to mention jeans with flag patches of the sort that had regularly led to flag desecration prosecutions twenty years earlier. A 1994 *Los Angeles Times* article suggested that fervor for flag-design articles was still going strong, with available items including shirts, vests, throw pillows, headbands, book bags, and even pasta ("flag-shaped riscotti in tomato red or white," although not blue, as "blue food seems to gross out even patriots").[8]

Aside from boosting the sale of flag-design clothing, the Gulf War also sent the sales of actual flags skyrocketing upward from levels that had already been stimulated by the flag burning controversy. Thus on July 4, 1990, a few weeks after the defeat of the flag desecration constitutional amendment in Congress, the owner of the Capital Flag Company of Oklahoma declared, "This year has been our biggest so far [for flag sales]." A few days after American planes began bombing Iraq in mid-January 1991, a spokesman at the Annin Flag Company in Roseland, New Jersey, reported that telephone orders had jumped from four hundred to over one thousand a day and that "every [flag] retailer I have talked to says they are swamped." In mid-February, the spokesman said, "We had good inventories when the fighting began three weeks ago, but that's been wiped out and now we're working on a five- or six-week backlog of orders."[9]

Along with an explosion of flag fashions and flag sales, the early 1991 period of the Gulf War and its immediate aftermath also witnessed a massive increase in general flag displays. On March 9, the *New York Times* published a huge and compelling front-page photograph that captured the enormous prominence and emotionalism of the flag displays that accompanied the war: against the backdrop of a huge flag, a black soldier returning from the Gulf was pictured being hugged by his daughter while he grasped a small flag in his hand that almost seemed to be part of the embrace. Another large *New York Times* photograph, published on June 15, perhaps best illustrated that many flag displays associated with Gulf War patriotism would have been illegal under the FPA and many state flag desecration laws: it depicted a huge flag, which weighed seven tons and was larger than a football field, being displayed on the grounds of the Washington Monument in celebration of Flag Day and the American victory in the Gulf. Although the flag was clearly placed on the ground because there was no other feasible way to display it, it would have been banned under the FPA provision which outlawed maintaining flags on the ground.

Numerous other Gulf War patriotic flag displays also would have raised serious legal questions had flag desecration laws still been in effect. For example, the

February 1, 1991, *Ann Arbor News* contained a huge picture of a flag at Deerfield High School in Michigan with the slogan, written across the stripes of the flag, "DEERFIELD SUPPORTS OUR TROOPS," and so covered with yellow ribbons designed to express support for American soldiers in the Gulf that they covered virtually all of the flag's stars and thus "defaced" the flag. Among the scores of other unorthodox Gulf War displays that might well have raised legal questions had flag desecration laws remained in effect was a huge "living flag" created by 3,600 people wearing colored T-shirts in San Diego (what if someone moved or wore the wrong color?); a flag created out of colored light-bulbs (what if some burned out?); and a flag painted on the windows of a college dormitory (what if the window was opened or broken?).[10]

In contravention of the voluntary 1942 congressional flag code and many state flag desecration laws in effect before 1989, many athletic teams initiated the practice during the buildup to and the outbreak of the Gulf War of wearing flag patches on their uniforms (indeed, so did American troops who served in the Gulf War, in the 1990 Panama invasion, and in Somalia in 1992–94, despite the obvious risk that such flags would be "defaced" by dirt and blood, among other substances). As *Sports Illustrated* noted in its February 25, 1991, issue: "There is hardly a pro or college team in the land that hasn't made some symbolic gesture in support of the U.S. forces. Flag decals and patches are everywhere, from the helmets of NFL (National Football League) players to the backboards of NBA (National Basketball Association) arenas, from the shoes of a high school wrestler to the jersey of Waad Hirmez, the Iraqi-born soccer star of the San Diego Sockers."

In some cases, as with respect to college teams that almost uniformly began wearing flag patches, the practice was in clear violation of National Collegiate Athletic Association rules baring wearing any decorations on uniforms; similarly, during the Gulf War the New York City Police Department and even the United Parcel Service modified their rules concerning uniforms to allow employees to wear small flag pins, and several colleges, including Cornell University and the University of Maryland, waived ordinary regulations barring the display of flags from student dormitories. As an official at Cornell explained, "In light of the situation in the Persian gulf, it is clear that banning American or other flags is not something any of us feels comfortable doing."[11]

In many other instances not associated with the Gulf War during the post-*Eichman* period, flags were also used in unorthodox ways that might have raised legal questions had flag desecration laws remained intact. For example, on September 1, 1992, the *New York Times* published a front page photograph depicting a flag being used in emergency conditions to hold up a glucose bag being used to treat a survivor of Hurricane Andrew in Florida. Pop star Madonna urged young people to vote in 1990 by appearing in an MTV video wearing only red underwear and wrapped in a flag, promising that "if you don't vote, you're going to get a spankie." The Committee for National Health Insurance repeatedly advertised its calls for health reform in the *New York Times* by showing a flag cut into ten pieces, each of which was labeled with a perceived problem in the existing health care system. American tennis player David Wheaton was depicted in a prominent photograph published in the July 2, 1991, *New York Times* wearing a flag headband to stop sweat from interfering with his vision, and numerous American athletes who participated in the 1992 Olympics wore skimpy uniforms decorated with flag colors and designs or celebrated their victories by wearing flags as capes or shawls. Gay activists protesting lack of funding to combat AIDS regularly replaced the field of stars with skulls and crossbones in the early 1990s. Rescue workers at the disastrous April 1995 Oklahoma City bombing of a federal building in which over 160 people were killed appeared on national television wearing flag-design headbands. Even President Bush was involved in acts that almost certainly would have violated most pre-1989 flag desecration laws: in February 1992, he gave visiting Russian president Boris Yeltsin a pair of Texas cowboy boots and a silver belt buckle adorned with Russian and American flags; and in October 1992, during the election campaign, he was photographed wearing a flag-decorated jacket, as well as being greeted by cheerleaders wearing skimpy flag-design halter tops and shorts.[12]

Flag Desecration in the Post-Eichman Era

Perhaps the most widespread assumption or prediction made by those who opposed the Supreme Court's 1989–90 rulings legalizing flag desecration was that flag burnings and similar incidents would increase and that the perpetrators of such acts would go unpunished. These predictions proved just as wrong as did predictions that flag desecration would remain a burning issue after Congress defeated the constitutional amendment in 1990 and that its legalization would diminish Americans' love for the flag. During the five years following the June 1990 *Eichman* ruling, only about three dozen instances that could be broadly construed as flag desecration to express political protest were reported in the general press, about the same number of such incidents reported during the fewer than eight months when flag desecration was technically illegal under the FPA between late October 1989 and mid-June 1990. Furthermore, about half of these incidents occurred as protests against two highly unusual events: the American buildup and entry into the Persian Gulf War during the fall and winter of 1990–91 and the acquittal in April 1992 of Los Angeles police accused of beating black motorist Rodney King. One of the most fervent opponents of flag desecration, Supreme Court chief justice William Rehnquist, was one of the few people who accurately predicted the results of the Supreme Court rulings that he bitterly dissented from. In an unusual public comment before a meeting of lawyers and judges in August 1990, Rehnquist declared, "There are not many people in this country who have burned flags, but now that it has finally been established as legal, there will be far fewer."[13]

If predictions that flag burnings would escalate in the wake of the *Eichman* ruling and the defeat of the constitutional amendment proved inaccurate, the same proved true of the logical expectation that those who engaged in flag desecration after 1990 would not suffer legal or other penalties. In fact, of the three dozen broadly construed political protest flag desecration incidents reported after mid-1990, almost half led to arrests and another 25 percent led to noncriminal reprisals or threats. In at least eight cases, prosecutions were initiated under flag desecration laws that had presumably been struck down by the Supreme Court's 1989–90 rulings, and in another ten or so cases other, often highly dubious, charges were brought although the real "crime" appears to have been flag desecration. In almost all of these cases the charges were eventually either dropped or those charged were acquitted, but the message that flag desecration would continue to bear a heavy legal cost had still been delivered.

Apparently, the only post-*Eichman* incident in which an explicit flag desecration prosecution ultimately (if almost certainly unconstitutionally) led to a conviction came in a 1991 case in Cortland, Ohio, where Tracy McLellan was sentenced to fourteen days in jail for theft, disorderly conduct, criminal trespass, and flag desecration after police arrested him for tearing a flag from a church flagpole and attempting to sprinkle gasoline on it. In contrast to the Ohio incident, in Texas, Midland County district attorney Mark Dettman was unsuccessful at every legal step, all the way up to the United States Supreme Court, in attempting to prosecute Robert Lynn Jimenez under the 1989 Texas flag desecration law, which had been law modeled on the federal FPA and was similarly designed to circumvent the *Johnson* ruling. Jimenez was arrested in February 1990, while the FPA was still in effect, for allegedly writing and painting obscenities and "satanic" symbols on Texas and American flags, but legal proceedings against him commenced only in March 1991, after the *Eichman* ruling struck down the FPA and almost certainly invalidated the Texas law also. At Jimenez's pretrial hearing in Midland County Court on March 15, 1991, Midland County Court judge James Fitz-Gerald declared, "I'm required, as far as I know, to follow the Supreme Court's decisions" and, without hearing any evidence, dismissed the prosecution on the grounds that the 1989 Texas law was in fact unconstitutional, at least as applied to Jimenez. Subsequently, a three-judge panel of the Eighth District Texas Court of Appeals rejected Dettman's appeal from Fitz-Gerald's dismissal of the Jimenez prosecution, and the Texas Court of Criminal Appeals and the United States Supreme Court both refused to hear further appeals.[14]

In one especially odd post-1990 flag desecration prosecution, Somerset, Pennsylvania, district justice Jon Barkman dismissed charges in October 1993 that had been brought under state law against local artist Lisa Mostoller. Mostoller had covered a portion of a flag with a black cloth painted with the words "Laurel Arts Pirate Ship" to advertise an attraction at an annual festival of the arts. Barkman declared that Mostoller, who had recently been declared Outstanding Person of the Year by the Somerset County Chamber of Commerce, had not intended to desecrate the flag and that his decision was not based on constitutional grounds.

Perhaps the most bizarre of the post-*Eichman* flag desecration prosecutions also came from Pennsylvania, where Mark Cox was arrested in Youngsville in June 1991 for allegedly ripping down several American flags from a bridge display and slapping a woman passerby who had chastised and slapped him for tossing the flags. After pleading guilty to charges of harassment of the passerby and insult to the state and national flags, in the expectation that he would only be fined, Cox was instead ordered by Warren County judge Robert Wolfe to pay a $500 fine, to serve a jail term of nine to twenty-three and a half months, to undergo alcohol counseling, and to read and write a book report about *Man Without a Country,* a fictionalized account about a man who, after denouncing the United States, was banished and required to spend the rest of his life without a homeland aboard ships on the high seas.[15] Judge Wolfe told Cox that he would read the book report to determine if writing it "rehabilitates your attitude towards the flag." In response to the sentence, Cox's mother lamented, "It's not right. There's murderers, there's rapers out there, then there's Mark." Cox served a total of almost four weeks in jail before he was released on parole while he appealed. Warren County officials eventually agreed to drop the flag insult allegations after a Pennsylvania appeals court overturned his convictions in late 1992, without ruling on their substance, on the grounds that Cox had not been given adequate legal assistance and advice at his original trial.

In another case with a similar flavor, Barry Carpenter was convicted of flag desecration in Russellville, Alabama, in early 1991 after police arrested him while he was distributing leaflets opposed to the Persian Gulf War outside the local post office. Carpenter was originally detained for "littering," desecrating a monument—the post office—by chalking antiwar slogans on the post office sidewalk, and endangering the welfare of his child (by getting himself arrested and therefore leaving no one to care for her) and was subsequently charged with flag desecration when the police discovered a flag in Carpenter's coat pocket, which was alleged to be soiled and in a very "disorderly" and "wadded" condition. After two appeals, Carpenter's conviction was thrown out on the grounds that the applicable state law required that acts of illegal flag desecration had to be performed in "public." Carpenter won an out-of-court settlement after he sued Russellville officials for a variety of offenses, including false imprisonment and malicious prosecution.[16]

In addition to these eight cases in which alleged flag desecrators were tried under state flag desecration laws which were almost certainly unconstitutional after the *Eichman* ruling, in about ten additional post-*Eichman* cases civilians were arrested under other charges, such as arson or inciting to riot, which in most cases appear to have been pretexts for punishing them for acts of flag desecration. Apparently in only one of these cases, plus one case involving a soldier tried under the Uniform Code of Military Justice, did a conviction ultimately result. In the others, the charges appear to have been dropped or the cases were ultimately dismissed in the courts.

Among the latter cases, disturbing the peace charges originally brought against two anti–Gulf War protesters involved in a flag burning in St. Louis on March 24, 1991, were dropped after they filed a complaint alleging false arrest and complaining that police had stood by while they were assaulted by hostile onlookers. In Oberlin, Ohio, two protesters, who had been originally investigated by the FBI for possible violation of the FPA for burning a flag in January 1990 (before the *Eichman* ruling) to denounce the American invasion of Panama, were acquitted in August 1990 of charges of receiving stolen property (the flag) and criminal damage to someone else's property, which had first been alleged only after the June *Eichman* ruling.[17]

In Los Angeles, police arrested five RCYB members for arson, inciting a riot, and resisting arrest on July 8, 1990, after they were attacked in MacArthur Park by onlooking VFW members who succeeded in grabbing away from them flags that they were attempting to burn. More than a dozen Los Angeles police stood by while the melee occurred; they rejected RCYB demands to arrest the VFW members while defending their arrests of the flag burners on the grounds that municipal codes banned burning anything in the park. Repeated attempts to obtain information from the Los Angeles Police Department concerning the ultimate disposition of this case proved unsuccessful, which suggests that in all likelihood the case was not pursued.[18]

In New York City, charges of violating a municipal ordinance which outlawed setting a fire on any city property, brought against a man named Donald Payne, who was alleged to have burned a flag on three separate occasions in July 1990 outside a city courthouse during a highly publicized trial, were ordered dropped by a Manhattan Criminal Court judge in January 1991 on the grounds that his acts posed no threat to the peace or public safety and were a form of political speech protected by the Supreme Court's flag desecration rulings. Because the city did not allege that Payne had been disorderly, had blocked traffic, or otherwise threatened any possible government interest in "preventing a public disturbance," the judge declared, "it appears that the primary interest" in prosecuting him was to "suppress the defendant's politically charged acts of burning the flag," a motivation that was "inconsistent with the First Amendment" under the *Johnson* ruling.[19]

In Cleveland, RCP member Cheryl Lessin was charged with a felony count of inciting to riot during a flag burning protest rally on August 10, 1990, against American policy leading up to the Persian Gulf War. She was convicted by a jury and sentenced to a year in prison based on the testimony of two Cleveland police officers who, in contradiction to the testimony of several other witnesses, claimed that Lessin had run through a crowd of bystanders shoving people, throwing punches, and shouting obscenities; one of the officers admitted that he had ordered Lessin's arrest with the words, "She admitted burning the flag, arrest her." In October 1993, the Ohio Supreme Court overturned Lessin's conviction by a 4-3 vote on the technical grounds that the trial judge had failed to adequately instruct the original jury that her "disgraceful and irreverent action" in burning the flag was a constitutionally protected form of free speech that could not by itself be construed as proof that Lessin had incited violence, and that therefore it was "impossible to say with any degree of certainty that her burning of the United States flag was disregarded by the jury in reaching its verdict." On March 21, 1994, the United States Supreme Court refused Ohio's request to consider an appeal from this ruling, and subsequently Cleveland officials decided not to exercise their option of retrying the case with amended jury instructions.[20]

Of all of the post-*Eichman* flag desecration incidents that led to arrests under other charges, only two led to convictions that were not overturned subsequently. In September 1991, the U.S. Army Court of Military Review upheld the conviction of soldier Samuel Wilson, who had been convicted by a court-martial under the Uniform Code of Military Justice for disobeying a lawful order and dereliction of duty for blowing his nose on a flag. Wilson's sentence included a bad-conduct discharge, confinement, forfeiture of pay for four months, and reduction in rank. The review court in effect held that, although soldiers enjoyed First Amendment rights, including the right of symbolic expression, the *Johnson* and *Eichman* rulings did not fully apply to them because military needs "may warrant regulation of conduct that would not be justified in the civilian community," in particular because "military necessity, including the fundamental necessity for discipline, can be a compelling government interest warranting the limitation of the right of freedom of speech."[21]

The only civilian flag desecration case prosecuted under other charges during the five years following the Eichman ruling that resulted in a non-overturned conviction stemmed from a New York City protest against the American buildup to the Persian Gulf War which, ironically, involved the same Shawn Eichman of the earlier landmark Supreme Court decision which bore her name. On September 11, 1990, Eichman and fellow RCP supporter Joe Urgo were arrested while standing on top of a military recruiting center in Times Square, after they had climbed the building with a ladder, dripped motor oil and red-dyed corn syrup (to simulate blood) on the building in order to suggest that the United States was willing to spill blood to protect its oil interests in the Middle East, and attempted to burn the American flag that was flying over the building (according to the protesters, it would not catch fire because it was so caked with soot from flying in the polluted air of downtown New York). Federal officials at first charged the two protesters with arson for seeking to burn down the recruiting center, then replaced that with charges of depredation to federal property, reckless endangerment and burglary, and subsequently replaced the burglary charge with an allegation of arson for seeking to burn the federally owned flag (under the federal arson statute invoked, the same ten-year maximum penalty applied either for attempting to burn a federal flag or attempting to burn down a federal building, although the maximum penalty under the 1968 and 1989 federal flag desecration laws was one year in prison).[22]

Eichman and Urgo were convicted by a jury on March 23, 1991, on the charges of arson and depredation and were subsequently sentenced to two years probation and two hundred hours of community service. The extremely light sentence may have been partly influenced by an unusual letter sent to the judge by one of the jurors that stated that all of the jurors who spoke on the subject agreed that the prosecution would never have occurred "if it were not for the action involving the flag" and that "no matter how the government couches the language, the case seems pretty obviously a flag burning case." On February 13, 1992, a three-judge panel of the Second Circuit U.S. Court of Appeals unanimously upheld the convictions and no further appeal was made in the case.

In addition to the dozen or so post-*Eichman* arrests of individuals in flag desecration-related incidents, in other instances perceived flag desecrators during the post-June 1990 period suffered a variety of forms of extralegal harassment or persecution although they were not formally arrested or prosecuted. In at least four incidents, art exhibits involving alleged flag desecration touched off controversies, including threats and reprisals. The most serious of the art exhibit controversies substantially contributed to the demise of one of Alaska's leading art galleries, the twenty-one-year-old Anchorage Visual Arts Center (VAC). As part of a spring 1992 exhibit on what ultimately turned out to be the ironic theme of censored art, the VAC included a reprisal of "Dread" Scott Tyler's infamous "flag on the floor" exhibit, which had sparked a major controversy when it was displayed in Chicago in early 1989. Although the VAC was already in serious financial trouble at the time of the exhibit, controversy over the Tyler exhibit dealt VAC a final blow, as the mayor of Anchorage announced that he would cut off further city funding for VAC and the gallery's landlord called in overdue rentals and evicted a number of artists who had studios in the building's basement.[23]

In two instances during the height of Persian Gulf War fervor, opposition to the widespread display of flag patches and pins led to nonprosecutory reprisals against perceived political dissidents. In one highly publicized case, Seton Hall University basketball player Marco Lokar, an Italian citizen, resigned from his team and left for home with his pregnant wife in February 1991 after he was repeatedly booed by fans and received threats because he refused to wear the flag patch that all his teammates wore. Another Gulf War incident erupted when Warren County, New York, defense lawyer Kurt Mausert won Queensbury town justice Michael Muller's agreement in February 1991 to have a county prosecutor remove a flag pin he was wearing in court on the grounds that it might prejudice the jury against Mausert's client. State Supreme Court justice John Dier quickly overturned the ruling and in addition ordered that Mausert be banned from the ranks of lawyers henceforth allowed to defend indigent clients in Warren County and that a judicial review be conducted of Justice Muller. In February 1992, a panel of New York State's highest court overruled Dier, held that Justice Muller had acted properly, and additionally held that Dier had no authority to order reprisals against Mausert.[24]

In another flag incident that sparked extralegal reprisals and which occurred during the peak of Gulf War fervor, nine high school students at the somewhat misnamed Baltimore City College were briefly suspended for burning a flag in a courtyard outside the school's cafeteria in January 1991. According to Principal Joseph Antenson, the students were suspended "because of unauthorized activity that could endanger the safety of students, not because of the flag burning."[25]

In another Persian Gulf War period school flag burning incident, University of Wisconsin at River Falls (UWRF) lecturer Jeffrey Gerson became the center of a storm when he burned a flag on March 11, 1991, during an American politics class. According to Gerson, he burned the flag as a "teaching tool" and as a "pedagogical" rather than a "personal act," during a class discussion of Supreme Court rulings on flag desecration. Gerson immediately became the target of verbal threats and the focus of numerous phone calls and letters from protesting students and Wisconsin citizens. Among the critics was UWRF chancellor Gary Thibadeau, who said Gerson had exercised "extraordinarily bad judgment" and used "offensive and insensitive" teaching methods, and a mob of student protesters, who marched on March 14 to a building where Gerson was teaching, carrying flags and fire extinguishers and loudly singing the national anthem, recited the Pledge of Allegiance and chanted "U.S.A." and "can [fire] Gerson" outside the windows of his class. A month later, Gerson, who was teaching on a one-year contract, was informed that he would not be rehired for the following year. In an interview in April 1992, political science chairman Richard Brynildsen declared that the decision not to rehire Gerson had already been made before the flag burning incident occurred and was related to a redefinition of Gerson's teaching position, but he conceded that he could "probably not convince a lot of people of this."[26]

Two of the most bizarre of the post-*Eichman* flag desecration controversies that did not involve government prosecutions nonetheless resulted in prolonged legal proceedings in which perceived flag desecrators won court battles against what they argued were attempts to discriminate against them. In one of these cases, the Old Glory Condom Corporation, which billed its products as "Condoms with a Conscience," sought to register as a trademark with the U.S. Patent Office a flaglike image in the shape of an unfurled condom bearing the slogan "Worn with Pride, Country-Wide," which decorated the exterior packaging of its condoms (the condoms themselves were ordinary latex condoms in single colors of red, white, or blue, with no flags on them). Along with the flag design, the condom packaging featured an "Old Glory Pledge" which promised to donate a portion of all profits to AIDS research and which declared, "We believe it is patriotic to protect and save lives."[27]

Patent Office attorney Rachel Blue rejected the request to register the trademark on May 30, 1991, on the grounds that it included "immoral or scandalous matter" that "would be perceived as a disparagement of the American flag" and would "scandalize or shock" the general public, which would be "offended" by the use of "a sacrosanct symbol" associated with "courage and patriotism" to promote items "associated with sex." The legal basis for the ruling was an arcane and rarely enforced provision in the patent laws that banned trademark registrations consisting of "immoral, deceptive or scandalous matter," which might disparage or bring into "contempt" persons, "institutions, beliefs or national symbols."

In January 1992, Old Glory lodged an appeal with the Patent Office's Trademark Trial and Appeal Board on the grounds that the denial amounted to a violation of its free speech rights "based solely on the political content" of its logo. Following a public hearing in May 1992, the Patent Appeal Board overruled the refusal to register the logo in March 1993. The Board declared that the flag-condom logo was "in no way" scandalous, pointed out that trademark registration of designs using the flag had been "sufficiently common that there can be no justification for refusing registration," and even applauded Old Glory for its evident "seriousness of purpose" in expressing the view "that the use of condoms is a patriotic act."

Perhaps the most bizarre and prolonged post-*Eichman* flag desecration controversy involved a dispute over a mural depicting a burning flag at Elk Grove High School in Elk Grove, California, which ended only after the mural was painted over on the order of school officials after nearly three years of contention, months of litigation, prolonged debates by the local school board, and the suspension of almost fifty students. The furor originated in the fall of 1991, when school officials invited student organizations to brighten up the school's walls by painting them with murals reflecting their groups' interests. A wide variety of murals subsequently graced the school's walls without eliciting any objections from school officials, even though some of them included potentially controversial contents, including a mural from the African-American club that portrayed black militants such as Malcolm X and communist leader Angela Davis.[28]

However, when students of the Model United Nations/Junior Statesmen Club proposed to celebrate the Bill of Rights by depicting a burning flag along with textual references to civil liberties, including the *Johnson* case, principal Paula Duncan refused to authorize it on the grounds that a mural on school walls could "easily be perceived as an endorsement of flag burning" and "many people in our community—and students as well—will find a mural depicting our flag in flames to be offensive." Ironically, the students who proposed the mural repeatedly declared that they were seeking to celebrate American freedoms rather than to support flag burning. Thus, MUN/JS member Jackie Limbo explained, "Putting up this mural shows patriotism. We love the rights that were given to us. We want to show others that they have these rights too."

After a year of fruitless negotiations by the students with Duncan and a 6-0 vote by the local school board in February 1993 to uphold her authority to forbid the mural, eight MUN/JS students obtained in May 1993 a preliminary injunction forbidding school officials from further blocking the mural from Sacramento County Superior Court judge Ronald Robie. Robie acted on the grounds that the school had not objected to other murals with controversial content and therefore to ban the flag burning mural would amount to imposing political censorship in a forum (the school's walls) that had been established as a protected area for expression. "Instead of giving the students a printing press, the school gave them a wall," he noted, adding that it was a "sad commentary on an extraordinary experiment" that school officials had created such an open arena for expression and then banned a mural that had been designed to celebrate freedom of expression. Although school officials subsequently lost an appeal to the California Appeals Court and the mural was finally painted in September 1993, in February 1994 the school board voted to ban all permanent murals in the schools as of July 1994. Forty-eight students who subsequently walked out of school to protest the new policy were suspended from school for three days. The mural was painted over on August 5, 1994.

The Resurrection of the Flag Desecration
Constitutional Amendment in 1995

During the four years following congressional defeat of the proposed constitutional amendment to forbid flag desecration in June 1990, the only substantial effort to revive it was undertaken by the American Legion. Shortly after the amendment's defeat, the Legion organized a drive that was originally designed to obtain, by May 1991, nonbinding "memorializing" resolutions to Congress in support of an amendment from at least thirty-eight state legislatures, the minimum required to ratify an amendment following the needed congressional endorsement of a two-thirds vote in both houses. Although the Legion failed to meet its original goal (by May 1991, only twenty-one legislatures had passed memorializing resolutions), by April 1995 forty-nine legislatures (all but those in Vermont) adopted such resolutions, with sixteen legislatures acting during the Persian Gulf War period of early 1991. Typical of the rhetoric advanced on behalf of the memorializing resolutions was New York Democratic state assemblyman Ronald Tocci's declaration during legislative debate that the flag was "not just a symbol or an icon" but "the embodiment of everything that America stands for."[29]

In August 1994 the Legion's campaign to revive the amendment, which it termed the "quiet revolution," was formalized and made public with the organization, under Legion sponsorship, of the Citizens Flag Alliance (CFA), a coalition of about ninety civic, ethnic, and veterans organizations with a claimed membership of over twenty-seven million people (including, for example, the Knights of Columbus, the Elks, Moose International, the Air Force Association, and the

Polish American Congress). Although the CFA was technically independent of the Legion, Legion domination of it was apparent: CFA president Dan Wheeler had formerly edited the Legion's magazine; the CFA was funded with over six million dollars from the Legion; its original board of directors was composed almost entirely of prominent Legion members; and its original staff and office space was provided by the Legion.

The CFA's arguments were essentially identical with those offered by amendment backers in 1989 and 1990, including the contentions that flag desecration was "conduct," not "speech" that went "too far" in offending the sensibilities of Americans concerning the "sacred" symbol of the nation; that other forms of dissent would still be protected by the First Amendment; and, above all, that most Americans detested such behavior and should, in a democracy, be allowed to work their will. In its inaugural publication, the CFA declared:

> We cannot accept the [Supreme] Court's decision which allows the U.S. flag to be set on fire, spit upon and trampled as a form of political expression protected by the guarantees of free speech. We believe that such acts ARE NOT speech, but are, instead examples of violent, destructive, and despicable conduct, which recognize no values or morals, and are incompatible with civilized society.

The CFA also published a list of suggested responses for common objections to the amendment: for example, to counter arguments that the amendment would create a "slippery slope" for subsequent erosion of constitutional guarantees, such as outlawing burning copies of the Constitution, it declared that when the Supreme Court "says [the flag] is just a colorful piece of cloth and has no more significance than a dust rag, that's a 'slippery slope' that upsets Americans" and that nothing else was analogous to flag burning because "there is no other act that arouses the same sense of outrage"; to claims that flag desecration did not destroy the flag's symbolic power, the CFA responded that "while it's hard to get your arms around the precise harm done," the destruction of even one flag "promotes nothing worthwhile" and "tears at the fabric of our nation" and in any case most Americans "think that harm is so great that flag desecration should be a crime"; and in response to the comment, "We've studied this issue thoroughly and think it's a bad idea to amend the constitution just to stop flag burning," the CFA response was, "Talk to the average guy on the street about this issue and he will tell you that he wouldn't burn a flag himself and he thinks it's wrong to do it. That's it in a nutshell. The Supreme Court can make it legal, but nothing can make it right."[30]

In early 1995, following the Republican triumph in the 1994 congressional elections, CFA congressional allies in both houses formally introduced the revived constitutional amendment, which proposed that "Congress and the states shall have power to prohibit the physical desecration of the flag of the United States." By May 1995, 274 representatives and 54 senators had announced their support for the proposed amendment (compared to 255 representatives and 58 senators who voted for the amendment in June 1990, and compared to 290 representatives and 67 senators required for a two-thirds majority). On May 24, the HJC subcommittee on the Constitution held hearings on the amendment, and on the following day it forwarded the proposal to the full HJC with the support of the seven Republican members and over the opposition of the five Democrats on the subcommittee. During the subcommittee deliberations, Republican Representative Gerald Solomon predicted that the amendment would "be ratified faster than any other constitutional amendment" in American history if Congress endorsed it and termed flag desecration "not speech or expression" but only a "hateful tantrum." However, conservative Republican Clint Bolick, vice-president of the Institute for Justice, urged the subcommittee not to strike a blow against "freedom" by endorsing an act of "constitutional desecration" that would be "far more regrettable" than flag desecration.[31]

Although it was endorsed by forty-nine state legislatures, and the early sponsorship of the revived amendment by over 50 percent of both houses of Congress and the results of a 1995 Legion-sponsored Gallup Poll indicating 75 percent public support all seemed to suggest that the amendment might have clear sailing in Congress and afterward in the states, other indications suggest that backing for the amendment lacked intensity and that substantial opposition to it existed. For example, although the CFA announced in the fall of 1994 a goal of obtaining twenty million signatures on petitions in support of the amendment by Flag Day (June 14) 1995, as of late April it claimed less than five hundred thousand such signatures. CFA publications repeatedly declared that the "biggest obstacle" to its success was "apathy," in particular the need to convince Congress that there was widespread, intense public demand for an amendment: in January 1995, for example, CFA President Wheeler, in communications to the CFA membership, stressed that Congress needed to hear that the amendment was "important to the people of the United States," declared that "individual, personal apathy" was the main obstacle to success, and warned that "doing nothing is, in effect, a vote for keeping flag desecration legal." Even CFA lobbyist Jim McAvoy conceded in March 1995 that the flag desecration issue had been "totally off of Congress's and the media's radar screens, and we have to bring it back to the point where people are taking it seriously."[32]

While the Legion/CFA campaign did ultimately obtain support from forty-nine state legislatures, at various times between 1990 and 1995 at least four state legislative chambers rejected requests for such endorsements and in several others 20 percent more of state legislators voted against them. Thus, Legion-sponsored resolutions were defeated in the Virginia Senate in February 1991, in the Nebraska and Kansas houses in April 1991, and in the Vermont House in February 1995. Although such measures passed overwhelmingly in some state legislatures (for example, by 92-1 in the Kentucky House and 89-8 in the Iowa House, both in early 1995), they passed only over strong opposition in other state legislatures, for example, in early 1991 by votes of 36-23 in the Oregon House, by 33-26 in the Wyoming House, and by 25-10 in the Arkansas Senate.[33]

Amendment opponents spoke out vigorously in many of the state legislative debates. For example, in the North Dakota House, Democratic Representative Bruce Anderson, who voted against a resolution which passed by a 79-26 vote, declared that while it was "abhorrent to watch someone burn the flag," that the issue was not "about the flag, it is about liberty. The flag is what we stand for, and what we stand for is liberty." In Vermont, where the House rejected endorsing the amendment by 76-69 and subsequently passed a resolution urging respect for the flag by 86-59 while warning that banning flag desecration would "diminish the very freedoms and liberties for which the flag has stood for over 200 years," even the state's Republican attorney general opposed the amendment, warning against tampering "with the constitutional cornerstone of our democracy, the First Amendment."[34]

Early expressions of editorial opinion in 1995 suggested continuing overwhelming disdain for an amendment in the nation's press. CFA president Wheeler lamented in the March 24, 1995, issue of organization's newsletter, *CFA Highlights,* that after "meeting with editors of more than a dozen daily newspapers . . . none could clear the shroud from their eyes" created by "misinterpretation of our First Amendment." The general themes of editorial opposition to the amendment in 1995 were similar to those expressed five years earlier, including that forbidding flag desecration would sacrifice substantive freedoms to protect a symbol of liberty, that flag desecration was so rare that an amendment was completely unwarranted, and that reviving the flag controversy would only divert the nation's attention away from its real problems. Thus, the March 27 *Portland Oregonian* declared that flag burning had been "all but invisible in recent years" and that the Constitution should not be "amended so lightly and for so little reason"; the February 26 *Chicago Tribune* proclaimed that compared to crime, poverty, taxes, and the federal deficit flag desecration was an insignificant problem and that the proposed amendment would elevate "intolerance to the highest value, in defiance of the American tradition of permitting all views to be expressed"; and the March 8 issue of *Newport News* (Virginia) *Daily Press* opined that the amendment would "chip away at that freedom undermining the value of the symbol" and that the flag was adequately "protected by the respect and love the overwhelming majority of Americans have for it."

The American Bar Association and leading civil liberties spokesmen also indicated unyielding opposition to the revived amendment in 1995. Thus ABA president George Bushnell argued that American soldiers had not fought "just to protect the flag" but to ensure for all Americans "the fundamental principles upon which this nation was built." People for the American Way executive vice-president Elliot Mincberg said that the revived amendment would dishonor the flag "by undermining the freedom it represents," while radical lawyer William Kunstler termed the proposal an "absolute outrage." Northwestern University law professor Stephen Presser, a supporter of CFA, conceded in an article in the CFA's March 24 newsletter that "most of the legal academy perceives the idea [of a flag desecration amendment] as pernicious at best, and lunacy at worst."[35]

One aspect of the early 1995 debate that differed from the 1989–90 controversy was that it was conducted partly via the Internet, a worldwide computer network. In early 1995 an Arizona scientist named Warren Apel created a "flag burning home page" on the Internet which voiced his objections to the proposed amendment and featured a picture of a flag that, when "clicked" on by Internet users, turned into the image of burning flag. Apel warned his readers that they should "proceed at your own risk" before clicking, as "burning a flag—even a virtual one—may soon be considered a heinous criminal act." In response to Apel, a Dallas computer consulting firm created a "Save Old Glory from Flames" Internet site, which termed flag burning an idea "which should be ALL WET," featured a picture of a fire extinguisher, and declared, "Tell a grieving service widow that it's a good idea to have the right to set ablaze the symbol which covered her husband's casket, or ask a veteran of Iwo Jima if he minds your immolating the flag for which he risked his life, and you're likely to get more than fiery debate!"

Some Afterthoughts

In reporting on the *Johnson* decision, the British newsmagazine the *Economist* termed it a "routine reaffirmation of free speech." Constitutional law professor Rodney Smolla declared that the only "surprise" about the ruling was that four Supreme Court justices dissented from such a clear affirmation "of the principle that speech may not be proscribed merely because it is offensive to mainstream sensibilities." A 1992 encyclopedia of historic U.S. court cases begins its discussion of *Johnson* by declaring that it "ought to have been a relatively simple case involving freedom of expression." In assessing the 1989–90 flag desecration controversy, and in particular the fact that enormous amounts of the time and energies of all three branches of the government were devoted to this subject because of one 1984 flag burning, Democratic representative Don Edwards lamented, "To think that a nincompoop in Dallas, Texas, could do something that could trigger this reaction is rather distressing." Whether Gregory Lee Johnson is a "nincompoop" or not, certainly the massive reaction to a single flag burning and its legalization by the Supreme Court, displayed both by the American political elite and the American public, suggests some rather "distressing" things about the health of the American body politic in general as the twentieth century nears its end. Although this reaction clearly demonstrates that flag burning, as a form of symbolic political protest, is unlikely to generate any significant public support, in a peculiar way the American political system may very well owe Johnson considerable gratitude for exposing some fundamental and distressing realities about itself.[36]

Whatever one's view of the wisdom or advisability of burning flags, such behavior is unquestionably a form of political expression that has no concrete adverse consequences, as even the 1990 *Eichman* Supreme Court dissenters acknowledged. The frequency of such behavior, at least until politicians began advocating overturning the 1989 *Johnson* ruling, was minimal during the post–Vietnam War period, and in any case, as *Washington Post* columnist Judy Mann has pointed out, "When it happens the sum total of the damage is a burned flag. No one is deprived of liberty or justice." Every bit of evidence from both the Vietnam War and 1989–90 flag desecration controversies suggests that, rather than diminishing the symbolic value of the flag in the eyes of the vast majority of Americans, flag burnings have exactly the opposite effect; surely few individuals Americans have done as much for patriotism in recent times as Gregory Lee Johnson. But even if mass flag burnings were to become an everyday occurrence, such actions would case no real harm and indeed would probably provide a service to the political leadership by informing them that political grievances were spreading among the population and needed attention. In any case, sending flag abusers to jail is hardly going to turn them into patriots convinced of the wonders of American liberties or to produce any other positive effects. In contrast, had several hundred "mainstream" Americans conducted mass flag burnings to protest repression of dissent in the United States during World War I, the excesses of the post–World Wars I and II "red scares," or the forced evacuation and detention of more than one hundred thousand Japanese-Americans without criminal charges or trials during World War II, their act might have compelled a reevaluation of such policies and, as a result, the American flag would fly more freely and proudly today (in practice, of course, the very perceived "extremism" of burning flags tends to confine such acts to political fringe groups and individuals whose acts mostly antagonize, rather than to more "respectable" protesters whose acts would have far greater impact).[37]

Because burning the flag is a form of harmless, if to many highly obnoxious, political expression, and as Justice Brennan has noted, the right to such expression is the "bedrock" principle of American democracy the First Amendment was designed to protect, the real significance of the 1989–90 flag desecration controversy (and earlier such disputes) lies in the reaction to Johnson's action (and that of earlier flag desecrators) rather than in anything that he (or they) did. This is a true case, in other words, of "we have met the enemy and it is us." As has been discussed at great length above, the 1989–90 flag desecration controversy was considerably whipped up, augmented, and prolonged by press sensationalism and by politicians and other political elites—including Democrats and their civil libertarian allies such as Professor Tribe and the ACLU, who supported a law they did not really believe in as a means of blocking an amendment—who were, in many cases, at least substantially motivated by cynical political considerations. But press sensationalism and political pandering over the flag issue would have been effective only had there been a responsive audience, and thus part of the critical deeper significance of the 1989–90 flag controversy (and earlier such disputes) lies not so much in that the issue was exploited but that it was so exploitable.

Certainly part of the reason for the massive adverse public reaction to the *Johnson* ruling was simply the same lack of knowledge, understanding, and support of the basic principles of American democracy that public opinion polls have repeatedly demonstrated (an ignorance that, of course, reflects poorly on the American education system and on the failures of the American political leadership and the civil liberties community to remedy such failings). For example, a December 1991 poll of over five hundred Americans revealed that only one-third could correctly identify the Bill of Rights and only 9 percent could accurately describe its original purpose as limiting potential federal abuse of individual rights. But going beneath the surfaces of such polling data and facile interpretations of public reaction to the *Johnson* ruling—that Americans apparently are full of pride and support for their country—the public response ultimately reflected extraordinarily deep and widespread insecurities and doubts about the fundamental health of the country (which similarly existed during the Vietnam War period and during the 1895–1910 height of the original flag desecration controversy, when the Flag Protection Movement's promoters were fearful that their traditional elite roles were about to be swamped by radicalism, immigration, urbanization, and industrialization).

Certainly, the massive political and public reaction that occurred in 1989–90 in response to one insignificant flag burning—what the Supreme Court in *Johnson* termed "one gesture of an unknown man"—is not a sign of national self-confidence but exactly the opposite. The insecurity reflected in the 1989–90 flag desecration controversy is unquestionably rooted in the same sense of America "in decline," both internationally and domestically, that played a key role in the 1992 election defeat of President Bush. For example, polls taken in the late 1980s and early 1990s have generally indicated that over 50 percent of Americans think the nation is "on the wrong track," and a 1992 poll indicated that 75 percent were concerned that their children would live less well than they did. In mid-1992, a distinguished panel sponsored by the Carnegie Endowment for International Peace reported that "it is a long time since America has been so uneasy about itself and so uncertain about where to go next."[38]

In international terms, despite the seeming American triumphs in the 1991 Gulf War and in the Cold War with the collapse of communism in the Soviet Union and Eastern Europe in 1989–91, the continuing trauma of Vietnam and other recent embarrassments for American foreign policy (such as the 1979–81 Iran hostage affair, the 1986 Iran-Contra revelations, and the embarrassing ineffectiveness of American foreign policy in Somalia and Bosnia during the post-1990 period) and, above all, the obvious comparative slide of the United States in the world economy, have clearly, both in fact and in perception, reduced the almost-unchallenged American military and economic world dominance of the 1945–65 period. This decline has been especially apparent during the post-1980 period, when America, formerly the world's leading creditor nation, became the world's leading debtor nation (net foreign debt was a $364 billion surplus in 1982 but a $412 billion deficit in 1990), when the rate of growth in American productivity dropped drastically from previous levels and lagged well behind that of other industrialized nations, and when the American gross national product, which as a share of the total world economy had been well over 30 percent in the mid-1950s, slumped to about 20 percent.

Numerous measures comparing American economic and social health to those of other countries reflect similar declines in recent years; for example, the United States had the world's twelfth lowest infant mortality rate in 1960, but was only twenty-second in 1987, and although American banks dominated the list of the wealthiest world banks in the 1960s, not a single American bank was among the top twenty-five world banks in 1991. According to a 1991 *New York Times* survey, a majority of Americans feel that Japan will be the world's leading economic power in the twenty-first century, and the *Los Angeles Times* reported in early 1990 that its surveys had revealed a nation "mired in an extraordinary funk," with many Americans perceiving "a nation inexorably losing ground to foreign competition, slowly surrendering affluence built in better days."[39]

In relating such developments to the 1989–90 flag controversy, University of Michigan history professor Terrence McDonald notes that while in the twentieth century "it's always been a good idea for a politician to wrap himself in the flag," the apparent "resurgent nationalism" displayed over the flag desecration issue was "linked to the perceived decline in American power in relation to the rest of the world" because "when reality gets too hard to handle, you can fall back on symbols of nationhood." Similarly, the *Economist* suggested a comparison with the fact that "Britain become particularly flag-happy when it felt its first intimations of decline as a power late last century" and noted that "a country sensing others climbing past it tends to mark with particular flag-waving the little victories that buck the trend."

Indeed, in retrospect, it is hard to avoid the conclusion that, at least to some extent, the 1991 Gulf War was "intended therapeutically," in the words of conservative columnist George Will, designed partly "to restore American confidence" and "banish 'the Vietnam syndrome.'" President Bush presented the American military victory in the war in such terms, declaring, for example, "By God, we've kicked the Vietnam syndrome once and for all," that the war had brought a "renewed sense of pride and confidence here at home" and "buried forever" the "specter of·Vietnam in the desert sands of the Arabian peninsula," and that American soldiers had "helped this country liberate itself from old ghosts and doubts." In short, the same fears of international decline that led to massive flag waving during the Gulf War, touched off spontaneous chants of "USA! USA!" when the end of the war was announced during a hockey match in New York's Madison Square Garden, and led to the general response which a *Washington Post* article summarized as "Hooray for us! We kicked butt!" helped to foster the massive negative public response to the *Johnson* ruling, which amounted symbolically to pouring salt into an already deeply wounded national pride.[40]

Just as fears of international decline helped to make Americans extraordinarily sensitive in 1989–90 to the idea that dissidents could burn flags with impunity, a perceived parallel domestic decline and seeming unraveling probably contributed even more to the collective expression of insecurity that was reflected in the 1989–90 flag controversy. In comments that were echoed again and again by politicians and commentators during this period, Senator Paul Sarbanes noted, "Contrary to the past when people could anticipate that they would do better over their lifetime and their children would do even better, now they face stagnation and even decline in their income." Similarly, a Gallup Poll official stated, "The general idea in America that kids can live better than their parents—people just don't think that's working anymore. It's giving up the American dream to some extent." Thus over 50 percent of Americans aged fifteen to twenty-four who were polled in early 1992 said that America's best days had passed. Relating this growing mood to the flag controversy, University of California at San Diego sociologist Richard Madsen points out that the flag dispute reflected a "great insecurity about our own values and unity. Many people have a sense of America in decline, a sense of intractable problems from drug abuse to the environment. Under these conditions, people get doubly upset when the flag is desecrated." Michael Lerner, the editor of *Tikkun* magazine, linked what he termed the pro-flag "pathology" to an even more general and diffuse sense of alienation, pain, frustration, and "desperate search for communities of meaning and purpose" in America, arguing that the real "commotion" was not about the flag but the "loss of the idealized community that the flag represents."[41]

Although it is impossible to document anything as abstract as a feared loss of an idealized community, study after study has indicated that the general rate of American economic growth, as well as the health of the average American's pocketbook, has either stagnated or declined since about 1973, following thirty years of rapid growth, and that families with children and the relatively young, poor, uneducated, and unskilled have been especially adversely affected. Median family income in 1992, for example, was slightly below that in 1973 (with a 7 percent decline for families with children), and average hourly wages, weekly earnings, and household purchasing power, adjusted for inflation, all declined during the 1980s (thus average hourly wages decreased 17 percent for those without a high school diploma and 10 percent for those with no more than a high school education between 1979 and 1989). The percentage of full-time workers who earned low wages (defined as less than $12,000 in constant 1990 dollars) increased from 12 percent to 18 percent during the same period, and for all working men aged twenty-five to thirty-four, inflation-adjusted income declined 20 percent between 1969 and 1989. For the first time in five decades, the rate of American home ownership declined during the 1980s (from 66 to 64 percent overall and from 60 to 52 percent among those aged thirty to thirty-four). Average mortgage payments as a percent of income grew from 21 to 33 percent between 1967 and 1989, the number of weeks of median household earnings required to buy a new car grew from nineteen to twenty-five weeks between 1980 and 1989, and the rate of college tuition increases outstripped growth in median family income fivefold between 1980 and 1987. Only the wealthiest 20 percent of families have enjoyed any significant economic improvement during the post-1973 period, with the result that the gap between rich and poor has widened to record post–Great Depression levels after almost fifty years of steady lessening: total net worth of the wealthiest 1 percent (840,000) of American households doubled from 18 to 37 percent of total national wealth between 1976 and 1989, thereby exceeding, in the latter year, the total net worth of the poorest 90 percent (84 million households).[42]

Numerous other data reflect other declines in economic and social health during the 1980s, indicating, for example, that for the 1989–91 period a record number of Americans were receiving food stamps and other welfare benefits, lacked health insurance, and were being incarcerated (between 1980 and 1990, the number of prisoners jailed for more than a one-year period more than doubled from three hundred thousand to seven hundred thousand, while the number of Americans declaring bankruptcy similarly doubled between 1984 and 1990). In late 1992, an index of overall American social well-being developed by the Fordham University Institute for Innovation in Social Policy, based on measures of sixteen different social problems including employment, homicide, and child abuse, indicated that America's social health was at its lower level since the index was developed in 1970, having fallen from a rating of 72 (on a scale of 100) in 1976 to 42 in 1990. The director of the study, who termed it a "sort of Dow Jones [index] of the national soul," concluded that the study revealed that "something is coming loose in the social infrastructure."[43]

Evidence directly tying together the general perceptions of America in decline domestically and outrage over the legalization of flag burning is not difficult to find. For example, a visitor to the American revolutionary battlefield site at Concord, Massachusetts, told a reporter shortly after the *Johnson* decision, "The country is torn by crime and drugs. We really should have something to rally around." A letter writer who protested a "flag on the floor" art exhibit in Cleveland in 1991 used virtually identical words, declaring, "In a time of social unrest, crime, poverty and low morale, there are few things left to hold onto nowadays." Veterans who protested the original 1989 Chicago "flag on the floor" exhibit passed out leaflets that referred to the "REAL AMERICA," when "riots were unthinkable," "when a boy was a boy, and dressed like one," and when "you weren't made to feel guilty for enjoying dialect comedy." In the minority report of ten members of the HJC supporting a constitutional amendment to overturn the *Johnson* ruling, the congressmen stated that Americans should be "required" to respect the flag and declared, "In this day and age, when it seems that perversion is accepted and morality a taboo religion, perhaps this small mandate for freedom is not asking too much!"

Columnist Ray Kerrison lumped the Supreme Court decision in with what he termed the "step by step" dismantling of "nearly all the institutions, beliefs, practices and safeguards of the past 200 years" and lamented that there was nothing surprising about it in a "climate" in which "family life is in shreds," marriage is a "take-it or leave-it proposition," the "school system is poisoned with destructive social aberrations," and "religion is not only mocked and ridiculed incessantly on radio and TV, but these attacks are subsidized in the arts by federal and state governments." Similarly, a letter writer to the *New York Times* declared, after referring to the *Johnson* decision, that "America is in a free fall" like a truck "plummeting downhill in pitch darkness with no brakes, no headlights to illuminate our vision of where the road is heading." *Houston Chronicle* columnist David Wilson attacked the *Johnson* ruling as expressing a "national failure of self-esteem" that would hasten the "disintegration of national coherence and unity" and lamented that, if in fact America was "a decadent great power whose fall is assured by the rushing tides of history," then the Supreme Court's decision "will nudge it a bit."[44]

To many conservatives, the flag desecration controversy symbolized everything they felt had gone wrong in American society, and, especially because flag burning was still associated with anti–Vietnam War protest, it also symbolized all of what they perceived as excesses of the 1960s. Thus Senator John McCain (R-Ariz.) reported in July 1989 that his constituents were especially angry over the *Johnson* ruling because it was "reopening that resentment that Middle America felt toward the anti–Vietnam War protesters." Conservative columnist Cal Thomas associated the *Johnson* ruling with "protecting pornography" that "inspires serial killers," "tolerance of marijuana," which had "paved the way for crack cocaine," and even Elvis Presley, who had "opened a musical door through which heavy metal and garbage-mouth groups walked." He characterized enacting a flag desecration amendment as "an opportunity to say that enough has finally become enough." Antifeminist spokeswoman Phyllis Schlafly called for preserving the flag to "help give us a national identity" in the face of "so many demonstrators who trample on patriotism, religion, family, decency, Western civilization and U.S. traditions."

Conservative columnist Pat Buchanan, who unsuccessfully ran for president in 1992 on a platform of fighting a "culture war" against the aftereffects of the

1960s, called for passing a flag desecration amendment as part of the fight against "moral pollution" of those who had brought the United States "flag burning, abortion, pornography, affirmative action, quotas," and other developments that had cast "aside as so much trash the deepest sentiments, traditions and beliefs of the American people." Representative Henry Hyde (R-Ill.) perhaps best summarized the view of cultural conservatives on the flag desecration issue when he told the HJC on June 19, 1990: "Those who are shocked, revolted and frustrated by the excesses of the counterculture, the pornography and obscenity that inundates our entertainment industry, the drugs, the AIDS explosion, the high abortion rate, view flag burning as one more slap in the face of millions of veterans who found enough values in America to risk their lives in combat. People resent the vulgarization of their country. . . . I once saw a bumper-sticker that said, 'Honk if you believe in anything!' That says it all for some people."[45]

Aside from reflecting a collective public insecurity about the state of the country, the very nature of the 1989–90 flag controversy suggests some of the reasons for that insecurity: namely, that the American political leadership and the American press in the post–Vietnam War period has far too often been consumed with symbols rather than substance and, either out of inability or unwillingness, has far too often preferred engaging in ultimately nonproductive and often divisive media mongering about nonissues rather than tackling real problems. The amount of time and energy devoted by American political elites in 1989–90 to debating flag desecration—and even more the sudden disappearance of this issue into oblivion (at least for four years)—reflects a political system which, as the 1988 presidential campaign demonstrated with George Bush's similar use of symbolic nonissues like the Pledge of Allegiance, has increasingly emphasized smoke and mirrors above real political issues, even while the health of the society and body politic has rapidly declined. In short, like Nero, the American political leadership has fiddled, more consumed with one burning flag than with cities that have been steadily decaying, and occasionally, as in Los Angeles in 1992, quite literally burning.

Although certainly the American people as a whole cannot escape some responsibility for the failures and neglect of their leaders, ultimately the American political leadership sets the tone and must bear the bulk of the blame for the erosion of the quality and fairness of American life during the past two decades. But if diverting public and political attention away from real issues and pandering to the public's worst instincts has been, in general, a far too often instinctive reaction of American political leaders in the late twentieth century, a far more serious fault, and one with even greater potentially disastrous consequences for the nation, is that they apparently have little or no faith in or understanding of the most basic democratic principles, those of a "free marketplace" of ideas and of tolerance of even the most unpopular and offensive political dissent. This fundamental democratic lesson was elaborated with unequaled eloquence by Justice Jackson in the 1943 *Barnette* flag salute case: "If there is any fixed star in our constitutional constellation, it is that no official, high or petty, can prescribe what shall be orthodox in politics, nationalism, religion or other matters of opinion or force citizens to confess by word or act their faith therein." It is a sad commentary that in 1989–90, during the two-hundredth anniversary of the Bill of Rights, the American political leadership still needed to learn this lesson and, even more important, to reflect it in their daily actions and words. As a *New Republic* columnist wrote in August 1989, "It's a terribly insecure nation that makes such an unholy fuss about some minor nut burning the flag," and it's an even sadder commentary that in the American political leadership it appears that there is "no one eloquent enough to make people weep with gratitude that we live in a country where people are free enough to burn the flag."[46]

★

ADDENDUM:
THE REVIVED STRUGGLE
OVER THE FLAG DESECRATION
AMENDMENT IN 1995

January 9, 1996. After the text of this volume was originally completed in late May 1995, major developments occurred with regard to the revived proposed constitutional amendment to authorize "Congress and the states" to "prohibit the physical desecration of the flag of the United States." (The operative language of the 1995 amendment was identical to that considered in 1989–90, but the controversial preamble of the 1989–90 version was deleted from the 1995 text.) In late June, the House of Representatives endorsed the amendment by 312-120, far surpassing the required two-thirds "supermajority" for constitutional amendments. However, in a cliffhanger vote in the Senate on December 12, the amendment, now shorn by its sponsors of the original reference to authorizing "the states" as well as Congress to ban flag desecration (in a last gasp effort to pick up additional votes), failed by 63-36, falling just three votes short. Although this still marked a significant increase from the 51 and 58 Senate votes received in 1989 and 1990, respectively, the Senate action effectively killed the amendment for the 1995–96 Congress. However, its backers promised to make the amendment an issue in the 1996 elections and to reintroduce it when the new Congress reconvenes in 1997.

What was particularly striking about the amendment's greater success in 1995 than in 1989–90 was that the entire controversy received far less press coverage, public debate, and congressional hearings and debate than five years previously; that the Clinton administration opposed it whereas the Bush administration had earlier backed an amendment; that public opinion appears to have been considerably less aroused and less favorable toward an amendment than in 1990; and that there were only a handful of reported flag burnings in the country during the two years preceding the 1995 congressional votes, whereas a wave of flag burnings had marked the period between the 1989 and 1990 votes.

The crucial differences between 1989–90 and 1995 were that the 1994 elections returned a conservative Republican majority to both houses of Congress for the first time in forty years and that supporters of the amendment had the highly organized backing of the American Legion and the CFA, whereas amendment opponents (beyond the editorial pages of the overwhelming majority of the nation's newspapers), especially in Congress, were relatively unorganized, both compared with amendment proponents in 1995 and with amendment opponents in 1989–90. One clear sign of the better organization among amendment proponents in 1995 was that Senate offices surveyed in December 1995 uniformly reported, regardless of party, region, or their position on the amendment, that the overwhelming percentage of their mail and phone calls supported it, and that the vast majority of pro-amendment communications obviously resulted from the CFA's campaign rather than citizens acting on their own initiative.

Thus, Victoria Streitfeld, press secretary for Senator Bill Bradley (D-N.J.), who became a special target for CFA efforts after he indicated that he was reconsidering his 1990 opposition to the amendment, reported receiving 8,800 letters on the issue, with over 90 percent favoring the amendment. Tom McMahon, press secretary for Senator Howell Heflin (D-Ala.), as well as a spokeswoman for a midwestern Republican senator who asked to remain anonymous, both reported similarly overwhelming support for the amendment among the more than 4,000 communications each of their offices received. However, a spokesman for Senator Christopher Dodd (D-Ct.) was typical in reporting that, while communications were about five to one for the amendment, those opposed were "usually a more thought out personal letter whereas the others are more form letters."

Republican members of Congress and their staffs repeatedly pointed to the CFA's efforts as critical to both reviving the amendment in 1995 and nearly getting it passed. Thus, Kathryn Hazeem, Republican chief counsel of the HJC subcommittee on the Constitution, which held a May 24, 1995 hearing on the issue, said during a December 1995 interview that

> the CFA and Legion folks were very helpful and were very much in
> tune with grassroots support. They did a good job because it's very
> difficult on an issue like this—there's not a lot of money or business

interests involved, it's not like telecommunications where billions of dollars are at stake. There's a lot of sentiment in the country, but you have to get that sentiment pointed in the right direction and let members know that people care about that and they were able to do that. This is something that you could say is priceless.

Hazeem added that in 1990 Republicans "very much took for granted that this would be an easy victory and were crowing about 30-second sound bites, but did not really do the work that was required to make it happen," whereas in 1995 Republicans not only worked harder, but amendment opponents "had many more issues to deal with" than in 1990, when Democrats had controlled Congress and had "much more significant resources to dedicate to opposition, including both congressmen and staff. But I really think the difference was the organization at the grassroots in terms of contacting members."

Similarly, Jim Wilkinson, press spokesman for House majority leader Dick Armey (R-Tex.), said during a December 1995 interview that, "Veterans groups were working it hard. It's an issue that resonates in America and members basically were affected by a lot of grassroots support. It's hard to stare a wounded vet in the face and say you ought to be able to burn the flag. Veterans groups were constantly holding our feet to the fire on it. They were advertising everywhere, were organizing letter-writing campaigns. Vets were coming by every office on the [Capitol] Hill." A key Senate Republican source also interviewed in December concurred, declaring that the CFA "really concentrated and focussed their efforts on building support and getting commitments to get this through. I believe they accelerated their efforts because it was a Republican Congress, and they were very active." This source added that at least in the Senate "this vote more than a lot of others was a personal vote for a lot of members. I haven't seen many issues that touch people as personally as this one."

Asked to explain why the amendment had fared so well in the House in June but failed in the Senate in December, Hazeem said that "the first body to act has a little bit of the pressures off. They don't have quite the sense that this is on the verge of becoming law and feel maybe the other body [i.e., the Senate] will fix it." Wilkinson similarly said, "A lot of times in Congress it's real easy to schedule a political vote and get on the record with something you think isn't going to become law and that was an easy vote back then [in June in the House]. A lot of those votes then were probably from people who said it probably won't ever get to the states for ratification, so why not, it's an easy yes vote." Along the same lines, a well-placed Senate Republican source said in another December 1995 interview,

"There is some sense that the Senate always moderates things and especially this year, we're sort of a safety valve. A flag constitutional amendment is in some ways an easy one to vote for politically, especially when you have a whole other house to go through." Another key Senate Republican staff source interviewed in December added that the fact that all members of the House had just run for office eight months earlier (and thus were all impacted by the perceived conservative 1994 electoral tide) and all would have to run again in 1996, whereas both of these were true for only one-third of senators, "has to have had some effect." When asked if another explanation for the different outcomes in the House and Senate might have been that public opinion polls showed increased support for President Clinton and decreased support for the Republican-controlled Congress in the interim, this source said he tended to "think not. I think people decided on what they thought was the right thing to do when they decided to oppose it." (In December 1995, Clinton's popularity rate topped 50 percent for the first time since February 1994, while approval of Congress dropped below 30 percent in for the first time since the 1994 elections.)[1]

Beyond the CFA's highly-organized efforts, the general public appears to have been considerably less exercised over the flag desecration issue in 1995 than in 1989–90. While the American Legion reported that its sponsored 1995 Gallup poll revealed more than 75 percent support for an amendment, the *Washington Post* reported July 19 that its own poll found that only 51 percent backed an amendment and that 48 percent said the Constitution should be left alone "even if that means flag burning stays legal." Meanwhile, the ABA reported 64 percent of the respondents it surveyed in 1995 initially favored a flag desecration amendment, but when told such an amendment would be the first in American history to restrict freedom of political protest, supporters dropped to 38 percent, and 52 percent indicated opposition. Another sign suggesting that the CFA had not really stirred up massive enthusiasm for the amendment was that although in 1994 it had set a goal of obtaining 20 million signatures supporting the amendment by June 1995, even three months later than that it could claim barely over one million.[2]

Despite these signs strongly suggestive of less-than-massive popular support for the amendment, the CFA unquestionably out-organized its opponents at the grassroots level in 1995 (having had about a year's headstart before opponents realized that there was a serious chance the amendment would pass) and amendment proponents on Capitol Hill also clearly had far better organization than did their congressional antagonists. To give the most striking example, whereas the Republican congressional leadership strongly supported the amendment in 1995 (as in 1989–90), the Democratic congressional leadership, which had put forth highly effective organized opposition to the amendment in 1989–90, failed to even make such a stance a matter of party policy in 1995, although their own president had formally taken such a position. In fact, numerous members of the Democratic congressional leadership, including chief Senate Democratic Whip Wendell Ford of Kentucky, Senate Democratic Policy Committee members Harry Reid of Nevada and Jay Rockefeller of West Virginia, deputy House Democratic whips Bill Richardson of New Mexico and Chet Edwards of Texas, and even House Democratic leader Richard Gephardt (who had voted against the amendment in 1990 and bitterly attacked President Bush in 1989 for backing it for partisan reasons), voted for the amendment in 1995. The result, as one highly-placed Senate Democratic source put it in a December 1995 interview, was that there was "no sort of organized, orderly campaign against" the amendment among congressional Democrats. This was especially true in the House, where, as PAW public policy director Leslie Harris stated in another December interview, "Some Democrats saw a fait accompli and saw voting against it as a suicide mission."

Gephardt never offered any public explanation for his turnabout, but most observers speculated along the lines offered by HJC constitutional subcommittee counsel Hazeem in a December 1995, interview: "He wants to run for president?" In a late 1995 interview a top Gephardt aide reported, on condition of anonymity, that in 1990 Gephardt had held "out a great deal of hope that there was a statutory solution looming on the horizon" and had voted for one, but "with the passage of time it was increasingly clear that there was not likely to be a statutory solution satisfactory to the Supreme Court and that in combination with an extreme public outcry in favor of the amendment led him to change his position." Molly Rowley, assistant press secretary to Senate Democratic leader Thomas Daschle of South Dakota, confirmed in a December 1995 interview that widespread reports that Daschle had not made opposition to the amendment a "party issue" were "absolutely correct," because, while he personally strongly opposed the amendment as an infringement on free speech, "he thought it was an issue of conscience and that people should not be pressured to vote one way or another." Rowley added that there had been only one other issue during the previous year (lifting the arms embargo on Bosnia) on which Daschle had taken a similar approach.

Along with the Democratic congressional leadership, the press and flag desecrators expressed relatively little interest in the issue in 1995. If the press went overboard in covering the flag desecration controversy in 1989, in 1995 large segments of the press went to the other extreme (at least in their news coverage, if not in their editorial opposition), leaving much of the American public ignorant of the fact that the First Amendment was in grave danger of being altered for the first time in American history. Thus ASNE president William Ketter lamented in an October 13, 1995, *Christian Science Monitor* column that the press was suffering from "apathy" in covering the issue, a complaint that was spectacularly demonstrated by the sketchy and often inaccurate coverage of the four substantial days of Senate debate on the amendment in early December. For example, the *Washington Post,* which normally covers congressional activity microscopically, almost completely ignored the debate until the actual Senate vote, and the same pattern of virtual noncoverage was widespread in the press, with the result that the vast majority of Americans could not have known before the vote that the issue was even being debated in the Senate. In December 1995 interviews, PAW public policy director Harris declared, "The press has been asleep at the wheel," and Ketter agreed, stating that "a lot of people [in the press] took their eye off the ball and didn't realize the amendment was moving forward and getting a lot of populist support."

Along with the press, flag desecrators clearly also had lost interest in the controversy by 1995: only about ten flag desecration incidents were reported nationwide between mid-1994 and late 1995 (and most of these were only reported in local news accounts and none were apparently organized by any radical groups such as the RCP). For example, flags were burned during a Honolulu protest demanding sovereignty for Hawaii in January 1995; burned flags were mysteriously discovered near the city halls of Twentynine Palms, California, and Hays, Kansas, in March and June 1995, respectively; and about twenty flags were taken and burned from a cemetery in Bloomington, Indiana, in June 1995. In April 1995, after an Hispanic high school student in suburban Chicago burned a flag at his home and displayed the remnants inside his school locker to protest racial discrimination in American history, white students angrily confronted him and organized a mass recital of the Pledge of Allegiance; the school administration seized the flag tatters; and conciliation specialists from the U.S. Justice Department visited the school to head off rising tensions and rumors of a impending "rumble" between Hispanic and white students. Subsequently the flag-burning student agreed to make a videotaped statement expressing regret for his actions, which was shown to the student body and apparently calmed the situation. According to the school principal, "We will be better off because of this incident. In the long run, it will foster harmony and understanding among the students."[3]

In Pittsburgh, two teenagers were arrested under the state's patently unconstitutional flag desecration law for burning a small flag on the University of Pittsburgh campus in March 1995, while in Moore, Oklahoma, a similar arrest was effected in September 1995 against a teenager who used an old flag he had kept in his car as an oil dipstick. In both of these cases, prosecutors eventually dropped the cases as nonviable due to the Supreme Court's 1989–90 flagburning rulings. In the Oklahoma case, Cleveland County Assistant District Attorney Lee Cates declared, "As reprehensible as most of us may find it to be, there's clearly a long line of appellate decisions protecting an individual's right" to use the flag in an unorthodox manner and "we're bound by that." ACLU attorney C. S. Thornton, who undertook to defend the accused teenager, noted in a December 1995 interview that news reports indicated that at first police officers were unsure whether a crime had been committed but made an arrest after dispatchers uncovered a flag desecration law still officially on the state statute books. He related, "I told them I was not aware that the Moore Police Department was employing dispatchers who moonlighted as constitutional scholars."[4]

In the only 1994–95 flag desecration incident associated with violence, Palomar College student David Phillips, a protester against a California proposition designed to reduce services to illegal immigrants, was attacked by fellow demonstrators when he snatched a flag away from someone who was about to burn it near the San Marcos City Hall. Phillips had his wallet stolen, was struck several times, and was left with a swollen jaw and aching back before police shielded him from further assaults and hustled him away in a squad car. Phillips was subsequently given a "True American Hero Award" by a San Diego veterans group and was presented with a flag that had flown over the U.S. Capitol by Representative Randy Cunningham (R-Calif.).[5]

In perhaps the most bizarre flag desecration controversy of 1995, Representative Pete King (R-N.Y.) and a group of veterans bitterly demanded at a December 18 news conference the removal of a seven-foot spherical sculpture by artist Donald Lipski entitled, "Flag Ball," which had been on outdoor display since 1992 at the C. W. Post Campus of Long Island University. The "Flag Ball," which was composed of bolts of actual flag fabric covering a core of Styrofoam and batting, was attacked by King and the veterans at the news conference as a "disgrace," an "anti-American piece of trash," and a "mockery of the ideals our nation was founded upon and of the servicemen and women who fought and died to protect those ideals." The news conference was held in front of the sculpture, with the result that the sculpture was photographed and widely reproduced in the local news media, thereby giving the image far greater distribution than it had ever obtained before.

Apparently nobody had taken umbrage at the flag sculpture until a visitor from Vermont wrote in 1995 to King, the American Legion, and Long Island University Press president David Steinberg to complain about it. Shortly before his press conference, King wrote to Steinberg to urge removal of the flag and to complain that "you seem more interested in pseudo-intellectual modern 'artist' Donald Lipski's need for self-expression than you are with good taste, decency and reverence for the American flag." In a letter dated December 19, Steinberg rejected King's demand for the exhibit's removal, declaring that devotion to the flag was not about "the piece of cloth as much as the precious values for which it serves as a symbol," and terming the "flag ball" and Lipski's other flag-based artworks "an extraordinarily serious effort to explore the flag in any number of different manifestations." Steinberg suggested, moreover, that Lipski's work was far less disrespectful to the flag than its appearance "on all manner of sports gear, footwear, and in other advertisements" that were "truly desecrating the symbol for which Americans have lived and died" and whose "central purpose" seemed to be the "manipulation of its potent symbolism to increase sales and, therefore, profits, just as politicians of all persuasions have always used" the flag "to confer upon themselves a special patriotic status."

Lipski told reporters and stated in a December 1995 interview, as the controversy flared, that he had already been considering moving his exhibit to a permanent indoor display before the coming winter since he was pleased with the way the flags had weathered ("they are starting to look really perfect") but wanted to protect his creation from further deterioration. Lipski denied that the sculpture was "in poor taste" but rather had gotten "more poignant and powerful" as a "celebration of democracy," especially because "what it stands for doesn't get tattered at all" and "if anything, it's saying that we live in a country where the government doesn't make laws limiting how people can express themselves." Lipski added that the fact that "different people can see such different things in the work is testament to the magic of art" and the idea that "out of all the materials in the world something could be labelled as illegal for me to use strikes me as un-American."[6]

Aside from the fallout of the Republican electoral victories in 1994, the efforts of the CFA, and the disorganized state of congressional opposition to the amendment, another factor in the greater success of pro-amendment forces in 1995 may have been that the two most important American civil liberties organizations, PAW and the ACLU, appeared to have been less active, or, at any rate, to have maintained a far lower profile in their anti-amendment efforts in 1995 than five years earlier. One highly placed Senate Democratic source interviewed in December 1995 said that the role of the "public interest community [i.e., PAW and the ACLU]" during the 1995 controversy had been "non-existent," with the result, along with the lack of organized Democratic opposition to the amendment, that while "the CFA are no shrinking violets, there's no push back." PAW and ACLU spokesmen interviewed in December responded to this perception by conceding that they had been somewhat surprised and overwhelmed by the financing and organization of the CFA, but they also maintained that a "low profile" strategy had been a deliberate one, while behind the scenes they had exerted enormous and ultimately successful efforts to lobby key congressmen and encourage newspapers and respected conservatives to occupy the public spotlight in opposing the amendment.

Outgoing PAW public policy director Harris, in an interview conducted one day before the climactic December 12 Senate vote, when the outcome was still highly uncertain, said that her organization had felt that it had won the fight against the amendment in 1990 and "it was over. We really deluded ourselves by having gone up against Goliath last time and prevailed, and didn't realize it could come back and stomp us." When the issue re-emerged in 1995, Harris recounted, "I was stunned and couldn't believe it would happen again," especially because "nothing happened in [the] 1990 [elections] after all those threats and bravado." Once the amendment began to move through Congress in the spring, Harris continued, civil liberties groups such as the PAW were forced to fight on numerous fronts, including, in addition to the $5 million CFA-financed flag desecration campaign, proposals to limit abortion rights, to impose censorship on the Internet, and to legalize prayer in public schools, with the result that "resources have been spread very, very thin" and her organization had been "pulled in a million directions." Harris added that another reason for the greater success of the amendment forces in 1995 was "the failure of progressives to organize the grassroots across the board."

Diane Rust-Tierney, chief legislative counsel and associate director of the ACLU's Washington office, and head ACLU lobbyist against the amendment, in an interview conducted immediately after the Senate voted, agreed with Harris that the simultaneous emergence of numerous perceived serious civil liberties threats had thinned their resources, but she rejected any suggestion that the ACLU had not mounted an aggressive campaign. She said the ACLU's anti-amendment efforts had involved "all aspects" of the organization, "both in Washington and in the national office," including working with newspaper editorial boards, contacting major contributors, mobilizing the organization's "grassroots network," and putting forth the ACLU's opposition on the Internet. She said that while the ACLU made a "concerted effort" in the House, it focused its attention on the Senate

> where felt we had better prospects. Our major strategy was holding our
> people [i.e., those expected to oppose the amendment in the Senate],

which is what we ended up doing. There, was a strategy which was important, particularly given the politics of the situation, that we put forward, to highlight those without an axe to grind, editors and congressmen and conservative thinkers, so ACLU spokesmen weren't featured but we participated in the coalition [with PAW and the ABA] that set the strategy. We're all stretched thin and maybe we weren't covering as in the past when we had the luxury of having fewer issues to cover but we put in the work institutionally that was necessary to get the job done. There are times when, as the saying goes, 'You can get anything you want to get done in Washington as long as you don't take the credit.' Our view was not to be the issue, but the most important thing was to protect the constitution. We sought to get the message out with as many voices as we could and the proof [of success] is in the pudding.

At least publicly, the profile of the ABA and the ASNE against the amendment was considerably higher in 1995 than that of the ACLU and PAW. In a December 1995 interview, ASNE president Ketter declared that his organization considered opposition to the amendment its "foremost effort on the legislative front this year" and viewed the amendment as a threat to the "fundamental liberty" of the "public's right to express themselves" and "not just a press matter." The ASNE circulated information opposing the amendment to its more than 850 member newspapers and urged them to editorialize and lobby in Congress against it, repeatedly attacked the amendment in its trade magazine, *The American Editor,* and wrote to all members of Congress attacking it as a "unnecessary infringement of the First Amendment's free speech covenant with the American people." ABA president George Bushnell repeatedly issued statements and held news conferences to oppose the amendment while Irene Ensellem, ABA senior legislative counsel, led the organization's lobbying effort on Capitol Hill. In a December 1995 interview Ensellem said that, like the ACLU, the ABA "didn't focus a lot of attention on the House because I saw this as a wasted effort and wanted to focus on the Senate, where there was a more cohesive group [of congressmen] working [against the amendment]."[7]

Why the Amendment Flared Up Again

Especially given the paucity of recent flag burnings, general American insecurities and fears and the desire of amendment backers to make a symbolic statement rejecting perceived trends toward national moral and social disintegration were unquestionably a major impetus behind the amendment drive in 1995, just as five years earlier. Between 1990 and 1995, a general sense that the country was in crisis intensified, as was reflected in the rejection of President Bush's 1992 re-election bid, followed by the 1994 ousting of the long-standing Democratic congressional majority. Numerous measures of American well-being and public opinion reflected this growing sense of crisis. For example, in October 1995, Fordham University scholars reported that, based on sixteen different measures, America's social health had dropped, on a scale of 0 to 100, from 78 to 41 between 1973 and 1993, and that in 1993 the lowest scores ever were recorded for six measures, including children in poverty, average weekly earnings adjusted for inflation, and the gap between rich and poor Americans. The director of the study, Dr. Marc Miringoff, declared, "Behind these numbers, there's a lot of insecurity, a lot of frustration." In an October 1995 cover story published in *The Atlantic Monthly,* two public policy analysts reported a decline of 45 percent between 1970 and 1995 in their own combined measure of more than twenty economic indicators, which they dubbed the "genuine progress indicator."[8]

A study of "leading cultural indicators" published in 1994 by former secretary of education William Bennett reported a wide variety of discouraging trends between 1960 and the early 1990s, including a 500 percent increase in violent crime, a tripling of teenage suicides, a doubling in the divorce rate, and an increase of over 400 percent in illegitimate births; Bennett concluded that unless such "exploding social pathologies are reversed, they will lead to the decline and perhaps even to the fall of the American republic." In November 1995, the American Medical Association reported that a rising tide of sexual assaults and family violence (including about four million annual reports of abuse of children and women) was devastating the nation's physical and emotional well-being; in the same month, the National Conference of Catholic Bishops characterized the nation as suffering from a "sense of economic insecurity and moral decline." An astonishing December 1995 Gallup poll reported that 16 percent of respondents (projected to the entire population, the equivalent of about 42 million people) feared that they might become homeless, and a variety of other 1995 polls reported that a majority of Americans were gloomy about the future, foresaw a worse standard of living for the next generation, and felt that the country generally was "on the wrong track." In short, just as the flag is the primary symbol of American identity, the perceived need to outlaw flag desecration no doubt reflected a sense that the country is undergoing a national identity crisis that threatens disintegration, and that something must be done to remedy this, even if only symbolically.[9]

Backers of the amendment often publicly backed it in terms that support this analysis. For example, HJC chairman Henry Hyde (R-Ill.) declared that "what is at work here is something larger than the flag itself," and termed the amendment "an effort by mainstream Americans to reassert community standards" and "a popular protest against the vulgarization of our society." Representative James Traficant (D-Ohio) explained that the entire controversy was not "about the flag debate" but rather "about pride, it's about respect, it's about values." In explaining his switch from opposing the amendment in 1990, conservative representative Charles Stenholm (D-Tex.) cited a "deep concern about a growing, negative and disrespectful national attitude."[10]

In congressional testimony and a published article, Northwestern University law professor Stephen Presser said that the amendment would allow the American people to establish a "baseline of decency, civility, responsibility and order," to "reconstruct a dangerously fractured sense of community," and to reverse a trend in constitutional interpretation toward concern "only with the gratification of individual desires and the expansion of individual license" at the cost of sufficient concern for "community responsibility and self-restraint." Similarly, Harvard law professor Richard Parker urged the SJC to support the amendment partly on the grounds that "the bonds that hold us together" appeared to be "disintegrating." In a June 27 *Denver Post* column, Ken Hamblin supported the amendment because "enough is enough" and because liberals such as those who opposed the amendment were responsible for a "corrosive impact" on "American morality and the principles of basic decency and respect."[11]

The SJC majority began its published argument for the amendment by declaring, in a tone sounding remarkably like that of the original turn-of-the-century flag protection movement:

> We live in a time where standards have eroded. Civility and mutual respect are in decline. Nothing is immune from being reduced to the commonplace. Absolutes are distrusted. Values are considered relative. Rights are cherished and constantly expanded, but responsibilities are shirked and scorned. . . . At the same time, our country grows more and more diverse. . . . The American flag is the one symbol that unites a very diverse people in a way nothing else can, in peace and war. . . . Failure to protect the flag inevitably loosens this bond.

SJC chairman Hatch, who managed the amendment on the Senate floor, repeatedly argued for it in similar terms. He began Senate debate by complaining that the country was being "increasingly bombarded by coarse and graphic speech and by angry and vulgar discourse," and lamented that

> Drugs, crime and pornography debase our society to an extent that no one would have predicted just two generations ago. . . . There are no limits. Anything goes. . . . We have no monarchy, no state religion, no elite class—hereditary or otherwise representing the Nation and its unity. We have the flag. . . . the American flag forms a unique, common bond among us. . . . This debate concerns our judgment about what values are truly at stake. It is about our sense of national community. . . . We are fighting for the very values that the vast majority of the American people fear we are losing in this country. . . . The Senate must decide whether enough is enough. . . . Have we gotten so bad in this country that no values count?[12]

William Detweiler, national commander of the American Legion, the spearhead of the renewed amendment drive, urged support for it in a February 11 letter to the *Washington Post* by expressing concern that "Americans today harbor real doubts about what we stand for as a nation and who we are as a people" and declared that while the amendment wouldn't "erase all the doubts Americans have about the future" or even "send the stock market into a rally . . . . it's a start." In congressional testimony, Detweiler declared that the amendment would send "a clear message that unacceptable, anti-social conduct that is inarticulate and repugnant need not be tolerated." He made especially clear that many amendment backers viewed it as an almost purely symbolic statement about perceived threats to American unity and patriotism, rather than a response to any real threat to the flag itself, by declaring that flag burning was "a problem even if no one ever burns another flag."[13]

The 1995 Rise and Fall of the Flag Desecration Amendment

Following the May 25 7-5 endorsement of the proposed amendment by the HJC subcommittee on the Constitution, after one day of hearings with nine witnesses (compared to four days of hearings in 1989 with twenty-six witnesses), House Republican leaders, confident of victory with over 270 of the needed 290 votes already pledged to the CFA campaign, quickly moved it to a House floor vote. On June 7, the full HJC backed the amendment by a straight party-line 18-12 vote, and on June 28, in what the Associated Press termed a "gesture timed for the

Fourth of July holiday," the full House endorsed it 312-120, two dozen votes more than the required two-thirds majority and an increase of fifty-eight votes over those backing the amendment in 1990 (including those of sixteen representatives, among them Gephardt and a dozen other Democrats, who abandoned their 1990 positions). Republicans supported the proposal 219-12, while Democrats opposed it 107-93 and the sole House independent voted against it. In the 1995 vote, 47 percent of all House Democrats backed the amendment, compared to 37 percent in 1990; while 73 percent of the entire House backed the amendment in 1995, only 65 percent of those who had voted on the issue in 1990 did so, but 80 percent of those elected since 1990 voted affirmatively. The House vote followed only three hours of debate allowed by the Republican majority (compared to a debate lasting twice as long scheduled in 1990 by the-then Democratic majority), during which Republican leaders displayed copies of 49 state legislative resolutions and a three-foot stack of citizens' petitions urging favorable action.[14]

Civil liberties spokesmen complained in interviews conducted in December 1995 that the amendment was deliberately rushed through the House to prevent opponents from effectively organizing. Thus, ABA senior legislative counsel Ensellem said, "It really went through the House at breakneck speed" and "it was very difficult to organize anything because of the speed at which it went through." PAW public policy director Harris said that the speed of the House passage proved a lesson in "how a majority party that wants to make things happen could ram it through." Harris added that House Democrats were still shell-shocked from the 1994 elections and "pulled their punches," feeling they were faced with "a lot of moving trains and that they couldn't stand in front of every one of them." In response to such complaints, chief HJC subcommittee counsel Hazeem declared, in a December 1995 interview, with reference to past House and HJC consideration of the issue in 1989–90, "We had dealt with this issue many times. We were not dealing with a blank slate. When you're going to lose you always want more time." Similarly, Jim Wilkinson, press spokesman for House majority leader Armey, said during another interview, "This isn't that complicated an issue. You're either for it or you're against it. It's not like figuring out the tax code. It's an important amendment to the Constitution, but they [opponents] knew all year long it was coming."

On June 6, one day before the full HJC recommended approval of the amendment to the House, a SJC subcommittee held a one-day hearing on it, listening to eleven witnesses (compared to five days of SJC hearings and thirty-four witnesses in 1989–90). The Clinton administration formally opposed the amendment at the hearing, although with arguments that placed little stress on free-speech issues.

Assistant Attorney General Walter Dellinger, who had strongly opposed the amendment on free speech grounds before Congress in 1989–90 while a professor at Duke Law School, testified that President Clinton had outspokenly supported a law to outlaw flag desecration as Arkansas governor in 1989, had a personal "abhorrence" of "all forms of flag desecration," felt the *Johnson* ruling was "wrongly decided," "has a commitment to the protection of the flag," and "would have agreed with Justice [Hugo] Black," who had declared in his dissent in the *Street* case that, "It passes my belief that anything in the Federal Constitution bars a State from making the deliberate burning of the American flag an offense."

Nonetheless, Dellinger declared that Clinton was "reluctant to tamper with the Constitution" and added that there was no need to conduct a "first-time edit of the Bill of Rights in the absence of any meaningful evidence that the flag is in danger of losing its symbolic value," especially given the lack of recent flag burnings. Dellinger also declared that the amendment would "create legislative power of uncertain dimension to override the First Amendment and other constitutional guarantees" and run "counter to our traditional resistance, dating back to the time of the Founders, to resorting to the amendment process. For these reasons, the proposed amendment—and any other proposal to amend the Constitution in order to punish a few isolated acts of flag burning—should be rejected by this Congress."[15]

Commenting on Dellinger's unwillingness to make a spirited free speech attack on the amendment, civil liberties columnist Nat Hentoff, writing in the July 18 *Village Voice,* declared that he "used to know" Dellinger as "an authentic constitutional scholar who vigorously defended the Bill of Rights," but that as assistant attorney general Dellinger had "become a Clinton apologist." (Dellinger spoke for hours during interviews for this book in 1991 about his 1989 congressional testimony and expressed regret that he had not been more forthright in attacking the FPA on free speech grounds, but he failed to respond to repeated telephone requests for an interview about his 1995 testimony.)

According to Clinton administration and congressional sources interviewed in 1995, Clinton personally made the decision to oppose the amendment in consultation with the White House Office of Legal Counsel, and Dellinger's testimony was cleared with the White House before it was given and deliberately worded to avoid the implication that Clinton had any sympathy for flag desecrators. White House spokesman Mike McCurry told reporters on June 29, following House endorsement of the amendment, that Clinton "loves the American flag" and "also loves the Constitution," that the flag is a "symbol of our republic, but the Constitution is the soul of our republic," and "the President doesn't believe that you tinker with the soul for something symbolic." Shortly before the climactic

December 12 Senate vote, McCurry declared that while Clinton "feels strongly about the flag as a symbol of this country," he opposed any effort to "tamper with the Constitution," since "the guys in the powdered wigs had it about right in 1792, and there's good reason why in 200-plus years we have not amended the Bill of Rights, which is what this legislation [amendment] would do." However, McCurry added the bewildering comment that Clinton favored providing "some federal protection, adequately structured" for the flag, such as a criminal statute that "would provide penalties for flag burning," although the 1990 Supreme Court *Eichman* ruling had made crystal clear that such an approach was a constitutional impossibility.[16]

Following Dellinger's July 6 testimony, on July 20 the full SJC voted 12-6 to recommend Senate passage of the amendment, with ten Republicans and two Democrats supporting and six Democrats opposing it. Senate Republican majority leader Dole kicked off his fall campaign for the Republican presidential nomination with a speech to the American Legion in early September promising a prompt Senate floor vote on the amendment. However, CFA executive assistant Jennifer Zeller and Senate Republican sources confirmed during interviews in early December that Dole's original plan to have an early October floor vote was postponed at the CFA's request because they lacked the needed votes. As early as mid-June, in fact, the highly respected *Congressional Quarterly* reported that thirty-four senators, enough to defeat the amendment, either had declared their opposition to the amendment in 1995 or had voted against it in 1990 and that it therefore appeared doomed in the Senate.[17]

However, in the fall several Democratic senators who had opposed the amendment in 1990, including Barbara Milkulski of Maryland, Bill Bradley of New Jersey, and Joshua Lieberman of Connecticut, indicated that they were rethinking their positions, and for a brief period it appeared that the amendment could pass the Senate, especially since the resignation of Oregon Republican Bob Packwood reduced the required two-thirds majority from 67 to 66. In early September, *Congressional Quarterly* reported that "both sides agree that they will win or lose by one or two votes." In October the CFA began a $1 million-plus campaign of TV ads targeted at a dozen wavering senators, including Milkulski, Bradley, Lieberman, and Republicans Arlen Specter of Pennsylvania and Mitch McConnell of Tennessee (who had both supported the amendment in 1990).[18]

CFA representatives bluntly threatened political reprisals against senators who failed to support the amendment. SJC chairman Hatch, who spearheaded the Senate drive for the amendment, publicly declared, "Veterans groups are out for blood. Those who don't vote for it are going to be sorry." When Senator

John Kerry (D-Mass.), a Vietnam veteran, announced in early December that he would oppose the amendment because the flag was merely a "symbol of this country" while the Bill of Rights was "the substance of our rights and freedoms," Massachusetts CFA chairman and past American Legion national commander Jake Comer, who had headed up a Veterans for Kerry group during his 1990 reelection campaign, said that the CFA would follow Kerry "all over the state. We are not going to let this thing die." When McConnell announced in early December that he would oppose the amendment because it would "rip the fabric of the Constitution at its very center," and because "as conservatives we should be skeptical of tinkering with the Bill of Rights and restricting freedom even in the cause of patriotism," CFA spokesman Marty Justis declared that McConnell, who was facing a 1996 reelection contest, had engaged in a "disappointing flip-flop" and had "been in Washington too long."[19]

On December 5, Dole suddenly announced plans to begin debate on the amendment the next day, with the stated hope that voting would occur on December 7, the anniversary of the 1941 Japanese attack on Pearl Harbor. CFA officials claimed that they had sixty-seven pledged votes at a December 6 news conference; however, at the same time the *Congressional Monitor,* a daily newsletter published by *Congressional Quarterly,* reported that only sixty-one senators were committed to the amendment, that thirty were pledged against it, and that eight were undecided. In interviews conducted on the verge of the vote, which was ultimately held on December 12 (largely due to delaying tactics by Senator Jeffrey Bingaman [D-N.M.]), insiders on both sides privately reported that the lineup had become 62-33, and that the fate of the amendment rested on the four remaining undecided senators, Milkulski, Bradley, Lieberman, and Specter, all of whom came under massive lobbying pressure from both sides. Ultimately, all four senators voted as they had in 1990 and thus amendment backers obtained only 63 votes, three short of the required two-thirds, while opponents obtained 36 votes. Amendment opponents seriously feared that they would lose as late as twenty-four hours before the December 12 roll call began, while after the vote CFA spokeswoman Susan Ridge said, "We went in this morning feeling very confident about it and watched it unravel . . . before our eyes."

Forty-nine Republicans and fourteen Democrats supported the amendment, while thirty-two Democrats and four Republicans voted against it. Fifty-one supporters of the amendment in 1995 had previously voted for it as members of the House or Senate in 1990, twenty-nine opponents had voted against it previously in 1990, and two opponents in 1995 (Republican McConnell and Democrat Kent Conrad of North Dakota) switched from "yes" in 1990 to "no" in 1995. Among senators who had never voted before on the amendment, twelve supported it (including all of the freshmen Republicans) and five voted against it.[20]

As a futile last-minute effort to round up additional votes for the amendment, SJC chairman Hatch won unanimous Senate consent to drop the "states" provision from the text that had been approved in the House, in response to repeated criticisms that the provision would lead to fifty-one different federal and state definitions of "flag" and "desecration." In asking that the "states" provision be deleted, Hatch declared that he "did not want to make this concession" but "sometimes compromise is necessary in order" to achieve the "task of trying to assemble 66 votes." According to a key Republican Senate staff source interviewed in December, "no deals were made in advance," but the deletion of the "states" provision was designed to "pick and solidify support" for the amendment, and it "may have solidified some but it didn't pick up."[21]

Before the critical 63-36 Senate rejection of the final form of the amendment, two alternative proposals were also rejected. One, introduced by former SJC chairman Joseph Biden (D-Del.) was a revived version of his proposed "content-neutral" constitutional amendment of 1990, designed to authorize a federal flag desecration law, but only one which would outlaw the burning, mutilating, or trampling of the American flag under all circumstances, with the sole exception for the disposal of "worn or soiled" flags. Biden's proposal was a response to the open declaration by backers of the revived 1989–90 amendment that they wanted to authorize the outlawing (in the words of the SJC majority) of only "the contemptous or disrespectful physical treatment of the flag," such as "placing the words 'Down with the fascist Federal Government' or racist remarks on the flag," while still allowing "respectful" damage to the flag, such as a soldier who wanted a flag cremated with his remains or who wanted to print on a flag flown in battle "the name of his unit and location of specific battles, in honor of his unit, the service of his fellow soldiers, and the memory of the lost." Biden argued that this approach impinged on First Amendment rights "in a way never before permitted in our nation" and would take "us down an unchartered and very perilous path" by violating the "very basic notion" that the government could not discriminate on the basis of the content of expression, since it did not make the "act of flag burning the crime" but rather the "*message* behind the act the crime." Under the revived 1989–90 amendment, Biden declared, the states might well jail "the fringe artist displaying the flag on the floor of an art museum" while "giving its blessing to the veteran who displays the flag on the ground at a war memorial." On the other hand, he maintained, his amendment, while admittedly impacting "first amendment values" and restricting "expressive conduct," would "protect the flag while not doing damage to core free speech values—by prohibiting all abuse of the flag without regard to the message intended by the abuser," and protecting the "flag as treasured symbol—not as vehicle for disagreeable speech." Biden's approach garnered virtually no support, however, as the vast majority of senators either opposed any tinkering with the First Amendment or wanted to be able to discriminate among those who damaged flags on the basis of their perceived attitude toward it: his proposal was crushed in the Senate by 93-5 and had no real impact on the overall debate.[22]

The second rejected alternative to the revived 1989–90 amendment, proposed by Senator McConnell, may well have significantly contributed to the amendment's defeat. McConnell's proposal, entitled the "Flag Protection and Free Speech Act of 1995," was a statutory rather than constitutional one, which would have outlawed damaging flags "with the primary purpose and intent" or the knowledge that such acts were "reasonably likely" to "produce imminent violence," as well as punishing the theft and destruction of a flag owned by the federal government and the theft and destruction on federal land of a flag belonging to another person. McConnell declared that his proposal would "result in the swift and certain punishment for those who commit the contemptible act of defacing the flag, but leave the first amendment untouched." However, McConnell's opponents argued, quite cogently, that: (1) his proposal would not impact most flag burnings, which usually involved the destruction of flags owned by the flag desecrator and generally did not occur on federal land; (2) inciting violence and theft were already illegal; and (3) providing special protection for flags (rather than treating theft of flags and inciting violence with flags under existing general laws against theft and incitement to violence) might well fail the Supreme Court's guidelines in *Johnson* and *Eichman* suggesting that no special legal category could be created to protect the flag where symbolic speech was involved. While the McConnell proposal was overwhelming rejected by 71 to 28, it nonetheless may have provided "political cover" for senators wary about not only amending the Constitution but also being unable to claim that they had cast at least some sort of vote for protecting the flag; certainly it was no coincidence that twenty-six of the twenty-eight senators who backed the McConnell proposal voted against the revived 1989–90 amendment, and without this alternative to vote for, as Biden publicly suggested, some of them might have felt forced to support the amendment.[23]

The amendment's narrow defeat left some of its backers bitterly disappointed, threatening political revenge and promising to bring it back to Congress no later than 1997. CFA president Wheeler proclaimed in a press release, "We'll be back. We'll see you in [the] November [1996 congressional elections]." In an interview conducted the morning after the amendment's defeat, Wheeler expressed pride that the CFA "over a period of 21 months took the issue from not being on the radar screen whatsoever—when I talked to Congress at first they looked at me as though I'd just beamed down from the mother ship." But he also expressed considerable bitterness, blaming the Senate defeat on the McConnell proposal, complaining that it gave "political cover to those" who "wanted to hide behind a statute" and "wanted to say they could protect the flag but also wanted to protect the First Amendment, which was the same dodge used in 1989." Wheeler added:

> What members of Congress are doing is lying to American people about this issue. It's not possible to [protect the flag] with a statute and they're preying on the ignorance of the American people and talking legal mumbo-jumbo. At least they should have the integrity to say they don't think it's important enough to provide constitutional protection for the flag. We did find out it's a real misnomer for many member of Congress to put the words "the honorable" in front of their name, not because of the way they voted but because of the way they indicated they were going to vote and didn't do it. We know who the people are and they know who the people are. We're going to make sure the people know what the facts are when they go to the polls in November. This [CFA] campaign was an exercise in the right of people to govern themselves and I think the people who became involved learned a little bit more than they wanted to about the way the government works.

Wheeler added that the CFA had already told congressional leaders that "the only way you're going to get this off your agenda is to pass [the amendment]," and that Clinton's announced support for a flag-desecration statute was "disingenuous" because "he graduated from law school, his wife graduated from law school, they both know the only way to protect the flag with a statute is to [first] pass an enabling amendment."[24]

Immediately after the Senate vote, SJC chairman Hatch blamed Clinton, whom he termed "the leader of the opposition," for its failure, declaring that Clinton "won this vote and the American people lost," and that had Clinton supported the amendment, "I have no doubt we would have prevailed." While conceding that the "current Senate" would probably not endorse the amendment, Hatch added, "This amendment is not going to go away. The American people are not going to allow it." Similarly, House Veterans' Committee chairman Bob Stump (R-Ariz.) termed Clinton's opposition the "decisive factor" in the Senate's action, declared that the president had "demonstrated his contempt for America's

26 million veterans," and promised to continue to work for passage of the amendment. A key Senate Republican staff source interviewed in December also blamed Clinton for the defeat, declaring that "a desire not to embarrass the president operated on the Democratic side," especially since Dellinger's June 6 SJC testimony had laid down such an "extremely hard line" position against the amendment that obviously represented a "considered position" by the Clinton administration. He added, "The president's opposition when you need two-thirds is significant. The President has an inevitable effect on a fight like this, however quiet he's been publicly about it. If he had come out in favor, I think we would have won." In another December interview, Dennis Shea, legal counsel to Senate leader Dole, explained the amendment's defeat as simply resulting from the fact that, "We just didn't have the votes," because efforts to sway swing senators "bore no fruit." He added, "We need four more votes and if we pick up more Republican seats [in the 1996 elections] it's more likely to come back [in 1997]."[25]

Ironically, while some Republican leaders blamed Clinton for the amendment's failure, opponents very likely would have pointed the finger at Clinton had the Senate endorsed it, since, aside from Dellinger's SJC testimony and Clinton press secretary McCurry's brief statements, the president appears to have exerted no personal effort concerning the issue. Multiple White House and congressional sources on both sides of the issue interviewed in December 1995 reported no signs of any presidential phone calls or other personal lobbying, or even that Clinton had made defeating the amendment a high priority. Thus, a high-level Democratic Senate source said, "Clinton has not weighed in on this," and chief ACLU lobbyist Diane Rust-Tierney concurred, declaring that while the Dellinger testimony was a "beautifully written strong statement" against the amendment, "in general administration policy has been to keep the president above the fray of battle and on this amendment it followed this general strategy." A key Senate Republican staff source agreed with this assessment, although he evaluated it somewhat differently: "The president wanted to get the advantage of defeating the amendment while standing in the tall grass. He knows where the American people are on this, so he wanted to defeat it without necessarily having the spotlight on him."

Opponents of the amendment expressed satisfaction with the defeat, but many warned that the vote had been perilously close and that the danger was not over. Thus ACLU executive director Ira Glasser said that while the vote was a "victory for free speech, the fact that it was so close is deeply troubling." Speaking a day before the Senate defeat, at a time when the outcome was still unclear, PAW public policy director Harris said, "The idea that a handful of flag burnings would precipitate amending the First Amendment is really stunning. It reflects an atmosphere of fear and repression that I don't think American is about. I'm worried about the future. You can't separate this from a larger move towards censorship in this country." The December 14 *Chicago Tribune* said the thirty-six opponents of the amendment deserved credit for "recognizing the grotesque irony of mutilating the Bill of Rights to safeguard the flag," but that the margin of victory had become "dangerously close." The December 14 *Minneapolis Star-Tribune* said it was "hard to work up a lather of glee" over the defeat because the vote "came just three votes short of constitutional sabotage" and lamented that those who favored the amendment "seem to be firmly, unaccountably bewitched by the notion that cherishing freedom entails curtailing it. . . . There is indignity in discovering that 63 percent of this nation's senators feel greater fondness for colored cloth than for an indispensable abstraction called liberty."[26]

The 1995 Debate over the Constitutional Amendment

Most of the key arguments made on both sides of the 1995 amendment debate echoed those of 1989–90. Arguments stressed by opponents included that the amendment was a frontal attack on free speech and the Bill of Rights; that it would harm America's ability to serve as a worldwide model of freedom; that it was motivated by political considerations; that it confused the flag's symbolism with the substantive freedoms it represented; that there was no flag-burning problem to solve; that focusing attention on the issue would only encourage flag burners and divert attention away from real problems; that the amendment would create a "slippery slope" for future erosion of constitutional rights; and that the amendment's failure to define "flag" or "desecration" would create legal chaos and endless litigation, especially since (before the "states" provision was deleted by Senate amendment backers) each state might come up with its own definition.

Far more than in 1990, most opponents of the amendment attacked it on basic ideological grounds: that it was a frontal assault on free speech. There was far less emphasis in 1995 on the totemic, or sacred and untouchable character (as opposed to the content), of the Constitution as a counter-icon to the sacred flag. For example, among congressional opponents of the amendment, the twelve-member Democratic HJC minority attacked it as detracting from the American system of "unfettered political expression" and declared that it would harm America's international human-rights standing, since if the nation was to "maximize our moral stature in matters of human rights," it was "essential that we remain fully open to unpopular dissent, regardless of the form it takes." Similarly, five members of the SJC minority declared, "If our system of government and our society is to continue to define freedom and democracy throughout the world, it must, as a threshold be a system open to free and diverse debate—that is what separates us from oppressive nations across the world."[27]

The most eloquent congressional attack on the amendment on free-speech grounds came from Senator John Glenn (D-Ohio), who as a decorated Marine combat pilot in both World War II and Korea, and as the first American astronaut to orbit the earth, was a certified American hero and played a role in providing "political cover" to other senators much like that played by Senator Robert Kerrey in 1989. Glenn's December 8 Senate oration made all of the free-speech arguments that scores of other amendment opponents also made, but with considerably more eloquence, and he was subsequently quoted or cited in many newspaper accounts, as well as in editorials attacking the amendment. Preceding his remarks by stating that "until today, I have tended to hold my tongue" because "it is no fun being attacked or being labeled as unpatriotic or a friend of flag burners," Glenn declared that "nobody" had fought "any harder" or loved the flag more than he; but, he added, the flag only symbolized American freedoms but "is not the freedoms themselves," of which the most important included the individual liberty to "express ourselves freely and openly and independently, no matter how out of step that may be with the feelings of the majority." He added that the "only way" the country's fabric could be weakened was not by the acts of a "few misguided souls burning our flag," but by "retreating from the principles that the flag stands for," which would "do more damage to the fabric of our nation than a thousand torched flags could ever do." Glenn declared that "those of us" who remembered and cared deeply about the nation's sacrifices "on behalf of freedom" were especially responsible for opposing the "political mud merchants" and "those who would deal in demagoguery on this issue," adding:

> It would be a hollow victory indeed if we preserve the symbol of our freedoms by chipping away at the freedoms themselves. Those who have made the ultimate sacrifice for our flag did not give up their lives for a red-white-and-blue piece of cloth. They died because of their allegiance to the values, rights and principles represented by that flag.

Glenn warned against "even the potential of a tiny crack in the Bill of Rights" that would restrict free expression and might "be a tiny opening that could possibly be followed by others." He declared that "if America is truly going to be the land of the free, you and I must prove [by taking the political risk of opposing the amendment] that it is still the home of the brave."[28]

In the House, the most eloquent opposition to the amendment on free-speech grounds came from a Republican, Wayne Gilchrest of Maryland, who declared that while he personally deplored flag desecration, as a Vietnam veteran he had come to realize that the "right to be obnoxious, to be unpatriotic" was in fact "the essence of what we fought for" and that "freedom means the freedom to be stupid just as surely as it means the freedom to be wise" and "no government should ever be so powerful as to differentiate between the two." Gilchrest added that amendment proponents were "confusing the flag with what it symbolizes," and that the amendment would allow governments to "coerce respect" for the flag that is "the symbol of freedom from government coercion."[29]

Among other congressional amendment opponents, Representative Cardiss Collins (D-Ill.) declared it made no sense to "canonize the symbol by utterly destroying what it represents," and Senate Democratic leader Tom Daschle asked, "Do we really hold the symbol more important than the principle it represents?" and answered his question by declaring, "The flag is important," but "our basic freedoms . . . are clearly more important." Senator Chuck Robb (D-Va.) opposed the amendment because "the acid test of any democracy is the ability to speak out and protest our government without fear of being arrested. The amendment goes to the heart of that freedom." Noting that amendment backers had made clear that they wanted to be able to prosecute dissident flag burners while protecting the right of veterans to burn worn flags, Senator Russell Feingold (D-Wisc.) declared that the amendment really was targeted at "disrespectful" expression and ultimately at "what somebody is thinking when they burn the flag. It is about the content of their mind." Almost all of the congressional opponents of the amendment simultaneously bitterly attacked flag burners: Senator Frank Lautenberg (D-N.J.) termed flag burning "an ugly, despicable and cowardly act," while Representative William Clinger (R-Pa.) termed flag burners "twisted lowlifes" and "pathetic individuals" who engaged in "cheap theatrics" and whose "sorry causes" would only be given stature by a passing a constitutional amendment, which would "turn a fool's act of cowardice into a martyr's civil disobedience, and encourage more dimwits to burn the flag."[30]

A number of Democratic opponents of the amendment charged that its backers sought primarily political gains. Thus, Senator Kennedy termed the amendment a "troubling and unprecedented effort to politicize the Constitution" that would treat that "enduring charter of our nation and our liberties" as a "bill-board on which to plaster the bumper-sticker slogan of the moment." Senator Dale

Bumpers of Arkansas said amendment proponents were engaged in "sheer politics," designed to embarrass those who opposed it via a "30-second political spot," which suggests they are "not patriotic." Bumpers added that "it takes a little courage" to oppose the amendment, but "courage is in very short supply," especially as evidenced by the fact that there were "a lot of Senators who will take you aside and deplore this amendment" but vote for it "because they do not want to have to go home and talk to their constituents." Senator Barbara Boxer said the real question was, "Do we stand behind Speaker Newt Gingrich and the House of Representatives? Or do we stand behind the founding fathers? I, for one, choose to stand with the founding fathers, Thomas Jefferson, James Madison and Ben Franklin."[31]

Many amendment opponents argued that it would foster future erosions of American liberties, divert attention away from more pressing and real problems, and fail even to increase respect for the flag, since patriotism and love of country could only be brought about by education and solving the country's problems, rather than by mandate. Thus, Senator Paul Simon (D-Ill.) declared it ironic that forbidding flag desecration would be enshrined in the Constitution if the amendment were enacted, "while if you burn [a copy of] the Constitution nothing happens. Should we then have another amendment for that? And perhaps another amendment for anyone who would burn the Bible? Where does this stop?" Representative Jose Serrano (D-N.Y.) declared, "If this flag could speak to us, it would probably tell us to stop this silly debate and to do what it stands for," such as feeding hungry children, caring for the elderly, and abolishing racial prejudice. Referring to Republican proposals to cut veterans' benefits, Representative Pat Williams (D-Mont.) warned during the June 28 House debate that the House was scheduled to vote the next day to cut veterans' benefits by billions of dollars, and termed the amendment a "duck, a dodge, a camouflage," and a "dupe, a ruse, a subterfuge," which essentially told veterans not to worry that "they do not have any veterans' nursing homes," because "the Republicans are going to save the flag for them." Representative David Minge (D-Minn.) declared that educating Americans about the flag's significance, "rather than mandating respect, is the only true and enduring reverence our flag deserves," and termed the amendment "a gesture to provide political cover for my colleagues who are financing tax cuts on the backs of veterans." Representative Thomas Foglietta (D-Pa.) declared that the best way to "pass on to our children our reverence for our country" was to spend every day in Congress "living up to the highest ideals of democracy," including preserving freedom of speech, while colleague William Clinger (R-Pa.) said he was most struck by a letter from a constituent who had written, "If the day ever comes when we must ensure patriotism by statute, it will already be too late for our country."[32]

Many of these arguments were endlessly repeated in massive and virtually unanimous opposition to the amendment voiced by the nation's editorial writers, columnists, and cartoonists (press opposition was so pervasive that one key Senate Republican staffer interviewed in December characterized it as "virtually herd-like," adding, "I got a kick out of people saying how heroic it was to vote against the amendment, since these are people who are going to get ten honorary degrees and be lauded by the chattering class—the law professors, editorial writers and opinion makers and molders"). Senator Herb Kohl (D-Wisc.) could have spoken about any state when he declared that "across my home state, from the *Milwaukee Journal-Sentinel* to the *Eau Claire Leader-Telegram* to the *Appleton Post-Crescent* to the *LaCrosse Tribune*," newspapers had expressed the firm belief that the amendment was "a bad idea."[33]

In *Newsday* columns published on July 13 and December 13, Robert Reno complained that in an era of "promiscuous promises" made by politicians, "nobody is promising a decent economic growth rate, the one cure for the stagnant wage levels that are driving national discontent," but instead voters were being offered "snake oil" solutions like the flag-desecration amendment in order to "distract people from what really ails them." Moreover, Reno wrote, the amendment would "reduce respect for the flag to a compulsory act, and by punishing disrespect thereby equates things that ought to be natural and freely given with illegal parking, the dumping of old tires in a public park or building an outhouse in the front yard in violation of zoning and health codes." In a cartoon published in the December 24 *Oakland* [County, Mich.] *Press,* a warmly dressed congressman was depicted strolling past two homeless men sitting behind a trash can fire declaring, "What a relief! For a minute, I thought you were burning a flag!" Writing in the July 3 *Nashville Business Journal,* editor Roger Shirley termed the amendment "political pandering to a bogus issue" and a "monumental waste of time and resources," which amounted to "tinkering with the First Amendment" and threatened to create "an unparalleled slippery slope [paving the way for further limitations on freedom of speech], one with a huge cesspool at the bottom." In a June 29 *Chicago Tribune* column, Eric Zorn termed the House action a desecration of the flag that exceeded that of flag burners because, given its symbolic nature, the flag could only be desecrated abstractly, and then "only by lawmakers, judges and other officials when they profane and defile that for which it stands."

Free speech arguments played a central role in the opposition to the amendment by civil liberties groups and the press. Thus, in a June 6 letter to members of the House, PAW declared that "it would be the most hollow form of patriotism to coerce reverence for national symbols" while "undermining the very free speech rights that the symbol represents." ASNE president William Ketter declared that at a time when "a large part of the world is awakening to the first tastes of personal freedom and democracy in the wake of the collapse of communism," it was "absolutely crucial" that the "United States exerts its leadership as the nation among all others that has led the way in demonstrating that governments and their citizens need not fear freedom of thought and expression." ABA president George Bushnell declared that those who favored the amendment were seeking, for short-term political gain, to "chip away at the guarantees contained in the Bill of Rights" and appeared willing to go "blindly down the path of restricting political speech that we find repugnant and distasteful," ignoring the fact that "there are principles that are worth much more than votes in the next election." Bushnell especially attacked Senate Republican leader and declared presidential candidate Dole for allowing his "political ambitions" to outstrip "his decency as an individual." ACLU executive director Ira Glasser, in a June 28 statement following House endorsement of the amendment, declared that "false patriots" had "dishonored the flag," and in "proposing to begin to unravel the First Amendment, they desecrate what the flag represents and what millions of Americans have died to defend."[34]

Free speech arguments were also central to the massive opposition to the amendment by editorial writers, cartoonists, and columnists. A July 7 *Atlanta Journal* column by Joanne Jacobs attacked the amendment because "our heritage is liberty and our tradition is tolerance for freethinkers, mavericks, loonies and louts," and the flag "does not represent obedience to central authority, mindless conformity, coerced patriotism," but rather "flies over a big, bickering country that is not threatened by dissidence, only strengthened." The *Sacramento Bee* declared on July 3 that passage of the amendment was a "dreadful way to honor a document [the Constitution] and a group of statesmen who were fighting repressive government" and warned that "free speech is indivisible" and therefore "once we limit it for certain forms of expression, it makes it that much easier to limit it again, and again, and again." The June 30 *Cincinnati Post* declared that the amendment would "do more to injure the spirit of American liberty than all the kerosene-pouring America-haters put together," especially since the American spirit of liberty would survive "without a singe" even if "subversive vandals" were to "burn every flag in the country." Numerous editorial cartoons also attacked the amendment on free-speech grounds: For example, the *Denver Post* depicted a Republican elephant setting fire to the Bill of Rights with a cigarette lighter labelled "flag-burning amendment," while the *Washington Post* portrayed a man wearing a "congressional politics" button shredding the Bill of Rights while standing atop a flag.[35]

Many press comments similarly complained that amendment proponents were motivated primarily by cheap political motives. Thus, the June 28 *Atlanta Constitution* said the amendment would violate basic constitutional rights, all for the purpose of gaining votes by championing constitutional "thou shalt nots" to halt America's "supposed slide into social decay." The June 30 *San Francisco Chronicle* declared that the founding fathers "must be spinning in their graves" at the "embarrassing spectacle of posturing patriots in Congress seeking to flaunt their love of the American flag" by "mouthing chauvinist platitudes and rushing to save the Stars and Stripes in time for the Fourth of July recess." Writing in the June 28 *Russellville* (Arkansas) *Courier,* columnist Joe Spano termed the issue one made to "order for bellowing, butt-bussing, chauvinistic, demagogic, fulsome, hypocritical, pusillanimous, screeching, shallow, smarmy, speechifying, supercilious politicians." The *Eau Claire Leader-Telegram* declared on June 18 that the amendment was being fostered by "politicians without the guts or the brains to solve what really ails this country" but who know that

> they can fool many voters simply by using the flag as a political prop and making flowery speeches about patriotism, love of country, etc. . . . What a legacy to leave to our children: "Hey, kids, we've mortgaged your future in the name of special interests and for our convenience, but we've protected the flag with an amendment. Pretty smart, huh?" . . . Burning the American flag won't solve anything, but neither will outlawing burning of the flag while the nation it represents crumbles underneath it.

The *New York Times,* in editorials published on June 12 and December 7, referred to amendment supporters as "professional patriots" who sought to protect the flag from "the virtually nonexistent danger of physical desecration"; it added that the flag's "deep meaning derives from the broad tolerance built into the Constitution even for a tiny minority that is unwilling to share the reverence the rest of the nation awards it" and therefore the only real threat to it came from "a band of flag wavers" who failed to respect "the freedoms for which the flag stands." *Newsday*'s editorials of June 14 and July 4 termed it "abhorrent" that some amendment proponents sought to "manipulate Americans' deep love of the flag for their own political gain" by using a "diffuse sense of public anxiety and anger" to "erode bedrock principles—the right of free expression and of political dissent."

Far more than in 1989–90, amendment opponents argued that flag burning was an extremely rare event and therefore a nonproblem, especially as there were no indications that Americans were losing their love for the flag. Thus, Senator Kerrey declared that the "community's revulsion at those who burn a flag" had successfully "contained the problem without the government getting involved," and that love of the flag should come from "the force of our conscience" rather than the "force of the police" or the fear that "we are afraid something bad is going to happen to us if we desecrate [it]." Five dissenting SJC Democrats declared that an amendment "to 'protect' a flag which is already protected by the unwavering respect of an entire nation is unwarranted, ill conceived" and "does unprecedented damage to the Constitution and the very principles the flag symbolizes," especially since "a handful of dissidents each year cannot shake the devotion of the American people to the Flag."[36]

Amendment opponents repeatedly pointed to studies suggesting that fewer than forty-five flag burnings had been reported in all of American history prior to the 1989–90 controversy and that only about three dozen flag desecration incidents could be uncovered by the Congressional Research Service for the 1991–95 period. Thus, Senator Glenn termed the amendment "a solution looking for a problem to solve," while Representative Gary Ackerman (D-N.Y.) asked what great threat required passing the amendment: "Are our constituents jumping out from behind parked cars, waving flags, and burning them at us so we cannot get to work? . . . Or is it a blue, white and red herring to use our beloved national symbol as a partisan pawn by petty politicians for their personal partisan purposes?" *Philadelphia Tribune* columnist Camillo Gonsalves wrote on July 4 that "Today, one is as likely to see someone spontaneously combust as to see a burning flag," and he termed the House endorsement of the amendment an act that "has shamed the flag and that which it represents more than a thousand incinerations of Old Glory ever could." Conservative *Washington Post* columnist Charles Krauthammer wrote on July 1 that the House, in endorsing the amendment, had responded "smartly to the national flag-burning emergency—a grand total of five or six cases a year" at the cost of endangering the freedoms the flag symbolized. "If this is conservatism," he declared, "liberalism deserves a comeback." The *Los Angeles Times,* in June 8 and October 15 editorials, termed the amendment drive a "sign of national insecurity," reflecting a "gross overreaction" provoked by the "childish behavior of a few" that threatened to erode "one of the Constitution's most noble and vital protections." It added, "Congress takes an oath to uphold the Constitution—not the flag."[37]

Some conservative critics of the flag amendment opposed it partly on the grounds that it would only encourage publicity seekers to burn flags. Thus, conservative lawyer Bruce Fein wrote in the June 5 *Legal Times* that the incidence of flag desecration had "plummeted to the submicroscopic" with the end of "media infatuation" with the issue after 1990, but that banning flag desecration might "actually encourage such dishonorable and juvenile behavior in the hope of earning free speech martyrdom, assisted by an easily beguiled mass media desperate to discover an O. J. Simpson sequel [a reference to the sensational murder trial that mesmerized the nation in 1995]." In a July 10 *U.S. News & World Report* column, another conservative critic of the amendment, John Leo, declared that "the only absolutely certain way to revive the flag-burning instinct among American misfits is to pass an amendment forbidding it."

Another issue repeatedly stressed by amendment opponents was that, at least as originally drafted, it would allow each state to come up with its own definition of "flag" and "desecrate," with the resultant certainty of years of subsequent confusion and litigation. For example, the HJC Democratic minority report argued that the "untested meaning and scope" of the amendment's language would "inevitably lead to confusing and inconsistent law enforcement and adjudication, and it will likely be decades before the court system could even begin to sort out the problems." Similarly, an editorial in the July 3 *St. Louis Post-Dispatch* warned of an impending "nationwide legal nightmare" if the amendment succeeded. This position was seemingly strongly supported by a March 1995 report by the nonpartisan Congressional Research Service, which reported that forty-eight states retained on their statute books wildly varying flag desecration laws (presumptively unconstitutional under the Supreme Court's 1989–90 rulings but presumably legally restored if the 1995 amendment passed). For example, the Texas law defined "flag" as confined to objects that were "capable of being flown from a staff" and specifically excluded representations of flags in paintings, photographs, clothing, or jewelry; furthermore, it limited improper use of the flag to anyone who intentionally "damages, defaces, mutilates or burns [it]". On the other hand, the Wisconsin law banned casting "contempt" upon the flag in any manner and defined "flag" as "anything which is or purports to be the Stars and Stripes," specifically including a "copy, picture or representation" of the flag.[38]

Congressional amendment opponents had a satirical field day as they repeatedly attacked the alleged vagueness of the terms "flag" and "desecration" in the text. Representative Pat Schroeder declared that the proposed amendment was so loosely written that some state might criminalize "canceling a postage stamp with a flag on it," while Representative Jack Reed (D-R.I.) queried if men's boxer shorts with a flag motif would constitute desecration. Senator Bumpers asked if a flag-desecration ban would apply to swizzle sticks with flags on them in cocktail bars or to July 4 newspapers with flag reproductions, "every one of them going into the trash before sundown." Senator Glenn asked about "small paper flags on a stick we hand out to children at political rallies" that "are often tossed on the floor or in a garbage can at the conclusion of an event." Senator Kerrey warned that if the amendment were passed, state laws would be so diverse that "one may have to get from AAA [the American Automobile Association] information about what the various flag ordinances are from State to State," and that the flag would become an object of increased political controversy, rather than an object of increased respect. Representative Jose Serrano (D-N.Y.) asked if a flag-desecration ban would apply "if you wear a soccer shirt with the American symbol on it and you sweat it up or you are a terrible soccer player?"[39]

During the June 28 House floor debate, Representative Ackerman displayed a varied array of flag merchandise, including pantyhose, boxer shorts, plates, suspenders, pinwheels, and slippers, while asking questions such as whether blowing one's nose in a flag-design napkin would constitute desecration ("Violating the Constitution is nothing to sneeze at"). Referring to a disposable flag-design flashlight, Ackerman asked, "Can you dispose of it or do you have to give it a decent burial if it dies?" He continued: "How about flag socks? Do you violate the flag when you make them? When you buy them? When you wear them? Does it matter if your feet are clean or dirty? And what happens if different states pass different statutes? Do you have to check your socks at the border?"[40]

In a more serious vein, former Berkeley law professor Robert Cole warned that the amendment threatened an "unpredictable but certainly serious range of prohibitions, presently unconstitutional, on uses of flags in art, theater and other contexts," with the certain result that "artists, performers and producers will be prosecuted for the crime of being irreverent to a flag." The strongest attack on the alleged deficiencies of the amendment's wording in the House of Representatives came from Representative John Bryant (D-Tex.), who termed the amendment's failure to define "flag" and "desecration" "unreasonable" and "unworkable" during the June 28 House floor debate, and resulting primarily from proponents' haste to pass it "before the July Fourth recess, so you could all go home and say, 'Look what I did and look what those other bad guys wouldn't go along with.'" However, his proposal to return the amendment to committee with instructions that Congress alone provide a definition of "flag," and that the forbidden acts be restricted only to "burning, trampling, soiling or rending" it (with the term "desecration" entirely deleted), was rejected by a vote of 369-63[41]

Curiously, no one questioned whether a special June 14 Flag Day display on the Washington Monument grounds would constitute a case of "desecration" under the proposed amendment: It consisted of a 83-by-56-foot, 18,500-pound cake replica of the flag, with red, white, and blue icing covering strawberry and blueberry pie filling, smothered in 3,600 pounds of whipped topping, which was carved up and eaten by tourists without incident or arrest. Nonetheless, as in 1989–90, the 1995 flag desecration debate provided endless fodder for satirical newspaper columnists. In the March 26 *Atlanta Constitution,* Tom Teepen wrote that to protect the nation's symbolic integrity it would soon become necessary to "make it unconstitutional to draw funny hats on pictures of sitting presidents, joke about George Washington's wooden teeth, make Uncle Sam look bad in editorial cartoons or call the Founding Fathers the First Dads." In a July 1 *New York Times* column, Russell Baker suggested that next Congress might propose an amendment to "make it a crime to desecrate home and mother," but added that such a proposal might fail because "too many mothers nowadays belong to the single-mother variety" and that "for Congress, that's pushing motherhood beyond the limit." *Arizona Republic* columnist Charles Levendosky asked on July 7, "Will the flag be desecrated if you sit down while wearing your flag pants? . . . Is burning a virtual flag in the cyberspace of the Internet desecration?" *Newsday* columnist Robert Reno asked on December 13, "What happens to people who store a flag improperly so that it gets eaten by moths?" and "What happens if your house burns down and you save the TV set instead of the flag? . . . What if somebody makes a patriotic movie depicting flag burners as drooling, wicked libertines? Will the flag-burning scenes all have to be animated or will even artificially portrayed desecration be impermissible?"[42]

Time magazine columnist Barbara Ehrenreich wrote on July 3 that if the amendment were passed, some time in the future "a man innocently wearing flag-motif briefs may cross a state line only to find himself hoisted up the nearest flagpole and saluted by troops of Boy Scouts." She added that wearing flag-design underwear might turn "even a small lapse of personal hygiene" into a "punishable offense." In a similar vein, *Washington Post* columnist Jonathan Yardley suggested on July 3 that lawyers would welcome the flag amendment for the "everlasting profit" it would yield them as the courts sought to determine if there was any "legal or moral distinction between burning the flag" and using it on clothing, which, among other things, covered one's "private" and "at times malodorous" body parts.

San Francisco Chronicle satirist Arthur Hoppe suggested in his July 5 column that Congress might next turn to ban desecration of "apple pies and hot dogs, not to mention eagles, dads, McDonald's, Uncle Sam and possibly 1953 Chevrolets." In a June 17 *Atlanta Constitution* column, John Head, supposedly looking back from the vantage point of the year 2015, recalled that after passage of the flag desecration amendment, the Constitution had been amended so many times that it "got to be as fat as a New York phone book." In its July 8 issue, the British newsweekly *The Economist* declared that by endorsing the amendment, the House of Representatives had "got down to the really serious stuff" and suggested including among the forbidden acts "allowing your dog to desecrate a flag-pole" and "rolling a person in the flag when he/she is one fire." Writing in the September 18 *Nation,* Jamin Raskin and Michael Anderson asked what would happen if "postmodern Magritte-ists [a reference to the surrealist artist] paint perfect flag copies but make them an inch too wide" and write "THIS IS NOT A FLAG" across them.

One new argument by amendment opponents that emerged in 1995 was that its spirit contradicted the claimed desire of the newly elected Republican congressional majority to lessen governmental power and intrusion into citizens' private lives and conservatives' criticism of attempts to impose "politically correct" limits on free expression, such as that which offended racial minorities. For example, in a June 14 *Washington Post* column, Roger Pilon, director of the Center for Constitutional Studies at the conservative/libertarian Cato Institute, attacked Republican amendment backers as hypocrites because they purported to be dedicated to "liberty and limited government," yet were desecrating the core value of liberal democracy, namely "the right of the individual to be free" to "do what one wishes short of violating the rights of others." A cartoon published in the June 26 *Ann Arbor News,* referring to Republican attempts to limit environmental regulations, portrayed a Republican elephant wrapping himself in the flag while declaring, "You many now desecrate the air, the land and the water . . . but *not* the flag." A July 4 *Newsday* editorial declared that past constitutional amendments such as the Bill of Rights had usually sought to expand personal liberties, but that the "new conservatives would reverse course" with the flag amendment, steering the nation "toward less freedom, fewer liberties, less tolerance." Writing in the July 17 *Indianapolis Business Journal,* Don Feder declared that the real point of the amendment was to safeguard the "sensibilities of veterans and other patriotic Americans," but that this was exactly what the "politically correct crowd" was criticized for by conservatives when they sought to impose "totalitarian speech codes" on college campuses that punish people for "hurtful words" which might "aggravate and agitate various minorities." From the far Left, RYCB spokesman Gregory Lee Johnson, the defendant in the landmark 1989 Supreme Court case, posted a July 4 Internet statement that termed the amendment part of the Republicans' "cruel 'Contract On America' war on the poor, blacks, youth, and working people," which was part of a "whole shut 'em up, lock 'em up, deport 'em official atmosphere," reflecting a "sick and dying empire clutching at its symbols which rest on genocide and slavery."

Several critics of the amendment maintained that its backers were also violating traditional tenets of conservatism by seeking to amend the Constitution for trivial reasons and by blurring the traditionally sharp American distinction between the sacred and the secular. Thus, Representative Schroeder, noting that the Republican leadership was also backing constitutional amendments to impose congressional term limits and to balance the budget, complained that amendment backers were "beginning to treat the Constitution as a rough draft." Stanford University law professor Kathleen Sullivan warned in the fall 1995 issue of *The American Prospect* that what she termed "constitutional amendmentitis" would violate numerous well-established constitutional principles, such as stability and limiting constitutional provisions to broad general statements of policy, and that the flag amendment specifically would violate basic principles of free speech and thus set a precedent for subsequent civil liberties erosions. Two Illinois theologians warned in the autumn 1995 issue of the *Journal of Church and State* that the use of the term *desecration* in the amendment suggested the institution of a "new religion of the flag as object of final loyalty" and warned that it threatened to establish a "blasphemy exception" to the First Amendment. Cal Thomas, a prominent conservative commentator who had supported the amendment in 1990 as a means of saying that "enough has finally become enough," similarly attacked it in 1995 for placing the flag "in a category and context that is idolatrous" and coming "pretty close" to forcing the population to "worship or devote ourselves to the flag as we might a religious symbol or being."[43]

In response to the arguments of amendment opponents, its backers maintained that flag desecration was a form of "conduct," not speech, which could be banned without infringing upon Americans' rights to voice their opinions in an endless variety of other ways; that public opinion overwhelmingly favored providing special protection for the nation's unique symbol; that flag desecration was so heinous that it was irrelevant how frequently such acts occurred, especially since flag burnings were often widely publicized and viewed by millions; that the states and federal government could be trusted to come up with reasonable definitions of "flag" and "desecration"; and that giving to the states as well as the national government the power to ban flag desecration was perfectly consistent with the principles of American federalism and democracy. For example, CFA president Daniel Wheeler suggested that the "definition" issue was a smokescreen to distract the public and declared, "We trust the common sense and good intentions of the American people and their elected representatives." Similarly, chief House amendment sponsor Gerald Solomon (R-N.Y.) said that during the past not one state had "abused" its power to define "desecration" in state statutes, and Representative Duncan Hunter (R-Calif.) said it was "absolutely appropriate" for the state legislatures to "participate in protecting the flag" and they "did a great job of it prior" to the *Johnson* ruling. CFA spokesman Marty Justis said that the amendment was aimed only at cloth flags suitable for flying and thus would clearly not include flag clothing, and Senator Hatch declared that no one in Congress was "going to go beyond reason in protecting the flag," and that the flag could be protected "without infringing upon scarves or swimming suits or sweaters or ties or any number of other items which can be worn with great pride." However, another leading amendment proponent, Representative Charles Canady (R-Fla.), told the HJC on June 7 that, "There are circumstances in which a state legislature or the Congress could find that clothing would involve the desecration of the flag."[44]

The SJC majority declared that the terms "physical desecration" and "flag" were no more vague that numerous other terms in the Constitution, including "probable cause," "cruel and unusual punishment," and "due process of law"; however, it conceded that "there is some flexibility in the [state] legislative bodies" in defining "flag," suggesting that they might choose to include "something a reasonable person would perceive to be a flag," even if it had "48 stars, or 12 or 14 stripes." Nonetheless, the SJC majority declared that the past history of enforcement of state statutes demonstrated no "insuperable problems of administration, enforcement and adjudication" and rendered no basis for "the parade of horribles" posed by amendment opponents who suggested the states might ban "things such as bathing suits, paper cups, and napkins with a picture of the flag." The SJC majority added that such arguments reflected a "fundamental mistrust of the people, acting through their elected officials, to enact reasonable" laws and that the flag "belongs to the people of the several States as well as to the American people as a whole." Therefore, it continued, to restore to the states their pre-1989 power to ban flag desecration "reflects the basic constitutional principle of federalism," and it posed no problem "if Utahns, for example, want to ban only burning and trampling on the flag as a means of casting contempt on it, and New Yorkers or Congress or both wish to also ban defacing and mutilating the flag."[45]

On the "free speech" issue, CFA president Wheeler declared that the proposed amendment would not "curtail speech in any way" but only outlaw "despicable physical acts intended to offend," which were "not what the Constitution's framers had in mind." Similarly, Rose Lee, a representative of the Gold Star Wives organization of veterans' widows, termed flag burning not free speech but a "terrible, physical act" that was a "slap in the face of every widow who has a flag [from her husband's coffin] just like mine." She added that it was a "dishonor to our husbands and an insult to their widows to allow this flag to be legally burned." *Arkansas Democrat-Gazette* editorial page editor Paul Greenberg, writing on July 6, declared that the American people "just can't seem" to be talked, orated, lectured, "or condescended and patronized out of" the concept that "burning the flag is burning the flag, not making a speech," although the nation's "intelligentsia" have explained "to us yokels again and again that burning the flag" was not "an action, but speech."[46]

Representative Floyd Spence (R-S.C.) maintained that flag desecration no more amounted to free speech than did "throwing a bomb into a building," while his Republican colleague Marge Roukema of New Jersey compared it to "throwing blood on the U.S. Capitol, painting a swastika on a synagogue, or defacing a national monument." Representative Solomon declared that "people outside the [Washington] beltway, you know, real, down-to-earth people say this amendment would not violate their right to free speech," especially since the flag is "what makes us all Americans, regardless of where we came from."[47]

Representative James Quillen (R-Tenn.), who had strongly urged passage of the 1968 federal flag desecration law, declared, "Our flag is a part of the soul of America, not merely a piece of cloth," while his Democratic colleague James Manton of New York similarly declared that flag desecration was "not just a simple expression of free speech" but rather a "profound and brutal attack on the very soul and history of our country." Senator Heflin, a twice-wounded World War II marine, declared:

> Nothing quite approaches the power of the flag as it drapes those who died for it—or the power of the flag as it is handed to the widow of that fallen soldier. The meaning behind these flags goes far beyond the cloth used to make the flag . . . . Allowing the burning of that flag creates a mockery of the great respect so many patriotic Americans feel for the flag. . . .We have trivialized so many symbols and values in America that we don't have anything that is sacred. I think the flag should be sacred.

Senator Hatch rejected arguments that flag desecration did not harm the flag's symbolic power because "our very refusal to take action" to protect it "clearly devalues it," and "as a practical matter, the effect, however unintended, of our acquiescence equates the flag with a rag, at least as a matter of law, no matter what we feel in our hearts."[48]

Most amendment backers also rejected arguments that enacting it would either alter the First Amendment or pave the path toward future erosions of popular expression. Thus, Solomon declared that "our goal is not really to change the Constitution" but rather to "restore the Constitution to the way it was understood until the 1989 *Johnson* ruling." Senate Majority Leader Dole said the amendment was intended "not to amend the Bill of Rights, not to change the first amendment, but to correct the Supreme Court's own red-white-and-blue blunder." SJC chairman Hatch similarly declared that the amendment did not, in fact, "amend" the Constitution, but only reversed "two Supreme Court decisions which have misconstrued the first amendment," whose protections had in any case never been absolute, with numerous exceptions for expressions such as those considered libelous, obscene, or threatening to public peace and order. He added that freedom of expression had remained "extremely robust" when flag desecration statutes were in force before 1989. "During the nearly 100 years" that Congress and the states had flag protection laws, Hatch continued, "we seemed, somehow, to avoid the descent into tyranny," yet some amendment critics claimed that the amendment would "herald a new dark age," even though "numerous other methods of protest including marches, rallies, use of placards, posters, leaflets and much more clearly remain available."[49]

Hatch rejected numerous other criticisms of the amendment, terming opposition to the amendment by professors as "arcane," characterizing the ABA's position as "thoughtless and intemperate outbursts," and labeling some of his antagonists' arguments "absurd," "overblown," and "ridiculous" (at one point he also termed them "garbage," but this remark was excised from the transcript of his remarks published in the *Congressional Record*). Hatch specifically rejected the claim that Congress had more important problems to solve, declaring that congressional time was spent "in so many desultory ways that do not amount to a hill of beans" that it was "about time we spent time on something this significant." In fact, Hatch maintained, the real question was "why would we take so much time debating this when we ought to pass it without even much of a debate?" With regard to the argument that love of the flag was meaningful only when not mandated, Hatch declared that not even amendment opponents "would agree that their respectful treatment of the flag meant something less at 9:59 A.M. June 21, 1989, than it did one minute later when the Court announced its *Johnson* decision." He sarcastically noted that during the pre-*Johnson* period, opponents of the amendment had made no effort to save America "from its decline and fall into totalitarianism" threatened by flag desecration laws and, in particular, had not "lifted one finger to plug this gaping hole in our freedom by trying to repeal" the 1968 federal law. Hatch also noted that many amendment opponents had voted for the 1989 FPA and asked, "How can they argue that a statute which bans flag burning does not infringe free speech, and turn around and say that an amendment which authorizes a statute banning flag burning does infringe free speech?" To argue that flag burners should be persuaded they were wrong rather than prosecuted could be just as logically applied to murderers and marijuana smokers, Hatch argued, adding, "There is no danger of a slippery slope here because there is no other symbol of our country like the flag. We do not salute the Constitution or the Declaration of Independence." Similarly, Senator Larry Craig (R-Idaho), termed the "slippery slope" argument "hogwash," because the flag's "uniqueness absolutely prevents this effort from being extended to anything else."[50]

Amendment backers especially stressed that the American people had made clear, via opinion polls and the forty-nine state-legislative resolutions supporting the amendment, that they wanted it, and that in a democracy the public will should be honored. Thus, Hatch told the June 6 SJC subcommittee hearing, "There is more wisdom, judgment and understanding on this matter in the hearts and minds of the American people than one will find on most editorial boards, law faculties and, regrettably, in the Clinton administration." Northwestern University law professor Stephen Presser wrote in the June 19 *Chicago Tribune* that the level of popular support for the amendment was "unprecedented" and "anyone who believes in popular sovereignty" should back it. CFA president Wheeler declared that passage of the amendment would reflect the "real freedom guaranteed by our great Constitution," namely "the right of the people to decide what kind of government they want and what kind of laws they will live under."[51]

Amendment proponents repeatedly argued that protecting the flag was especially owed by the nation to its veterans. Representative Sonny Montgomery (D-Miss.) proclaimed, "Over one million Americans have died in defense of this flag and we owe it to them to adopt this amendment," while Representative Michael Flanagan (R-Ill.) declared that the flag "represents the souls of departed American heroes who fought so valiantly to protect it over the last 200 years." Representative Thomas Barrett (D-Wisc.) said the flag should be protected because it was the "embodiment of all that the brave men and women of our country have fought, sacrificed and laid down their lives for," and that desecrating it insulted "every patriotic American." Senator Charles Grassley (R-Iowa) said that especially since Congress was cutting veterans programs, "the least we can do" would be to pass the amendment "out of respect" for their service to the nation.[52]

Amendment proponents rejected the argument that flag desecration did not occur frequently enough to warrant action. The SJC majority declared, "If it is right to empower the American people to protect the American flag, it is right regardless of the number of such desecrations," just as "if murder rarely occurred" there would still be reason to outlaw it. Hatch argued that this was especially so because "when a flag desecration is reported," especially in the media, "tens upon tens of millions of people read or learn of them. . . . The impact is far greater than the number of flag desecrations." Hatch repeatedly made this point during the December Senate debate while standing before national television cameras in front of a huge full-color picture of a flag burning, thereby accomplishing precisely what he said was especially harmful (particularly since the national, as opposed to local, news media had overwhelmingly long stopped reporting flag desecration incidents). Senator Jon Kyl (R-Ariz.) argued that amendment opponents could not "have it both ways," arguing on the one hand that flag burning was a "nonproblem because it is hardly ever done" but on the other claiming that forbidding such conduct "would be the biggest travesty and impingement on free speech to be visited upon" the Constitution and the nation.[53]

Amendment backers repeatedly returned to the theme that action was needed as a response to a general crisis in American values and growing threats to American unity. Thus, Representative Stephen Buyer (R-Ind.) urged support for it because the American people were telling the Congress, "We are upset with the direction of the country," and his colleague Christopher Smith (R-N.J.) said that the flag remained the "best symbol of solidarity," and unity under it "affords us the unique opportunity to maintain a harmonious multicultural superpower." In a report replete with patriotic poetry and oratory, the SJC majority declared that the flag represented "in a way nothing else can, the common bond shared by the people of this Nation, one of the most heterogeneous and diverse in the world." Representative Toby Roth (R-Wisc.) said the amendment should be passed because "nothing is sacred in America anymore," while Senator Grassley termed the amendment drive a reflection of the "rediscovery of core American values, like respect for authority" and a rejection of the "counterculture" values of the 1960s and the "antiauthoritarian attitude" and "anti-Americanism" that had flourished then.

In his June 9 *Denver Post* column, Mike Rosen declared that while a traditionally tolerant nation could theoretically indulge those who hated it and burned its flag, the country simply should not because flag desecration "offends us so deeply that we simply won't permit it. This is our right as a society." In a January 31, 1995, *Boston Globe* column, Jeff Jacoby lumped the Supreme Court's rulings on flag desecration together with a variety of other alleged high court rulings that had "emptied" the Constitution of its "original understanding and replaced it with the values of the intellectual and cultural class they belong to—values never shared by most Americans," thereby frequently making its rulings "feel like assaults on mainstream sensibilities." As a result of the Court's alleged misinterpretations of the First Amendment and usurpation of the Constitution's intent that local communities make decisions for themselves, Jacoby continued, such communities had been "stripped of their right to make rules, enforce standards and encourage faith," and "laws for maintaining civilized and restrained behavior" had been struck down.[54]

On January 8, 1996, the United States Supreme Court handed down a decision (or, more technically, a nondecision), that essentially indicated its desire to avoid touching the flag desecration issue anymore, even with a ten-foot legal pole. In the case of *Troster v. Pennsylvania State Department of Corrections*, the Court declined to hear an appeal from the federal Third U.S. Circuit Court of Appeals, which in turn had declined to intervene in the case of a Pennsylvania prison guard threatened with the loss of his job because he objected to wearing an American flag patch on his uniform on free-speech grounds. According to Yale Kamisar, a University of Michigan law professor widely regarded as one of the nation's leading constitutional scholars, who was interviewed the day after the Court's refusal to hear the case, its action suggested that, especially given the "heavy fire" the Court had come under in the wake of its 1989–90 flag desecration rulings, that the justices were not "excited about getting involved in a case that might well get a lot of possibly confusing and misleading media cover." However, he added, "Who knows why" the Court refuses to take cases.

The prison guard in this case, Dieter Troster, a German-born naturalized American who served in Vietnam during his twenty years in the U.S. Army before becoming first a trainee and eventually a sergeant at the State Correctional Institution at Greensburg, had refused to comply with a 1993 Pennsylvania Corrections Department regulation mandating the wearing of such patches by prison guards on the grounds that while he revered the flag and the "principles it symbolizes," he viewed the compulsory wearing of a flag patch as desecrating and debasing the flag because it stood for freedom from state-coerced speech. Pennsylvania officials defended the mandated wearing of the patch as promoting "the image of a professional corrections force, something important to the overall operation and security of its prisons," although it did not explain how the prison system was able to function before requiring the patch in 1993.

After Troster, whose work record had been exemplary, defied the order, he was suspended for five days in 1994 for gross insubordination but was allowed to remain on the job while challenging the regulation in court. However, a federal trial judge ruled in March 1994 that the flag patch display did not "compel expression" and therefore did not violate the First Amendment; the judge added, however, that he was "not overwhelmed by the state's argument" and that it did not "appear that mass insurrection among inmates or corrections officers would break out if the patch" were not required. In September 1994, the appeals court also declined to support Troster, declaring that while the prison system had run "smoothly" before the compelled wearing of the flag patch and that it was "sympathetic" to Troster's "genuine patriotism as well as with his predicament," it could not agree that the "mere act" of wearing the patch "constitutes an expressive or communicative" use of the flag, partly because the flag "has various and somewhat imprecise ideas associated with it," and therefore it viewed neither the mandated wearing of the patch nor Troster's refusal to comply as raising First Amendment issues. According to Professor Kamisar, such a conclusion was clearly "dead wrong," although he suggested the decisive issues in the appeals court ruling involved upholding prison discipline, even though the court placed no stress on this aspect of the case.

Although technically the Troster case arguably raised different issues than those decided in the Supreme Court's 1943 compulsory flag salute *Barnette* ruling and in the 1989–90 *Johnson* and *Eichman* decisions, in the real legal world these prior rulings clearly suggested that mandatory wearing of a flag patch constituted compelled expression that was in collision with the First Amendment. Therefore, the Supreme Court's refusal to intervene must realistically be interpreted in light of Supreme Court Justice Stevens's public declaration in August 1990 that the Court should never have taken the *Johnson* case to begin with, and had it restrained itself, it would have saved the nation "a lot of ink and a lot of heartache." But also in the real legal world, the Supreme Court's refusal to intervene in the case meant that Troster faced the prospect of losing his job because his self-professed beliefs in the principles for which the flag stood would not allow him to wear it under orders.[55]

★

APPENDIX

Four Key Documents Relevant to the 1989-90 American Flag Desecration Controversy

---

The 1968 Federal Flag Desecration Law (18 U.S.C. §700[b] [1988]).

Be it enacted by the Senate and House of Representatives of the United States of America in Congress assembled, That Chapter 33 of title 18, United States Code, is amended by inserting immediately preceding section 701 thereof, a new section as follows:

"§ 700. Desecration of the flag of the United States; penalties

"(a) whoever knowingly casts contempt upon any flag of the United States by publicly mutilating, defacing, defiling, burning, or trampling upon it shall be fined not more than $1,000 or imprisoned for not more than one year, or both.

"(b) The term 'flag of the United States' as used in this section shall include any flag, standard, colors, ensign, or any picture, representation of either or of any part or parts of either, made of any substance or represented on any substance, of any size evidently purporting to be either of said flag, standard, colors, or ensign of the United States of America, or a picture or a representation of either, upon which shall be shown the colors, the stars and the stripes, in any number of either thereof, or of any part or parts of either, by which the average person seeing the same without deliberation may believe the same to represent the flag, standard, colors, or ensign of the United States of America.

"(c) Nothing in this section shall be construed as indicating an intent on the part of Congress to deprive any State, territory, possession, or the Commonwealth of Puerto Rico of jurisdiction over any offense over which it would have jurisdiction in the absence of this section."

Text of the Texas Penal Code Provision
(Desecration of Venerated Object Law,
Texas Penal Code §42.09, Vernon 1974))
used to prosecute Gregory Lee Johnson for the
August 22, 1984, burning of a flag
at the Dallas City Hall.

§42.09 Desecration of Venerated Object

(a) A person commits an offense if he intentionally or knowingly desecrates:

(1) a public monument;

(2) a place or worship or burial; or

(3) a state or national flag.

(b) For purposes of this section, "desecration" means deface, damage, or otherwise physically mistreat in a way that the actor knows will seriously offend one or more persons likely to observe or discover his action.

(c) An offense under this section is a Class A misdemeanor [with a maximum sentence of one year in jail and a $2,000 fine].

Complete Text (including preamble) of
constitutional amendment sponsored by President Bush
to legalize forbidding flag desecration
in response to the Supreme Court's
Texas v. Johnson *ruling.*

JOINT RESOLUTION

Proposing an amendment to the Constitution of the United States authorizing the Congress and the States to prohibit the physical desecration of the flag of the United States.

Whereas the flag of the United States of America is a national symbol of such stature that it must be kept inviolate;

Whereas the physical desecration of the flag should not be considered constitutionally protected speech; and

Whereas physical desecration may include, but is not limited to, such acts as burning, mutilating, defacing, defiling or trampling on the flag, or displaying the flag in a contemptuous manner: Now, therefore, be it

Resolved by the Senate and the House of Representatives of the United States of America in Congress assembled (two-thirds of each House concurring therein), That the following article is proposed as an amendment to the Constitution of the United States, which shall be valid to all intents and purposes as part of the Constitution when ratified by the legislatures of three-fourths of the several States within seven years after the date of its submission for ratification:

ARTICLE—
"The Congress and the States shall have power to prohibit the physical desecration of the flag of the United States."

Text of the Flag Protection Act of 1989,
Public Law No. 101-131, 103 Stat. 777
(amending 18. U.S.C. §700 [Document One]).

Be it enacted by the Senate and House of Representatives of the United States of America in Congress assembled,

SECTION 1. SHORT TITLE

This Act may be cited as the "Flag Protection Act of 1989".

SEC. 2. CRIMINAL PENALITES WITH RESPECT TO THE PHYSICAL INTEGRITY OF THE UNITED STATES FLAG

(a) IN GENERAL.—Subsection (a) of section 700 of title 18, United States Code, is amended to read as follows:

"(a)(1) Whoever knowingly mutilates, defaces, physically defiles, burns, maintains on the floor or ground, or tramples upon any flag of the United States shall be fined under this title or imprisoned for not more than one year, or both.

"(2) This subsection does not prohibit any conduct consisting of the disposal of a flag when it has become worn or soiled."

(b) DEFINITION—Section 700(b) of title 18, United States Code, is amended to read as follows:

"(b) As used in this section, the term 'flag of the United States' means any flag of the United States, or any part thereof, made of any substance, of any size, in a form that is commonly displayed."

SEC. 3 EXPEDITED REVIEW OF CONSTITUTIONAL ISSUES

Section 700 of title 18, United States Code, is amended by adding at the end the following:

"(d)(1) An appeal may be taken directly to the Supreme Court of the United States from any interlocutory or final judgment, decree, or order issued by a United States district court ruling upon the constitutionality of subsection (a).

"(2) The Supreme Court shall, if it has not previously ruled on the question, accept jurisdiction over the appeal and advance on the docket and expedite to the greatest extent possible."

★

NOTES

Abbreviations Used in Footnotes

AFA: American Flag Association, Circular of Information (date is given in each citation)

ALI: American Law Institute, Model Penal Code and Commentaries (Philadelphia: American Law Institute, 1980)

AP: Associated Press

Cal. Rptr.: California Reporter

CQ: Congressional Quarterly

CR: Congressional Record

DAP: Document(s) in author's possession

F.: Federal Reporter

F. Supp.: Federal Supplement

GLJ: Trial Transcript, *Texas v. Johnson,* No. MA844601 3-H/J, County Criminal Court, Dallas County, Texas, Nov. Term, 1984 (unpublished, DAP)

HJC 1915: House Judiciary Committee, "Desecration of the Flag," 63d Cong., 3d sess., Feb. 10, 1915

HJC 1967: House Judiciary Committee, Hearings on H.R. 271 and Similar Proposals to Prohibit Desecration of the Flag, 90th Cong., 1st sess., Serial No. 4, 1967

HJC 1967a: *House Report No. 350,* "Penalties for Desecration of the Flag," 90th Cong., 1st sess., June 9, 1967

HJC 1989a: House Judiciary Committee, *Hearings on Statutory and Constitutional Responses to the Supreme Court Decision in Texas v. Johnson,* 101st Cong., 1st sess., Serial No. 24, 1989

HJC 1989b: House Judiciary Committee, Transcript of Meeting of July 26, 1989 (unpublished, DAP)

HJC 1989c: House Judiciary Committee, Transcript of Meeting of July 27, 1989 (unpublished, DAP)

HJC 1989d: *House Report No. 231,* 101st Cong., 1st sess., 1989

HJC 1990: House Judiciary Committee, Transcript of Meeting of June 19, 1990 (unpublished, DAP)

House Brief 1990: Brief for the Speaker and Leadership Group of the U.S. House of Representatives, Amici Curiae, in the Supreme Court of the United States, Oct. Term, 1989, *U.S. v. Eichman,* No. 89-1433, Apr. 1990.

JA 1990: Joint Appendix, in the Supreme Court of the United States, Oct. Term, 1989, *U.S. v. Eichman,* Probable Jurisdiction Noted Mar. 30, 1990

N.E.: Northeastern Reporter

N.W.: Northwestern Reporter

S.Ct.: Supreme Court Reporter

S.E.: Southeastern Reporter

S.W.: Southwestern Reporter

SAR: Sons of the American Revolution, National Yearbook (year is given in each citation)

SCW: National Flag Committee of the Society of Colonial Wars in the State of Illinois, Misuse of the National Flag of the United States of America (Chicago, 1895)

Senate Brief 1990: Brief for the United Senate as Amicus Curiae in Support of Appellant, in the Supreme Court of the United States, Oct. Term, 1989, *U.S. v. Eichman,* Nos. 89-1433 and 89-1434, Apr. 1990

SJC 1989a: Senate Judiciary Committee, *Hearings on Measures to Protect the Physical Integrity of the American Flag,* Serial No. J-101-33, 101st Cong., 1st sess., 1989

SJC 1989b: Senate Report 101-152, *The Flag Protection Act of 1989,* 101st Cong., 1st sess., Sept. 29, 1989

SJC 1989c: Senate Report 101-162, *S.J. Res. 180,* 101st Cong., 1st sess., Oct. 6, 1989

SJC 1990: Senate Judiciary Committee, *Measures to Protect the American Flag,* Serial No. J-101-77, June 21, 1990.

SMAC 1904: Senate Military Affairs Committee, "Desecration of the American Flag," 58th Congress, 2d sess., Report No. 506, Jan. 29, 1904

TR1 1990: Transcript, Motion to Dismiss Hearing, Feb. 14, 1990 before U.S. District Judge Barbara Rothstein, Seattle, Washington, *U.S. v. Haggerty,* No. CR89-315R (unpublished, DAP)

TR2 1990: Transcript of Hearing, Feb. 22, 1990, before U.S. District Judge June Green, Washington, D.C., *U.S. v. Eichman,* Nos. 89-0419, 89-0420, 89-0421 (unpublished, DAP)

U.S.: United States Reports

U.S.C.: United States Code

WCPD: Weekly Compilation of Presidential Documents

Note: Citations to legal sources follow the standard form for legal citations. Thus, a citation to 189 P.2d 341 (1989) would indicate a reference to the case beginning on page 341 of volume 189 of the Pacific Reporter, second series, covering cases reported in 1989. A citation to 189 P.2d 341, 343 (1989) would indicate a reference to the same case and especially to information contained or quoted on page 343 therein.

Preface

1. *CR* (1989), p. H5503.

2. *CR* (1990), p. S8685.

3. Arnold Loewy, "The Flag Burning Case: Freedom of Speech When We Needed It Most," *University of North Carolina Law Review* 68 (1989): 174; *Texas v. Johnson,* 491 U.S. 397, 414 (1989); *W.Va. Bd. of Education v. Barnette,* 319 U.S. 624, 641–42 (1943).

4. *Barnette,* 632–33; Alexander Meiklejohn, *Free Speech and Its Relation to Self-Government* (New York: Harper, 1948), 27.

5. *Kime v. U.S.,* 459 U.S. 949, 953 (1982); *CR* (1989), p. S8106.

6. *Stromberg v. California,* 283 U.S. 259 (1931); *New York Times,* Dec. 9, 1989, Apr. 29, 1990; *Detroit Free Press,* Feb. 8, 1993.

7. SJC 1990, p. 113.

8. *Chicago Tribune,* Mar. 16, 1989.

9. *U.S. News & World Report,* May 29, 1989, p. 54; Wilbur Zelinsky, *Nation into State* (Chapel Hill: University of North Carolina Press, 1988), pp. 196, 243.

10. Fariborz Nozari, *Flag Desecration and Related Number of People Arrested* (Washington, D.C.: Library of Congress Law Library, 1989); Nozari, *Flag Desecration: A Legal Survey* (Washington, D.C.: Library of Congress Law Library, 1990).

11. Bernhard Bleise, "Freedom of Speech and Flag Desecration: A Comparative Study of German, European and United States Laws," *Denver Journal of International Law and Policy* 20 (1992): 471–91; Peter Quint, "The Comparative Law of Flag Desecration: The United States and the Federal Republic of Germany," *Hastings International and Comparative Law Review* 15 (1992): 613–38 (quotation at p. 632); *Los Angeles Times,* Mar. 24, 1993; AP, Mar. 1, 1991; *Rocky Mountain News,* June 29, 1990. In 1978 (after the death of Franco), a Spanish prosecution against an eighteen-year-old actor who was accused of "insulting the flag" culminated in a one-year jail term (*New York Times,* Nov. 19, 1978).

12. Steven Kale, "The Monarchy According to the King: The Ideological Content of the Drapeau Blanc, 1871–1873," *French History* 2 (1988): 399–426; Frederik Ohles, *Germany's Rude Awakening: Censorship in the Land of the Brothers Grimm* (Kent, Ohio: Kent State University Press, 1992), 35; *Los Angeles Times,* Oct. 1, 1993; Nishimura Hidetoshi, "Flag and Anthem, Symbols of Distress," *Japan Quarterly* 35 (1988): 152–56. The translated texts of all German flag desecration laws dating from 1871 can be found in *State v. Turner,* 474 P.2d 91, 9–97 (1970).

13. Harry Saker, *The South African Flag Controversy, 1925–1928* (Capetown: Oxford University Press, 1980); Erich Eyck, *A History of the Weimar Republic,* vol. 2 (New York: Atheneum, 1970), 66–68; *Christian Science Monitor,* May 5, 1992; *The Guardian* (Manchester), Jan. 4, 1992; *Los Angeles Times,* Dec. 12, 1993, Oct. 6, 1995; Stanley Karnow, *Vietnam: A History* (New York: Viking, 1983), 279–311; Walter LaFeber, *The Panama Canal* (New York: Oxford University Press, 1979), 136–40; *Christian Science Monitor,* July 2, 1990; *New York Times,* Oct. 18, 1992, Apr. 6, Oct. 8, 1993, May 8, 1994.

14. *New York Times,* Jan. 27, 1993; *Washington Post,* June 30, 1993; *Ann Arbor News,* Nov. 25, 1992, Jan. 27, 1994.

Chapter 1: The Pre-1984 Origins of the American Flag Desecration Controversy

1. By far the best source on early cultural attitudes toward the flag is Scot Guenter, *The American Flag: 1777–1924: Cultural Shifts from Creation to Codification* (Rutherford, N.J.: Fairleigh Dickinson University Press, 1990), 1–66. For the Betsy Ross director's quote, see *Washington Times,* July 4, 1989.

2. Geo. Henry Preble, *Origin and History of the American Flag* (Philadelphia: Nicholas Brown, 1917), 459–60, 471–76, 480–81; Guenter, *American Flag,* 64; James Parton, *General Butler in New Orleans* (New York: Mason Brothers, 1864), 352–53, 607–9.

3. See Guenter, *American Flag,* 88–114; Boleslaw Mastai and Marie-Louise D'Otrange Mastai, *The Stars and the Stripes: The American Flag as Art and as History from the Birth of the Republic to the Present* (New York: Knopf, 1973), 208.

4. SCW, pp. 16, 21, 26.

5. Guenter, *American Flag,* 133–35; Stanley Jones, *The Presidential Election of 1896* (Madison: University of Wisconsin Press, 1984), 291–93; Mary Dearing, *Veterans in Politics: The Story of the GAR* (Baton Rouge: Louisiana State University Press, 1952), 460–62; Lawrence Goodwyn, *The Populist Moment* (New York: Oxford University Press, 1978), 280–82.

6. Charles Kingsbury Miller, *Desecration of the American Flag and Prohibitive Legislation* (Chicago, 1898), 3; Miller, *Desecration of the American Flag* (Chicago, 1902), 2.

7. *New York Times,* Mar. 27, June 2, 3, 1916, Mar. 3–10, 13–15, 1917.

8. Wallace Davies, *Patriotism on Parade: The Story of Veterans' and Hereditary Organizations in America, 1783–1900* (Cambridge, Mass.: Harvard University Press, 1955), 354–55. The fears expressed by the organizations that spearheaded the FPM were widespread in the United States during the late nineteenth and early twentieth centuries. For example, see generally John Higham, *Strangers in the Land: Patterns of American Nativism, 1860–1925* (New York: Atheneum, 1970) and Robert J. Goldstein, *Political Repression in Modern America: From 1870 to the Present* (Boston: G. K. Hall, 1978), 1–60.

9. SAR 1900, p. 94; Miller, *Desecration and Legislation,* 4, 11; Miller, *Desecration,* 1–2; *American Monthly* (magazine of the Daughters of the American Revolution), 1899, pp. 903–4, 906; SAR 1898, pp. 82–83.

10. Charles Kingsbury Miller, *The Crime of a Century: Desecration of the American Flag* (Chicago, 1900), 1, 4–5; AFA 1909–13, pp. 47–48.

11. Miller, *Desecration and Legislation,* 11–12; Miller, *Crime of a Century,* 5, 7.

12. *New York Times,* June 15, 1923; *American Monthly* (1907): 460.

13. For a listing of states with the dates (often including month and day as well as year) of passage of flag desecration laws up to 1905, see Peleg Harrison, *The Stars and Stripes and Other American Flags* (Boston: Little, Brown, 1906), 383; a complete list of the year of original passage of all state flag desecration laws is included in "Flag Burning, Flag Waving and the Law," *Valparaiso University Law Review* 4 (1970): 362–67. For collections of the texts of early state flag desecration laws, see SMAC 1904, pp. 4–12; AFA 1903–4, pp. 10–24; AFA 1905–6, pp. 29–76; SAR 1912, pp. 112–17; AFA 1909–13, pp. 69–91; HJC 1915, pp. 10–15; SAR 1915, pp. 126–31; Bernard Kosicki, *Commercial Use of National Flags and Public Insignia* (Washington, D.C.: U.S. Department of Commerce, Trade Information Bulletin 438, 1926). Congressional action on flag desecration legislation can be gleaned by examining the *Congressional Record*'s annual indexes for passage of legislation by subject.

14. *Halter v. Nebraska,* 205 U.S. 34 (1907), 35–37, 41–43, 45.

15. The data in this and the following paragraphs are primarily based upon an examination of news stories indexed in the *New York Times Index.*

16. *Ex Parte Starr,* 263 *Federal Reporter* 145, 146–47 (1920); *State v. Peacock,* 25 *Atlantic Reporter* 2d 491, 493 (1942); *Street v. New York,* 394 U.S. 576 (1969).

17. *New York Times,* June 29, 1914, Apr. 4, 15, 21, 25, June 21, July 7, 1917.

18. *New York Times,* Sept. 29, 1922, Sept. 16, 1925, Oct. 21, 1930.

19. On World War I, see H. C. Peterson and Gilbert Fite, *Opponents of War, 1917–18* (Seattle: University of Washington Press, 1957), 45–46, 152–53. On red flag laws, see Robert Murray, *Red Scare* (New York: McGraw-Hill, 1964), 233–34; Zechariah Chafee, *Free Speech in the United States* (New York: Harvard University Press, 1941), 159–63, 362–66; Julian Jaffe, *Crusade against Radicalism: New York during the Red Scare* (Port Washington, N.Y.: Kennikat, 1972), 80–82; *New York Times,* May 8, 1913; and especially Elmer Million, "Red Flags and the Flag," *Rocky Mountain Law Review* 13 (1940–41): 47–60.

20. In general, on the flag saluting controversy, see David Manwaring, *Render Unto Caesar: The Flag Salute Controversy* (Chicago: University of Chicago Press, 1962), and Leonard Stevens, *Salute! The Case of the Bible vs. the Flag* (New York: Coward, McCann, and Geoghegan, 1973).

21. *Minersville School District v. Gobitis,* 310 U.S. 586, 595–96 (1940); Stevens, *Salute!* 11–16; Goldstein, *Political Repression,* 261; Manwaring, *Render unto Caesar,* 166, 183.

22. *Stromberg v. California,* 283 U.S. 359 (1931); *West Virginia Board of Education v. Barnette,* 319 U.S. 624, 641–42 (1943).

23. *Street v. New York,* 394 U.S. 576 (1969); *Johnson v. Texas,* 109 S. Ct. 2533, 2544 (1989); *U.S. v. Eichman,* 110 S. Ct. 2404 (1990).

24. Guenter, *American Flag,* 236–37.

25. ALI, pp. 411, 415; *Handbook of the National Conference of Commissioners on Uniform State Laws and Proceedings of the Annual Conference,* 1966, pp. 176, 427.

26. See, generally, David Prosser, "Desecration of the American Flag," *Indiana Legal Forum* 3 (1962): 159–237, on the role of the Central Park flag burning in sparking the Vietnam War flag desecration controversy.

27. *CR* (1967), p. 16304; Scot Guenter, "The Hippies and the Hardhats: The Struggle for Semiotic Control of the Flag of the United States in the 1960s," *Flag Bulletin* 130 (1989): 137.

28. *Time,* July 4, 1970, pp. 14–15.

29. HJC 1967, p. 118; *New York Times,* June 21, 1967.

30. The complete text of the 1968 law is reprinted in the appendix to this book.

31. *CR* (1967), pp. 11727, 16481; HJC 1967, pp. 105, 211.

32. HJC 1967, pp. 46, 70–71.

33. *CR* (1967), pp. A2728, 9911, 11977, 16484.

34. HJC 1967, pp. 70–74, 94, 133, 185; *New York Times,* June 21, 1967.

35. *Washington Post,* June 21, 1967; *CR* (1967), p. 16483; *Newsweek,* July 3, 1967, p. 29; *New York Times,* June 7, 1967.

36. HJC 1967a, pp. 17–21; *Washington Post,* May 10, June 14, 1967.

37. *Commonweal,* Oct. 18, 1968, p. 77; *Christian Century,* June 14, 1967, p. 772.

38. A compilation of flag desecration laws in effect in 1967 is published in HJC 1967, pp. 324–46. Changes can be determined by examining updated lists of the penalties provided in state flag desecration laws published in "Flag Burning, Flag Waving and the Law," *Valparaiso*

University Law Review 4 (1970): 362–67; Dennis Tushla, "Flag Desecration: The Unsettled Issue," *Notre Dame Lawyer* 46 (1970): 218–20; and James Hall and Walter Albano, *Selected Decisions on Flag Use, Flag Desecration and Flag Misuse* (Washington, D.C.: Congressional Research Service Report 81-126A, May 18, 1981), 53–224. For estimates concerning prosecutions, see *Christian Science Monitor,* Mar. 15, 1973 and *Art in America,* May 1972, p. 51.

39. Data in this and following paragraphs are primarily based on the author's WESTLAW search of reported state and federal flag desecration cases; all cases turned up by the WESTLAW search were surveyed, as were all other relevant reported cases that were referred to in these cases or other sources. Although some reported cases may have escaped the attention of the author, it seems unlikely that they amount to more a few.

40. *Deeds v. State,* 474 S.W.2d 718 (1971); *Sutherland v. Dewulf,* 323 F. Supp. 740, 745 (1971).

41. *Crosson v. Silver,* 319 F. Supp. 1084, 1086, 1087 (1970); *U.S. v. Crosson,* 462 F.2d 96 (1972); *Crosson v. U.S.* 409 U.S. 1064 (1972).

42. *State v. Saionz,* 261 N.E.2d 135 (1969); *State v. Liska,* 291 N.E.2d 498, 499 (1971); *State v. Nicola,* 182 N.W.2d, 870, 872 (1971).

43. *Parker v. Morgan,* 322 F. Supp. 585, 586–87, 588, 590 (1971); *Long Island Vietnam Moratorium Committee v. Cahn,* 437 F.2d 344, 348, 349 (1970).

44. *State v. Waterman,* 190 N.W.2d 809 (Iowa 1971); *People v. Cowgill,* 78 Cal. Rptr. 853 (1969); *State v. Mitchell,* 288 N.E. 2d 216 (Ohio 1972); *State v. Saionz,* 261 N.E. 2d 135 (Ohio 1969); *Franz v. Commonwealth,* 86 S.E. 2d 71 (Va. 1972); *People v. Vaughan,* 514 *Pacific Reporter* 2d 318 (Colo. 1973); *State v. Saulino,* 277 N.E. 2d 580, 583 (Ohio, 1971); *State v. Kasnett,* 283 N.E. 2d 636, 637, 539 (Ohio, 1972); *State v. Kasnett,* 297 N.E. 2d 537, 538 (Ohio, 1973).

45. "Who Owns the Stars and Stripes?" *Time,* July 6, 1970, pp. 8–15; "New Glory?" *Newsweek,* June 15, 1970; "Decalomania over the American Flag," *Life,* July 19, 1989, 32–33; *New York Times,* June 21, 1967, Jan. 10, July 5, 1971; *Time,* July 6, 1970.

46. *New York Times,* May 5, 1968, May 22, July 8, 1970, Aug. 3, 1974; *Boston Globe,* Apr. 3, 8, Nov. 18, 1970.

47. *Deeds v. State,* 474 S.W. 2d 718 (1971); *Dallas Times Herald,* May 22, 26, June 23, 24, 25, 1970; *Dallas Morning News,* June 23, 24, 25, 26, 1970.

48. *Stromberg v. California,* 283 U.S. 259 (1931); *W.Va. Board of Education v. Barnette,* 319 U.S. 624 (1943); *Thornhill v. Alabama,* 310 U.S. 88 (1940); *Cox v. Louisiana,* 379 U.S. 536 (1965); *Tinker v. Des Moines Indep. Community School Dist.,* 393 U.S. 503 (1969).

49. *Cox v. Louisiana,* 379 U.S. 536, 555 (1965); *U.S. v. O'Brien,* 391 U.S. 367, 376 (1968).

50. *U.S. v. O'Brien,* 391 U.S. 376–77 (1968).

51. Randolph Collins, "The Constitutionality of Flag Burning," *American Criminal Law Review* 28 (1991): 913.

52. *Street v. New York,* 394 U.S. 576 (1969).

53. *Brandenburg v. Ohio,* 395 U.S. 444, 447 (1969); *Chaplinsky v. New Hampshire,* 315 U.S. 568, 572 (1942); *Cohen v. California,* 403 U.S. 15, 26 (1971); *Schacht v. U.S.,* 398 U.S. 58 (1970).

54. *Smith v. Goguen,* 415 U.S. 566 (1974); *Spence v. Washington,* 418 U.S. 405 (1974).

55. *Spence v. Washington,* 418 U.S. 411–12, 414.

56. For example, see the cases cited in footnotes 66 and 68, below.

57. *Smith v. Goguen,* 415 U.S. 566, 602–3 (1974); *Spence v. Washington,* 418 U.S. 405, 420–21 (1974).

58. *Smith v. Goguen,* 415 U.S. 566, 590–91 (1974).

59. For a collection of the texts of state flag desecration laws in effect in 1981, see Hall and Albano, *Selected Decisions,* 53–220. This paragraph and much of the material in the following paragraphs is based on a comparison of this collection with the collection published in HJC 1967, pp. 324–46.

60. On the ALI model code provisions, see ALI, pp. 416–17, 420.

61. Texas Penal Code Ann. §42.09 (Vernon 1974). The complete text of the Texas law is reprinted in the appendix to this book.

62. For general information on the RCP, upon which this and the next several paragraphs are largely based, see Harvey Klehr, *Far Left of Center: The American Radical Left Today* (New Brunswick, N.J.: Transaction, 1988), 92–96; and A. Belden Fields, *Trotskyism and Maoism: Theory and Practice in France and the United States* (New York: Praeger, 1988).

63. *New York Times,* May 2, June 18, 22, 1980.

64. *Los Angeles Times,* May 2, 1983; *Nation,* Apr. 19, 1980, p. 452; *Detroit News,* Mar. 18, 1980.

65. See the following paragraphs and their footnotes for details and sources concerning some of these incidents.

66. *Atlanta Journal,* Nov. 30, 1979, Sept. 18, 1980, Mar. 7, 20, 1984; *Atlanta Constitution,* Nov. 30, 1979, Sept. 18, 19, 1980; *Monroe v. State,* 295 S.E. 2d 512 (1982); *Monroe v. State Court of Fulton County,* 571 F. Supp. 1023 (1983); *Monroe v. State Court of Fulton County,* 739 F. 2d 568 (1984); *Bowles v. State,* S.E. 2d 250, 252 (1983); *Bowles v. Georgia,* 465 U.S. 1112 (1984); *Bowles v. Jones,* 758 F. 2d 1479 (1985).

67. *Monroe v. State Court of Fulton County,* 739 F. 2d 558, 572, 574, 575 (1984).

68. The Greensboro press provided extensive coverage of the arrest and trial. For example, see *Greensboro* (N.C.) *Daily News,* Mar. 28, May 1, June 17, 18, July 22, 1980; *Greensboro News and Record,* June 23, 1989. The legal trial of the case can be found in *U.S. v. Kime,* Cr-80-95-G, U.S. District Court for the Middle District of N. Carolina, June 12, 1981 (unpublished, DAP); *U.S. v. Kime,* No. 81-5160 (L), U.S. Court of Appeals for the Fourth Circuit, Jan. 28, 1982 (unpublished, DAP); *U.S. v. Kime,* 459 U.S. 949 (1982); Brief of Appellents, *Kime v. U.S.,* No. 81-5160 (L) and 81-5161, in the U.S. Court of Appeals, Fourth Circuit, Sept. 28, 1981 (DAP), pp. 7, 10, 11, 12, 21, 31.

69. *U.S. v. Kime,* 459 U.S. 949, 950, 953, 954, 956 (1982); for examples of press coverage, see *Washington Post, Los Angeles Times, Dallas Times Herald, New York Times,* and *Greensboro Daily News,* all for Oct. 19, 1982.

70. For examples of news coverage, see stories published on Aug. 23, 1984, in the *Dallas Times Herald, Dallas Morning News, New York Times, Los Angeles Times, Washington Post, Chicago Tribune, Detroit Free Press, Ann Arbor News,* and *Washington Post.* This and the next paragraphs are based on the trial transcript (GLJ) in the author's possession, on these newspaper sources, on the author's interviews with Johnson and his lawyers in 1990 and on biographical material on Johnson published in *People,* July 10, 1989, pp. 98–100 and in *Creative Loafing* (Tampa), July 22, 1989, pp. 1–5.

Chapter 2: The Texas Trials
of Gregory Lee Johnson, 1984–1988

1. GLJ, pp. 843, 847. Biographical information on Judge Hendrik and the lawyers was supplied during interviews with each of them in 1990.

2. Information in this chapter on Johnson's trial in Dallas in December 1984 is drawn from the trial transcript (GLJ), on coverage of the trial in the *Dallas Times* and the *Dallas Morning News* for December 10–14, and on interviews with the participants.

3. Appellant's Brief on Appeal in the Court of Appeals for the Fifth Supreme Judicial District of Texas at Dallas, Texas, *Johnson v. Texas,* Appeal No. 05-85-00318-CR, July 8, 1985; Appellant's Supplemental Brief on Appeal Post-Submission (in the same case).

4. Brief for the Appellee, the State of Texas (in the same case as in note 3 above), July 8, 1985, 17, 18, 19–20; *Deeds v. State,* 474 S.W. 2d 718 (1971); *State v. Farrell,* 223 N.W. 2d 270 (1974), cert denied, 421 U.S. 1007.

5. *Johnson v. State,* 706 S.W. 2d 120, 123 (1986).

6. Appellant's Motion for Rehearing and Rehearing En Banc (in the same case as in note 3 above), Feb. 7, 1986.

7. Appellant's Petition for Discretionary Review in the Court of Criminal Appeals for the State of Texas, *Johnson v. Texas,* Appeal No. 05-85-00318-CR, Mar. 26, 1986.

8. Appellant's Brief on Petition for Discretionary Review in the Court of Criminal Appeals for the State of Texas, *Johnson v. Texas,* No. 0372-86, Apr. 9, 1987.

9. State's Brief in Response to Appellant's Brief in Support of Appellant's Petition for Discretionary Review (in the same case as in note 8 above).

10. Brief of Amicus Curiae Texas Civil Liberties Union (in the same case as in note 8 above), Sept. 16, 1987.

11. *Johnson v. State,* 755 S.W. 2d 92 (1988).

12. Ibid., 98.

13. Motion for Rehearing (in the case referenced in note 8 above), May 3, 1988, p. 20.

14. State's Motion for Rehearing and Brief in Support Thereof (in the case referenced in note 8 above), Apr. 29, 1986.

15. On Petition for Writ of Certiorari to the Texas Criminal Appeals in the Supreme Court of the United States, Oct. Term, 1967, *Texas v. Johnson,* July 26, 1988.

16. Respondent's Brief in Opposition (in the case referenced in note 15 above), No. 88-155, Sept. 28, 1988.

Chapter 3: The Flag Controversy Moves to Center Stage,
August 1988–June 1989

1. A comprehensive chronology of the 1988 Pledge of Allegiance controversy is contained in Whitney Smith, "The American Flag in the 1988 Presidential Campaign," *Flag Bulletin* 128 (1988): 176–95. The Kaufman quote is from *Kusso v. Central School District No. 1,* 469 F. 2d 623 (1972), cert. denied, 411 U.S. 832 (1973). The Massachusetts Supreme Judicial Court opin-

ion is printed as Opinion of the Justices, 363 N.E. 2d 251 (1977). See also John Concannon, "The Pledge of Allegiance and the First Amendment," *Suffolk University Law Review* 23 (1989): 1019–47.

2. Smith, "American Flag," 184; *Wall Street Journal,* Sept. 20, 1988; *Time,* Oct. 3, 1988, p. 16; Scot Guenter, "Bush, Dukakis and the Pledge," *Flag Bulletin* 128 (1988): 161; Elizabeth Drew, *Election Journal: Political Events of 1987–1988* (New York: Morrow, 1989), 340, 344; Jack Germond and Jules Witcover, *Whose Broad Stripes and Bright Stars? The Trivial Pursuit of the Presidency, 1988* (New York: Warner, 1989), 11, 460; Sidney Blumenthal, *Pledging Allegiance* (New York: HarperCollins, 1990).

3. Smith, "American Flag," pp. 182, 184, 185; *Newsweek,* Sept. 26, 1988, p. 12; *Time,* Sept. 5, 1988, p. 33; *New York Times,* June 26, 1989.

4. Smith,"American Flag"; Drew, *Election Journal,* 267, 275, 285; *Washington Post,* Oct. 13, 1988; *Los Angeles Times,* Sept. 21, 1988; Guenter, "Bush, Dukakis and the Pledge," 165; Witcover, *Whose Broad Stripes,* 408; *U.S. News & World Report,* Oct. 3, 1988, p. 20; *Time,* Oct. 3, 1988, p. 16.

5. *U.S. News & World Report,* Oct. 3, 1988, p. 14; *New Republic,* Sept. 26, 1988, p. 13; *Newsweek,* Sept. 5, 1988, p. 35; *Wall Street Journal,* Sept. 20, 1988; Smith, "American Flag," p. 186; Drew, *Election Journal,* p. 275.

6. Witcover, *Whose Broad Stripes,* 461; Blumenthal, *Pledging Allegiance,* p. 292; Smith, "American Flag," pp. 184–85.

7. *New York Times,* June 26, 1989.

8. Among the more useful general accounts of the Feb.–Mar. 1989 SAIC Scott Tyler "flag on the floor" controversy, see Steven Dubin, *Arresting Images: Impolitic Art and Uncivil Actions* (New York: Routledge, 1992), 102–34; Elizabeth Hess, "Capture the Flag: Is Dread Scott's Flag-Piece Art, Treason or Both," *Village Voice,* Apr. 4, 1989, pp. 25–31; Jean Fulton and Benjamin Seaman, "The Flag Fracas," *New Art Examiner,* May 1989, 30–32; *New York Times,* June 11, July 3, 1989; Sylvia Hochfield, "Flag Furor," *Art News,* Summer 1989, 43–47; *Los Angeles Times,* Mar. 13, 1989; SAIC Student Newsmagazine, Mar. 1989; *Chicago Sun Times,* Aug. 13, 1989. For Tyler's own account, see Dread Scott Tyler, "Speakeasy," *New Art Examiner,* June 1989, 13–15. For accounts by SAIC officials, see Anthony Jones (SAIC president), "Stars and Bras: A Report from the Trenches," *Academe,* July–Aug. 1990, 18–23; Carol Becker (SAIC associate dean), "Art Thrust into the Private Sphere," *Art Journal,* Fall 1991, 65–68.

9. *Chicago Tribune,* Feb. 26, 1989; *Village Voice,* Apr. 4, 1989.

10. *Village Voice,* Apr. 4, 1989; *Chicago Tribune,* Mar. 15, 1989; *Morton Grove* (Ill.) *Champion,* Apr. 13, 1989; *Chicago Sun Times,* May 4, June 30, 1989.

11. *Village Voice,* Apr. 4, 1989; *Chicago Sun Times,* Mar. 2, 3, 11, 1989; *Detroit News,* Mar. 19, 1989; *Rosemont* (Ill.) *Suburban Times,* Mar. 15, 1989.

12. *Chicago Sun Times,* Mar. 3, 1989; *Art News,* Summer 1989, 44.

13. *New York Times,* July 3, 1989; *Chicago Sun Times,* Mar. 12, 1989.

14. *Chicago Weekly Reporter,* June 18, 1989; *Columbia* (S.C.) *State,* Mar. 13, 1989; *Detroit News,* Mar. 19, 1989; *Village Voice,* Apr. 4, 1989, p. 28; Tyler ledgerbook copies provided by Tyler to the author (DAP).

15. *New Art Examiner,* May 1989, pp. 30, 32; *Chicago Tribune,* Mar. 13, 1989; *Chicago Sun Times,* Mar. 10, 1989; *Harrisburg* (Ill.) *Register,* Mar. 10, 1989.

16. *Newhall* (Calif.) *Signal,* Mar. 3, 4, 7, 1989; *Los Angeles Times,* Mar. 7, 8, 1989.

17. *Chicago Tribune,* Mar. 9, 15, 1989; *Chicago Sun Times,* Mar. 9, 1989; *Laporte* (Ind.) *Herald-Argus,* Mar. 17, 1989; *Vernon Hills* (Ill.) *Review,* Mar. 16, 1989; *Lake Zurich* (Ill.) *Courier,* Mar. 16, 1989; *Joliet* (Ill.) *Herald News,* Mar. 17, 1989; *Morton Grove Champion,* Apr. 1, 1989; *Harrisburg Register,* Mar. 15, 1989.

18. *Chicago Sun Times,* Mar. 17, 1989; *Southtown* (Chicago) *Economist,* Mar. 17, 1989; *Norridge* (Ill.) *News,* June 21, 1989; *Pontiac* (Ill.) *Leader,* Mar. 16, 1989; *Hammond* (Ind.) *Times,* June 15, 1989; *Darien* (Ill.) *Dupage Doings,* June 16, 1989.

19. *Chicago Sun Times,* May 25, July 20, Aug. 13, 1989; *Windy City Times* (Chicago), July 27, 1989; *Chicago Tribune,* June 1, 1989; *New City* (Chicago), July 6, 1989; *Norridge News,* June 21, 1989; *New York Times,* June 11, 1989.

20. *New York Times,* Mar. 17, 1989; *Charlotte Observer,* Mar. 17, 1989; *CR* (1989), pp. S2793–94, H547–48.

21. *Chicago Sun Times,* Mar. 23, 1989; *Wheaton* (Ill.) *Times-Press,* May 4, 1989; *Decatur* (Ill.) *Herald-Review,* May 28, 1989; *Woodstock* (Ill.) *Northwest Herald,* July 21, 1989.

22. SAIC Student Newspaper, Mar. 1989, p. 3; *Chicago Sun Times,* Mar. 22, 1989; *Miami Herald,* Mar. 4, 1989; *Daily Californian* (University of California student newspaper), Feb. 17, 1989.

23. *New Republic,* Jan. 23, 1989, p. 8; *Miami Herald,* Mar. 5, 1989.

24. *Miami Herald,* Mar. 5, 1989.

25. *Editorials on File,* Aug. 1988, pp. 968–76.

26. Lewis article, as reprinted in *Warren* (Ohio) *Tribune-Chronicle,* Apr. 2, 1989; *Chicago Tribune,* Mar. 16, 1989.

27. Brief for Petitioner in the Supreme Court of the United States on Writ of Certiorari to the Texas Court of Criminal Appeals, Oct. Term, 1988, *Texas v. Johnson,* No. 88-155, Nov. 10, 1988.

28. Motion for Leave to File Brief Amici Curiae and Brief Amici Curiae of the Washington Legal Foundation [WLF], Veterans of Foreign Wars [and five other organizations] in Support of Petitioner (in the case referenced in note 27, above), Dec. 1, 1988; Brief of the Legal Affairs Council [LAC] as Amicus Curiae (in the case referenced in note 27, above).

29. *Washington Times,* Dec. 9, 1988; HJC 1989a, pp. 220, 221, 227, 230.

30. DAP; *Spy,* Sept. 1990; *Newsday* (New York), Jan. 6, 1991.

31. For a biographical sketch of Cole, see *New York Times,* June 22, 1990.

32. Brief for Respondent (in the case referenced in note 27, above), Jan. 25, 1989.

33. Brief Amicus Curiae of the American Civil Liberties Union [ACLU] and the Texas Civil Liberties Union [TCLU] in Support of Respondent, Jan. 25, 1989; Brief for Jasper Johns [and fifteen other artists] Amici Curiae, in Support of Respondent, Jan. 25, 1989; Brief of the Christic Institute [and twenty other civic, political, professional and trade union organizations], as Amicus Curiae in Support of Respondent, Jan. 25, 1989 (all in the case referenced in note 27 above).

34. Petitioner's Reply Brief (in the case referenced in note 27, above), Feb. 22, 1989.

35. Official Transcript, Proceedings before the Supreme Court of the United States, *Texas v. Johnson,* #88-155, Mar. 21, 1989.

36. *Chicago Sun Times,* Mar. 20, 1989.

37. *Progressive,* Feb. 1989, p. 8; *Nation,* Mar. 20, 1989, p. 370; *Newsday,* Mar. 20, 1989; *USA Today,* Oct. 18, 1988; *Village Voice,* Apr. 4, 1989, p. 27.

38. DAP.

39. *Chicago Tribune,* Mar. 22, 1989; *Dallas Morning News,* Mar. 22, 1989.

40. Papers of Justice Thurgood Marshall, Box 553, folder 5, Box 454, folder 1, Box 462, folder 2, Box 453, folder 4, Box 478, folder 5, National Archives, Oct. Term, 1988.

41. See the June 22, 1989, news accounts in *Washington Post, New York Times, Los Angeles Times,* and *Washington Times.*

42. *Texas v. Johnson,* 491 U.S. 397, (1989).

Chapter 4: The Immediate Post-Johnson Flag Firestorm

1. *Newsday,* July 2, 1989; *Newsweek,* July 3, 1989, p. 18; *CR* (1989), pp. S8098, S8105–6, H3234, H3390.

2. WCPD, June 26, 1989, p. 960, July 3, 1989, pp. 982–85; *CR* (1989), pp. S7189, S7458, H3239, H3880–H3438.

3. *New York Times,* July 4, 1989; *Detroit News,* July 3, 1989; *St. Louis Post-Dispatch,* June 29, July 1, 10, 27, 1989; *Austin-American Statesman,* July 11, 1989; *Newark Star-Ledger,* July 11, 1989; *Los Angeles Times,* July 14, 1989; *CR* (1989), pp. S8054, S8977, S9062, S10825, S10918; *The Record* (Hackensack, N.J.), July 17, 1989; *Washington Post,* July 3, 1989; *Dallas Morning News,* July 14, 1989; *San Antonio Light,* July 7, 1989; *Columbus Dispatch,* July 26, 1989; *Cleveland Plain Dealer,* July 12, 1989; *Atlanta Constitution,* July 13, 1989.

4. For additional polls with similar results, see *Newsday,* July 2, 1989, and *Arizona Republic,* July 10, 1989.

5. *CR* (1989), p. E2622; *USA Today,* June 23, 1989; *San Jose Mercury-News,* June 23, 1989; *Dallas Morning News,* June 23, 1989; *Richmond News-Leader,* July 4, 1989.

6. WCPD, June 26, 1989, p. 960, July 3, 1989, pp. 982, 985, 1008; CBS Evening News, June 28, 1989; *Washington Times,* June 23, 1989; *CR* (1989), p. H3004; *Washington Post,* June 23, 1989.

7. *Atlanta Constitution,* June 29, 1989; *Milwaukee Sentinel,* July 4, 1989.

8. *Atlanta Constitution,* July 21, 1989; *Sacramento Bee,* Sept. 3, 1989; *Chicago Sun Times,* Sept. 4, 1989; *CR* (1989), pp. H3235, S7189.

9. *Indianapolis Star,* June 23, 1989; *Boston Globe,* July 2, 1989; *Washington Post,* July 9, 1989; *CR* (1989), pp. E2303, H3237, S7189.

10. *Washington Post,* June 23, 1989; *Los Angeles Times,* June 23, 1989; *Boston Globe,* July 2, 1989; SJC 1989a, p. 432; *CR* (1989), p. H3422.

11. *New York Daily News,* June 25, 1989; *Sacramento Bee,* Sept. 3, 1989; *CR* (1989), pp. H3236, 3433, S7188.

12. *Newark Star-Ledger,* July 13, 1989; SJC 1989a, pp. 354, 377, 430; HJC 1989a, pp. 10, 13.

13. *CR* (1989), pp. H3532, S7189; *Atlanta Constitution,* July 5, 1989; *Washington Post,* June 30, 1989; *Los Angeles Times,* June 30, 1989.

14. *New York Times,* June 23, 1989; SJC 1989a, p. 15.

15. HJC 1989a, pp. 90–91; *CR* (1989), p. S7189.

16. *CR* (1989), p. S7188; *Los Angeles Times,* June 30, July 9, 1989; *Christian Science Monitor,* July 6, 1989; *Newark Star-Ledger,* July 11, 1989; SJC 1989a, p. 500.

17. *CR* (1989), pp. S9062, S10825, S13724; *Christian Science Monitor,* July 6, 1989.

18. *CR* (1989), pp. S7589, H3381–96, H3403–10, H3426–33.

19. *CR* (1989), pp. H3407–13, H3434, H3509–16.

20. *CR* (1989), p. E2279; *Washington Times,* June 23, 1989.

21. *USA Today,* June 22, 1989; *Washington Times,* June 22, 1989; *Ann Arbor News,* July 4, 1989; *CR* (1989), pp. S9062, E2542; *Dallas Morning News,* July 14, 1989; *Miami Herald,* July 3, 1989; *Columbia State, New York Post,* and *New York Daily News,* June 23, 1989; *Newsday,* July 2, 1989.

22. *Miami Herald,* July 3, 1989; *St. Louis Post-Dispatch,* June 23, 1989; *San Francisco Chronicle,* July 5, 1989; *New York Daily News,* June 23, 1989; *Newsday,* July 2, 1989.

23. *Washington Post,* June 23, July 9, 1989; *CR* (1989), p. H3135; *People,* July 10, 1989, p. 99.

24. *People,* July 10, 1989, pp. 99–100; *Newsday,* June 22, 1989; *USA Today,* June 22, 1989; *Chicago Sun Times,* June 23, 1989.

25. *San Francisco Examiner,* June 23, 25, 1989; *San Francisco Chronicle,* June 23, 1989; *Chicago Tribune,* June 23, 1989; *New York Daily News,* June 24, 1989; *New York Post,* June 26, 1989; *New York Times,* June 26, 1989.

26. *Janesville Gazette,* June 25, 1989; *Indianapolis News,* June 28, 1989; *Indianapolis Star,* Aug. 11, 1989; *Findlay Courier,* June 30, 1989; *Boston Globe,* July 1, 1989; *Cleveland Plain Dealer,* June 30, 1989.

27. *Boston Globe,* July 2, 15, 1989; *USA Today,* July 5, 1989; *Dallas Morning News,* July 5, 1989; *Springfield* (Mass.) *Union News,* July 4, 1989; *Washington Post,* July 5, 10, 1989; *Chicago Tribune,* July 5, 1989; *New York Daily News,* July 29, 1989; *Iowa City Press-Citizen,* July 4, 1989; *Daily Iowan* (University of Iowa), July 5, 1989; *Des Moines Register,* July 4, 1989; *Austin-American Statesman,* July 5, 1989.

28. *Salt Lake City Tribune,* July 3, 21, Aug. 24, 1989; *Deseret News,* July 20, 21, Aug. 2, 24, 1989.

29. *New York Post,* July 5, 1989; *Newsday,* July 5, 1989; *Village Voice,* July 18, 1989; *New York Times,* July 8, 1989; *Arkansas Gazette,* June 29, 1989; *Arkansas Democrat,* July 5, 6, 9, 1989; *Memphis Commercial-Appeal,* July 7, 1989.

30. Alan Schlein, "Pols, Reporters, Wave White Flag on Flagburning Story," *News/Inc.* (Sept.–Oct. 1989): 71; *Rocky Mountain News, Chicago Tribune, Newsday,* and *New York Daily News,* July 21, 1989; *Newark Star-Ledger,* Aug. 7, 1989.

31. *Washington Times,* July 6, 1989.

32. *San Jose Mercury-News,* June 29, 1989; *Manchester Union Leader,* June 22, 1989; *Atlanta Constitution,* July 5, 1989; *Gary Post-Tribune,* July 13, 1989; *St. Louis Post-Dispatch,* Sept. 9, 1989; *New Haven Register,* July 21, 1989; *Washington Times,* June 23, 1989; *Memphis Commercial-Appeal,* June 23, 1989; *Reno Gazette-Journal,* June 23, 1989; *Houston Chronicle,* June 24, 1989; *Boston Globe,* July 2, 1989.

33. *Boston Globe* and *Los Angeles Herald-Examiner,* July 2, 1989; *Rocky Mountain News,* June 28, 1989; *Record,* June 30, 1989.

34. *CR* (1989), pp. H3384, H3414.

35. *Richmond News-Leader* and *New York Daily News,* July 4, 1989; *USA Today,* July 3, 5, 1989; *Record,* June 30, 1989; *Austin-American Statesman,* July 4, 1989.

36. *Springfield* (Mass.) *Union News* and *Los Angeles Times,* July 3, 1989; *Time,* Aug. 7, 1989, p. 23.

37. *Atlanta Constitution,* Aug. 8, 1989; *CR* (1989), p. E4012; *Seattle Times,* Feb. 18, 1990.

38. *USA Today,* July 3, Aug. 12, 1989; *San Francisco Chronicle,* July 5, 1989; *Washington Post,* July 23, 1989; *Los Angeles Times,* July 19, 1989; *CR* (1989), p. H3517.

39. *Boston Globe,* July 2, 1989; *Atlanta Constitution,* June 30, 1989; *St. Louis Post-Dispatch,* June 27, 1989; *Record,* July 7, 1989.

40. *Atlanta Constitution,* July 1, 6, 1989; SJC, 1989a, p. 120; *Detroit News,* Nov. 7, 1989.

41. SJC 1989a, p. 25; *Columbia* (S.C.) *State,* June 23, 1989.

42. *Wheaton* (Ill.) *Daily Herald,* July 3, 1989.

43. SJC 1989a, p. 506; *Atlanta Constitution,* Sept. 24, 1989; *Los Angeles Times* June 29, 1989.

44. *Dallas Morning News,* July 4, 1989.

45. *Christianity Today,* Sept. 8, 1989; James Wood, "Making a Nation's Flag a Sacred Symbol," *Journal of Church and State* (Autumn 1989): 379–80.

46. *Melbourne Age,* July 17, 1989; HJC 1989a, pp. 420–21.

47. SJC 1989a, pp. 22, 504; *Progressive,* Aug. 8, 1989, p. 7; *St. Louis Post-Dispatch,* June 29, 1989.

48. *Ann Arbor News,* July 2, 1989; *New York Times,* July 1, 1989.

49. *Austin-American Statesman,* July 7, 1989.

50. *Houston Post,* July 21, 1989.

51. *Economist,* July 1, 1989.

52. Schlein, "Pols, Reporters," 71.

53. *San Francisco Examiner,* June 27, 1989; HJC 1989a, pp. 36, 242; *CR* (1989), p. S8487; "This Week with David Brinkley" (ABC), July 2, 1989; *U.S. News & World Report,* July 10, 1989; NBC Evening News, Aug. 16, 1989.

54. *Los Angeles Times,* July 13, 1989; *Ann Arbor News,* Oct. 15, 1989.

55. WCPD, July 3, 1989, pp. 1006–8; CBS Evening News, June 30, 1989.

56. The complete text of the constitutional amendment is reprinted in the appendix to this book.

57. WCPD, July 3, 1989, p. 998; *St. Louis Post-Dispatch,* June 29, 1989; *Boston Globe,* June 29, 1989; *Washington Times,* June 29, 1989.

58. *Newsday* and *Salt Lake City Tribune,* July 1, 1989; *Philadelphia Inquirer,* June 30, 1989.

59. *USA Today,* June 23, 1989; *Newsday,* July 1, 1989.

60. WCPD, June 26, 1989, pp. 959–60; *National Journal,* July 8, 1989, pp. 1758–59.

61. *CQ,* June 24, 1989, p. 1547; WCPD, July 3, 1989, pp. 982, 991; *National Journal,* July 8, 1989, p. 1758

62. SJC 1989a, p. 22.

63. *Washington Post,* Oct. 20, 1989; *Newsday,* July 7, 1989; *San Jose Mercury-News,* June 29, 1989; Nat Hentoff, "The Atwater Flag Sting," *Progressive,* Nov. 1989, pp. 12–14; "Bushwaterism," *New Republic,* July 17–26, 1989, pp. 5–6.

64. *Washington Post,* June 24, 1989; *National Journal,* July 8, 1989, pp. 1758–59; *New York Times,* July 7, 1989; NBC Evening News, June 27, 1989; *Mercury-News,* June 29, 1989; *Christian Science Monitor,* July 10, 1989; *Austin-American Statesman,* June 25, 1989; AP story, July 28, 1989; *New York Times,* July 24, 1989; *Denver Post,* June 29, 1989.

65. *Houston Chronicle,* June 24, 1989; *New York Times* and *Honolulu Star-Bulletin,* June 25, 1989.

66. *Honolulu Star-Bulletin,* June 25, 1989.

67. *Rocky Mountain News,* June 29, 1989; DAP; *CR* (1989), pp. H3238–39, H3329, H3380–H3439; NBC Evening News, June 30, 1989.

68. *Washington Post,* June 28, 1989; SJC 1989a, p. 515; HJC 1989a, p. 24.

69. *Springfield* (Ill.) *State Journal-Register,* June 28, 1989; *Rocky Mountain News,* June 29, 1989; *Lexington Herald-Leader,* June 30, 1989; *Los Angeles Times,* July 14, 1989; CBS Evening News, July 13, 1989.

70. *Rocky Mountain News,* June 29, 1989; *Columbia* (South Carolina) *State,* June 23, 1989; *Boston Globe,* June 27, 1989; *San Francisco Examiner,* June 27, 1989; *Los Angeles Times,* July 2, 1989; *Newark Star-Ledger,* July 11, 1989; *Wilkes-Barre Times Leader,* June 18, 1990.

71. *Concord* (N.H.) *Monitor,* June 29, 1989; *Houston Post,* July 6, 8, 1989; *Austin-American Statesman,* June 29, July 6, 1989; *San Antonio Light,* July 6, 7, 1989.

72. *St. Paul Pioneer Press,* July 1, 1989.

Chapter 5: The 1989 Congressional Flag Desecration Debate: To Overturn Johnson by Law or by Constitutional Debate

1. HJC 1989a, p. 173; SJC 1989a, pp. 392, 499.

2. Robert Cwiklik, *House Rules* (New York: Villard, 1991), 174; HJC 1989a, pp. 228, 232–33, 257, 316.

3. HJC 1989a, p. 10.

4. *Record,* July 4, 1989.

5. HJC 1989a, p. 358.

6. *Washington Post,* July 22, 1989; *Progressive,* Nov. 1989, p. 12.

7. HJC 1989a, pp. 192–94, 219, 230.

8. *Legal Times,* July 17, 1989; *New York Times,* Aug. 8, 1989.

9. *Seattle Times,* Oct. 14, 1989; *Dallas Morning News,* June 29, 1989.

10. *New York Times,* Aug. 1, 1989; *San Francisco Examiner,* July 4, 1989.

11. *Los Angeles Times,* June 29, 1989; *Dallas Morning News,* July 29, 1989; SJC 1989a, p. 52.

12. SJC 1989a, pp. 34, 249; HJC 1989a, pp. 5, 354; *CR* (1989), p. S7189.

13. *New York Times,* June 23, 1989; *Houston Post* and *Washington Post,* June 24, 1989; *Newsday,* June 28, 1989.

14. *Ann Arbor News,* June 24, 1989; *San Francisco Chronicle,* June 26, 1989; *Dallas Morning News,* June 28, 1989; AP, Oct. 13, 1989; *USA Today,* July 12, 14, 1989; *CR* (1989), p. S7965.

15. *Texas v. Johnson,* 491 U.S. 397, 414, 415, 418 (1989).

16. Ibid., 403, 411, 412; *Smith v. Goguen,* 415 U.S. 566, 591.

17. *CR* (1989), pp. S7457–58; HJC 1989a, p. 10.

18. *CR* (1989), p. S7457; *Texas v. Johnson,* 491 U.S. 397, 416–17 (1989).

19. SJC 1989a, pp. 157: HJC 189a, pp. 124, 130.

20. *Washington Post,* July 25, 1989.

21. SJC 1989c, p. 4.

22. House Brief 1990, p. 16.

23. SJC 1989b, p. 13; SJC 1989c, p. 30.

24. For this and the next few paragraphs, see SJC 1989a, pp. 151–57, 164–67, 181–89, 202, 537, 541; HJC 1989a, pp. 52–55, 102–4, 118–28, 134, 138.

25. *Atlanta Constitution,* July 6, 1989; *Chicago Tribune,* July 5, 1989.

26. SJC 1989a, pp. 157, 540–57; HJC 1989a, pp. 33, 37, 48, 74, 81, 197.

27. HJC 1989a, p. 52; SJC 1989a, pp. 137, 147; *CR* (1989), p. S13429.

28. HJC 1989a, p. 41; SJC 1989a, pp. 57, 97, 561.

29. SJC 1989a, pp. 90, 97, 134; ABC News Nightline, June 29, 1989; ABC News This Week with David Brinkley, July 2, 1989.

30. This and the following paragraphs are based on an examination of state statutory provisions dealing with flag desecration, plus a variety of newspaper sources, such as *Ann Arbor News,* July 3, 1989; *New York Times,* July 7, 1989; *Harrisburg* (Pa.) *Patriot-News,* July 14, 1989; *Richmond Times-Dispatch,* July 2, 1989; *Arkansas Democrat,* July 15, 1989; *Arkansas Gazette,* July 15, Nov. 8, 1989; *Dover (Del.) State News* and *Annapolis Capital,* June 12, 1990.

31. SJC 1989a, pp. 16–17.

32. HJC 1989a, p. 201.

33. *National Journal,* July 8, 1989, p. 1759; Judith Waldrop, "The Patriotic Sell," *American Demographics,* July 1990, p. 6.

34. HJC 1989a, p. 202.

35. Ibid., pp. 169, 174; SJC 1989a, p. 115.

36. HJC 1989a, pp. 3, 47, 170, 171, 193, 199, 232, 360; SJC 1989a, p. 125.

37. SJC 1989a, pp. 68, 116–17, 123; HJC 1989a, pp. 170, 171, 190, 193, 198.

38. HJC 1989a, pp. 21, 127, 142–43; SJC 1989a, p. 232.

39. HJC 1989a, pp. 66, 103–4, 110, 115–16, 127, 135–40; SJC 1989a, pp. 151–52, 159–60, 173, 179, 199–200, 569.

Chapter 6: The 1989 Decline and Fall of the Constitutional Amendment and the Passage of the Flag Protection Act

1. *Washington Times,* June 23, 1989; *Honolulu Star-Bulletin,* June 25, 1989; *San Jose Mercury-News,* June 29, 1989; *Rocky Mountain News,* June 29, 1989; Cwiklik, *House Rules,* p. 76; *Los Angeles Times,* June 29, 1989; *Washington Post,* July 1, 1989.

2. *Detroit News,* July 3, 1989; HJC 1989a, p. 280.

3. HJC 1989a, pp. 242–51; *American Legion Magazine,* Aug. 8, 1989; DAP.

4. *Record,* Sept. 1, 1989; *U.S. News & World Report,* Oct. 30, 1989; SJC 1989a, p. 430; *VFW Magazine,* Oct. 1989; DAP.

5. *San Francisco Chronicle,* July 5, 1989; *Ann Arbor News,* Aug. 18, 1989.

6. *Washington Post,* June 28, 30, July 9, 1989; *New York Times,* July 3, 1989; *New York Post,* June 23, 1989.

7. SJC 1989a, p. 25; *New York Times,* Oct. 18, 1989.

8. *New York Times,* July 7, 1989; *Washington Times,* June 29, 1989; *New York Daily News,* Aug. 16, 1989; *Record,* July 26, 1989.

9. *CR* (1989), pp. S8102–3.

10. HJC 1989a, pp. 370, 376; *Los Angeles Times,* July 15, 26, 1989; *Christian Science Monitor,* July 18, 1989; *New York Post,* July 20, 1989; SJC 1989a, p. 253; *Washington Times,* Sept. 22, 1989; *New York Times,* Oct. 18, 1989.

11. *Record,* Aug. 30, Sept. 15, 1989; *Jersey* (Jersey City, N.J.) *Journal,* Aug. 29, 1989.

12. *San Antonio Light,* Sept. 2, 4, 17, 1989.

13. *Warren* (Ohio) *Tribune-Chronicle,* Sept. 6, 1989; *Daily Penn* (University of Pennsylvania student newspaper), Sept. 14, 15, Oct. 11, 12, 1989; *Philadelphia Inquirer,* Sept. 15, 16, 1989, Mar. 23, 1990; *New York Daily News,* Sept. 15, 1989.

14. *New York Times,* Aug. 18, Sept. 3, 1989; *Ann Arbor News,* Sept. 10, 1989.

15. *Ann Arbor News,* Sept. 10, 1989; *Washington Post,* Oct. 18, 1989; SJC 1989a, pp. 256, 296, 490.

16. HJC 1989a, pp. 2, 45, 376.

17. HJC 1989a, p. 239; SJC 1989a, p. 414, 514; *CR* (1989), pp. S8749, S9182.

18. *CR* (1989), pp. S12655, S13733.

19. Ibid., p. H5562; *CR* (1990), pp. H4087–88.

20. DAP; *Austin-American Statesman,* July 2, 1989; *Washington Post,* Aug. 5, 1989; *Newsday,* June 28, 1989; *Boston Globe,* June 29, 1989.

21. *Legal Times,* July 23, 1990; *United States Law Week,* Nov. 6, 1990; DAP; *CR* (1989), pp. S13747–51; SJC 1989a, pp. 646–48.

22. *Los Angeles Times,* June 22, 1989; SJC 1989a, pp. 732–39; *CR* (1989), p. S13651.

23. *New York Times,* Oct. 18, 1989; AP, Oct. 20, 1989; *Washington Post,* Oct. 20, 1989; *U.S. News & World Report,* Oct. 30, 1989, p. 14.

24. R. Neil Taylor, "The Protection of Flag Burning as Symbolic Speech and the Congressional Attempt to Overturn the Decision," *Cincinnati Law Review* 38 (1990): 1056–57; Charles Tiefer, "The Flag Burning Controversy of 1989–1990," *Harvard Journal on Legislation* 29 (Summer 1992): 366.

25. *Report of the 41st Annual Meeting of the ABA* (1918), p. 82; Goldstein, *Political Repression,* 363–64; SJC 1989a, pp. 633–43; DAP.

26. *Newark Star-Ledger,* Aug. 4, 6, 11, 1989; *Houston Chronicle,* Aug. 10, 1989.

27. *CR* (1989), p. S7965; AP, July 14, 1989.

28. This and the next several paragraphs are all based on HJC 1989b, 1989c, 1989d.

29. *CR* (1989), p. H5562.

30. *New York Times,* Sept. 13, 1989; *Washington Post,* Sept. 13, 1989; *Los Angeles Times,* July 26, Sept. 13, 1989.

31. The House debate can be found in *CR* (1989), pp. 5497–514. The Fitzwater quote is from *New York Times,* Sept. 13, 1989.

32. The material on the SJC debate and findings is based on *Ann Arbor News, Washington Times,* and *Los Angeles Times,* all Sept. 22, 1989; *CQ,* Sept. 23, 1989; SJC 1989b; SJC 1989c.

33. *Los Angeles Times,* Oct. 4, 6, 1989. The Senate debate is in *CR* (1989), pp. S12572–626, S12650–55.

34. *Washington Post,* Oct. 6, 1989.

35. The House debate is at *CR* (1989), pp. H6989–97.

36. WCPD, Oct. 15, 1989, pp. 1539, 1543.

37. *CR* (1989), p. S13733; AP story, Oct. 20, 1989; *New York Times,* Oct. 20, 1989.

38. *CR* (1989), pp. 13511–12, 13520; *U.S. News & World Report,* Oct. 30, 1989.

39. DAP; SJC 1989a, p. 49; *U.S. News & World Report,* Oct. 30, 1989.

40. WCPD, July 31, 1989, pp. 1171, 1174, Aug. 28, 1989, pp. 1263–64, Sept. 11, 1989, pp. 1323–24, 1327, Oct. 9, 1989, pp. 1507–8; *Record,* July 26, 1989; *Los Angeles Times,* Oct. 20, 1989; *New York Times,* Oct. 19, 20, 1989.

41. The Senate debate is at *CR* (1989), pp. S13418–33, S13503–21, S13607–53, S13721–33. For Mitchell's comments, see AP, Oct. 18, 1989; *New York Times,* Oct. 20, 1989.

Chapter 7: The Flag Protection Act and the Federal District Courts, October 1989–February 1990

1. WCPD, Oct. 26, 1989, p. 1619.

2. *San Francisco Chronicle* and *Oakland Tribune,* Oct. 28, 1989; *Daily Californian,* Oct. 30, 1989; *Ft. Collins Coloradoan,* Oct. 28, 1989.

3. *National Law Journal,* Nov. 20, 1989; *Seattle Post-Intelligencer,* Oct. 28, Nov. 1, 2, 1989; *Seattle Times,* Oct. 29, 30, 31, 1989; *Washington Times,* Oct. 30, 31, 1989; *University of Washington Daily,* Nov. 11, 1989; JA 1990, pp. 40, 79.

4. DAP.

5. JA 1990, pp. 55–56; AP, Oct. 30, 1989; *USA Today* and *New York Daily News,* Oct. 31, 1989.

6. *CR* (1989), pp. S14371, S14472, E3774; *Time,* Oct. 23, 1989; *New York Times,* Nov. 11, 1989.

7. *Washington Post, New York Times, Washington Times, Seattle Times,* and *Post-Intelligencer,* all Oct. 31, 1989; *University of Washington Daily,* Nov. 3, 1989.

8. *New York Times,* Nov. 1, 1989; *Chicago Tribune,* Nov. 11, 1989; *Chicago v. Aubin* et al., in the Circuit Court of Cook County, Illinois County Dept., Chancery Division, No. 89 CH 8763, Oct. 31, 1989, made permanent Mar. 2, 1990.

9. *Chicago Sun Times* and *USA Today,* Nov. 1, 1989; *Atlanta Constitution,* Nov. 2, 1989; *Ann Arbor News,* Nov. 1, 1989.

10. *Legal Times,* July 23, 1990.

11. *CR* (1989), pp. E3803, E3929; *CQ,* Nov. 25, 1989, p. 3247.

12. *Post-Intelligencer,* Nov. 29, 30, 1989; DAP.

13. DAP; *Denver Post,* Nov. 4, 1989; *Telluride Times-Journal,* Nov. 2, 1989.

14. *San Francisco Examiner, San Francisco Chronicle,* and *Oakland Tribune,* all Nov. 4, 1989; *Daily Californian,* Nov. 6, 10, 1989.

15. *Record,* Nov. 9, Dec. 1, 1989; *Princeton Metro Times,* Nov. 9, Dec. 1, 1989; *New Jersey Home News,* Nov. 9, 1989; *Trentonian,* Nov. 10, 12, 1989; *Trenton Times,* Nov. 16, 1989; *Newark Star-Ledger,* Dec. 1, 1989, *New York Times,* Dec. 4, 1989.

16. *Meridian* (Conn.) *Record-Journal,* Nov. 18, 1989; *Middletown* (Conn.) *Press,* Nov. 17, 18, 1989; *Hartford Courant,* Nov. 18, 1989.

17. *Cleveland Plain Dealer,* Jan. 26, 1990; *Antioch Observer,* Jan. 18, 1990; *Elyria* (Ohio) *Chronicle-Tribune,* Jan. 6, 8, 9, 25, 1990.

18. *Santa Rosa* (Calif.) *Press-Democrat,* Dec. 6, 8, 9, 1989; *Sonoma* (Calif.) *Index-Tribune,* Dec. 15, 1989, Jan. 30, 1990.

19. *San Francisco Examiner,* Jan. 19, Feb. 2, May 21, June 12, 1990; *Oakland Tribune, Mercury-News,* and *San Francisco Chronicle,* all Feb. 8, 1990; *Editor & Publisher,* Jan. 13, 1990; DAP.

20. *Record,* Nov. 13, 1989; *Hartford Courant,* Dec. 28, 1989.

21. *U.S. v. Eichman et al.,* U.S. District Court for the District of Columbia, Cr. Nos. 89-419/420/421 JLG, Defendants' Memorandum in Support of Motion to Dismiss, Dec. 5, 1989; Government's Memorandum in Opposition to Defendants' Motion to Dismiss, Jan. 12, 1990 (in the same case).

22. *CR* (1989), pp. S16239, H6992; CQ, Nov. 11, 1989; Motion of the Speaker and Leadership Group of the U.S. House of Representatives in Opposition to Defendants' Motion to Dismiss, Jan. 26, 1990 (in same case as cited in note 21, above); Memorandum of the U.S. Senate as Amicus Curiae in Support of the Constitutionality of the FPA, Jan. 12, 1990 (in the same case as cited in note 21, above).

23. *Legal Times,* May 14, 1990.

24. Defendants' Reply Memorandum in Support of Motion to Dismiss (in the same case cited in note 21, above).

25. TR1 1990; TR2 1990.

26. *U.S. v. Haggerty,* 731 F. Supp 425 (1990); *U.S. v. Eichman,* 731 F. Supp. 1123 (1990).

Chapter 8: The Supreme Court and Flag Burning, Round Two, *March–June 1990*

1. *Atlanta Constitution, Washington Times, Dallas Morning News, New York Times, USA Today,* all Feb. 23, 1990.

2. DAP; *Seattle Times,* Feb. 15, 22, 1990; *Washington Post* and *USA Today,* Feb. 23, 1990.

3. *Post-Intelligencer* and *Seattle Journal-American,* Feb. 22, 1990; *Dallas Morning News,* Feb. 23, 1990; *Washington Post,* Mar. 6, 1990.

4. *Washington Post,* Mar. 14, 1990; *U.S. v. Eichman,* in the Supreme Court of the United States, Oct. 1989, Motion to Expedite Statements and to Establish Expedited Schedule for Brief and Argument, Mar. 1990.

5. *Washington Post,* Mar. 14, 1990; *Dallas Times Herald,* Mar. 7, 1990.

6. Jurisdictional Statement, Mar. 1990 (in the same case cited in note 4, above).

7. Appellees' Opposition to Motion to Expedite Consideration (in the same case cited in note 4, above).

8. DAP; Memorandum of Appellees in Response to Jurisdictional Statements (in the same case cited in note 4, above).

9. Brief for the Speaker and Leadership Group of the U.S. House of Representatives in Support of Jurisdictional Statements, Mar. 15, 1990 (in the same case cited in note 4, above).

10. *CR* (1990), p. S2731.

11. The House debate is in *CR* (1990), pp. H1018–33.

12. *New York Times, Washington Post,* and *Dallas Morning News,* all Mar. 31, 1990; *CR* (1990), p. S3592.

13. *Washington Post,* Apr. 4, 10, 1990.

14. *New York Times,* May 1, 1990.

15. *U.S. v. Eichman,* Nos. 89-1433 and 89-1434, Brief for the United States, Apr. 1990, in the Supreme Court of the United States.

16. Brief of the Southeastern Legal Foundation, Inc.; Brief for Senator Joseph R. Biden, Jr.; Brief of Gov. Mario M. Cuomo; Senate Brief 1990; House Brief 1990 (all amicus briefs in the case cited in note 15, above).

17. Brief for Appellees (in the case cited in note 15, above). Amicus briefs in support of the appellees are described in the next paragraphs. Their formal titles are Brief Amicus Curiae of the ACLU [and three other organizations]; Brief of People for the American Way [and five other organizations]; Brief for Jasper Johns [and fifteen other artists]; Amicus Brief of the NAACP; Brief of the Association of Art Museum Directors [and thirty-three other organizations]; and Brief of the American Bar Association.

18. Reply Brief for the United States (in the case cited in note 15 above); Official transcript, Proceedings Before the U.S. Supreme Court (in the case cited in note 15 above).

19. *Newsday,* May 13, 1990; *National Law Journal,* May 14, 1990.

20. *Newsday,* May 13, 1990; *National Law Journal,* May 14, 1990.

21. *Newsweek,* May 21, 1990; *Legal Times,* July 23, 1990; *CR* (1989), p. S13650; *United States Law Week,* Nov. 6, 1990.

22. *New York Times,* June 22, 1990; *Legal Times,* July 23, 1990.

23. Lyle Denniston, "Flag Burning Cases Tip First Amendment Scales," *American Lawyer,* Sept. 1990, pp. 89–90; *Legal Times,* May 14, 1990.

24. *Los Angeles Times* and *Legal Times,* both May 28, 1990.

25. *Legal Times,* May 28, 1990.

26. May 14, 1990, evening news broadcasts on ABC, NBC, and CBS; May 14 reports in *New York Times, Washington Post,* and *Los Angeles Times.*

27. *Minneapolis Star-Tribune,* June 22, 1989; *St. Paul Pioneer Press,* Feb. 27, 1990; *U.S. v. Cary,* 897 F. 2d 917 (1990); *U.S. v. Cary,* 111 S.Ct. 288 (1990); *U.S. v. Cary,* 920 F. 2d 1422 (1990).

28. *Dallas Times Herald,* Mar. 9, 1990; (University of) *Indiana Daily,* Apr. 2, 1990; *New York Times,* May 9, 16, 1990; *Washington Times,* May 22, 1990; *Detroit News,* Apr. 4, 1990.

29. *Daily Texan* (University of Texas), *Dallas Times Herald, Austin-American Statesman,* all Apr. 18, 1990; *Chicago Tribune,* May 17, 1990.

30. *Chicago Tribune,* Apr. 27, 1990.

31. *Philadelphia Inquirer,* Feb. 23, 1990; *Newsday,* Dec. 16, 1989; *New Orleans Times-Picayune,* May 29, 1990; *Wall Street Journal,* June 5, 1990; *Atlanta Constitution,* Feb. 6, 1990; *Denver Post,* Feb. 22, 1990.

32. *U.S. v. Eichman,* 496 U.S. 310 (1990).

33. *Seattle Times,* Nov. 20, 1990.

Chapter 9: Flag Burning: The Sequel, June 1990

1. WCPD, June 18, 1990, pp. 935, 937–39; *New York Times* and *Boston Globe,* both June 12, 1990.

2. *Washington Times, Washington Post, Dover State News,* and *USA Today,* all June 12, 1990; *Dallas Morning News,* June 20, 1990; *Newsweek,* June 25, 1990; *Los Angeles Times,* June 12, 17, 1990.

3. *New York Times,* June 15, 1990; *Seattle Post-Intelligencer,* June 14, 1990; *Washington Times,* June 18, 1990; *Philadelphia Inquirer,* June 17, 1990; *Wilkes-Barre Times-Leader,* June 18, 1990; *Harrisburg Patriot,* June 14, 1990; *Cleveland Plain Dealer,* June 17, 1990.

4. *New Orleans Times-Picayune,* June 13, 1990; *Chicago Tribune,* June 22, 27, 1990.

5. CBS Evening News, NBC Evening News, *Washington Times, Boston Globe, Dallas Morning News, Des Moines Register,* and *USA Today,* all June 12, 1990; *Seattle Times,* June 11, 1990; *National Law Journal,* June 25, 1990.

6. *St. Louis Post-Dispatch, Omaha World-Herald, USA Today,* and *Wall Street Journal,* all June 12, 1990; *Washington Post,* June 14, 1990.

7. *New York Times,* June 13, 1990; National Public Radio, June 14, 1990; ABC Evening News, June 19, 1990.

8. *Newsday,* June 12, 1990; *CQ,* June 16, 1990; *Philadelphia Inquirer,* June 17, 1990.

9. *CR* (1990), pp. S7670, S7693, H4059; SJC 1990, pp. 20, 50–51.

10. *CR* (1990), pp. S7694, S7920, H3430, H3999; *Indianapolis Star,* June 20, 1990; SJC 1990, pp. 29, 50–52.

11. *CR* (1990), pp. S7849, S7921, S8245; SJC 1990, pp. 52, 64; HJC 1990, p. 9.

12. *CR* (1990), p. S8245.

13. Ibid., H4087.

14. *CR* (1990), pp. S8632, S8661, S8736.

15. DAP; *Washington Post,* June 13, 14, 20, 1990; SJC 1990, p. 174.

16. *CR* (1990), pp. S8700, S8704, S8719.

17. Ibid., H4089–91, H4093–94.

18. HJC 1989a, p. 3.

19. *Wall Street Journal,* June 12, 1990; *CQ,* June 16, 1990; NBC Evening News, June 13, 1990.

20. *St. Louis Post-Dispatch,* June 12, 1990; *Cleveland Plain Dealer,* June 12, 1990; *Ann Arbor News,* June 16, 1990; *Rocky Mountain News,* June 15, 1990; *CR* (1990), pp. H3427, H4016, H4061, H4079, H40987, S8665, S8729.

21. *Detroit News* and *Dallas Morning News,* both June 12, 1990; *Washington Post,* June 19, 1990; *CR* (1990), p. H4046.

22. *CQ,* June 16, 1990; *Ann Arbor News,* June 13, 1990; *New York Times,* June 12, 1990; *CR* (1990), pp. S8211–12.

23. *CR* (1990), p. E2037; *National Review,* July 9, 1990; *Boston Globe,* June 17, 1990.

24. *CR* (1990), pp. S7928, S8639.

25. SJC 1990, pp. 112–20; *CR* (1990), p. H4018.

26. *CR* (1990), pp. H4079, S8212; SJC 1990, p. 11.

27. SJC 1990, p. 139–40; *CR* (1990), pp. H3427, H4002–3, H4054, H4058, H4065, H4070, H4079; *Ann Arbor News,* June 12, 1990.

28. Andre Codrescu, *The Hole in the Flag: A Romanian Exile's Story of Return and Revolution* (New York: Avon, 1991).

29. Robert Scheer, "Freedom to Burn," *Playboy,* Mar. 1990, p. 51; *Christian Science Monitor,* June 20, 1990.

30. SJC 1990, pp. 10, 30.

31. *Washington Post,* June 12, 13, 1990; *Wall Street Journal* and *USA Today,* both June 12, 1990; *CQ,* June 16, 1990; DAP.

32. AP, June 11, 18, 1990; *Atlanta Constitution,* June 15, 1990; *New York Times,* June 17, 1990.

33. *Detroit Free Press,* June 22, 1990; *Detroit News,* June 14, 1990; *Miami Herald,* June 13, 1990; *CQ,* June 16, 1990; *New York Times,* June 17, 1990.

34. *Los Angeles Times,* June 12, 14, 1990; *Houston Post* and *Chicago Tribune,* both June 14, 1990; NBC Evening News, June 21, 1990; *New York Times,* June 25, 1990.

35. *CQ,* June 16, 1990; *New York Times,* June 13, 1990; *Philadelphia Inquirer,* June 17, 1990; HJC 1990, p. 36; *Washington Post,* June 19, 1990.

36. *CR* (1990), pp. H4000, S7932; *USA Today,* June 22, 1990.

37. *Washington Post,* June 19, 1990; *USA Today,* June 12, 1990; CBS Evening News, June 12, 1990; *CR* (1990), pp. S7925, S8297, S8647, S8796, S8662, H4003.

38. *CR* (1990), p. H4013.

39. *St. Louis Post-Dispatch,* June 15, 1990; *CQ,* June 16, 1990; *New York Times,* June 17, 1990; *USA Today,* June 22, 1990; *Atlanta Constitution,* June 24, 1990; *Ann Arbor News,* June 22, 1990.

40. On the Democratic task force, see *CQ,* June 23, 1990.

41. WCPD, June 18, 1990, pp. 935, 937–39, 944, 949–50, June 25, 1990, pp. 973–74, 987; *CQ,* June 23, 1990.

42. DAP.

43. *New York Times, Washington Post,* and *Los Angeles Times,* all June 15, 1990.

44. *National Journal,* June 30, 1990.

45. Ibid.; *New York Times,* June 22, 1990; *Newsweek,* July 2, 1990; *CQ,* June 23, 1990.

46. *USA Today* and *New York Times,* both June 20, 1990; *Washington Post,* June 19, 1990; DAP.

47. *CR* (1990), pp. H3837–38.

48. DAP.

49. *Wall Street Journal,* June 18, 1990; *Columbus Dispatch,* June 17, 1990; *CR* (1990),   pp. S8732–34.

50. *Boston Globe,* June 15, 1990; *Denver Post,* June 25, 1990; *Chicago Tribune,* June 14, 1990.

51. *Washington Post,* June 14, 1990; *New York Times,* June 15, 1990; *Washington Times,* June 18, 1990.

52. *CR* (1990), p. H4085.

53. *Washington Post,* June 19, 1990.

54. *New York Times* and *Chicago Tribune,* both June 21, 1990; *Cleveland Plain Dealer,* June 24, 1990; *Miami Herald,* June 21, 1990.

55. *Christian Science Monitor,* June 21, 1990; *CR* (1990), pp. S8648, S8658, S8662.

56. *Christian Science Monitor,* June 13, 1990; DAP; *ASNE Bulletin,* July–Aug. 1990.

57. *National Journal,* June 23, 1990; *Los Angeles Times,* June 24, 1990; *Newsweek,* June 25, 1990; *Chicago Tribune,* June 15, 1990; *New York Times,* June 14, 15, 1990; *Seattle Times,* June 13, 1990; *Dallas Morning News,* June 14, 1990; *Seattle Post-Intelligencer,* June 15, 1990; *St. Louis Post-Dispatch,* June 14, 1990.

58. *Detroit News,* June 17, 1990; Tom McNichol, "Flag Flambé: The American Legion's Special Recipe for Tattered Old Glories" (Washington, D.C.) *City Paper,* May 18, 1990, pp. 12–15.

59. *Baltimore Sun, Washington Times, Dallas Morning News,* and *Philadelphia Inquirer,* all June 20, 1990; *CR* (1990), p. H4087.

60. *CR* (1990), pp. H4053, H4058; *New York Times,* June 23, 1990.

61. *CR* (1990), pp. H4016, H4070.

62. Ibid., H4043–44.

63. Ibid., H4048–50; *Dallas Morning News,* June 23, 1989; *New York Times,* June 23, 25, 1990; Cwiklik, *House Rules,* 235–27; *Illinois Daily Herald,* June 23, 1989.

Epilogue and Afterthoughts: The Flag Desecration Controversy in the Post-Eichman Era, Mid-1990 to Mid-1995

1. *Ann Arbor News,* July 9, 1990; *New York Times,* July 13, 1990.

2. *USA Today,* June 22, 1990; *Boston Globe,* June 23, 1990.

3. *CQ,* Nov. 24, 1990; *New York Times,* Nov. 8, 1990.

4. Voting statistics in this and the following paragraphs are drawn from *The World Almanac of U.S. Politics, 1991–93 Edition* (New York: Pharos Books, 1991).

5. *Washington Post,* August 26, 27, 1992.

6. *Chicago Tribune,* Aug. 8, 1990.

7. *Seattle Times,* June 14, 1991; *Time,* July 9, 1990.

8. *New York Times,* Jan. 20, Feb. 11, 1991; *Advertising Age,* Feb. 11, 1991; *Los Angeles Times,* June 30, 1994.

9. *Tulsa World,* July 4, 1990; *Detroit Free Press,* Jan. 14, 1991; *New York Times,* Jan. 31, Feb. 12, 1991.

10. *Ann Arbor News,* Jan. 30, Feb. 11, 12, 13, 1991.

11. *New York Times,* Mar. 3, 4, 1991; *Ann Arbor News,* Feb. 12, 1991; *Time,* Feb. 25, 1991.

12. *New York Times,* Apr. 19, Oct. 21, 1992; *Ann Arbor News,* Feb. 2, 23, Aug. 3, 8, 9, Oct. 11, 1992.

13. *Miami Review,* Aug. 8, 1990.

14. *Warren* (Ohio) *Tribune-Chronicle,* July 11, 1991; *Dallas Times Herald,* Mar. 9, 1990; *State v. Jimenez,* 828 S.W. 2d 455 (1992); 113 S.Ct. 317 (1992); DAP.

15. *Johnstown Tribune Democrat,* Sept. 1, 1993; *Warren* (Pa.) *Times Observer,* Nov. 9, 1991, Jan. 16, Oct. 1, 1992; *Harrisburg Patriot,* Nov. 24, 1991; DAP.

16. AP, Feb. 12, 1991; *Carpenter v. State,* 597 So. 2d 737 (1992); DAP.

17. *St. Louis Post-Dispatch,* Mar. 25, 26, 1991; *Cleveland Plain Dealer,* Jan. 26, 1990; *Oberlin (Ohio) Review,* Sept. 7, 1990; *Elyria Chronicle-Telegram,* Jan. 8, July 7, Aug. 28, 29, 1990; *In These Times,* Feb. 21, 1990; DAP.

18. *Los Angeles Times,* July 9, 1990.

19. *New York Law Journal,* Jan. 17, 1991.

20. *Cleveland Plain Dealer,* Aug. 11, 31, Oct. 23, 24, 30, Nov. 12, Dec. 9, 1990, Apr. 24, 1992, Oct. 28, 1993; *State v. Lessin,* 620 N.E. 2d 72 (1993).

21. *U.S. v. Wilson,* 33 M.J. 797 (1991).

22. *Newsday,* Sept. 12, Oct. 7, 1990, Mar. 26, June 5, 1991; *Downtown* (New York City), Sept. 26, 1990, Jan. 23, 1991; *Rockland County* (N.Y.) *Journal-News,* Dec. 23, 1990; *U.S. v. Eichman,* 756 F. Supp. 143 (1991); *U.S. v. Eichman,* 957 F. 2d 145 (1992).

23. *Los Angeles Times,* Oct. 6, 15, 1990; *St. Louis Post-Dispatch,* Nov. 6, 1990; *Cleveland Plain Dealer,* Nov. 14, 1991; *Anchorage Daily News,* May 19, 24, 1992; *Anchorage Times,* May 20, 22, 1992; *Artweek,* Dec. 3, 1992; *Art in America,* Mar. 1993; *Artnews,* Mar. 1993.

24. *New York Times,* Feb. 14, Mar. 23, 1991, Feb. 18, 1992; *Washington Post,* Feb. 14, 1991.

25. *Baltimore Sun,* Jan. 18, 1991.

26. *Eau Claire Leader-Telegram,* Mar. 12, 13, 14, 15, Apr. 25, 1991; *River Falls Journal,* Mar. 21, 1991.

27. *Cape Cod Times,* Nov. 28, 1991; *Boston Globe,* Oct. 27, 1991; *Washington Post,* May 20, 1992, Mar. 9, 1993; DAP.

28. *Sacramento Bee,* Feb. 12, 17, Apr. 17, July 4, Sept. 3, Oct. 15, 1993, Feb. 3, 8, 23, 24, 1994; *Elk Grove Citizen,* Apr. 21, 30, May 21, 1993; *ACLU News* (Northern California), May–June 1993, July–Aug. 1993.

29. For a complete listing of dates when state legislatures passed memorializing resolutions, see the newsletter of the Citizens Flag Alliance, *Highlights,* April 28, 1995.

30. For basic information on the CFA, including the quoted material, see its inaugural publication, *Protecting the U.S. Flag: A Historical Prospectus* (1984), and its newsletter, *CFA Highlights,* published periodically beginning in January 1995.

31. *Los Angeles Times* and *New York Times,* both May 26, 1995.

32. *Chicago Tribune,* Mar. 4, 1995; *CFA Highlights,* Jan. 5, 14, 1995.

33. *Oregon Statesman-Journal,* Mar. 16, 1991; *Richmond Times-Dispatch,* Feb. 22, 1990; *New York Times,* Feb. 14, 1995; *Arkansas Democrat,* Feb. 5, 1991; *Wyoming State Tribune,* Jan. 25, 1991; DAP.

34. *Bismarck Tribune,* Mar. 19, 1991; *New York Times,* Feb. 14, 1995.

35. AP, May 25, 1995; *USA Today,* Mar. 22, 1995; *Chicago Tribune,* Mar. 1, 1995.

36. *The Economist,* July 1, 1989; Rodney Smolla, "Free Speech Afire with Controversy," *Trial,* Dec. 1989, p. 49; John Johnson, *Historical U.S. Court Cases, 1690-1990: An Encyclopedia* (New York: Garland, 1992), 521; *CR* (1989), p. H4044.

37. *Washington Post,* June 30, 1989.

38. *New York Times,* Dec. 15, 1991, July 23, 26, Sept. 7, 1992.

39. *New York Times,* Sept. 2, Dec. 3, 1991, Sept. 22, 1992; *Ann Arbor News,* Jan. 27, 1990, Sept. 8, 23, 1992.

40. *Boston Globe,* July 2, 1989; *Economist,* Aug. 12, 1989; *Ann Arbor News,* Jan. 12, Feb. 28, Mar. 3, 18, 1992; *New York Times,* Mar. 1, 2, 1991.

41. *New York Times,* Mar. 17, Sept. 7, 1992; *Newsday,* July 2, 1989; *Tikkun,* Sept.–Oct. 1989, pp. 8–9.

42. *New York Times,* Dec. 16, 1990, Aug. 16, Sept. 2, 1991, Jan. 7, Apr. 2, 15, May 12, 14, Sept. 4, 1991; *Ann Arbor News,* Sept. 22, 1991, Mar. 2, July 7, 1992. For in-depth background to these and similar data, see generally Kevin Phillips, *The Politics of Rich and Poor: Wealth and the American Electorate in the Reagan Aftermath* (New York: Harper, 1991); Donald Barlett and James Steele, *America: What Went Wrong?* (Kansas City, Mo.: Andrews and McMeel, 1992); Robert Samuelson, "How Our American Dream Unraveled," *Newsweek,* Mar. 2, 1992, pp. 32–39; "What Happened to the American Dream," *Business Week,* Aug. 19, 1991, pp. 80–85.

43. *New York Times,* July 5, Aug. 2, 7, 11, Oct. 5, 1991; *Ann Arbor News,* Jan. 17, 1992.

44. *Boston Globe,* July 2, 1991; *Cauldron* (Cleveland State University student paper), Nov. 21, 1991; HJC 1989d, p. 22; *New York Post,* June 23, 1989; *New York Times,* July 2, 1989; *Gary Post-Tribune,* July 4, 1989; *Houston Chronicle,* June 30, 1989.

45. *New York Times,* July 2, 1989; *New York Daily News,* Aug. 12, 1989; *USA Today,* July 24, 1989; *New York Post,* July 2, 1989; *Washington Times,* June 18, 1990; HJC 1990, p. 20.

46. *New Republic,* Aug. 14, 1989.

Addendum: The Revised Struggle over the Flag Desecration Amendment in 1995

1. *New York Times,* Dec. 14, 1995.

2. *Ann Arbor News,* Aug. 4, 1995; CFA *Highlights,* Sept. 15, 1995.

3. *Honolulu Star-Bulletin,* Jan. 11, 1995; *Desert Trail* (Twentynine Palms, Calif.), Mar. 2, 1995; *Cleveland Plain Dealer,* June 22, 1995; *Indianapolis Star,* June 9, 1995; *Chicago Tribune,* Apr. 6, 1995.

4. *Pittsburgh Post-Gazette,* Mar. 13, 1995; *Daily Oklahoman,* Sept. 16, 19, 1995; *Tulsa World,* Sept. 20, 1995.

5. *San Diego Union Tribune*, Nov. 3, 4, 1995.

6. *New York Daily News, Newsday*, both Dec. 19, 1995; DAP. In mid-January 1996, vandals severely damaged Lipski's "flag ball" sculpture. Long Island University officials removed it from its display site and placed it in a storage building while Lipski decided what to do (*Newsday,* Jan. 22, 23, 1996).

7. *American Editor*, July, Nov., 1995; DAP.

8. *New York Times*, Oct. 15, 1995; Clifford Cobb, "If the GDP is Up, Why is America Down?" *Atlantic Monthly*, Oct. 1955, 60.

9. William Bennett, *The Index of Leading Cultural Indicators* (New York: Simon & Schuster, 1994); *New York Times*, Nov. 5, 7, 1995; *Ann Arbor News*, Nov. 5, Dec. 29, 1995.

10. *Reuters*, June 7, 1995; *CR* (1995), pp. H6408, H6425.

11. *Chicago Tribune*, June 19, 1995; CFA *Highlights*, June 1, 14, 1995; *CR* (1995), p. S8297.

12. *SJC Report* 104–148, "Senate Joint Resolution 31," 104th Cong., 1st sess., Sept. 27, 1995, pp. 24–25; *CR* (1995), pp. S18039–40, S18043, S18282.

13. AP, June 6, 1995; *St. Louis Post-Dispatch*, June 7, 1995.

14. AP, *New York Times*, both June 8, 1995; AP, *New York Times, Washington Post, Los Angeles Times*, all June 29, 1995.

15. AP, June 6, 7, 1995; *New York Times* and *Los Angeles Times*, both June 7, 1995; *Washington Post* and *Washington Times*, both June 6, 1995.

16. U.S. Newswire Transcript of White House press briefing, June 29, 1995; *New York Times, Washington Post, Los Angeles Times*, Dec. 13, 1995.

17. Reuters, July 20, 1995; *Atlanta Constitution*, Sept. 9, 1995; *Arizona Republic*, June 19, 1995.

18. *CQ*, Sept. 2, 1995; *Atlanta Constitution*, Nov. 29, 1995; *USA Today*, Nov. 20, 1995.

19. *Atlanta Constitution, Boston Globe, Kentucky Post*, all Dec. 7, 1995; *Washington Post,* Dec. 5, 1995; *Lexington Herald-Leader,* Dec. 6, 1995.

20. *CQ*, Dec. 9, 1995; Reuters and *Congressional Monitor*, both Dec. 6, 1995; *USA Today* and *St. Louis Post-Dispatch* both Dec. 7, 1995; AP and *Albany Times-Union* both Dec. 12, 1995.

21. *CR* (1995), pp. S18325–26, S18351.

22. SJC Report 104–148, "Senate Joint Resolution 31," 104th Cong., 1st sess., Sept. 27, 1995, pp. 39–40, 55–63; *CR* (1995), pp. S18316–22, S18352, S18391.

23. *CR* (1995), pp. S15338–39, S18264–68, S18322–23, S18282–86, S18356–60, S18374–75, S18378, S18393; *Lexington Herald-Leader*, Dec. 13, 1995.

24. *New York Times*, AP, *Washington Post, Cleveland Plain Dealer, Lexington Herald-Leader,* Reuters, *Chicago Tribune, USA Today, Miami Herald*, all Dec. 13, 1995.

25. *CR* (1995), p. 18395; PR Newswire, Dec. 12, 13, 1995.

26. AP, Dec. 12, 1995.

27. House of Representatives Report 104–151, "Flag Desecration," 104th Cong., 1st sess., pp. 17, 19; SJC Report 104–148, "Senate Joint Resolution 31," 104th Cong., 1st sess., Sept. 27, 1995, p. 74.

28. *Columbus Dispatch*, Dec. 7, 1995; *Pittsburgh Post-Gazette* and *Rocky Mountain News*, Dec. 9, 1995; *Cleveland Plain Dealer*, Dec. 9, 12, 1995; *CR* (1995), pp. S18276–80; *Philadelphia Inquirer*, Dec. 12, 1995; *Akron Beacon-Journal*, Dec. 13, 1995.

29. *CR* (1995), p. H6421; *Atlanta Constitution, Detroit Free Press, New York Times,* all June 29, 1995.

30. *CR* (1995), pp. H6417, H6432–33, S18257–58, S18281, S18379, S18393.

31. *Los Angeles Times,* June 7, 1995; *CR* (1995), pp. S18061–62, S18381.

32. *CR* (1995), pp. H6419, H6422, H6428, H6432, H6434.

33. *CR* (1995), p. S18346.

34. DAP; *Editor and Publisher,* July 8, 1995; *Denver Post,* June 17, 1995; AP, Aug. 4, 1995.

35. *Denver Post,* July 4, 1995. The *Washington Post* cartoon is reprinted in the July 1 issue of *Editorials on File,* p. 820.

36. *CR* (1995), pp. S1873–74; SJC Report 104–148, "Senate Joint Resolution 31," 104th Cong., 1st sess., Sept. 27, 1995, pp. 65, 79.

37. Robert J. Goldstein, "Two Centuries of Flagburnings in the United States," *The Flag Bulletin* 34 (Mar.–Apr. 1995), 65–76; DAP; *CQ,* Dec. 16, 1995; *CR* (1995), p. H6438.

38. House of Representatives Report 104–151, "Flag Desecration," p. 21; Vastine Davis Platte, "Flag Desecration and Flag Misuse Use Laws in the United States," Congressional Research Service Report 95–182 A, Mar. 29, 1995.

39. *Miami Herald,* Dec. 7, 1995; *New York Times,* June 8, 29, 1995; *Washington Post,* June 8, 1995; CR (1995), pp. S18062, S18273, S18279, H6419.

40. *CR* (1995), p. H6439.

41. *San Francisco Examiner,* July 2, 1995; DAP; *CQ,* July 1, 1995; *CR* (1995), pp. H6437, H6445.

42. Gannett News Service, June 14, 15, 1995.

43. *New York Times,* June 8, 1995; *World,* May 6, 1995; *New York Daily News,* Aug. 12, 1989.

44. *CFA Highlights,* July 1, 1995; *Christian Science Monitor,* June 9, 1995; Reuters, June 7, 1995; *CR* (1995), pp. H6438, H6441–42, S18255, S18326.

45. SJC Report 104–148, "Senate Joint Resolution 31," 104th Cong., 1st sess., Sept. 25, 1995, pp. 30–33.

46. *USA Today,* May 16, 1995; *CFA Highlights,* June 1, 1995.

47. *CR,* (1995), pp. H6426, H6432.

48. *CR,* (1995), pp. H6410–11, S18042, S18353–54.

49. *CR,* (1995), pp. H6404, S18042, S18086.

50. *CR,* (1995), pp. S81041–43, S18343, S18352–53, S18359.

51. *New York Times,* June 7, 1995; *USA Today,* May 16, 1995.

52. *CR* (1995), pp. H6407, H6422, H6424, S18275, S18356.

53. Senate Judiciary Committee, Report 104–148, "Senate Joint Resolution 31," 104th Cong., 1st sess., p. 37; *CR* (1995), pp. S18042, S18261, S18391.

54. Senate Judiciary Committee, Report 104–148, "Senate Joint Resolution 31," 104th Cong., 1st sess., pp. 2, 9; *CR* (1995), pp. H6423, H6429, H6442, S18355.

55. AP and Reuters, both Jan. 8, 1996; *Troster v. Pennsylvania State Dept. of Corrections,* 65 F.3d 1086 (1995); *Chicago Tribune,* Aug. 8, 1990.

★

INDEX

Names preceded by an asterisk (*) were interviewed by the author during the research for this book; otherwise undocumented statements attributed in the book to them are based on these interviews. Flag desecration incidents, prosecutions, and laws occurring in specific states and localities are indexed under the state in which they occurred; thus, a flag burning in Cleveland referenced in the book will be indexed under Ohio.

BURNING THE FLAG

was composed in Times Roman
using Quark Express 3.31 for Macintosh
at Books International Inc.,
printed by sheet-fed offset
on 50-pound Supple Opaque Natural Recycled stock,
notch case bound with 88-point binder's boards
in ICG Kennett book cloth,
and wrapped with dustjackets printed in
two colors 100-pound enamel
by Thomson-Shore, Inc.;
designed by Donna Hartwick;
and published by
The Kent State University Press
Kent, Ohio 44242